PSYCHOLOGY AND LAW

PSYCHOLOGY AND LAW
Research and Application

SECOND EDITION

Curt R. Bartol
Anne M. Bartol
Castleton State College

Brooks/Cole Publishing Company
Pacific Grove, California
a division of International Thomson Publishing Inc.

Brooks/Cole Publishing Company

A division of International Thomson Publishing Inc.

© 1994 by Brooks/Cole Publishing Company.

Printed in the United States of America

10 9 8 7 6 5 4

Library of Congress Cataloging-in-Publication Data

Bartol, Curt R., 1940–

    Psychology and law: research and application / Curt R. Bartol,
Anne M. Bartol. — 2nd ed.

       p. cm,

    Rev. ed. of: Psychology and American law. c1983.

    Includes bibliographical references and index.

    ISBN 0-534-16320-3

    1. Psychology, Forensic. 2. Evidence, Expert—United States.
3. Criminal psychology—United States. I. Bartol, Anne M.
II. Bartol, Curt R., 1940– Psychology and American law.
III. Title.

KF8922.B37 1994

345'.001'9—dc20

[342.50019]   93-39459

                                             CIP

Sponsoring Editor: Ken King, Marianne Taflinger

Editorial Assistant: Gay Meixel, Virge Perelli-Minetti

Production Coordination: Joan Marsh, Lisa Berman

Production Editor: Jim Love

Production Assistant: Debi Maronay

Manuscript Editor: Heather Bennett

Interior Design: Jim Love

Cover Design: Laurie Albrect

Art Direction: Jim Love

Interior Illustration: Margot Koch

Composition and Make-up: Publishers Design Studio, Inc.

Cover Printing: Phoenix Color Corporation

CONTENTS

PREFACE

PSYCHOLOGY AND LAW: RESEARCH AND APPLICATION is intended to be a textbook for the behavioral-science student who has limited knowledge about, and minimal experience with, the legal system. The text has three additional purposes.

First, the text tries to help the student to become skillful at discriminating between knowledge that is well supported and misinformation based upon unwarranted assumptions and popular myths. Such skill requires the student to develop a healthy skepticism about unverified statements presumed to be valid simply because they are offered by "experts" who exude self-confidence.

Second, the text tries to help the student realize that scientific knowledge is not absolute in the sense of offering established fact or "ultimate truth." Rather, it is tentative, fallible, and developing. Throughout the book, the research will be qualified by such cautionary phrases as "the weight of the evidence," "research to date," and "thus far the evidence seems to indicate." In many areas, students also will be reminded that "more research is needed" before something can be established with confidence.

Third, the text approaches psychology as fundamentally a scientific enterprise with the primary mission of creating or continually reconstructing testable theory, a process that allows psychologists to progress steadily toward understanding human behavior. Much of what we have learned so far can be applied to the legal process. However, the field of psychology and law should continue to work toward systematizing and synthesizing valid and significant research findings about law-related behavior into viable, testable theory. When this is done, psychological knowledge will have become evenly applicable to legal issues.

It would be unrealistic to claim that this text will bridge the enormous gap between psychology and law. Law is a practical, conservative, and traditional endeavor that is strongly influenced by moral, social, and political pressures. And, perhaps for good reason, representatives of the law view the science of psychology with suspicion and skepticism, convinced that psychology must prove its worth in "meaningful" application before it can be accepted and trusted. Psychologists, on the other hand, often view law as cloaked in unsupported assumptions and maddeningly unresponsive to the findings of science. When questions of treatment are at issue, the law is sometimes regarded as obstructionist. Nonetheless, psychology and law continually interact with one another and should seek mutual respect, if not common ground.

The text tries to cover as much of the legal system as possible, but within the confines of available psychological research and current interest. Since the first edition was published in 1983, research and interest in psychology and law has exploded. This is reflected both in the literature and in the increasing numbers of undergraduate and graduate courses in the area. Some of the

material presented here may become dated within two years after publication. Even as we go to press, new articles are appearing and new court decisions are being announced. However, the principles and strategies of scientific psychology will remain the same, and the need for unifying theoretical statements will persist.

In this second edition, both new features and substantive material have been added. First, the title has been changed to reflect the desirability of establishing a connection between research and practice. Key concepts and terms are emphasized with bold type within the chapters and are in the new glossary at the end of the book. Students are also given questions to ponder at the end of each chapter.

Substantively, we have added considerably more material on civil matters throughout the text, including updated information on involuntary civil commitment. A chapter on family law has been added, which deals with issues relating to the psychology of abortion, adoption, custodial options in divorce, mediation, and juvenile justice. Because of the growth in knowledge concerning research on the jury, the psychology of the jury has been divided into two chapters. Additionally, we have added more material on the interaction between psychology and criminal justice, such as treatment of mentally disordered inmates, psychological assessments of various competencies relating to the criminal process, and issues relating to the insanity defense.

In this revision, a concentrated effort has been made to improve the material from a student perspective. Students in Curt Bartol's psychology and law courses have been closely involved in this revision in many ways. For example, during the last two years of the revision process, the book was closely examined in seminars that strongly encouraged critical comments from students. During these seminars, students were required to submit weekly written explanations of what they would like to see added or otherwise changed. The students responded to this task with excitement and competence. Discussions were lively and extremely helpful.

Three themes continually emerged through this process. First, students liked the scholarly tone of the book. They said they did not like to be "talked down to" and were adamant that, as long as the material was clearly written, maintaining a scholarly style was important. Second, students liked boxed-in material, but did not find great interest in reproduced newspaper clippings of sensational stories. They preferred legal or research materials that enhanced the content. The boxes, therefore, were carefully selected to avoid popularized content. Third, students were very interested in exploring career choices. This edition reflects more of this interest, with a conscious effort made to explain what psychologists working in a legal setting actually do.

Acknowledgments

We are grateful to Professors Phoebe Ellsworth, Leo Alex NcCandlish, John Monahan, Steve Penrod, Lita Schwartz, and the numerous other anonymous reviewers who provided invaluable comments and guidance throughout the various phases of this revision. Many students also made significant contributions. However, special thanks are due to the following students who carefully read the text and provided extensive commentary from a student perspective. They were: Gina Bartol, Kevin Bowes, Susan Carreira, Ryan Clement, Marc Daigneault, Kim Douglas, Laurie Dursza, Jennifer Forsey, Jackie Gralnick, Keoki Hansen, Joanna Harrison, Michelle Hudson, Tom Hussey, Irina Klein, Michelle Larocque, Rachel Madsen, Sean Nary, Tammy Nelson, Alison Pearce, Becky Pregger, Jennifer Rogert, Kyle Snow, Kevin Souza, Lori Thompson, Cathy Jo Vickers, and Dave Wilbur.

We also appreciate the competence, efficiency, patience, and sense of humor of the many individuals who were involved with the technical aspects of publishing this book. Years ago, Ken King gently persuaded us that a new edition was long overdue. Our new editor, Marianne Taflinger, was extremely helpful and encouraging during the writing and submission of the manuscript. Heather Bennett is a copyeditor par excellence. She worked on the manuscript with care and thoughtfulness, and offered numerous suggestions for improving the clarity of the writing. Joan Marsh and Lisa Berman orchestrated the production with great professionalism. Finally, we were consistently impressed with the speed and efficiency of Jim Love and his staff at Publishers Design Studio, who helped us survive the whirlwind of the last few weeks of production. Illustrator Margot Koch and production assistant Debi Maronay deserve special thanks.

Anne M. Bartol also wishes to thank the faculty at the School of Criminal Justice, State University of New York/Albany, for its commitment to excellence in graduate education. Particularly noteworthy are the teaching and scholarship of James R. Acker, Hans Toch, Fred Cohen, and Terence Thornberry, each of whom in his own way demonstrates an intelligent and humane approach to the challenges facing criminal justice. Although their individual perspectives may not always be reflected in the text, they will have a lasting influence.

Curt R. Bartol
Anne M. Bartol

REVIEWERS

Dr. David Dunning	*Cornell University*
Dr. Phoebe Ellsworth	*University of Michigan, Ann Arbor*
Dr. William W. Finger, Ph.D.	*Dayton Veterans Affairs Medical Center, Wright State University*
Dr. Robert Mauro	*University of Oregon*
Dr. Leo McCandlish	*University of Texas*
Dr. John Monahan	*University of Virginia*
Dr. Lita Linzer Schwartz, Ph.D.	*The Pennsylvania State University at Ogontz*
Dr. Vicki L. Smith	*Northwestern University*

CHAPTER ONE

INTRODUCTION

THIS BOOK IS ABOUT PSYCHOLOGICAL KNOWLEDGE as it pertains to law. It is difficult to be more precise, because the field of psychology and law is very broad, extremely diverse, and expanding rapidly. Most of the research has been published in the last decade, and virtually all over the past twenty years (Melton, 1992). Anything dealing with law is within its bailiwick and is fodder for empirical study and practical application. As a result, researchers have examined issues ranging from the capacity of adolescents to consent to medical treatment to the effect of media publicity on juries in criminal trials. Practitioners are consulting with lawyers, working in court clinics, evaluating children for custody decisionmaking, and offering a wide range of testing and counseling services to law enforcement, corrections, and social agencies.

Despite this extensive and exciting involvement, Psychology and Law is a vessel without moorings. Its very diversity defies a neat definition of the field. As Melton (1992, p. 382) notes, "…it has no explicit perspective whatsoever that guides the choice of topics for research—a deficit that, without remediation, will doom the field to little continuing influence on legal scholarship and policy and that indeed will leave persistent questions about why the field exists at all." Students and professionals in the discipline report that it is somewhat frustrating to work in an area that is ill-defined and constantly changing (Hafemeister, Ogloff & Small, 1990). Furthermore, as in any rapidly developing field, there are identity squabbles, often between those who believe psychologists should be cautious in communicating information to the law and those who believe psychology should be actively involved in bringing about social change.

Psychology and Law is clearly in a state of flux. New paradigms, or models, are being proposed as a means of structuring the field and recognizing some of its frustrations (e.g., Monahan & Walker, 1988; Wexler, 1990b; Wexler and Winick, 1991). These new models, which will be integrated throughout the text, testify to their sponsors' commitment to the continuing development of the field. The book is written in this spirit of confidence that psychology has a great deal to offer to law—and students are invited to share in the excitement.

Psychology is defined as the science of human behavior. The definition of law is more evasive. "The question, 'What is law?' haunts legal thought…" (Vago, 1991, p. 6). For the present, we will adopt a very broad definition of law as a process of producing and applying a body of written rules governing society, recognizing that this definition, like all others, is far from perfect. Viewing law as a process, however, encourages us to think of it as continually subject to change and interpretation, a critical feature in the interaction of law and psychology. In a later chapter we will discuss various classifications of law, which make its study more manageable. The study of psychology and law itself can be approached from many angles, and divided and subdivided

many ways. Haney (1980) has suggested a perceptive approach, which we adopt and integrate throughout the text. He believes it is useful to distinguish three relationships: psychology *in* the law, psychology *and* the law, and psychology *of* the law.

PSYCHOLOGY *IN* THE LAW

The psychology *in* the law relationship has been the most common and may be the source of much of the malaise within the discipline. In this relationship, representatives of the law take the initiative. They call on psychology when they need it, or when they perceive it will give them an advantage. After gaining the psychologist's testimony or acquiring the relevant psychological knowledge, they dismiss the psychologist and the relationship is terminated. In this context, psychology is applied within the restrictions of the standard legal process. The law asks specific, narrow questions that psychologists are required to answer within a legal context. Thus the "law side" of the relationship not only controls the scope of the issue, but also translates the meaning of answers provided by the "psychology side." The nature of this relationship limits the impact psychology can have on law and its beliefs about human behavior. "We'll call you when we need you," asserts the legal system, and psychologists conform to that role. It should be emphasized that not all judges and lawyers take such a narrow view. Many court officials see considerable value in psychology beyond its usefulness as a way to gain an advantage in the courtroom.

It should not be assumed that psychology has no influence within that legal context, however. Quite the contrary. When mentally disordered individuals are involved, for example, studies show a high rate of agreement between the recommendations of psychologists and the final decisions of those who sought their input. The point is that the psychology *in* the law relationship does not permit the full potential value of psychological knowledge to be communicated. The next relationship, psychology *and* the law, is far more likely to do this.

PSYCHOLOGY *AND* THE LAW

In this relationship neither psychology nor law dominates. Rather, psychology is viewed as a separate discipline examining and analyzing various components of the law from a psychological perspective and developing psychological research and theory. With the execution of well-designed studies and the thoughtful formulation of theory to tie the results of these experiments together, psychology can develop an impressive body of knowledge relevant to the legal system. Are the numerous legal assumptions about human behavior empirically supported? For example, can decisionmaking by jurors really be unaffected by information they are told to disregard? Are eyewitnesses, so heavily relied upon in the criminal courts, generally accurate in their recollection of events surrounding a crime? Do mentally disordered individuals have the ability to make decisions in their own best interest? What are the limitations of psychological tests used by employers to screen prospective employees? In the psychology and law relationship, psychology tries to answer these questions and communicate them to the law. Ideally, then, the relationship is truly interdisciplinary. Even if the legal system does not change in the direction of the scientific evidence, the body of psychological knowledge remains intact.

Wexler and Winick (1991; Wexler, 1990b, 1992) argue that psychology and law, particularly mental health law, has not yet become truly interdisciplinary. Mental health law is that subset of the law that deals with individuals who are or are suspected to be mentally disordered (Wexler, 1981). It covers such issues as insanity, the administration of psychoactive medication, and the involuntary civil commitment of the mentally disordered, to name but a few. Noting that mental health law has developed as a "rights oriented" approach which has now reached a stalemate,

■ 1.1: *FINDING COURT CASES AND OTHER LAW*

PEOPLE UNFAMILIAR WITH LAW AND LEGAL RESEARCH are often hesitant to approach legal materials, feeling deterred by the apparent "mystique" surrounding American law. Actually, researching many topics is a straightforward process. Most libraries have general source materials about the U.S. Supreme Court and the American judicial system. Many also have law dictionaries (including the indispensable *Black's Law Dictionary*), legal encyclopedias, and the multi-volume publication *Words and Phrases*, which gives legal definitions for certain terms and refers the reader to cases which helped define them. The *Index to Legal Periodicals* refers us to journal articles on a case or topic. All of these are examples of secondary legal authorities.

Primary legal authorities are the constitutions, statutes, regulations, and court decisions themselves. Sizeable libraries have at least some of these on hand. The *Supreme Court Reporter* and *U.S. Reports*, for example, both contain complete decisions of the U.S. Supreme Court. It is a simple process to locate a case, given its name (e.g., *Miranda v. Arizona*) and a cite (384 U.S. 436). We have only to go to volume 384 of *U.S. Reports* and the case will be at page 436. The same principle is used to record lower court cases. Decisions of federal appellate courts are found in the *Federal Reporter* (e.g., 465 F.2d 496). The *Federal Supplement* holds federal district court cases. State court decisions are found in state reporters and regional volumes.

Without the case name, and with only a general subject area to research, the process becomes more involved, but it is still manageable. In this situation, a student makes use of a limited subject index at the back of the case reporter or one of several special indexes, often called case digests.

The American Digest System, used in American law libraries, makes use of a "key number" system developed by West Publishing Company. Law is divided into seven main classes, each class into subclasses, and each subclass into topics. When a case is received for indexing, each point of law covered in the case is isolated and summarized in a headnote, which is then assigned a topic and a key number. Although the system sounds complex, it is relatively simple once the researcher has located the current digest, which will then refer him or her to appropriate cases on the subject of interest. Law libraries and university and college libraries subscribe to computerized data search services, including LEXIS and WESTLAW, simplifying the researcher's task even more.

James Acker (1990) offers many other useful suggestions to people about to embark on legal research. As he notes, "Law collections may appear hopelessly byzantine at first glance; yet even a passing familiarity with legal reference materials quickly leads to facility with their use and opens up a magnificent storehouse of information" (p. 215). ■

Wexler and Winick call for a new paradigm which would recognize law's potential as a therapeutic agent. Acknowledging that an emphasis on legal rights was vital in the early years of modern mental health law, Wexler (1992, p. 29) suggests that "a nearly exclusive emphasis on this approach is both risky and, after twenty years, sterile." Wexler and Winick do not suggest that therapeutic considerations should hold precedence over legal considerations; rather, they ask for a truly interdisciplinary relationship whereby decisions are fully informed by the findings of psychological research. We will return to the Wexler and Winick suggestions in a later chapter, because they represent some of the most current thought in the continuing struggle to define the relationship between psychology and law.

Legal reform predicated upon sound psychological principles will not occur with ease. Law's practices are built upon a foundation of long tradition and conservative attitudes toward innovation. More importantly, law is often skeptical about psychology and its history of favoring individual differences over equal application of the law. However, it is precisely this mutually independent psychology and law relationship that holds promise for improvement in both disciplines.

PSYCHOLOGY OF THE LAW

The third relationship, psychology *of* the law, represents a more abstract approach to law as a determinant of behavior. How does law affect society and how does society affect law? How successful are laws and the consequences for their violation in controlling and altering human behavior? For example, does the death penalty deter violent crime? Why are some laws embraced, some tolerated, and others resisted? What factors explain discretion in the enforcement of laws? The psychology of law poses and grapples with these questions.

A recent contribution in the area is the book *Crimes of Obedience* (Kelman & Hamilton, 1989), which identifies social psychological factors that operate in individuals who commit crimes under the direction of some higher authority. Another is Tyler's (1990) *Why People Obey the Law*, an incisive examination of psychological principles associated with legal behavior. The authors of each of these books try to understand why individuals both defy and conform to the law.

This book includes material relevant to all three relationships, but will focus on the **psychology *and* law model**. It is *not* a "how to" book, although it sometimes describes how psychologists do their work. It will not train you to testify in court, prepare a profile of a serial murderer, or decide which of two parents should be given custody of a minor child. It is a textbook designed to educate interested students about contemporary psychological knowledge that is pertinent to the legal system. It identifies unwarranted assumptions and misinformation about human behavior; but it also recognizes the limitations of psychological knowledge itself. The text's mission is to inform students about the relationship between psychology and law, encourage critical thinking about the two disciplines, communicate trends in psycholegal research, and suggest how the two disciplines might better understand and relate to one another.

The book requires the reader's basic understanding of the philosophy and methods of the behavioral sciences, because we will discuss many research studies applicable to the legal process. Despite the rapid growth of research in psychology and law, there is still a great need for well-designed and well-executed studies directed at the many legal assumptions about human behavior. There is an even stronger need for psychological theories which encompass and explain the results of this research.

Philosophy of Science

It is helpful to set the stage for a discussion of psychological research by touching on the philosophy of science. The work of philosopher Charles Peirce is instructive. Peirce outlined four general ways through which humans develop beliefs and knowledge about their world (Kerlinger, 1973). First, there is the **method of tenacity**, where people hold firmly to their beliefs about others because they "know" them to be true and correct, simply because they have *always* believed and known them to be true and correct. These beliefs are tightly embraced, even in the face of contradictory evidence: "I know I'm right, regardless of what others say or the evidence indicates."

The second way of knowing and developing beliefs is the **method of authority**. Here, people believe something because individuals and institutions in authority proclaim it to be so. If the courts over the years have said it is so, it is so. If a well-recognized and respected legal scholar makes an argument in favor of or against a proposition, that scholar's name is cited as authoritative evidence for the proposition's soundness or unsoundness. Education is partly based on this method of knowing, with authority originating from teachers, scholars, experts, and the "great masters" they cite. Elementary school children often quote the authority of their teacher as indisputable evidence in support of an argument; college students often assert, "It says so in the book." Attorneys cite precedence, the decisions of previous courts, to support their arguments. Tyler's (1990) research, however, suggests that this expressed allegiance to authority will not necessarily translate to action unless people believe in the legitimacy of the authoritative source.

The **a priori method** is a third way of obtaining knowledge. An idea is believed correct because "it only stands to reason" or because it can be logically deduced; experience has little to do with it. Parenthetically, the point of view that emphasizes *experience* as the way to knowledge is the *a posteriori* method, which—in Latin—means "from the most recent aspect or point of view." Early in the history of American Law, it was believed that judges or legislators did not make law, but were merely discovering the already existing law of nature, which inherently communicated what was right and wrong (Carter, 1979). Therefore, through logical thought and reasoned deduction, one would ultimately arrive at the universal truths of "natural law." Universal truths, such as what is fair and just, are believed by some to exist inherently in nature and in the minds of all of us, and are to be discovered through careful, logical thought.

The natural law argument has been replaced with a focus on **positive law**, sometimes referred to as "the law on the books." From this perspective, the logical thought and reasoned deduction results from research on primary sources, such as constitutions, court decisions, statutes, and administrative regulations. To a lesser extent, law is also derived from secondary sources, such as law reviews, legal treatises, social science journals, books, and other reference works. The *a priori* method based on positive law is the dominant approach to knowledge in the legal process. It is often tempered, though, by another line of reasoning, which emerged during the 1920s and 1930s as the legal realist movement (Melton, 1987) and which continues to have strong support today. The legal realist believes that cases should not be resolved exclusively *a priori*, or with reference to what happened in the past; rather, the law should take into consideration social reality. In other words, the law should be responsive to a society's needs and concerns at a particular time.

The fourth way of obtaining knowledge is the **method of science**, which is the testing of a statement or set of statements through observations and systematic research. On the basis of this systematic study, statements about natural events or processes are revised, reconstructed, or discarded. Science is an enterprise under constant change, modification, and expansion rather than an absolute, unalterable, fact-laden system. Science teaches us that there are few certainties in the natural world—only probabilities—and that we should base our decisions and expectations on "the best of our knowledge" at any particular time in history. The method of science is the dominant approach to obtaining knowledge in psychology.

Peirce's four methods of knowing provide a rough framework for determining the source of one's knowledge, and they will be useful guides throughout the remainder of the book. With the possible exception of the method of tenacity, each method has its place in the accumulation of knowledge, as long as we recognize which method we are using to obtain our knowledge and also understand the limitations of each. Authoritative sources and reasoning both are valuable contributors to our beliefs and opinions. The method of science, however, provides us with additional information about the "soundness" of our authoritative and logical knowledge, and it promotes a critical and cautious stylistic way of thinking about our beliefs.

Scientific knowledge, because it is based on systematic observations, hypothesis testing, and experiments, places itself permanently at risk of being shown to be incorrect, or **falsified**. It is constantly updated to account for observations and experiments, and it attempts to make predictions beyond our present experience. Ultimately, it seeks the underlying order of things. The method of science is a testable, self-corrective approach to knowledge that offers one of the most powerful sources available for the understanding of human behavior.

The science of human behavior has not been easily integrated into the legal system. Although psychologists and other social scientists began consulting with courts around the turn of the twentieth century, the first case where social science played an important role in the U. S.

Supreme Court's analysis, *Brown v. Board of Education*, did not occur until 1954 (Hafemeister & Melton, 1987). Even in this case, wherein the Court declared that "separate but equal" schools for African-Americans and whites were inherently unequal and therefore, unconstitutional, the extent to which the Court actually relied on the social science research brought to its attention remains a matter of scholarly debate (Hafemeister & Melton, 1987).

Basic Premises of Psychology

People hold many assumptions about human behavior, and the science of psychology tries to test the validity of these assumptions. Many forms of behavior have come under its scrutiny. An experimental or empirical psychologist studies organisms to understand, predict, and control (or, in the case of humans, to help them to control) their behavior. The methods of study vary greatly, from simple, direct observation in natural environments to complex experimental manipulations in laboratory settings.

THE EXPERIMENTAL METHOD

Many psychologists are convinced that human behavior can best be understood if researchers use the **experimental method**, which requires careful control and measurement. Often, these research psychologists bring the phenomenon to be studied into the laboratory, where conditions can be manipulated, monitored, and controlled, where many possible extraneous factors can be discarded, minimized, or accounted for.

One such experiment was conducted by a group of research psychologists (Davis, Kerr, Atkin, Holt & Meek, 1975), who wondered how the size of a jury affected its final decision. Traditionally, juries in England, Canada, and the United States comprise twelve persons, who are usually required to arrive at a unanimous decision. In the 1960s, states began to experiment with smaller jury sizes and with majority verdicts, especially in civil cases (Kalven & Zeisel, 1966; Wrightsman, 1977). Other countries regularly use trial juries of fewer than twelve persons (Saks & Ostrom, 1975).

Davis and his colleagues (1975) designed an experimental situation that simulated trial conditions, or a "mock trial" as it is called in the research literature. Various six- and twelve-person "juries" listened to a tape recording that contained an abbreviated version of the transcript of an actual trial. Some of the juries were instructed to come to a unanimous decision regarding guilt or innocence; other juries were told they must reach a two-thirds majority decision within the same time period. The twelve- and six-person juries generally arrived at the same decision (the defendant was found not guilty) whether or not they were forced to unanimity. The juries differed in group process, however. Specifically, unanimous juries (both six- and twelve-person) needed a larger number of poll votes and longer deliberation time before reaching a verdict. On the basis of this experiment, the researchers concluded that jury size does not appear to affect the final verdict, but does affect the length of time and the manner of arriving at the final decision. It is not clear, however, whether studies using simulated juries are generalizable to actual jury decisionmaking. We will cover this issue when we discuss a wide range of similar research on juries in Chapter 7.

QUASI-EXPERIMENTAL DESIGNS

Realistically, many real-world questions cannot be subjected to the experimental control and general confines of the laboratory. With respect to actual jury deliberations, for example, researchers cannot participate in or observe what goes on in the jury chamber. Nor can they assign real jurors deliberating a case to various conditions (say, by giving them different sets of jury instructions). The situational and juror demographic variables are beyond their control.

Researchers then must use designs that allow them to study subjects outside their direct control and to examine already existing conditions. These are called **quasi-experimental experiments**. For example, let's say a biopsychologist wants to examine the effect of lowering the legal level of blood alcohol content (BAC) for DUI on fatal traffic accidents. A "pure experimental method" would require a laboratory setting where subjects' blood alcohol level was manipulated and simulated driving scenarios were set up—to the point of permitting a fatal accident! Obviously, this is out of the question. The more realistic method is to work outside the laboratory, by: (1) examining a state law which lowered the BAC levels; (2) finding the number of fatalities that occurred *prior* to its enactment (pretest); and (3) comparing that to the number of fatalities that occurred *after* the law was enacted (posttest). The researcher also will try to control for other factors that may have affected the fatality rates, such as time of year or changes in sentencing laws. The method is not perfect, because the researcher cannot control for all other factors that might have affected the fatality rates. Thus, the quasi-experimental design is a pragmatic approach to research in an effort to collect the best data under less-than-ideal conditions (Leary, 1991).

SURVEY RESEARCH

Survey research involves obtaining information about people by asking them well-prepared questions, either orally or on written questionnaires. These questions ask respondents about their attitudes, beliefs, and typical ways of acting in various situations. Survey researchers almost always use sampling techniques, because it would be prohibitively expensive to question everyone in the population being studied. Thus, the researcher obtains a representative segment, a sample, through the process of randomization. Randomization ensures that each person in the relevant population has an equal chance of being selected for an interview.

Survey research is used more extensively by sociologists, political scientists, and economists than by psychologists. However, such research can be very helpful to psychologists trying to determine characteristic beliefs and attitudes of certain populations. Psychologists interested in the effects of pretrial publicity on jury verdicts, for example, may survey public opinion following news coverage of a case soon to go to trial. Constantini and King (1980, 1981) surveyed Californians about their knowledge of and attitudes toward three criminal cases. They found that respondents with greater knowledge were more likely to favor the prosecution (Carroll et al., 1986). In fact, they learned that this pretrial information was the strongest predictor of a respondent's decision-making about the case, regardless of other demographic or attitudinal characteristics. We cannot assume that the same effects would occur in an actual trial situation, however. In Chapter 10, we will discuss more research on the effect of pretrial publicity on juror decisionmaking.

VALIDITY

Psychological research deals extensively with the question of **validity**, which asks, are we measuring what we claim to be measuring? It is different from the question of reliability, which asks, would we get the same results if we used different examiners or if we measured this next week? Of the two concepts, validity is the more critical. Think of a yardstick on which the space intervals between the lines are not accurate. This yardstick is reliable: different persons using it would obtain the same measurement, and the same measurement would be obtained over different periods of time. It is not a valid instrument, however.

In psychological research, validity is subdivided into many forms, which will be discussed in Chapter 2. For the moment, we should distinguish between **external validity** (also called **ecological validity**) and **internal validity**. External or ecological validity refers to the degree of generalizability research findings have to other populations and other situations. Usually, the degree of external validity is approximated by conducting further research using different populations, at different times, and in different situations. External validity helps answer the question, to what extent can we safely conclude that these results remain consistent across time, place, and persons? (Note that we are not asking whether the methods we used to obtain the results would yield the same in other situations, which would be inquiring about reliability.) To use a jury research example once again, studies using video-taped re-enactments of actual court cases are likely to have more external validity than studies using a written description of a case and asking subjects to deliberate to reach a verdict, simply because they come closer to approximating reality. Recognizing this, University of Minnesota psychologist Steve Penrod has prepared a number of such videos for use in jury research. Therefore, although high external validity is difficult to obtain in the psychology and law area, efforts are continually made towards achieving it. It is important to do this, because the lack of external validity is a major reason for the conflicting and contradictory results commonly reported in the literature. Results in one study often do not generalize to another study trying to answer the same questions but conducted under a different set of circumstances.

Internal validity, on the other hand, deals with the level of confidence we can place in the results obtained in a particular study. In other words, how well done was the study? Did it have basic flaws in its design or in its data collection? Did it really address the question the researcher was trying to answer? Usually, the flaw is a **confounding variable** that makes it very difficult or impossible to conclude what explains the final outcome. A confounding variable is an extraneous variable that interferes with or clouds the research findings. For example, if we are interested in determining how well a psychological test predicts differences in performance between men and women in law enforcement, we must be careful that the groups have received the same kind of training. We must also be sure that their performance is evaluated using the same criteria. If we did not control for these training and evaluation variables, it would be foolhardy to assert that any performance differences between the two groups could be attributed to gender. In this example, training and evaluation become confounding variables.

Both external validity and internal validity are important criteria to use in determining the value of psycholegal research, and we will encounter them repeatedly as we review the research throughout the book. We should be aware, however, that the legal system sometimes uses the term "validity" in a different way than psychology uses it. As Schuller and Vidmar (1992) note, when courts ask whether psychological information is valid, what they really want to know is whether it is reliable. This is but one example of the numerous inconsistencies in vocabulary which challenge the student of psychology and the law.

Research Strategies

EVIDENCE

The psychologist-philosopher Joseph Rychlak (1968) posits that psychologists gather two types of evidence to help them arrive at knowledge and theories about human behavior. Evidence procured by using experimental methods is called **validating evidence**. It is the evidence or knowledge gained through careful, controlled research. A second type of evidence, most often gathered by

1.2: *VALIDITY AND RELIABILITY OF AN EQUIVOCAL DEATH ANALYSIS*

THE FOLLOWING MATERIAL WAS TAKEN FROM an article by Norman Poythress, Randy K. Otto, Jack Darkes, and Laura Starr that appeared in the January 1993 issue of *The American Psychologist.* The interested reader is urged to read the original article for a more complete description of the issues involved.

In 1989, a powerful explosion aboard the USS *Iowa* killed 47 persons. The U.S. Navy promptly began an intensive investigation to determine its cause, finally concluding that the explosion was caused by one person, Clayton Hartwig, who also died in the tragedy. During the investigation, information about Hartwig's habits, aspirations, lifestyle, and personality was gathered from his friends, family members, and shipmates. This information was turned over to the National Center for the Analysis of Violent Crime, a division of the Federal Bureau of Investigation (FBI), for a **reconstructive psychological investigation**, an attempt to develop a psychological image of a dead person (his or her personality, habits, intentions, dreams, motivations, lifestyle) while alive. The FBI prefers to call this process **equivocal death analysis** (EDA).

The U.S. House of Representatives Armed Services Committee, however, was not convinced that the conclusions reached by the Navy were the right ones and asked the American Psychological Association for help. The House Committee requested that the APA set up a panel of psychologists to provide independent evaluations of the Navy report and the claims advanced by the FBI. The APA panel found that the FBI "behavioral scientist experts" had told the House Committee, in absolute terms, that—through the mysteries of the EDA—they had concluded that Hartwig had acted alone and purposely caused the explosion. Most troubling to the APA panel was the absoluteness and conviction with which the FBI had presented its "facts." One of the special agents told the Committee that "... he could recall only three of forty-five cases (7 percent) in which he was unable to arrive at a conclusive opinion" (p. 9).

However, the APA panel could find no known research that has investigated the reliability or validity of the EDA. It is a method that appears largely based on speculation, hunch, bias, and perhaps folklore. In short, it appears to be largely based on the method of tenacity and has little, if any, scientific foundation. One of the special agents demonstrated a disturbing disdain for validity and science in general when he stated:

I certainly appreciate that wonderful academic approach to a practical problem. It is typical of what we find when we see people who have not had the experience investigating either crime scenes, victims, criminals and so forth in active, ongoing investigations...[I]n the field of psychology and psychiatry, there are existing raging arguments about the validity of the very techniques that exist. They won't be resolved in this world. So, to ask us to provide the validity is an exercise in futility (p. 9). ■

applied and clinical psychologists, is called **procedural evidence.** This is the information clinicians suspect to be correct based on their personal observations, assessments, and interpretations. Procedural evidence includes the elements of common sense, logic, and insight, and it results in a sense of conviction that a given hypothesis accounts for some observations and is useful. Clinicians have had considerable experience working with individuals in a clinical setting, and they use this expertise to form theory about human behavior. For example, police officers who have intervened in domestic disturbances have told clinicians it is wise to separate the disputants in a two-person confrontation (e.g., remove them to different rooms for a "cooling off" period). When one party is aggressing, however, very little validating evidence supports this practice (Sherman & Berk, 1984; Sherman, 1992). It is considered a temporary measure which does not solve the underlying conflict. Some research suggests that arrest of the offending party is a more effective measure for deterring him from future incidents (Sherman & Berk, 1984), but other research (Dunford, Huizinga, & Elliott, 1990) suggests that arrest is no more effective than separation or the officer's attempt at mediation. On the other hand, there is *procedural* evidence that both separation and arrest are effective if accompanied by additional intervention strategies, such as referring the victim to social services in the community and providing follow-up support.

The experiences of those working within the legal system and those who formulate policy, then, may also be considered procedural evidence. In this sense, clinical psychologists and professionals in other applied disciplines share common ground with participants in the legal system. Both gather procedural evidence. This shared method of science explains, in part, why judges and lawyers often prefer the testimony of clinicians to that of experimentalists.

The two types of evidence—procedural and validating—are interdependent in that they both contribute to our knowledge about human behavior. To reject one or the other severely limits the knowledge we can gain. Although it is sometimes difficult to draw a fine line between these two methods, because both may be methods of science, the distinguishing features between them are replicability and control.

REPLICABILITY

The method designed to gain validating evidence demands that the findings be replicable, or able to be repeated by others. **Replicability** requires that the descriptions of the variables studied and the procedures used to study them be precise and objective enough so that what was done is very clear. We sometimes call this "operationalizing." If researchers wish to study the effects of anxiety on test taking, for example, they must be extremely clear about what is meant by both terms (anxiety and test taking), and precisely what procedures and measurements were used to examine the relationship. These clear descriptions serve as checks on both external and internal validity and are required if the study is to be replicated.

CONTROL

Control refers to the attempts by the research to account for all variables with a potential influence on the relationship being investigated. For example, in the test taking anxiety study, the researcher must be certain that it is anxiety rather than some extraneous influence like intelligence, time of day, gender, age, or even room temperature that has a significant effect on test taking performance. These extraneous influences are called **secondary variables**. The researcher must also be careful to identify and measure the **independent** and **dependent variables**. The independent variable is the measure whose effect is being studied (in the above example, anxiety). The dependent variable (test performance), we might say, feels the effect. The dependent variable is the variable that is measured to see how it is changed by manipulations in the independent variable.

The independent variable in most scientific investigations is manipulated in a controlled fashion. In our example, the researcher might want to test the effects of three different levels of anxiety on test taking. This manipulation might require some procedure for inducing anxiety (however defined and measured), such as threatening the subjects with varying dire consequences for failing the exam. In one condition the subjects may be threatened with having to repeat the test in a much longer session, whereas in another they may be threatened by the knowledge that all grades will be posted. A third condition might involve no threat or consequence (potentially a no-anxiety condition), and individuals in this group would be considered the controls. The first two groups would be the **experimental** or **treatment groups**.

Procedural or clinical evidence may also be gathered in a similar manner, but in a majority of instances it is obtained with considerably less precise objective description and control. From a scientific perspective, its value rests principally in the hypotheses it generates. A **hypothesis** is a speculative explanation of behavior, and it implies prediction. In the domestic conflict situation referred to earlier, the procedural evidence that referral of victims to follow-up services is effective in preventing future incidents should generate a hypothesis that could be carefully tested through a controlled experiment.

Clinical Judgment Versus Statistical Prediction

The lines between procedural and validating evidence are often not as sharp as we have described them here. This point can best be illustrated by the long-standing debate over the predictive accuracy of clinical judgment—a form of procedural evidence—versus that of statistical or actuarial methods—forms of validating evidence. Clinical judgment is judgment based on professional and training experience. Clinically based predictions of behavior make use of social history, interviews, or other personal contacts, comments, and recommendations from others. Information from various psychological tests may or may not be included. This clinical material is then used to form an impression of what a person is like and how he or she might act in the future.

The **actuarial method** employs statistics to identify certain parameters about the person's background and behavior that have been found to be related to the behavior being predicted. These parameters might include age, measurable past behavioral patterns, gender, scores on psychological tests, and occupation. Once these parameters have been identified statistically, probabilities are offered, or critical cut-off points drawn, relative to the person's future behavior. This process is independent of the evaluator's personal bias or clinical intuition. For example, the actuarial method might predict, on the basis of background and past behavior, that an individual being considered for parole represented a 75 percent statistical probability of committing another criminal offense within two years. If the parole board has established an objective criterion that anyone with a 60 percent or higher probability will be denied parole, the actuarial method dictates a decision against parole. In ideal form, the actuarial method is highly objective and mechanical in both data collection and application. Realistically, however, subjective factors enter into many supposedly objective decisions. Prison records, for example, reflect not only the behavior of the inmate but also the discretionary exercise of power by correctional officers.

The conceptual difference between clinical judgment and the actuarial method also disappears, when the data collection and application become mixed. Hare (1985) and his colleagues (Hart, Kropp, & Hare, 1988; Serin, Peters & Barbaree, 1990; Hare, McPherson & Forth, 1988), have developed a "psychopathy checklist" which has been found to predict recidivism on parole. A prison psychologist might administer this test, but ultimately offer a clinical judgment based upon impressions garnered from interviewing the inmate and experiences with other similarly situated inmates in the past. Therefore, despite the carefully constructed test based on extensive research with accompanying statistical tables outlining accuracy probabilities in predicting recidivism, the psychologist's recommendation could be swayed by clinical hunch.

The opposite could also happen. Data collection might be predominantly clinical in nature, but the psychologist could ultimately rely on specific objective criteria in offering a prediction. For example, the psychologist might obtain vague responses to inkblots and other ambiguous stimuli or ask the individual to respond to hypothetical dilemmas (e.g., What would you do if you were on parole and got a chance to leave the country and start life over again?). However, in making a final recommendation, the psychologist might be swayed by the inmate's performance on the Psychopathy Checklist.

The debate over which method (in pure form) is superior in accuracy of prediction has existed at least since the mid-1920s (Sawyer, 1966). Thirty years later, Paul Meehl (1954, 1965) brought the controversy to the forefront. Meehl incurred the ire of many clinicians when he concluded, after surveying approximately two dozen studies comparing statistical with clinical predictions, that the statistical methods were clearly superior in predictive accuracy. Subsequent reviews (e.g., Mischel, 1968; Goldberg, 1968, 1970) also found that clinical wisdom was faulty when compared to objective methods of arriving at overall prognostic or diagnostic decisions. Yet, studies have shown that people have a remarkable disregard for statistical data when they make judgments about others (e.g., Kahneman & Tversky, 1973; Nisbett et al., 1976), preferring hunches, intuition, and case-specific information over statistical base rates and tables.

A series of three studies by Carroll (1980) illustrates this hesitancy to use statistical information. Carroll presented both actuarial data and clinical data to criminology students and actual parole board members and asked them to predict the likelihood that offenders would commit another crime while on parole. The actuarial data were base rates representing the probability of recidivism, such as "25 percent of these parolees committed another crime" or "75 percent of these parolees committed another crime." The clinical data were case descriptions such as those available to parole boards. The descriptions were presented in such a way that subjectively each parolee would be given a 50 percent chance of committing a new crime.

Carroll's first two studies indicated that both students and parole board members made their decisions based on the clinical, rather than the statistical information. That is, whether they were given a 75 percent probability rate or a 25 percent probability rate, the decisionmakers still gave the offenders a 50 percent chance of committing a new crime. A third study, however, indicated a greater use of statistical information. Carroll attributed this to the emphasis placed on the base rates; that is, the numerical and risk statements were reinforced with the presentation of each case, thereby increasing their saliency. The Carroll data demonstrated that decisionmakers do not have an aversion to actuarial data and will use such information if it is offered as directly related to the individual presented for judgment. We should note, however, that the external validity of the Carroll studies may be limited, because at no time were the subjects making real, life-affecting decisions.

As Carroll (1980) has noted, actuarial decisionmaking guides have been available to the criminal justice system since the 1920s, but were rarely used. In the late 1970s and 1980s, however, they came into vogue (Gottfredson & Tonry, 1987), particularly in predicting success on bail or on parole. Glaser (1987, p. 265) notes that "published studies in the criminal justice field have ... always found statistical predictions more accurate than case study predictions for the same samples of cases." Glaser himself had led the way with a call for a new approach to predict success on parole (1954) and development of prediction tables (1962). Yet statistical tables were not widely used until they were developed collaboratively by researchers and the officials who would use them (Glaser, 1987). This again reinforces the importance of taking into account both validating and procedural evidence.

Numerous legal questions have been raised about both statistical and clinical decisionmaking. Tonry (1987), who has summarized them concisely, believes the troubling issues are more ethical than legal, however. Courts have given wide berth to official actions based on prediction. "There are virtually no constitutional impediments to the use of prediction and classification devices in the criminal justice system.... The absence of controlling statutes and constitutional doctrines means that analyses of the appropriateness and use of predictions and classifications may be phrased in ethical and policy terms" (1987, p. 382–383).

CLINICIANS AND RESEARCHERS

The evidence-gathering distinction between clinicians and researchers within psychology parallels differences in their work settings and, to some extent, in their goals. Researchers are generally affiliated with universities as professors and researchers, or with various research institutions and laboratories. Both federal and state agencies and the private sector also make extensive use of experimental psychologists. The Federal Aviation Agency (FAA), for example, employs psychologists to test the effect of illumination on the readability of control panel dials. Corporations which market products to the general public employ them to test the effect of various advertising approaches.

Clinicians also may be affiliated with industry, often to offer consulting services in employee selection or counseling. Most, though, are in private practice or are associated with mental health agencies, court clinics, correctional institutions, law enforcement agencies, and social service agencies. Researchers and clinicians who specialize in various aspects of the law often call themselves "forensic psychologists." Although this is a generic term, those who work closely with law enforcement agencies usually prefer to be called **police psychologists** and those working in corrections prefer the title **correctional psychologist**. Increasingly, then, the term **forensic psychologist** is reserved for those who interact primarily with the judicial system. We will apply the terms in this manner throughout the text. The term forensic comes from the Latin word *forensis*, which literally means "of the market or forum." The word derives from the public forums of ancient Rome where the law courts were commonly held.

Clinical psychologists have a practical goal: to determine the nature of a problem and to develop an effective way of solving it. The police psychologist may be faced with developing a workable, valid method for the screening and selection of police candidates. The forensic psychologist may evaluate defendants for criminal courts or be asked by a law firm to advise its partners how to select a jury most favorably inclined toward their client. The correctional psychologist may provide psychological treatment for inmates or help in classifying them for both custody and treatment purposes.

Researchers, who are almost always psychologists at colleges and universities, have a more generalized goal, one common to all sciences: to amass enough knowledge about a phenomenon to be able to understand and predict it, with an accuracy rate substantially above chance. A researcher studying aggression in the laboratory tries to understand it enough to be able to predict when it will occur. Ideally, clinicians use the information obtained by the researchers, add it to their own procedural evidence, and also attempt to make predictions.

Before 1988, most psychologists in the United States were members of the American Psychological Association (APA), totalling 67,000 members. However, goal differences between researchers and practitioners (clinicians) prompted many of the researchers to form their own organization in 1988, the American Psychological Society (APS).

RESEARCH AND THE LEGAL SYSTEM

Researchers and clinical psychologists both have much to offer the legal system, as long as their information is presented accurately and with appreciation for the complexity inherent in human behavior. The **legal system**, as we are using the term here, refers to courts, both civil and criminal, law enforcement agencies, corrections, and a wide array of administrative agencies. Psychology's contributions will encompass not only direct services to the system but also relevant knowledge in such areas as group behavior, the ability to make decisions, personality typologies, stress, the causes and prevention of crime, and the treatment and remediation of criminal behavior. It is important to note that our legal system does not operate in an organized, sequential, and coordinated manner. Like many other "systems," it is plagued with disorganization, conflict, and ambiguity. On the other hand, the parts of the system are interdependent, and efforts to achieve some degree of organization continue.

Psychological Theory

As we noted earlier in the chapter, one of the frustrations of doing research in psychology and law is its lack of an anchor, which is partly due to the paucity of theories behind which to rally. Often we find a mass of studies in a given area with no unifying theme. Yet the basic goal of psychological research is theory development, not the unsystematic accumulation of facts. As the philosopher of science Thomas Kuhn (1970) observed, scientific history does not support the contention that science is doing research for its own sake without theoretical commitment. Scientific development depends upon at least "some implicit body of intertwined theoretical and methodological belief that permits selection, evaluation, and criticism" (Kuhn, 1970, pp. 16–17).

A **theory** is "a set of interrelated constructs (concepts), definitions, and propositions that present a systematic view of phenomena by specifying relations among variables, with the purpose of explaining and predicting the phenomena" (Kerlinger, 1973, p. 9). **Psychological theory**, therefore, purports to explain and predict human behavior. It offers a general explanation that systematically connects many different behaviors. Moreover, "a theory which is not refutable by any conceivable event is nonscientific" (Popper, 1962, p. 36).

Therefore, as a scientific explanation of behavior, a psychological theory must be able to be tested and falsified. The terms in any scientific theory must be as precise as possible, with their meaning and usage clear and unambiguous. Vague and imprecise theories are not falsifiable and hence cannot be tested scientifically. The advantage of vague theory is that it can live on, on borrowed time, without running the risk of being tested and found inadequate. Freudian and neo-Freudian theories are good examples, because they cannot be refuted by the methods of science. How can one "disprove" the existence of the unconscious, the basic element of Freudian theory? The concepts in Freudian theory, then, can remain unchallenged by empirical data. Testable theories, on the other hand, draw heavy empirical scrutiny and critical comment; many fall by the wayside, and nearly all experience extensive revision.

As a result, scientifically powerful and heuristic theories which have the capacity to lead us toward explanations and predictions of behavioral phenomena are under constant revision and reconstruction. To the lay person, they appear fragmented and complicated, and they communicate excessive tentativeness and caution. Untestable theories, on the other hand, offer generalizations which may provide insight into human dilemmas, but they are more philosophical than scientific exercises.

The position taken in this book is that the avenue toward explanation and prediction is paved with scientific theory, which promotes experiments, evaluation, and criticism. The development of scientific theory represents the greatest challenge to psychologists studying the legal system today.

Psychologists and Psychiatrists

In the pages ahead, we will review briefly how psychologists interact with the legal system and some of the problems connected with the many roles they take. Prior to any discussion of these roles, however, we must examine the differences between psychology and psychiatry, the two main professions which try to understand human behavior at the *level of the individual*. Other disciplines, such as sociology and economics, try to understand human behavior too, but these fields concentrate on the influence of social factors on group and individual action. In psychology, the starting point is the individual; in other social sciences, the starting point is society and its forces.

■ 1.3: *JENKINS v. U.S.*

Selected *Amicus Curiae* Briefs

THE BRIEF SUBMITTED BY THE AMERICAN PSYCHIATRIC Association in Jenkins emphasized the extensive medical training of psychiatrists, training which made them uniquely qualified to offer diagnoses of the presence or absence of mental illness. By contrast, the psychiatrists told the court, psychologists may be highly trained, but they are competent in a very specialized area, which does not include mental illness. They also suggested that the role of the psychologist was to be a helpmate to the psychiatrist.

The American Psychological Association emphasized that psychology is an established science. The brief delineated the ethical responsibilities and the intraprofessional standards that psychologists are expected to embrace. Like the brief of the psychiatrists, the APA brief expanded upon the years of training that culminate in the Ph.D., in particular the Ph.D. held by clinical psychologists.

Following are excerpts from each of the briefs.

American Psychiatric Association

Psychiatrists traditionally have been called upon by our Courts to give expert medical testimony concerning mental illnesses, the productivity thereof and their effects.

The question of whether a person not trained in medicine, not a Doctor of Medicine and *not* a doctor trained as a specialist in the diagnosis, treatment and care of the mentally ill, can qualify as a *medical* expert and give expert *medical* opinions concerning the diagnosis of specific mental diseases and the *medical* effects thereof is of grave concern to psychiatrists and their Association….

The clinical psychologist, like "teachers, ministers, lawyers, social workers and vocational counselors," all utilize their skills as aids only to the psychiatrist in his medical diagnosis, care and treatment of the mentally ill….

Reduced to simple terms, clinical psychology "remains simply one of the possible methods" to be selected by the psychiatrist in evaluating and treating a specific mental illness. Its use in any specific case is for the psychiatrist to determine….

While they (psychologists) are skilled in psychology, this does not qualify them to diagnose or to prescribe treatment and care for a specific mental illness. Traditionally, ultimate medical diagnosis, care and treatment for the mentally ill is reserved to the psychiatrist.

The American Psychiatric Association recognizes the clinical psychologist as a highly trained person in a special field of psychological examination. He can provide important relevant data, such as the result from M.A. and I.Q. tests, to the psychiatrist who has the final responsibility for medical diagnosis. But the psychologist, not being a qualified Doctor of Medicine with special training in the mental health field, cannot qualify as a medical expert in the diagnosis, treatment and care of the mentally ill.

American Psychological Association

From a scholarly discipline and science developed mainly in university centers, the result of psychological effort has become recognized as capable of application in many fields of activity….

The foundation stone, however, of all developments of the field continues to be a rigid adherence to the principles of science, to a belief in the value of empirical evidence and verification, and to the development of appropriate theory. These are some of the processes which differentiate the sciences from other approaches to the understanding of human behavior….

It is submitted that psychology in its present state of development is clearly an established science and…psychologists are clearly engaged in the practice of an established profession. It would obviously be foolish to assert that any psychologist is testimonially competent to express an expert professional opinion upon all questions relating to the science of psychology. In fact, the Association would oppose any such rule as being contrary to the professional standards to which it and its membership adhere. It is submitted, however, that a psychologist is clearly competent under well-established rules of evidence, to testify as an expert upon matters within the scope of his professional experience….

In the diagnosis of mental disease and mental defect, including the formulation of professional opinions as to causal relationships between mental disease or defect and overt behavior, a principal tool of the clinical psychologist is found in psychological tests….

Infallibility is not claimed for any psychological test, and no professional psychologist would assert that he could reach a valid diagnosis upon the basis of test results alone. However, the use of test results, in conjunction with a review of a person's history and evaluative interviews, can be extremely useful to the clinical psychologist in reaching informed opinions as to the nature and existence of mental disease or defect in a given subject and as to the causal relationship or lack thereof between such mental disease or defect and the subject's overt behavior. ■

Psychiatrists, like psychologists, are closely associated with law, primarily from a clinical perspective. In some areas, such as issues relating to insanity, psychiatrists are more visible than psychologists. Law-related research, however, tends to be conducted much more by psychologists. It should be emphasized that the following presentation is an *abbreviated* sketch of the two disciplines and their perspectives.

Clinical psychologists, along with psychiatrists, are trained to provide direct services to persons with emotional or behavioral problems. The "problems," of course, may be relatively minor and transitory; in fact, it is estimated that the vast majority of adjustment problems faced by individuals can be solved in relatively short time. Psychologists, especially clinical psychologists, are often confused with psychiatrists in the public mind. The distinction between the two fields is an important one to make, because a difference in fundamental approach will mean that the same problem is viewed differently and that alternative solutions may be found.

Psychiatrists are medical doctors (M.D.s) who specialize in behavioral disorders rather than physical illness. The American Board of Medical Specialties (ABMS) recognizes both a general specialty certification in psychiatry and two subspeciality certifications, child psychiatry and geriatric psychiatry (Zonana, Crane & Getz, 1990). As yet, there is no certification for a subspecialty called **forensic psychiatry**, although there are active attempts to get it recognized by the ABMS. A psychiatrist has experienced the rigors of three or four years of medical school followed by a four-year psychiatric residency, with training in the handling of psychiatric patients. The specific requirements of the residency depend on state, institutional, and professional standards, and to some extent on personal preference. All residencies, though, must include some education in law and psychiatry. Psychiatric residents also become familiar with the legal regulation of psychiatric practice, and learn to perform emergency certification for mentally disordered individuals who require involuntary hospitalization (Zonana, Crane & Getz, 1990). Traditionally, the training adopts the **medical model** approach to diagnosis and treatment, including strong reliance on drug treatment. This orientation is not surprising, considering the fact that medical school training has been in the basic biological sciences, such as anatomy, biochemistry, physiology, genetics, microbiology and cell biology (see Box 1.3).

According to the medical model, psychological abnormality is analogous to physical disease, and like physical disease, it is classified and treated. Thus, we get the term "mental *illness*." The many classifications are published in the "bible" of the psychiatric profession, its Diagnostic and Statistical Manual (DSM). The classifications are revised periodically and new disorders are added (see Box 5.2).

Exclusive reliance on the medical model has waned, however. While many practicing psychiatrists do not subscribe to the medical model approach, a sizeable number do accept some diagnostic categories as disease categories and treat the behaviors as symptoms of a mental disease, often through the use of psychoactive drugs, which exert a direct influence on the brain. As we will note at various points in the text, administration of these drugs over the objections of the patient is an important legal issue.

Psychology as a Profession

In 1991, there were over 500,000 psychologists worldwide, twice the number reported in 1980 (Rosenzweig, 1992). Most of the psychologists in the world are practitioners who are concerned with the application of psychology to human problems. Only 62,000 to 82,000 psychologists report research as their primary or secondary work activity, and this number is dropping significantly

■ 1.4: *GRADUATE TRAINING IN PSYCHOLOGY AND LAW*

JOINT PROGRAMS IN SOME ACADEMIC AREA AND LAW were established in the 1960s, allowing students to pursue a degree in law (Doctor or Jurisprudence, abbreviated J.D.), while simultaneously completing requirements for a graduate degree in another area, such as business, education, economics, and psychology (Hafemeister, Ogloff, & Small, 1990). The first Law and Psychology graduate program began at the University of Nebraska in 1974, and has persisted as the largest and most diverse program in the field (Melton, 1990). Eight other programs followed: Johns Hopkins Department of Psychology and the University of Maryland Law School (established in 1979), Hahnemann University Department of Mental Health Services and Villanova College of Law (1979), University of Arizona (1981), Stanford University (1982), University of Hawaii (1989), the University of Minnesota (1989), Widener University and the Delaware School of Law (1989), and the Northwestern University Law School and Northwestern Medical School (1990). The Widener-Delaware program awards the Psy.D. and the J.D. All the others award the Ph.D. (usually in Clinical Psychology) and the J.D. The prospective student in all the psychology and law graduate programs must be admitted to *both* the law school and the department of psychology. The University of Denver and the Catholic University of America offer a combined J.D.-Master of Arts (psychology) program. Of the nineteen who received the combined J.D.and Ph.D. degrees at Nebraska prior to 1990, six work currently within colleges and universities, three in private research centers, seven in public service, and three in private practice (Melton, 1990).

At this writing, only six universities offered graduate programs specifically in forensic psychology, most of which have a discernible slant toward corrections. Two are in Canada. Queen's University in Kingston, Ontario, offers a Ph.D. with a specialization in forensic psychology and correctional psychology within the clinical program that prepares students to become scientist-practitioners in the judicial, forensic mental health, and correctional systems. Queen's also offers a Ph.D. within the basic and applied sequence that prepares students to conduct program evaluation and research as well as provide psychological services to the criminal justice system. The other Canadian university is the University of British Columbia at Vancouver. In the U.S. the University of Alabama and Florida State University offer a Ph.D. with a strong emphasis on correctional psychology. At least eight universities offer a Ph.D. in psychology with a *concentration* in psychology and law: Simon Fraser University at Burnaby, British Columbia, State University of New York at Buffalo, the University of Kansas, the University of Kentucky, the University of Nebraska at Lincoln, the University of Illinois at Chicago Circle, Northwestern University, and the University of Virginia. The John Jay College of Criminal Justice of City University of New York offers a master's degree in Forensic Psychology. ■

(Rosenzweig, 1992). In the U. S., only 35,000 psychologists said they were involved in any research as of mid-1992.

Most of the psychologists in the U. S. and Canada have doctorate degrees. The vast majority have Ph.D.s, while others have the Psy.D. (Doctor of Psychology), a degree that concentrates more on the applied aspect than the research aspect of psychology. The median number of years of full-time study from the baccalaureate to the doctorate in the U. S. is 6.9 (Nixon, 1990).

The practitioners of applied psychology can be roughly subdivided into three specialties: clinical, counseling, and industrial-organizational psychology. A fourth specialty, **forensic psychology**—the application of psychological knowledge to the judicial system—is emerging, but there are still few graduate programs currently offering specific training in that area (Melton, 1987) (see Box 1.4). The American Board of Professional Psychology does award certification as a Diplomate in Forensic Psychology. This certification attests that an established organization of peers has examined and accepted the psychologist as being at the highest level of excellence in his or her field of forensic practice. The specialty is both clinical and research in orientation. Therefore, practitioners who regularly do psychological assessments for the court as well as researchers who frequently testify in court on various psycholegal issues are called forensic psychologists. As noted earlier, psychological practitioners within the law enforcement and corrections branches of the criminal justice system prefer to call themselves police or correctional psychologists, though some writers include them in the realm of forensic psychology.

Of the three specialties, clinical psychology is the most active in the legal system. The **clinical psychologist** generally has a Ph.D.—an academic degree requiring intensive study of research methods, psychological theory, assessment, and psychotherapeutic methods. In addition to academic training, the clinical psychologist typically experiences nine or twelve months of supervised internship in a clinical setting, where the theories and methods acquired in graduate training can be applied to human behavior problems. The **counseling psychologist** has received much the same training as the clinical psychologist, including the internship. In the past, the major distinction between the two was their focus. The counseling psychologist evaluated and treated adjustment problems, such as those relating to education, job, and personal relationships. The clinical psychologist evaluated and treated the more serious behavior problems. This distinction is rapidly becoming blurred, however, and there is now considerable overlap in their respective functions.

The **industrial-organizational psychologist** is routinely involved in personnel selection, human factors in machine and equipment design, executive development, consumer research, organizational working conditions, and retirement counseling. The training for this specialty usually involves a heavy emphasis on research design, statistics, knowledge of the research literature as it relates to organizations, and a one-year internship within a relevant organization.

Psychology and the Courts

Any of the specialties described thus far may include some contact with the judicial system. As we have noted, the forensic psychologist is most likely to have direct, day-to-day interaction with the courts. It is worthwhile at this point to comment upon what the science of psychology can offer the judicial system as well as on what it cannot.

Psychology cannot provide absolute truths or easy answers. Instead, it has many partial, often tentative answers embedded in probabilities. Research psychology is largely **nomothetic** as opposed to **idiographic** in scope. The idiographic approach emphasizes the intensive study of one individual. Nomothetic study focuses on the search for general principles, relationships, and patterns by examining and combining data from many individuals. Therefore, research psychologists are generally cautious in responding to questioners who demand simple, certain answers or solutions to complex issues. Moreover, the principles and theories proposed by psychology are confirmed only through the collection of consistent and supporting data, a process that is not only long and rigorous, but also punctuated by debate and competing interpretations. "History suggests that the road to a firm research consensus is extraordinarily arduous" (Kuhn, 1970, p. 15).

Courts, like psychology, are concerned with predicting, explaining, and controlling human behavior, but much of the relevant and extensive research available in psychology today is unknown to them, as well as to the legal system as a whole. Daniel Yarmey (1979, p. 10) notes that what Munsterberg, the first forensic psychologist, wrote in 1908 continues to hold today. Munsterberg claimed:

> The court would rather listen for whole days to the "science" of handwriting experts than allow a witness to be examined with regard to his memory and his power of perception…with methods…of experimental psychology. It is so much easier…to be satisfied with sharp demarcation lines… ; the man is sane or insane, and if he's sane, he speaks the truth or he lies. The psychologists would upset this satisfaction completely.

Courts, however, look for simple facts which are directly and specifically applicable to the case at hand. To some extent, the psychologist can provide some of these facts. For example, she or he can testify that a defendant achieved a certain score on a psychological test, that the psychologist has treated a defendant for a mental disorder, or that a child displayed distrust or fear of an adult. Many facts that the psychologist can testify to, however, are facts about research findings to date. Because of the complexity of human behavior and the nature of the scientific enterprise, however, these are necessarily tentative. Even more difficult is the issue of opinion testimony, which courts often seek from those who are recognized experts in their field. They might ask, for example, whether a person will be a good parent or whether an offender will be dangerous. Rarely can psychology provide these answers with a high degree of certainty.

The judicial process demands certainty, or at least the appearance of it, in the courtroom. Because scientific hypotheses and generalizations are not conclusive, they are held suspect by professional participants in the legal system. Authoritative experts who offer certainty are much preferred over empirical psychology and its cautious approach. As we will see in later chapters, those psychiatrists and clinical psychologists who are willing to make absolute statements and to offer strong opinions and conclusions often are the parties invited to consult in both criminal and civil cases. Many mental health practitioners too often have testified in line with the court's wishes, without emphasizing the caution and tentativeness required in light of present knowledge.

THE ADVERSARY MODEL

Research psychology, directed by theory, arrives at "truth" and scientific knowledge through the accumulation of data derived from experiments that emphasize precision, measurement, and control of an array of variables that may contaminate outcomes. Law, on the other hand, embraces an **adversarial process**, which assumes that the best way to arrive at truth is to have proponents of each side of an issue present evidence most favorable to their position and uncover flaws in the other side's. The contenders confront one another in the courtroom, where truth is tested and refined through the "fight" theory of justice (Frank, 1949). It is assumed that justice will prevail once each side has had the opportunity to present its version of the evidence to the decisionmaker—the judge or the jury. It is assumed, also, that "objective" truth about human behavior cannot be acquired from any single source. Instead, different accounts are sought which, when put together, allow for judgment within an acceptable margin of error.

The adversary model presents problems for forensic and research psychologists. Not only does it concentrate on one case at a time, but it also encourages lawyers to dabble in and out of the data pool and pick and choose whatever segment of psychological information they wish to present in support of their position. The lawyer may select only part of an experiment and present the material out of context. Even in cross-examination, the opposing lawyer may be unaware of the real context or of contradictory findings. This procedure allows distortion and misrepresentation of research findings, since the lawyer's main concern is to provide the decisionmaker with evidence that will be favorable to the lawyer's client. Therefore, by using legal skill—but without having to appreciate the goals of science—lawyers can cite almost any psychological data in the service of their positions. The adversarial model relies not necessarily on truth, but on persuasion (Haney, 1980). Adversary proceedings have the advantage of avoiding the dangers of unilateral dogmatism, but we cannot forget that the essential purpose of each advocate is to outwit the opponent and win the case (Marshall, 1972).

Most psychologists agree that the most desirable role for the psychologist as expert witness is that of an "impartial educator" (McCloskey, Egeth & McKenna, 1986). Many experienced psychologists, however, contend that this role is extremely difficult if not impossible to maintain. There are always pressures from the attorney who hires the psychologist. Most psychologists who agree to be expert witnesses are hired by the defense (Konecni & Ebbesen, 1986). Even when psychologists are court-appointed and are acceptable to both sides (as might happen during pretrial proceedings), the presiding judge may press them to provide dogmatic, "yes" or "no" answers or to offer opinions against their better judgment. To some extent, a more representative view of psychological research can be presented to the courts during the appellate process, when the interested parties file briefs outlining in detail the evidence supporting their position. As we will note and discuss in Chapter 4, the American Psychological Association has been very active in this brief-writing process. The process makes it more likely that a deciding court will have all available information at its disposal.

Psychologists and Criminal Justice

The criminal justice system is a bureaucracy comprising interacting parts or subsystems—law enforcement, the courts, and corrections (Cole, 1992). It comprises all the institutions, agencies, and processes that deal with violations of the criminal law, and it is by far the most heavily studied component of the legal system.

Psychologists are being used increasingly in the various segments of this criminal justice system, but exact statistics are difficult to obtain. The American Psychological Association (APA) formed a Task Force on the Role of Psychologists in the Criminal Justice System, and in 1980 published the results of an extensive survey of 203 psychologists principally employed in criminal justice settings (Clingempeel, Mulvey & Reppucci, 1980). Most of the psychologists (67 percent) had doctorates and considerable postdegree experience (average of 10.9 years). The respondents were predominantly white males (98.4 percent). Most positions involved work with adults rather than with juveniles.

A majority of the psychologists surveyed offered indirect or direct services to correctional institutions (70 percent). Other services were offered to courts (46 percent), probation departments (41 percent), parole agencies (31 percent), community correctional agencies (25 percent), and police agencies (17 percent). Psychological assessment and treatment of offenders were the most frequently provided types of service (75 percent and 74 percent, respectively). Assessment included testing, status appraisal, or prediction of dangerous or antisocial behavior. Other significant services were consultation with administrators (53 percent), personnel training (53 percent), and personnel screening and selection for the variety of criminal justice agencies (21 percent). Below, for illustrative purposes, we discuss briefly the work of police and correctional psychologists.

POLICE PSYCHOLOGISTS

Consider the following three scenarios:

■ Police officers and their spouses are attending a workshop on police marriages and the stress that is unique to these relationships. Participants role-play situations they encounter in their marriages. A consulting psychologist leads the subsequent discussion.

■ A staff psychologist in a metropolitan police department is summoned to talk with a person threatening suicide. Later in the day, the psychologist provides therapy for a police captain becoming increasingly disenchanted with his job and home life.

■ A police chief decides not to hire a police officer candidate, partly on the basis of the results of psychological tests that pointed to potential behavioral problems.

The above examples underscore the need for the services and skills of psychologists in law enforcement. Police are the first-line participants in the criminal justice system. These officers are the agents who interview witnesses and interrogate suspects, gather a large portion of the evidence in criminal cases, and use their discretionary powers in making arrests and handling potentially dangerous situations. Moreover, police officers are more likely to be eyewitnesses to a crime and even to influence society about the concept of justice. Psychology would be remiss if it failed to study law enforcement with the goal of improving the quality of its participation in the legal process.

In a recent survey of police psychologists (Bergen et al., 1992), the psychologists reported that about 37 percent of their time was spent counseling police officers and their families, and 32 percent was spent screening and selecting police personnel. The remaining time was divided between training (stress management, training seminars, crisis intervention techniques) and organizational development (morale boosting, shift-work management, community awareness). Most respondents to the survey had a Ph.D. (90 percent), with the remainder having Ed.D., Psy.D. or M.A. degrees. Most of the Ph.D.s were in clinical psychology (65 percent). The annual income of the full-time police psychologists ranged from $30,000 to $86,000, with a median income of $62,000. The results of the survey suggested that police psychologists are extremely satisfied with their work. Interestingly, women expressed more satisfaction with the work than their male counterparts, and the number of women entering this specialty seems to be increasing.

CORRECTIONAL PSYCHOLOGISTS

The correctional system is divided into two main components, institutional and community-based corrections. The former is what most people envision when they think of corrections: a tightly controlled living situation behind walls. As we will note in Chapter 13, however, there is great variation in the physical features of correctional institutions. Community-based corrections refers to the supervision of offenders in the community. It encompasses probation and parole, together with their many variants. Persons on probation and parole, for example, may be living in their own homes or in half-way houses, and may or may not be electronically monitored.

Correctional psychologists work closely with inmates, probationers, and parolees, administering a wide variety of psychological assessment techniques (intellectual, personality, aptitude, vocational and educational), interpreting results, and preparing comprehensive reports. They are also involved in the development, organization, and administration of individual and group therapy and other rehabilitative programs for treatment of a variety of behavioral problems. Correctional psychologists also offer counseling services to staff, particularly correctional officers who are in most direct contact with inmates.

Research psychologists often study the psychological effects of correctional systems on prisoner behavior. Topics include the general effect of imprisonment on special populations of offenders, such as the mentally disordered or the elderly; the effects of crowding; the effects of isolation; and the outcome of various rehabilitative programs. Interestingly, psychologists in this setting are often criticized for aligning themselves with prison administrators or failing to acknowledge the detrimental effects of incarceration (Roberts & Jackson, 1991).

Psychologists have been active in many facets of the correctional system for a long time, much longer than they have been in the courts or in law enforcement settings, but their track record of successful change, particularly in the institution, has not been remarkable. This is partly due to the nature of the beast: the correctional system teems with overworked, underpaid, and sometimes undertrained personnel. Its institutions are often outmoded and overcrowded; the working and living settings can be depressing. Psychologists working under these conditions are often confronted with ethical dilemmas which challenge their commitment to rehabilitation. In Chapter 13, we will discuss these and other complex problems.

Nevertheless, there is ample evidence of the positive impact of psychology on the correctional system. Despite earlier pessimistic reports about the outcome of treatment programs, some forms of psychological intervention are documented to be effective (Gendreau & Ross, 1991). Psychologist Hans Toch and his colleague Kenneth Adams (Toch & Adams, 1989a, 1989b), for example, have demonstrated that psychologists working in the correctional system can help prisoners cope with their environment and take concrete steps toward positive change. Likewise, Ted Palmer (1992) has proposed new intervention models which offer hope to those who are convinced that psychological rehabilitation is an essential component of corrections.

PSYCHOLOGY AND CRIMINAL BEHAVIOR

The cause of criminal behavior is elusive. A review of the major literature in criminology reveals that, until recently, psychology was not integrated sufficiently into the approaches taken to crime prevention and the treatment of offenders. The literature was predominantly sociological or psychiatric in perspective.

The caution which is often seen in psychology's approach to law is especially apparent when we focus on the understanding of criminal behavior. While a good grasp of criminal behavior requires combined research from all interested disciplines and from the various schools of theoretical thought within those disciplines, there is little reason to leave the work primarily to sociologists, psychiatrists, anthropologists, and legal scholars. Psychology offers another dimension that can illuminate the scientific puzzle of criminal behavior. Furthermore, psychology has the potential to contribute to the development of laws and policies concerned with crime prevention as well as appropriate sanctions once offenses have been committed. What is the likelihood that "shaming" a white-collar offender by heavily publicizing his crime will be effective in deterring him from committing additional crimes, for example? What psychological factors are at work when an individual reacts to that shaming? Cognitive-social examinations of crime, such as these, will be emphasized in this book, not only because they offer a contemporary psychological viewpoint, but also because they recognize the many complexities and variables involved in any human behavior.

Summary and Conclusions

This chapter has introduced readers to the goals of the book and to psychology as the science of human behavior. We have seen that, with caution and with appreciation for the complexity of human behavior, the various segments of the legal system can benefit substantially from psychological knowledge. The book will consider separately psychology's potential contributions to each sector—law enforcement, the civil and criminal courts, criminal behavior, corrections, and institutional confinement.

The legal system is highly pragmatic, conservative, and traditional in outlook and process. This is because law cannot respond to every *zeitgeist* on the horizon; if it did, it would risk losing its cultural, traditional, and moral bearings. Innovation and excessive creativity would promote legal fluidity, which would wreak havoc with consistency, structure, and orderliness. This is particularly true of the judicial system. Those who prefer an activist judiciary, however, say these are but excuses to delay needed change. From this viewpoint, the conservatism of the law may be an impediment to social progress.

Interestingly, psychology is often viewed with suspicion and skepticism from both of the above perspectives. In fact, the legal system as a whole utilizes segments of scientific or empirical findings only if advantageous. Therefore, it is unrealistic to expect that the scientific contributions of psychology, as outlined in this text, will be embraced eagerly. What we can hope for is a slow, gradual acceptance of some of the information psychology uncovers, reports, and consistently supports through well-designed research.

The three possible relationships between psychology and law were outlined. The psychology *in* law relationship, the one most typical today, will do little to advance psycholegal research or integrate it into the system. Here, law dictates to psychology what it wants and when it wants it, and law proceeds to interpret the material as it wishes. Psychology *and* law, which presumes an equal partnership between the two disciplines, is best suited to the advancement of psychological knowledge in relation to the legal system.

Psychology and the law arrive at "truth" in decidedly different ways. Truth for psychology is gained through the scientific methods of hypothesis testing, sound methodological construction, quantification, systematic observation, and an attempt at objective interpretation of the data. "Truth" is, of course, an ideal which is seldom reached.

Law, by contrast, relies on the adversarial process to discover truth. The ambiguity of the law encourages participants to present their best case in a persuasive fashion. If the law were clear and concise, the adversarial process would be severely undermined. Lawyers selectively choose precedent and current folklore or science to build their cases and present their clients in the most favorable light.

Science rarely provides firm conclusions. The social sciences offer only segmented, partial answers to complicated, but intriguing puzzles of human conduct. Nevertheless, there is much cause for optimism. With patience and a very high tolerance for ambiguity, psychology can become an increasingly valuable source of knowledge for the law.

Questions to Ponder

1. What career choices can you identify for someone with both a Ph.D. in psychology and a J.D. in law?

2. Why do you think the courts prefer clinical prediction over actuarial predictions? Would you prefer a physician's diagnosis and prediction of a serious disease over a computer diagnosis and prediction? Why?

3. If you were defendant in a murder case in which you pled not guilty by reason of insanity, who would you want to testify as expert witness on your behalf, a psychologist or a psychiatrist? Why?

4. Psychiatrists have long argued that psychologists should not be allowed to testify in court on issues of mental illness. Why do you think this is?

5. Give some examples of psychology *of* the law and contributions this area may make in the future.

PSYCHOLOGICAL ASSESSMENT, TESTING, AND THE LAW

PSYCHOLOGICAL ASSESSMENT AND PSYCHOLOGICAL TESTING have become indispensable to the legal system. Note that the two terms are not synonymous. **Psychological assessment**, which also may be called psychological evaluation, refers to *all* the techniques used to measure and evaluate an individual's past, present, or future psychological status. It usually includes interviews, observations, and various measuring procedures which may or may not include psychological tests. **Psychological testing**, then, refers specifically to the use of psychological measuring devices. A child custody assessment or evaluation, for example, might include: (1) mental status and biohistorical interviews of the adults and minor child(ren); (2) psychological testing of the child(ren) and possibly the adults as well; (3) observations of the interaction among the adults and the minor child(ren); and (4) assessment of significant others (Weissman, 1991). As Matarazzo (1990, p. 1000) states: "Psychological *assessment* ... is engaged in by a clinician and a patient in a one-to-one relationship and has statutorily defined or implied responsibilities."

Psychological tests are the measuring devices which are but one component of the assessment process. Tests come in different formats and have specified goals. Some are designed to measure intelligence (the so-called IQ tests), while others try to define aptitudes, interest patterns, and personality.

In criminal law, assessment and testing are important in *five* major areas. First, they play a major role in the arrest and pretrial process, when a psychologist may assess the mental status of a detainee or evaluate a defendant's competency to waive legal rights, plead guilty, or stand trial. Second, when a defendant raises an insanity or a diminished capacity defense, evidence obtained from evaluations of his or her mental state at the time of the crime is crucial. Third, assessment and testing are used to help courts determine a defendant's dangerousness to self or others. Fourth, the victim of the crime, especially if that victim is a child, may undergo assessment and testing to introduce evidence that a crime did indeed occur. Fifth, assessment and testing may provide invaluable information in the sentencing phase of a criminal trial, particularly when the judge is interested in knowing about an offender's amenability to rehabilitation. In sex offense cases, for example, a judge might order the offender to be examined to see whether he would be a good candidate for a rehabilitation program.

In civil cases, psychological assessment and testing have long been used to determine whether individuals are able to care for themselves or are in need of psychological treatment. Courts today must make judgments about the need for involuntary confinement in a mental institution or for treatment services within the community. To make appropriate decisions, they turn to psychologists and psychiatrists for guidance. Heilbrun (1992) notes that psychologists are increasingly asked to assess competencies to consent to medical treatment or research and to enter

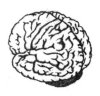

26

CHAPTER
TWO:
PSYCHOLOGICAL
ASSESSMENT,
TESTING,
AND THE
LAW

into a contractual relationship. They are participating in the disability determination process and the process of determining compensation for mental injuries. In family law, in addition to psychological assessment in child custody decisions, psychologists are consulted in abuse and neglect determinations and juvenile delinquency dispositions.

Increasingly, assessment and testing procedures are used to determine a parent's suitability as a custodian of minor children, to appraise a person's ability and capacity to make wills, or to determine an individual's eligibility for federal and state benefits on the basis of mental or emotional incapacity. Work-related personal injury litigation, through which plaintiffs seek compensation for an injury allegedly suffered on the job due to negligence on the part of an employer, is a rapidly growing area where assessment plays an integral part.

Personal injury suits need not be job related, of course. John Ziggle is an expert skier. At Killer Mountain, however, he loses control, allegedly because of exposed rocks on the trail, crashes into a tree, and becomes a paraplegic with substantial brain damage. John sues Killer Mountain, Inc., arguing that it was responsible for keeping the ski trail free of hazards. In cases such as this, the psychological assessment of brain injury and nervous system functioning—a field called **forensic neuropsychology**—has become almost indispensable (Doerr & Carlin, 1991). The forensic neuropsychologist, retained by the Ziggle family, examines John to evaluate the extent of his neurological disability and its long range effects on job opportunities and overall adjustment to society.

Neurological disabilities are not as straightforward as physical loss, such as the loss of a limb or an organ of sensation. Insurance companies have manuals already listing the usual compensation for the loss of a limb or eye. Neurological impairments, however, are far from clear-cut, and the assessment procedures are often expensive and time consuming. Part of the problem is that disability evaluators and insurance agents have little or no training in the recognition of neurological disorders (Glass, 1991). Another problem is that the psychological and cognitive changes are so subtle that they are sometimes difficult to detect.

Psychological assessment and testing are frequently used throughout the educational system, not only to measure intelligence and aptitude, but also to diagnose learning disabilities. They also appear in the screening and selection of personnel in business and industry, the military, and the criminal justice system. Some criminal justice agencies rely on psychologists to help make screening, selection, and promotional decisions. Law enforcement candidates and already employed personnel are often given psychological tests designed to depict their intellectual and emotional functioning. Metropolitan police departments have so far been at the forefront in studying and adopting such procedures, but there is a growing nationwide trend toward using psychological assessment in smaller and rural departments. The psychological assessment of correctional officers is less common, although there is little doubt that it could aid in the selection of competent, adaptable personnel.

The assessment and classification of prison populations has a history of mixed success (Gearing, 1979). Ideally, the psychological evaluation of prisoners should provide insights into the development and treatment of criminal behavior and some understanding of the psychological effects of short-term and long-term imprisonment. It should also help to determine and evaluate rehabilitative strategies.

This partial list of the various uses of psychological assessment illustrates its pervasiveness. Currently, we do not really know the amount or type of testing that goes on nationwide, particularly in forensic settings (Heilbrun, 1992). We must recognize, though, that there are numerous problems associated with assessment and testing in all of the areas discussed above, as will become clear in the pages ahead.

Generally, psychology's relationship with law *vis-à-vis* assessment is one of psychology *in* the law. Judges, lawyers, law enforcement, and correctional administrators use and interpret the information they have requested of examiners who are usually clinical psychologists and psychiatrists, seldom research psychologists. Some examiners, though, have such a long-standing, mutually respectful relationship with those who seek their services that the relationship could more accurately be termed psychology *and* the law.

Over the years, psychological assessment and testing techniques have generated a spectrum of social concerns and considerable legal scrutiny in both civil and criminal cases. In the civil arena, questions of unfair employment practices, discrimination, and invasion of privacy have been at the forefront. In criminal cases, the issue of self-incrimination has been extremely troubling.

One purpose of this chapter is to acquaint students with the many concerns society has or should have about assessment methods, particularly psychological tests. Another is to address misunderstanding about the strengths and weaknesses of tests and related procedures. The chapter is not intended to provide comprehensive information about specific assessment methods. It is merely a review, description, and evaluation of testing, including the major psychological concepts associated with it. Some of the more provocative issues surrounding the use of assessment within the legal system will be addressed.

Psychological Testing

Psychological tests have many limitations and flaws. If used properly, however, they can be important tools for evaluating intellectual functioning, measuring personality, and describing emotional or psychological status. Testing is a process of reducing the complexity of human behavior to a manageable set of variables, so that present behavior can be described and future behavior can be predicted. It is a complex enterprise, and procedures vary widely according to the population being tested and the preferred methods of the examiner. Testing basically involves the quantification of a *sample* of behavior obtained under standardized conditions, with the level of quantification and the degree of standardization varying from test to test. Some tests require a well-trained examiner and must be administered under such highly controlled conditions that they are similar to scientific experiments. Other tests are less standardized and may be given by an untrained examiner, sometimes to large groups.

There are approximately 2,000 different psychological tests on the market today. They may be grouped into eleven different categories, according to what they are measuring: (1) neuropsychological; (2) personality; (3) cognitive ability (intelligence); (4) educational; (5) achievement; (6) developmental; (7) reading; (8) sensory-motor; (9) speech and hearing; (10) vocational; and (11) the catch-all *other*, or unclassified category.

The four most important concepts to understand in psychological testing—and psychological assessment in general—are reliability, validity, normative distribution, and standard error of measurement. Any testing instrument should be judged according to each of those concepts.

RELIABILITY

Reliability refers to the consistency of measurement; a test is reliable if it yields the same results over and over again. A test's reliability may be measured in one of three ways. If different parts of the same test yield the same results, this is **internal consistency**. If the same test yields the same results when administered to the same person at two different times, this is **test-retest**

28

CHAPTER
TWO:
PSYCHOLOGICAL
ASSESSMENT,
TESTING,
AND THE
LAW

reliability. If the test produces the same results when scored or interpreted by different clinicians or examiners, it is high in **inter-judge reliability**. A highly reliable test will meet all three criteria, but in reality, psychological tests rarely produce the identical results again and again. A mathematical index, known as a **correlation coefficient**, is computed to determine the degree to which a test comes close to producing the same results.

The method of correlation was developed by Karl Pearson, a graduate student who sympathized with his mentor, Sir Francis Galton, a British scientist and statistician. Galton was trying to determine the relationship between the height of sons and fathers. He arranged their heights on a square table by using pins to represent each. The fathers' heights were on the x-axis and the sons' heights were on the y-axis. Once the pins were in place, Galton would stretch a silk thread diagonally across the center of the table until he thought the position of the thread approximated the middle point of all the data points represented by pins (Hull, 1928). These painstaking attempts to center the thread produced humorous contortions, with Galton alternately leaning over and sitting on the table. Once he had "eyeballed" the thread through the center of the pins, Galton would measure the angle by which the thread deviated from the vertical axis and then look up the tangent of this angle in a table. Since the tangent of a zero angle (angle showing no relationship) is zero, and since the tangent of the angle showing a perfect relationship is 1.00, these numbers made a decent index (or coefficient) of the magnitude of the relationship.

Suspecting that Galton's method was unduly difficult, Pearson developed the still-used mathematical formula for calculating the correlation coefficient, known as the Pearson product-moment coefficient of correlation, or Pearson's r.

Historical vignette aside, it is important to recognize a correlation coefficient as mathematical shorthand for describing the relationship one variable has to another. A correlation coefficient tells us two important things about a relationship: (1) its magnitude; and (2) its direction. The magnitude is expressed by a number (coefficient) ranging from .00 to 1.00, with 1.00 being a perfect correlation and .00 representing no relationship at all. You have probably had the experience of taking the Scholastic Aptitude Test (SAT), required for admission to most colleges and universities. If the correlation coefficient between the SAT and a student's subsequent GPA were 1.00, then we could predict with 100 percent accuracy a person's GPA on the basis of his or her score on the SAT. A zero correlation, on the other hand, would mean there was no relationship; that is, a person's SAT score would have no power in predicting GPA. Knowing the SAT score would produce no better prediction than guessing a student's GPA without knowing anything about that student. Reliability coefficients in the field of testing range somewhere between these two extremes. The actual correlation coefficient between the SAT score and subsequent GPA is believed to be approximately .50.

The correlation coefficient also communicates something about the direction of the relationship (same or opposite). Direction, expressed either by a positive (+) sign or a negative (−) sign, tells what happens to one variable if the other variable changes. If both change in the same direction, we have a positive correlation. Note, however, that the sign does not *specify* the direction. In other words, both variables could go down, but the sign would still be positive.

Let's continue to use SAT / GPA scores to illustrate. Assume the SAT / GPA correlation is +.80 (a higher than realistic correlation, as we have noted). This means either that high SAT scores predict high GPA or that low SAT scores predict low GPA. If the correlation is negative (e.g., −.80), we know that high SAT scores predict low GPA scores or that low SAT scores predict high GPA scores.

Psychological examiners prefer to use psychological tests that have the highest correlation possible (whether positive or negative). A test-retest reliability correlation of .90, for example, is usually regarded as solid evidence that subsequent administrations to the same individual would yield very similar results. Within legal contexts, it is not advisable to use a test with a test-retest reliability coefficient of less than .80 (Heilbrun, 1992). Generally, the lower the reliability, the poorer the validity. If the test is also high in inter-judge reliability and in internal consistency, the test has been well developed and solidly constructed.

When the attribute being measured is itself unstable over time, the correlation coefficient will be low. Compare, for example, measurements of intelligence and depression. Intelligence is expected to be a stable attribute over time. If Lucretia scores above average in December and below average in March, we can suspect that something is wrong with the testing instrument. If we were trying to measure a relatively unstable personality attribute like depression, however, we would expect to find different scores from one testing session to another. The fluctuations in scores would reflect mood changes or even significant life events that may have occurred between testing dates. Therefore, we would expect a relatively high correlation coefficient in the first example and a lower coefficient in the second, because of the differing nature of personal attributes being measured.

VALIDITY

The reliability of a test merely assures us that we have established a consistent procedure of measurement. Before a test can be meaningful and useful, however, it must also have **validity**, which tells us whether it measures what it is supposed to measure. For example, if a psychological test is designed to predict how well applicants will perform in law enforcement, we must have evidence that it in fact does predict this. If not, the test is meaningless, even though it may have very high reliability. Court decisions have barred the use of intelligence tests for the classroom placement of youngsters in school systems in Texas, California, and other states because they lacked demonstrated validity (Matarazzo, 1990; Elliott, 1987). They were not a "true measure" of a child's ability to succeed in a classroom setting. Despite a child's low score, he or she could do well if other factors, such as a teacher's special encouragement, were attended to. Although we discussed validity briefly in Chapter 1, we will study it in more detail here because it is *the* most important measure of testing. Like reliability, validity is usually expressed statistically through the computation of a correlation coefficient.

Among the more important forms or types of validity are concurrent and predictive, together called **criterion-related validity**. **Concurrent validity** is usually determined by comparing one test with another, already established one. For example, suppose we wished to determine whether a test we designed to predict success in law enforcement had concurrent validity. We would administer a test with an established track record of criterion-related validity and also administer our newly constructed test to a group of experienced police officers, and we would compare each person's scores on both tests. If the scores are similar, as determined by a high correlation coefficient (say, .80), we can conclude that our test has a high level of concurrent validity. Concurrent validity also may be established by determining whether our psychological instrument can obtain the same results as other, non-test criteria. For example, can the test results differentiate between poor and satisfactory police officers as rated by their supervisors? In this situation, we would correlate test results with on-the-job ratings provided by the supervisors. If the resulting coefficient is high, our test has good concurrent validity for distinguishing "good" police officers from "poor" officers.

Predictive validity is the degree to which a test predicts a person's subsequent performance on the dimensions and tasks the test is supposed to measure. If a test claims to be able to predict

30

CHAPTER
TWO:
PSYCHOLOGICAL
ASSESSMENT,
TESTING,
AND THE
LAW

which candidates develop into good or outstanding police officers, its predictive validity should be high, discriminating those who eventually perform well from those who do not. If there is empirical evidence that the instrument does have predictive validity, a test is a powerful device for the screening and selection of candidates prior to entry into law enforcement. Obviously, a device that could do this would save both the candidate and the agency valuable time as well as potential difficulty and embarrassment. For example, suppose we have a very high incidence of stress-related disorders within a particular group of police departments. The stress disorders are not only interfering with job performance, but also are resulting in a high turnover rate. In an effort to identify both the stressors and the individuals most prone to stress, the psychologist administers a battery of psychological tests before the officers are hired and follows them over a number of years, collecting supervisory reports, the officers' own self-reports on stress, and any other information pertaining to stress measures. The psychologist then correlates the pre-employment measures with reported and observed stress levels, paying particular attention to those officers who leave or who perform poorly on the job. If all goes well, the psychologist should be able to identify those tests that predict poor reactions (or good reactions) to stress, and use those tests in future screening of police officers for these departments. This same procedure can be applied to business and industry, identifying those who remain with the company and work out well and those who do not.

We should be careful to add a note of caution with respect to the above illustration, however. The best way to deal with stress among employees may not be to screen out ahead of time those who are most susceptible to it. Rather, the best way may be to improve working conditions, thus minimizing the opportunity for stress to appear. An important thing to remember about predictive validity, therefore, is that it predicts adaptability to the status quo, or to the situation as it exists. The ideal situation for productive employment may be quite different.

While psychometric (tests and measurement) experts have tried to perfect methods of establishing criterion-related validity, representatives of the legal system are often more interested in the issue of **content validity**. "Content-related validity involves essentially the systematic examination of the test content to determine whether it covers a representative sample of the behavior domain to be measured" (Anastasi, 1988, p. 140). In law enforcement, for example, it is recommended that the test content be related to what the officer will encounter on the job, thereby supposedly tapping pertinent skills found in traffic investigation or judgment and reasoning needed to handle domestic disturbances. In pre-trial situations, some defendants are administered tests to determine whether they are competent to stand trial. Some of the recommended tests ask the defendant to explain the judge's role and the role of the attorney.

When emphasis is placed on content validity in this way, the behaviors considered important must be fully described in advance, rather than defined after the test has been prepared. Further, as in the law enforcement context, successful behaviors specific to the various demands of the job must be identified and delineated. Often, this content-validation approach eliminates the use of standard psychological tests and replaces them with made-to-order tests that may be high in content validity but untested as far as reliability and criterion-related validity are concerned. In the area of assessing a variety of legal competencies, psychologist Thomas Grisso has made impressive strides in developing assessment instruments that are high in reliability, content, and criterion-related validity. There are obvious advantages to strengthening content validity, but care must be taken not to sacrifice the other criteria by which a test's strengths may be judged.

Very often, too, "face validity" is confused with content validity. Face validity refers not to what the test actually measures, but to what it *superficially* appears to measure (Anastasi, 1988). If a test "looks valid," or if it appears to measure what should be measured, it has face validity.

In reality, there may be no empirical support for these assumptions. Face validity does have some value, because examinees believe the exam is at least pertinent to the job for which they are applying. However, unless other types of validity are also ensured, a test has little overall worth.

So far we have considered criterion-related validity (both concurrent and predictive) and content validity. Many other types of validity are discussed in psychology, including ecological validity, temporal validity, substantive validity, structural validity, and as we noted in Chapter 1, external and internal validity. Two things are important to note about validity and its relationship to testing. First, it is a common fallacy that a significant relationship between a test result and a criterion is sufficient grounds for claiming the test is valid. Second, concurrent, predictive, and content validity under close scrutiny begin to merge into one fundamental form of validity, called **construct validity**.

To what extent does the test measure a theory or theoretical construct? This is the question with which construct validity is concerned. Many scholars in the field of psychometrics argue that construct validity is the most important determinant of a test's validity. As Guion (1977, p. 410) asserts: "All validity is at its base some form of construct validity … . It is the basic meaning of validity." Messick (1980, p. 1015) writes: "Construct validity is indeed the unifying concept of validity that integrates criterion and content considerations into a common framework for testing rational hypotheses about theoretically relevant relationships … . [It] provides a rational basis both for hypothesizing predictive relationships and for judging content relevance and representativeness." In essence, Messick is arguing that empirical relationships found between a test score and some isolated criterion do little to advance our understanding of the human processes underlying these test scores. Test results and their relationships to specific criteria, such as job performance or academic achievement, must be linked systematically to theory. "The simple demonstration of an empirical relationship between a measure and a criterion in the absence of a cogent rationale is a dubious basis for justifying relevance or use" (Messick, 1980, p. 1017).

Therefore, some authorities in the testing field argue that in order for a psychological test to be valid, it must do two things. First, it must demonstrate empirically established relationships between test scores and a behavioral criterion. Second, it must be built on theoretical constructs that explain the processes and personality structure it is attempting to measure. In addition to the empirical relationships found for concurrent, predictive, or content validity, therefore, true test validity requires the establishment of construct validity. The test should mean something. It should be linked to some theoretical rationale and explanation. Impressive correlation coefficients, standing alone, are not enough.

We should also realize that empirical verification of the reliability and validity for a particular test or assessment instrument may not be enough to convince a court of the soundness of the evidence it provides. For instance, when racial or gender discrimination is involved, a court may be inclined to disregard evidence obtained through the use of even well-validated tests (Heilbrun, 1992). Thus, the overall extended impact of the discrimination will outweigh the accuracy of the test itself. For example, in employment situations, even if the selection procedure is validated to screen out all the individuals who do not perform in an outstanding manner, a judgment may have to be made to allow otherwise-qualified minorities the opportunity to demonstrate outstanding performance. Also, for any kind of testing or assessment, there is always the danger that the instrument will provide an inaccurate or misleading representation of an individual, or groups of individuals. Finally, psychological tests should not be used by themselves to make decisions. The material they provide should be used in conjunction with other information.

32

CHAPTER
TWO:
PSYCHOLOGICAL
ASSESSMENT,
TESTING,
AND THE
LAW

NORMATIVE DISTRIBUTION

A test score by itself tells us little unless we know how other people have scored. Interpretation of results therefore requires that normative distribution—sometimes called norms—be developed before a test is put into general use. This is done by giving the test to a representative sample of the population for which that test is designed. The sample is called a **standardization** or **normative group**. The statistical position at which an individual scores within this normative group may be expressed in various ways, such as percentile rank or standard score. Knowledge about the standardization group is important because it enables the evaluator to determine if the results are generalizable to the individual or groups of individuals being tested.

STANDARD ERROR OF MEASUREMENT

Joseph Matarazzo (1990), in his Presidential Address to the American Psychological Association, warned that psychologists are increasingly being challenged on the concept of the standard error of measurement of their assessment tools when testifying in the courtroom. When potentially high damage awards are at stake in injury litigation, courts are keenly interested in how much error there is in a test score. Ironically, some are not so keenly interested when a person's liberty or even life are at stake in the criminal context.

The **standard error of measurement** (SEM), also called the standard error of a score, is an index of how much variation we can expect in a test score each time a person takes that same test. Let's assume that the SEM of a particular intelligence test is 5. If Lloyd receives a score of 110 on the test, the SEM informs us that we can expect Lloyd's score to vary between 105 and 115, 68 percent of the time or two out of every three times he takes the test.

Cognitive Assessment and Testing

When mental processes such as thinking, learning, perceiving, problem solving, and remembering are measured and evaluated, this is cognitive assessment. Ideally, the process combines interviewing, behavioral observation, and testing. Many cognitive "assessments," however, are more accurately called cognitive "tests," since they consist only of the use of an intelligence or IQ test.

COGNITIVE ABILITY TESTS (CATs)

One of the first reliable and reasonably valid cognitive ability tests was developed by the French psychologist Alfred Binet. In 1904, Binet and psychiatrist Theodore Simon were asked to design a test that could identify mentally defective children, who could then be taught effectively at a different pace than normal children. The resulting scale, consisting of thirty problems arranged in ascending order of difficulty, was called the Binet-Simon Scale. The test, which was revised shortly thereafter to establish satisfactory validity, attracted worldwide attention and was adopted and translated into many languages. In 1914, German psychologist William Stern suggested that Binet scores be expressed as a ratio of tested age (mental age score) over chronological age (actual age), multiplied by 100. A ten-year-old with a mental age of 15 would have an IQ of 150 ($^{15}/_{10} \times 100$), for example. Thus was born the intelligence quotient, known today as the IQ.

In America, L. M. Terman, a psychologist at Stanford University, revised and adapted the test to suit an American population. This revision became known as the Stanford-Binet. In 1985, an entirely new version of the Stanford-Binet was published. Items that were biased against ethnic groups or against males or females were replaced with neutral items. Traditionally, the Stanford-Binet was the most frequently used instrument to measure intelligence until clinical psychologist David Wechsler developed another group of cognitive ability tests (known as the Wechsler scales), beginning in 1939. The first version was known as the Wechsler-Bellevue Intelligence Scale, and it was primarily designed to measure the intelligence of adults. Later, Wechsler devised downward extensions of the Wechsler-Bellevue so that the intellectual functioning of children could also be measured. In 1955, the Wechsler-Bellevue was revised and renamed the Wechsler Adult Intelligence Scale (WAIS).

It should be noted that both the Stanford-Binet and the Wechsler series of scales have been updated and revised periodically, with the most recent versions having more culturally pluralistic norms. That is, the norms are based on a more representative sample of the general population, a feature that is not only right, but also very important to courts. The WAIS was revised in 1981 and is called the WAIS-R. The Wechsler Intelligence Scale for Children (WISC), first published in 1949, was revised in 1974 (WISC-R) and again in 1991 (WISC-III). The WISC-III is designed for ages six through sixteen. The Wechsler Preschool and Primary Scale of Intelligence (WPPSI), developed in the 1960s, is for children from four to six and one-half years old.

The Wechsler scales measure a wider scope of intellectual functioning than does the Stanford-Binet, which is primarily a verbal measure of intelligence. The Wechsler scales also tap both the verbal and behavioral components believed to be required in intellectual functioning. For example, the WAIS-R consists of eleven subtests, each of which is assumed to measure a particular ingredient of intelligence. Six of the subtests relate to verbal intelligence, while five are designed to tap behavioral or performance intelligence. Together, the eleven subtests provide a Full Scale IQ. The examiner is thus able to determine the Verbal IQ, the Performance IQ, and the Full Scale IQ. This approach treats intelligence as comprising a number of different abilities, rather than as one generalized ability.

Both the Stanford-Binet and the Wechsler scales are **individual cognitive ability tests**, designed to be administered to one examinee at a time by a highly trained examiner. Trained examiners are needed both because the standard of administration is complex and because behavioral observations add substantially to the assessment. Administration time varies, but the test is usually completed within one hour. Scoring, interpretation, and report writing usually take an additional two to four hours. Individual intelligence scales accordingly require considerable time and expense, features that have helped stimulate the less expensive, more efficient **group cognitive ability tests**.

Group tests generally are paper-and-pencil instruments devised to be administered to small or large *groups* of people. The convenience and economy of group tests have led to their use in schools and employment offices, in the selection and promotion of law enforcement personnel, and in many other mass-testing situations. The Otis Self-Administering Test of Mental Ability and the Army Alpha and Army Beta, developed during World War I to classify soldiers, are examples of the more commonly used group tests. Many other group cognitive ability tests have been developed. Among the more popular are the Otis tests, such as the Otis-Lennon School Ability Test; the Henmon-Nelson Tests; the Multidimensional Aptitude Battery; and the Cognitive Abilities Test (CAT). Administration, scoring, and interpretation usually do not require a highly trained examiner, and less interpretation and scoring time is needed than for individual tests.

While group tests provide a cognitive ability score generally comparable to individual tests (concurrent validity), they do not yield the rich behavioral observation and interpretation so characteristic of individual tests. Also, because of minimal face-to-face contact, the examiner has much less opportunity to establish rapport, obtain cooperation, and maintain the interest of

34

CHAPTER
TWO:
PSYCHOLOGICAL
ASSESSMENT,
TESTING,
AND THE
LAW

subjects, factors that may affect performance. Therefore, although group tests have undeniable advantages, their shortcomings cannot be overlooked. For thorough assessment, individual tests are more desirable, but because of their economy and practicality, group tests are administered more frequently. Most cognitive ability tests are designed to yield an average standard score of 100 and a standard deviation of about 15. A standard deviation is a statistical index that tells us how spread out the scores are around the average or mean score. An average of 100 and a standard deviation of 15 is based on the assumption that the population follows a normal distribution, where a majority of the examinees score somewhere around the middle and only a few score at the ends or poles of the distribution (see Figure 2.1). About 68 percent of the population falls between the IQ scores of 85 and 115. Approximately 95 percent scores between 70 and 130, and 99.72 percent between 55 and 145. A person who achieves an IQ score of 130 has scored higher than approximately 98 percent of the entire population.

As was noted earlier, some states have discontinued the use of cognitive ability testing in their school systems. In the legal context, results of cognitive ability tests are a critical component in the assessment of disabilities. Furthermore, they often appear in family law and criminal law contexts. A juvenile, for example, may be given a cognitive ability test and the results used to argue against his being transferred to an adult criminal court. Cognitive ability scores also appear in some reports of pretrial competency and sanity evaluations, pre-sentence investigation reports submitted to sentencing judges, and prison records.

Personality Assessment

The term "personality" means different things to different psychologists, but common themes run through their definitions. The definitions of most psychologists focus on some relatively enduring psychological attributes of a person which can differentiate that person from others. For example, almost all psychologists agree that some individuals are more anxious and tense than others across a variety of situations. In police work, it is commonly known that some officers respond to stress and life-threatening situations with greater levels of anxiety and agitation than others. They may also take longer to return to their usual day-to-day anxiety levels. Moreover, they consistently react this way under stressful conditions. The personality variable in this instance is anxiety, more commonly called nervousness.

For our purposes, personality will be defined as "the combination of all of the relatively enduring dimensions of individual differences on which [the person] can be measured" (Byrne, 1974, p. 26). Personality measurement may be divided into two broad approaches: projective and objective. These two techniques are distinguished principally by the clarity of stimuli used to obtain responses from subjects.

PROJECTIVE TESTS

Projective tests are designed with the assumption that personality attributes are best revealed when a person responds to ambiguous stimuli. Since projective techniques were developed by psychodynamically oriented theorists interested in plumbing the hidden depths of personality, projective tests generally try to measure unconscious dispositions. Since there is no established meaning to the stimuli, it is premised that the responses of subjects reveal significant features about their personalities. Some of these personality features—perhaps even most of them—may be unknown to the respondent.

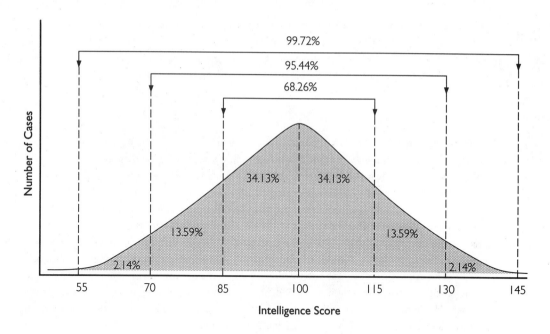

Figure 2.1 ■ *Distribution of intelligence scores in a normal curve.*

Some projective (ambiguous) test materials are very abstract, such as inkblots; others are more concrete, such as pictures of social situations. The most commonly used instrument representing the first category is the Rorschach, while the second category is represented best by the Thematic Apperception Test (TAT).

The **Rorschach** test, developed several decades ago by the Swiss psychiatrist Herman Rorschach, is administered by a trained examiner who presents a series of ten bilaterally symmetrical inkblots and asks the examinee to describe what each inkblot resembles or suggests. The response characteristics are used by the clinician as "signs" that reflect the individual's underlying personality dynamics. If you see a killer cyborg in an inkblot, for example, this is supposed to reveal something significant about your personality. Scoring and interpretation are complex tasks requiring different phases of administration and different levels of interpretation. Clinicians trained to administer projective tests rate the subject on areas such as anxiety, hostility, neurosis, organic brain damage, and psychosis.

At about the time the Rorschach was introduced, the American psychologist Henry Murray developed the **Thematic Apperception Test** (TAT), which consists of twenty-nine pictures on separate cards and one blank card. The cards are presented one at a time, and the individual is instructed to make up a story suggested by each picture, complete with plot and characters. The respondent tells what the situation is, what has led up to the situation, what the characters are feeling and thinking, and what the outcome will be.

The Rorschach and the TAT both have been heavily criticized for their lack of objectivity in arriving at subject ratings. Anastasi (1988) strongly questions the validity of projective tests and suggests that they may be as much a projection of the examiner's biases, perceptions, and theoretical orientations as they are of the examinee's personality attributes. Their usefulness in the legal system is highly debatable, particularly where substantial criterion-related validation is required, as when predicting which candidates will perform well in law enforcement, or whether

36

CHAPTER
TWO:
PSYCHOLOGICAL
ASSESSMENT,
TESTING,
AND THE
LAW

a defendant is dangerous. Extensive reviews of the research literature have failed to yield many encouraging signs for the empirical value or validity of projective tests (Maloney & Ward, 1976), and there is considerable evidence that other psychological instruments provide far more meaningful information for the assessment and prediction of human behavior.

OBJECTIVE TESTS

The other personality measure frequently used in clinical practice is the **objective test**. Basically, a test is objective to the extent that scorers can apply a scoring key and agree about the result. When all steps avoid bias on the part of the examiner who administers, scores, and interprets the tests, objectivity is assured (Mischel & Mischel, 1977).

The vast majority of objective personality tests have a "self-report" format, meaning that the subjects are expected to respond "true" or "false" to brief statements or descriptions referring to their behavior or attitudes. The most widely-used self-report test associated with the law is the Minnesota Multiphasic Personality Inventory (MMPI), a test given in many employment situations.

The original MMPI (first published in 1942) is an extensive (550 to 566 questions) paper-and-pencil inventory that requires respondents to answer true or false to questions about themselves. The items delve into a wide range of behaviors, beliefs, and feelings, some of them very personal in nature. Items on the original MMPI are also dated.

The objectionable content of the MMPI led to a class action suit in 1989 against the agency which used it as a screening measure before hiring applicants. The suit, *Soroka v. Hudson Security Co.*, was settled out of court in the summer of 1993. An estimated 2,500 job seekers who had taken the test over a four-year period were jointly awarded $1.3 million dollars. Another $60,000 was awarded to the four employment candidates specifically named in the suit. Interestingly, plaintiff Soroka had not been denied a job on the basis of test results. Rather, he argued that the personal nature of the questions caused him emotional distress both before and after he was hired.

Many psychologists have been unhappy with the original MMPI for other reasons as well as its offensive questions. The population used to establish the original norms was highly selective, and did not represent adults from different regional areas, cultural settings, and ethnic and racial groups. For years, however, professionals were reluctant to abandon the original MMPI because of the vast amount of irreplaceable data accumulated on it over years of research.

In 1989, after nearly seven years of research and development, the new MMPI-2 was published with national norms that are much more representative of the current population of the United States. In addition, item content was changed to modernize wording and eliminate invasions of privacy, sexist questions, and ambiguity. The format, administration, scoring and interpretation of the MMPI-2 are intended to be similar to the original MMPI, enabling clinicians to use the instrument in basically the same manner as its predecessor.

Criticism of the original MMPI's content is clearly warranted. Criticism of its validity, however, seems unjustified and demonstrates lack of knowledge about the instrument's design and intention. Because we may see the same type of attack on the MMPI-2, it is important to address this issue.

There is widespread misunderstanding of the original design and purpose of the MMPI, which has led to faulty application, particularly in the criminal justice system. Maloney and Ward (1976) and Dahlstrom (1972) point out that clinicians and researchers often confuse two types of assessment: that designed to identify abnormality and that designed to identify personality traits. The MMPI was designed to differentiate "abnormal" persons (as defined by society during the late 1930s and early 1940s) from "normal" persons. It was not intended to be a personality measure

■ 2.1: MMPI AND MMPI-2: KEY DIFFERENCES

THE ORIGINAL MMPI (the Minnesota Multiphasic Personality Inventory) was developed during the late 1930s and early 1940s at the University of Minnesota Hospitals by Starke R. Hathaway, a clinical psychologist, and J. Charnley McKinley, a neuropsychiatrist. Hathaway and McKinley developed the scale primarily as a diagnostic tool that would aid in the classification of psychiatric patients. To construct the scale, they identified a criterion group of patients at the University Hospitals who had been assigned a variety of psychiatric diagnoses. A control (or normative) group of non-psychiatric patients comprised friends and relatives visiting non-psychiatric hospital patients, as well as some high school students and administrators.

The MMPI-2 was published in 1989 after seven years of research and development. Many features of the MMPI-2 are highly similar to the original MMPI, but MMPI-2 differs in two important ways.

First, the *content* is different. The designers of the MMPI-2 eliminated outmoded words or idiomatic expressions. They also improved the grammar, punctuation, and general readability of the scale. In addition, the new questions are less intrusive into the personal lives of the respondents. Questions about religious beliefs, sexual behavior, and scatological habits are gone.

Second, the *normative sample* for the MMPI-2 is more representative of the general population in the U.S. In the first version the group was white, around 35, married, not generally educated beyond high school, and living in rural areas. The new sample represents all walks of life and a better distribution of ethnic or minority groups (81 percent white, 12 percent African-American, 3 percent Hispanic, 3 percent Native-American, and 1 percent Asian-American.

A special version of the MMPI for adolescents (MMPI-A) was released in August 1992. ■

---

which would provide information about personality traits. This misunderstanding has meant that many experiments examining the MMPI's effectiveness in predicting strong job candidates based on personality features have been poorly designed. In essence, the test is to be used to screen out inappropriate candidates, not screen in appropriate ones.

The MMPI has drawn more research attention than any other psychological test. The typical evaluation study relates to the use of the MMPI in law enforcement, because the test is widely used in police selection. Much of this research has assumed, however, that the MMPI has the power to appraise both emotional status *and* normal personality traits, ignoring the fact that psychopathological detection and personality description demand different methods of assessment. Tests that try to do both things seem destined for confusion and criticism; the MMPI is not such a test.

The reader should keep this point in mind when he or she reviews studies that try to evaluate the MMPI's ability to depict police personalities, or even to distinguish good police officers from bad ones.

PERSONALITY TRAITS: SPECIFIC OR GENERAL?

One of the active controversies in psychology today centers on whether personality characteristics are specific to certain situations or generalized across time and place. Is Brutus a timid person, or is he timid only under some conditions? This issue of specificity versus generality is especially relevant to psychological testing, because most testing procedures are predicated on the assumption that the attributes being measured are highly consistent.

Personality traits, which are more appropriately thought of as personality predispositions, can be understood only if both the person *and* the situation are considered. The expressions of a person's traits hinge on a given psychological situation (Mischel & Mischel, 1977; Bowers, 1973; Endler, 1973; Mischel, 1973). It is a generally held tenet in psychology that behavior results from

38

CHAPTER
TWO:
PSYCHOLOGICAL
ASSESSMENT,
TESTING,
AND THE
LAW

a complex interaction between these personality predispositions and the situation. Therefore, the degree of consistency in our personality depends to some extent on the situations in which we find ourselves.

There are two crucial aspects in determining the consistency of personality traits, **cross-situational** (or **trans-situational**) **consistency**, referred to above, and **temporal consistency**, or consistency over time. The latter asks, if a person behaves a certain way now, will he or she behave essentially the same way a month, a year, or even ten years from now, in similar situations?

Consistency over time has never really been in dispute (Mischel & Mischel, 1977). Few psychologists seriously doubt that our lives have temporal consistency and coherence. Most people see themselves and others as relatively stable individuals who exhibit similar behavior over time— at least in dealing with, or responding to, *similar* situations.

Cross-situational consistency is more involved. Some research suggests our actions are often highly specific to the particular situation and may in fact be unique to that situation. For example, a highly competent and efficient judge may be relaxed and witty in the courtroom on a day-to-day basis, but her demeanor may change noticeably when she sentences an offender to prison. In light of the seriousness of that situation, she may become tense and humorless, though still competent and efficient. However, research focusing on traits has also reported much consistency across situations (Bem & Allen, 1974). In general, evidence indicates that people both discriminate and generalize their behavior as they interact with situations. Some people are consistent in some areas of behavior, but not in others; some are consistent on some traits. It is quite clear, though, that none of us are consistent on all traits (Mischel & Mischel, 1977).

This intricate and highly individualistic interaction of personality and situation creates problems for psychologists interested in personality assessment. Until recently, personality research and theory building emphasized the person to the exclusion of the situation. Traditional personality assessment theory (called **trait psychology** or **psychodynamics**) assumed that stable personality traits or personality structures were the center of the individual's universe; once these attributes were delineated, accurate prediction of that person's behavior was almost guaranteed. Thus, to say someone had an aggressive personality was to imply a corresponding list of behaviors, most of them negative. We are now realizing, though, that the situation and the meaning of that situation for the person are critical variables. Therefore, rather than relying on a global conclusion that a police candidate has an "aggressive personality," an agency would do well to try to determine how the candidate handles himself or herself in various situations. It is unwarranted to attach negative connotations to a personality label. Aggressive behaviors are sometimes necessary in some instances, while inappropriate in others.

The above discussion emphasizes that accurate assessment and prediction require not only an evaluation of the person (as advocated by trait and psychodynamic perspectives), but also an evaluation of the psychosocial environment within which the behaviors we are trying to predict occur. Failure to consider the context of the behavior is destined to produce unwarranted conclusions.

In the remaining sections of the chapter we will focus on three types of tests from the eleven categories briefly described near the beginning of the chapter. Each of the three—neuropsychological, cognitive, and personality—will be described in the context of a given professional setting. Forensic neuropsychology, for example, is the setting associated with the first. The setting for the cognitive and personality tests will be police and, to a lesser extent, corrections psychology. There are two reasons for this law enforcement focus. First, a massive body of research on testing and assessment in the law has concentrated on law enforcement. Second, addressing issues on the selection and screening of law enforcement officers provides a bridge to Chapter 3, which deals with a variety of other issues in police psychology.

Forensic Neuropsychology

Neuropsychology studies and assesses the function and dysfunction of the human nervous system, particularly the **cerebral cortex**. In general, this discipline is concerned with the diagnosis and consequence of brain damage within a legal context. Forensic neuropsychology has developed almost exclusively within the realm of civil law, and, until recently, was largely neglected in the criminal law area (Martell, 1992). This is rapidly changing, particularly as criminal defendants raise defenses based on dysfunctions of the brain. The predominant application of forensic neuropsychology to date, however, has been in civil cases involving disability determination, worker's compensation, and personal injury cases (Martell, 1992).

The forensic neuropsychologist tries to answer three basic questions: (1) Is there brain damage? (2) What was the cause of this brain damage? And (3), what effects will this brain damage or dysfunction have on the behavioral, affective (emotional), and cognitive life of this individual? In the criminal context, the question becomes, what effect *did* the brain damage have on the individual's behavior?

Neuropsychological assessment techniques vary widely. They may include an evaluation of general intelligence, language, memory, attention, thought processes, perceptual-motor functioning, and/or emotional status. Two of the most widely-used test batteries for the detection of neuropsychological problems are the Halstead-Reitan and the Luria-Nebraska Neuropsychological Battery. In a survey of neuropsychologists, however (Guilmette & Faust, 1987), only 30 percent of the respondents said they used the Halstead-Luria regularly and 20 percent said they use the Luria-Nebraska regularly. A few (4 percent) indicated they use the Luria-Christensen battery with regularity. Many neuropsychologists apparently prefer to use various combinations of tests, depending on the individual being tested and the legal questions asked. Overall, no single test is adequate for the detection or diagnosis of all suspected brain damage, primarily because of the enormous complexity of the brain (Martell, 1992).

Brain injury can result from a variety of causes, including blows to the head (trauma), changes in oxygen supply (anoxia and hypoxia), drugs and alcohol, and toxins. Head trauma, of course, may result from a wide assortment of causes, ranging from traffic accidents to a brawl in a bar. Anoxia and hypoxia refer to a lack of oxygen, a condition that can cause irreparable damage to particular areas of the central nervous system in a relatively short period of time. Very often, the forensic questions in this area focus on neurological problems of an infant (such as cerebral palsy) as a result of possible professional incompetence during childbirth or during immediate aftercare.

Toxic injury to the brain can result from accidental or incidental exposure to elements in the outdoor environment, food or drink, medication, or features of the workplace (Leestma, 1991). Certain carpet fibers, for example, have been suspected to emit neurotoxins. Toxic injury can also result through willful consumption of substances with toxic consequences or as a result of willful criminal intent. Consumption of inappropriately prescribed drugs may result in nervous system damage, as may consumption of some illegal drugs or very heavy ingestion of alcohol.

Over the past twenty years, we have seen numerous illustrations of the harmful effects of toxic substances used indiscriminately, often by major corporations (Mokhiber, 1988). The "corporate roster of wrongdoing" ranges from highly publicized cases—Agent Orange, Love Canal, and Thalidomide—to less well known illustrations, and the public is rapidly becoming aware of the grave consequences of exposure to toxic materials. As a result, civil suits in this area have proliferated.

40

CHAPTER
TWO:
PSYCHOLOGICAL
ASSESSMENT,
TESTING,
AND THE
LAW

One of the major tasks for neuropsychologists making forensic assessments is to separate pre-existing brain dysfunctions from dysfunctions resulting from a current injury. Conditions that existed prior to the trauma in question are sometimes subtle, complicated, difficult to identify—even by those who know the individual well—and are more common than supposed (Tucker & Neppe, 1991). Another important task is to ensure that the examinee is not malingering (faking) or exaggerating. The ability of neuropsychologists to detect deception is currently a highly controversial area, with heated arguments on both sides (Martell, 1992). A third important objective is to make certain that indicators of neurological impairment gathered from neuropsychological assessment are not the result of other factors in an otherwise healthy individual. For example, the apparent impairment may simply be the result of advancing age.

As noted above, neuropsychology is increasingly employed in criminal cases, such as in evaluating the defendant's competency to stand trial or determining whether an insanity defense could be supported. The language "mental disease or defect" which appears in the law related to insanity is broadly interpreted to include not only psychological causes but neurological or physiological ones as well. In Chapter 5, we will be addressing these issues in more detail. Traditionally, the term "functional" has been applied to suspected psychological causes of mental disorder (such as reactive depression), and the term "organic" has been reserved for suspected or known neurophysiological causes of mental disorder due to trauma or disease. But clinicians today are finding it increasingly difficult to determine whether certain mental disorders, such as schizophrenia, are due primarily to functional or organic causes. Neuropsychology, therefore, is more likely to determine what *effect* known brain damage may have on the capacities and behavior of a defendant.

It should be stressed that the field of neuropsychology is new and developing very rapidly. Current knowledge of the immediate and long-term consequences of brain injury, especially if the injury seems minor or moderate, is limited. Nevertheless, forensic neuropsychologists are indispensable to the process of attempting to determine not only the direct physical effects of an injury, but the emotional effects as well.

Psychological Assessment in Law Enforcement

As mentioned earlier, a massive amount of research on the legal aspects of psychological assessment and testing has focused on the selection of law enforcement officers. This scrutiny was prompted by six different Presidential Commissions on Law Enforcement and Crime during the 1960s, all of which emphasized the value of properly selected law enforcement officers. Implicit in these recommendations was the pressing need for reliable and valid instruments that would evaluate the intellectual capacity, emotional stability, and personality characteristics of law enforcement personnel. Keep in mind, however, especially in the testing context, that it is important to distinguish between screening *in* and screening *out*. Screening in refers to identifying features that make an individual a good candidate for law enforcement; screening out refers to identifying "red flags," or characteristics that make the individual a risk. As will become clear, psychological testing thus far has had more success at screening out than screening in.

In 1967, the Task Force on the Police (President's Commission on Law Enforcement and the Administration of Justice) underscored the lack of adequate screening in most law enforcement agencies. Six years later, the National Advisory Commission on Criminal Justice Standards and

Goals recommended that every law enforcement agency "employ a formal process for the selection of qualified police applicants. This process should include a written test of mental ability or aptitude, an oral interview, a physical examination, a psychological examination, and an in-depth background investigation" (Spielberger, 1979, p. xi).

Law enforcement selection was traditionally based upon minimum (or maximum) standards of age, health, height, vision, hearing, physical fitness, weight, agility, and appearance. Whether these specifications related to actual job performance was generally unknown; the relationship was unexamined, but it was assumed. With the introduction of the Civil Rights Act of 1964 and federal guidelines such as those of the Equal Employment Opportunity Commission (EEOC), it became clear that many of these earlier criteria would be carefully scrutinized. Departments were prompted to reexamine their existing practices, to develop new ones, or to drop existing criteria of questionable validity. If they did not abide by the guidelines, they were leaving themselves open to EEOC compliance measures or to civil suits by aggrieved parties.

Selecting capable law enforcement officers is a demanding responsibility for law enforcement administrators. The presence of even a few undesirable officers is potentially damaging to both the agency itself and the population the agency serves. For example, one officer's overzealous behavior and poor judgment can result in psychological, social, and financial costs within the department and the community. Simply from a financial standpoint, every new officer who is terminated because of misconduct, incompetence, or dissatisfaction costs each law enforcement agency thousands of dollars in training and equipment. It is crucial, therefore, that carefully designed and valid screening devices be available, at least to screen out potentially problematic candidates.

Psychological devices used without adequate validation, however, very likely will, literally, have their day in court when lawsuits are filed by victims or by candidates who believe they were screened out of law enforcement work unjustifiably. To avoid costly litigation and embarrassment, law enforcement agencies must avoid using haphazard screening procedures and must support efforts to validate the methods they are using.

Recent research on law enforcement selection indicates agencies are using four broad measures or procedures in the selection process:

1. *Psychological tests*, including measures of intelligence, aptitude, attitudes, interest, and personality;

2. *Situational tests*, in which job behaviors are simulated or a candidate's behavior is observed in "test" situations;

3. *Background and physical data*, including education, performance on physical ability tests, indications of substance abuse, and prior criminal involvement;

4. The *interview*, which includes oral boards and possibly clinical data gathered by a psychologist or psychiatrist.

In the following sections, we will discuss the three measures which are directly related to the practice of psychology: psychological tests, situational tests, and the interview.

PSYCHOLOGICAL TESTING IN LAW ENFORCEMENT

Over the past three decades, various psychological devices have been tried in the law enforcement selection process. In the late 1970s, law enforcement agencies began to shift away from broad, largely unvalidated "intelligence" and "aptitude" tests and projective personality instruments.

42

CHAPTER
TWO:
PSYCHOLOGICAL
ASSESSMENT,
TESTING,
AND THE
LAW

These were replaced with objective personality measures, usually of a paper-and-pencil variety given to law enforcement candidates in a group setting. Two major surveys conducted during these years illustrate the shift.

In a survey of assessment techniques used in metropolitan police departments (Narrol and Levitt, 1963), 85 percent of the departments reported using objective tests specifically intended to assess aptitude for law enforcement work. However, the testing programs were described only vaguely, and the departments appeared to be using them as a symbolic gesture to appease the community rather than as empirically conceived instruments of valid selection. Most of the tests were little more than unstandardized cognitive ability tests of questionable design or validity. Concurrent or predictive validity—the measures of how the tests actually related to performance— were unknown or not even examined by most departments. Only 22 percent of the departments reported using "personality measures" in their selection process, and only one department reported doing any original research to determine the validity of the tests it used.

Nearly ten years later, Murphy (1972) surveyed 258 local law enforcement agencies employing at least 100 officers and 49 state police forces. While his data indicated no significant shift in the percentage of departments using psychological exams, he found a substantial shift away from questionable aptitude, intelligence, or projective tests. Instead, departments were adopting more standardized and somewhat more valid psychological measures of personality and emotional status. About 44 percent of the local police departments used "psychological examinations" to screen police candidates, but only 13 percent of the state law enforcement agencies used them. Although this percentage is considerably lower than that found in the Narrol and Levitt survey (85 percent), it is important to note that Murphy's questionnaire was worded differently. It specified "psychological tests," whereas Narrol and Levitt had asked to be informed of *any type* of examination.

Most of the tests reported in the Murphy study were objective, paper-and-pencil personality measures. The MMPI was by far the most common personality test used, with 48.75 percent of the agencies using it alone or in combination with other tests. Murphy also learned that 41.25 percent of the agencies used a "psychiatric interview" in the screening procedure.

Although many different assessment techniques are currently used in the screening, selection, and promotion of law enforcement officers, it is usually not known whether these testing procedures are valid predictors of effective on-the-job law enforcement performance (criterion-related validity) (Spielberger, 1979). This is a sobering fact, because any selection procedure should ultimately be validated. Empirical investigations evaluating relationships between initial selection standards (predictors) and the actual job performance of law enforcement officers should be undertaken, supported by attempts at determining construct validity.

Using psychological tests as predictors of effective law enforcement performance is problematic, partly due to the diversity and complexity of behaviors required of law enforcement officers. Their duties range from preventing and detecting crime to investigating accidents, intervening in disputes, handling domestic disturbances, and responding to a wide range of requests from the public. The smaller the department, the more varied the responsibilities of individual officers. It is not unusual to find a local, small-town law enforcement officer offering bicycle safety tips to an elementary school class and on the same day dealing with a violent domestic altercation. Because specialization is a luxury few small departments can afford, it is very difficult to establish objective performance criteria upon which to base predictions. Some officers may perform very competently on some tasks while failing at others. The officer who relates exceptionally well to adolescents may perform poorly in crisis situations involving very young children.

To account for the heterogeneity of law enforcement activities, screening devices must contain a number of predictors based upon a multitude of behaviors, and few are able to do this.

In addition, because law enforcement work differs substantially from one jurisdiction to another, a test may be adequate for a given department but not sufficient elsewhere. Rural or small-town law enforcement requires behaviors and talents different from those required by metropolitan or urban law enforcement work. Also, sheriff's departments often offer services different from those of municipal or state law enforcement agencies. Federal agents provide a wide range of additional duties, such as patrolling national borders, protecting government witnesses, and enforcing environmental laws.

Another obstacle to validating psychological tests is determining what precisely constitutes successful performance. Inter-judge agreement about performance ratings is often difficult to obtain, even within one department. What one supervisor considers superior performance in the field may be only average performance to another supervisor. Predictors of success, therefore, are elusive.

The wide scope of law enforcement, together with the urgent need for more vigorous and sophisticated methods of study, warns us that we should expect few solid conclusions in the research literature as to what are adequate predictors of success or failure in law enforcement work. As expected, the literature is littered with inconclusive or mixed results. This does not mean that reliable and valid psychological assessment is beyond reach. It may mean, though, that a successful testing program must be tailor-made to the needs of a particular agency.

Cognitive Assessment

One of the first U. S. studies on law enforcement selection was conducted in 1917 by psychologist Louis M. Terman, who gave an abbreviated form of his Stanford-Binet Intelligence Scale to thirty male applicants for police and firefighter positions in San Jose, California. He found that a large majority of the candidates were functioning near the dull normal range of intelligence; only three candidates obtained a cognitive ability score over 100, the score considered average for the general population! Terman concluded that police and firefighting positions attracted individuals of exceptionally low intelligence. He recommended that all candidates who scored below 80 be eliminated automatically from further job consideration. He also urged police administrators to keep the cognitive ability scores and compare them with later job performance, but apparently this was never done. As a result of Terman's project, an IQ score of 80 was established as an arbitrary score to indicate ability to perform police responsibilities.

A contemporary of Terman, psychologist Louis Thurstone, was also interested in the value of mental testing to police selection. Thurstone (1922) administered the Army Intelligence Examination (the Army Alpha) to 358 various ranking members of the Detroit Police Department. Officers at all ranks scored below average; in fact, the more experienced the police officer was, the lower was his intelligence. The average score for the 307 patrol officers was 71.44; the 34 sergeants averaged 54.71 and the 17 lieutenants 57.80. Like Terman, Thurstone concluded that law enforcement simply did not attract intelligent individuals. He further surmised that the more intelligent individuals who entered police service left for other occupations, where their ability and intelligence were presumably better recognized.

Fortunately, improvement in professionalism and in rewards of law enforcement work over the years began to attract significantly more intellectually capable individuals. In later studies, law enforcement officers obtained at least average intelligence scores (Matarazzo et al., 1964; Gordon, 1969). In a review of the literature, Poland (1978, p. 376) notes that "if police agencies can attract applicants with some college education, they have an applicant pool of above average intelligence." As encouraging as it may be to know that law enforcement personnel are not substandard intellectually, this tells us little about the relationship between intelligence level and actual job

44

CHAPTER
TWO:
PSYCHOLOGICAL
ASSESSMENT,
TESTING,
AND THE
LAW

performance. Is high intelligence a predictor of superb or even satisfactory functioning as a law enforcement officer?

In general, intelligence and ability tests have been useful predictors of *police academy* performance, but less reliable for predicting how well an officer actually performs in the field (Spielberger, Ward & Spaulding, 1979; Henderson, 1979). Studies using general cognitive ability tests like the Army General Classification Test, the Wonderlic, and the California Test of Mental Maturity, typically report correlations between test scores and academy grades in the .35 to .70 range, with the most frequent correlations clustering around .50 (e.g., Dubois & Watson, 1950; Hess, 1973; Mills, McDevitt & Tonkin, 1966; Mullineaux, 1955). However, there are few parallel correlations between intelligence measure and field performance, or between academy and field performance. McKinney (1973) reported that a tailor-made written examination used in Phoenix, Arizona, to select officers had value in predicting on-the-street job performance, but had much better predictive power when applied to police academy performance.

Personality Assessment

Fortunately, law enforcement selection procedures have now shifted from using poorly defined examinations of intelligence and vague assessments of personality dynamics to including more objective measures of personality that are able to provide criterion-related validation data. The most widely used objective personality inventory in the selection of law enforcement officers is the Minnesota Multiphasic Personality Inventory (MMPI), used as part of entrance requirements in many federal, state, and local agencies (Beutler et al. 1985; Inwald & Kenny, 1989; Shaw, 1986). Although we discussed the MMPI briefly earlier in the chapter, we will apply it specifically to the law enforcement context here.

Most MMPI research in law enforcement has been criterion-related validity of the concurrent variety, where the personality characteristics of already employed law enforcement officers are assessed and used to establish predictors of good performance. Typically, the test is administered to officers representing varying degrees of success in law enforcement work, with "success" determined by supervisor ratings. For instance, if a high percentage of officers evaluated by supervisors as "successful" respond to questions on a subscale of the MMPI differently than does a group of "unsuccessful" officers, that scale can be considered a good predictor of on-the-job performance. Research that examines individuals already in law enforcement has a critical limitation, however, because it ignores the characteristics of officers who were hired but dropped out because of hurdles along the way. Thus, significant segments of the population are missed. One of the reasons for using any screening device is to discover the potential drop-outs or failures as soon as possible.

Predictive validation is a more useful and vigorous research procedure than concurrent validation, but it is rarely implemented because of the time it requires and the percentage of the law enforcement budget it swallows. Predictive validation demands longitudinal study to decide how well initial assessments and standards predict a candidate's success or failure as a law enforcement officer. In this method, the MMPI is administered to candidates and, several years hence, the researcher determines which of the candidates "succeeded" in law enforcement.

Both concurrent validation and predictive validation studies of the MMPI's use in selection are confusing and ambiguous in their hypotheses, designs, results, and conclusions. Clear, cogent, or unequivocal conclusions and recommendations are rarely found in the existing literature. Some researchers have reported good, even exceptional results, while others have found little in the way of encouraging data. However, it should be emphasized that there is much to be gained through testing programs founded on well-designed and well-executed research. Valid psychological measures hold great promise for the efficiency and accuracy of personnel selection.

The Los Angeles Police Department reported one of the earliest attempts to use the MMPI as a selection tool (Rankin, 1959). The triggering event for this innovation was an incident in which law enforcement officers allegedly used unnecessary force and brutality toward suspects in their custody, a situation that, in some respects, sounds similar to the highly publicized 1991 case in which criminal charges were brought against four Los Angeles police officers relating to their behavior at an arrest. After the former incident, the LAPD instituted a candidate screening program to answer public criticism and to reduce future incidents. The program included the MMPI, the Rorschach, and a psychological interview. Unfortunately, procedural and statistical details about the program, as reported by Rankin (1959), were not sufficient to permit generalizations to other departments. Rankin said he rejected a substantial number of potentially "unsuitable" law enforcement officers on the basis of psychological test results. He posits that 11 percent of the 2,000 applicants screened over a six-year period were rejected for "psychiatric reasons." Rankin only assumed, however, that vaguely defined psychiatric problems would lead to unsatisfactory job performance. Later research on the MMPI attempted to demonstrate this association, with little success.

Over the years, some studies have reported a weak or nonexistent relationship between MMPI scores and job performance (Gottesman, 1975; Henderson, 1979; Kent & Eisenberg, 1972; Spielberger, Spaulding & Ward, 1978). Others have reported moderate relationship between some performance standards and one or more of the MMPI subscales (Azen, Snibble & Montgomery, 1973; Blum, 1964; Colarelli & Siegel, 1964; Hooke & Kraus, 1971; Marsh, 1962; Matarazzo, Allen, Saslow & Weins, 1964; Nowicki, 1966; Rankin, 1957).

In recent years, George Hargrave and Deirdre Hiatt (Hargrave & Hiatt, 1987; Hiatt & Hargrave, 1988b) have tried to identify a relationship between MMPI scores and various measures of performance. In one study (Hiatt & Hargrave, 1988a), the MMPI profiles of officers who had been involved in serious disciplinary actions were compared with a matched group of officers who had not been involved in such actions. Several subscales were identified as decent predictors of disciplinary actions. Furthermore, the problem officer was twice as likely to have a T-score above 70 on at least one of the MMPI subscales.

A few predictive validation studies also have been done. Beutler et al. (1985) followed officers from three different agencies (a community college security department, a large university security department, and a large urban police department) over a two-year period. The researchers reported that suspensions were strongly related to certain score elevations on the MMPI, but they did not specify which scales. In another project (Beutler, Nussbaum & Meredith, 1988), eleven officers were followed over a four-year period to see if their MMPI profiles changed significantly as a result of their experience in the field. They concluded that they had, but again did not specify the changes. Hiatt and Hargrave (1988b) followed fifty-five urban officers over a three-year period and discovered that the unsuccessful group had higher mean scores on eleven of the thirteen MMPI scales, although only two were statistically significant.

In a longitudinal study spanning thirteen years, Bartol (1991b) followed 600 police officers over their careers to see who would be rated unsuccessful in small-town law enforcement. Officers who "failed" were most often described by their supervisors as immature and inappropriate. They were frequently reprimanded for such behaviors as excessive and inappropriate use of authority in dealing with the public. They had frequent accidents with police vehicles, demonstrated inappropriate use of firearms and other equipment, and showed little commitment to police work. Supervisors said they had serious concerns as to whether these officers could be counted on or trusted in times of crisis or emergency situations. A combination of three MMPI scales emerged

46

CHAPTER
TWO:
PSYCHOLOGICAL
ASSESSMENT,
TESTING,
AND THE
LAW

as a powerful predictor of eventual failure in three-quarters of the officers who had received poor ratings. The combination, called the "immaturity index," may generalize to other police departments as a help in identifying those officers who do not succeed in law enforcement. Although the immaturity index needs further research attention, the study demonstrates that the MMPI and the MMPI-2 might be valuable tools in the screening and selection of law enforcement officers if we focus on establishing predictive validity.

Now that the MMPI has been purged of its offensive questions, the test should continue to be useful. The test samples over 500 self-report behaviors, is the prototype of personality testing, and has stimulated nearly 4,000 research articles examining its strengths and weaknesses. According to Maloney and Ward (1976, p. 342), "Problems, critics, and rivals notwithstanding, the MMPI will probably continue to be a dominant force in the field. This is primarily due to the vast wealth of accumulated data and 'wisdom' that it possesses."

Other Screening Devices

The California Psychological Inventory (CPI) was empirically developed from the MMPI and is similar in that personality dimensions are scored and plotted to produce a personality profile. Whereas the MMPI is keyed to detect psychopathology, however, the CPI describes normal personality patterns. Constructed between 1956 and 1960, the CPI consists of fifteen scales that measure such personality dimensions as achievement, dominance, responsibility, and sociability. Three validity scales measure test-taking attitudes. The test has 480 items that require a true or false answer. The item content is less distasteful to the respondent and has not evoked charges of invasion of privacy that were seen with reference to the original MMPI.

The CPI has not been extensively used in the screening and promotion of law enforcement, however, partly because the instrument has received mixed reviews (Sherman, 1979). Three main criticisms have been made. First, the test has so many scales that it provides too much data for a clinician to integrate effectively. Second, there are no suggested standards for interpreting CPI profiles and response patterns. Finally, several of the scales are repetitive, measuring similar personality characteristics.

Some researchers have reported good success with the CPI (e.g., Spielberger, Spaulding & Ward, 1978) and have suggested it should be considered for use in screening programs. Hogan (1971) examined the personality characteristics of three classes of police cadets and state police officers with one year's experience. Staff and supervisory ratings served as the criterion measures. Hogan cross-validated the concurrent "prediction" of the supervisory job-performance ratings with scores on the CPI and found that the CPI scales which related to intelligence, self-confidence, and sociability discriminated highly rated officers from those less highly rated. Nevertheless, although the CPI may hold promise as a screening tool, there are too few supportive studies to recommend its widespread use.

SITUATIONAL TESTING

Because psychological tests administered to law enforcement candidates have not demonstrated high predictive validity, some police psychologists have constructed test situations that resemble as closely as possible the working conditions actually encountered in police work. Proponents of such situational tests argue that paper-and-pencil intelligence and personality tests do not require candidates to do anything that approximates actual police work. Situational tests were used extensively by the American, British, and German militaries during World War II to select officers and special services personnel. Although there were few data to support the value of these tests in predicting success (Murray et al.,

1948), they have a strong intuitive appeal and remain popular today.

Chenoweth (1961) was among the first to suggest that situational tests be used for the selection of police officers. Later, Diliman (1963), R. B. Mills and his colleagues (1966, 1969, 1976), and Tagatz and Hess (1972) began to explore the use of such tests through research.

Diliman (1963) reported the first application of situational tests to police screening in a study involving a police force in Albuquerque, New Mexico. He devised two situations typical of police work in that city, one requiring an officer to interview an uncooperative hit-and-run suspect, the other requiring the officer to deal with a man stopped for speeding in the process of driving his pregnant wife to the hospital. Police academy recruits were used as subjects. In each situation, the recruit's responses were taped and rated by a group of judges, who scored the responses for both frequency and dominance. Frequency referred to the actual number of responses made by the recruit, and dominance to the overriding or "repetitive theme" of the recruit's response pattern. As a criterion measure, the recruits were ranked by the commandant of the academy according to their potential as police officers. The relationships between frequency and dominance of responses and the commandant's ratings were highly significant for the first situation, but considerably less so for the second.

In light of the inconsistent relationship between academy performance and field perform-ance frequently reported in other studies (e.g., Spielberger, 1979), the usefulness of this situational study to the selection of police officers is questionable. It is not even known whether frequency and dominance of responses contributes to successful police work. Also, it is unwise to rely on one person's assessment (the commandant's, for example) of who will and will not become a successful officer.

The only other published attempt to apply situational tests to police selection was reported by Robert Mills and his colleagues in Cincinnati (Mills, McDevitt & Tonkin, 1966). The Mills group constructed scenarios of a variety of situations commonly encountered in some aspect of police work. The overall results were discouraging and did not support the value of situational tests for selection of police officers.

Situational tests can be time-consuming and expensive, particularly when they involve role-playing as opposed to asking candidates what they would do in a given situation. They require special equipment, technical, and professional assistance. More importantly, there is little guaran-tee that the tests, though apparently job-related, have any value in predicting who will succeed in law enforcement and who will not. Moreover, candidates cannot be expected to know how to handle situations until they receive the proper training. The notion that test content which appears job-related increases the validity of the test is misguided. On the contrary, there is evidence that carefully-selected paper-and-pencil exams are more accurate in assessing and predicting good police officers. Unfortunately, the preference for job-related content over apparently less relevant but predictive tests is not uncommon in personnel selection.

THE INTERVIEW

The interview has not been found to be a particularly valid device for discriminating or predicting which candidates will become successful police officers (Stotland & Berberich, 1979; McDonough & Monahan, 1975; Landy, 1976). In fact, contrary to what would be expected in light of its widespread use, the interview is not a particularly helpful tool for making screening decisions, even outside law enforcement (Fisher, Epstein & Harris, 1967; McKinney, 1973). Interviews prob-ably test the potential compatibility of an employer and a prospective employee rather than subsequent job performance per se. Indeed, some researchers have suggested that, if it is to be

48

CHAPTER
TWO:
PSYCHOLOGICAL
ASSESSMENT,
TESTING,
AND THE
LAW

used to screen police candidates, the interview should be considered a rapport builder and an educating medium for the candidate, rather than an evaluating device (McDonough & Monahan, 1975). Moreover, reliability between oral interviewers (the degree to which the interviewers agree with one another about an applicant's ability to succeed) is also poor (Stotland & Berberich, 1979). Despite these facts, oral examinations or interviews continue to be among the most commonly used police candidate selection methods.

Recent research emphasizes the need to consider differences in interviewers (Miner, 1992). Some interviewers seem to be better at predicting than others, and a few appear to have a very good record of identifying successful employees (Dreher, Ash & Hancock, 1988). Furthermore, structured interviews can also enhance prediction if used properly. A **structured interview** is one in which questions are standardized and the responses are recorded in a systematic manner (Miner, 1992). The interviewer asks questions that have been shown to predict job performance and records the answers according to a standardized checklist. Structured interview procedures have been found to be twice as valid as unstructured interviews (Miner, 1992; Wiesner & Cronshaw, 1988; Wright, Lichtenfels & Pursell, 1989). Thus, recent findings indicate that a carefully trained interviewer, following a valid structured interview format, may add to the predictive accuracy of screening and selection in law enforcement.

CONCLUSION

In the early 1970s two writers concluded that with few exceptions the quality of research pertaining to police selection was poor and of limited use (Kent & Eisenberg, 1972). The same conclusion, again with some exceptions, can be offered today. Predictive (as opposed to concurrent) and construct validation for police selection are desperately needed. Research examining officers already on the police force must be evaluated cautiously, for such concurrent studies ignore the potential and characteristics of applicants who dropped out along the way. A theory to explain why given behaviors are predictive of good performance while others are predictive of unsatisfactory performance is also desirable.

It is clear that no one procedure or variable, by itself, is powerful enough to predict on-the-job performance. This includes the most commonly used instrument, the MMPI, although it has more support in the empirical literature than any other single test. Furthermore, the task of predicting successful law enforcement performance or even identifying some factors associated with it is complicated, because law enforcement duties are multidimensional and highly variable from one agency to another. As a result, agencies often become discouraged and eschew predictive validation methodology, shifting to job-related validation. This last trend was noted by Kent and Eisenberg (1972) and continues today.

In selecting screening devices, police administrators should look for testing instruments that are able to predict the probabilities of success in law enforcement prior to entry. It is probably unrealistic to expect administrators to evaluate construct validity also, but the psychologist involved in the screening process should certainly be aware of it. The administrator should also be aware of probabilities—the number of "hits" an instrument is expected to make compared to "misses." The hits come into two categories: those that allow rejection of poor candidates (screening out) and those that allow the retention of good ones (screening in). Misses also come in two categories: those that failed to identify poor candidates and those that rejected potentially good candidates. When cost considerations are important, it is more critical that an instrument be able to identify as many poor candidates as possible, while still not rejecting a large number of potentially good candidates. There is no fast rule about which cut-off score to use in selection.

This is an administrative decision that hinges upon the social, psychological, and material costs the agency is willing to risk.

PSYCHOLOGICAL ASSESSMENT OF CORRECTIONS OFFICERS

Corrections officers have the unenviable task of maintaining control of inmates, who are sometimes hostile and dangerous, in a psychologically adverse environment. The ideal officer relies on appropriate judgment, authority, and compassion and is able to manage the stress generated by daily work in a closed, potentially life-threatening environment. If correctional personnel lack the necessary personal attributes and coping skills, the consequences can range from mere ineptitude on the job to severe exacerbation of tension, risks, disruptions, and violence. An effective program of psychological assessment to obtain suitable candidates for these working conditions is crucial.

Ben Crouch (1991) discusses six main problems faced by today's correctional officers in their dealings with inmates, administrators, and co-workers. First, officers experience role conflict and ambiguity while attempting to strike a balance between the need to maintain security and the desire to participate in inmates' rehabilitation. Second, they are constantly in danger of physical attack, making fear and uncertainty a daily reality. Third, corrections officers experience a sense of diminished control, and many perceive a lack of support from prison administration. Fourth, Crouch notes, the aforementioned three problems may produce considerable psychological stress. A fifth problem is adjustment to racial and sexual integration within the ranks. Racism, when present, divides the force, and many officers are convinced that women do not belong in the correctional setting, despite evidence that women and men can do the job equally well. Finally, deviance among some officers, including assaults on inmates, theft, and trafficking in contraband, contributes to a less-than-ideal work setting.

Goldstein (1975) surveyed requirements for corrections officer positions in the U. S. Forty-two of the forty-six responding states indicated they screened applicants "to identify those emotionally and psychologically unfit for corrections work." The states reported a wide variety of screening procedures, including personal interviews, medical exams, written tests and background checks. Few of these procedures were validated. In fact, according to Inwald, Levitt, and Knatz (1980, p. 2), "less than a dozen studies have been done analyzing the relationship between predictor measures and subsequent performance (in the correctional system), and, for a variety of reasons, the results have been less than enlightening."

Inwald and her colleagues (1980) launched a comprehensive attempt to screen correctional officers in the New York City Division of the State Department of Corrections and follow up their job performance. The candidates took the MMPI, were interviewed and rated by an experienced corrections officer, and again interviewed by a counseling psychologist. Inwald found that strong negative psychological evaluations can predict problems on the job. The follow-up revealed a "trouble variable," identified by the presence of one or more of the following: a) at least one disciplinary action; b) at least one corrective interview; c) at least three or more separate absences; d) three or more separate times late to work. Inwald and her colleagues concluded that if one or more of the above behaviors appeared, the officer would probably have some difficulty continuing to work in a correctional institution.

Several political and practical realities hinder empirical studies in the correctional setting, Inwald suggested. She also noted that there is a high attrition rate among corrections officers (one out of six leave within ten months of being hired) and considerable pressure for departments to maintain full staffs. Therefore, supervisors or peers are reluctant to evaluate negatively, even if

50

CHAPTER
TWO:
PSYCHOLOGICAL
ASSESSMENT,
TESTING,
AND THE
LAW

officers are performing at a substandard level. This need to give officers every chance to succeed develops into an internal code of solidarity and mutual protection among officers and supervisors. Inherent in this code is the assumption that an officer who "blows the whistle" on another will eventually encounter problems of his or her own: no backup support. This internal code, together with the usual suspicions toward mental health personnel, often prevents the researcher from obtaining performance data.

The above presentation of psychological assessment methods in law enforcement and corrections has highlighted problems frequently encountered in the evaluation process and has touched upon the nature of employment in criminal justice settings. In the next chapter we will discuss psychological characteristics of policing in more detail, and in Chapter 13 we will return to the correctional setting. Psychological assessment also pervades the judicial process, as will be illustrated in many of the chapters ahead.

At this point, it is important to mention legal issues relating to testing in admission, educational placement, hiring, promotion, transfer, and termination practices. These issues reflect growing concerns about the limitations and potential of psychological tests. As a result, legislatures and courts have examined closely the use of psychological assessment, particularly centering on discriminatory practices. We will begin with the Civil Rights Act of 1964, the major federal law which has had widespread implications for employment testing, and discuss Supreme Court cases involving that legislation. An important amendment, the Civil Rights Act of 1991, will also be covered.

Testing in Employment

In the Civil Rights Act of 1964, Congress addressed the broad spectrum of discriminatory practice in its many forms. Specifically relating to employment, under Title VII of the Civil Rights Act it is illegal to discriminate against an individual or class of individuals on the basis of race, color, gender, religion, or national origin. The law (with its subsequent amendments) makes it clear that employees and prospective employees are protected against discrimination related to hiring and promotion. As a result, psychological tests which lack adequate validation data or which base classification and cut-off scores on norms developed from a culturally advantaged population are particularly susceptible to lawsuits. When the Civil Rights Act was first passed, many psychological tests, especially of the cognitive ability (IQ) variety, came under heavy social and legal attack.

Along with the Civil Rights Act, Congress created the Equal Employment Opportunity Commission (EEOC), a federal administrative agency which issues guidelines to employers and generally oversees employment practices to assure that they are in compliance with the law. Among the EEOC's guidelines is the need to demonstrate the job-relatedness of employment tests. The guidelines pertain to any test used to select, transfer, promote, train, refer, and retain employees. It should be noted that state statutes may address the testing issue as well.

If an employer wishes to use a test to screen out or screen in applicants for a position, that test must have been "validated," or shown to be predictive of relevant job behavior. For example, an employer may promote an employee to a position after she or he has scored higher than others on a skills test, which has been demonstrated to predict success at that position. If the company limits a training program to individuals who have "passed" an *unvalidated* test, however, it is subject to being sued and must be ready to demonstrate that the test predicts success in the training program. It is important to note that the EEOC guidelines do not reject the use of properly validated tests designed to help place people into positions requiring certain skills. They do discourage the use of tests that discriminate against individuals without evidence that the tests are predictive of success in the program.

THE SUPREME COURT AND EMPLOYMENT DISCRIMINATION

Since the passage of the Civil Rights Act of 1964, the U. S. Supreme Court has heard many cases involving job discrimination issues. In a landmark case that directly addressed psychological assessment, *Griggs v. Duke Power Co.* (1971), the Court interpreted Title VII to forbid employment practices which might seem neutral on their face, but which resulted in a "disparate impact." Therefore, even if an employer did not have an intention to discriminate, if it could be demonstrated that the employer's hiring or promotion practices had a disproportionate impact on members of a protected group, the law was violated. Once disparate impact was demonstrated, the employer would then have to prove that there was a legitimate business need to continue with the practice.

In *Griggs*, fourteen African-American employees at a steam station owned by Duke Power Company challenged the legality of general ability exams used to hire and promote. Prior to Title VII, the company had openly discriminated against blacks, assigning them only to the labor detail, where the highest-paid laborer earned less than the lowest-paid white worker in other departments. Faced with Title VII and the EEOC guidelines, the company allowed blacks to transfer if they had a high school diploma (and only 12 percent of blacks in the state did) or could pass two psychological ability and aptitude tests, the Wonderlic Personnel Test and the Bennet Mechanical Comprehension Test. None of these criteria had been shown to measure the ability to learn to perform a particular job. New employees, furthermore, were required to score satisfactorily on two additional aptitude tests.

The petitioners in the *Griggs* case contended that the tests made a disproportionate number of blacks ineligible for a better job. Lower courts rejected their claims because there was no proof that the company intended to discriminate. The U. S. Supreme Court, however, ruled that the intent was not the important factor. Even if a practice does not seem unfair, if discrimination is the effect, intent is not needed.

> (G)ood intent or the absence of discriminatory intent does not redeem employment procedures or testing mechanisms that operate as built-in headwinds for minority groups and are unrelated to measuring job capability .... Congress directed the thrust of the (Civil Rights) Act to the *consequences* of employment practices, not simply to motivation. More than that, Congress has placed on the employer the burden of showing that any given requirement must have a manifest relationship to the employment in question.

The case was a landmark one for two major reasons: 1) It allowed employees to support claims of discrimination by showing disparate impact, an easier task than showing intent to discriminate; and 2) It required the employer to prove that a test which had a disparate impact nonetheless predicted job performance and was thus a legitimate business practice. The burden of proof, then, fell heavily on the employer's shoulders.

The *Griggs* case was cited frequently in *Albermarle v. Moody* (1975), in which again a class action suit on behalf of African-American employees was initiated. Albermarle, a company that transformed wood into various paper products, had been administering the Wonderlic Personnel

52

CHAPTER
TWO:
PSYCHOLOGICAL
ASSESSMENT,
TESTING,
AND THE
LAW

Test and the Revised Beta Exam to prospective employees for skilled-labor jobs. When the *Griggs* decision was announced, Albemarle hired an industrial psychologist to study the job relatedness of its testing program. Although the psychologist performed a concurrent validation between the tests and present employee performance, the U. S. Supreme Court was not satisfied that this met the guidelines established by the EEOC.

Noting that the EEOC's guidelines were based on those of the American Psychological Association, the Court found the psychologist's validation study defective. Among the problems, the Court noted that the study had failed to specify the particular skills needed for the jobs. The test also was not predictive of performance on all of the jobs. Furthermore, the psychologist's procedure relied on subjective and vague supervisory ratings. With its *Albemarle* decision, the Court made it clear that it would not take an employer's word that a test had been validated. Furthermore, the Court seemed to be looking for evidence of construct validity as well as concurrent validity. The very process of validation would be scrutinized.

A year after *Albemarle*, in *Washington v. Davis* (1976), the U. S. Supreme Court drew a distinction between suits brought under EEOC guidelines and those brought on constitutional grounds. African-American police candidates in Washington, D.C., had argued that a test developed by the Civil Service Commission and used extensively in the federal system violated their Fifth Amendment right to due process and equal protection of the law. "Test 21," as it was called, measured verbal ability, vocabulary, and reading and comprehension skills. It had been demonstrated to predict success in Washington's police training program.

The trial court in the case had determined that the test did indeed have a discriminatory impact, producing a disproportionate number of white to African-American officers. With that evidence, the court had then addressed the question of whether the test predicted job performance. It did not, but it did predict success in the training program, a criterion that the district court found acceptable.

The Washington Court of Appeals reversed the district court's ruling. Finding that Test 21 had a discriminatory impact on African-Americans, regardless of whether there was a discriminatory purpose. Applying a *Griggs* standard, the appeals court then determined that the absence of validating evidence based on job performance, rather than success in the training program, was a critical factor which rendered the test unconstitutional.

The U. S. Supreme Court, however, found error in the appeals court's application of the Title VII standard. Title VII suits did not require the "strict scrutiny" that suits alleging a violation of the Constitution required. Disproportionate impact against a racial group was not irrelevant, the Court said. However, "Standing alone, it does not trigger the [constitutional] rule that racial classifications are to be subjected to the strictest scrutiny and are justified only by the weightiest of considerations" (426 U. S. 228). The Court then agreed with the district court that the evidence of a relationship between test scores and success in the training program was sufficient to support continued use of the test.

A new Supreme Court in the 1980s dealt with employment discrimination in a very different manner. Between 1986 and 1991, the Rehnquist Court issued nine rulings that had the collective effect of making it more difficult for employees to win discrimination suits against their employers. The most highly publicized of the decisions, *Ward's Cove Packing Company et al. v. Atonio* (1989) prompted Congress to take action within the Civil Rights Act of 1991, an amendment to the Civil Rights Act of 1964. The 1991 law, among other things, clarifies provisions regarding disparate impact actions.

Although the *Ward's Cove* case (see Box 2.2) did not involve psychological assessment, it is worthy of note because the decision had an impact on any employment practice which was

■ 2.2: *FISHY EMPLOYMENT PRACTICES?*

WARD'S COVE PACKING COMPANY had for many years employed Filipinos and Alaskan natives in its seasonal salmon canning operations. The *cannery* jobs, as the Supreme Court noted in its 1989 decision, were intense, requiring workers to eviscerate fish, pull eggs, clean fish, and "operate at a rate of approximately four cans per second." Also available were *noncannery* positions which were both skilled and unskilled. They included machinists, engineers, quality control persons, record keepers, kitchen help, deckhands, carpenters and carpenter's helpers. Filipinos and Alaskan natives, who made up close to half the salmon canning industry, were almost invariably placed in the cannery positions, which paid less. Thus, nearly all cannery workers were non-white. Furthermore, they were housed in separate dorms and ate in separate mess halls, practices which, in the words of the dissenters, resembled a "plantation economy" and amounted to overt and institutionalized discrimination.

In his own separate dissent, Justice Stevens noted other problems as well. The more desirable noncan-nery jobs were seldom advertised, and there was no promotion to them from the cannery ranks. The intensity of the work precluded on-the-job-training which might help a cannery worker move up in the ranks. Even without additional training, however, cannery workers had demonstrated that they were qualified for advancement. In a footnote, Justice Stevens noted that some cannery workers had college training. Some later became professionals: architect, Air Force officer, graduate student in public administration.

As noted in the text, the Court majority placed a heavy burden on the workers to prove the practices of the company had a disparate impact. The dissenters, in their concluding paragraph, directly chastised the Court majority. "Sadly, this [decision] comes as no surprise. One wonders whether the majority still believes that race discrimination—or, more accurately, race discrimination against nonwhites—is a problem in our society, or even remembers that it ever was" (490 U. S. 662). ■

---

allegedly discriminatory. The case was a massive blow to employees bringing a disparate impact suit for a number of reasons. Most critical of these was a major shift in the burden of proof, back to the employees. By a 5-4 vote, the Court ruled that plaintiffs had to identify each objective and subjective employment practice that had the alleged disparate impact and prove that it did. Once the disparate impact was demonstrated, the burden would be shifted to the employer to produce evidence of need to continue the practice. Then, once again, the burden would be shifted back to the plaintiffs, who would have to *disprove* the employer's claim that the practice was based on legitimate neutral business considerations.

If the employees could not disprove the employer's claim, they would have still one more option. They could persuade the court that an alternative employment practice could also meet the employer's legitimate business needs. The Court was not encouraging about the likelihood of a plaintiff being able to do that, however. The alternative proposed by the employees had to be equally effective, and cost could be taken into consideration. "[T]he judiciary should proceed with care before mandating that an employer must adopt a plaintiff's alternative selection or hiring practice ..." (490 U. S. at 661).

The Court majority did not believe requiring the employees to do all of this would be unduly burdensome. The four dissenters in the case disagreed (see Box 2.2), noting that the additional requirements placed on employees were not in keeping with the spirit of the Civil Rights Act of 1964.

Two years later, Congress agreed with the dissenters. In its 1991 Amendment to the Civil Rights Act, Congress made the following points clear. First, once the plaintiff has demonstrated disparate impact, the burden is on the employer to prove the practice is job related and necessary. The plaintiff does not then have to disprove the employer's claim. Second, if the plaintiff demonstrates that an alternative business practice is available and the employer refuses to accept

54

CHAPTER
TWO:
PSYCHOLOGICAL
ASSESSMENT,
TESTING,
AND THE
LAW

it, the law is violated. Finally, employees are still required to prove that each challenged practice has a disparate impact. However, "if the complaining party can demonstrate to the court that the elements of [an employer's] decisionmaking process are not capable of separation for analysis, the decisionmaking process may be analyzed as one employment practice."

It is important to keep in mind that the above discussion refers to "disparate impact" rather than "intentional discrimination." The latter, not surprisingly, is extremely difficult to prove. In employment discrimination cases relating to psychological assessment, where predictive validation is a critical issue, a disparate impact claim is more likely to be at issue than a claim of intentional discrimination. Employees could produce statistical data that a psychological test, even if validated, effectively prevented them from being promoted. However, *intentional discrimination* will come into play if the employer adjusts the scores, establishes different cut-off scores, or otherwise alters the scores, practices also prohibited by the Civil Rights Act of 1991.

THE AMERICANS WITH DISABILITIES ACT OF 1990

In 1990, Congress passed what has become known as the Americans with Disabilities Act (ADA), which became fully effective two years later, in July of 1992. The ADA is the most far-reaching public law since the Civil Rights Act of 1964, affecting all levels of state and local governments, about 5 million private businesses, and some 43 million Americans defined by the law as physically or mentally disabled. The ADA prohibits employers from discriminating against any disabled persons who can perform the essential functions of the jobs they hold or desire to hold. Because the law is so new, numerous questions about its application have yet to be answered. The ADA does not spell out clearly who qualifies as disabled, for example, although it specifically excludes from that category persons with sexual disorders, compulsive gamblers, kleptomaniacs (persons with a compulsive need to steal), pyromaniacs (those with a compulsive need to set fires), homosexuals, and persons with disorders resulting from current illegal use of drugs. The exclusion of homosexuals reflects current recognition that homosexuality is not a mental disorder. Because the specific types of psychological or mental disorders covered by the law are not clear, courts are very likely to be faced with the need to interpret the law in the years ahead.

The ADA prohibits oral questions or questionnaire items pertaining to past medical history or otherwise eliciting information about disabilities. This raises a problem with respect to many psychological tests. Some items on the MMPI and the MMPI-2, for example, ask about medical history or center around medical or health problems. Does this mean that the MMPI cannot be used, or does it mean only that those items which delve into medical history must be deleted? The ADA further prohibits using qualification standards, employment tests, or other selection criteria that screen out individuals or a class of individuals with disabilities unless the standard, test, or other selection criteria is shown to be job-related and is consistent with business or occupational necessity. It could be argued, for example, that the ability to run is critical to work as a corrections officer, and that a person confined to a wheelchair could be screened out of such a position on that basis. On the other hand, the person should not be screened out of working as a counselor or a classification specialist in that prison.

According to the ADA, test procedures and materials must also be administered in such a manner that the test results accurately reflect the applicant's or employee's skills, aptitudes, or other relevant abilities that are necessary for the job. This suggests that hiring agencies will be expected to adapt testing procedures if they impede performance of persons with a disability. For example, we might begin to see more braille versions of self-administered paper-and-pencil tests.

The ramifications of the ADA for psychological testing and assessment are enormous and will draw considerable legal attention in the years to come. There is no question that a public law protecting Americans with disabilities from discrimination is long overdue. The ADA will, however, intensify conflicts between mental health professionals and lawyers. Key questions at this point are how a mental disorder is to be defined and which diagnostic labels will be most likely to qualify people as disabled. We can expect to see increasing challenges to the validity of these labels and the instruments and methods used to produce them.

Testing in Education

Testing affects most of us in some way, but the effect is most pervasive in the American educational system. More than 250 million commercial standardized tests designed to measure ability, achievement, and perceptual, emotional, and social competencies, as well as interest patterns, are administered annually in our schools (Bersoff, 1979).

For years, the use of these educational and psychological tests went unchallenged. Prompted by various interest groups, courts in the 1960s began to scrutinize the cultural and social validity of a wide range of testing practices in both the educational setting and in the employment policies of various private companies and public agencies.

One landmark case, *Hobson v. Hansen* (1967), questioned the propriety of using standardized tests to place a disproportionate number of minority children into the lower academic tracks and middle-class white children into higher ones. In *Hobson*, the federal appellate court condemned the practice of rigid, poorly conceived group classifications on the basis of group tests lacking sensitivity to minorities. The court found that the skills measured by the test instruments were not innately intellectual but rather were acquired through cultural experience gained in home, community, and school. Once labeled, the child would move along a predetermined track, perpetuating the classification and leaving little opportunity to alter it.

Bersoff (1979, p. 50) writes, "With one blow ... [the] decision in Hobson severely wounded two sacred cows, ability grouping and standardized testing." Perhaps the gravest blow came from the court's insistence that educational grouping must be based on tests that measure *innate* ability. The quest for culturally fair tests which might truly measure such ability has not been successful. Behavior is a result of the ongoing interaction between cultural-social experience and neurophysiological predisposition and capacity. One component cannot be isolated and measured independently of the other. The jurisprudential demand could not be met, and psychological testing within the nation's school systems faced extinction.

Amid the controversy, psychologists tried to educate the public and the courts about what psychological tests can do. They argued that standardized tests are useful to some extent in predicting future learning. The correlation coefficients of validity between test scores and academic performance are modest, but they are significant and generalizable. Moreover, achievement tests generally demonstrate good content validity and do measure how well students have acquired the skills taught in the school system. Nevertheless, psychologists were hard pressed to justify tests if they were used to discriminate against minority students.

Another landmark case, *Larry P. v. Riles* (1972), questioned the use of individual cognitive ability tests and the existence of special classes for the academically or intellectually handicapped. In 1971 the parents of black children attending San Francisco schools filed a class-action suit charging discrimination in the educational placement of their children. Children scoring 75 or lower on a cognitive ability test were placed in special educable mentally retarded (EMR) classes.

56

CHAPTER
TWO:
PSYCHOLOGICAL
ASSESSMENT,
TESTING,
AND THE
LAW

The parents presented affidavits from black psychologists who had retested the children and found them to score above the 75 cut-off point. The black examiners, while administering the same tests as the previous white examiners, tried to establish rapport during the testing and reworded test items in a way which was consistent with the children's social and cultural background. Of course, altering the testing procedure contaminates the internal validity of the test results, rendering the scores questionable for comparison purposes. Yet, the point made by the black examiners cannot be ignored.

The court decided that the defendants (the San Francisco School System and the California Department of Education) could meet the challenge initiated by the suit by showing "a minimally reasonable relationship between the practice of classification and the goal of placement" (Bersoff, 1979, p. 72). The problem then became: What constitutes a "reasonable relationship"? What correlation coefficient would satisfy the court's expectations? As noted by Donald Bersoff, validity correlations that psychologists find acceptable (often around .30 to .40—lower than acceptable coefficients) may not satisfy the expectations of the courts. In *Merriken v. Cressman* (1973, p. 920), for instance, it was ruled that "when a program talks about labeling someone as a particular type and such a label could remain with him for the remainder of his life, the margin of error must be almost nil … ." "Nil" implies an unusually high correlation, probably ranging between .90 and a perfect correlation of 1.00. Few if any psychological tests demonstrate validity of this magnitude.

Riles, which was ultimately resolved by the California Supreme Court, was a long and difficult case because of the numerous important issues raised about the potentially discriminatory classifications in testing and about labeling within the educational system. The case, which produced two federal decisions, took over seven years to settle. The first decision, known as *Riles I* (1972), was concerned only with the propriety of a preliminary injunction to suspend classification on the basis of existing methods of testing the children. *Riles II* (1979) was far more wide ranging, because the court found that the cognitive ability tests used for classification were culturally biased in favor of white children and therefore discriminatory. The court required that the tests used for classification purposes be shown to have clear validity and be appropriate for use with minority children. As Bersoff (1981, p. 1048) explained, "tests would have to be correlated with relevant criterion measures; that is, IQ scores of African-American children would have to be correlated with classroom performance." He adds that, given the stringent criteria outlined by the court, "it is unlikely that any of the currently used cognitive ability tests are valid, which casts doubt on the continued utility of traditional evaluations using psychology's storehouse of standardized ability tests." Even recent restandardizations of the Wechsler and Stanford-Binet scales using a representative population of African-American children have failed to satisfy the court's standard of validity.

Psychologists have argued that the conclusions reached in *Riles II* reflect considerable misunderstanding and ignorance of psychological testing and psychometric theory (Bersoff, 1981; Reschly, 1987). The case of *PASE v. Hannon* (1980), however, was more unsettling. In it, the court ruled that the cognitive ability tests used by the school system in question did not discriminate against African-American children, a conclusion reached in a highly subjective and unscientific manner. The judge cited each question on the Wechsler and Stanford-Binet scales and then cited every acceptable response to each item. He decided for himself on the basis of this "analysis" which items were culturally biased. In his judgment, only eight items on the WISC/WISC-R and one item on the Stanford-Binet met his "criterion" for bias.

The ultimate resolution of the status of psychological testing and its utility in educational placement appears far down the road. The confusion is at least partly due to lack of knowledge about testing and psychometric theory which occurs both in the legal system and in psychology itself. Psychologists must realize, however, that legitimate questions of acceptable social policy are also at issue. In the opinion of many observers, a psychological test which correlates strongly with academic performance but has a discriminatory impact on a minority group of students has no place in our educational system.

Many of the legal problems encountered in testing could be eliminated, or at least reduced, if test designers and users understood and systematically described the behaviors they were measuring, the tasks to which those behaviors were demonstrably related, the conditions for the instrument's proper use, and the known distortions and potential risks involved (Schwitzgebel & Schwitzgebel, 1980). Before concluding that a test measures "intelligence," one should know a) the precise behavioral definition of the intelligence to be tapped by that test; b) the specific behaviors included; c) what tasks or performances the behaviors are related to; and d) the inherent dangers and possibility of the test having a discriminatory impact. This would presuppose knowledge about a test's reliability and validity, the methods used to establish its norms, and the standardization procedures. In addition, it must be recognized that a test samples a very small segment of behavior under restrictive and artificial conditions. Unfortunately, a large portion of existing published tests would fail to meet many of these guidelines.

This does not mean that all tests, including cognitive ability tests, are meaningless and useless. We must know what a test can and cannot do, and we must apply it to appropriate populations cautiously and scientifically. With this approach, valid psychological tests can be used to our advantage and to the advantage of the population we are assessing. Shortcuts can bring social damages to consumers in the same manner that a hastily marketed drug may harbor potential physiological damage.

So far, judicial concern about the discriminatory potentials of testing in the educational and employment fields has focused almost exclusively upon ability or intellectual testing, both group and individual. Personality testing has yet to be challenged seriously, although its susceptibility to challenge is extremely high. Personality testing is plagued by vagueness and excessive levels of subjective interpretation backed by little empirical support. Construct validation would be helpful, because this form of testing appears to be a good candidate for considerable legal attention in the near future.

Summary and Conclusions

The goal of psychological assessment is to reduce the complexity of human behavior to a manageable set of variables so that present behavior can be appraised and some parameters of future behavior can be predicted. As such, assessment can be a valuable tool to the psychologist consulting with courts, law enforcement, the correctional system, and business and industry. The most rapidly developing form of assessment is performed by forensic neuropsychologists, who study and assess the functioning of the human nervous system. In both civil and criminal courts, reports of neuropsychological assessments are becoming more commonplace. This chapter has emphasized the testing services provided to law enforcement agencies, specifically with reference to the screening and selection of personnel. The principles, concepts, and problems discussed in law enforcement screening and selection can be generalized to psychological assessment and testing in other arenas.

An understanding of the basic principles of reliability, validity, standard error of measurement, and normative distribution is crucial if one is to evaluate any testing program. Too many agencies

58

CHAPTER
TWO:
PSYCHOLOGICAL
ASSESSMENT,
TESTING,
AND THE
LAW

have initiated testing programs without any evidence that the instruments they are using are valid or reliable.

The primitive state of the art of test validation in law enforcement and corrections must be emphasized. To date, the data are inconclusive. There is a great demand for predictive validation studies: those that will help administrators detect, prior to hiring an individual, whether that person is likely to succeed in the position. At present the very definition of "success" is open to interpretation; thus far, the criterion most often applied is the favorable evaluation by a supervisor. The importance of construct validity as the unifying concept and fundamental rationale for psychological assessment must also be stressed.

Various screening devices are available, with varying limitations and strengths. In view of the inconclusive nature of the research in this area, it is important to note that, as yet, no *one* test or variable is powerful enough to predict on-the-job performance. At present the most frequently used screening device is the MMPI, but the traditional methods of using that test have been no more validated than methods of using other tests.

The quality of present selection and promotional procedures in law enforcement is substandard and in need of more careful scrutiny. Lack of interest on the part of psychologists partly explains the poor quality. Other factors include the limited available research upon which to base decisions and plan programs, and unfamiliarity with and a general ignorance about assessment validation.

Finally, the legal questions about psychological testing practices in both educational and employment screening and placement remain unsettled and are likely to appear repeatedly in future litigation. Many of them can be eliminated, however, with better understanding of what psychological tests can and cannot do and with empirical study to determine whether the instruments are doing what they are designed to do.

Questions to Ponder

1. Why is the topic of validity so important in psychological assessment, especially as it pertains to legal issues?

2. Do you think psychological assessment is necessary for screening applicants for positions of public safety? What procedures can you think of that might replace psychological testing?

3. The interview is used extensively in the selection of applicants for most employment positions. Can you think of ways it could be improved in the selection process?

4. Do you think you can predict what your best friend will do in most—if not all—situations? Why or why not?

5. What are the drawbacks of using only one psychological test in an assessment procedure?

CHAPTER THREE

THE PSYCHOLOGY OF LAW ENFORCEMENT

 HE RELATIONSHIP BETWEEN PSYCHOLOGY AND LAW ENFORCEMENT has developed so steadily and rapidly over the past thirty years that a chapter on this topic seems insufficient. As law enforcement departments have become more professional, law enforcement administrators better educated, and the public has demanded more accountability, the role of psychologists as consultants to law enforcement has increased substantially. Additionally, research psychologists have delved into areas directly related to law enforcement work, such as screening of candidates—which was discussed in the previous chapter—crisis intervention techniques, and stress management for law enforcement officers. Also on the increase is the number of research papers focusing on psychology and law enforcement presented at the Annual National Convention of the American Psychological Association (APA). Many of these presentations are sponsored by APA divisions 18 (Psychologists in Public Service) and 41 (Psychology and Law).

This chapter will examine some of the law enforcement areas in which both research and practicing psychologists have been the most active. We begin by exploring the empirical evidence for the "police personality," addressing the question, "Does law enforcement work attract people with distinguishable behavioral patterns or specific personalities?" Next, we turn to the issue of women in law enforcement work. Women make up nearly 10 percent of the law enforcement force nationwide (Martin, 1991). Their unique contributions and the particular obstacles they encounter will be discussed.

Next, we shift to discretionary behavior in law enforcement and how "occupational socialization" affects this behavior. Finally, we will focus on the many dimensions of stress and its relationship to law enforcement. Stress has an important influence on the attention, memory, and decisionmaking not only of first-line participants in the criminal justice system—the law enforcers—but also on the participants at all levels of the criminal justice process. Neither witnesses, plaintiffs, defendants, judges, nor lawyers are immune to its effects. Although we will concentrate on stress as it affects law enforcement officers, the material covered is generalizable to human beings in a variety of occupational and social situations.

The Police Personality

The public's perception of law enforcement officers ranges over a broad spectrum of images. Some people associate them with the rigid, dogmatic institutions that perpetuate social injustices in favor of the financially, politically, and socially powerful. Others feel that the police

CHAPTER
THREE:
THE
PSYCHOLOGY
OF
LAW
ENFORCEMENT

are unappreciated, caring individuals trying to protect the community from the onslaughts of crime. Some scholars have promoted the image of the typical law enforcement officer as an authoritarian, cynical, politically conservative, socially and psychologically insensitive person. By contrast, the entertainment media have been instrumental in encouraging images of free-wheeling, unorthodox cops who, in the face of political and organizational pressures, unrelentingly pursue criminals to the end, even if it means losing their jobs, or violating the civil rights of citizens. Often, novice officers and police academy recruits model these media characters, but they soon learn through the socialization process that this image is unrealistic.

What, then, is the "police personality?" Is there such a thing? Does law enforcement attract certain types of people? To provide a framework for our discussion, we will adopt the classification scheme proposed by Lefkowitz (1975), who identified and evaluated two trends in the theoretical writing and existing research on the police personality. He labeled these trends "Trait Syndrome I" and "Trait Syndrome II" to reflect the personality style being examined by the researchers.

TRAIT SYNDROME I

Trait Syndrome I includes behavioral indicators of social isolation and secrecy, defensiveness and suspicion, and cynicism. It is based on the common observation that law enforcement officers generally associate with their "own kind" and develop values and interests that correspond closely to those exhibited by their in-group. Law enforcement officers are often said to party, go fishing, and attend sports events together. This promotes social isolation from individuals outside police-related occupational groups and encourages secrecy about law enforcement work. It is unclear whether this socio-occupational isolation results from pressures encountered in law enforcement work or the law enforcement training program, or whether it is a feature of the personality structures of the people drawn to law enforcement. That is, would these individuals be just as socially isolated if involved in different occupations? Whatever the origin, isolation and secretiveness seem to promote mutual misunderstanding between law enforcement and the public (Lefkowitz, 1975).

Lefkowitz cites research indicating that law enforcement officers not only feel misunderstood by the public, but also rate this as one of the major problems they face (e.g., Olson, 1973; Opinion Research Corporation, 1968). Interestingly, when the public is asked for its views about law enforcement officers, those views are not as negative as the officers believe (Lefkowitz, 1975, 1977).

According to Trait Syndrome I research, law enforcement officers are suspicious of citizens (Matarazzo et al., 1964; Mills, 1969; Rhead et al., 1968; Roberts, 1961; Verinis & Walker, 1970) and sometimes even of each other (Westley, 1956). However, the factors contributing to this high level of suspiciousness have not been carefully identified. As with isolation, it is not known whether suspicious personalities are drawn to law enforcement work or whether suspicion develops as a consequence of the job experience.

CAREER-STAGE RESEARCH

Niederhoffer (1967), who studied New York City police officers, argues that urban officers go through stages of **anomie** and **cynicism** during their careers. Anomie, a term developed by the French sociologist Emile Durkheim and later refined by the American sociologist Robert Merton, means alienation from one's society and traditional culture. Anomie is described by Niederhoffer as a loss of faith in people, a feeling of alienation from society at large, and a turning toward the police organization as the principal hope for social salvation. He sees cynicism as a way of adapting to the frustrating feelings brought on by anomie. In police officers, cynicism is characterized as "...diffuse feelings of hate and envy, impotent hostility, and the sour grapes pattern" (Niederhoffer,

1967, p. 99). **Impotent hostility** springs from the inability to express hostility against society; a police officer must remain calm, even when spat on. The **sour grapes** behavior pattern describes the feelings of police officers that desired but unattainable goals are really not all that important or valuable. For instance, college-educated patrol officers may find that their expectations of promotion are not fulfilled, and try to convince themselves that promotion really does not mean all that much to them. On the other hand, non-college-educated officers may rationalize that higher education is not necessary.

Niederhoffer contends that cynicism—which comprises any or all of the above elements—is discernible at all levels and in all fields of law enforcement. He postulates there are two kinds of police cynicism: One is directed *toward society*; the other is directed *toward the police organization* itself. The first is characteristic of police at all levels, running from the patrol officers to the police chief. It is the attitude that most people are basically weak or even evil and would commit crimes if they knew they could get away with it. Cynicism toward the police organization is most often found in the patrol officer and is much less likely to affect the higher ranking officers. Niederhoffer explains that it is less likely in the ranking officer because he or she hopes to transform and eventually control the system. The patrol officer, on the other hand, develops a greater degree of frustration with the criminal justice process. Daily encounters with crime and victimization are more likely to promote frustrations about the ineffectiveness of the "system."

According to Niederhoffer, police cynicism passes through four distinct stages of development. The first stage, which he calls **pseudo-cynicism**, is most recognizable among recruits at the police academy. Although they express cynical *attitudes* to mimic their police models at the academy, they can barely conceal the idealism and commitment they actually feel. **Romantic cynicism**, the second stage, is reached during the first five years of the police career. Although Niederhoffer does not define the precise behavior, it appears that the most idealistic, young members of the force are the most disillusioned by the reality of police work and hence most vulnerable to this type of cynicism. The third stage, **aggressive cynicism**, gradually builds until it becomes most prevalent during the tenth year of service. According to Niederhoffer, it corresponds to a resentment which is best expressed by the catch phrase, "I hate citizens," and it results in a diffuse hostility toward society and the department. The fourth stage, **resigned cynicism**, occurs during the last few years of a police career. It is demonstrated by acceptance of the job situation and capacity to come to terms with the flaws of the criminal justice system. This final stage is viewed by Niederhoffer as the successful resolution of a career marked by much dissatisfaction and conflict.

Niederhoffer observes that, for the first few years of a police career, cynicism increases in proportion to the length of service. It then tends to level off sometime during the fifth and tenth years of service. He believes cynicism is learned as part of a socialization process typical of the police occupation, a process estimated to take about five years.

Reiser (1973) has hypothesized a similar process, the **John Wayne Syndrome**, which begins early in the career of a law enforcement officer and lasts for three to four years. This behavior pattern is characterized by coldness toward others and emotional withdrawal, authoritarian attitudes, cynicism, overseriousness, and a black-or-white, inflexible approach to daily problem solving.

Violanti (1983) identifies four law enforcement career stages quite similar to Niederhoffer's: (1) the alarm stage (0–5 years); (2) the disenchantment stage (6–13 years); (3) the personalization stage (14–20 years); and (4) the introspective stage (20 years and over). In the **alarm stage**, the new officer experiences "reality shock," which is realization that law enforcement work is different than what is learned at the academy. After about five years, the **disenchantment** stage sets in and continues until midcareer (12–14 years). During this stage, bitter disappointment develops when

62

CHAPTER
THREE:
THE
PSYCHOLOGY
OF
LAW
ENFORCEMENT

mid-career officers realize that pressures and demands of law enforcement work far outweigh their ability to respond effectively. At the end of mid-career (14–20 years), Violanti believes officers go through a **personalization stage**, in which they focus more on their personal goals before retirement and pay less attention to the goals of the law enforcement agency. This stage represents a kind of "mid-life crisis" for officers, at which point they evaluate whether they are where they want to be professionally. Finally, at around twenty years of service, an **introspective stage** emerges. The officer "looks back on earlier years as the good old days" and becomes secure and settled in the job. It is at the introspective stage that dissatisfaction and boredom sets in, and performance correspondingly drops. According to Violanti, this pattern is one of the reasons why officers normally retire after twenty years of service.

Niederhoffer's theory and the twenty-item questionnaire of police cynicism he developed has generated more research than any other theory of police attitude and career change. Much of the research has examined the cynicism scale's reliability and validity, but the research has not found the scale particularly promising so far (Lefkowitz, 1975; Anson, Mann, & Sherman, 1986; Langworthy, 1987). One thing does appear clear: The scale is multidimensional and measures a number of things besides cynicism (Regoli, Crank & Rivera, 1990). The lack of research support for the scale's reliability and validity, however, does not mean that Niederhoffer's theory of cynicism is unsupportable. Rather, it may mean the scale is seriously flawed but that the theory itself remains untested.

TRAIT SYNDROME II

Trait Syndrome II encompasses behaviors that generally carry the label "dogmatic" or "authoritarian." The authoritarian personality is displayed through rigid adherence to and an overemphasis on middle-class values; uncritical acceptance of authority figures; a firm belief in strong punishment and discipline for those who violate social values and laws; and a generalized tendency to think in rigid, oversimplified categories that generate black-and-white answers to social and psychological problems. Authoritarian personalities are hypothesized to show a strong desire to associate themselves with powerful people, to be cynical about the motives and purposes of others, to be superstitious, and to disapprove of free emotional lives or displays of emotion (Adorno et al., 1950).

Trait Syndrome II is also not well supported by the research, however. Although components of the authoritarian personality often exist in many law enforcement officers, the existence of a pervasive authoritarianism in most law enforcement officers has not been substantiated.

Authoritarianism is usually measured by an attitudinal scale called the California F-Scale. After reviewing the literature in the area up to 1974, Lefkowitz (1975, p. 11) concluded that police officers "have scored, almost without exception, as not particularly authoritarian or dogmatic on the F-Scale, D (Dogmatism) Scale, and modifications of same." Later research continued to support this conclusion (Conser, 1980). For example, British studies have consistently reported that police recruits are no more authoritarian than control groups gathered from the general population (Reiner, 1992). However, there is some evidence that, although there is a "liberalizing effect" of law enforcement training, experience in the field does seem to develop authoritarian attitudes (Reiner, 1992).

OTHER REPRESENTATIVE RESEARCH

A study by C. Abraham Fenster, Carl F. Wiedemann, and Bernard Locke (1977) is representative of much of the traditional research on the police personality. Over 700 male subjects were divided into four groups, depending on whether they had law enforcement experience or a college background. All were comparable in age (with an average age in the late twenties). A variety of group mental and personality tests were administered to all subjects, and comparisons were made between the scores of the four groups. However, as in most studies on the police personality, little theoretical rationale was offered as to why these particular tests were selected, nor was validity information described. Several of the tests used have notoriously questionable validity and weak theoretical bases for their construction—important points to consider in assessing the research.

Results showed that law enforcement officers demonstrated significantly lower neuroticism scores (reactivity to stressful events) than the nonpolice groups. In addition, they obtained lower authoritarian scores and slightly higher intelligence scores. The authors concluded that this officers sample "may represent a superior subsample of the general population" (p. 104), and that the officers were better adjusted psychologically than the nonlaw-enforcement groups. Overall, there was little evidence for particular law enforcement personality traits.

A study by Carol Mills and Wayne Bohannon (1980) illustrates a trend toward better research design and a more vigorous attempt to link test scores with theory. The Mills-Bohannon project tried to identify those personality characteristics associated with high supervisory ratings on leadership and overall suitability for law enforcement work. Further, the study was designed to test two predictive models of law enforcement effectiveness and leadership (viz., Hogan, 1971; Gough, 1969).

The measuring instrument used to delineate personality characteristics was the empirically constructed California Psychological Inventory (CPI). Forty-nine male Maryland state police officers with one year's experience served as subjects. Each subject was rated by two supervisors on a seven-point scale for leadership and "overall suitability for police work." There was a good amount of inter-judge reliability (.78) between the two supervisory ratings for each subject.

The results showed that the Hogan model of police effectiveness was significantly better able to predict leadership than Gough's model. Hogan's model uses the four CPI personality variables of social presence, self-acceptance, achievement via independence, and intellectual efficiency to predict law enforcement performance. Social presence refers to the personality trait of being poised and self-confident in personal and social interaction. Self-acceptance refers to a tendency to feel competent, combined with a capacity for independent thinking and action. Achievement via independence denotes motivation to achieve in settings where autonomy and independence are encouraged. Intellectual efficiency refers to the ability to think clearly and planfully.

The results of the Mills-Bohannon study *suggest* that the personality requirements for successful law enforcement leadership are the above described four traits in combination, although caution is advised when generalizing to other law enforcement agencies in other states and other countries (ecological validity). Also, the vagueness of the personality traits is troublesome, because it renders them susceptible to multiple interpretations. For example, what precisely does "the ability to think clearly and planfully" mean, and in what context?

There is evidence to suggest that law enforcement officers in general tend to be conservative, conventional, and concerned with maintaining the status quo (Lefkowitz, 1975). Hence, at least one component of the authoritarian personality is supported in the research literature. This conventional outlook appears to be fostered by para-military regulations and rules of conduct expected by some law enforcement agencies. Beyond this conservative aspect, the "average" law enforcement officer seems to display personality characteristics similar to those of the "average" population—normal and free of pathology.

Very little research has been directed at motivations for pursuing a law enforcement career (Stotland & Berkerich, 1979; Lefkowitz, 1975). One frequent conclusion is that job security is the

64

CHAPTER
THREE:
THE
PSYCHOLOGY
OF
LAW
ENFORCEMENT

greatest attraction of law enforcement work (Gorer, 1955; Niederhoffer, 1967; Reiss, 1967). This motivation seems to be more characteristic of white candidates than of members of ethnic minority groups (Hunt, 1971).

It should not be surprising that the research on the police personality continues to be equivocal and inconsistent. As we learned in Chapter 2, individual behavior (personality) and situational context intermingle. The search for consistent behaviors must consider what kind of consistency (temporal or cross-situational) is being measured, and in what context. The fact that some researchers report law enforcement officers to be authoritarian or cynical while others do not underscores this interaction. Some law enforcement agencies expect their officers to assume an authoritarian role, while others do not. Some agencies look for applicants who already "fit the mold," while others anticipate that the young officers will acquire appropriate roles through peer pressure or occupational experience. It is entirely possible that law enforcement behavior is shaped more by agency-appropriate roles the officer is expected to assume than by the officer's own personality variables. In other words, the occupational socialization process may override individual differences or personality styles. Furthermore, individuals regarded ineffective by one police department are often seen as effective in another (Bartol, 1991; Bartol & Bergen, 1992). It seems that law enforcement agencies have "personalities" roughly analogous to individual personalities, and that these "organizational personalities" may play a critical role in predictions of job success and failure. In this sense, the psychological characteristics of law enforcement officers as measured by personality inventories may be irrelevant to success in law enforcement.

In conclusion, it does not appear productive to search for any entity called the "universal police personality" that characterizes, even in part, the person who becomes a law enforcement officer. It may be more appropriate to limit one's research conclusions to the specific law enforcement agency in which the subjects are employed. Research findings on the "personality" of law enforcement officers may reveal more about the characteristics and expectations of the law enforcement agency than about the people within it.

Women in Law Enforcement

The first full-time, sworn woman officer in the United States was Alice Stebbins Wells, who was appointed policewoman in Los Angeles in 1910 (Buwalda, 1945; Higgins, 1961). Although her duties were primarily to supervise young women and girls in places of public recreation, such as dance halls, theaters, and skating rinks, she was the first to be called a *policewoman* by an organized police department. Other women were in law enforcement in this country long before 1910 but they were appointed as "matrons," restricted to taking care of detained women and girls.

Wells' appointment received widespread national recognition and drew front page stories, often critical and accompanied by negative caricatures. However, Wells utilized her unique position to become a prime mover in the policewomen's movement, and helped form the International Association of Policewomen in 1915 (More, 1992). Today the organization is known as the International Association of Women Police (IAWP).

Other departments were slow to accept women in law enforcement. When they did, they were generally restricted to desk jobs, even working as clerks, secretaries, and dispatchers. They worked with juvenile cases or supervised women detainees. They were also charged with identifying community "moral hazards" and presenting them to community leaders and civic groups for action (Buwalda, 1945). Patrol work and investigation were left to men. Law enforcement administrators did not believe women had the physical strength or stamina, or the psychological temperament to exert forceful authority over adults.

It took twenty more years before women gained law enforcement positions at the state level. In May 1930, Lotta Caldwell and Mary Ramsey were enlisted into the Massachusetts State Police, the first women to gain entry into a state police or highway patrol agency (Higgins, 1961). In 1972, the first two women graduated from the FBI Academy and were sworn in as special agents (Horne, 1975).

The 1930 U. S. census listed 1,534 women employed in law enforcement, and by 1940 this number increased slightly to 1,775 (More, 1992). In 1960, the census showed the number increased to 5,617, a figure which still represented only 2.3 percent of the total officers nationally (Martin, 1980). Today, women are entering law enforcement at an increasing rate. Between 1971 and 1978, the proportion of women entering law enforcement more than doubled (2 percent to 4.2 percent), and between 1978 and 1986, the proportion more than doubled again (4.2 percent to 8.8 percent) (Martin, 1991). Researchers have also found that women are making progress in acquiring promotions and administrative positions, although they encounter continuing resistance from supervisors (Martin, 1989, 1992). Still, women remain a small minority in law enforcement nationwide. Interestingly, the same situation holds in Great Britain. Despite the British Sex Discrimination Act of 1975 that led to abolition of separate police divisions based on gender and other discriminatory practices, only 10 percent of all police officers in England and Wales are women (Reiner, 1992). Beliefs in the physical and emotional unsuitability of women in law enforcement continue to reign.

Much of the contemporary research (beginning in the 1970s) on women in law enforcement has concentrated on comparing job performance of men and women to determine if women can physically and psychologically handle the rigors of law enforcement work, particularly patrol assignments. This research has consistently found that women can do law enforcement work at least as effectively as men in large metropolitan departments (Pendergrass & Ostrove, 1984; Feinman, 1986; Balkin, 1988) and small-town departments (Bartol, Bergen, Volckens & Knoras, 1992). Despite the growing research that continually finds women can do law enforcement work, women officers still face many obstacles and stressors. Interestingly, one of the greatest barriers to accepting women into law enforcement does not come from the public but from male officers, particularly male supervisors (Wexler & Logan, 1983; Bartol et al., 1992).

Researchers have studied how women adapt and adjust to the barriers and gender discrimination found in male dominated police culture. Some writers (e.g., More, 1992; Berg & Budnick, 1986) have asserted that female officers go through adjustment stages, running from the honeymoon stage, to the ambivalent stage, to the transition stage. Another approach is to try to identify the various methods by which women adapt to law enforcement work.

Judie Gaffin Wexler (1985) has identified four role styles adopted by women in law enforcement: neutral-impersonal, feminine, semimasculine, and mixed. The largest number of women officers in her sample adopted the **neutral-impersonal** style, adopting a business-like attitude toward their male colleagues. Women who followed this style wanted to be treated with respect as full and equal members of the work group, and they shunned special treatment from colleagues or administrators. Wexler found, however, that the women in this group believed they had to approach some aspects of law enforcement work differently than their male counterparts traditionally would. For example, they believed that force was often not necessary in accomplishing certain goals, such as making arrests. Wexler also discovered that women who adopted the neutral-impersonal style typically did not do much socializing with their male colleagues, and half of them described their relationships with the male officers as distant and tenuous.

66

CHAPTER
THREE:
THE
PSYCHOLOGY
OF
LAW
ENFORCEMENT

The **semimasculine** style was defined by Wexler as a tendency to be professional and to do the job well, all the while believing that they would not be totally accepted as equals in this male-dominated profession. The women adopting this style did expect to be treated as individuals, however. In contrast to the neutral-impersonal officers, the semimasculine officers believed that they could be accepted as individuals by socializing with the male officers, by joking with them, going out after work for drinks, and cheering for, or participating in, departmental sports teams.

Women who adopted what Wexler called the **feminine** style put more emphasis on the fact that they were women in the physical sense. "Being attractive at work was important to them" (Wexler, 1985, p. 752). Interactions with male officers often carried a sexual undertone, in which they used their femininity to gain acceptance. Women in this group accepted or desired special treatment from colleagues or supervisors, and also accepted male protectiveness on the job. Wexler observed that women who followed this style were really not accepted in the informal work group and they were not taken seriously enough by the male officers for information to be shared with them.

The **mixed** style is characterized by selective utilization of all three styles, with no particular style dominating. These officers wanted to get respect by hard work and interpersonal distance, but they often resorted to a combination of conscientious hard work, flirting, and teasing to reach their goals. They also wanted to be treated as equals and refused special treatment.

While Wexler's research is interesting, it is unfortunate that she chose the term "feminine" to refer to women who appear to use their sexuality on the job. As we will see shortly, other researchers have identified "feminine" characteristics in law enforcement that transcend this physical emphasis. It is also important that research examining styles not be limited to one gender or to relationships with colleagues. An interesting study might focus on gender differences in style in patrol work and on which approach is most effective in the eyes of the public. However, we are likely to find that most effective police officers—male or female—use a variety of styles, depending on the situation. Some preliminary data have indicated, in fact, that women as a group use multiple styles or strategies in various situations (Bartol & Urzillo, 1993). Similar research on male officers would be helpful.

Current research does suggest that the style of law enforcement utilized by women as a group may be more effective than styles employed by men as a group. For example, many law enforcement administrators and a large segment of the public believe that female officers are better able than male officers to defuse a potentially dangerous or violent situation (Weisheit & Mahan, 1988; Balkin, 1988; Bell, 1982). Interestingly, the police chief of Madison, Wisconsin, was quoted as saying he believed that female officers made his police department a "kinder, gentler organization" (McDowell, 1992, p. 72).

A recent study by Johnson (1991) underscores observations that women as a group have a "gentling effect" when dealing with the public. Johnson focused on gender differences in job strain. Specifically, she looked at "internal burnout," characterized by feelings of being emotionally depleted on the job, and "external burnout," characterized by feelings of being emotionally hardened by the job and lacking compassion for citizens. While there were no significant gender differences in self-described internal burnout, men showed a greater tendency to report feelings of external burnout. Johnson concluded that the relatively low external burnout rate of women officers was perhaps a result of their less-aggressive and more gentle policing style. Johnson found in her interviews that they spoke about the compassion they brought to the job, as well as their strong preference for dealing with the public verbally and psychologically rather than physically.

These research discoveries, along with consistent findings that women are perfectly capable of meeting the physical and emotional demands of law enforcement work, suggest that the future for women in law enforcement should be bright. It is important, however, that the quality of their

■ 3.1: *GUILTY IN L.A.*

THE EYES OF THE NATION WERE ON LOS ANGELES on April 17, 1993, when a federal jury announced its verdicts in the case of four police officers accused of violating the civil rights of a criminal suspect, Rodney King. In court, jurors over a six-week period heard testimony from fifty-four witnesses. They also saw an incriminating home video of officers repeatedly delivering blows with batons and stomping on King, who lay on the ground, having been apprehended following a high-speed chase. Both the defense and the prosecution used the videotape to their advantage. When the video showed King trying to get up off the ground, for example, the prosecution said he was trying to get away from the lethal blows; the defense said he was out of control on drugs and resisting arrest.

The jury convicted two of the four officers. Sergeant Stacey Koon, in command during the incident, was found guilty of intentionally allowing unreasonable force to be used on a suspect in custody. Officer Laurence Powell, who had been shown on the tape inflicting the most serious blows, was convicted of using unreasonable force to violate a suspect's civil rights.

Many police administrators remarked that the King incident and the verdicts did not change policy in departments which "did things right" in the first place. Law enforcement officials as well as citizens were outraged by the police behavior they saw displayed on the videotape. Nevertheless, to many residents of inner cities, the King beating was not an isolated incident; it was one that happened to be recorded. The guilty verdicts reminded law enforcement officers that accountability to the public is a critical feature of their work. ■

work not be measured by a male yardstick but rather be judged on its own merit (see Tavris, 1992). This could lead to a new definition of effective policing. It is equally important that we encourage both male and female officers to develop qualities associated with success in law enforcement work.

Law Enforcement Discretion

"Discretion involves the ability to act on the basis of personal judgment, uncontrolled by prearticulated rules of law" (Nimmer, 1977, p. 257). It is the central ingredient in the day-to-day activities of the law enforcement officer, who deals directly and frequently with the public. Because of their enormous discretionary latitude, there is considerable variability among law enforcement officers in how they apply the written law (Reiss, 1992). Moreover, these discretionary decisions are generally not seen by the public, but only by the law enforcement officers and the accused (Reiss, 1992). Discretion is more important in the lives of local law enforcement agents than federal agents, because procedures and rules are more clearly spelled out at the federal level (Bennett-Sandier et al., 1979).

Most students of and participants in the criminal justice process consider discretion both indispensable and impossible to eliminate. It is a reality at all levels of the system (Cole, 1992). The maxim "squeeze out discretion here and it will emerge there" (Wilkins, 1979, p. 46) is widely accepted.

The discretionary behavior of law enforcement officers depends on a number of factors, including the nature of the offense at issue. Generally speaking, the more serious the act the less latitude there is for discretionary action by the law enforcement officer (Gallagher, 1979). Although an officer's actions appear to be strictly prescribed (Lefkowitz, 1977), the police have considerable discretion in handling such matters as moving traffic violations, minor juvenile offenses and family disturbances, exhibitionism, and drunkenness, but very little in handling homicides, aggravated assaults, rapes, or robberies.

68

CHAPTER
THREE:
THE
PSYCHOLOGY
OF
LAW
ENFORCEMENT

Discretion is also influenced by community concerns. If the community places great pressure on law enforcement to eliminate prostitution in a given area of the city, or to keep intoxicated persons off the streets, the scope of discretionary behavior is somewhat narrowed.

Other limiting factors are the officer's frame of mind at the time he or she investigates a given offense and the perpetrator's reaction to the officer (Gallagher, 1979). If the officer has encountered recent personal difficulties, he or she is apt to be less generous in handling minor violations. If the offender is hostile to the officer, an escalation effect may occur, in which each challenging remark or action is met with increased action by the other party. In the juvenile context, for example, research has shown that officers are more likely to take into custody juveniles who either challenge their authority or who are overly (and suspiciously) deferential (Lab & Whitehead, 1989).

AN ARCHIVAL STUDY

Sarah Berk and Donileen Loseke (1980–81) have examined characteristics of law enforcement discretion in handling domestic disturbances. Using an **archival** method of data collection, in which they relied on previously recorded events, Berke and Loseke studied law enforcement reports of domestic disturbances forwarded to the district attorney's unit of the Santa Barbara, California, Family Violence Program.

To increase internal validity, the researchers analyzed only those 262 law enforcement reports which had enough detailed information to convey a relatively complete picture of the domestic incident. However, by increasing internal validity the researchers lost some external validity. That is, by using only the most complete law enforcement reports in their analysis, they neglected a sizeable portion of the total reports available. This limits the extent to which the results can be generalized to law enforcement discretion in other domestic disputes.

"Domestic" was defined as those incidences "where the principals were adults involved in a heterosexual 'romantic' or conjugal relationship prior to, or at the time of, the incident" (p. 326). Therefore, two kinds of relationships qualified for analysis: (1) legal ones, as indicated by marriage, separation, or divorce; or (2) relationships which constituted a sharing of a residence, such as a common-law marriage or a live-in arrangement. "Disturbance" was defined by the law enforcement reports. Various events qualified, but most included physical violence or threats of violence, property damage, and verbal arguments.

The researchers were primarily interested in determining what specific characteristics found in domestic disturbances contributed to the law enforcement decision to arrest one of the parties. In the reports, a wide variety of notations were made by the law enforcement officer in describing each incident. The notations were assumed to identify the critical dimensions of law enforcement decisionmaking and, therefore, formed the basis of a law enforcement discretion model proposed by Berk and Loseke.

The dependent variable in this study was whether an arrest was made. The independent variables were determined on the basis of demographic and notation material earmarked and coded for statistical analysis.

Results indicated that four variables exerted a significant effect on law enforcement arrest. The strongest was whether one party (always female) was willing to sign an arrest warrant against the other party. Thus, if the woman refused to sign, an arrest was unlikely. Two other significant variables were whether the male was intoxicated and whether there was an allegation of violence by the female. However, these two independent variables were significant only when both parties were present at the time the law enforcement officer arrived on the scene.

The fourth variable exerting a significant effect on the officers' decisionmaking was whether the woman in the household or someone else had called the police. If the woman had done so, the probability of an arrest decreased. The researchers speculated that the person or party who alerted the police was an index of the severity of the disturbance. If neighbors, friends, or social service personnel called police, the officers may have believed the disturbance was out of hand and represented a more serious incident. If the woman called the police, they may have believed the incident was less serious.

The results of the Berke and Loseke study suggest that encouraging officer discretion in domestic violence situations is problematic, unless officers have received specialized training in handling this type of case. Domestic violence, to be discussed again in Chapter 11, is a complex issue which requires an appreciation for factors such as a) why a woman would change her mind about wanting an arrest; b) why she puts up with a punishing situation; and c) the power differential between the parties. Because officers often have not received extensive training, some observers suggest that police discretion in domestic situations should be limited.

The Berk-Loseke project also demonstrates how police discretion can be studied in a realistic setting through archival study. (We will return to the many advantages of archival research in a later chapter.) However, the degree of generalizability of this study to police decisionmaking in other domestic disturbances is limited because of the attention given to internal validity over external validity. The study suggests the influence of some variables on decisions to arrest in cases where a detailed and full report is filed. Potentially, other variables may also exert powerful effects on decisions to arrest if we analyze all police reports, including the less informative ones. Additionally, qualitative research in which officers are asked directly what contributes to their decisions to arrest would yield valuable information.

A FIELD STUDY

Another example of law enforcement discretion research using a different methodology was conducted by Donald Black (1971). In this study, arrest was again the dependent variable, but it was related to a much broader scope than domestic disturbances. The independent variables included the suspect's race, the seriousness of the alleged crime, the evidence available in the field setting, the complainant's preference for law enforcement action, and the social relationship between the complainant and the suspect. Black wanted to discover which of the independent variables emerged as significant factors in the officer's decision to arrest or not to arrest.

The data were collected through "systematic observation" of police-citizen transactions in three major cities during the summer of 1966. In comparison to the Berk and Loseke study, which was archival and not contaminated by any obtrusive measure or observer, the Black investigation utilized a data collection method with potential to affect the results. That is, the presence of observers might alter the event being investigated. Black used thirty-six researchers who recorded observations of encounters between patrol officers and citizens. The observers' training and supervision was approximately the same in all three metropolitan locations. They accompanied the police officers on all work shifts, but most of the observation time was spent when police activity was highest, especially on weekend evenings.

Over 5,700 incidents were observed and recorded, but only about 5 percent of them were used in the study analysis. Again, as in the Berk-Loseke study, a concerted attempt was made to insure internal validity, somewhat to the detriment of external validity. Incidents in which there was no opportunity for an arrest, such as when the suspect had left the scene prior to police arrival or when no apparent crime had been committed, were deleted from the analysis. Traffic

70

CHAPTER
THREE:
THE
PSYCHOLOGY
OF
LAW
ENFORCEMENT

encounters and incidents that could "invisibly distort or otherwise confuse the analysis" were also excluded. The final data were gathered predominately from encounters with blue-collar adults suspected of criminal conduct, and they represented only a small amount of the total encounters observed.

Although caution and skepticism are advised, the data do provide some clues about the discretionary decisionmaking of police officers working in metropolitan police departments. Results revealed that a majority of the police-citizen encounters were *reactive* rather than *proactive*. Specifically, most encounters were citizen initiated rather than police initiated. On an average evening shift, for example, there were six citizen-initiated encounters for every one police-initiated contact. These results suggest that a major portion of criminal-law enforcement activity depends on citizens, not the police.

Arrest practices also depended heavily on the preferences of citizen complainants. When a citizen's eyewitness account linked a suspect to a crime, an arrest resulted in fully 75 percent of the cases in which the citizen specified a preference for an arrest. On the other hand, when the complainant preferred that no arrest be made, the police went along with this request 90 percent of the time. One conclusion which can be drawn from these data is that the complainant's preference may be a more powerful situational motivator for arrest than the evidence itself.

The probability of arrest increased as the intimacy of the relationship between the complainant and the suspect decreased. The more familiar the complainant and the suspect were to one another, the less likely was it that the suspect would be arrested. Further data showed that the probability of an arrest also increased when a suspect exhibited disrespectful behavior toward police. For legally serious crimes (felonies), police arrested 40 percent of the respectful suspects compared to 69 percent of the disrespectful suspects. For less serious crimes (misdemeanors), the police arrested 43 percent of the well-mannered and 71 percent of the disrespectful suspects.

The Berk-Loseke and Black investigations provide some information about the discretionary behavior of law enforcement officers in making arrests. There is little doubt that much more data collection must be done, using different research approaches and samples of behavior. The two projects illustrate the two most common methodological approaches to the study of law enforcement behavior, archival and field study.

DISCRETION IN THE CONTEXT OF THE LEGAL SYSTEM

Along with the factors already mentioned, law enforcement discretion is influenced by feedback the officer receives from the legal system itself, from peers, supervisory personnel, the prosecuting attorney, the judge, and other agents of the system. As Saks and Miller (1979, p. 74) have noted, "It is the behavior of other actors in the system that regulates the behavior of any given actor, not the written law."

The prosecuting attorney's strategy in handling a case is often dictated by the anticipated behavior of judge and defense. Judges make decisions that often serve as messages to the police and prosecutors about how to handle future cases. Prosecuting attorneys also give messages to the police about what will "go" in court and what is a legitimate case. Among these is the message that excessive zeal in arresting and charging perpetrators of minor offenses will overload the system. Such behavior may also generate public outcry that police should "catch the criminals and stop harassing the citizens."

An officer usually learns how to use discretion by modeling more experienced officers. Heavy peer pressure about the "right way" to do things and handle incidents appears to be

■ 3.2: *PSYCHIC DETECTIVES*

IN DISCUSSIONS OF UNUSUAL INVESTIGATION techniques, the use of psychics for help in solving crimes has always been controversial. Law enforcement agencies routinely deny their use to any great extent (Broughton, 1991). However, off the record, they will admit using psychics as an adjunct to traditional investigative procedures in major, hard to solve cases (Hibbard & Worring, 1982; Lyons & Truzzi, 1991). The extent to which psychics actually *help* solve a crime is largely unknown, though anecdotal evidence indicates they sometimes do.

Richard Broughton (1991) describes a tragic 1987 case in New Orleans. André Daigle and his friend were leaving a poolroom when a woman neither man knew asked for a ride home. Daigle volunteered and was never heard from again. He was reported missing the next morning by his family. His sister, who lived in California, consulted a psychic. When asked about Daigle, the psychic apparently felt pains around her head and was able to point out on a map of Lousiana where Daigle's body could be found. The sister called the family, and they rushed to the location. On the way, they saw Daigle's truck pass them on the highway, but Daigle was not inside. The two men in the truck were arrested for auto theft. While in custody, one of them confessed to the brutal murder of Daigle. The woman who had asked for a ride had taken Daigle to an apartment where the two men bludgeoned him to death by blows to the head. Daigle's body was found in the location identified by the California psychic.

Although this is an interesting and dramatic example, Broughton reports that most psychics provide inaccurate or misleading information that rarely yields fruitful results. Most of the time, it seems to be a hit-or-miss proposition. Some self-proclaimed psychics are simply frauds. Even psychics with a good track record of working with law enforcement officials often miss the mark. However, when police are desperate for leads, a psychic may produce something helpful. ■

---

continually exerted, and excessive deviance from the norm is usually not tolerated. Unfortunately, the norm in some departments or among some working groups of officers may be legally inappropriate. The officer who uses discretion in an atypical way may be inviting occupational and social sanction from colleagues, occupational termination, or even prosecution. Alternately, his or her actions may be neutralized by the actions of others, such as a supervisor or the prosecuting attorney.

Behavior that stays within the limits of the law enforcement officer's legally and departmentally defined role will be interpreted by outside observers as legitimate discretion (Saks & Miller, 1979), while behavior that exceeds these limits will be considered deviant. Therefore, discretion is partly based on the judgment of the individual, but also partly (perhaps even largely) based on the department's code of expected conduct. Experienced officers show the rookies strategies to use and the rookies model the veterans. In many instances, the "war stories" of the veteran cop offset the training and strategies presented by the police academy; in most instances, instructors who are also well-seasoned officers are given greater credibility than college professors. It is occupational socialization, therefore, which probably has the most influence on the development of discretionary behavior at the gateway to the legal system.

The discretionary behavior of each law enforcement officer, then, because it is partly dependent on the strategies and codes adopted by each particular department, is sometimes independent of the written law. In the larger departments, the strategies and codes to be adopted may be dictated more by subgroups within the department than by any efficient organizational unit. These unwritten rules are in turn partly determined by behavior of other participants in the judicial system, such as the prosecuting attorneys, the defense attorneys, the trial judge, the appellate judge, and even the probation and parole officers. In some cases the capacity of the correctional system dictates the discretion used by the first-line participants. An officer who knows the local jail is overcrowded may hesitate to arrest a belligerent reveler and detain him

72

CHAPTER
THREE:
THE
PSYCHOLOGY
OF
LAW
ENFORCEMENT

overnight. When traffic court dockets are full, an officer may issue a stern warning rather than a citation to appear in court.

In sum, the criminal justice system functions with interdependence among its components, and the discretionary behavior used by one component affects other components. In addition, as Saks and Miller (1979, p. 79) have observed, "actors closest to the borders of a system are least influenced by the system's norms and sanctions. It may therefore be predicted that judges have the least ability to deviate; police have the most."

Psychological Stress in Law Enforcement

For several decades law enforcement work was believed to rank among the top of all occupations in the amount and variety of stress it promotes. But stress—and its accompanying arousal—is not only germane to law enforcement; it is also pertinent if we seek to evaluate eyewitness testimony and victim accounts of traumatic incidences. Also, any empirical study of criminal behavior requires major attention to stress and physiological arousal. Although our focus will be on the stress faced by law enforcement officers, the principles outlined could be applied to all other actors in the legal system.

DEFINITION

Stress was first used as an engineering term referring to any external force directed at a physical object (Lazarus, 1966). It was introduced into the life sciences in 1936 by endocrinologist Hans Selye (Appley & Trumbull, 1967), who became one of the world's leading researchers on biological stress. Selye directed most of his attention to effects of biological stress on the physiological and biochemical functions of the living organism. He defined stress as "the nonspecific response of the body to any demand" (Selye, 1976, p. 15). Thus, the bodily reaction is presumed to be generalized, with the whole body system as a unit engaged in reducing or eliminating "agents" which cause stress. The agents, which Selye called **stressors**, may be external to the organism (exogenous) or within the organism (endogenous), and they may develop from a virus, physical injury, or disease-causing agent.

For our purposes here, we will suggest that psychological stress occurs when a stimulus initiates a response which does not lead to greater perceived or actual control over the stimulus. The behavioral pattern of the person involved is relatively unique, but it typically involves sympathetic activity in the autonomic nervous system and a restriction in the range of cues which are used to guide behavior. In other words, stress as a response involves physiological arousal and a reduction in the ability to use environmental guides (Easterbrook, 1959). To keep the discussion short, we will focus attention briefly on the input-output factors and skip the behavioral strategies for coping, unless they relate directly to law enforcement.

The input elements are the stressors or the stimuli which a person considers stressful—the stimuli or events which are evaluated as threatening, frustrating, or conflicting. The output element is the person's reaction or response. In psychology, the most common response is called **anxiety**, a term often used interchangeably with **stress reaction**. Anxiety is an unpleasant emotional state marked by worry, fear, anger, apprehension, and muscular tension, and manifested in behavior. Thus, the anxious person may stammer or display other speech disturbances, may chainsmoke, display irritability, avoid a situation, or assume any number of other behavioral postures, all of which may be responses to stressors.

We should distinguish briefly here between two types of anxiety (Spielberger, 1966). **State anxiety**, common in humans, is an emotional reaction to a specific situation. We have all been anxious in the face of certain stressors. If we are anxious in many or most situations, however, the arousal is labeled **trait anxiety** and thus is regarded by behavioral scientists as a personality variable. In trait anxiety, the person perceives threatening stimuli across a wide variety of situations.

MEASUREMENT OF STRESS

To conduct effective research on stress and bring it out of the realm of speculation, it would be helpful if behavioral scientists were able to measure it. Ideally, this calls for methods of discovering both how much stress a person is going through at a particular time and how much cumulative stress the person has faced. However, there is yet no satisfactory, objective way to measure psychological stress. We can measure it only indirectly through behavioral responses and physiological reactions to it.

Physiological reactions encompass a wide range of bodily changes, including changes in blood pressure, muscle tension, brain activation, skin conductance, heart rate, blood biochemistry, urinary levels of epinephrine, fatty acid mobilization, and hormone levels. Sophisticated equipment can monitor accurately any changes in these variables when stressors are introduced. Some biopsychologists argue cogently that these physiological indices are the most quantifiable and therefore the most precise procedures for measuring the effects of psychological stress. Consequently, much of the contemporary research concerned with stress factors has used these measures. The measures have two general shortcomings, however. First, they consider, in large part, only the immediate stress reaction; the cumulative reaction, which would be more reflective of the amount of stress a person is experiencing, is largely out of reach. Second, in working with human subjects, researchers generally deal with stress that is artificial, in the sense that it is induced in a laboratory setting. This lab-induced stress must also be restricted because of ethical considerations.

Some researchers have relied on subjective methods or **self-reports** to attempt to measure stress. In this self-report method, people tell researchers what feelings they are experiencing or have experienced, what they think precipitated these feelings, and in some instances what they are doing to adjust. However, due to individual differences in how one appraises stress conditions, comparable, quantifiable data are often difficult to obtain unless the researcher sets up objective, standardized questionnaires limiting the variety of responses.

A number of standardized questionnaires have been developed in an attempt to measure subjective appraisal of psychological stress elicited by various stimuli and everyday events. One of the best known is the Social Readjustment Rating Scale (SRRS) designed by Thomas H. Holmes and his colleagues (Holmes & Rahe, 1967; Holmes & Masuda, 1974), who identified forty-three events that most people experience as stress situations (stressors). Groups of subjects then rated each situation according to the amount of change or adaptation needed to adjust to it. This resulted in each situation being assigned a number of "life change units" (LCUs). The intensity and duration of change accompanying the event, rather than how desirable or undesirable the event itself was, determined its rank value. For example, getting married earned a high LCU rating while a minor traffic accident, though presumably less desirable, was believed not to require much change.

When people take the SRRS, they are simply asked to indicate whether or not each event has occurred in their lives and if so, when. Their own assessment of the stress related to the event

74

CHAPTER
THREE:
THE
PSYCHOLOGY
OF
LAW
ENFORCEMENT

is not considered. Life Change Units (LCUs) are summed, and when their values add up to 150 or more over a one-year period, the person is said to have "life crises." Holmes and Rahe (1967) have hypothesized that the greater the magnitude of LCUs the greater the probability that physical or psychosomatic disease will result from the stress of readaptation.

Although some research on the SRRS is promising (e.g., Rahe, Mahan & Arthur, 1970; Holmes & Masuda, 1974), the scale is not an accurate predictor of stress reactions. Some behavioral scientists (e.g., Brown, 1974) have pointed out numerous methodological and conceptual flaws in its design and development. One of the major shortcomings is its inability to take into account individual differences in subjective appraisal of the stress in life's events. A $90,000 mortgage is unlikely to be of equal stress to everyone who assumes it.

James Sewell (1983) has developed a stress scale for law enforcement that is an offshoot of the SRRS. The scale, called the Law Enforcement Critical Life-Events Scale (LECLES), lists 144 events that may be stressors for officers, from the pursuit of a traffic violator to the death of another officer in the line of duty. The officers were asked to indicate on a scale of 1 (no stress) to 100 (extremely high stress) the stress they experienced when confronted with each event. Sewall found that the most stressful event for the officers was the violent death of a partner in the line of duty (rated on average 88), followed by dismissal (85) and taking a life in the line of duty (84) (More, 1992). Although the LECLES has some of the same shortcomings as the SRRS, it recognizes that some occupations add their own unique stressors to the usual stressors faced by people on a day-to-day basis.

In summary, stress is measured a) by delineating a set of stressful situations and assuming that individuals confronted with them experience stress; and b) by assessing the person's appraisal of and response to a class of stressors. Most current research has focused on immediate physiological reactions to specific stressors in humans, studied under laboratory conditions. The long-term effects of stressors are still unknown. Attempts to rectify this have prompted the development of standardized questionnaires to determine the effects of life-event changes on adaptation and illness, but as yet conclusive data have not emerged. Behavioral measures, usually subsumed under the heading "anxiety," have lost some popularity, but the term anxiety is still used to signify a generalized response pattern to stress.

Occupational Stressors in Law Enforcement

Since the mid-1970s, considerable research interest has been directed at stress among males in metropolitan or urban law enforcement, often with the implicit assumption that law enforcement work is the most stressful of all occupations (Malloy & Mays, 1984). However, persons in many occupations may argue that they face more physical danger than law enforcement officers. Construction workers, miners, stunt pilots, and demolition workers are all exposed to potential death and physical injury. Paramedics and other medical personnel, though less likely to be exposed to physical harm, contend that theirs is as stressful as any occupation. However, perhaps few occupations encounter the *variety* of stressors (e.g., physical, psychological, social) as consistently as law enforcement work.

A number of studies have compared police work with other occupations on measures of health and social problems, such as disease, suicide, and divorce. Malloy and Mays (1984) carefully analyzed several studies often cited as good illustrations of the high personal costs of law enforcement. They concluded that these studies failed to demonstrate that police work is any more stressful than a number of other occupations. Terry (1985) has also observed that the issue of stress among law enforcement officers may be overstated. Furthermore, it is not clear to what extent the stressors listed by law enforcement officers affect their job performance. The literature in industrial/organizational psychology, however, clearly suggests that stress and job performance are inversely related; that is, the higher the stress, the lower the satisfactory job performance. For example, Miner (1992, p. 156) writes, "Performance—whether measured by supervisor ratings, organizational perceptions of effectiveness, or job performance on job-related examinations—has repeatedly been found to decrease with increasing levels of stress." To date, however, the police stress literature is lacking in assessments of the impact of stress on performance (Sewell, Ellison & Hurrell, 1988; Malloy & Mays, 1984).

There are, nevertheless, some educated guesses about the nature of the relationships among law enforcement experience, stress, and job performance. These hunches may be placed into three major categories: (1) the positive linear hunch; (2) the curvilinear hunch; and (3) the negative linear hunch. Niederhoffer's research (1967) illustrates the **positive linear hunch**. He supposes that as law enforcement experience increases, self-reports of stress should correspondingly increase, provided the individual remains a patrol officer (as opposed to being promoted to administrator). According to Niederhoffer, therefore, we can expect job performance to decrease with experience. John Violanti (1983) represents the **curvilinear hunch**. He hypothesizes a curvilinear relationship between stress and experience, with stress increasing during the first 14 years of experience, decreasing after 14 to 20 years of experience (the personalization stage), and increasing again prior to retirement (after 20 to 25 years of experience). Following Violanti's position, we would predict an inverted **U**-shaped function, with job performance low and stress high in an officer's early years, performance at its best in the middle years with stress low, and performance declining while stress increases toward the end of the officer's career. The **negative linear hunch** is represented by Ezra Stotland (Stotland, 1986, 1991; Stotland, Pendleton & Schwartz, 1989), who predicts that as job experience increases, job stress will decrease. Correspondingly, we would expect job performance to increase with experience.

Unfortunately, research examining these three relationships is sparse. Curt Bartol (1991b) has reported on preliminary data from 869 small-town officers followed over 13 years' experience. The data suggest that job performance (as evaluated by supervisors) increases with experience, while both self-reported and supervisory-reported stress decreases. This tentative finding provides support for the negative linear hunch. On the other hand, Bernie Patterson (1992), using data from nearly 4,500 police, correctional, and probation/parole officers, found some curvilinearity for law enforcement and probation/parole officers, but not for correctional officers. When only first-line officers were considered (in contrast to ranking officers), a linear pattern did emerge, with stress increasing as experience increased. This pattern suggests a positive linear hunch. It is obvious that much research needs to be conducted before we can disentangle these complex relationships.

TYPES OF POLICE STRESS

A common strategy employed in the police stress literature is to divide the stressors identified by urban or metropolitan police officers into four major categories: organizational, external, task-related, and personal (Kroes, Margolis & Hurrell, 1974; Wexler & Logan, 1983). **Organizational** stressors generally refer to the policies and practices of the police department itself. They include poor pay, excessive paperwork, insufficient training, inadequate equipment, weekend duty, shift

76

CHAPTER
THREE:
THE
PSYCHOLOGY
OF
LAW
ENFORCEMENT

work, limited promotional opportunities, poor supervision and administrative support, and poor relationships with supervisors or colleagues. Several surveys have reported shift work as a major occupational stressor (Eisenberg, 1975; Hilton, 1973; Kroes, 1976; Margolis, 1973). Shift work not only interferes with sleep and eating habits, but also with family life. Moreover, irregular hours often preclude social get-togethers and family activities, a job characteristic that socially isolates the law enforcement officer even more. Also, the organizational structure of large police departments often promotes office politics, lack of effective consultation, nonparticipation in decision-making, and restrictions on behavior (Cooper & Marshall, 1976).

Task-related stressors refer to the nature of police work, such as inactivity and boredom, situations requiring the use of force, responsibility of protecting others, the use of discretion, the fear that accompanies danger to oneself and colleagues, dealing with violent or aggressive individuals, making critical decisions, frequent exposure to death, continual exposure to people in pain or distress, and constant need to keep one's emotions under close control.

External stressors include frustration with the courts, the prosecutor's office, the criminal process, the correctional system, the media, and public attitudes. For example, for every hundred felony arrests, forty-three are typically dimissed or not prosecuted (Witkin, 1990). Moreover, many law enforcement officers feel court appearances are excessively time consuming, and they are often frustrated over judicial procedures, inefficiency, and court decisions. It has also been suggested that one of the predominant stressors confronting law enforcement officers is alienation (Niederhoffer, 1967). Jirak (1975) found that alienation due to perceived lack of support from political groups, the press, courts, and the public was a dominant stressor for New York City law enforcement. He also found that feelings of alienation usually increased throughout an officer's career, reaching a peak about the fifteenth year of service, at which point they decreased, apparently due to anticipated retirement. This trend was also reported by Lotz and Regoli (1977). Law enforcement-community relations are presumed to be important contributing factors to feelings of alienation (Skolnick, 1973). In a survey study by Chappell and Meyer (1975), only 2 percent of U. S. police officers polled believed the public held them in high esteem. Related to this is the often reported role conflict between what law enforcement officers think they should be doing (e.g., crime detection and arrest) and what the public believes they should be doing (e.g., protecting citizens, settling family disputes, chasing unleashed dogs) (Wilson, 1968).

Personal stressors involve marital relationships, health problems, addictions, peer group pressures, feelings of helplessness and depression, and lack of achievement. In a survey conducted by Kroes, Margolis, and Hurrell (1974), seventy-nine of the eighty-one married police officers interviewed felt that the nature of their work had an adverse effect on their home life. More specifically, the officers thought that police work gave a negative public image to their family, that their spouses worried regularly about their safety, that they took the tremendous pressures of the job home, that it made them less able to plan social events, and that the job inhibited nonpolice friendships. A survey of 100 police spouses—all women—(Rafky, 1974) revealed that nearly one-fourth were dissatisfied with their husbands' careers and that particular aspects of the job resulted in frequent family arguments.

Although the media often depict high divorce rates and general marital unhappiness among law enforcement officers, documentation is very difficult to obtain. One extensive study by the National Institute of Occupational Safety and Health (NIOSH), however, does reveal some evidence that the divorce rate is high for law enforcement officers and that marital problems are a chief reason for leaving the force. The NIOSH study (cited by Blackmore, 1978) polled 2,300 officers in twenty-nine departments around the United States and found that 22 percent of the law enforcement officers in the sample had been divorced at least once (compared to a national divorce rate of 13.8 percent among urban white males [1970 census]). The NIOSH study also revealed a 26 percent divorce rate for officers married before joining the force, compared to an 11 percent rate for those who married after joining. Officers also reported that marital problems are the prime cause of quitting the force before retirement.

Hageman (1978) found evidence that as length of service increases, marital unhappiness and discontent also increase. Because no comparison was made with marriages in the general population, it is not clear whether the increasing disenchantment was directly due to length of service. However, the study did report that the increasing "emotional detachment" of the officer was one of the primary factors in marital conflict. Without additional documentation, though, it is unwise to assume that interpersonal relationships are more problematic for law enforcement than for other occupational groups.

SOURCES AND INTENSITY OF STRESS

Kroes et al. (1974), using semi-structured interviews, found that perceived sources of stress for Cincinnati male police officers were largely organizational in nature. Task-related stressors did not emerge as a major source of stress, contrary to what is commonly supposed (e.g., Somodevilla, 1978). In one of the few studies examining stress in smaller departments, Crank and Caldero (1991) investigated self-reported stress in eight medium-sized Illinois municipal police departments ranging in size from 40 to 100 sworn full-time officers. The researchers passed out a questionnaire to officers present at roll-call for all shifts. Their study focused on one item in the questionnaire requesting officers to write a statement "about what you think is your greatest source of stress, and why" (p. 341). Only six of the 162 officers were identified as women, precluding a meaningful comparison by gender. More than two-thirds (68.3 percent) of the respondents perceived the organization as their principal source of stress, reflected particularly in problems with superior officers (usually their immediate supervisors). The second most frequent stress source identified was task-related (16.2 percent), followed by the court system, an external source (7.2 percent). Level of stress intensity was not measured.

While sources of stress are usually reported in the police literature, stressor intensity is often ignored. Officers are asked to say what stresses them, but not to indicate the level of stress they experience. Therefore, it is seldom clear whether their lists represent common complaints of people performing a difficult job, or whether they detail serious threats to health, social adjustment, job performance, or longevity. Post-shift conversations among officers often resonate with complaints about the absurdities of the day with the courts, supervisors, the public, and the media. We can surmise that generalized complaints reach the status of serious stressors, however, when performance is adversely affected.

Malloy and Mays (1984) assert that longitudinal studies are necessary if the research on police stress is to progress to a more sophisticated level. They suggest that there may be an as yet unidentified personality feature that might forecast susceptibility to stress in police candidates. Malloy and Mays urge researchers to adopt the Davidson and Neale (1982) model, termed the Diathesis-Stress paradigm. *Diathesis* refers to a personality or constitutional predisposition toward a given condition, abnormality, or ability.

A study conducted by Curt Bartol and his colleagues (1992) examined the stressors and problems faced by officers in small-town municipal law enforcement. The study examined: (1) whether female and male officers in the same department experience the same stressors; (2) how stressors affect performance; and (3) whether there are identifiable predictors of susceptibility to police-related stress. Performance was measured by supervisory evaluations of eleven behaviors believed to be critical for adequate performance in small-town or rural law enforcement. Stress was

78

CHAPTER
THREE:
THE
PSYCHOLOGY
OF
LAW
ENFORCEMENT

measured both by observations of supervisors and the officers' self-reports. Predisposition susceptibility to stress (diathesis variables) was measured by MMPI scores obtained at the time of initial
screening, prior to any law enforcement experience.

External stressors emerged as the category small-town police officers, both men and women,
found most stressful, followed closely by organizational stressors. Based on written comments of
the officers, the "liberal" attitude of the courts, dealing with the prosecutors who are "always playing
let's make a deal," and "constantly being in the public eye" were among the leading specific external
stressors. Specific organizational stressors included constant politics within the department, lack of
recognition for good work, inadequate retirement plans, insufficient personnel to do the job effectively, and colleagues not carrying their fair share of the load. The perceived stress caused by the
job itself (task-related) was significantly less than external or organizational stress, a finding also
reported by Crank and Caldero (1991).

Interestingly, the study found that women and men experienced the same stressors, to a
large extent. The one exception was for task-related stress, with female officers finding more stress
in this area than male officers. Nevertheless, the higher level stress reported by female officers did
not translate into poor performance. This finding suggests that women may be more sensitive and
empathetic in their policing than their male counterparts. Women indicated they are strongly
affected by the tragedy, pain, and death they encounter in police work. In fact, five female officers
noted that frequently encountering abused and dead children was one of the most stressful aspects
of the job. A similar finding was reported by Wexler and Logan (1983). Female officers also
reported more stress than their male counterparts as a result of the sense of responsibility they
have for the lives and safety of the public as well as for the safety of their police colleagues.

DIFFERENCES FOR SMALL-TOWN LAW ENFORCEMENT

Whether the stresses faced by small-town police officers (communities with a population of less than
50,000 and away from an urban sprawl) are similar to metropolitan or urban police remains an
unanswered question. Informal discussions with rural officers in Maine (Sandy & Devine, 1978)
suggested that there may be four stressors unique to small-town or rural patrol. Three are task-related:
security, working conditions, and inactivity. The fourth, social stress, is external. **Security stress** factors
center around the extreme sense of isolation experienced by officers confronting incidents in the field,
including domestic disturbances. Rural and small-town officers usually work alone, without readily
available backup. Moreover, contributing to perceived lack of security is the belief that many homes in
rural areas contain a collection of firearms purchased either for protection, hunting, or both. **Stressful
working conditions** include the small salary and marginal benefits, and inadequate equipment and
resources. Finally, **inactivity** can be a significant stressor. Sitting alone in a cruiser at night while a small,
isolated town closes down can be stressful. **Social stressors** in the rural context stem from the absence
of anonymity officers experience, both on and off patrol. Like those of other residents of a small
community, the habits and behaviors of law enforcement officers are open to public scrutiny. Moreover,
the rural officer may be reminded "who's paying your salary." Officers frequently refer to this phenomenon as the "fishbowl effect." Also, according to Sandy and Devine (1978), a majority of small-town
and rural officers have been born and raised within the community. Enforcing the law against people
they have known all their lives often produces dilemmas that may be highly stressful.

GENDER DIFFERENCES

Women entering the male-dominated occupation of law enforcement are likely to face an array of
stressors not usually experienced by men (Yarmey, 1990), including sexual harassment, negative

attitudes of male officers and supervisors, working as the sole female officer, and lack of role models. Wexler and Logan (1983) interviewed twenty-five women patrol officers in a large metropolitan police departments in Northern California. They found that the officers mentioned organizational stressors and stressors associated with being women in male-dominated departments most often during interviews. Inadequate training, rumors about them within the department, and lack of promotional opportunities were the organizational stressors mentioned most frequently. Negative attitudes of the male officers, lack of role models, and group blame (one poorly performing woman officer prompts men officers and the general public to generalize to all women officers) were the second group of stressors mentioned repeatedly. These findings prompted Wexler and Logan to add a fifth category, called "female-related stressors," to those previously identified in the literature. The Wexler and Logan study did not include a control group of male officers and did not measure the intensity of the perceived stress.

Another study examining the stress experienced by female officers was conducted by Pendergrass and Ostrove (1984). They surveyed police employees (sworn officers, police technicians, and civilians) on stress in police work and its health consequences. The study focused on both self-reported physiological and psychological/behavioral consequences of stress. However, the researchers, because of the "high disparate group numbers," did not statistically analyze the data, but simply listed mean scores. Therefore, it is difficult to determine whether there were actual gender differences in the officers' experiences of stress.

WORKLOAD AND STRESS

With the exception of extreme and sudden life-threatening situations, it is reasonable to assume that no stimulus is a stressor to all individuals exposed to it (Appley & Trumbull, 1967). Whether stress develops depends greatly on how the person perceives and appraises the stimulus, in combination with other personality variables. Therefore, the conditions analyzed above are not invariably stressors for all law enforcement personnel. Also, the same individual may enter into a stress condition in response to one presumably stressful situation and not to another. Accordingly, a great variety of different environmental conditions are capable of producing stress.

For example, Stotland (1991) makes a connection between workload and stress. He divides law enforcement careers into two categories, depending on the amount of fast-moving action they experience on a daily basis. Those officers who are exposed daily to shootings, crime, drugs, and violent incidents are called **high-workload** officers. Contrary to what might be expected, these individuals maintain a steady level of job performance (neither going up or down to any great extent) and remain largely unaffected by police department politics or supervisory evaluations. **Low-workload** officers are exposed to fewer violent and high-paced incidents, but may experience more stress. They serve the community by engaging in more ordinary tasks, such as we would find in small, low-crime communities. However, such concerns as their appearance and courtesy with the public are important both to them and the department, and their performance is highly influenced by supervisory evaluations. Therefore, they strive to improve their performance throughout much of their careers. High-workload officers, on the other hand, are more concerned with "doing their thing" and strive to do a good job by their own standards rather than the standards of the supervisor sitting behind the desk.

In light of the above data about stress in law enforcement work, it is not surprising that police departments are increasingly hiring full-time police psychologists or psychological, counseling, and psychiatric professionals to consult on difficult cases and to offer their services to individual officers. Delprino and Bahn (1988) reported that 53 percent of police agencies studied

80

CHAPTER
THREE:
THE
PSYCHOLOGY
OF
LAW
ENFORCEMENT

used counseling services for job-related stress. About one-third of these agencies also hired psychologists to provide relevant workshops and seminars. In addition, many family support groups are appearing throughout the country, frequently at the instigation of police spouses who band together to discuss and solve common problems (Brandreth, 1978).

When Adaptation Fails

In this section we will consider some of the more common maladaptive patterns found among the general population and relate them to law enforcement personnel. The reader should be forewarned that law enforcement is one of the most difficult professions about which to gather information regarding failures to adapt. Unfortunately, most of the data are based on anecdotal or incomplete clinical or agency information. This procedural information is valuable, but it should be balanced with validation evidence in the form of experimental studies, which are to this point lacking.

ALCOHOLISM

It has been reported by various sources, but not confirmed, that approximately 20 to 25 percent of law enforcement officers have a serious alcohol abuse problem (Hurrell & Kroes, 1975; Somodevilla, 1978). Furthermore, alcohol abuse appears to be more common among older, more experienced law enforcement officers, over age forty, with fifteen to twenty years of service (Unikovic & Brown, 1978). Although some police departments would concur with these statistics, many others would deny them. Some preliminary data reported by Pendergrass and Ostrove (1986) suggest that law enforcement officers may be heavier consumers of alcohol than the general population. The drinking problems appear to get worse during retirement (Violanti, 1992). We have little evidence of the extent of substance abuse other than alcohol, however. In light of the temptations offered to law enforcement officers by drug traffickers, abuse of illegal substances would not be surprising. However, much work needs to be done before conclusions can be advanced in either this or the alcohol abuse issue.

BURNOUT

Burnout is a common phenomenon within the helping professions as well as those which both help and control, such as law enforcement, the judiciary, and juvenile and adult corrections. Burnout was first identified and defined in this way by Herbert Freudenberger (1974): "...to fail, wear out, or become exhausted by making excessive demands on energy, strength, or resources" (p. 159). Burned-out individuals feel emotionally drained or exhausted, depressed, and exhibit irritability and negative, cynical attitudes toward people they work with. They feel unhappy about themselves and are dissatisfied with their accomplishments on the job. Eventually, burnout may lead to increased tardiness, absenteeism, and lapses in job performance. The scale most commonly employed to measure burnout is the Human Service Inventory (formerly the Maslach Burnout Inventory) (Maslach & Jackson, 1981).

Burnout appears to develop through three stages. In the first, emotional exhaustion, the individual has little energy or verve left for the job. The second stage, depersonalization, is characterized by a cynical, insensitive attitude toward others. Burned-out professors become cynical and negative toward students, burned-out social workers become distrustful and insensitive toward clients, burned-out nurses feel unappreciated by patients, supervisors, and the organization, and burned-out law enforcement officers become cynical and noncaring toward the public. The third phase is marked by feelings of low personal accomplishment, where the individual begins to feel that rewards and achievement no longer accompany the job. Because the person no longer thinks that what he or she does really makes a difference in the scheme of things, the person stops trying.

POST-SHOOTING TRAUMATIC REACTIONS

This syndrome (PSTR) represents a collection of psychological reactions that occurs after a law enforcement officer shoots someone in the line of duty. The pattern is especially apparent when the victim dies. Fortunately, many law enforcement officers complete their careers without ever firing a weapon in the line of duty. Still, in the U. S., about 3,600 individuals are shot at annually by law enforcement officers (More, 1992). Of that total, 600 are killed, 1,200 are wounded, and 1,800 are shot at but missed (More, 1992). Although a widely recognized phenomenon, PSTR has not been subjected to well-executed empirical research. As Zeling (1986, p. 410) writes, "The study of post shooting trauma is illustrative of a concept in police psychology that is widely accepted yet has little empirical support."

Solomon and Horn (1986) conducted a self-report survey of eighty-six law enforcement officers who had been involved in a shooting and found some common psychological effects both during and after the shooting incident. One of the strongest psychological phenomena experienced by these officers was perceptual distortion during the incident. Eighty-three percent of the officers experienced time distortion during the shooting. Most of them said that time seemed to slow down to a point where everything was happening in slow motion. One officer remembered thinking, "How come I'm moving so slowly?" On the other hand, a minority of officers thought everything speeded up during the event. Fifty-six percent of the officers reported visual distortions, and 63 percent experienced auditory distortions. The most frequent visual distortion was "tunnel vision": the officer became so focused on one object that everything else at the scene went unnoticed. This phenomenon is frequently experienced by victims of a terrifying event as well. Some officers reported seeing everything more intensely and in greater detail than normal. Auditory distortions centered around not hearing sounds (such as the shots fired), or hearing them less clearly or more intensely.

Following the incident, officers experienced a number of reactions. The five most common were a heightened sense of danger, anger, sleep difficulties, isolation/withdrawal, and flashbacks. Officers who were shot or observed other officers get shot often lost their sense of invincibility and began to perceive their job as more dangerous than they originally thought. Anger at the victim of the shooting, at the department, at colleagues, or at society in general for having to shoot someone, was the second most frequent reaction. Officers had difficulty both falling asleep and staying asleep because of thoughts of the episode. Many of the officers also needed to withdraw for a while to get their thoughts together and to work through what had happened. The fifth common reaction was the reoccurrence of thoughts of the scene intruding into the officer's daily life.

Solomon and Horn found that reactions varied widely in intensity. About 37 percent of the officers described their reactions as mild, 35 percent as moderate, and 28 percent as severe. The variance in intensity of these reactions is similar to that reported by Stratton, Parker and Snabbe (1984). The researchers (Solomon & Horn; Stratton, et al.) also agree that intensity of reaction depends partly on the perceived "fairness" of the shooting incident. "Being outnumbered, having a limited field of fire due to bystanders, going against a shotgun when armed with a revolver, and

82

CHAPTER
THREE:
THE
PSYCHOLOGY
OF
LAW
ENFORCEMENT

having to shoot someone who points an unloaded weapon (unknown to the officers), are examples of factors affecting the 'fairness' of the situation" (Solomon & Horn, 1986, p. 390). The more "fair" the officer perceived the incident, the less intense the psychological trauma experienced.

Other clinicians have reported a variety of symptoms or reactions to PSTR, but their observations are based on cases they encountered during their work as police psychologists. Systematic research with carefully designed methodology is badly needed in this area.

DEPRESSION

Behavioral scientists often divide depression into two major categories: endogenous and reactive. **Endogenous depression** refers to features believed to be precipitated by biochemical or physiological imbalance. It is commonly held that a predisposition to this type of depression is transmitted genetically. Drugs such as lithium have been successful in rectifying the imbalance and substantially alleviating the depression. Endogenous depression, however, is believed to account for only a small proportion of depressive features. In recent years, there has been a good deal of criticism of physicians and psychiatrists who almost blanketly prescribe drugs for depressive reactions.

Reactive depression, which is due to stress from a traumatic event or a series of negative events, is far more common. Loss of a loved one, loss of a job, loss of self-esteem, or a series of small failures can all precipitate reactive depression, which appears to have no fundamental physiological cause. Reactive depression, then, is essentially a psychological phenomenon directly related to psychological stress, and it affects law enforcement personnel (and the general population) far more often than endogenous depression does. When we refer to depression henceforth, it will be considered a maladaptive response to psychological stress rather than a condition caused by biological or physiological imbalance.

We often think of depression as a mood disorder. In fact, its symptoms do include apathy and disinterest, sometimes verbally expressed. It is also highly cognitive, in the sense that a person has thoughts and feelings of helplessness or hopelessness. ("What's the use of trying?" "Life is not worth living." "I can't do it.") Although these mood-cognition symptoms are probably the most important indicators, other things also signify depression. There are, for example, behavioral and somatic manifestations. The depressed person may withdraw socially, may procrastinate at tasks, may overeat or undereat consistently, and may not be able to perform his or her role. There also may be gastrointestinal disturbances or sleep problems.

Any or all of the three modes—somatic, mood-cognition, and behavioral—may exist in the individual. Note, however, that the mode or severity of the depression is not necessarily indicated by the frequency of behavioral or bodily symptoms. Thus, it is possible for a person to be very severely depressed and only manifest it cognitively. In fact, research by Martin Seligman (1975) has indicated that how people feel about themselves and their competence in relation to their environment (especially the social environment) appears to be the most crucial indicator of how widespread and intense their depression will be.

Antecedents of Depression

There is growing support for the view that reactive depression is partly a learned reaction to life events. One of the most crucial antecedents of depression seems to be a lack of mastery over one's environment, or a feeling that one has little control over what happens to oneself (Seligman, 1975). With successive failures over an extended period of time, a person "learns" that his or her behavior does not seem to have any or much effect on events in his or her life. This learned helplessness may begin as early as childhood, because children are especially susceptible to feelings of not being able to control their lives. If a child is not provided with sufficient opportunity to exercise some decisionmaking and competence building skills, that child may be unable to achieve the mastery expectations that are so important in later life.

Acquisition of social skills is another important element for gaining control of one's situation. Conversing with others on a give-and-take basis without monopolizing the discussion is an example of a social skill for which the person receives approval from others. Lack of social skills reduces the opportunity for the child—and later the adult—to receive recognition, while allowing more time to be preoccupied with negative personal thoughts.

Thus, in some instances the antecedents of depression occur in childhood, where the individual has first learned helplessness and inability to adapt to stress. The helplessness may become a pattern continued into adulthood. Depression, therefore, happens as a result of poor social and adaptation skills, and not vice-versa. However, depression does not always begin in childhood. The adult who meets a long series of personal failures which seem to accent personal incompetence may have sufficient cause to encounter feelings of helplessness and depression.

Depression is also often preceded by difficulty in adapting, not only to major stress events (which require "coping" and which may occur very rarely), but also to less dramatic but routine stressors. For example, among the most consistently reported stressors as antecedents of reactive depression are consistent arguments with a spouse or otherwise disturbed interpersonal relationships. McLean (1976) calls these sources of small, repetitive personal and social frustrations *microstressors*. He theorizes that the basis for much reactive depression is an accumulation of these microstressors, which may be present in the lives of many people. That is, depression may not be primarily a result of a heavy or serious failure or loss (called a macrostressor), but rather of an accumulation of many small failures and frustrations. McLean cites six specific sources of microstressors:

1. *A reduction in behavioral productivity.* A retiree with nothing to do can experience considerable strain. Sometimes activity is deliberately reduced because there seems little reward for undertaking it.

2. *Lack of interpersonal communication.* Communication with others allows us to obtain personal feedback, essential for our self-esteem. Thus, the macrostress which invariably occurs with the loss of a loved one can be compounded by the microstress that can occur if the surviving mate becomes isolated from other personal contacts.

   Law enforcement officers often complain that only other police personnel understand the nature of their job. It is not uncommon to find in many cases that their after-hours contacts are restricted to a close circle of friends who are in the same line of work. Part of this is also due to the reinforcement they get from one another. The nature of the law enforcement job often produces interpersonal isolation from other members of society, however. This lack of communication with others, especially with spouse or family, is potentially a good foundation for depression.

   Many police personnel are familiar with the John Wayne Syndrome (discussed earlier), named after the strong law-and-order image that the actor portrayed. New and naive officers are especially likely to display characteristics of the syndrome, a pattern usually lasting three or four years. It is believed to help the new officer adapt to the demands of the job. Because of the tendency to take the work so seriously, however, and the almost complete identification with the police role, officers with that syndrome are often distant and cold toward spouse and children (Chandler & Jones, 1979). The John Wayne syndrome, then, can produce considerable microstress.

84

CHAPTER
THREE:
THE
PSYCHOLOGY
OF
LAW
ENFORCEMENT

3. *Lack of goals in one's life.* It is important for all of us to set attainable and realistic goals. Not having such goals formulated can be a source of considerable discomfort.

4. *Inadequate social interaction (distinguished here from the interpersonal* communication *factor mentioned above).* Here McLean is referring to inadequacy in dealing with others. If a person is brusque and offensive toward others, for example, that person's interactions will be inadequate and unsatisfactory, and microstress will probably result. This differs from lack of communication in which an individual may have adequate social interaction skills but may choose not to exercise them.

5. *Decisionmaking and problem solving difficulties.* When people are unable to make adequate decisions or solve small everyday problems, this becomes a stressful situation.

6. *Lack of cognitive self-control.* If the person ruminates frequently about failures or shortcomings, microstress is likely to occur.

If we accept McLean's theory, the above are all sources of microstress and may eventually produce depression. Whether a person does indeed become depressed as a result of these series of microstressors appears to depend on at least three factors: (1) the degree, chronicity, and pervasiveness of the stress experiences; (2) the adaptation skills available to the person to reduce the stress; and (3) the nature and number of compensating positive experiences under the individual's control. In this connection, it is important to remind ourselves that law enforcement officers are very likely bombarded with both macrostressors and microstressors. Whether the officer actually perceives them as stressors has much to do with how chronic they will become. In many instances, the stress situations are built into the job. Therefore, it is especially important that adaptation skills and compensating positive experiences be available, else depression may set in.

Reactive depression appears to develop in four discernible stages. First, the individual faces repeated goal frustration in a variety of significant areas and/or a series of minor but consistent stressors. Second, lacking satisfactory adaptation skills, the individual feels little control over the environment. Third, because lack of control is habitual, the individual anticipates more of it in the future. At this point, the depression has set in. Finally, it is manifested in the somatic, mood-cognition, or behavioral symptoms discussed earlier.

SUICIDE

The ultimate behavioral manifestation of depression is suicide. Although other factors can lead to suicide (e.g., terminal illness, killing oneself for a cause), the bulk of suicide appears to be precipitated by feelings of hopelessness and helplessness (Bedrosian & Beck, 1979). Statistics in this area are misleading, because it is often difficult to tell whether a person's death was suicidal or accidental. For example, car accidents and drownings are sometimes suspected to be self-induced. There are probably many suicide attempts that are thwarted by relatives or friends and that go unreported. About 30,000 official suicidal deaths are reported per year in the U. S. (approximately 12.8 out of every 100,000 inhabitants). Because of the likely under-reporting, however, the actual number is believed to be between 50,000 and 100,000 (Comer, 1992; Rosenhan & Seligman, 1984). It is also estimated that about 600,000 persons in the U. S. and more than 2 million people throughout the world attempt to kill themselves each year, a phenomenon known as parasuicide (Comer, 1992). When successful suicide rates are examined, the following facts emerge:

1. The male rate is three times greater than the female (Mears & Gatchel, 1979; Rosenhan & Seligman, 1984; McIntosh, 1991). However, women make about three times as many suicide attempts as men.

2. Men commonly kill themselves by violent and lethal means, especially with firearms (Haas, 1979). Women most commonly use drugs, especially barbiturates (Haas, 1979). This may explain to some extent why men are more successful at suicide than women.

3. The suicide rate for whites in the U. S. is twice as high as that for African-American or other racial groups (Comer, 1992; McIntosh, 1991).

4. Suicide deaths increase linearly with age (Haas, 1979). That is, the rate is much higher among the aged, even though there are reported increases in adolescent suicides.

When we narrow the statistics to police suicide, which is of particular interest here, we find that data are extremely difficult to obtain. To date, less than a dozen published studies are available. Kroes (1976) suggests that many departments fail to report police suicides because of the stigma (the blot on the police image). Survivors do not report them because of possible loss of insurance benefits. There are frequent assertions in the literature that the actual rate is two to six times higher than the rate for other occupations (Stratton, 1978; Blackmore, 1978; Somodevilla, 1978). Vena, Violanti, Marshall, and Fiedler (1986) report that police officers commit suicide three times more often than other municipal workers. Violanti (1992) reports that the suicide rate of police officers after retirement is about the same as the rate for working officers. The disabled officer, however, appears to have the highest rate of all. In an often cited, but unfortunately outdated study, police officers in 1950 were found to have the second highest suicide rate of thirty-six occupations in the United States, with only self-employed manufacturing managers and proprietors having a higher rate. The actual rate for police officers was 47.6 per year per 100,000 officers (Labovitz & Hagedorn, 1971).

The most heavily cited research on police suicide was conducted by Friedman (1967), who studied in detail the cases of ninety-three New York City officers who were believed to have committed suicide between January 1, 1934 and January 1, 1940. He concluded that the annual suicide rate during the six-year period was 80 per 100,000. Heiman (1975) reports rates during the same years of 48 per 100,000 in Chicago; 51.8 per 100,000 in San Francisco; 17.9 per 100,000 in St. Louis; and 0 per 100,000 in Denver.

Data reported by Heiman (1975) for the period 1960–73 was a New York rate of 19.1 per 100,000, a substantial decrease from the figures described above. Danto (1976) reported only twelve suicides among Detroit police officers from 1968 through 1976.

Dash and Reiser (1978) compared incidents of police suicide with a national rate, which in 1975 was about 12.6 per 100,000, including both men and women. Studying the Los Angeles Police Department over a seven-year period, they found a rate of 8.1 per 100,000. That figure was also below the California average, which was 16 per 100,000 for both genders together during the same year. More recently, David Lester (1992) sent questionnaires to the National Central Bureaus of all participating nations in INTERPOL, asking for information on the number of suicides among law enforcement officers, 1980–89. Surprisingly, Lester found that many countries did not collect data on police suicide. For those that did, Lester found that the suicide rate for law enforcement officers was not consistently higher (or lower) than the suicide rate for men in general within that country.

What do these statistics tell us? Very little in the way of definitive information. In spite of assumptions or sketchy reports of high suicide rates among police officers, there is little systematic research evidence to support this. Recent evidence, in fact, suggests that the rates may be lower than the national average for males. Any conclusions we make can only be speculative. More detailed research and better reporting systems are needed.

86

CHAPTER
THREE:
THE
PSYCHOLOGY
OF
LAW
ENFORCEMENT

If suicide rates for law enforcement personnel are indeed lower than in the past, this may be due to a number of factors, such as a more sophisticated screening procedure and rigorous evaluation at times of hiring, increased use of stress-awareness training, greater use of psychological or psychiatric consultants in police departments, and better police training, enabling officers to feel more competent at their jobs. On the other hand, the few studies available may show decreasing rates because police suicides are too often unreported by departments and by families.

PSYCHOPHYSIOLOGICAL DISORDERS

The symptoms of psychophysiological disorders are highly similar to those of physical diseases. The basic distinction between the two is made on the basis of cause. Psychophysiological disorders are caused primarily by psychological factors, such as stress, while physical illnesses are caused by non-psychological agents, such as viruses or faulty diet. The DSM-III-R (*Diagnostic and Statistical Manual of Mental Disorders, Third Edition, Revised,* 1987) now labels psychophysiological or psychosomatic disorders "psychological factors affecting physical condition." We will continue to use the less cumbersome psychophysiological disorders.

While the literature on law enforcement often asserts that there is a high rate of psychophysiological disorder among law enforcement officers, documentation and well-designed research to substantiate the claims continue to be noticeably lacking. Much of the information, again, is based on procedural evidence alone. For example, it is not unusual to find statements such as "cardiovascular disorders and other health problems are very frequent and psychosomatic illnesses in general are rampant in police work" (Somodevilla, 1978, p. 111) or "the increase in emotional problems, heart trouble and other physical ailments related to job stress among police is alarming" (Hagerty, 1976, p. 9). Neither source cites a research project to validate these observations.

Certainly, if law enforcement is a highly stressful occupation, we should expect a relatively high incidence of psychophysiological disorders. Available research addressed at examining this issue is sketchy, fragmented, and often poorly designed. Nonetheless, the few studies that have emerged do *suggest* a positive relationship between job stress and psychophysiological disorders. Jacobi (1975) reported that law enforcement officers in his survey submitted disability claims at a rate six times greater than other employees. Fifty percent of the claims involved high blood pressure and another twenty percent lower back pains. Studies by the Los Angeles County Sheriff's Department and the U. S. Department of Health, Education, and Welfare suggest that law enforcement officers are among the highest occupation in stress related to physical disorders, when compared with other occupational groups of similar age (Thomas, 1978). The Los Angeles study revealed that the three leading causes of nonaccidental disability retirement among law enforcement officers were cardiovascular disorders, back disorders, and peptic ulcers. It will be instructive, therefore, if we examine more closely some of these disorders, together with the available research.

The categories of psychophysiological disorders commonly reported in the general population include:

1. skin disorders, such as hives, acne, eczema, and an assortment of other rashes;

2. musculoskeletal disorders, such as tension headaches, muscle cramps, and some forms of arthritis;

3. respiratory disorders, such as bronchial asthma;

4. cardiovascular disorders, such as hypertension (high blood pressure), heart attacks, paroxysmal tachycardia (palpitations of the heart), vascular spasms, migraine headaches;

5. gastrointestinal disorders, such as peptic ulcers, chronic gastritis, colitis, and indigestion; and

6. psychoneuroimmunology disorders, where effectiveness of the body's immune system is reduced by stress, thus rendering the person more susceptible to viral and bacterial infections.

Musculoskeletal, cardiovascular, and gastrointestinal disorders appear to be the most commonly reported among law enforcement officers, and we will pay closer attention to them. However, before we do, the reader should be aware of several considerations.

First, it is often believed that persons afflicted with psychophysiological symptoms are not actually suffering physical ailment or discomfort, but that the symptoms are "all in the mind." The assumption is that the person is imagining or malingering. This is a misconception. Psychophysiological disorders differ from physical illnesses only in cause, as we mentioned above. They may be accompanied by pain or tissue damage, and in many cases they may cause permanent physical handicap, tissue alteration, or death.

Second, the formation of psychophysiological disorders appears to be extremely complex, with physical, social, and psychological factors interacting in a complicated way with organic and neurological predispositions. Although it is hypothesized that certain stress factors acting on some part of the body over a long period of time might develop symptoms of a particular psychophysiological disorder, it is quite well established that there are wide individual differences in what part of the body shows the disorder, to what intensity, and for how long (Ursin et al., 1978). Some individuals, because of their biological makeup and personality, may be particularly susceptible to ulcer formation under stress, while others may be highly prone to develop cardiovascular disorders.

Third, personality factors that have been continually linked to psychophysiological and general health issues in the literature include feelings of helplessness, lack of personal control, and pessimism. Conditions of helplessness and lack of control in experimental animals have often precipitated an assortment of psychophysiological disorders (Seligman, 1975; Weiss, 1968, 1970, 1971; Ursin et al., 1978). Obviously, setting up similar experimental conditions with human subjects would not be condoned. However, if we are allowed to generalize the findings to the human organism, we conclude that a sense of self-mastery is an important factor in maintaining health.

Finally, the studies reported in the next section only suggest a potential relationship between the psychological stress found in law enforcement work and physical disorders which might be psychophysiological, in that a portion of the cause is not strictly organic or biological. Psychological stress does not necessarily directly cause physiological disorders in law enforcement officers. For example, physical stress brought on by sitting in a patrol car for extended periods, poor eating habits, and little opportunity for rest while off duty, might be more potent causes of the reported physical ailments. Much more work needs to be done before we can conclude that the psychological stress inherent in law enforcement employment often leads to psychophysiological disorders.

Cardiovascular Disorders

Numerous disorders are related to the heart and blood vessels. In this section we shall consider briefly only three: coronary heart disease (CHD), high blood pressure, and migraine headaches. As is true for all psychophysiological disorders, the relationship between them and the occupational stress of law enforcement has only been minimally examined. Research does consistently show, however, that the cardiovascular system is highly susceptible to stress in relation to its reactivity and activation. In fact, Selye (1976) has said that psychological stress is among the most frequent causes of cardiovascular disease.

As Selye notes, many studies demonstrate a relationship between clinical hypertension and psychological tensions arising from interpersonal relationships in the family or at work. Acute,

88

CHAPTER
THREE:
THE
PSYCHOLOGY
OF
LAW
ENFORCEMENT

intense "mental arousal" is often involved in cardiac failure. He comments, "There appears to be little doubt that emotional stress is one of the most frequent factors in the development of high blood pressure, congestive heart failure or cardiac infarction in predisposed patients" (1976, p. 768). Moreover, cardiovascular dysfunction appears to be closely related to the organism's available options for adaptation (Seligman, 1975). That is, if the organism appraises the situation as hopeless, the likelihood of cardiovascular dysfunction may be greatly increased.

Behavioral scientists (e.g., Friedirian & Rosenman, 1974; Glass, 1977) have carefully studied the relationship between CHD and certain personality types. These personality types have been simply labeled A, B, and C. The Type A personality pattern is competitive, achievement-oriented, driving, constantly preoccupied with job deadlines, and has a high sense of time urgency and restlessness. Type A is believed to be a style of responding designed to assist the individual to adapt to stressful life events which could threaten the sense of environmental control and mastery (Glass, 1977). Type B individuals manifest the opposite pattern of behavior; they generally respond to life in a less hurried fashion. Type C is characterized as having the same features as Type B, but with an added element of chronic anxiety, which promotes over-reaction to stress. As you might expect, Type A is hypothesized to have the highest susceptibility to cardiovascular disorders. However, although research has shown Type A to have an unusually high cholesterol level, a shortened blood clotting time, and some tendency for CHD (Selye, 1976), extensive research by David Glass (1977) indicates the relationship is much more complex than that. Personality variables are not the only element to consider when seeking causal factors for CHD. Situational variables, for example, such as the frequency and intensity of stressful life events, appear to play a very crucial role.

Do law enforcement officers have Type A personalities? Research by Caplan and his colleagues (Caplan et al., 1975) indicate they do not, if we can generalize from his small sample of 111 police officers. Few other research projects have closely examined this personality variable with law enforcement officers, and thus generalizable statements cannot be made. However, it would be interesting to examine potential differences for high-workload officers compared to low-workload officers.

Do law enforcement officers tend to be plagued by high levels of cardiovascular problems? Richard and Fell (1975) report that law enforcement officers are admitted to hospitals for cardiovascular disorders at a much higher rate than other occupations. Kroes et al. (1974) cite some evidence that hypertension is the second most frequently reported major health problem among law enforcement officers. Grenick (1973) also reports several findings of import:

1. A survey of heart index (measures such as heart rate, blood pressure, electrocardiogram, and blood chemistry) found that one-fourth of the officers studied were in a category of medium-to-high risk for coronary heart disease.

2. Fifteen percent of the officers had levels of cholesterol which rendered them twice as prone to coronary heart disease as persons in the general population.

3. The onset of coronary strain appeared to occur early in the officers' careers.

    A later LEAA-funded study showed that officers under thirty-nine years of age tended to be of average risk for coronary heart disease (Gettman, 1978), while middle-aged officers were of higher-than-average risk.

The available research, therefore, does suggest a relationship between CHD and hypertension, but the nature of this relationship is undefined. Additionally, we do not know how it compares with other occupational groups and the population in general when age and other related variables are controlled.

Migraines

Although at least fifteen categories of headaches have been delineated, among the most frequently experienced headaches are migraine and muscle-contraction or tension headaches (Bakal, 1975). The tension headache will be discussed in the musculoskeletal section.

Migraines are characterized by aching, throbbing pain, often coincident with the pulse beat, and usually on one side of the head. Migraine headaches occur with regularity within families, which suggests that they may be hereditary to some extent (Bakal, 1975). Approximately 12 million Americans suffer migraines, and two-thirds of them are women (Comer, 1992).

The physiochemical basis of migraine appears to center on the constriction and dilation of blood vessels. It is generally accepted that migraine is associated with blood-vessel constriction in the brain during the preheadache, and vessel expansion in the brain during the headache phase (O'Brien, 1971, 1973; Dalessio, 1972). Moreover, there has been good success in treating migraines with procedures emphasizing blood-vessel volume changes, such as biofeedback of finger temperature (Bakal, 1975). Through biofeedback, finger temperature can be raised during the headache phase, thereby increasing the blood volume to the peripheral regions (fingers and toes) and reducing the blood volume (vasodilation decrease) in regions of the brain.

Both migraines and tension headaches appear to be principally triggered by psychological stress (Bakal, 1975). The relationship between migraines and the occupational stress of law enforcement has received minimal attention, however. Kroes (1976) reported that headaches were the second most frequently listed minor health problem mentioned by law enforcement officers in an interview survey, but it is impossible to tell whether these were migraine or tension headaches, or both. Blackmore (1978) learned that law enforcement officers are plagued by unusually high rates of migraine. However, hard data are again difficult to obtain and, as with all other psychophysiological disorders, conclusions cannot be drawn. Despite the paucity of research available, the frequency of reported migraines in law enforcement in comparison to other stress-inducing occupations leads to the suspicion that the problem is a very real one.

Ulcers

These are usually caused by excessive flow of the stomach's acid (especially hydrochloric acid), which eventually destroys portions of the stomach lining (gastric ulcer) or the upper part of the small intestine or duodenum (peptic ulcer). Causal agents may include diet, various diseases, and psychological stress, but stress, working in combination with neurological predispositions, is believed to be a principal factor (Lazarus, 1966; Comer, 1992).

Ulcers, common in the general population, may be "quiet" in the sense that they cause no pain or discomfort and remain unnoticed (Mears & Gatchel, 1979). Most often, though, people feel discomfort ranging from a burning sensation to severe pain accompanied by nausea and vomiting. If the ulcer involves damage to blood vessels in the walls of the stomach, vomiting of blood may occur. If this becomes excessive, there is the possibility of hemorrhaging and even death.

Research strongly indicates that ulceration is most likely to occur under stress, when people feel events are unpredictable or aversive and out of their control (Seligman, 1975; Weiss, 1968, 1970, 1971; Ursin et al., 1978). Thus, persons who feel they have little influence over their fates are more likely to develop peptic ulcers than those who perceive themselves as more in control of their lives. However, we must continue to keep in mind the added factor of biological predisposition, without which stress probably will not be manifested in an ulcerative condition.

Since the job demands of law enforcement work are often unpredictable and ambiguous, especially for the less trained officer, we would expect a high incidence of ulcers. After studying 2,300 officers in twenty departments, Blackmore (1978) reported that law enforcement officers

90

CHAPTER
THREE:
THE
PSYCHOLOGY
OF
LAW
ENFORCEMENT

are among the highest of all occupations in reporting stomach disorders, especially ulcers. Kroes, Margolis and Hurrell (1974) found that 32 percent of law enforcement officers interviewed reported gastrointestinal disorders, a significantly higher rate than the general population.

This is hardly enough information to conclude that the situation is representative of law enforcement officers as a whole, however. More data are needed. Specific figures remain unavailable, and we know little about the course of the reported ulcerations. Such factors as length of time on the job before the ulcers occurred and personality and background characteristics of the individuals must be uncovered. Until this is done, we face the quagmire of suspecting something must be true without having validating evidence to confirm the suspicion.

Musculoskeletal Disorders

There is little doubt that stress causes muscular tension (Selye, 1976). In fact, muscular tension is a component of the reaction to stress clinically referred to as "anxiety." Chronic or sustained muscular tension is directly related to a wide variety of muscular aches and pains, including tension headaches and backaches.

Tension or muscle-contraction headaches appear to arise from sustained tension of skeletal muscles about the face, scalp, neck, and shoulders (Martin, 1972). It is usually experienced as sensations of tightness and persistent band-like pain located bilaterally in the back or front of the head or both (Bakal, 1975).

Back pain arises from a wide variety of causes, one of which may be muscular tension in reaction to stress. This is especially true for low back pain (Gentry, Shows & Thomas, 1974), a problem apparently encountered frequently in law enforcement (Kroes, 1976).

Unfortunately, no published studies are available that have examined tension or musculoskeletal disorders in law enforcement compared to other occupational groups. Most of the claims of high incidence are reported informally or anecdotally and are often subject to multiple interpretations.

Summary and Conclusions

Although it is a commonly held assumption that law enforcement officers are conservative, rigid, dogmatic, or insensitive, the existence of a "police personality" characterizing individuals who go into law enforcement work has yet to be supported. Police officers as a group exhibit personality characteristics not unlike those of the general population. There is evidence that many officers display one component of the authoritarian personality—namely, conservatism—but it is unclear whether this feature is developed on the job or whether law enforcement work attracts individuals with a conventional, cautious approach to the world.

With increases in the number of women in law enforcement, researchers have begun to examine both what they contribute and how they adapt to a traditionally male occupation. It is clear that women can do law enforcement work. Psychological research also suggests that they adopt different styles of policing. We should be careful not to limit such research to female officers; styles of male officers should be scrutinized as well. An even more promising area of research, however, is the discovery that many women bring to the job characteristics such as communication skills which are desirable in all law enforcement officers, male or female. Furthermore, because many of the obstacles to women's advancement in law enforcement relate to attitudes of male officers, it would be helpful to apply attitude-change research to address this problem.

Police officers are the first-line participants in the criminal justice process. As such, they often determine what cases will reach the courts and the correctional system. Their ability to exercise discretion effectively becomes an important aspect of their work. We saw in this chapter that discretion, especially with respect to minor offenses, is both encouraged and shaped within the law enforcement network. This occupational socialization, which teaches each officer the acceptable way to exercise judgment, is one of the implicit realities within criminal justice. Discretion is also affected by the acts of other participants in the system, such as various attorneys, the judge, supervisors, and even the victim and alleged perpetrator of a crime.

Since psychological stress seems to appear with more intensity in law enforcement than in other occupational groups, much of this chapter was devoted to examining that phenomenon. We first adopted a definition of stress that encompasses: (1) the initial perception of a stimulus as potentially harmful; and (2) the strategies an individual adopts to adapt to the resulting discomfort. There is no completely satisfactory, objective way to measure psychological stress, although physiological and subjective methods are often used. In general, an attempt is made to measure the individual's appraisal of a situation and his or her response to it.

Stress in law enforcement can develop from a variety of situations, some seemingly minor (microstressors) and others far more taxing (macrostressors). It is a generally accepted maxim that a series of microstressors can be as debilitating as one major catastrophe. Alienation from society, police community relations, role conflict, job unpredictability, and interpersonal relationships were all listed as possible sources of microstress. Just because an officer experiences these difficulties, however, does not mean that his or her job performance will suffer. Situational and personality variables help determine the severity of the stress. Often, a person's general feelings of competence or motivation to overcome a crisis will lessen the intensity of stress. Individual differences in nervous system characteristics also account for the differential effects of stress-producing stimuli.

Surprisingly, little research has examined the relationship between age of law enforcement officers and job performance. What little research has been done has yielded inconsistent results (Spielberger, Ward & Spaulding, 1979). Based on their extensive review of the literature on predictors of job performance, Spielberger et al. (1979) were forced to conclude that: "Until more definitive research is available, the usefulness of age as a predictor of on-the-job performance cannot be determined" (p. 14). There is, however, no shortage of speculation about the relationship between age and job performance. Sims (1982), for example, asserts—without supportive data—that age and years of experience have a negative relationship with job performance in small-town and rural police. In fact, he supposes that turnover rate and tenure of rural officers can be accounted for largely by decreased job performance as a result of age.

Niederhoffer supposes that an officer's job performance should decrease in a linear fashion as a direct result of job experience and age, unless the officer is promoted to a higher rank. However, Niederhoffer's hypothesis was developed on urban, male officers. Whether this hypothesis holds for small-town or rural officers, or women, is largely untested.

The research examining the relationship between perceived job stress and job experience is relatively extensive, although contradictory. Whether perceived stress follows a linear pattern of decreased stress as a function of experience, or a **U**-shaped relationship, with intermediate experience associated with the most stress, is at the heart of the controversy. Violanti (1983) was one of the earliest researchers to report a **U**-shaped relationship between job experience and perceived stress in police officers. Using a random sample of 500 police officers from 21 departments in western New York State, he found that police officers with the least and most job experience reported less stress than did officers of intermediate lengths of job experience. Dividing the officers into his four career stages, Violanti found that officers in the alarm stage and in the introspective stage reported less stress than officers in the disenchantment and personalization stages (intermediate career points). Stotland and his colleagues (Stotland, 1986, 1991; Stotland,

92

CHAPTER
THREE:
THE
PSYCHOLOGY
OF
LAW
ENFORCEMENT

Pendleton & Schwartz, 1989) investigated the relationship between self-reported job stress and job experience in a metropolitan police department in Oregon. Stotland predicted a linear relationship, with increased job experience reducing stress, and consequently increasing job performance. The data supported their hypothesis. Over time, patrol officers' degree of ability to cope with their jobs improved significantly, and their performance improved correspondingly.

We discussed examples of what can occur when an individual fails to adapt satisfactorily to stress. Alcoholism, suicide, depression, and psychophysiological problems were examined individually. It is important to note that, although law enforcement officers are often assumed to exhibit these failures to adapt, there are not enough data to support this assumption. Although it is difficult to obtain information about police alcoholism, illegal substance abuse, depression, suicide, and psychophysiological problems, we have no reason to believe they occur more frequently in law enforcement than in the general population.

Questions to Ponder

1. Why do you think the myth of the police personality has so much resilience?

2. What must individuals in law enforcement and other helping professions do to prevent burnout? To what extent should (a) administrators and (b) members of the public be involved?

3. Good judgment is an important attribute for a successful career in law enforcement. Can good judgment be taught? What are some ways to measure it in a screening procedure?

4. If you were embarking on a law enforcement career, would you prefer small-town, suburban, or metropolitan law enforcement? Why? What would be advantages and disadvantages of working in the community in which you were raised?

5. Research shows that women and men can do law enforcement work equally well. If women made up one-half of the law enforcement community nationwide, how would law enforcement work change?

Psychology and the Courts: An Overview

 N THIS AND THE FOLLOWING FOUR CHAPTERS we will begin to apply psychology to issues dealing with the courts. The present chapter introduces the reader to the court system, different categories of law, and discusses the judicial process in both criminal and civil law. We will then highlight fundamental issues in both psychology and law that create special challenges to those attempting to span the boundaries between the two disciplines. These include issues of free will and determinism, the predictability of human behavior (particularly dangerousness), and the role of the psychologist as expert witness.

Organization of the Courts

The court system in the United States is a dual system, federal and state. Article III, Section I of the U. S. Constitution establishes one Supreme Court and "such inferior Courts as the Congress may from time to time ordain and establish." Congress subsequently established four additional levels of the federal court system: magistrate's courts, district or trial courts, special district courts, and courts of appeals (Figure 4.1). These federal courts have authority over matters arising from violations of federal laws, including violations of rights guaranteed by the Constitution.

State courts often parallel the federal structure, but there is wide variation in the numbers and levels of courts within each state. Some states, for example, have few specialized courts and no intermediate appellate court. Others have a variety of specialized courts (e.g., traffic, small claims, and family courts).

The term **jurisdiction** is used to refer to the authority given to a particular court in resolving a dispute. Jurisdiction is best understood as "the geographic area, subject matter, or persons over which a court can exercise authority" (Abadinsky, 1991, p. 134). Occasionally, two or more courts may have the authority to hear a case. An employer who refuses to promote a handicapped employee, for example, may be violating both federal and state statutes. In this situation, the person filing suit (the plaintiff) may have the choice of filing in the federal or state court. Likewise, in the criminal context, one incident may represent an alleged violation of both federal and state law. The highly publicized videotaped beating of a criminal suspect by four Los Angeles police officers in 1991, discussed in Chapter 3, illustrates this very well. Officers were first tried and acquitted of aggravated assault in a state district court. Then, they were charged with intentionally violating the constitutional rights of a citizen (by using excessive force while he was in custody), a federal offense. They were again tried, this time in federal court. Two were convicted and two were acquitted (see Box 3.1).

CHAPTER
FOUR:
PSYCHOLOGY
AND
THE
COURTS:
AN
OVERVIEW

FEDERAL COURTS

The jurisdiction of federal courts is set forth in Article III, Section 2 of the U. S. Constitution:

The judicial Power shall extend to all Cases, in Law and Equity, arising under this Constitution, the Laws of the United States, and Treaties made, or which shall be made, under their Authority;—to all Cases affecting Ambassadors, other public Ministers and Consuls;—to all Cases of admiralty and maritime jurisdiction;—to Controversies to which the United States shall be a Party;—to Controversies between two or more States—between a State and Citizens of another State;—between Citizens of different States;—between Citizens of the same State claiming Lands under Grants of different States, and between a State, or the Citizens thereof, and foreign States, Citizens or Subjects.

In all Cases affecting Ambassadors, other public Ministers and Consuls, and those in which a State shall be Party, the supreme Court shall have original Jurisdiction. In all the other Cases before mentioned, the supreme Court shall have appellate Jurisdiction, both as to Law and Fact, with such Exceptions, and under such Regulations as the Congress shall make.

Congress over the years has passed a vast array of laws which are often interpreted or tested in federal courts. Laws relating to the protection of the environment, employment discrimination, health regulation, crime control, safety in the workplace, and broadcasting are but a few examples. Although Congress has also created administrative agencies such as the Nuclear Regulatory Commission (NRC), the Federal Communications Commission (FCC), and the Occupational Safety and Health Administration (OSHA) to enforce these laws, the federal courts have the ultimate power to resolve disputes arising out of agency decisions. Thus, the work of federal courts today is both varied and overwhelming. In the period 1960–83, cases filed in federal district courts more than tripled, from roughly 80,000 to 280,000 per year (Posner, 1985).

District or trial courts carry most of the workload in the federal system. There are ninety-four U. S. District Courts, at least one in each state. Some states have two or three, and California, Texas, and New York each have four U. S. District Courts. U. S. District Courts also are located in

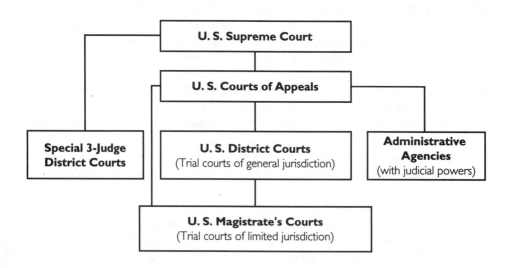

Figure 4.1 ■ *The U. S. federal court system. Specialized courts, such as the Court of Claims, are not included.*

Puerto Rico, the Northern Mariana Islands, Guam, the District of Columbia, and the Virgin Islands. Additionally, Congress has created special district courts, which are three-judge courts to be convened only when necessary. Comprising two district judges and one appeals court judge, these special courts rule on issues relating to the Voting Rights Act of 1965 and the Civil Rights Act of 1964, as well as their respective amendments. They also deal with apportionment cases.

At the next level, the United States is divided into thirteen geographically defined jurisdictions or circuits, each with a U. S. Court of Appeals. These federal appellate courts comprise between three and fifteen judges, who meet both in panels of three and, in major cases, as a whole (*en banc*). The primary purpose of a Court of Appeals is to review decisions made by the federal district courts within its jurisdiction. Courts of appeals also review cases heard by specialized courts, such as tax courts, and the various federal administrative agencies. Therefore, criminal defendants or litigants who have lost their cases in a district court or before an agency such as the FCC may have their cases reviewed by the Court of Appeals in their circuit.

Although the appellate process may be quite slow, in matters in which time is of the essence or in which political interests are at stake it may occur very quickly. In 1992, an American citizen returned from France with the French "abortion pill" RU-486. Because it was an unapproved drug in the U. S., the tablets were seized by customs officials. A federal district court upheld the woman's right to bring the drug into the U. S., on the basis of the woman's right to privacy and a compassionate-interest doctrine. Courts have allowed American citizens in the past to carry nonapproved drugs into the country when such drugs are deemed critical to their health (e.g., experimental AIDS drugs). In this case, the woman's victory was short-lived: An appeals court on the same day overruled the lower court. Within a week, the U. S. Supreme Court had also rejected the woman's plea to have the drug returned to her.

It is important to note that appellate courts do not conduct trials, because their function is to rule on matters of law, not fact. They ask, "Was the law applied properly?" rather than, "Did he do it?" We might illustrate with a hypothetical situation. Moe is arrested and charged with kidnapping the child of a prominent political figure. When his case comes to trial in a U. S. District Court, he chooses not to testify, exercising his Fifth Amendment right not to incriminate himself. The prosecutor, in closing arguments to the jury, suggests that Moe must be guilty because of his failure to testify, and the presiding judge does not admonish the jury to disregard the comment. Moe is convicted. Moe's lawyer appeals the conviction on the basis that the prosecutor's comment prejudiced the jury and deprived her client of his Sixth Amendment right to a fair trial. The appeals court, then, is asked to determine whether the law (in this case, involving instructions to the jury) was properly applied. The federal appeals court determines that the law was not properly applied and sends the case back for a new trial.

While federal appeals courts must rule on all cases properly presented to them for review, the highest court in the land, the U. S. Supreme Court, has much more discretion. The Supreme Court consists of nine Justices appointed for life by the President, with the advice and consent of the U. S. Senate. One of the nine is designated Chief Justice by the President, and the Court is usually referred to collectively by the name of that individual—for example, the Rehnquist Court. The Supreme Court begins to meet on the first Monday of October each year and usually continues in session until June. Although what the Court *may* hear is defined by Congress, the Justices are given nearly complete control of their docket because they can refuse to hear and review cases. The cases the Justices select are usually those believed to address important, unanswered questions. A petitioner or appellant requests review by filing a series of legal documents summarizing the facts of the case, the decision of the lower court, and setting forth an argument as to why the Court should hear the case. In addition, the U. S. Supreme Court, like other federal

96

CHAPTER
FOUR:
PSYCHOLOGY
AND
THE
COURTS:
AN
OVERVIEW

appellate courts, may receive *habeas corpus* **petitions** on behalf of individuals who believe they are improperly confined (e.g., in a mental institution or prison). A writ of *habeas corpus* requests a judicial determination of the legality of an individual's custody or confinement. Sometimes, the Court hears from indigents who are not represented by lawyers. These *in pauperis* **petitions** have been the source of landmark rulings.

About 5,000 appeals are filed with the U. S. Supreme Court each year, but most are denied either because the subject matter is not proper or is not of sufficient importance to warrant full Court review, or because the Court does not have enough time to review all cases presented to it. These refusals, called denials of *certiorari*, may include a brief statement explaining why the decision of the lower appellate court must stand or may be made without comment. On the average, the Court agrees to hear about 150 to 200 cases each year. At least four of the nine Justices must vote to hear a case, a decision which results in the issuance of a **writ of certiorari**.

STATE COURTS

As noted earlier, state courts follow roughly the same pyramidal structure as the federal courts, with one highest appellate court. Some states choose to call their highest court something other than State Supreme Court, however. Massachusetts's court of last resort, for example, is the Supreme Judicial Court, and New York's highest court is the New York Court of Appeals. In Texas, in addition to the Texas Supreme Court, there is a special court of last resort for criminal cases, the Court of Criminal Appeals. The process and administration of these state courts vary widely, as do the state laws under which they operate.

State courts have a general, unlimited power to decide almost every type of case, subject only to the limitations of state law. While Posner (1985) asserts that the rate of growth in federal courts is surpassing that in most state courts, it is in the state court, primarily the trial courts, that most of the judicial business in American society begins and ends. According to a recent estimate, over one million cases were heard by trial courts in the U. S. during one year (Flanagan & Maguire, 1991). The higher or appellate state courts were created to deal with questions of law which arose in the lower courts, often during the trial process.

Classifications of Law

As we noted in Chapter 1, few scholars are able to propose a definition of law which will satisfy everyone. There is less disagreement when scholars discuss classifications or types of law. Law is classified both by its *content* and by its *origin*.

CONTENT CLASSIFICATIONS

The traditional content classifications are two-category distinctions between civil and criminal law, or between substantive and procedural law. Increasingly, scholars prefer to use terms which specify content even more clearly, such as education law, mental health law, environmental law, family law, medical law, and public health law.

The distinction between civil and criminal law rests primarily on the disputive versus punitive nature of a case. In **civil law**, two or more parties (litigants) approach the legal system seeking resolution of a dispute. The **plaintiff**, the person bringing the case, is hoping for some remedy from the law. Although the remedy may include fines or punitive damages, the concept of punishment is not the main purpose of civil law. It is designed to settle disputes, or to make the victim whole through monetary awards or injunctive relief. An injunction, in this context, is court order to one party to cease some activity, such as using an unvalidated psychological test. **Criminal law**, on the other hand, involves an alleged violation of rules deemed so important that the breaking of these rules incurs society's formal punishment, which must be imposed by the criminal courts. An important component of criminal law is the need to have the rules stated clearly by a legislative body. To be a crime, an action must be defined as such in the statutes and the appropriate punishment for violation of that rule must be specified, at least within a given range.

Although it may not seem difficult to discern criminal from civil law, the lines between the two are sometimes blurred. In most states, for example, if a juvenile allegedly violated the criminal law, he or she will most likely be brought to a juvenile or family court, which is considered a civil rather than a criminal setting. Likewise, a mentally disordered individual who allegedly broke the criminal law may be committed to a mental institution through civil proceedings, rather than led through the criminal courts. This is most likely to occur for minor crimes or because the person has been found incompetent to stand trial and the criminal charges dismissed. Disputes between private persons or organizations, such as a breaches of contract, libel suits, or divorce actions, are clearly cases at civil law. The government also may be a part of a civil suit, either as plaintiff or defendant. However, when the government fines a corporation for dumping hazardous waste, the fine may be either a civil or a criminal penalty. When Michael Milken, Dennis Levine, Ivan Boesky, and their coterie broke rules of the Securities and Exchange Commission (SEC) against insider trading, they were committing criminal offenses.

Cases at civil law are often more complex and difficult than those at criminal law, and the legal territory is more likely to be uncharted. The notorious Agent Orange case, for example, in which approximately 16,000 Vietnam Veteran families sued Dow Chemical and six other chemical companies for exposing them to the toxic effects of a defoliant made of dioxin, took nearly twenty years to settle in the federal courts. Because most cases in the courts are civil rather than criminal, the backlog of civil disputes is very high, and the process of achieving settlement is tedious. Additionally, there is no guarantee that the judgment in a civil case will be enforced. This fact has spurred a nationwide movement toward alternative dispute resolution (ADR), where parties attempt to arrive at a solution for their dispute with the help of a trained mediator rather than proceeding with the court process (Wohlmuth, 1990). ADR is discussed again in Chapter 11 (see Box 11.1).

A case at criminal law is brought by, or in the name of, some legally constituted government authority at either the federal, state, or local level. In bringing a criminal law case to court, the proper government authority (called the prosecution) accuses a defendant (or defendants) of a specific violation of law as defined by statute. Like civil cases, criminal cases are backlogged, but the courts are expected to handle them as expeditiously as possible to insure that the due-process rights of the defendants are not abridged. This is one of the reasons why the plea bargaining process, by which defendants admit guilt—usually to a lesser offense and in exchange for a lighter sentence—has become an essential feature of the criminal process. On the other hand, innocent persons may be tempted or pressured to plead guilty to avoid the uncertain outcome of a trial.

Another way of classifying law by content is to divide it into substantive and procedural categories. **Substantive law** defines the rights and responsibilities of members of a given society as well as the prohibitions on their behavior. For example, the Bill of Rights in the U. S. Constitution sets forth fundamental rights of citizens, such as freedom of speech and the right to be free from unreasonable search and seizure. State and federal statutes which define and prohibit

98

Chapter
Four:
Psychology
and
the
Courts:
An
Overview

fraud, embezzlement, murder, rape, assault, arson, burglary, and other crimes against personal safety and property security are also examples of substantive law. Still others are court decisions asserting that citizens should be free from the effects of unwanted psychoactive drugs.

Procedural law outlines the rules for the administration, enforcement, and modification of substantive law in the mediation of disputes. In a sense, procedural law exists for the sake of substantive law. It is intended to give defendants in a criminal case and litigants in a civil case the feeling that they are being fairly dealt with, and that all are given a reasonable chance to present their side of an issue before an impartial tribunal (James, 1965). State laws that specify the documents to be filed and the hearings to be held in child custody disputes are examples of procedural law.

Classifying by Origin

Another common method of classifying law is to look for its sources, such as constitutions, statutes, court decisions, rules of administrative agencies, and treaties. With the exception of treaties, the sources of law exist at both the federal and state (including municipal) levels.

Constitutional law is that related to the U. S. Constitution and the constitutions of individual states. It provides the guidelines for the organization of national, state, and local government, and places limits on the exercise of government power (e.g., through a Bill of Rights). Thus, in a psychology-related U. S. Supreme Court decision, the Court announced that before a prison inmate could be transferred to a mental institution, he or she had a constitutional right to challenge that transfer in a hearing (*Vitek v. Jones*, 1980). This decision also illustrates the making of procedural law, because the Court outlined minimum requirements for conducting those hearings.

The law that emerges from court decisions is sometimes referred to as **case law** or "judge-made" law. It has developed from **common law** (local customs formed into general principles) and through precedents set in previous court decisions. Case law may involve the interpretation of a statute. If the legislature of a given state passes a law including a provision that psychiatrists are to conduct evaluations in child custody cases, for example, a court may be asked to interpret whether the legislature intended "psychiatrist" as a generic term which could also cover psychologists.

The principles outlined in the court's written decision become precedent under the doctrine *stare decisis* (to stand by past decisions) and are perpetuated, unless a later court chips away at or overturns a principle. *Stare decisis* is more a matter of policy than a rigid rule to be mechanically followed in subsequent cases dealing with similar legal questions. The principle is extremely important, however, for it encourages stability, predictability, and the orderly development of the law.

Statutory law refers to written rules drafted and approved by a federal, state, or local law-making body. Examples range from far-reaching legislation such as the Civil Rights Act to local ordinances prohibiting trash burning. Statutes are what most people mean when they refer to "law." They outline what factors entitle a person to initiate a civil suit, for example, or what crimes will be considered felonies or misdemeanors. An example of a statute relating to psychology is one in which the legislature ordains that all law enforcement candidates must pass a psychological test before they can be hired.

Administrative law is created and enforced by representatives of the numerous administrative agencies of national, state, or local governments. Examples of such agencies at the federal level are the NRC, the FDA, the FCC, and the ubiquitous Internal Revenue Service (IRS). These and other agencies have been delegated broad rule-making and enforcement powers by Congress. Additionally, every state assigns agencies to create, administer, and enforce laws such as those pertaining to zoning, public education, and public utilities. Examples of state agencies that relate to psychology are departments of mental health and licensing boards, which oversee the quality of services provided by professionals.

The Judicial Process

The judicial or court process in both criminal and civil cases can be divided into four major stages: pretrial, trial, disposition, and appeals. Illustrations of what contemporary psychologists, both practitioners and researchers, can contribute at each of these stages abound.

During the pretrial stage, psychologists may be asked to evaluate the mental state of individuals charged with crimes, help attorneys in selecting a jury which will be most sympathetic to their side, or interview children in a custody dispute. Their assessments, and sometimes their expert testimony, is then used in a wide range of pretrial proceedings including court hearings. During the trial stage, psychologists again testify on matters such as criminal responsibility, eyewitness testimony, or the emotional state of a litigant, one claiming Post-Traumatic Stress Disorder (PTSD), for example. Clinical psychologists report on their evaluations of an individual; research psychologists may be asked to testify about the empirical evidence relating to a given disorder. Psychologists also may be part of the trial team, consulting with attorneys on such matters as jury selection or the testimony of witnesses, including opposing mental health experts.

Psychologists enter the disposition stage particularly in the criminal process, where sentencing judges may rely on their recommendations to choose between alternatives such as prison or probation accompanied by community treatment. In some states, psychologists testify at death penalty hearings, usually in relation to mitigating circumstances which an offender wishes to raise.

In a study of ninety-one young offenders sentenced to death, for example, Robinson and Stephens (1992) found evidence that most were profoundly disadvantaged. Approximately one-third had psychological disturbance, and another third had some mental disability. There was extensive evidence of disruptive family histories, indigence, and substance abuse as well. A psychologist examining a young offender convicted of a capital crime, aware of this research, would look for these factors and report their presence to a sentencing judge or jury. The judge or jury would then weigh this information, along with other mitigating and aggravating circumstances, to decide whether to impose the death penalty.

During the appellate stage, psychologists may be involved in filing *amicus curiae* briefs, may provide treatment to offenders or litigants, or may do additional assessments or conduct research to be brought to the attention of an appeals court. Because of psychology's intense interest in the judicial process, each of these phases can be discussed in detail, together with some illustrative research studies. Unless otherwise specified, the following relates to both civil and criminal cases.

PRETRIAL STAGE

The process in a criminal case begins when a crime is reported and investigated and evidence begins to accrue. For federal crimes and some state violations, **grand juries** review evidence gathered by the prosecutor and decide whether there is enough to prosecute. In this sense, they are a screening mechanism to protect their fellow citizens from prosecution based on insufficient evidence. An **indictment** is a grand jury's written statement outlining reasons why an individual should be charged. Grand jurors are also empowered to gather their own evidence, independent

100

Chapter
Four:
Psychology
and
the
Courts:
An
Overview

of the prosecutor. Here, they may issue a **presentment** recommending that one or more individuals be charged.

In the absence of a grand jury, the prosecutor brings an accused person directly to court. With or without a grand jury, however, a defendant is arraigned. The **arraignment** is the court proceeding during which a defendant is formally charged with an offense, notified of her or his rights, and asked to enter a plea. At this point, it is not unusual for people charged with minor offenses to plead guilty and receive an immediate fine or sentence. A plea of guilty is a waiver of the fundamental constitutional right against self-incrimination (the right to remain silent). It should be noted that this guilty plea can be entered at any subsequent stage of the process as well.

If the defendant pleads not guilty, the judge must decide on conditions of release (amount of bail, release on recognizance, release to the custody of a third party). Denial of bail (preventive detention) is increasingly common when an individual is deemed dangerous to society. This bail decision is made after consideration of the nature and circumstances of the offense, the background of the accused, and recommendations from the prosecutor or other relevant individuals. If a bail amount is set and cannot be posted, or if the individual is denied bail, he or she is placed in or returned to jail.

A not-guilty plea sets the trial process in motion. The next step is one or more pretrial hearings, during which witnesses, arresting officers, and other parties may present evidence. Numerous decisions may be made during these pretrial hearings. They include whether evidence is admissible; whether a trial should be moved because of extensive pretrial publicity; whether a youth should be transferred to juvenile court; and the aforementioned issue of whether bail should be denied because of the alleged dangerousness of a defendant. The juvenile transfer and dangerousness issues represent two pretrial situations in which practicing psychologists are most likely to be involved.

During the pretrial hearing or hearings, and between these and the trial, extensive negotiating and plea bargaining often take place, with the result that criminal cases rarely get to the trial stage. In some jurisdictions, as many as 90 percent of the defendants charged with crimes plead guilty at the outset or change to guilty pleas before trial date (Cole, 1992).

The pretrial process in *civil* cases parallels the above. When one citizen sues another, however, there are no grand jury indictments or formal charges. Instead, a complaint outlining the alleged wrong and the desired remedy is filed by the plaintiff, the defendant receives a summons, and the defendant has a time limit in which to respond. As in criminal cases, there may be extensive negotiation between parties before they see the inside of a courtroom. Unlike criminal cases, however, speedy trials are not at issue, and years may elapse before a case comes to trial. It has been estimated that 75 percent of all civil cases are settled between the time a complaint is filed and the trial date (Abadinsky, 1991).

The **discovery process** is an important component of the pretrial process in both criminal and civil cases. It requires each side to make available information at its disposal to the other side while the cases are in preparation. A prosecutor in a criminal case, for example, is obliged to make known exculpatory evidence to the defense. Rubin (Hurricane) Carter, the world middle-weight boxing champion who spent eighteen years in prison for a crime he did not commit, was freed partly because the prosecutor had failed to tell the defense that another person had confessed to the crime.

As part of the discovery process, depositions may be required. These are sworn statements from witnesses, including expert witnesses, usually responding to questions from attorneys. Some psychologists have commented that the grilling they receive during a deposition proceeding can be more extensive than cross-examination during the trial itself. Furthermore, because most cases are settled before trial, psychologists are more likely to be deposed than to testify in court.

In both criminal and civil cases, trials follow a similar pattern, beginning with jury selection, unless the verdict will be rendered only by a judge (called a **bench trial**). This is followed by opening arguments, two rounds of presentation and cross-examination of witnesses for both sides, summations, judges instructions to the jury, jury deliberation, and verdict.

The role of psychologists during the trial stage, particularly their testimony as expert witnesses, has received extensive attention. It is not unusual to hear this role disparaged, as in the comment "If you look hard enough, you'll find a shrink willing to testify to anything." We will be discussing this perception and the resultant battle of experts later in the chapter. It is important to note, however, that both clinical and research psychologists make contributions at the trial stage.

Research psychologists, for example, have valuable information to convey to courts relative to the issue of pretrial publicity, particularly in criminal cases. The Sixth Amendment to the Constitution guarantees criminal defendants the right to a speedy public trial by an impartial jury of their peers. The First Amendment guarantees the press the right to be unhampered by the government in gathering and reporting news. In a line of decisions, (e.g., *Sheppard v. Maxwell*, 1966; *Nebraska Press Association v. Stuart*, 1976; *Richmond Newspapers, Inc. v. Virginia*, 1980) the U. S. Supreme Court has attempted to balance these two constitutional rights.

Psychological research also has uncovered extensive information about attitude formation and jury behavior, human perception and memory, and the credibility of child witnesses. These and other trial-related topics will be discussed in separate chapters on the psychology of the jury and the psychology of evidence.

DISPOSITION STAGE

The third stage of the judicial process is most relevant to criminal cases, since it requires that a judge or jury impose a sentence or other penalty upon a convicted offender. In the civil process, when a verdict favors the plaintiff, a judgment is handed down, specifying the remedy to be borne by the defendant. The standard civil case does not involve the psychologist once this has occurred. It should be noted, however, that the juvenile process, which is civil, also may involve a "sentence," which is technically called a **disposition**, and that clinical information is often used in this context.

It is at the disposition stage that a decision is made whether to incarcerate the individual and for how long and, in death penalty cases, whether to impose the ultimate penalty. Psychologists may be consulted by the probation officer preparing a pre-sentence investigation report. This is a document submitted to the judge that includes background data on the offender and other information considered helpful to the sentencing judge. The judge also may request, or grant an attorney's request for, a psychological evaluation of the offender's amenability to rehabilitation. For example, a judge may sentence a child molester (pedophile) to probation with the condition that he participate in a community-based sex-offender treatment program, after having heard from psychologists that the offender would be a good candidate for such a program.

The involvement of psychiatrists and psychologists at the sentencing stage of death penalty cases has received a good deal of attention. In *Penry v. Lynaugh* (1989) the Supreme Court ruled that, before an offender is sentenced to death, he or she has the right to present and have considered all the mitigating evidence. Penry, who had a mental age of six and one-half and a childhood marred by abuse, had been sentenced to death without having had these facts taken into consideration. The court did not say that the death penalty should not have been imposed; it merely stated that Penry's mental age and history should have been brought to the jury's attention.

102

CHAPTER
FOUR:
PSYCHOLOGY
AND
THE
COURTS:
AN
OVERVIEW

A minority of death penalty states also require some prediction of "future dangerousness" of the offender, a standard which is generally thought to necessitate the input of an examining clinician. Many psychologists have been reluctant to participate in the prediction of dangerousness, particularly when it involves death penalty cases.

The presence of mental disorder is a commonly raised mitigating factor in such cases. White (1987) refers to this as the "mental status defense." He identified a variety of factors associated with a successful mental status defense, or, in other words, information that spared an offender the death sentence. These include the direct testimony of a clinician, a diagnosis of psychiatric disorder, a history of treatment and/or hospitalization (or, lacking that, family history of such), and objective evidence of mental disability (test scores, brain scans). Gender differences also appear to influence the success of mental status defenses: a woman is more likely to be spared death on the basis of mental disability than a man, and the presence of women on the sentencing jury is more likely to result in a successful mental status defense for both male and female offenders.

APPELLATE STAGE

During the appeals process a higher court reviews the findings of a lower or trial court on matters of law. The basis of an appeal may involve psychology directly: for example, a father appealing a custody decision may argue that the one psychologist who interviewed his child did not have the credentials outlined in the statutes. The major involvement of psychology in the appellate process, however, involves the filing of *amicus curiae* (friend of the court) briefs. An *amicus* brief is a document filed by interested parties other than those directly involved in the case. Bersoff and Ogden (1991, p. 950) summarize five purposes of the *amicus* brief: 1) to supply information not readily available to the parties in the case; 2) to develop arguments that one party has been able to present only in summary form; 3) to make arguments that one party has been unable to make because of lack of resources; 4) to fill a void by making arguments that one party prefers not to make; and 5) to address the broad social implications of a decision.

James Acker (1990a), reporting the results of an analysis of briefs filed in 200 Supreme Court criminal cases over a 25-year period, found *amicus curiae* briefs prepared by social scientists were more the exception than the norm. Although Acker was not referring only to psychological briefs, his results are relevant. In his sample of cases, "the vast majority of social science authorities cited in the Court's decisions had been located through the Justices' own efforts, rather than through prior discussion in the briefs or otherwise" (p. 40). When briefs did cite research evidence, they had been prepared by lawyers, government officials, or interested groups other than those possessing expertise in the social sciences. Only a handful had been prepared on behalf of scientifically competent organizations, and this handful "demonstrate dramatically that such organizations can make an important contribution to the transmission of social science information to the Justices..." (p. 40). Acker concluded that Supreme Court Justices can go astray in their interpretation of research results if not guided by competent social scientists.

In a separate analysis of death penalty cases from his original sample, however, Acker (1991) discovered that social scientists were more likely to be directly involved but not likely to be influential. They had filed briefs in 34 percent of the cases (compared to 13 percent of criminal cases overall). Their research, however, was cited significantly more often in footnotes than in the text of the Court's opinions, and also cited significantly more often by dissenters than in the majority opinion. Liberal Justices used social science data more than conservative Justices. Acker concluded that, at least for that sample of death penalty cases, social science evidence had little impact on the final decision.

HARPER, A WASHINGTON STATE PRISONER, REFUSED to take antipsychotic drugs after having voluntarily taken them for a six-year period. The Washington State Supreme Court ruled that a judicial hearing was required before prisoners could be given antipsychotic drugs against their will. The state successfully appealed that ruling to the U. S. Supreme Court. In an *amicus curiae* brief, the APA supported Harper:

"Because antipsychotic drugs have grave effects, inherent potential for abuse and an actual history of indiscriminate use by the psychiatric profession, forcible administration of these drugs requires review by an independent decisionmaker in a matter comporting with due process," the APA brief noted.

The brief-writer observed that the drugs "have powerful effects on a person's ability to think and feel, and on his sense of self." In a surprisingly strong statement, it was added that the drugs "also *cause* disabling, incurable and often unpredictable disorders, including akathisia ... dystonia ... and neuroleptic malignant syndrome, a condition that can be fatal."

"Forced drugging should occur only if a reasonably independent and unbiased decisionmaker concludes that it is warranted, based upon evidence from diverse professionals (such as internists and psychologists) who have no vested interest in using antipsychotic drugs. Forced drugging is warranted only if the prisoner is incompetent or imminently dangerous, if the medication is likely to be effective, if non-drug therapies have been objectively explored, and if forced medication is truly needed for the welfare of the prisoners or others." ■

The American Psychological Association (APA) has aggressively pursued its responsibility to inform the courts about relevant research evidence. As of 1990, the APA had filed twenty-eight *amicus curiae* briefs in U. S. Supreme Court cases and approximately the same number in lower federal and state courts (Bersoff & Ogden, 1991). Additionally, individual psychologists have joined other concerned social scientists in filing briefs, as was the case in the landmark desegregation case *Brown v. Board of Education* (1954). According to Donald Bersoff, former legal counsel for the APA, the organization's briefs have "embraced a wide variety of constitutional and civil rights issues about which psychology has significant and pertinent information" (Bersoff & Ogloff, 1991, p. 950). These issues have included the forced medication of inmates (see Box 4.1), the effects of employment discrimination, the civil commitment of minorities, sexual behavior in the privacy of one's home, sex stereotypes, and death penalty cases involving predictions of violent behavior.

Thomas Grisso and Michael Saks (1991) warn psychologists against being discouraged when judicial decisions seem in conflict with social science evidence. They note that the U. S. Supreme Court's expertise in constitutional analysis and other information must be considered. Grisso and Saks also argue that the Court has not directly *rejected* social science evidence, but rather has often based its decisions on other grounds. They emphasize that it is important for psychology to continue informing the Court about the findings of research in order "to provide a safeguard against judicial use of erroneous presumptions about human behavior. With this as a criterion for judging success, psychology has reason to take heart" (Grisso & Saks, 1991, p. 208).

Psychology and the Courts: Special Issues

Thus far, we have provided an overview of the structure and process of courts and have given illustrations of psychology's participation in the judicial process. We have not, however, answered the fundamental question of why psychologists believe they have expertise to offer. To

CHAPTER
FOUR:
PSYCHOLOGY
AND
THE
COURTS:
AN
OVERVIEW

address that question, it is necessary to consider issues in psychology and law that prompt psychologists to contribute to the judicial process.

FREE WILL VERSUS DETERMINISM

Law is a normative enterprise that considers nearly all persons completely responsible for most of their behaviors and often for the natural and probable consequences of those acts (Morse, 1978a, 1978b). Both criminal and civil law are rooted in the concept that individuals are masters of their fate, the possessors of free will and freedom of choice. As one federal appellate court put it, "[O]ur jurisprudence...while not oblivious to deterministic components, ultimately rests on a premise of freedom of will" (*U. S. v. Brawner*, 1972, p. 995). Law does acknowledge that individuals are influenced to some extent by various biological, psychological, and environmental forces, but resists the notion that these forces determine how individuals behave.

Psychology, on the other hand, is more likely to argue that antecedent events—prior experiences or situations—determine individual behavior. According to this thesis, human behavior is governed by causal laws and free will is undermined. Psychological determinism in its extreme form, **hard determinism**, asserts that all behavior is determined by antecedent stimuli or events and that all human behavior, therefore, is lawful. Concepts such as free will or moral responsibility are meaningless. If the relevant laws are understood, behavior is also highly—if not completely—predictable. This perspective is best represented by the writings of B. F. Skinner and Sigmund Freud. Although hard determinists are very much in the minority, most psychologists (especially research psychologists) subscribe to the view that some degree of determinism plays a substantial role in human behavior. This position is called **soft determinism**.

This is not the same as saying that human behavior is predictable, for it is unlikely that we will ever know all of the antecedent circumstances. It is also not to say that the concept of freedom is an illusion. According to soft determinism, human behavior is determined, but this determination is not incompatible with free will (Sappington, 1990). That is, soft determinism believes that people do make conscious choices between different causes of action, and that these choices do affect their lives (Sappington, 1990, p. 20). Although determinism is at the heart of traditional psychology, psychologists have held spirited debates in an effort to reconcile that notion with the idea of freedom of action (e.g., Bandura, 1989; Sappington, 1990; Tageson, 1982; Rychlak, 1979).

Research psychologists must assume at least a soft deterministic position—that there are *lawful* causes of human behavior—in order to understand why human beings do what they do. Research on simulated juries, for example, assumes some degree of lawfulness in human conduct which has relevance to real-life juries and courtroom trials. Otherwise, all social science research as we now know it would be meaningless.

The free will-determinism debate will reappear in the next chapter, when the special issue of criminal responsibility is discussed. However, the reader should realize at this point that while law—especially criminal law—embraces free will, psychology—especially research psychology—is steeped heavily in the deterministic tradition. In this sense, a "mentally normal" person who commits a criminal act with intent is blameworthy in the eyes of the criminal law. Most psychologists would argue that the person's past and present social environment play a major role in the criminal action, and thus that "blameworthiness" is not that clear-cut.

PREDICTION OF HUMAN BEHAVIOR

Although the law embraces the concept of free will, it ironically often asks psychologists to predict what an individual will do in the future. Norval Morris and Marc Miller (1985) identify three kinds of predictions. The first, **anamnestic prediction**, is based on how a *particular* person acted in the past in similar situations. For instance, every Saturday afternoon when it is sunny John takes his dog for a long walk, after having mowed his lawn. The neighbors can *usually* predict John's dog walking when these conditions are met (sunny, Saturday, lawn mowed). The second, **actuarial prediction**, is based on how *groups* of individuals with similar characteristics have acted in the past. Insurance companies have compiled extensive statistics on who has traffic accidents, for example. These statistics show that twenty-year-old males who have mediocre academic records and drive Trans-Ams have a very high probability of being involved in a traffic accident within a two-year period. If Skip falls into this group, he will pay much higher insurance rates than Beth, a twenty-year-old woman with an outstanding academic record, and a five-year-old station wagon. The thing to remember is that actuarial prediction is based on *statistics* compiled on *certain groups* of people. The third predictive method is **clinical** or **experience prediction**. This is prediction based on experience dealing with a certain clientele. A clinical psychologist may assert: "Based on my experience in dealing with this kind of person, I predict that he will violate the law in a violent manner within twelve months." Of the three types of prediction, clinical prediction is the most intuitive and subjective.

Interestingly, the courts have generally responded most favorably to clinical predictions. However, it must be emphasized that a wide range of professionals make "clinical" predictions, including correctional counselors and case managers, social workers, and probation/parole officers. Therefore, we will use the term "practitioner" as an all-encompassing term that will include not only psychologists and psychiatrists, but all human service professionals who make predictions of human behavior within the judicial context.

Prediction is a deterministic enterprise, because past events, or antecedents, are assumed to cause future events. As we noted previously, though, it is unlikely we can identify all these antecedents. Yet requests for clinical prediction are common. Courts ask practitioners to foresee whether an individual will harm society, whether an adolescent will function as an independent adult, whether a juvenile will continue offending, whether a person will benefit from a rehabilitation program, whether a defendant will be able to participate in the trial process, and whether one parent will be better able than another to meet the needs of a child in a custody suit.

In requesting the above, courts assume that practitioners, especially psychologists and psychiatrists, are more accurate in their judgments of human behavior than are lay persons or those without psychological training. This presumption of accuracy and expertise in understanding and predicting others is based upon faith in the special qualifications professionals have acquired through training, experience, and the development of rules and strategies for interpreting human data.

The available research (e.g., Wiggins, 1973; Litwack & Schlesinger, 1987; Dawes, Faust & Meehl, 1989; Faust & Ziskin, 1989; Cooper & Werner, 1990), however, does not support the legal assumption of a direct relationship between training (or experience) and accuracy in *clinical prediction*. Highly trained and experienced practitioners are often no more accurate in their predictions of a variety of human behaviors than nonclinicians or less trained and inexperienced practitioners (Ziskin & Faust, 1988). Even in instances when highly experienced practitioners did demonstrate greater accuracy in judgment than totally inexperienced laypersons, brief supplementary training tended to equalize their levels of performance (e.g., Goldberg, 1968).

As noted in Chapter 1, the accuracy of actuarial prediction is higher than either anamnestic or clinical prediction. Meehl's research (1954, 1957, 1965, 1977, 1986) is again illustrative. In 1954, Meehl found only twenty studies which had compared the accuracy of clinical judgment to that of statistical or actuarial methods. The criterion variables studied by researchers included success

105

PSYCHOLOGY
AND
THE
COURTS:
SPECIAL
ISSUES

106

CHAPTER
FOUR:
PSYCHOLOGY
AND
THE
COURTS:
AN
OVERVIEW

in academic or military training, recidivism and parole violation, and recovery from psychosis. Eleven of the twenty studies showed relative superiority of statistical methods over clinical judgments in accuracy of prediction. Eight were classified as ties: neither clinical judgment nor statistical prediction was superior. The results of one study were unclear, but further examination revealed that this investigation, too, qualified as a tie. Of the twenty studies reviewed, there was not a single example of clinical judgment exceeding statistical methods in accuracy of predicting human behavior.

In 1957, Meehl was able to review twenty-seven additional studies on the issue. Seventeen indicated that statistical methods were superior to clinical judgment. Ten were evaluated as ties. Again, not one study revealed superiority of clinical judgments over the statistical methods.

By 1965, Meehl had evaluated fifty more studies. The criterion variables now included continuance in psychotherapy, response to shock treatment, psychiatric diagnosis, job success and satisfaction, and even medical diagnoses. The box score now read thirty-three in favor of statistical methods, seventeen ties, and one in favor of clinical judgment. However, the one study showing the superiority of clinical judgment was later determined to be also a tie. The results clearly support the superiority of statistical methods, or at the very least, their equivalence to clinical judgment.

In 1986, Meehl judged the evidence in favor of actuarial prediction over clinical prediction to be stronger than ever. He writes, "There is no controversy in social science which shows [so many] studies coming out so uniformly in the same direction as this one...it is time for a practical conclusion." And again in 1989, Meehl writes, "I find, on reading what I wrote almost 20 years ago, that there is little to change on the basis of theoretical arguments or empirical evidence that have appeared since that time" (p. 540).

More recently, Robyn Dawes, David Faust, and Paul Meehl (1989) reviewed nearly 100 comparative studies in the social sciences. They conclude: "In virtually every one of these studies, the actuarial method has equalled or surpassed the clinical method, sometimes slightly and sometimes substantially" (p. 1669).

Stephen Gottfredson (1987) asserts that those on the statistical side of the argument would not be disappointed with the research in the criminal justice field either. Actuarial methods have consistently outperformed mental and correctional case workers on predictions of recidivism, for example. " [T]he best predictors of parole violation are the age of first conviction, number of past convictions, and number of prison violations; the subsequent 'knowledge' gained in a parole interview simply *decreases* accuracy in predicting who will remain outside of jail" (Dawes, 1989, p. 464).

Clinical and practicing psychologists maintain, however, that the research designs of the studies Meehl and others evaluated were faulty (many were), or that only fragments of the total data available to psychologists working in the field were used, or that the research data do not apply to them. Nearly four decades ago, clinical psychologist Robert Holt (1958, p. 1) lamented: "Clinical students in particular complain of a vague feeling that a fast one has been put over on them, that under a great show of objectivity, or at least bipartisanship, Professor Meehl has actually sold the clinical approach up the river." This observation still holds today. The work of Meehl and others is often not taken seriously by clinical or practicing psychologists.

Implicit in the concerns of the practitioners is that the prediction of human behavior requires, ultimately, the human ingredients of integration, experience, cognitive processing, and judgment of a wide range of input data. Essentially, it takes humans to predict and understand the complexity of humans. Humans are able to take into account the unique, the unexpected, and the mysterious workings of other human minds. The presumption is that computers and statistical tables based on mathematical probabilities cannot possibly consider individual differences properly. Computers and actuarial methods are nomothetic, not idiographic. Despite these arguments,

■ 4.2: DR. DEATH

THE FORENSIC (AND PROSECUTION) PSYCHIATRIST Dr. James Grigson is known as "Dr. Death" throughout the Texas criminal justice system because of his uncanny ability to sway juries toward the death penalty. He has a practice of telling juries that he can "guarantee" that a defendant will kill again, and the jury in most instances believes him (Rosenbaum, 1991). "He'll take the stand, listen to a recitation of facts about the killing and the killer, and then—usually without examining the defendant, without ever setting eyes on him until the day of the trial—tell the jury that, *as a matter of medical science*, he can assure them the defendant will pose a continuing danger to society ..." (Rosenbaum, 1991, p. 210).

Dr. Grigson's constant claims of extreme accuracy in predictions of dangerousness gained him a reprimand from the American Psychiatric Association, which submitted a brief in *Barefoot v. Estelle* (1983). Dr. Grigson testified, without having examined Thomas Barefoot, that he could diagnose the man "within reasonable psychiatric certainty" as "a fairly classical, typical, sociopathic personality disorder." He classified Barefoot in the "most severe category" of sociopaths (on a scale of one to ten, he considered Barefoot "about eleven"), and testified that there was no known cure for this condition (Monahan & Walker, 1990). He further testified that if Barefoot were released to society, or even kept in the general prison population, there was a "one hundred percent and absolute" chance that he would commit future acts of violence (Monahan & Walker, 1990).

In its *amicus curiae*, the American Psychiatric Association wrote that predictions of long-term future dangerousness were not as accurate as Dr. Grigson claimed; in fact, two out of three predictions made by psychiatrists on this matter were wrong. Dr. Grigson did not take the reprimand from the APA seriously, maintaining that he was better qualified than any member of the APA committee because his predictions are based on his unmatchable data base (Rosenbaum, 1991).

Grigson's self-confidence and personal charm have captivated journalists as well as jurors. According to one court expert (personal communication) who has opposed him a number of times, Grigson is "the consummate master of persuasion. What he says is not nearly as important as how he says it."

Grigson claims to have examined 12,000 criminals, including 1,400 murderers and 391 capital-murder defendants. He further points out that he does not invariably predict that the defendant will be dangerous in the future, and has done so in only 60 percent of death penalty cases (Rosenbaum, 1991). Once he makes the prediction, however, he is absolutely certain of the accuracy of his decision. ■

---

however, clinical judgment has yet to be redeemed; it has not demonstrated its superiority over actuarial methods in any criterion variable targeted for study (Dawes, Faust & Meehl, 1989; Faust & Ziskin, 1989). The fact remains that when the same input data or predictor variables are given to an individual using statistical tables or formulae and to a clinician, and when each is asked to make specific predictions, the clinician continually fails to achieve a higher "hit" ratio than the person using the statistical procedure.

Years of clinical experience do not seem to increase accuracy either. Howard Garb (1989) summarized the research on clinical experience and accuracy of judgment and concluded that there is *no* relationship. It did not matter whether the clinician had twenty years of experience or one, accuracy was about the same in both cases. Garb did find, however, that training and education improved prediction.

During the 1980s, researchers shifted from studying accuracy of prediction to studying the *process* of prediction, essentially, the decisionmaking process. That is, what data combination rules or strategies do practitioners use in making their judgments? Are the data combinations of practitioners qualitatively and quantitatively different from computer or statistical models? Many practitioners argue that clinical processing is inaccessible or private, and therefore not subject to logical or empirical analysis. They argue too that the process is so complex that they are unable to verbalize the cognitive operations that enter into data combination, and so cannot create computer analogues.

Nevertheless, the research literature consistently shows that, compared to actuarial methods,

108

CHAPTER
FOUR:
PSYCHOLOGY
AND
THE
COURTS:
AN
OVERVIEW

clinical prediction is fraught with biases, misconceptions, and just plain inaccuracy. Practitioners, urged on and supported by the judicial system, continue to believe in the predictive accuracy of the time-honored method of experienced-based intuition. It may feel more "human," but the injustices possible when legal decisions are based on these inaccurate predictions urge a careful reevaluation of its use.

WHY CLINICAL PREDICTIONS MISS THE MARK

The process psychologists and other practitioners use in arriving at predictions is not well understood, but available research suggests that they use far less data and are much more simple in their data combinations than they believe (Wiggins, 1973; Jones, 1977; Dawes, Faust & Meehl, 1989; Faust & Ziskin, 1989). Moreover, the instruments and methods for obtaining human data or predictor variables are, as we discovered in Chapter 2, not often designed to uncover the behavioral indicators relevant to the criterion variables. In addition, practitioners have considerable difficulty distinguishing relevant from nonrelevant information and are at loss in determining how much weight to give the information in making their judgment (Dawes, Faust & Meehl, 1989). Statistical techniques, on the other hand, such as multiple regression and discriminant analysis, identify predictive variables, eliminate nonpredictive ones, and weight the predictive variables in accordance with the informational contribution to the conclusion.

Further, the interpersonal skills and prejudices of the practitioners may be as much a limitation of data collection as the instruments employed (e.g., Truax & Mitchell, 1971; Mischel, 1981; Dawes, Faust & Meehl, 1989). Practitioners use these limited data to estimate a person's status with respect to given hypotheses and then use their favorite theoretical model as a basis for prediction. In most instances, the practitioners base their inferences on perceived "regularities" that have been observed in the past between predictor variables and the criterion variables, and this process tends to be an art more than a science. That is, practitioners rely too heavily on intuition and the "unusual case," and this violates the statistical rules of prediction in systematic and fundamental ways (Kahneman & Tversky, 1973).

The well-cited and classic critique of the clinical field of assessment and prediction is a monograph by Walter Mischel, *Personality and Assessment* (1968), which raises incisive questions about the tendency of practitioners to use a small number of behavioral signs to categorize people into fixed slots. Mischel demonstrates that the assessor's favorite theoretical biases enter very clearly into appraisals of other people's functioning. These status determinations in turn are used to predict specific behaviors (such as dangerousness) and to make important decisions about others' lives. Mischel's justified concern is that even highly trained and experienced practitioners infer, generalize, and predict too much from too little information, and they do so in a way that is disconcertingly similar to the personal judgment of nonpractitioners. In addition, the "expert" judgments of practitioners—like everyone else's judgments—are subject to strong biases that often produce serious distortions and oversimplifications in their conclusions about behavior.

For example, practitioners have a strong tendency to attribute causality to a person's personality rather than to the circumstances in which the person acts. This well-ingrained clinical proclivity for underestimating the importance of situational determinants and overestimating the importance of the actor's personality was noted as long ago as 1943 (Ichheiser, p. 151). Called **fundamental attribution error**, it is a common tendency found in people when they are attributing a cause to another person's behavior. Specifically, fundamental attribution error refers to a powerful tendency to explain another person's behavior in terms of dispositional or personality (internal) factors rather than situational or environmental (external) factors. For example, when correctional counselors

109

PSYCHOLOGY
AND
THE
COURTS:
SPECIAL
ISSUES

were asked to explain why inmates had committed crimes that put them in prison, the counselors attributed the causes almost exclusively to dispositional factors or personality factors (such as "meanness" or "laziness") rather than environmental factors, such as upbringing, socioeconomic status, living environment, or social forces (Saulmier & Perlman, 1981).

There also appears to be a curious need for humans, including practitioners, to favor subjectively vivid but unreliable data over more complete empirical but pallid information, regardless of one's theoretical leaning (Mischel, 1979; Kahneman & Tversky, 1973; Nisbett & Borgida, 1975). This preference for subjective information over objective data is reflected in the continuing popularity of inkblots and other projective instruments in clinical practice, in spite of extensive data showing them to be unreliable and fundamentally invalid (Anastasi, 1988). Researchers cautioning their clinical colleagues about these instruments are often ignored or told that public pressure forces practitioners to address complex problems and provide at least a semblance of a solution. Alternatively, they are told they simply do not understand the complexity of human behavior and the value of projective instruments.

Research also consistently reveals that people, even professionals who should know better, tend to shun statistical data in favor of interview impressions or face-to-face information, (Gottfredson & Gottfredson, 1988; Fong, Lurigio & Stalans, 1990). The expectations of the referral source also potentially influence the accuracy of clinical judgment. For example, referrals from the court may communicate to the assessor, explicitly or implicitly, some desired direction or conclusion. It is possible that a sizeable number of practitioners slant their assessments to some extent to meet the expectations of the court. If the court expects a practitioner to recommend counseling for an offender, this expectation may be communicated to the evaluator in some manner and may influence the report delivered.

Finally, another reason practitioners are inaccurate in their clinical predictions is that they rarely receive feedback about their judgments. They make predictions but often do not learn the outcome. A fundamental principle of learning is that a student should receive information about his or her performance, an opportunity rarely provided to practitioners.

The foregoing discussion should not be construed as asserting that accurate assessment and predictions about human behavior are impossible. It does warn about the severe limits on the range and level of clinical prediction that can be expected in light of our present knowledge about human behavior. Furthermore, the research also shows that statistical training, designed to promote a deeper understanding of statistical concepts, can provide a set of valuable inferential tools to improve decisionmaking and predictions substantially (Fong, Lurigio & Stalans, 1990). In addition, Thomas Litwack and Louis Schlesinger (1987) argue that the research on predictions of violence and dangerousness of previously violent people have not really given practitioners a chance to "show their stuff." These scholars contend that practitioners *can* predict reasonably accurately under some circumstances. "…[T]he issue is not simply whether mental health professionals can predict violence, but, rather, what types of predictive statements can they offer, with what type of certainty, with what types of patients, under what types of circumstances" (p. 233).

Contemporary psychological research (e.g., Kenrick & Stringfield, 1980; Bem & Allen, 1974; Mischel, 1979) indicates that although people display some consistency across situations, it is an error to assume that even most of their behavior is consistent. In fact, research suggests that behavior is inconsistent across diverse situations but consistent across time (temporal consistency) in highly similar situations (Mischel, 1973). That is, people are apt to act the same way when the situations are very similar; in different situations, though, much behavior is not consistent. Therefore, any faith in generalities based on traditional personality types or traits is misplaced. As Endler and Hunt (1969, p. 20) remark, behavior "is idiosyncratically organized in each individual."

110

Chapter
Four:
Psychology
and
the
Courts:
An
Overview

The unreliable status assessments and the inaccurate clinical predictions so frequently offered by practitioners—their years of training notwithstanding—may also be blamed, in part, on limited access to a small, nonrepresentative sample of behavior during an artificial, stressful interview or testing session. The best source of information about past, present, and future behavior appears to be an individual herself (Mischel, 1968; Kenrick & Stringfield, 1980; Bem, 1967, 1972; Monson & Snyder, 1977). She has more data at her disposal, along with direct access to the publicly unobservable affective and cognitive elements that instigate and control behavior. We should note, though, that this is far different from the subjective information derived from some projective tests. In those tests, examiners are interpreting an individual's "story," not taking into account his or her self-reported behavior. A secondary source of information is someone who knows her well and has had the opportunity to observe her in a variety of situations (Kenrick & Stringfield, 1980). These individuals, often family members or close friends, can corroborate the information she provides. However, they are usually not aware of what behaviors she considers consistent or inconsistent.

Therefore, the accurate assessment and clinical prediction of human behavior appears to require careful study of the interaction of a specific behavior and the psychosocial environment in which it occurs. Accurate assessment and prediction also require, of course, a good understanding of the contaminative influence of personal biases and hunches, along with a willingness to rely on statistical and empirical data concerning the criterion behavior.

PREDICTION OF DANGEROUS BEHAVIOR: RISK ASSESSMENT

There is a lengthy history of the law relying on predictions of dangerousness, dating at least as far back as the sixteenth century (Morris & Miller, 1985). Today, the prediction of dangerousness—sometimes called **risk assessment**—is one of the most important issues in both criminal and civil matters worldwide (Steadman et al., 1993). Courts are particularly interested in a psychological or psychiatric assessment of whether a person is dangerous in the sense of being violent or *physically* harmful to others. This question commonly arises in the criminal context (see Box 4.2). Predictions of dangerousness are sought in the civil context as well, however, specifically with reference to the mentally disordered. In most states, when a court is deciding whether to commit an individual to a mental institution, the criterion of dangerousness to self or others must be met. In fact, the courts have placed greater reliance on clinical predictions of dangerousness than the organizations of psychology and psychiatry generally feel comfortable with (Monahan & Shah, 1989; Morris & Miller, 1985). John Monahan and Henry Steadman (in press) assert that estimating whether or not the mentally disordered will commit harm will remain one of the core issues in mental health law, well into the foreseeable future.

Studies consistently show that behavioral scientists and practitioners are unable to specify the type or even severity of harm an individual may cause, or even to predict with "reasonable accuracy" the probability of harm occurring. When it comes to dangerous behavior, actuarial methods fare only slightly better than clinical ones because the concept of dangerousness is so ambiguous.

The ability to identify persons who will engage in dangerous or violent behavior may be expressed in several ways. One frequently used index is the ratio of **false positives** to **true positives**. False positives are persons who are labeled dangerous, but who do not engage in dangerous behavior after release from custody, or during a specified period of time. True positives refer to persons predicted to be dangerous who show the prediction to be correct. Thus, if a practitioner predicts all ten persons of a selected population will demonstrate dangerous behavior—defined as violent behavior—within a two-year period, and six of the ten follow the prediction, that practitioner can

111

Psychology
and
the
Courts:
Special
Issues

claim a 60 percent rate of true positives and a 40 percent rate of false positives.

We may also have a ratio expressed as **false negatives** to **true negatives**. False negatives are persons predicted not to engage in dangerous behavior but who do. True negatives, on the other hand, refer to those persons predicted not to engage in dangerous conduct who do not (see Figure 4.2). Therefore, if a practitioner predicts that none of the population of ten will exhibit dangerous behavior over a period of time, and six do, we then have a 60 percent rate of false negatives and a 40 percent rate of true negatives.

It is obvious that it is more to the advantage of the practitioner to predict inaccurately that someone *will* engage in violence than to inaccurately predict the person will *not*. Practitioners who fail to protect the community by not detecting those who eventually engage in violence will pay a heavy social and professional price compared to practitioners who overpredict future violence. Not surprisingly, then, most studies indicate that current techniques for predicting dangerous behavior result in overprediction (Monahan, 1976, 1978, 1981; Monahan & Shah, 1989; Wexler & Scoville, 1971). At a minimum, the most sophisticated methods yield 60 to 70 percent false positives (Rubin, 1972; Kozol, Boucher & Garofalo, 1972; Wenk, Robison & Smith, 1972). The high level of false positives has "…led many to call for an end to the 'dangerousness standard' in both civil and criminal commitments" (Monahan & Shah, 1989, p. 550).

To illustrate some of the problems inherent in risk assessment of potentially violent individuals, let's examine an oft-cited project undertaken by the California Department of Corrections Research Division in 1965. The department tried to develop a violence-prediction scale for parolees based on predictor variables such as age, commitment offense, number of prior commitments, opiate use, length of imprisonment, and institution of release. Ernst Wenk, James Robison and Gerald Smith (1972) describe three studies which resulted from this massive project.

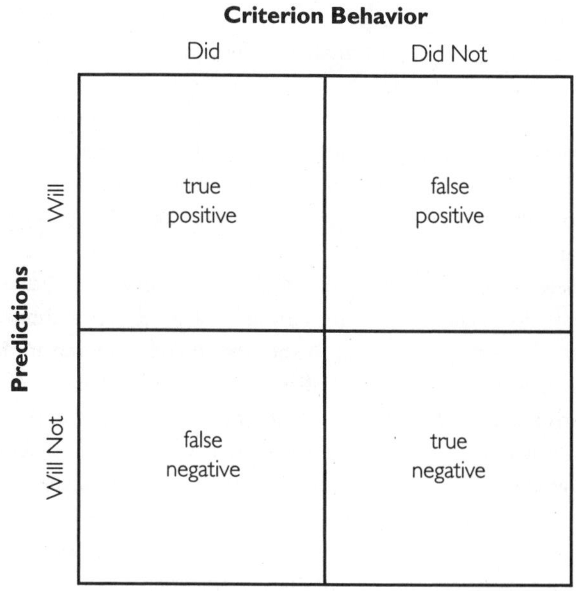

Figure 4.2 ■ *Four possible outcomes of predictions.*

112

CHAPTER
FOUR:
PSYCHOLOGY
AND
THE
COURTS:
AN
OVERVIEW

In the first study, predictor variables were used to divide the parolees into groups. About 3 percent were classified "most violent," and 14 percent of these most violent individuals actually violated parole by engaging in a violent or potentially violent act, compared to 5 percent of the parolees in general. Although the most violent group was shown to be nearly three times more *likely* than the other groups to break parole by involvement in violence, it should be emphasized that a majority (86 percent) of those parolees did not actually engage in violence while on parole. (Of course, it is possible that many did become involved in violence which was neither detected nor recorded.)

In the second study sponsored by the California Department of Corrections, Parole and Community Services Division, all parolees released were classified into one of six categories, according to past aggressive behavior. Categories ranged from the most seriously aggressive category (those who had committed one or more acts of major violence) to the lowest level of aggression category (no recorded history of aggression). These classifications were based on offender histories and psychiatric evaluations of violence potential. The study revealed that those parolees evaluated as most potentially aggressive (two highest groups) were no more likely to be violent than the least potentially aggressive groups (two lowest groups). The rate of actual violence for the potentially aggressive groups was 3.1 per thousand, compared to 2.8 per thousand for the least potentially aggressive groups—an insignificant difference.

In the third project, Wenk and his colleagues (1972) followed a sample of 4,146 youthful offenders admitted to the Reception Guidance Center at Deuel Vocational Institute, California, during the years 1964 and 1965. The study was primarily aimed at determining which background data were most useful in predicting violence during a fifteen-month parole period following the young offender's release from confinement. During the follow-up period, 104 (or 2.5 percent) of the youths became involved in a violation of parole because of violent (assaultive) behavior.

In an effort to discover the predictive variables of dangerousness (violent behavior), Wenk et al. (1972) combined and divided the background data in a variety of ways. One analysis revealed that general recidivism (any violation of parole) and violent recidivism (violation of parole by violence) were highest for multiple offenders (those who had been admitted to the correctional facility on several occasions). In another analysis, offenders who exhibited a history of "actual" violent behavior (which may or may not have resulted in legal custody or confinement) were three times more likely to be involved in violent recidivism during the fifteen-month parole period. Although this is an impressive finding, the authors admonish that if they were to make predictions based on the same background data, they would be accurate only once in twenty times (95 percent false positives), since only a tiny proportion of the parolees with violent backgrounds had a violent violation during parole.

It appears, therefore, that at least two out of every three persons predicted to do harm on the basis of our present ability to analyze predictor variables will not engage in dangerous activity during the period of prediction. The moral and social question then becomes: How many false positives—how many harmless persons—are we willing to sacrifice to protect ourselves from one violent individual?

Norval Morris and Marc Miller (1985), analyzing conclusions from the research literature, agree that current most accurate long-term predictions of violent behavior show one true positive for every two false predictions. Morris and Miller find this to be a reasonably high rate of accuracy. However, we must remember that the populations used to make these dangerousness predictions often represent skewed samples of humanity—usually institutionalized or incarcerated individuals who have committed past violent actions. Specifically, practitioners are quite likely to evaluate for the court persons with a strong propensity for violence. In this light, predictions of dangerousness that have a hit rate of 33 percent and miss the mark 67 percent of the time over the long haul are not all that impressive.

■ 4.3: *TARASOFF v. REGENTS*

IN LATE 1969 A YOUNG CALIFORNIA WOMAN WAS murdered by a man who two months earlier had confided his intention to kill her to his psychologist. Although the psychologist, who was employed by the University of California, notified campus police of the death threat, he informed no one else but his supervisor. Police questioned the patient but did not detain him. At that point the supervisor directed that no further action be taken. After the murder, the woman's parents sued the university, the psychologists, and the police for failing to confine the man and for not warning the family.

Following are excerpts from the decision by the California Supreme Court, which ruled that the therapist did not exercise reasonable care to protect the woman. Police, on the other hand, were not held responsible.

We shall explain that defendant therapists cannot escape liability merely because [the woman] herself was not their patient. When a therapist determines, or pursuant to the standards of his profession should determine, that his patient presents a serious danger of violence to another, he incurs an obligation to use reasonable care to protect the intended victim against such danger. The discharge of this duty may require the therapist to take one or more of various steps, depending upon the nature of the case. Thus it may call for him to warn the intended victim or others likely to appraise the victim of the danger, to notify the police, or to take whatever other steps are reasonably necessary under the circumstances ....

As a general principle, a "defendant owes a duty of care to all persons who are foreseeably endangered by his conduct, with respect to all risks which make the conduct unreasonably dangerous ....

Defendants contend ... that imposition of a duty to exercise reasonable care to protect third persons is unworkable because therapists cannot accurately predict whether or not a patient will resort to violence. In support of this argument amicus representing the American Psychiatric Association and other professional societies cites numerous articles which indicate that therapists, in the present state of the art, are unable reliably to predict violent acts; their forecasts, amicus claims, tend consistently to overpredict violence, and indeed are more often wrong than right. Since predictions of violence are often erroneous, amicus concludes, the courts should not render rulings that predicate the liability of therapists upon the validity of such predictions ....

We recognize the difficulty that a therapist encounters in attempting to forecast whether a patient presents a serious danger of violence. Obviously we do not require that the therapist, in making that determination, render a perfect performance; the therapist need only exercise "that reasonable degree of skill, knowledge, and care ordinarily possessed and exercised by members of [that professional specialty] under similar circumstances ....

Within the broad range of reasonable practice and treatment in which professional opinion and judgment may differ, the therapist is free to exercise his or her own best judgment without liability; proof aided by hindsight, that he or she judged wrongly, is insufficient to establish negligence.

In the instant case, however, the pleadings do not raise any question as to failure of defendant therapists to predict that [the patient] presented a serious danger of violence. On the contrary, the present complaints allege that defendant therapists did in fact predict [he] would kill, but were negligent in failing to warn.

We realize that the open and confidential character of psychotherapeutic dialogue encourages patients to express threats of violence, few of which are ever executed. Certainly a therapist should not be encouraged routinely to reveal such threats; such disclosures could seriously disrupt the patient's relationship with his therapist and with the persons threatened. To the contrary, the therapist's obligations to his patient require that he not disclose a confidence unless such disclosure is necessary to avert danger to others, and even then that he do so discreetly, and in a fashion that would preserve the privacy of his patient to the fullest extent compatible with the prevention of the threatened danger. ■

Three major factors contribute to overpredictions of dangerousness. First, the **base rate** of dangerous behavior is very low. Base rate, in this context, refers to the proportion of persons within some specified population who engage in a criterion behavior during some specified period

114

CHAPTER
FOUR:
PSYCHOLOGY
AND
THE
COURTS:
AN
OVERVIEW

of time. For example, if the annual base rate of violent behavior in a given group is 10 percent, this means that ten out of every 100 persons in that group would exhibit such behavior within a year's time. The base rate for violent behavior tends to be exceedingly low; few persons commit violent acts within a given time frame. Therefore, trying to predict future behavior with reasonable accuracy, even using sophisticated methods, is like looking for needles in a haystack.

A second major factor is the fact that psychiatrists and psychologists are less likely to be criticized or held responsible for any damages suffered by inmates or mentally disordered individuals during confinement than they are for releasing people who turn out to be violent. In essence, it becomes a choice between being accurate and being safe from social sanction. Practitioners could be more accurate if they predicted less dangerousness, but they would not then be protected from lawsuits and the wrath of society. Therefore, practitioners prefer to be safe than right, or worse, wrong.

Significant in this context is the *Tarasoff v. Regents of the University of California* (1976) case. The California Supreme Court held that, in certain circumstances, when a therapist determines that a patient is a serious danger to another, that therapist has a duty to protect the intended victim against such danger (See Box 4.3). Subsequent decisions from other jurisdictions have differed widely in their degree of agreement with *Tarasoff*. In the nearly twenty years since that case, some state courts have adopted it, some extended its reach, some have restricted it, and others have declined to follow it (Perlin, 1991). In spite of these disparate legal standards, many practitioners have interpreted the "spirit" of *Tarasoff* as national standard of practice. That is, it is assumed to be the professional responsibility of the clinician to take *reasonable* steps to protect a "reasonably identifiable victim" (and in some jurisdictions the duty is expanded to include even non-identifiable victims) when clients make serious threats. John Monahan (in press) posits that the "duty to protect" is a fact of professional life of nearly all American clinicians and that the requirements of *Tarasoff* eventually may be extended to clinical researchers as well.

Wexler (1991, p. 10) suggests that the requirement might be turned into a therapeutic tool with potential beneficial effects. The clinician's contact with the person allegedly in danger might result in joint therapy, contributing significantly to the original patient's treatment. Perlin (1991, p. 127) maintains that mental health practitioners have learned to live with *Tarasoff* and have found sensitive solutions for dealing with the requirements of that case. Nonetheless, it is widely believed that Tarasoff-type requirements have had the unanticipated effect of encouraging practitioners to overpredict dangerous behavior (Turklebaum and Parry, 1992), although there is little direct empirical evidence to support this.

A third factor contributing to overprediction is the lack of clarity in the concept of dangerousness. There is no agreement on precisely what behaviors should define the term. Courts have tried to limit it to a propensity to "attack or otherwise inflict injury, loss, pain, or other evil" (Steadman, 1976, p. 57). In addition, it is often believed that the dangerous act must occur "in the community in the reasonably foreseeable future" and that any prediction of dangerousness must be based on a "high probability of substantial injury" (Rubin, 1972, p. 399). Steadman (1976) observes that these terms are insufficient for legal application and, more distressingly, that the courts rarely press expert witnesses to explain and document the reliability or validity of their measuring instruments. If courts did press, they would likely find that many psychiatrists and psychologists rely on hunches, speculation, vague clinical judgment, and theoretical prejudice.

Monahan (1981, p. 43) suggests that the term "violent behavior" is preferable to dangerousness, because it can be more clearly defined as "acts characterized by the application or overt threat of force which is likely to result in injury to people." He is, of course, recommending that we narrow our focus to include only acts designed to injure others physically.

The belief that dangerousness should be limited to acts intended to do physical harm to others is not held by all courts, however. The Maryland Court of Appeals, in *Director of Patuxent Institute v. Daniels* (1966), ruled that "one who is a menace to the property of others fits within the definition of a danger to society." In *Jones v. U. S.* (1983), the U. S. Supreme Court permitted the inference that an individual convicted of attempted petit larceny—a misdemeanor—was dangerous. Society holds that potential harm to property may be considered dangerous, although to a lesser degree than potential harm to body. Although some states have rejected property harm as an indicator of dangerousness, a majority still include it. The issue of dangerousness continues to pervade the interaction of psychology and the courts and shows little sign of being resolved. It will reappear at several points in the chapters ahead.

115

THE
PSYCHOLOGIST
AS AN
EXPERT
WITNESS

THE CONFIDENTIALITY ISSUE

The obligation to maintain confidentiality in the patient/therapist relationship is fundamental. If you entrust the most intimate details of your life, such as your fears or bizarre behaviors, to a clinician, you expect that these will not be repeated outside the clinical setting. That confidentiality is not absolute, however. We have already referred to the clinician's duty to protect third parties who may be in danger. In many states, practitioners also are required by law to report evidence of child abuse encountered in their practice to appropriate parties, which may include law enforcement or social service agencies. Court-requested evaluations, which may require practitioners to forward written reports to a range of judicial actors, are clearly not confidential (although in a criminal context practitioners are required to notify the person of this fact). In the civil context, reports are routinely sent to requesting agencies, such as schools or employers. Persons signing a waiver of confidentiality form often do not realize that such reports may cross the desks of a variety of clerical and administrative personnel.

Many ethical questions are raised, then, with respect to psychologists working with the courts. Perlin (1991) has discussed cogently the many problems which he attributes to the power imbalance between the psychologist and the individual he or she is assessing or treating. The psychologist or other mental health expert, Perlin notes, is employed by someone other than that individual. He also recognizes that the individual may suffer harm as a result of the psychologist's participation in the evaluation process.

The Psychologist as an Expert Witness

Despite the discouraging state of the art with reference to prediction of behavior, psychologists are able to provide useful and relevant information in other contexts which can help judges and juries make legal decisions. Few areas of psychology and law, however, have received as much attention as the use of psychologists as expert witnesses in courtroom settings. Often, the attention has been negative. In a recent critique of expert testimony in the courtroom, for example, Saks (1990) refers to mental health professionals as "imperial experts" who see themselves as "temporary monarchs" in the courtroom.

In most jurisdictions, lay witnesses can testify only to events that they have actually seen or heard firsthand. Opinions and inferences are generally not admissible (Schwitzgebel & Schwitzgebel, 1980). Expert witnesses, on the other hand, testify to facts they have observed directly, to tests they may

116

CHAPTER
FOUR:
PSYCHOLOGY
AND
THE
COURTS:
AN
OVERVIEW

have conducted, and to the research evidence in their fields. Moreover, the opinions and inferences of experts are not only admissible, but often sought by the courts.

There is considerable debate about the wisdom of offering opinion, however, particularly when it concerns a case's "ultimate issue." Should the expert be asked for an opinion about whether the defendant was indeed insane (and therefore not responsible) at the time of his crime? Or asked whether a particular mother is a fit parent? Or asked whether a patient is competent to refuse medical treatment?

Slobogin (1989) has summarized the arguments for and against allowing such testimony, and notes that "the available research strongly indicates that judges, lawyers, and juries all want ultimate-issue testimony from the expert" (p. 263). Nevertheless, he cautions that courts be extremely wary of its use, allowing it only if it can be rigorously tested through the adversarial process. As Slobogin points out, critics see "ultimate issues" as moral judgments, and although experts are surely capable of offering considered opinion, moral judgment is not their field of expertise. Furthermore, critics fear the undue influence of the expert on the fact finder. "This danger is exacerbated," Slobogin remarks, "if the willingness of the expert to provide an ultimate conclusion and the eagerness of the fact finder to hear it minimize efforts to examine the basis of the conclusion; the opinion on the ultimate issue may come to assume disproportionate weight relative to the underlying facts in the mind or minds of the fact finder because the facts are not developed, or are not properly emphasized" (p. 261).

Smith (1989) identifies three possible sources of error in such ultimate-issue testimony, and notes that these commonly occur in expert testimony. First, the expert may misunderstand the law and thus reach the wrong conclusion. This often happens, for example, when a mental health expert testifies about a person's competency to stand trial (a legal construct to be discussed in the next chapter). Second, the expert may apply hidden value judgments rather than scientific principles, such as might occur if a psychologist were to testify that a mother is not a fit parent because she works nights. Finally, the expert may arrive at the wrong conclusion in order to produce a desired result. A psychologist might conclude that an individual should be institutionalized, despite the fact that he does not meet the criteria for institutionalization. Those who favor testimony on the ultimate issue, however, argue that judges often depend on it, and that such testimony can be carefully controlled, particularly by means of effective cross-examination.

In order for an individual to qualify as an expert, courts require that he or she possess technical or other scientific knowledge which will assist the trier of fact (judge or jury). Until recently, many federal and state courts also required that the expert's evidence be "generally acceptable" to the scientific community, a standard known as the *Frye* test after a 1923 federal court decision. In a 1993 decision, *Daubert v. Merrell Dow*, the U. S. Supreme Court dropped the general acceptability standard in favor of a more liberal standard outlined in the Federal Rules of Evidence (see Box 10.2). The Court's decision effectively makes federal judges gatekeepers who must rule on the "reliability" and "relevance" of scientific testimony. In a footnote, the Justices said they were referring to *evidentiary* reliability, which they likened to trustworthiness. "In a case involving scientific evidence, evidentiary reliability will be based upon scientific validity."

It is important to note, however, that psychologists themselves argue that research evidence in some areas is transferred to the courtroom prematurely. This criticism has been leveled frequently at research on eyewitness testimony (e.g., Konecni & Ebbesen, 1986; Yuille, 1989), rape trauma syndrome (Frazier & Borgida, 1992), and issues relating to child custody determinations (Bolocofsky, 1989). On the other hand, proponents of expert testimony in these areas argue persuasively that carefully conducted research, yielding consistent results, is available and should be communicated to the courts (Loftus, 1991; Melton, 1987). The 1993 *Daubert* case supports this latter view.

■ 4.4: *SURVIVING THE WITNESS STAND*

IN HIS CONCISE AND WITTY BOOK, *Testifying in Court* (1991), psychologist Stanley L. Brodsky offers sage advice to clinicians testifying as expert witnesses.

In one chapter, Brodsky mentions four "fluency-initiating gestures" that are particularly relevant to courtroom testimony:

1. Vary the loudness of the voice. As Brodsky notes, an audience quickly adapts to speech at a fixed loudness level, and thoughts can easily stray.

2. Speak slowly. Fast talking typically characterizes anxiety and communicates that the speaker is not in control. Most of us would agree that, although there are exceptions, people who talk fast are not effective in getting their messages across.

3. Stress syllables, changing the pitch or volume for certain syllables. Brodsky gives examples of people who are or were very effective at this, including sportscaster Howard Cosell, commentator Paul Harvey, and President John F. Kennedy. We might add former Texas Congresswoman Barbara Jordan, who uses this fluency initiating gesture to perfection.

4. Ease into your breath pattern. Breathe in, begin to exhale, then speak. "That point in the exhalation allows the greatest calmness and control.... Witnesses should get the stream of exhaled air moving before responding" (p. 117). ■

Part of the "expert" problem for psychologists working with the courts stems from a fundamental confusion about the differences between psychology and psychiatry. Many courts continue to prefer psychiatrists to psychologists as clinical experts (Yuille, 1989). We referred to professional differences in Chapter 1, noting in particular the training emphasized by each profession. Compounding the problem is the fact that psychology is a broad discipline that encompasses widely diverse specialties. Doctoral level clinical or forensic psychologists qualify best as expert witnesses on matters associated with mental disorder, because they have been trained in assessing, diagnosing, treating, and researching mental illness or behavior problems at a level comparable or superior to psychiatric training, even as it relates to the effects of certain drugs on behavior (psychopharmacology). The training received by doctoral level psychologists also often includes the assessment and diagnosis of brain damage and other neurological dysfunctions.

As we have repeatedly noted, however, research psychologists can qualify equally well as experts if the legal questions posed relate to their area of expertise. A social psychologist with expertise in small-group behavior might testify on the effects of group dynamics on the individual, for example, or a developmental psychologist might testify on the competency of an adolescent to make medical decisions.

SURVIVING THE WITNESS STAND

"The courtroom is a place best reserved for those who are brave, adventuresome and nimble-witted." This comment (Schwitzgebel & Schwitzgebel, 1980, p. 241) summarizes well the perils inherent in cross-examination and the discomfort almost guaranteed the expert witness. The professional literature contains ample advice for psychologists daring enough (some say foolhardy enough) to approach the witness stand. Poythress (1979), for example, suggests that good preparation for the psychologist intending to be an expert witness should include thorough experiential learning in mock trial situations, observations of experienced expert witnesses, and specific course work or field placements in forensic settings.

Courtroom testimony, if punctuated by vigorous cross-examination, can be a punishing

118

CHAPTER
FOUR:
PSYCHOLOGY
AND
THE
COURTS:
AN
OVERVIEW

experience even when the expert witness is fully prepared, however. This is especially true in the behavioral sciences, where complexity is compounded by incomplete information. Conflicting testimony by two psychologists, two psychiatrists, or one of each confuses the courts and the public and can undermine the credibility of both professions (Yarmey, 1979). The underlying reason for cross-examinations, of course, is to "...reverse the substance or impact of a witness's testimony" (Brodsky, 1991, p. 1).

Differences of opinion between and within professions should not necessarily be interpreted as error or misinformation. The "collision of experts" is partly due to the complexity and ambiguity of the issues about which they are commenting. Problems and inconsistencies may also be due to differences in training and philosophy. In some cases, the confusion arises when medical and psychological testimony is so replete with professional jargon and with esoteric, empirically unsupported speculation that the testimony is nearly, if not completely, useless to the court. In other cases, problems stem from inadequate preparation or poor communication between the expert witness and the lawyer who has called that witness to testify. Also, as any experienced judge or trial lawyer knows, it is often easy to obtain psychiatric or psychological testimony to support either side of a case. In many of these cases, the so-called battle of experts is not even remotely edifying (Meehl, 1977).

Opposing experts are not always the norm, however. In many cases—particularly in pretrial criminal proceedings and involuntary civil commitment proceedings—there is only one clinical expert. This may happen because the court has appointed a clinician agreeable to both sides or because one side is unable to pay for the services of an expert witness. It should be noted, though, that indigent defendants who are pleading not guilty by reason of insanity in a death penalty case have a constitutional right to psychiatric assistance in the preparation of their defense and at sentencing (*Ake v. Oklahoma*, 1985).

Psychologists represent the science of behavior. They would be well advised, regardless of whether they are opposed by other experts, to be familiar with the behavioral research literature directly related to the legal issue upon which they will testify. Because psychologists represent the science of behavior, they would be well advised to be familiar with the behavioral research literature directly related to the legal issue upon which they will testify. They should also be prepared to substantiate the reliability and validity of any assessment instruments and procedures used in arriving at their conclusions. Writing about "survival on the witness stand," Stanley Brodsky (1977) notes that this preparation is essential. When experts are able to defend their specific theories, methods, and conclusions, their testimony becomes much more credible. In a more recent book, *Testifying in Court*, Brodsky (1991) advises prospective *and* experienced expert witnesses about the labyrinths of testifying. It should be required reading for anyone interested in issues surrounding expert witnesses.

Singer and Nievod (1987) note—as does Brodsky—that establishing a communicative relationship between the expert witness and the attorney early in the legal process is essential. "Some attorneys stereotypically view psychologists as soft thinkers, lacking in discipline, while psychologists often regard attorneys as narrowly focused, rigid, and inflexible. These stereotypes result from a failure to understand the other's professional needs at the outset of the consultation" (p. 530). Singer and Nievod also urge psychologists not to be persuaded to enter the courtroom without advance notice and sufficient preparation time. This occurs with surprising frequency and typifies the relationship psychology *in* the law described in Chapter 1. Finally, they (1987) warn that a psychologist's work products, such as interview notes, correspondence, and tape recordings relating to the case will be made available to attorneys for both sides under the rules of discovery. "Only wisdom and personal preference can dictate how extensively to maintain case records. There is no one way. If the psychologist takes few notes, an opposing attorney may attempt to characterize these notes as skimpy, careless, or the work of a cursory effort."

Summary and Conclusions

This chapter had two main purposes. The *first* was to provide an overview of the American court system and the judicial process, and to introduce the various categories of law. It is important that the reader become familiar with judicial concepts, terms, and process in order to understand the material that is to follow in later chapters.

The *second* purpose was to review how both law and psychology approach the fundamental problem of predicting human behavior. Determinism is a key issue. Do human beings follow the laws of the universe, where antecedent or past events dictate behavior? Or do they behave according to their future goals, dreams, hopes, and ambitions? If humans are lawful, they are ultimately predictable, a position often assumed by research psychology. If humans have free will and they decide on their courses of action through goals, they are largely unpredictable. Most psychologists take an intermediate approach, a position referred to by Sappington (1990) as "libertarianism."

Psychological research during the 1970s and early 1980s indicated that mental health experts were not accurate in predicting dangerous behavior. Actuarial methods were somewhat better than clinical methods, but still fell short in overall accuracy. However, many of these studies had methodological shortcomings. We also explored some of the psychological reasons for the inaccuracy of clinical prediction, including biases, prejudices, cognitive shortcuts, fundamental attribution error, and the fact that some of the behavior practitioners try to predict occurs so infrequently. Social psychologists have found that all of us have a strong tendency to take cognitive shortcuts, simplify complex problems, and accept the first reasonable solution that comes along (Saks & Krupat, 1988). We are stingy at mental work—according to a hypothesis called the **cognitive miser model**—and practitioners, regardless of their training and experience, are no exception. Yet, the judiciary expects and needs some indication of what certain individuals are apt to do in the future. This is especially true when it comes to dangerousness. Unfortunately, a vast majority of recent research has focused on predictions of *institutional* violence and have generally neglected *community* violence (Davis, 1991; Monahan & Steadman, in press). Some exceptions will be noted in the next chapter.

Finally, there is every reason to believe that with coordinated research, improved empirical methodology, and a sophisticated recognition by practitioners of the myriad pitfalls in prediction, we can significantly improve our predictive efforts. Monahan and Shah (1989, p. 550) write, "There is a guarded optimism in the field that it may be possible to improve the validity of clinical predictions of violence, and much promising research is currently underway."

Questions to Ponder

1. Your sister wants to be a psychologist working closely with the courts. List and discuss the duties she could perform in that capacity and tell her what type of academic preparation would be most helpful.

120

CHAPTER
FOUR:
PSYCHOLOGY
AND
THE
COURTS:
AN
OVERVIEW

2. What are illustrations of actuarial and clinical prediction other than those discussed in the chapter? If you were applying for a job, would you prefer that the hiring decision be based on actuarial or clinical data, and why?

3. Discuss the problems associated with the prediction of dangerousness in the criminal context. Should someone be punished for behavior he or she *might* exhibit?

4. What might explain the fact that judges often want an opinion from an expert witness, even though the final decision is left to the judge?

5. Discuss the concepts psychology *and* law and psychology *in* law as they related to expert testimony.

COMPETENCIES AND CRIMINAL RESPONSIBILITY: ASSESSMENTS FOR THE CRIMINAL COURTS

PSYCHOLOGISTS ARE INCREASINGLY BEING ASKED TO ASSESS a variety of competencies or abilities associated with the criminal process. After making these assessments, which are generally followed by a written report, the psychologist may be asked to testify as an expert witness. Some evaluations relate to mental states of witnesses. A psychologist might assess the ability of a child victim to recollect the crime accurately, for example, or meet with a rape victim and offer expert testimony on the psychological trauma she has experienced. Most assessments for criminal courts are of criminal defendants, however. Grisso (1986, p. 3) summarizes these as follows.

> They include the defendant's capacities: (1) to waive rights to silence and counsel 'knowingly, intelligently, and voluntarily,' prior to questioning by law enforcement officers; (2) to plead guilty; (3) to dismiss counsel, or to conduct one's own defense without benefit of counsel; (4) to stand trial (i.e., to function in the role of defendant in the trial process); (5) to possess the requisite cognition, affect, and volition for criminal responsibility (i.e., the insanity defense); (6) to serve a sentence; (7) to be executed (i.e., to undergo capital punishment).

When courts, both criminal and civil, inquire into an individual's "competency," the courts are looking for specific functional abilities. Applebaum and Grisso (1988, 1991) are involved in a continuing project to develop and test specific instruments for measuring these abilities in a variety of legal contexts. They identify four sets of abilities most often incorporated into legal standards. "These are the abilities to communicate a choice, to understand relevant information, to appreciate the situation and its consequences, and to rationally manipulate relevant information" (Grisso & Applebaum, 1991, p. 378). This emphasis on functional abilities, rather than upon mental disorder per se, is significant. As will become apparent throughout this and the following chapter, a diagnosis of mental disorder alone is not enough to demonstrate that a person is legally incompetent.

Although assessment of any of the above competencies may involve the psychologist, competency to stand trial and insanity evaluations have traditionally received the most research attention and consequently are highlighted here. In recent years, the controversial issue of assessing an offender's mental competency to be executed has raised numerous ethical and legal questions. The Supreme Court has ruled—*Ford v. Wainwright*, 1986—that it is unconstitutional to execute someone who is so mentally disordered that he or she cannot understand what is happening. That topic will be discussed in Chapter 13.

Competency to stand trial and **insanity** often confound the public. A long line of research shows psychiatrists and clinical psychologists, lawyers, judges, and legislators also have misconstrued the concepts (Simon & Aaronson, 1988; Melton et al., 1987). We will examine each one

122

CHAPTER
FIVE:
COMPETENCIES
AND
CRIMINAL
RESPONSIBILITY:
ASSESSMENTS
FOR THE
CRIMINAL
COURTS

separately, discuss how it is used in the judicial system, and point out problems associated with this use. The special verdict "Guilty But Mentally Ill," adopted in some states in response to frustrations with the insanity defense, will also be discussed.

Competency to Stand Trial

Competency to stand trial and insanity refer to a defendant's mental capacities at two different points in time. Specifically, competency to stand trial is concerned with the individual's capacity at the time of the trial preparation and the trial itself to understand the charges and legal proceedings, and to be able to communicate with his or her attorney. Therefore, competency to stand trial is restricted to the present and the foreseeable future. Furthermore, at any point during the trial, the presiding judge may order an evaluation of the defendant's competency.

The U. S. Supreme Court has ruled that defendants are *competent to stand trial* if they have "sufficient present ability to consult with their lawyer with a reasonable degree of rational understanding...and a rational as well as a factual understanding of the proceedings..." (*Dusky v. U. S.*, 1960, p. 402). In other words, competency to stand trial is the ability to play the role of defendant (Grisso, 1986; Szasz, 1960). *Insanity*, on the other hand, is the legal term for lack of criminal responsibility at the time of the crime, as the result of a mental disorder. It should be emphasized that both terms—insanity and competency to stand trial—are *legal*, not mental health concepts. The court determines who is insane or who is incompetent, not the mental health practitioner or clinician. In reality, however, as we will note later in the chapter, judges rely very heavily on the opinion of mental health practitioners.

A judge's finding that an individual is incompetent to stand trial (IST) means that the defendant is so cognitively, emotionally, or physically impaired that it is unfair to continue the criminal process. At this point, the criminal process is held in abeyance until the defendant once again becomes competent or, alternately, the case is dismissed. A finding that the defendant was insane, by contrast, absolves the defendant of guilt. The defendant does not necessarily go free, however. In fact, persons found not guilty by reason of insanity on average spend at least as much time in a mental institution as they would have spent in prison if convicted (Golding & Roesch, 1987). This could change, however. In a 1992 decision, *Foucha v. Louisiana*, the U. S. Supreme Court ruled that insanity acquittees may not be held in psychiatric facilities once they are no longer "mentally ill." Foucha was acquitted of burglary but sent to a psychiatric hospital, where he spent four years. He was then deemed "cured," but still dangerous because of an antisocial personality (which is not a mental illness). The Court ruled he should be released.

We should emphasize again that a diagnosis of a mental disorder per se does not render an individual either incompetent to stand trial or insane. A person with a depressive disorder, for example, may be perfectly capable of understanding the proceedings and helping her attorney. On the other hand, another person could be so severely depressed that he withdraws from the situation and refuses to communicate. As Grisso (1986, p. 95) remarks, "Although psychopathological symptoms by themselves are not synonymous with legal incompetency, they are certainly relevant for pretrial competency determinations."

Symptoms associated with a diagnosis of a mental disorder may also interfere with a person's competency to plead guilty. Recall that the vast majority of criminal cases are settled by way of a plea bargain. It has been argued that pleading guilty, in light of its consequences, requires sharper functional ability than going through trial (Halleck, 1980). The U. S. Supreme Court, in *Westbrook v. Arizona* (1966), noted that it was possible for a defendant to be competent to stand trial but not competent to plead guilty or waive other constitutional rights. Despite this, the failure to monitor guilty pleas more carefully appears to be one of the factors contributing to the influx of mentally disordered persons in jails and prisons (Steadman, McCarty & Morrissey, 1989).

It is important to note, also, that a defendant may be sane, or criminally responsible at the time of the crime, but found incompetent at the trial stage. In 1992, hotel magnate Leona Helmsley began serving a prison sentence for tax evasion; her elderly husband Harry, who *may* have been equally criminally responsible, was found incompetent to stand trial and remains free. Another example is the negligent driver who kills a pedestrian, is charged with vehicular manslaughter, and is so emotionally distraught as a result of the tragedy that he cannot help his attorney in the preparation of a defense.

The psychologist is most likely to be asked to evaluate a defendant for competency very early in the criminal proceedings. Typically, at the defendant's arraignment or shortly thereafter, a motion is made by either the defense lawyer or the prosecutor to inquire into the defendant's competency. Numerous factors can trigger this inquiry. The arresting police officer *may* have noticed bizarre behavior, for example, or the person may have attempted to commit suicide while detained in jail. Research has found that competency evaluations are also precipitated by previous psychiatric hospitalizations as well as psychologically irrelevant factors, including political motives, a defense lawyer's wish to "buy time," and homelessness (Nicholson & Kugler, 1991). The presiding judge also has authority to raise the competency issue at any time. Most requests for competency evaluation are neither denied by the judge nor challenged by the opposing attorney (Roesch & Golding, 1987).

It is estimated that 25,000 criminal defendants nationwide, or about one in fifteen, are evaluated for their competency to stand trial each year (Nicholson & Kugler, 1991; Whitcomb & Brandt, 1985). That competency inquiry has been called "the most significant mental health inquiry pursued in the system of criminal law" (Stone, 1975, p. 200). In a line of decisions (e.g., *Dusky v. U. S.*, 1960; *Pate v. Robinson*, 1966; *Drope v. Missouri*, 1974), the U. S. Supreme Court has made it clear that the conviction of an incompetent defendant violates due process of law.

Although some researchers have predicted that by the mid-1990s the majority of competency evaluations will be conducted in outpatient settings or in jails (Roesch & Golding, 1987), a common practice in most states is to send defendants to a mental institution for anywhere from fifteen to ninety days for inpatient evaluation (Nicholson & Kugler, 1991). Researchers find that judges and lawyers often distrust outpatient evaluations, believing they cannot adequately assess a defendant's competency (Melton et al., 1985). In an extensive study conducted in Canada, Menzies (1989) found that even defendants sent to an outpatient clinic did not escape hospitalization. Almost one in three were hospitalized for a thirty-day evaluation following their appearance at an outpatient clinic.

COMPETENCY EVALUATION

Although competency to stand trial and insanity are often interrelated (Golding & Roesch, 1987), they require separate assessments and determinations. Commentators (e.g., Grisso, 1988; Saks, 1990) often remark that psychiatrists and clinical psychologists fail to focus on the limited issue of a defendant's competency to stand trial. Instead, they travel into irrelevant conceptual terrain in their competency reports as well as in their courtroom testimony. Some examiners concentrate on the defendant's

CHAPTER
FIVE:
COMPETENCIES
AND
CRIMINAL
RESPONSIBILITY:
ASSESSMENTS
FOR THE
CRIMINAL
COURTS

dangerousness, for example (Grisso, 1988; Menzies, 1989) or on the defendant's state of mind at the time of the offense, which is critical to the insanity issue but not the competency issue. Some statutes and courts nurture this misinterpretation by requiring or allowing a **dual-purpose evaluation** of both the defendant's competency to stand trial and mental state at the time of the offense.

Statutes rarely prescribe the method of evaluation. As a result, how competency is assessed depends upon the examiner's training and theoretical orientation. Some prefer only the clinical interview, while others choose the interview in combination with projective or objective testing instruments. Still others use a wide-ranging assessment procedure which includes psychological tests, interview information, observation, and extensive background and social history. When an evaluation has been completed, the examiner transmits to the court and often to attorneys, a report which most routinely will include a recommendation as to the defendant's competency. The great majority of competency decisions are made on the basis of one clinician's assessment (Melton et al., 1987) and without direct testimony from that clinician. Furthermore, judges rarely disagree with the clinician's recommendation, particularly if the clinician believes the defendant is incompetent. After reviewing a number of studies on this matter, Melton and his colleagues (1987, p. 72) noted that "whomever examining mental health professionals characterize as incompetent is likely ultimately to be found incompetent."

There is a wide variety of professional literature advising clinical psychologists and other examiners how to conduct evaluations for the courts (e.g., Grisso, 1986, 1988; Shapiro, 1990; Weiner & Hess, 1987). Regardless of the specific procedures or techniques used, however, it is helpful for psychologists conducting competency evaluations to keep three points in mind. First, they must have a thorough understanding of the referral: Who raised the competency issue and why? What specific questions did the referring agent pose? Were there questions about the intellectual or neurological functioning of the defendant? Second, if tests are used, they should be those specifically designed for competency assessment and for which reliability and validity data have been established. These competency assessment instruments will be discussed shortly. Third, the examiner must be able to develop a connection between the data collected and the referral questions and to communicate the relationship clearly to the court, both in writing and—if necessary—orally. The report must be free of psychological jargon and extraneous material. It should be concise, make reference to specific behaviors, and be cautious in setting forth interpretations. The clinician also should remember that the decision as to whether a defendant is competent to stand trial is to be made by the presiding judge.

COMPETENCY ASSESSMENT INSTRUMENTS

Approximately four of every five defendants evaluated for competency to stand trial are ultimately found competent (Grisso, 1986; Nicholson & Kugler, 1991). This evidence, together with concerns that defendants often are hospitalized needlessly during the evaluation process, led to the development of screening instruments for the quick identification of those who are "obviously competent." The earliest work in this area was a brief checklist (Robey, 1965), which was soon superseded by guidelines proposed by McGarry and his colleagues at the Harvard Laboratory of Community Psychiatry (1974). The Harvard researchers developed two instruments specifically designed to direct clinicians toward relevant defendant behaviors. One instrument, the *Competency Screening Test* (CST), produces a summational score of competency to stand trial. The defendant is asked to complete twenty-two sentences (Example: "When I go to court the lawyer will..."), and each response is scored 0, 1, or 2. A total score below 20 usually raises questions about the defendant's competency. The instrument's major advantage is its ability to screen out quickly the clearly competent defendants, so that more time-consuming examination can be directed at those defendants whose competency is questionable.

The second instrument, the *Competency Assessment Instrument* (CAI), is designed to assess all possible legal grounds for a finding of incompetence. The instrument consists of thirteen "ego functions" or observable groups of behaviors related to a defendant's ability to cope with and understand the trial process. One item, for example, is the defendant's "quality of relating to attorney." Each of the thirteen functions is scored on a scale ranging from 1 (total incapacity) to 5 (no incapacity). There is no recommended minimal score, so assessors are left to make their own recommendations about the defendant's competency.

Golding, Roesch and Schreiber (1984) have developed the *Interdisciplinary Fitness Interview* (IFI), a structured interview "designed to assess both the legal and psychopathological aspects of competency" (Roesch & Golding, 1987, p. 386). A key feature of the IFI is its interdisciplinary nature; it encourages joint interviewing by a clinician and a lawyer. Also appearing on the scene are the *Georgia Court Competency Test* (GCCT) and its revision (GCCT-MSH). These last are rapid, quantitative measures of competency involving seventeen and twenty-one questions, respectively.

There is a rich store of reliability and validity studies directed at competency screening and assessment instruments (e.g., Jones & O'Toole, 1981; Nicholson et al., 1988a, 1988b) and commentators urge their continuing development (e.g., Grisso, 1986; Nicholson & Kugler, 1991). Nevertheless, the instruments do not seem to be widely used, and some clinicians remain guarded (e.g., Shapiro, 1990). When competency assessment instruments are used, they supplement traditional clinical methods, particularly the clinical interview (Roesch & Golding, 1987). Steadman and Hartstone (1983, p. 44) attribute the failure to use screening instruments to the "preference for clinical assessment within the medical profession over a more statistical approach implicit in the instruments." They add, "The extent to which this also is indicative of judicial recalcitrance is uncertain." As psychologists become more involved in competency evaluations, however, the likelihood that forensic instruments will be devised and used should increase.

THE INCOMPETENT DEFENDANT

As noted above, a minority of defendants evaluated for competency to stand trial are found incompetent. In his widely cited study of these defendants, Steadman (1979, p. 30) described them as a socially marginal group "with much less than average education and few useful job skills. Most have few community ties, either through employment or family. An unusually high proportion have never married." Nicholson and Kugler (1991), who analyzed thirty studies on competency to stand trial which had been conducted over a twenty-year period, reported that the strongest correlates of incompetency were not demographic but rather clinical in nature. Demographic data include factors such as age, gender, employment, and marital status. Clinical data include information about psychological functions. Specifically, in Nicholson and Kugler's summary, defendants found incompetent to stand trial: (1) performed poorly on tests specifically designed to assess legally relevant functional abilities; (2) were diagnosed psychotic; and (3) had psychiatric symptoms indicating severe psychopathology. This finding is not surprising, since, as we noted, judges rarely disagree with the clinical examiner's recommendation (Melton et al., 1987).

The relationship between competency status and crime charged appears erratic and varies widely according to jurisdictions. Some research has found incompetent defendants charged predominantly with violent crimes, or at least felony offenses (e.g., Steadman, 1979; Roesch & Golding, 1980; Williams & Miller, 1981). Nicholson and Kugler's examination of thirty studies, however, indicated that the type of offense "likely bears a stronger relation to the decision to refer

126

CHAPTER
FIVE:
COMPETENCIES
AND
CRIMINAL
RESPONSIBILITY:
ASSESSMENTS
FOR THE
CRIMINAL
COURTS

[for a competency evaluation] than it does to the decision about competency itself" (p. 366). More than half of the competency evaluees had been charged with violent crimes, but less than a third of those ultimately found incompetent were in that category.

Until 1972, a defendant found IST could face lifetime confinement in a mental institution. It was not uncommon for the defendant to be committed for an indefinite period of time, supposedly until rendered "competent." Some studies have reported that about 50 percent of those found incompetent under these procedures spent the rest of their lives confined in an institution (Hess & Thomas, 1963; McGarry, 1971). It was also estimated that these defendants comprised between 40 percent (Steadman & Cocozza, 1974) and 90 percent of the population in mental institutions (Committee on Psychiatry and Law, 1974).

In the 1972 case *Jackson v. Indiana*, however, the U. S. Supreme Court ruled that persons found incompetent to stand trial may be involuntarily confined only for the reasonable period of time necessary to determine whether there is a substantial probability of their becoming competent to stand trial in the foreseeable future. If the defendant was not likely to gain competency in the foreseeable future, civil commitment proceedings must be initiated or the defendant must be released. (Civil commitment, the subject of the next chapter, carries due-process protections that make it more difficult to place a person in a mental institution.) The Supreme Court in the *Jackson* case left it to states to determine what are reasonable amounts of time to strive for competency and how to evaluate the likelihood that competency would be achieved. Although the *Jackson* decision should have stopped the indefinite confinement of persons found incompetent to stand trial, approximately half the states continued to allow this almost ten years later (Roesch & Golding, 1979). Today, persons found IST with little likelihood of being restored to competency often have their cases **dismissed without prejudice**, which gives the prosecutor the option of reinstituting charges in the event that person does regain competency. Incompetent defendants also may be committed to mental institutions through involuntary civil commitment proceedings. If incompetent defendants are accused of serious crimes and there is strong interest in bringing them to trial, they are often given **psychoactive drugs** to stabilize their mental condition and render them competent. Psychoactive drugs are "those drugs that exert their primary effect on the brain, thus altering mood or behavior, or that are used in the treatment of mental disorders" (Julien, 1992, p. xii).

DRUGS AND INCOMPETENT DEFENDANTS

Do criminal defendants have a constitutional right to refuse these drugs? That issue, which was debated extensively during the 1980s, has yet to be resolved. In general, courts have not been sympathetic to incompetent defendants wishing to avoid psychoactive drugs. The leading cases are those announced by federal courts of appeals. In *U. S. v. Charters* (1988) the court ruled that an incompetent defendant could be forced to take antipsychotic drugs against his will at the discretion of medical personnel, providing judicial review of the medical decision is available. The influential D. C. Court of Appeals ruled in 1992 (*Tran Van Khiem v. U. S.*), that a murder defendant found incompetent to stand trial could be treated with psychoactive drugs against his will, because the government's interest in bringing him to trial was greater than the defendant's interest in avoiding the effects of the drugs.

The U. S. Supreme Court has not taken a direct stand on the issue. It has, however, affirmed the right of a defendant claiming insanity to be free of psychoactive drugs *during his trial* (*Riggins v. Nevada*, 1992), unless it could be shown that there was no alternative to medicating the defendant (see Box 5.1). The majority opinion noted that the Court was deciding only the issue of involuntary medication *during trial*. Justice Kennedy (118 L. Ed 2d 479, 495), however, in a concurring opinion, suggested that forcing drugs to make a defendant *competent to stand trial* would also violate due

■ 5.1: SYNTHETIC "SANITY" AT TRIAL: RIGGINS v. NEVADA

RIGGINS, A DEFENDANT CHARGED WITH MURDER, was being held in pretrial detention when he complained of hearing voices and having difficulty sleeping. He was prescribed the antipsychotic drug Mellaril along with the anti-convulsant drug Dilantin, both of which he had taken in the past. The drugs had the effect of stabilizing his behavior, and he was found competent to stand trial.

Riggins then raised an insanity defense. He asked the court to suspend the Mellaril during his trial because it infringed upon his freedom and would impede his ability to help his lawyer. Moreover, he argued that the jury should observe him in his natural, unmedicated state, as he had been at the time of the crime. The district court judge refused his request without explaining why. Riggins was tried while on medication, convicted, and sentenced to death.

The U. S. Supreme Court ruled, in a 7-2 decision, that the trial judge had been too quick to reject Riggins's request. Forcible administration of medication into a nonconsenting person's body was a deprivation of due process, the Court said. Therefore, the state had to demonstrate an overriding justification for the drug. Moreover, it had to demonstrate that no less intrusive alternative was available. Since there was a possibility that Riggins's defense was impaired by the administration of Mellaril, the Supreme Court remanded the case for further proceedings. ■

process. He was particularly worried that side effects would impair the defendant's ability to assist his attorney. According to Justice Kennedy:

> These potential side effects would be disturbing for any patient; but when the patient is a criminal defendant who is going to stand trial, the documented probability of side effects seems to me to render involuntary administration of the drugs by prosecuting officials unacceptable absent a showing by the State that the side effects will not alter the defendant's reactions or diminish his capacity to assist counsel.

Justice Kennedy doubted that the State could easily make such a showing, given the present understanding of the properties of psychoactive drugs.

Little is known about how institutionalized, incompetent defendants are treated, other than by means of psychoactive drugs. Wexler and Winick (1991, p. 314) posit that "treatment is probably rarely tailored to the specific abilities needed to be competent to stand trial. It probably has as a goal the treatment of the patient's psychopathology, rather than the short-term goal of restoration to trial competency, or more appropriately to competency to perform the specific trial-related task the defendant has been found unable adequately to do." In fact, a survey of 128 forensic facilities disclosed that over half did not treat incompetent defendants any differently than the general mentally disordered population (Siegel & Elwork, 1990).

As a result of their discovery, Siegel and Elwork developed a standardized treatment approach specifically designed to restore defendants to competency. It included both traditional mental health therapy and exercises geared to criminal defendants. The researchers used videotapes, problem-solving group sessions, and various techniques to teach defendants courtroom procedures and how to interact with lawyers and other participants (Elwork, 1992). The approach highlights the need for mental health experts to integrate both legal and psychological considerations into their practices (Elwork, 1992).

Wexler and Winick (1991, p. 315) recommend a treatment plan "detailing the kinds of treatment attempted and proposed and the anticipated outcome." In keeping with their paradigm of "therapeutic jurisprudence" discussed in Chapter 1, Wexler and Winick would allow incompetent defendants substantial choice in the type of treatment they receive to bring about their restoration to competency.

CHAPTER
FIVE:
COMPETENCIES
AND
CRIMINAL
RESPONSIBILITY:
ASSESSMENTS
FOR THE
CRIMINAL
COURTS

Insanity

To paraphrase a key federal case, if a person chooses to do evil through the exercise of his or her free will, that person must bear **criminal responsibility** (*U. S. v. Brawner*, 1972). Conversely, the *absence* of criminal responsibility absolves a person of guilt. The public is acquainted with this principle in law primarily through the insanity defense, because extensive publicity often accompanies a claim that a person who clearly committed an illegal act was not responsible. Criminal defendants may also use other, less-publicized defenses to argue that they should not be held criminally responsible. If you empty your employer's cash register because someone is holding your loved one captive at point of gun, waiting for you to return with cash, you might use *duress* as a defense. If you are hypnotized and ordered to do the same, your defense might be *unconsciousness*.

The often-used but not entirely representative illustration of an insanity case is the acquittal of John Hinckley, who in 1982 shot and wounded then-President Ronald Reagan and critically injured his press secretary, James Brady. Although Hinckley clearly fired the weapon, he was found not guilty by reason of insanity. The verdict, which outraged and confused the public, was nonetheless consistent with the federal insanity statutes in effect at that time. We will return to the Hinckley case shortly.

Despite the publicity which often accompanies them, cases which invoke the insanity defense are rare. Unfortunately, there are few nationwide or state data on defendants who plead not guilty by reason of insanity (NGRI). As Steadman et al. (1993) note, we know far more about insanity acquittals than about pleas. The information we do have suggests that defendants raise the issue in only about 1 percent of all felony cases (Callahan et al., 1991; Simon & Aaronson, 1988).

Insanity defense rates vary dramatically among jurisdictions. For example, McGinley and Pasewark (1989) report that in Colorado, 44 percent of insanity defendants were successful, while rates in Michigan, Maine, Minnesota, and Wyoming were 7 percent, 4 percent, 3 percent, and 2 percent, respectively.

In an eight-state study involving nearly 9,000 defendants who pleaded NGRI, Callahan et al. (1991) found an acquittal rate of 25 percent. They also found that only 7 percent of the acquittals were handed down by juries. Similarly, Beohnert (1990) found that 96 percent of defendants found insane had gone before a judge, not a jury. These findings highlight the crucial role of the mental health expert at the pretrial stage of a criminal case. As Simon and Aaronson note (1988, p. 9):

> ... in most instances where the insanity defense is successfully invoked, the available evidence of the defendant's abnormal mental state points so overwhelmingly to a conclusion of insanity that the prosecutor agrees not to formally contest the defense. Instead, prosecutors usually enter into a formal or tacit agreement for an acquittal by reason of insanity. Almost always, this decision is based on a report of the federal or state psychiatrists that the defendant meets the criteria for insanity.

Interestingly, 15 percent of the acquitted defendants in Callahan's study had not themselves raised the insanity defense, suggesting that they were considered so disordered that an insanity verdict was essentially imposed upon them. A comparison of successful and unsuccessful defendants indicated that those being found not guilty by reason of insanity tended to be older, female, better educated, and single. They were also considered extremely disturbed, with a large majority having prior hospitalization.

Another common assumption is that insanity acquittees "get off easy." Recall that these individuals are most often institutionalized, and usually for at least as long as they would have been confined had they been found guilty of a crime (Golding & Roesch, 1987). Whether *Foucha v. Louisiana* (1992) will change this remains to be seen. With respect to insanity acquittal as a function of the seriousness of the offense, the literature is mixed. Steadman (1985) found that murder and assault represented slightly over half of the offenses for which an NGRI verdict was returned in two states, Michigan and New York. In other states and in the District of Columbia, the crimes of insanity acquittees were less serious. Callahan and her colleagues (1991), however, found that nearly 15 percent of the insanity acquittees they studied had been charged with murder, and most of the rest had been charged with violent or potentially violent offenses.

INSANITY STANDARDS

Just as mental disorder does not equal IST, neither does mental disorder equal insanity. As mentioned previously, it is possible for a person to be diagnosed with a disorder and still be criminally responsible. Horace, charged with tax evasion, is known to have an obsessive-compulsive disorder, displayed in his need to stroke every doorknob in sight. The mere presence of his disorder does not mean he is not responsible for his crime. Some serious mental disorders, however, such as paranoid schizophrenia, are widely believed to rob their victims of rational thought (Grisso, 1990). In short, a defendant is not acquitted *because* he or she has a mental disorder. Rather, all excuses are basically founded on two criteria: irrationality and compulsion (Morse, 1986). If it can be established that a person was not in control of his or her mental processes (irrationality), and/or was not in control of his or her behavior (compulsion) at the time of an offense, then there are grounds for absolving that person of some or all responsibility for the offense. Not all jurisdictions accept both of these criteria, however.

In order to help judges and juries decide whether someone accused of crime was indeed insane, a variety of tests have been established in the law. These tests vary widely among the states, but they usually center around one of three general models: the **M'Naghten Rule**, and the **Durham Rule** (named after court cases), and the **ALI Rule** (proposed by the American Law Institute in its Model Penal Code). A modified form of this last test, called the **Brawner Rule**, was in use in the federal courts when John Hinckley was acquitted. Today, the federal courts abide by a substantially "tougher" test. A minority of states also recognize an **irresistible impulse test**.

M'NAGHTEN RULE: THE RIGHT AND WRONG TEST

This most frequently used rule to determine legal sanity is derived from the "wild beast" test pronounced by the English courts in 1724 (Marshall, 1968). According to this rule, individuals were not responsible for their actions if they "could not distinguish good from evil more than a wild beast" (Leifer, 1964, p. 825). The assumption was that it is ability to reason that distinguishes humans from beasts. In 1760, the words "right and wrong" were substituted for "good and evil" (Soboloff, 1958).

The M'Naghten Rule originated in mid-nineteenth century Britain. In 1843, Daniel M'Naghten believed he was being persecuted by the Tories, England's right-wing political party. He identified his major persecutor as Prime Minister Robert Peel. Traveling to London for the sole purpose of assassinating Peel, M'Naghten shot into the Prime Minister's carriage. His plan might have succeeded but for the fact that Peel was riding in Queen Victoria's carriage. Peel's secretary, Edward Drummond, died from the bullet intended for Peel.

There was no question that M'Naghten had committed the act, but the issue raised at the lengthy trial was his mental state at the time of the homicide. On the basis of new psychiatric insights derived from the writings of Isaac Ray, M'Naghten was found "not guilty by reason of

130

CHAPTER
FIVE:
COMPETENCIES
AND
CRIMINAL
RESPONSIBILITY:
ASSESSMENTS
FOR THE
CRIMINAL
COURTS

insanity." The decision was not based on the traditional right-from-wrong moral test in use at that time, but rather on the presumption of a defect of reasoning due to "mental unsoundness" which "embraced his criminal act" (Finkel, 1988). After hearing testimony from medical experts, the prosecutor decided not to press for a guilty verdict, the presiding judge halted the trial, and directed the jury to find M'Naghten insane (Finkel, 1988). In other words, because M'Naghten was apparently "mentally ill," it was assumed that he was not responsible for his actions.

Faced with public outcry and Queen Victoria's anger, the British House of Lords asked common court judges to examine the insanity issue. "In effect, the judges had to account for a perceived miscarriage of justice" (Simon and Aaronson, 1988, p. 13). The Queen's anger was understandable, because there had also been three attempts on her own life, although not by M'Naghten. One of these attempts had produced the "irresistible impulse" test, which held that an individual was not responsible "if some controlling disease was…the acting power within him which he could not resist" (*Regina v. Oxford*, 1840, p. 950.) The irresistible impulse test was rejected by English courts approximately twenty years later (Simon & Aaronson, 1988), but it has survived in states where it is believed that some defendants, because of mental disorder, were not able to control their actions.

Reexamination of the insanity issue, after M'Naghten was found not guilty, led to the development of a new standard by which to judge insanity claims. The common court judges reaffirmed the sixteenth-century **right-from-wrong test** of morality and determined that, had he been tried under that standard, M'Naghten could not have been absolved of responsibility. It is this test, and ironically not the test under which M'Naghten was acquitted, which is the basis of the present M'Naghten Rule.

Through the years the rule has been interpreted and clarified by various criminal and appellate courts. It is now generally recognized to state that a defendant is not responsible if he or she committed an unlawful act "while labouring under such a defect of reason, from disease of the mind, as not to know the nature and quality of the act he was doing; or, if he did know it, that he did not know he was doing what was wrong" (Brooks, 1974, p. 135). The M'Naghten Rule emphasizes the *cognitive elements* of (1) being aware of what one was doing at the time of an illegal act, or (2) knowing or realizing right from wrong in the moral sense. The test recognizes no *degree* of incapacity. The apparent simplicity of the rule may be a key to understanding why it continues to be popular, even though there has been extensive debate on the meaning of the word "know" (Finkel, 1988; Simon & Aaronson, 1988).

For a time, the rule was accepted as the principal standard of criminal responsibility in virtually every American jurisdiction (Saks & Hastie, 1978). However, it was also attacked by several schools of psychiatric and psychological thought, because it was too narrow and not in keeping with current theory and practice. Psychiatrists, who were then the main examiners in matters of criminal responsibility relating to mental states, said it was impossible to convey to the judge and jury the full range of information they obtained from assessing the defendant's responsibility if responsibility was framed solely in terms of cognitive impairment.

THE DURHAM RULE: THE PRODUCT TEST

In 1954, apparently motivated by widespread discontent with the restrictiveness and moral tone of the M'Naghten Rule, U. S. Court of Appeals Judge David Bazelon drafted what was to become the Durham Rule (*Durham v. U. S.*, 1954), sometimes called the "product rule" or "product test." Although Judge Bazelon's opinion is most often associated with this rule, it had for over a century been in operation in New Hampshire, where it was originally framed by a judge who was a friend of Isaac Ray (Finkel, 1988).

The Durham Rule states that "an accused is not criminally responsible if his unlawful act was the product of a mental disease or mental defect" (Brooks, 1974, p. 176). The rule, therefore, focuses more on mental disorder itself than on the cognitive element of "knowing" the rightness or wrongness of a specific action. The Durham Rule was later clarified in *Carter v. U. S.* (1957), which held that mental illness must not merely have entered into the production of the act, it must have played a necessary role.

Bazelon hoped that the new rule would give psychiatrists the latitude to talk freely about the defendant, whereas before they had to testify within the stricter confines of M'Naghten. By bringing the rule for criminal responsibility up to date with psychiatric theory, it was assumed that the ascription of criminal responsibility would be more "scientific."

Soon after the Durham Rule was adopted, however, its broad scope became its major shortcoming and eventually its downfall. Since definitions of "mental illness" are often vague and subjective, the rule, according to many jurists, gave wide discretionary power to psychiatry. During the time that Durham was in effect, some critics asserted that psychiatrists defined mental illness so broadly that it could be applied to most offenders. Anyone who committed an antisocial act could be viewed as mentally ill: the forbidden act was a product of the disorder. Applied in this way, the Durham Rule could be and was used to exculpate large numbers of offenders who had previously been held responsible.

The rule also created havoc among legal scholars, clinicians, and social and behavioral scientists who tried to define "mental disease" or "defect" and to determine what acts were "products" of such conditions. Expert testimony, not surprisingly, reflected this confusion. Ironically, the Durham Rule was supposed to insure that juries would be able to make more informed decisions about criminal responsibility. Yet psychiatrists were often pressed to offer their opinions on the ultimate issue of insanity. Furthermore, such testimony became so technical and abstruse that the juries were left with little choice but to go along with the experts. As Finkel (1988, p. 37) quips, "…the psychiatrist was freer to jargonize." Eventually, the Durham Rule became so unmanageable that it was discarded by most of the jurisdictions that had adopted it. Some states replaced it with the ALI Rule, while others returned to some variant of M'Naghten.

THE ALI AND BRAWNER RULES

In 1972, in *U. S. v. Brawner*, Judge Bazelon himself, writing for the District of Columbia Court of Appeals, ended eighteen years of unhappy experiment with the Durham Rule. The court adopted, however, with some modification, the 1962 draft of the Model Penal Code Rule formulated by the American Law Institute (hereafter referred to as the ALI Rule). According to this ALI Rule (Section 4.01):

(1) A person is not responsible for criminal conduct if at the time of such conduct as a result of mental disease or defect he lacks substantial capacity either to appreciate the criminality (wrongfulness) of his conduct or to conform his conduct to the requirements of the law.

(2) … the terms "mental disease or defect" do not include an abnormality manifested only by repeated criminal or otherwise anti-social conduct.

While adopting this ALI Rule, the D. C. Court of Appeals modified it slightly by specifying that "mental disease" or "defect" must be a condition which *substantially* (a) affects mental or emotional processes or (b) impairs behavioral controls. Note that the measure of degree is placed, not on the capacity itself, but on its effect on the emotions or behaviors. Therefore, *Brawner* permits

132

CHAPTER
FIVE:
COMPETENCIES
AND
CRIMINAL
RESPONSIBILITY:
ASSESSMENTS
FOR THE
CRIMINAL
COURTS

exculpation based on either *cognitive* or *control incapacity*. Note also that the two elements in the rule encompass the two fundamental legal criteria for insanity we discussed previously: *irrationality* and *compulsion*. The control incapacity component resembles the irresistible-impulse test which is based upon the defendant's alleged inability to control behavior, whatever might have been his or her cognitive capacity.

Significantly, the *Brawner* court accepted what has come to be called the **caveat paragraph** of the ALI Rule which excludes abnormality manifested only by repeated criminal or antisocial conduct. This provision was intended to disallow insanity for psychopaths (more precisely, sociopaths), who persistently violate social mores and often the law. Under the ALI rule, psychopaths cannot claim that their abnormal condition is a mental disease or defect.

The two rules discussed here are so similar that they are often combined and discussed as the ALI-Brawner Rule. It was the standard in federal courts when John Hinckley was tried and determined not guilty by reason of insanity.

INSANITY DEFENSE REFORM ACT

The insanity defense was subject to major legal changes in the 1980s, partly precipitated by the Hinckley case, which ironically had many similarities to the case of Daniel M'Naghten. Like M'Naghten's, Hinckley's acquittal provided fuel for extensive debate among members of the public, politicians, and professional groups. Amid public clamor to abolish the defense completely, Congress passed the **Insanity Defense Reform Act of 1984**, which kept the defense in the federal law but modified it in important ways. Essentially, Congress made it more difficult for persons pleading not guilty by reason of insanity in the federal courts to be acquitted.

Among the major changes were: (1) a shift in the burden of proof; (2) elimination of the volitional prong; (3) alteration of the verdict form; and (4) a limit on the role of the expert. Each of these major changes is explained below.

Under the new law, federal defendants claiming insanity have to prove that, "as a result of severe mental disease or defect, [they were] unable to appreciate the nature and quality or the wrongfulness of [their] acts." Prior to this change, once the defendant introduced evidence in support of insanity, the burden was on the prosecution to persuade the jury that the defendant was not insane. The defendant must now prove that he or she is legally insane by clear and convincing evidence rather than by the more lenient preponderance of the evidence (see Box 5.2). This often means that if the prosecution presents strong and impressive evidence against an insanity defense, the standard of proof is unlikely to be met.

Congress's elimination of the **volitional prong** means a defendant will now have trouble claiming an *inability to conform* his or her conduct to the requirements of the law. Thus, it becomes more difficult to establish the compulsion or irresistible-impulse component of the defense. A man who *appreciates* that an act is wrong, therefore, but is unable to control himself by virtue of a mental disorder, would not be absolved of criminal responsibility. Critics of this change have noted that defendants with some so-called compulsive mental disorders such as pyromania and kleptomania would not qualify for insanity acquittal (Simon & Aaronson, 1988).

The verdict handed down to successful insanity acquittees is now not guilty *only* by reason of insanity, a seemingly minor but symbolically significant change which implies resistance to absolving the defendant: the defendant would be guilty if not for the mental state. Expert witnesses are no longer allowed to give an opinion as to whether the defendant had the required mental state at the time of the criminal act. By not allowing the expert witness to testify to the ultimate issue in a case, the courts have tried to eliminate "the confusing spectacle of competing expert witnesses" (Radwin, 1991).

■ 5.2: UNANSWERED QUESTION: WHAT IS REASONABLE SCIENTIFIC CERTAINTY?

EXPERT WITNESSES CAN EASILY BE ENTRAPPED by lawyers if they stray too far from their clinical expertise. A good illustration of this is the temptation to translate scientific certainty into legal certainty (Brodsky, 1991).

In criminal law, the prosecutor has the burden of proving the defendant's guilt: As we have seen, a defendant also may have a burden, as in insanity cases. In civil law, the plaintiff has the burden of proving that he or she suffered harm and that the defendant was negligent. The law also identifies a standard or degree of certainty for meeting this burden.

Most people are familiar with the standard "beyond a reasonable doubt," which is required in all criminal cases. The prosecutor must prove every element of a crime beyond the reasonable doubt of the judge or jury. Although this standard is difficult to define, it may be expressed in the juror's comment, "I have to be 99 percent sure."

Less stringent standards are "clear and convincing evidence" and "preponderance of the evidence." The precise standard used will vary according to the nature of the case and the rule in force in a given jurisdiction. The clear and convincing standard is most likely to be used in involuntary civil commitment, when mental illness and dangerousness must be proved. Some states, however, may require that these be proved beyond a reasonable doubt. Preponderance, the least rigid of the standards, is most likely to be used in civil suits.

Brodsky advises expert witnesses to avoid the rugged terrain of legal standards. The best approach, he argues convincingly, is for clinicians to say (always confidently), that their testimony is based on reasonable scientific certainty. It is then up to the court to decide how well reasonable scientific certainty fits into the legal standard being applied in any one case.

"Burdens of proof and degrees of defined certainty are legal concepts. Do not accept, define, or incorporate them into clinical, psychological, or scientific testimony (unless you *really* know what you are doing)" (Brodsky, 1991, p. 17). ■

The new federal law prompted many states to join others which had already begun to restrict the insanity defense. At this writing, three states—Idaho, Montana, and Utah—have effectively abolished the insanity defense. This does not preclude a defendant from being acquitted due to mental disease or defect, however. Even if a severely mentally disordered defendant is unable to claim insanity, judges and juries can take his or her abnormal mental state into consideration in determining culpability.

It is widely believed that statutes making the insanity defense more difficult to support will result in fewer such defenses. Steadman et al. (1993) have documented this in their study of two states, Georgia and New York. They found that, after the passage of statutes shifting the burden of proof to the defendant, the rate of NGRI pleas declined. Furthermore, for those defendants who pursued an insanity defense, severe psychiatric diagnoses (e.g., schizophrenia or other psychosis) "almost became a prerequisite for success" (p. 44).

GUILTY BUT MENTALLY ILL

In response to disenchantment with the insanity defense, some states have introduced a new verdict form, **Guilty But Mentally Ill (GBMI)**. Michigan was the first to adopt this in 1975, after a controversial state Supreme Court decision, *People v. McQuillan* (1974). The Michigan court had ruled that it was unconstitutional to automatically institutionalize defendants found NGRI. Recall that the legal state of insanity does not necessarily follow from mental disorder, even serious mental disorder. The court ruled, therefore, that a hearing on present mental state must be held before a person could be hospitalized. At the time, state institutions held nearly 270 insanity acquittees who had been hospitalized without hearings (Simon & Aaronson, 1988). Sixty-four of these persons were released after hearings in which they were found "presently sane." One

134

CHAPTER
FIVE:
COMPETENCIES
AND
CRIMINAL
RESPONSIBILITY:
ASSESSMENTS
FOR THE
CRIMINAL
COURTS

promptly murdered his wife and another committed two rapes (Simon & Aaronson, 1988, p. 188). Public sentiment against the insanity defense, therefore, prompted the passage of a statute designed to restrict it.

By 1992, eleven other states had followed Michigan's lead. The GBMI option is intended as an alternative to, not a substitute for, the verdict NGRI. It allows jurors a "middle-ground" verdict in the case of allegedly insane defendants; a way of reconciling their belief that a defendant "did it" with their belief that he or she "needs help." Therefore, although states differ in the standards and procedures associated with the GBMI verdict, what all have in common is an apparent wish to reduce the number of insanity acquittals, hold the defendant blameworthy, but still recognize the presence of a mental disorder. Thus, the statutes usually include a provision for psychiatric treatment—although the statutes do not *guarantee* that this treatment will be provided.

Research on GBMI laws has found that they may not have accomplished their intended purpose. Early reports in Michigan, for example, found that insanity acquittals remained stable while guilty verdicts declined. Many of the GBMI defendants would otherwise have been found guilty (Smith & Hall, 1982). A national survey by Hugh McGinley and Richard Pasewark (1989) reports that the frequency of the insanity plea has *not* decreased in the states that have adopted the alternative GBMI. Evidence is now beginning to accumulate that defendants who would have been considered indisputably insane before the GBMI option are now being convicted under the new verdict form (Golding & Roesch, 1987). Callahan et al. (1992) found that GBMI individuals received longer sentences and were confined longer than "sane" defendants convicted of similar crimes. They concluded that the GBMI verdict form did affect the rate and number of insanity acquittals and would probably make the insanity defense a less appealing option.

There is also evidence that those being found GBMI are no more likely to be given psychotherapy or rehabilitative services than other mentally disordered defendants in the prison system, partly because GBMI legislation was rarely accompanied by increased appropriations for treatment (Klofas & Weisheit, 1986). Morse (1985) notes that this is constitutionally unacceptable, because convicted offenders have a constitutional right to adequate treatment (*Estelle v. Gamble*, 1979). Furthermore, using a striking analogy, Morse (1985, p. 804) argues that adding "but mentally ill" to the guilty verdict is ridiculous:

> Is the verdict "guilty but herpes" sensible or necessary to ensure medical treatment of inmates suffering from herpes? Even without the special verdict, simple humanity and the federal Constitution require that all prisoners who are ill— whether physically or mentally—must receive minimally adequate treatment.

Although GBMI statutes have remained on the books in a minority of states, more research is needed to determine their effect on both the insanity defense and on the treatment of those mentally disordered defendants who become caught in the criminal justice system. At this point, however, it is tempting to agree with Slobogin (1985), who asserted that the GBMI verdict is "an idea whose time should not have come."

CLINICAL ASSESSMENT OF SANITY

Defendants wishing to raise the insanity issue are constitutionally entitled to their own independent mental health expert to help in the preparation of their defense (*Ake v. Oklahoma*, 1984). An indigent defendant whose mental state is in question, therefore, has a right not only to a court-appointed lawyer, but also to a court-appointed psychiatrist or clinical psychologist.

The role of the psychiatrist or psychologist in an insanity case is essentially to "postdict." That is, the examiner is asked to assess a person's mental state at the time of the crime. She or he must determine what sort of disturbances existed at the behavioral, volitional, and cognitive level and clarify how those disturbances relate to the criminal act (Golding & Roesch, 1987).

Insanity evaluations are widely regarded as much more complex than competency evaluations (Melton et al., 1987). It is exceedingly difficult to determine what another human being was thinking or feeling at the time of a crime, an event that usually happened weeks, months, or even years previously. Considering the many biases and cognitive distortions that experts have, it is highly debatable whether *any* expert can make a decent post-hoc assessment at all. Furthermore, if there is a distinct process for evaluating mental state at the time of the crime, it is shrouded in mystery, because there is a paucity of research on the techniques used by clinicians. Additionally, few systematic studies of how and why they reach their decisions and arrive at their recommendations exist (Grisso, 1986; Homant & Kennedy, 1987).

Some commentators suggest that traditional clinical procedures are limited in their applicability to the insanity construct. Gary Melton et al. (1987), for example, believe that mental health professionals should function more as investigative reporters than as traditional clinicians, garnering stores of information from the defendant and from third-party sources. Slobogin, Melton, and Showalter (1984) developed a loosely structured interview technique which allows the examiner to obtain relevant information about mental state within a legally relevant framework. Golding and Roesch (1987, p. 422), two prominent forensic psychologists, have applauded and expanded upon this technique, suggesting that detailed inquiries "should enable an examiner, within the limits of current knowledge of psychopathology, to produce a meaningful psychological autopsy of the defendant's states of mind during the entire legally significant period."

Rogers and his colleagues (1981, 1984) have approached insanity evaluations from a different perspective, recommending the use of scales to rate the defendants on a number of characteristics, including, for example, psychopathology and cognitive control. Their continuing research in this area (Rogers et al., 1984a, 1984b) has produced impressive reliability coefficients. Nevertheless, as with the instruments for assessing competency to stand trial discussed earlier, there is resistance to using the nontraditional measures.

As in competency-to-stand-trial situations, the assessment may or may not be followed by courtroom testimony, either in a pretrial hearing or during a trial. Recall, however, that "successful" insanity defenses are most likely to occur in the case of persons who are so floridly disordered that prosecutors do not even challenge the issue (Simon & Aaronson, 1988). A diagnosis of some serious mental disorder and an opinion from an examiner that an insanity defense could be supported often lead the court to enter a decision of not guilty by reason of insanity.

THE NEED FOR THE INSANITY DEFENSE

In a persuasive presentation of the issues concerning the abolition of the insanity defense, John Monahan (1973) posits that two separate issues are involved in efforts to justify the defense. If two questions can be answered affirmatively, the insanity defense is acceptable. First, does a belief in responsibility for one's actions really have an effect on one's behavior? If yes, does the existence of an insanity defense in the criminal justice system contribute to the individual's belief in personal responsibility? While we have solid research support to answer affirmatively Monahan's first question concerning the behavioral effects of belief in responsibility, we have very little empirical support in either direction for his second question. Will citizens become more responsible if the need for responsibility is emphasized by the existence of the insanity defense?

John Monahan himself finds little logical or empirical support for the argument that citizens need the insanity defense, but he does find compelling justification for asserting that the law needs

136

CHAPTER
FIVE:
COMPETENCIES
AND
CRIMINAL
RESPONSIBILITY:
ASSESSMENTS
FOR THE
CRIMINAL
COURTS

it. To function adequately, our present system of legal principles requires the free-will concept, rather than a strict adherence to the deterministic position of behaviorists. Specifically, Monahan contends that the elimination of the insanity defense would lead to the complete acquittal of increasing numbers of abnormal offenders and would eventually result in a legal system based upon nonexistent treatment procedures and unfounded faith in our ability to predict dangerousness. A legal system of this sort would leave the citizen at the mercy of politically chosen "experts" with full *parens patriae* power. In sum, "the consequences are too uncertain and too potentially disastrous to recommend abolition" (Monahan, 1973, p. 738).

Diagnosing Abnormal Behavior

Historically, and especially during the past century, determining what constitutes abnormal behavior has been a medical enterprise dominated almost exclusively by psychiatrists. Many psychiatrists do subscribe to a **disease** or **medical model**. This model, which considers abnormal behavior mental illness, states that "psychiatric illnesses are similar in important respects to illnesses treated in general medicine" (Lickey & Gordon, 1991, p. 353). Classification and treatment schemes are applied to mental disorders just as they are to physical disease. Diagnosis, therefore, is a critical component.

Terms associated with the medical model—such as *sick, treatment, patient, hospital, disease*—permeate even the scientific study of abnormal psychology. The public, the courts, the media, and the behavioral and social scientists and practitioners all use these terms with regularity. Abnormal behaviors are called *symptoms* and are allegedly due to some internal malfunction or disease. The disease or medical model continues to influence our present theories, classifications, and treatment of abnormal or deviant behavioral patterns.

It should be emphasized that there are many perspectives on how or why mental disorders occur, as well as on the best ways to treat them. For example, many clinicians today view abnormal behavior principally as a product of faulty learning experiences. The behavior represents an unsuccessful attempt to cope with or adapt to the environment. Observable behavior and the factors which encourage it are emphasized. This contrasts with the traditional psychodynamic approach of looking for unconscious and conscious motivational states or biochemical imbalances. Psychology and psychiatry both embrace within their own ranks diverse views of the causes and perpetuation of abnormal behavior, however. There is no *scientifically* agreed upon definition of abnormal behavior among representatives of either discipline.

A diagnosis is a label placed on a pattern of behavior that deviates from the norm, presumably because of some mental, attitudinal, or motivational defect or faulty learning experience. In diagnostic classifications (see Box 5.3), the norm is often sociocultural (what is socially appropriate or culturally expected). If, upon entering an elevator, you stand facing the back wall of the elevator rather than turn around to face the door, your behavior is "abnormal" according to most social standards or expectations. Whether your behavior is considered abnormal enough to generate a diagnostic label (e.g., psychotic, neurotic, or personality disorder) usually depends upon two factors, both of which rely on clinical judgment. First, what are the motives behind your behavior? Second, to what extent does the unusual behavior cause distress to you or to those around you? The elevator behavior may be a symptom of a serious disorder or it may simply be a sign of eccentricity.

Representatives of the legal system routinely expect diagnoses and clinicians routinely supply them, even in evaluations of competency to stand trial. In sanity evaluations, diagnoses are the norm. Even though a verdict of insanity is a "moral judgment" (Slobogin, 1989), its foundation is some mental disorder. Specifying that disorder, then, becomes a critical issue.

Clinical psychologists are usually advised not to include diagnoses in competency reports (Grisso, 1986), and many prefer not to offer psychopathological diagnoses in sanity reports either (Golding & Roesch, 1987). The same reluctance can be seen among psychiatrists in the midst of increasing demands from the legal system to render formal diagnoses (American Psychiatric Association Task Force, 1992).

Some critics have argued that imposing a diagnosis on a defendant distracts the fact finder from the duty to view both competency to stand trial and insanity as legal, not psychiatric or psychological constructs (Melton et al., 1987; Golding & Roesch, 1987). Other critics argue that diagnoses are inherently subjective and unreliable (Ziskin & Faust, 1988). Early research examining the ability of highly trained and experienced clinicians to diagnose or even characterize persons consistently failed to demonstrate even minimal inter-judge reliability (e.g., Spitzer & Fleiss, 1974; Goldberg & Werts, 1966; Golden, 1964; Little & Schneidman, 1959; Soskin, 1959; Kostlan, 1954; Meehl, 1959). However, more recent research on the DSM-III-R indicates that the reliability of diagnosis has improved significantly (American Psychiatric Association Task Force, 1992). (See Box 5.3 for an elaboration of the DSM.)

The radical psychiatrist Thomas Szasz (1960, 1968) contends that mental illness itself is a myth and that the standards by which persons are defined as disordered should be psychosocial, ethical, and legal, but not medical. In Szasz's opinion, only confusion results from the use of "mental illness" to characterize both disorders of the brain and deviations of behavior, thinking, and emotion due to nondisease-related causes. More soberingly, he argues, thinking of mental abnormality as illness promotes abuses by psychiatry and the use of medical terminology to deprive persons of their civil liberties through involuntary hospitalization, confinement, incarceration, or other coercive techniques. "Mental illness" erroneously justifies the use of various medical

138

CHAPTER
FIVE:
COMPETENCIES
AND
CRIMINAL
RESPONSIBILITY:
ASSESSMENTS
FOR THE
CRIMINAL
COURTS

"psychotherapeutic" techniques, like drug therapy, psychosurgery, and electroconvulsive therapies, Szasz claims. Furthermore, he believes the medical-psychiatric profession has held on to the inaccurate and scientifically unsupported concept of mental illness to control and dominate the assessment, care, and disposition of the unfortunate many whom it labels "mentally ill."

Szasz is increasingly seen as an iconoclast, but he was never alone. A similar conclusion was reached by Hardisty (1973), who charged that psychiatry employs the words *mental illness* to achieve social purposes and to maintain power in influencing legal determinations of mental states. Mazer (1978, p. 98) adds, "The concept of mental illness gives psychiatrists the power to determine who is normal and who isn't, to dictate how persons ought to think, feel and behave in different situations." Stephen Morse (1978a) adopted a viewpoint not unlike that of Szasz, recommending that the legal system use the term "crazy behavior" rather than the medical jargon now surrounding "mental illness" and its many variants. As we noted above, Morse was listed among those who argued against the insanity defense. In 1985, he reconsidered his earlier position, conceding that a small number of individuals fundamentally incapable of behaving in a rational manner should be excused for their behavior. Morse still resists the "mental illness" term, however. He has proposed a new test for insanity, which obviates the need for a diagnosis and places the insanity issue squarely in the hands of the judge or jury. He would acquit a defendant when he or she is "extremely crazy and the craziness so substantially affected the criminal behavior that the defendant does not deserve to be punished" (Morse, 1985, p. 820).

Mental disorder, crazy behavior, mental illness, or *abnormal behavior,* the terms all refer to unusual behavior expressed through either thinking processes (cognition), feelings (affect), actions (behavior), or a combination of these. Abnormal behaviors are elusive primarily because individual behavioral patterns are unique and resist neat classifications. Normal or abnormal behavior is a product of an elaborate interaction between the person's biological and psychological predispositions and the enormous variety of environmental factors that act upon that person. Contemporary behavioral and social research continually underscore the infinite complexity and uniqueness of human behavior, to the point of raising the serious question: Can even broad generalizations of personality be meaningful? (Mischel, 1973). It appears that the most realistic approach to describing human behavior is to examine each person's behavior in relation to his or her particular context.

Special Conditions and Unique Defenses

Over the past decade, a number of unique defenses based on mental, neurological, and physiological conditions have been attempted in both criminal and civil courts, with varying degrees of success. Among these conditions are Post-Traumatic Stress Disorder, the XYY abnormality, amnesia, Rape Trauma Syndrome, Battered Child Syndrome, Battered Woman Syndrome, Holocaust Survivor's Syndrome, sexual addiction, and Multiple Personality Disorder. In criminal cases, defendants may claim to have been affected by these conditions in an effort to absolve themselves completely of criminal responsibility or to support a claim of **diminished capacity** or **diminished responsibility**. The conditions may also be raised at criminal sentencing, when the judge or jury hears evidence offered in mitigation. On the other hand, evidence of these mental states in *victims* of crime may be used by the prosecution as evidence that a criminal act occurred. Likewise, in civil cases, these new mental conditions may be raised by either plaintiffs or defendants.

139

SPECIAL
CONDITIONS
AND
UNIQUE
DEFENSES

In recent years, for example, rape victims and victims of child sexual abuse have increasingly initiated civil suits against their aggressors. In such cases, evidence of Rape Trauma Syndrome or Child Abuse Syndrome, if admitted into court, can be very relevant.

It is important to acknowledge at the outset the continuing controversy in both law and psychology with respect to defenses based on these special conditions. They are neither widely accepted nor widely successful, although some have been received better by courts than others. Steven Morse (1986, p. 186) even advocates that we "call a halt to studies that implicitly or explicitly legitimate creating distinct legal doctrines and approaches for distinct behavioral conditions." The material in this section outlines the scientific and clinical knowledge of the causes, effects, and legal acceptance of these conditions, which are often disorders. However, for some, their reliability and validity have yet to be satisfactorily demonstrated within the scientific or clinical communities; the jury is still out with respect to research findings. In the following pages we will discuss those conditions that have received the most attention from researchers, practitioners, and legal scholars.

POST-TRAUMATIC STRESS DISORDER (PTSD)

According to the *Diagnostic and Statistical Manual* (DSM-III-R, 1987, Section 309.89), **Post-Traumatic Stress Disorder** (PTSD) is the result of "a psychologically distressing event that is outside the range of usual human experience (…simple bereavement, chronic illness, business losses, and marital conflict [are inside that range])." The precipitating event would be markedly distressing to almost anyone, and is "usually experienced with intense fear, terror, and helplessness." PTSD is an umbrella term which has been applied to war veterans, survivors of the Holocaust, and victims of rape, child abuse, spousal abuse, and sexual harassment. There is debate, though, about whether these types of PTSD really should be considered "disorders," as we will note shortly.

The traumatic event which precipitates PTSD may be experienced alone, such as a rape, or it may be experienced in the company of others, such as a flood, hurricane, plane crash, or war. The event is so psychologically distressing that the person takes a very long time to recover, and sometimes never recovers completely. Interestingly, symptoms seem to be more severe and longer in duration if the trauma is perceived by the victim as human made (rape, child abuse, combat) rather than a natural catastrophe (earthquake, flood, hurricane, forest fire) (American Psychiatric Association, 1980). Moreover, some events are more likely to lead to PTSD than others. For example, deliberate human cruelty—such as torture, incarceration in a concentration camp, or a mass killing—is more likely to engender PTSD than a car accident or an accidental fire.

Studies report that between 1 and 2 percent of all Americans suffer from PTSD (Sutker, Uddo-Crane & Allain, 1991). This statistic is not surprising, considering the fact that there remain alive 11 million veterans of World War II, 5 million veterans of the Korean conflict, over 3 million survivors of the Vietnam War, and more than 500,000 Operation Desert Storm returnees (Sutker et al., 1991). In addition, an estimated 1 million refugees have resettled in the United States since 1975, many of them victims of brutal political torture. Finally, countless Americans have been victimized by criminal acts or have experienced major disasters of some sort (Sutker, Uddo-Crane & Allain, 1991).

Most of the current research and clinical commentary on PTSD has focused on Vietnam combat veterans. What is now recognized as Vietnam Stress Syndrome has been observed in combat veterans for a long time; it used to be called "shell shock" or "battle fatigue." In 1980, the American Psychiatric Association blessed it with a diagnostic label falling under the general category of anxiety disorders. It has been estimated that about 31 percent of Vietnam combat veterans experience formally diagnosable symptoms of PTSD at some point during their lifetimes

140

CHAPTER
FIVE:
COMPETENCIES
AND
CRIMINAL
RESPONSIBILITY:
ASSESSMENTS
FOR THE
CRIMINAL
COURTS

(Kulka, et al., 1990; Monahan & Walker, 1990). The lifetime prevalence of PTSD is about 31 percent among male and 27 percent among female Vietnam veterans (Kulka et al., 1991).

Characteristic symptoms of veterans and other persons suffering from PTSD include "flash-backs" of the traumatic event which disrupt daily living. These may appear in the form of recurrent dreams or nightmares, or as painful, intrusive, repetitive memories of the event. A diminished responsiveness to the external world, a kind of psychological "numbing," is also a common symptom soon after the traumatic event. A third sign is a feeling of alienation or detachment from others and considerable difficulty in forming close, meaningful relationships. Other symptoms include excessive autonomic arousal, such as over-alertness, being easily startled, or having diffi-culty falling asleep or concentrating, and extreme avoidance of reminders of the trauma. Persons suffering from PTSD tend to be irritable and agitated, and often go from job to job. Some Vietnam veterans suffering from PTSD even sleep with their guns. Headaches, problems with memory, and lack of concentration appear to be especially common complaints (Sutker et al., 1991).

There has been a longstanding debate about the validity and accompanying symptoms of Post-Traumatic Stress Disorder. There is little doubt that highly traumatic events can produce psychological problems in many individuals, but the extent to which resulting PTSD can be used as an excusing condition for crime and reprehensible conduct is open to question.

PTSD has been used to support a defense of not guilty by reason of insanity, though not all the cases involved violence (Monahan & Walker, 1990). In some instances, PTSD has been used as an excusing condition for drug trafficking. Evidence that a criminal defendant suffers from PTSD is more likely to diminish responsibility than it is to absolve the defendant of responsibility altogether. Such evidence is often considered as a mitigating circumstance at sentencing.

The presence of PTSD in the victim has also been introduced into evidence to support the contention that a crime did indeed occur or, at the sentencing stage, to support a harsher sentence. In rape cases, for example, the defendant may contend that sexual activity was consensual. The prosecution may try to counter this defense by introducing evidence that the victim suffers from Rape Trauma Syndrome, which is regarded by some (though not everyone) as a type of PTSD (Frazier & Borgida, 1992).

In psychological parlance, a **syndrome** is a collection of thoughts, feelings, and behaviors that are believed to be held in common by individuals experiencing a given situation, such as the common symptoms of Vietnam Stress Syndrome discussed above. Studies have found that many rape victims experience a wide range of symptoms after the rape, including depression, social maladjustment, fear and anxiety, sexual dysfunction, hypervigilance, nightmares, and irritability. Although there has been extensive research in the area of victim reactions to rape, courts remain divided on the issue of admitting expert testimony in this area. Complicating the issue of obtaining meaningful data, also, is the fact that few rape cases go to trial. Frazier and Borgida (1992) have provided an excellent review of the legal literature in this area, specifically as it relates to questions which haunt the courts.

BATTERED WOMAN SYNDROME

The term *Battered Woman Syndrome* (BWS) is attributed to Lenore Walker, a psychologist who specializes in research and counseling on domestic abuse. Walker first introduced it in 1979 based on information derived from her clinical experience with 110 victims of domestic violence (Walker, 1979). She later reported on extended interviews with 435 battered women (Walker, 1984), iden-tifying a variety of features or "psychological sequelae" often shared by women who have been physically and psychologically abused over a period of time by the dominant male figure in their lives. These include, but are not limited to, feelings of learned helplessness (Seligman, 1975); the development of survival rather than escape skills (e.g., appeasing the batterer rather than planning to leave); traditional beliefs about marriage, such as the dominance of the male; low self-esteem, and feelings of depression. It is important to note that Walker did not associate characteristics such as emotional disturbance or masochism with the syndrome.

The Battered Woman Syndrome has been used primarily in criminal courts, in defense for women accused of killing their mates. Proponents argue that a sufferer with battered woman syndrome is in continuing fear of immediate and severe bodily harm, and thereby should be excused for killing an abusive spouse. The desirability of a self-defense claim over an insanity claim in this situation should be obvious: Self-defense exculpates the defendant, while a finding of not guilty by reason of insanity may result in commitment to a mental institution.

It is important to note that there is resistance to considering this a category of PTSD, and even to the use of the word *syndrome* in this context (e.g., Browne, 1987; Gillespie, 1989). Terms like *disorder* and *syndrome* imply a pathology or deficiency in the woman who is the victim of abuse. Additionally, the applicability of the learned helplessness concept to abused women has also been challenged (Schuller & Vidmar, 1992). With more attention brought to domestic violence and more options open to its victims, studies show that victims are taking active steps to leave abusive situations and otherwise help themselves (Browne, 1987; Dobash & Dobash, 1979). Walker herself has stressed that learned helplessness can be prevented by "psychologically strengthening the potential victim" and reversed by "empowerment through additional competence training and skill building activities" (Walker, 1989, p. 697).

Walker reported a three-stage cycle of violence that accompanies Battered Woman Syndrome: a tension-building stage, an acute battering incident, and a loving and contrition stage, in which the batterer apparently expresses regret about the assaultive behavior and vows to change his ways. Battering relationships are said to revolve through these three stages, although a couple may remain in the first stage, where only minor assaults occur, for years. A woman qualifies for the Battered Woman Syndrome when she has experienced the complete cycle at least twice (Walker, 1979). Her recent work suggests also (Walker, 1990) that the third stage tends to disappear as the relationship progresses. Since battering behavior accelerates in both frequency and intensity over time, tension-building becomes more common while love and contrition declines. Women are thus more in danger the longer the relationship continues, unless intervention occurs.

Research on domestic violence indicates that the great majority of battered women remain in lifelong abusive relationships, learn to leave, or are killed by their abusers. In other words, battering relationships do not generally get better. Leaving such a relationship is a psychologically complex process (Walker, 1990) and frequently involves obtaining restraining orders against the batterer. These legal orders may be readily available, but they have numerous limitations and are difficult to enforce. In a careful analysis of restraining orders, however, Chaudhuri and Daly (1992) have demonstrated that they can be valuable tools for curtailing domestic violence.

A small minority of abused women kill their abusers. It is they who come to court attention as criminal defendants. Although Battered Woman Syndrome evidence is increasingly being admitted into the trials of women who kill their abusers (Schuller & Vidmar, 1992), it is rarely successful in bringing about an acquittal (Browne, 1987; Ewing, 1990). In a review of eighty-five trials in which BWS was introduced, the defendant was found guilty of murder or manslaughter in 70 percent of the cases (Ewing, 1987).

When a defense attorney seeks to introduce such evidence, she or he hopes that the expert will convey critical information to the judge and jury. Specifically, the expert must educate these triers of fact about BWS, including the crucial information that the victim believes she is always

141

SPECIAL
CONDITIONS
AND
UNIQUE
DEFENSES

142

CHAPTER
FIVE:
COMPETENCIES
AND
CRIMINAL
RESPONSIBILITY:
ASSESSMENTS
FOR THE
CRIMINAL
COURTS

in danger of imminent death or grievous bodily harm from which she is unable to escape. As a result, the action she takes is a reasonable response—qualifying her for self-defense. Some courts also allow the expert to give an opinion as to whether the woman on trial suffers from the syndrome. If this opinion evidence is not allowed, jurors are left to decide for themselves.

The need for and wisdom of using an expert witness in these situations has been extensively reviewed (e.g., Acker & Toch, 1985; Ewing, 1987; Schuller & Vidmar, 1992). Hans Toch and James Acker (1985) question whether experts do have special information "beyond the ken" of jurors, arguing that the evidence of juror misconceptions is not overwhelming. After reviewing the literature, Schuller & Vidmar (1992) agree, although not completely. "...[J]urors are misinformed on some aspects of wife abuse and...some jurors are likely to be more misinformed than others. Nevertheless, the surveys have not found overwhelming endorsement of the 'myths' about abuse" (p. 283). They add that, on the whole, "women, and individuals who hold equalitarian sex-role attitudes, who are more educated, and who are younger seem to hold less negative attitudes toward battered women and are more disapproving of the use of force in marital relationships" (p. 283).

What of the impact of such testimony on jury deliberation and jury verdicts? Schuller and Vidmar (1992) noted that there is insufficient evidence to support the idea that the testimony of an expert convinces a jury to absolve a woman of guilt, though it may influence jurors to reduce the crime from murder to manslaughter. The most important factors in a self-defense verdict, however, are the characteristics of the jurors, the couple, and the circumstances of the case.

Schuller and Vidmar (1992) also question the reliability of the diagnosis Battered Woman Syndrome and its applicability to the wide range of women who are abused. Noting that studies to date are limited to interviews with women in clinics or shelters, they suggest that this may not be a representative pool. Furthermore, the limitations of expert testimony may outweigh its benefits. Rather than focusing on the reasonableness of a woman's actions under her particular situation, the presence of the mental health expert encourages the jury to associate the case with insanity or diminished capacity.

MULTIPLE PERSONALITY DISORDER

The existence of multiple personality disorder is open to question, and it is sometimes referred to as the "UFO of psychiatry" (Ondrovik & Hamilton, 1991). According to the DSM-III-R, **Multiple Personality Disorder (MPD)** is characterized by the existence within an individual of two or more distinct personalities, each of which may be dominant at any given time (American Psychiatric Association, 1987).

MPD is certainly a popular topic. In the past 10 years, over 350 articles, chapters, and books have been written on the disorder, mostly in the popular press or pop media (Dunn, 1992). Beginning in 1988, the journal *Dissociation* has produced a steady flow of articles related to all aspects of MPD.

Although MPD became officially recognized by the American Psychiatric Association in 1980, the existence of MPD is debated by the psychological and psychiatric communities, and very much doubted by the legal community. Jill Radwin (1991, p. 355) writes, "As much as this disorder is debated and doubted in clinical circles, the legal world sees the disorder as sensational." Moreover, the public perceives MPD as nothing more than a bit of theatrics (Radwin, 1991). Therefore, to establish an insanity plea on the basis of MPD is extremely difficult.

The disorder confounds both the law and the layperson alike. The law assumes the integrity of the individual, that there is within each human body one person with whom society may interact (Slovenko, 1989). To the ordinary citizen, the existence of several personalities within one person

143

SPECIAL
CONDITIONS
AND
UNIQUE
DEFENSES

seems incomprehensible and suspect. Most of us would acknowledge, though, that we have different "personalities" that are reserved for the situation at hand. The way we act at home is often significantly different from the way we act with our coworkers, for example. As Slovenko (1989, p. 707) notes: "Chief Justice William Rehnquist of the Supreme Court waxes eloquent in his opinions, but he acts like a child when he goes out to lunch with his law clerks."

Multiple Personality Disorder, however, is more than just reacting differently to different people and in different situations. *If* it exists, it is clearly a dysfunctional phenomenon. The personalities are nearly always discrepant and often opposites. "For example, a quiet, retiring spinster may alternate with a flamboyant, promiscuous, bar [habitué]" (American Psychiatric Association, 1987, p. 270). Transition from one to another is usually sudden (often within seconds) and unexpected, and is often precipitated by psychosocial stress or social stimuli (American Psychiatric Association, 1987). The person (the original personality) is usually unaware of the existence of the other personalities, but the other personalities (subpersonalities) may be well aware of each other as well as of the original personality.

Reported cases of MPD have historically been extremely rare, but between 1980 and 1989 the number of cases diagnosed in the United States rose significantly, from 200 to at least 6,000 (Slovenko, 1989). Part of this dramatic increase is probably due to the American Psychiatric Association officially recognizing the disorder in 1980. The disorder generally begins in childhood, usually before age nine, and is generally found in persons who have been abused (often sexually) or have suffered another form of severe emotional trauma in childhood. It appears, then, that MPD may be a way of coping with past traumatic experiences. Approximately 75 to 90 percent of those said to have MPD are female (American Psychiatric Association, 1987). Interestingly, about half of the thirty-two women on death row have been diagnosed as having MPD, although it is unclear whether the diagnosis was rendered before or after conviction (Slovenko, 1989).

Hypnosis is the primary tool used in the diagnosis of multiple personality (Slovenko, 1989). In fact, research suggests that persons with MPD are so susceptible to hypnosis that self-hypnosis may be the primary etiological factor in MPD (Rosenhan & Seligman, 1984). That is, MPDs may enter a self-induced hypnotic trance as they assume their different personalities. Hypnosis is also used to expose fraudulent MPD claims. The notorious serial murderer Kenneth Bianchi, known as the Hillside Strangler, insisted that another personality had taken over his body and murdered at least a dozen women over a one-year period (1977–78). The murders were given wide publicity because of their brutality and sadistic quality. The victims were young, attractive women who were raped and strangled, and whose nude bodies were conspicuously displayed on the hillsides of the Los Angeles area.

Bianchi, whose career ambitions included being a police officer and a psychologist, maintained under hypnosis that his alter personality "Steve Walker" had done the killings. Using MPD as the foundation for his claim, Bianchi pleaded NGRI under the state of Washington's M'Naghten Rule. (The last two murders for which he was arrested took place in Bellingham, Washington). The court (*State v. Bianchi*, 1979) appointed a team of six experts to determine if Bianchi really was more than one person. If the experts could agree, the insanity defense might prevail. The team, led by psychiatrist Martin Orne (Orne, Dinges & Orne, 1984), was able to refute Bianchi's claim through careful examination of his past and skillful analysis of his behavior under hypnosis. For example, the team discovered that "Steve Walker" was the name of a psychologist whose credentials Bianchi forged to set up his own psychological practice in Los Angeles several years earlier. Orne, a leading expert in hypnosis, was also able to establish that Bianchi was not in a deep state of hypnosis throughout the investigation but was acting the part. In addition, although Bianchi knew the "textbook version" of MPD, probably from his extensive reading in psychology,

144

CHAPTER
FIVE:
COMPETENCIES
AND
CRIMINAL
RESPONSIBILITY:
ASSESSMENTS
FOR THE
CRIMINAL
COURTS

he did not know all the subtle clinical features of the disorder recognized by the experts. The team concluded that Bianchi was a psychopath rather than a multiple personality disorder. Bianchi then pleaded guilty in order to avoid the death penalty.

As in PTSD, the existence of MPD in *a victim* may be a factor in a criminal or civil trial. Ondrovik & Hamilton (1991) discuss the case of Sarah, a 26-year-old Wisconsin woman believed to have as many as forty-six distinct personalities. Sarah met a 29-year-old male (D. X.) for coffee one June day. During their meeting, she allegedly switched to several different personalities, including Jennifer, who apparently had voluntary sexual intercourse with D. X.

D. X. was charged with sexual assault. Testimony by the prosecution's expert witnesses established that Sarah was suffering from MPD and thus was regarded as "mentally ill" as defined by the Wisconsin Penal Code. Because the Wisconsin sexual assault statute prohibits sexual intercourse with mentally ill persons, D. X. was found guilty of second-degree sexual assault, even though he testified he was unaware of Sarah's condition.

D. X. retained new defense counsel after the conviction and filed a motion for new trial, claiming that the court was in error in failing to grant the motion for an independent psychiatric examination of Sarah. A new trial was granted but the state moved to dismiss the case, claiming that Sarah has been victimized enough.

As we saw in the Bianchi case, defendants claiming MPD most often try to establish an insanity defense, especially since it was successful in 1978 in *Ohio Department of Mental Health v. Milligan* (Radwin, 1991). Billy Milligan claimed he had twenty-four separate personalities and was found not guilty by reason of insanity in criminal charges of raping three women near the Ohio State University campus. However, due to the public outrage over Milligan and other publicized acquittals, it is currently very difficult to succeed at achieving a NGRI ruling in most jurisdictions (Radwin, 1991). In fact, some state statutes (Georgia, Hawaii, Ohio) now state that a claim of MPD is not enough to establish legal insanity. In addition, as we have stressed previously, neither psychologists nor psychiatrists are convinced, as a group, that MPD is a viable disorder. Many believe MPD is nothing more than very good acting or a well-rehearsed collection of roles we all assume from time to time, depending on the situation we find ourselves in.

AMNESIA

Amnesia refers to complete or partial memory loss of an incident, series of incidents, or some segment of life's experiences. Amnesia is not simply forgetting a name, a date, an incident, but is reserved for *severely* impaired ability to remember old material or to acquire and retain new material. If the memory loss involves past or old material, the disorder is called **retrograde amnesia** (retro means backward). If the memory loss is largely confined to the acquisition and retention of new material, it is called **anterograde amnesia** (antero means forward). Beyond these two major divisions, there are several subclassifications based on the person's behavioral characteristics, the specific brain mechanism involved, and the suspected etiology. The four most common subclassifications are: (1) chronic organic amnesia, (2) functional retrograde amnesia, (3) multiple personality amnesia, and (4) limited amnesia (Schacter, 1986). **Chronic organic amnesia** is associated with a wide range of neurological damage due to physical head trauma (such as a car accident), disease (Alzheimer's), or organic dysfunction (such as the result of a stroke). **Functional retrograde amnesia** refers to memory loss due to severe psychological or emotional trauma, such as being the victim of a violent crime. **Multiple personality amnesia** is restricted to memory deficits specifically observed in individuals with MPD. **Limited amnesia** refers to "a pathological inability to remember a specific episode, or small number of episodes, from the recent past" (Schacter,

1986a, p. 48). It may be produced by emotional shock, alcohol intoxication, head injury, or epileptic seizure. Thus, limited amnesia is not chronic (ongoing) nor does it involve extensive memory loss. Rather, the loss is temporary and usually for a specific event or incident.

The courts have *not* been particularly receptive to amnesia as a viable element in either the insanity defense or as a condition that promotes incompetency to stand trial (Rubinsky & Brandt, 1986). One basic rationale for this "hard line" approach to amnesia is the suspicion that the defendant may be feigning amnesia. It is relatively easy to claim a blackout of reprehensible behavior. Social psychologists have identified a strong tendency to attribute positive things that happen to us to our ability and personality, and to attribute negative things to something outside ourselves or events beyond our control. This phenomenon is called **self-serving bias**. Thus, some people blame alcohol for the reprehensible things they do at a party or the abuse they inflict on their spouse. They can further avoid blame by claiming a lack of memory for the incident. However, the courts have not been very sympathetic to defendants who rely on strategies supported by a self-serving bias. For example, in cases involving alcohol intoxication, the courts continue to hold the person blameworthy since he or she should have known, at the outset, the risks involved in drinking alcohol.

Attempts to use amnesia as the foundation of an insanity plea have met with strong resistance from the courts. For example, one court held that "insanity is the incapacity to discriminate between right and wrong while amnesia is simply the inability to remember" (Rubinsky & Brandt, 1986, p. 30). Thus, amnesia per se fails to qualify as a mental disorder that robs a person of the ability to differentiate between right and wrong.

Amnesia due to acute alcohol intoxication is the most commonly invoked excusing condition in criminal cases (Rubinsky & Brandt, 1986). Interestingly, 30 to 65 percent of persons convicted of homicide claim they cannot remember the crime (Schacter, 1986b). Most of these offenders said they were heavily intoxicated at the time. People who have committed other violent crimes make similar claims. There is some intriguing evidence that memories developed during acute alcohol intoxication appear to be state-dependent (Rubinsky & Brandt, 1986). That is, memories of what happened under acute intoxication can often only be retrieved if the person returns to a similar intoxicated state.

A major problem for the practitioner and the judicial system is distinguishing genuine—especially limited—amnesia from simulated amnesia. At this point in our knowledge, this is extremely difficult—if not impossible—to do. Furthermore, the psychiatric and psychological communities simply do not know enough about amnesia to make it a meaningful concept for judicial application. Attempts at building a defense centered on amnesia have therefore been largely unsuccessful.

THE PREMENSTRUAL SYNDROME (PMS)

The belief that there is a relationship between menstruation and crime, particularly violent crime, has been around for some time, but it has never been convincingly documented. Available studies have been seriously flawed and inconclusive. In an extensive review of the research data, Harry and Balcer (1987) write, "Despite what seems to be substantial interest in the topic, we conclude there is no scientific support for an association between any phases of the menstrual cycle and criminal behavior" (p. 318).

The **premenstrual syndrome** refers to the cyclic physiological and accompanying psychological changes that occur four to seven days prior to the onset of menstruation. Although there is much controversy about whether PMS merits a full diagnosis as a "syndrome" (Sommer, 1983),

145

SPECIAL
CONDITIONS
AND
UNIQUE
DEFENSES

CHAPTER
FIVE:
COMPETENCIES
AND
CRIMINAL
RESPONSIBILITY:
ASSESSMENTS
FOR THE
CRIMINAL
COURTS

the frequent observation that some physiological and psychological changes do occur in some women is rarely questioned. Common complaints include increased tension, irritability, depression, moodiness, anxiety, swelling and water retention in the extremities, abdominal and breast tenderness, fatigue, and severe headaches. It should be emphasized that PMS is not considered a mental disorder and that it is "... conceptually incorrect and disrespectful to women to claim that it should be" (Morse, 1986, p. 101).

Two classic studies were the first to make the connection between PMS and violence in women. The first was conducted by Morton and colleagues in 1953 in a New York correctional facility for women. The Morton study was originally designed to evaluate the effects of treatment for relief of premenstrual tension in inmates. Almost as a sidebar to the main study, Morton mentioned that 62 percent of a sample of 249 female prisoners had committed violent crimes (murder, manslaughter, and assault) during their premenstrual week. Another 17 percent of the sample had committed violent offenses during menstruation.

The Morton study, however, had several troubling aspects. The percentages of crimes were indicated for four cycle-phases (premenstrual week, midcycle, menstruation, and the end of period), but the lengths of these phases were not provided (Horney, 1978). Furthermore, no statistical analyses were reported, nor were there any explanations of how data were gathered (Horney, 1978).

The second study was conducted by Dalton (1961), who interviewed 156 newly convicted women in British prisons on their first weekend after sentencing. Dalton utilized a retrospective calculation method (Horney, 1978). That is, she identified the date of offense, then asked women for information about their menstrual cycles. She then calculated back to where they were in their cycles at the time of the offense. The menstrual cycle was divided into seven four-day periods. Menstruation was represented by days 1 through 4, while the premenstrual period (which she called the premenstruum) was indicated by days 25 through 28. Therefore, in a normally distributed population, incidents would have only a 14.3 percent probability of occurring in any one period of time.

Dalton found that 22 percent committed their crimes during their premenstruum and another 26 percent during menstruation. In the Dalton study, however, there was little evidence of an association with violent crime. Menstruation seemed to be of greater importance in crimes of theft (56 percent during pre- or menstruation) and prostitution (44 percent). The relationship was particularly strong for first-time offenders compared to repeat offenders. Dalton concluded: "The analysis shows that there is a highly significant relationship between menstruation and crime. This could mean that the hormonal changes cause women to commit crime during menstruation and the premenstruum and/or that women are more liable to be detected in their criminal acts during this time" (Dalton, 1961, p. 1753). She further speculated that PMS could play a major role in crimes of violence, even though 155 of the 156 crimes in the sample she studied were clearly nonviolent.

There are serious methodological problems with the Dalton study as well. For example, relying on a one-time estimation of self-reported menstrual cycles is fraught with potential for error, particularly since research indicates that time of menstruation is not that salient for women (Horney, 1978). Furthermore, Dalton was extremely vague in describing her method of retrospective calculation (Horney, 1978; Harry & Balcer, 1987). Not all women experience 28-day cycles. Perhaps most damaging is that no one to date has been able to replicate the Dalton findings (Harry & Balcer, 1987).

Despite the lack of systematic evidence to support the PMS-crime connection, PMS has been successfully raised as a mitigating condition in a small number of cases in England. Abplanalp (1985) describes two such cases. In one, a woman was released on probation after she pleaded that she suffered from a hormonal imbalance due to her menstrual cycle. In another, a woman accused of killing her lover by running him down with her car successfully pleaded guilty to manslaughter on the grounds of diminished responsibility due to PMS. In the U. S., PMS as a defense has not been well received by criminal courts. A New York case that might have put the syndrome to the test was plea bargained before it reached the trial stage (Carney & Williams, 1983).

Summary and Conclusions

Competency to stand trial and insanity are legal concepts which often confound the public and mental health practitioners alike. Although insanity has received more public attention, far more individuals are affected by competency-to-stand-trial evaluations and determinations. Furthermore, although the chapter has focused on assessments of competency to stand trial, it is important to keep in mind that mental health practitioners assess a number of other functional abilities as well. These include competency to plead guilty, to waive the right to silence, to dismiss counsel, to be sentenced, and to be executed. Input (e.g., psychological assessments of mental status and ability to or interest in change) from mental health professionals frequently play an important part in the sentencing process.

In light of the fact that guilty pleas are so important in the criminal justice process, some observers believe that a defendant's competency to plead guilty is not scrutinized closely enough by the courts. This may contribute to the observation that an inordinate number of mentally disordered individuals are found in jails and prisons.

The mental health practitioner has a key role in the competency assessment process, because her or his recommendation is routinely accepted by criminal courts, particularly when a defendant is believed to be incompetent to stand trial. Defendants are judged IST when, because of present mental functioning, they are either unable to help their attorney mount a satisfactory defense, unable to understand the judicial process in which they are enmeshed, or both.

Research suggests that incompetent defendants, as a group, tend to be marginal members of society: unemployed, slightly older than most criminal defendants, with few family ties, and prior hospitalization records. There is some indication that defendants found incompetent to stand trial have been charged with less serious offenses, but this varies widely according to jurisdiction. When charged with serious crimes, incompetent defendants are usually hospitalized prior to their trials and given psychoactive drugs to render them competent to face the proceedings against them. Although the Supreme Court has not spoken directly to this issue, it has recently declared that a defendant pleading not guilty by reason of insanity had a right to refuse psychoactive medication during his trial.

Insanity focuses on the individual's functioning at the time of the alleged illegal act. Fewer than 1 percent of all criminal cases involve the insanity defense, and when the defense is raised, it rarely succeeds. Furthermore, an insanity defense, even when it succeeds, is no bargain: the amount of time spent in a mental institution is generally at least as long as the amount of time the offender would have served in prison had he or she been found guilty.

Nevertheless, public sentiment against the insanity defense continues to be strong. Consequently, the federal government and most states have made it more difficult for defendants pleading not guilty by reason of insanity, either by adopting more restrictive tests for insanity or by shifting the burden of proving insanity to defendants. During the 1980s, approximately twelve states instituted a new verdict form, "guilty but mentally ill." Early research indicated that GBMI laws

148

CHAPTER
FIVE:
COMPETENCIES
AND
CRIMINAL
RESPONSIBILITY:
ASSESSMENTS
FOR THE
CRIMINAL
COURTS

did not decrease the number of insanity defenses. More recently, researchers have learned that juries are beginning to choose the GBMI option over the insanity option and to convict defendants who previously would have been found insane (Golding & Roesch, 1987; Callahan et al., 1992). Some evidence (e.g., Steadman et al., 1993) suggests that in major cases, defense lawyers and prosecutors may be more willing to negotiate a GBMI outcome than go to trial. If these trends continue, more mentally disordered individuals will be sent to prisons which do not have the resources to deal with them.

In the past twenty years, we have seen the emergence of many special defenses based on psychological states. Although these have received considerable media attention, courts have been extremely cautious about recognizing their place in the law. Defendants claiming lack of responsibility, or diminished responsibility, on the basis of Post-Traumatic Stress Disorder, Multiple Personality Disorder, amnesia, or Premenstrual Syndrome, for example, have generally failed to elicit sympathy from the courts. Rape Trauma Syndrome, experienced by victims, is receiving extensive research attention, but courts are divided on the appropriateness of allowing expert testimony on this issue. Courts are slightly more inclined to accept expert testimony on Battered Woman Syndrome, perhaps because of the salience of domestic violence in contemporary society. Women who are battered are far more likely to be seriously injured or killed than they are to kill their abusers. Nevertheless, evidence of Battered Woman Syndrome does not generally convince juries to acquit criminal defendants (Browne, 1987; Ewing, 1990).

Questions to Ponder

1. Public attention often focuses on the insanity defense, but the issue of competency to stand trial is much more significant. Why?

2. From a legal point of view, what are the positive and negative aspects of the *Diagnostic and Statistical Manual*?

3. Does the law *really* need the insanity defense?

4. Why is the Guilty But Mentally Ill (GBMI) option so appealing to some compared to finding a defendant Not Guilty by Reason of Insanity (NGRI)? Discuss GBMI from the perspective of a psychologist, a defense lawyer, the victim of a crime, and a prison superintendent.

5. Why is it necessary to be cautious about accepting syndrome evidence in courts? Are some syndromes more substantiated and therefore more "acceptable" than others?

CHAPTER SIX

CIVIL COMMITMENT

MOST ADULTS IN OUR SOCIETY ARE AWARE that we face important decisions about the treatment of mentally disordered individuals who are unable to care for themselves in our communities. The media not infrequently bring attention to the plight of those homeless persons who are believed also to be mentally disordered. Urban dwellers encounter them on the streets, and virtually every small city has its familiar resident citizen who displays harmless but bizarre behavior.

In the first two-thirds of the twentieth century, until approximately the late 1960s, mentally disordered individuals who could not be cared for by their families or friends were very routinely committed to state mental institutions, where it was not unusual for them to remain throughout their lives. With increasing recognition of individual rights, however, the courts began to see involuntary commitment as a deprivation of the liberty guaranteed by the Constitution (Wexler, 1990a). Therefore, commitment of persons to mental institutions against their wills began to be restricted so that it could be accomplished only with careful attention to procedural safeguards.

An estimated 30 percent of all patients in public mental institutions are believed to have been committed involuntarily (Wexler, 1991). Every state and the District of Columbia allow this commitment, which is presumably in the best interest of the patient and, in some cases, for society's protection. Candidates for civil commitment, however, are disproportionately poor or indigent, uneducated, and unemployed or employed in low-status occupations. They do not seem to be disproportionately male or female, although some research suggests that the interaction between age and gender is significant. That is, older women and younger men are more likely to be candidates for civil commitment than older men and younger women (Hiday, 1988). Ethnic and racial minorities do not seem to be disproportionately represented.

Civil commitment laws identify the standards and procedures to be followed prior to and during commitment. They usually require both evidence of mental disorder or defect and some prediction that there will be negative consequences, such as harm to society or to the individual, if the person is not confined. The statutes provide for an adversarial judicial hearing and legal representation. Additionally, they generally require that less and sometimes **least restrictive alternatives** to hospitalization be considered, particularly when a person is not deemed dangerous. Before placing an individual in a mental institution, for example, the decisionmaker should consider whether a group home or carefully supervised community care would be better than institutional confinement. As we shall see, however, there is very often a gap between the law on the books and the law as it operates, or between *de jure* and *de facto* civil commitment proceedings (Turkheimer & Parry, 1992).

149

Historical Justification and Current Philosophy

The typical stay in a public mental institution is less than twenty-five days (Brooks, 1986), although a substantial number of individuals are continually at risk of re-commitment (Parry, 1990). Virginia Hiday (1988), reviewing the empirical research on civil commitment, observes that the more flagrant and widespread abuses of the past no longer occur. Nonetheless, many questions continue to be raised about the treatment that is received in mental institutions, including the rights of patients to refuse medications and the efficacy of various treatment options. Additionally, in light of policies supporting the supervision of the mentally disordered in community settings, research on the efficacy of this approach is beginning to appear. After a historical review of the justifications for involuntary civil commitment, we will address each of these issues separately.

PARENS PATRIAE

Parens patriae (literally, "parent of the country") is the doctrine in law which establishes the right of the state to substitute its (presumably benevolent) decisionmaking for that of individuals who are said to be unable to make their own decisions. It thus authorizes the state to make and enforce decisions believed to be in the best interest of those who cannot or will not protect themselves, even when they are causing no direct harm to others. It is important to note that the *parens patriae* doctrine is the basis of laws other than those relating to involuntary civil commitment. Statutes which presumably protect the interest of minors, for example, even in situations where they are detained for criminal charges (e.g., *Schall v. Martin*, 1984) are derived from this doctrine.

Although the state's intercession under *parens patriae* is presumed to be in the best interest of the individual, it is essentially coercive (Carroll, 1991), a fact which led to the creation of laws designed to protect individuals against abuse of government power. The question of the person's competency is at the basis of *parens patriae* power (Winick, 1991a). "Only the assumed incompetency of mental patients, not their illness, can justify the law's treating the mentally ill differently from others" (Winick, 1991a, p. 43). Winick argues that the more coercive the state's intervention, such as in overriding a patient's request to refuse medication, the more rigorously the state should be obliged to demonstrate the individual's incompetency.

To appreciate the crucial place of the *parens patriae* doctrine in mental health law, it helps to consider its ambiguous history, which dates back to ancient Roman law, where it was applied when the head of the family was believed incompetent and in danger of wasting his estate. The state was vested with the power to declare the person *non compos mentis* and commit him and the estate to the care of curators or tutors designated by the praetor. *Parens patriae* was a doctrine applied selectively to persons who had valuable property holdings and other wealth, rather than to the general population. Ironically, the wealthy today are *less* likely to be subjected to decisions based on a *parens patriae* rationale.

The concept was adopted from Roman law in the eleventh century by the Anglo-Saxon King Aethelred II and developed and expanded during the early years of Edward I's reign (1272–1307) (Kittrie, 1971). The doctrine was first codified in 1324 during the reign of Edward II in the statute *Prerogativa Regis*. It gave the king the power to protect the lands and profits of "idiots" and "lunatics" until their mental restoration (Cogan, 1970).

Scholars have debated whether *parens patriae* has been used throughout its history for

151

HISTORICAL
JUSTIFICATION
AND
CURRENT
PHILOSOPHY

humanistic purposes (Cogan, 1970) or primarily as a state fiscal policy to protect wealth and property (Halpern, 1974). Cogan (1970) notes that even under *Prerogativa Regis*, care was taken to limit the king's rights to the lands. For example, the king had *guardianship* of "natural fools," a term which referred to those mentally incapacitated from birth. He had only *unprofitable care* of "lunatics," those who lost their "wit" sometime after birth. Cogan (1970, p. 157) surmises that the distinction was made to prevent "enemies of the king from being declared lunatics and having the profits of their lands added to the King's treasury."

Some courts, though, have seen it differently and have noted that it was not only the king who could profit. In *State ex rel Hawks v. Lazaro* (1974), for example, *parens patriae* was called a state fiscal policy "conceived in avarice and executed without charity." Moreover, "while wellmeaning people frequently attempted to operate under it [*parens patriae*] for the benefit of their fellowmen, it has often been used as a justification for greedy actions on the part of relatives or for the removal of unwanted or troublesome persons."

In the United States, commitment of persons to mental institutions against their wills and for long periods can be traced to what has been called the "cult of the asylum" (Rothman, 1971) or "cult of curability" (Deutsch, 1949) during the nineteenth century. Prior to this time, bizarre-acting persons were kept in their own homes or turned into the streets, where many joined the ranks of vagrants and eventually were held in workhouses or jails. In some cases, bizarre "treatments" were attempted. Julien (1992) notes that persons displaying what would now be called schizophrenic behavior were treated by such methods as "twirling them on a stool until they lost consciousness or dropping them through a trap door into an icy lake" (p. 217).

In the nineteenth century, however, institutional confinement began to emerge as a first resort (Dershowitz, 1974, p. 803). It was now assumed that the supposedly safe, protective, and nonstressful environment of the asylum offered society's best treatment for "lunatics." Critics such as Rothman (1975) have argued, however, that institutionalization was more a matter of convenience than genuine concern for the well-being of the mentally disordered.

These commitments required no formalized showing of mental disorder, inability to care for oneself, or dangerousness to self or to others, although the certification of one or two medical doctors was generally required. Consider, for example, New York State's insanity statute, enacted in 1842, barely six years after the state legislature authorized the building of the Utica asylum. "All lunatics, not only the dangerous ones, were to be confined; and they were to be confined immediately upon the occurrence of the disease" (Dershowitz, 1974, p. 808). The statute not only allowed authorities to incarcerate the insane accused of committing deviant acts, but also urged them to "seek out the quiet insane as well so that they might be cured of their disease" (Dershowitz, 1974, p. 808). Medical superintendents claimed 90 to 100 percent cure rates for "insanity" (Deutsch, 1949; Dershowitz, 1974), without supporting evidence. These claims prompted courts to commit involuntarily numerous persons considered mentally disordered, even if only marginally so. We should note that the term "insanity" is used here in its clinical sense, not in the legal sense discussed in the previous chapter. That is, insanity here refers to mental disorder, not to lack of criminal responsibility at the time of a crime as a result of mental disorder.

One of the earliest American court cases illustrating the full implementation of *parens patriae* power was the 1845 decision of the Massachusetts Supreme Judicial Court, *In re Oakes*. Josiah Oakes, a 67-year-old widower and wharf builder from Cambridge, was committed by his family to McLean Asylum because he was laboring under a "hallucination of mind." His wife had died after a lengthy illness. According to the court record, upon the death of his wife, Oakes seemed unperturbed and did not demonstrate the emotions which could be expected from a person in his right mind. Moreover, he had begun to "manifest a change in character" about six years earlier when a young woman of "bad character" entered his life. His conduct at his wife's funeral showed a "perversion of mind," according to the record. It was also noted that his persistence in his intention to marry the young woman and his refusal to believe the evidence of her bad character were indicative of this perversion.

There was no record of a hearing during the initial commitment process, and Oakes petitioned the court for release, claiming that his family had committed him illegally. In January 1845 the Massachusetts court sat for two days to deliberate the case. Chief Justice C. J. Shaw, considered an "enlightened liberal" (Zilboorg, 1944), delivered the opinion, which kept Oakes confined and set considerable legal precedent (see Box 6.1).

Deutsch (1949, p. 422) referred to the Oakes case as "one of the most important decisions affecting the civil insane in the history of American jurisprudence." It outlined for the first time the justification and limitations implicit in common law concerning restraint of the insane. Not only did it support the institutionalization of persons considered dangerous to themselves or others, but also asserted the power of the state to detain individuals for remedial treatment against their will. Kittrie (1971, p. 66) comments that the Oakes case represents the "cornerstone of the fullfledged modern therapeutic state."

POLICE POWER

Parens patriae remained embedded in law until the 1960s. At that point, concern over the potential for abuse associated with extensive reliance on it as a basis for civil commitment led to the adoption of more restrictive laws. Sometimes called *libertarian* civil commitment statutes, they sought to limit the *parens patriae* authority of the state. The laws reflected the belief that involuntary civil commitment could be justified only on the basis of dangerousness, reflecting the police power of the state.

Police power refers to the obligation and responsibility of the state to protect the public from harm to persons or to property. It encompasses the state's power to make laws and regulations for the protection of public health, safety, welfare, and morals (Comment, 1972, p. 158). Thus, while *parens patriae* relates to protection of the individual and implies the state's remedial, therapeutic, and caregiving responsibilities, police power relates to protection of society. While *parens patriae* focuses on the individual's ability to make appropriate decisions concerning his or her welfare, police power revolves around the individual's dangerousness or potential threat to others. Commitment based on a *parens patriae* rationale requires a demonstrated inability to care for oneself; commitment based on a police power rationale requires predictability of dangerousness.

The distinction between *parens patriae* and police power becomes nebulous, however, in situations in which a person's actions are considered dangerous only to that person and not to society as a whole. A mentally disordered person who lives under a railroad trestle, forages through trash cans for food, and refuses to accept shelter for the impending winter season cannot really be considered a danger to society. Under the *parens patriae* doctrine, this person could be forcibly institutionalized; under police power, he could not. In order to get around this dilemma, some states adopted **grave disability statutes**, which recognized their responsibility to care for those who cannot care for themselves. Even these statutes, however, often require evidence that the person is presently dangerous to him or herself. We will discuss them in more detail shortly.

Another way of getting around the dilemma might be to expand the breadth of police power to include dangerousness to oneself. It is difficult to justify a police power rationale on these grounds, however. The law is already decidedly fickle with respect to the allegedly dangerous behaviors it prohibits. We permit overworking, overeating, and the use of alcohol and tobacco,

■ 6.1: *IN RE OAKES*

THE 1845 *OAKES* CASE WAS A LANDMARK DECISION in mental health law. Among its key points are the following:

- Society has a right to confine persons against their wills if they posed a danger to society or to themselves. ("[T]he right to restrain an insane person of his liberty is found in the great law of humanity, which makes it necessary to confine those whose going at large would be dangerous to themselves or others.")

- Insane people do not have free will and cannot decide for themselves what is in their best interest. ("It is a principle of law that an insane person has no will of his own.")

- The term of the involuntary commitment may be left to the discretion of a medical practitioner.

("The restraint can continue as long as the necessity continues. This is the limitation, and the proper limitation.")

- The distinction between insanity in civil and criminal proceedings is emphasized. ("The same rules do not apply to the same extent in this case [as] apply in the case of a person who has committed a crime, and is sought to be excused on the ground of insanity.")

- Hospitalization must be more likely to cure the individual of the "disease" of insanity than other alternatives. ("The restraint shall last ... until he experiences relief from the present disease of mind...*and* [as long as] the care which he would meet with at the hospital, would be more conducive to his cure than any other course of treatment.") ■

but we often do not permit riding motorcycles without helmets or the use of proscribed drugs. Behavior which is dangerous to oneself is routinely displayed by persons who are perfectly competent, and competent people routinely refuse to seek treatment, including psychological treatment.

THE EMERGENCE OF DUE PROCESS

Due process is, of course, a paramount consideration in involuntary commitment. The U. S. Supreme Court has continually pointed out that commitment to a mental institution "is a deprivation of liberty which the State cannot accomplish without due process of law" (e.g., *O'Connor v. Donaldson*, 1975, p. 580). Loss of liberty and privacy are clearly entailed in such a commitment. Also at stake may be dignity, one's job, living arrangements, and social relationships. The social stigma which accompanies presumed incompetence and emotional weakness is another factor to take into consideration.

As noted above, prior to the late 1960s people were routinely committed to mental institutions without the benefit of hearings or the assistance of counsel. All that was needed was certification by medical doctors that they were mentally ill, needed treatment, and that such a commitment was in their best interest.

In 1966, a federal court ruled that persons could not be involuntarily committed unless other less drastic alternatives were considered (*Lake v. Cameron*). In 1972, another federal court, emphasizing that due process must be carefully protected in civil commitment proceedings, mandated a range of procedures including notice, the opportunity to be heard, and the right to counsel (*Lessard v. Schmidt*). Following the *Lessard* decision, Wisconsin adopted a new mental health statute with procedural safeguards for involuntary commitment proceedings. What happened thereafter was significant. Faced with more restrictive criteria, the state apparently began to take the criminal commitment route. Since it could no longer easily hospitalize people who acted in a bizarre—but not dangerous—manner, the state arrested them on minor charges, found them incompetent to stand trial, and sent them for inpatient psychiatric care for up to sixty days.

In the one-year period after that law went into effect, the number of persons found incompetent to stand trial increased by 42 percent. Once their commitment time had expired, the criminal charges were dropped (Dickey, 1980).

During the 1970s, other states also began to make changes in their statutory schemes. By 1978, all but two had afforded greater protections for those faced with civil commitment (Turkheimer & Parry, 1992). Research on the implementation of these statutes, however, indicated that the Wisconsin experience was not atypical. In Iowa, for example, the legislature passed a new statute designed to limit the number of persons potentially subject to civil commitment (Bezanson, 1975). The law mandated that, prior to involuntary civil commitment, courts must find by clear and convincing evidence that individuals are (1) mentally ill; (2) incapable of making a decision regarding treatment; (3) amenable to treatment; and (4) likely to be dangerous to selves or to others (Stier & Stoebe, 1979). The statute also advocated that defense attorneys challenge the credentials of medical experts, question their diagnoses, offer rebutting expert testimony, and submit factual evidence refuting expert opinions (Stier & Stoebe, 1979). Despite the establishment of these more stringent requirements, an extensive study of the implementation of the new Iowa law found virtually no change in commitment proceedings from the pre-1975 practice of automatic involuntary commitment based on a recommendation by a physician or psychiatrist (Stier & Stoebe, 1979).

In most states, civil commitment includes both emergency detention and long-term involuntary commitment. Some states, such as California, provide for an initial 72-hour evaluation period, a 14-day period of intensive treatment, and long-term confinement up to 180 days. In California, persons gravely disabled, as opposed to dangerous, may be confined for a one-year period. Although statutes do not always refer specifically to re-commitment hearings, researchers are finding significant differences in both the patients involved and the procedures associated with these re-commitments (Parry et al., 1991), as we will see below.

Emergency detention is intended to protect individuals from imminent serious harm to themselves or to prevent injury to others. This short-term confinement presumably provides a "cooling off" period, rarely lasting more than fifteen days, during which the person recovers from immediate psychological agitation or during which arrangements are made for permanent disposition of the case. Before the 1970s, the only way patients could challenge this short-term detention was by **habeas corpus** petition to the courts. The statutory changes in the 1970s, however, drastically curtailed the length of time a patient could be held without a hearing, usually to forty-eight hours. In the Lessard case, the judge declared forty-eight hours the *maximum* time, stating that "such an emergency measure can be justified only for the length of time necessary to arrange for a hearing before a neutral judge at which probable cause for the detention must be established."

Long-term confinement, which once could mean a lifetime in an institution, has been curtailed in most states to a maximum six-month period after which a review of the patient's status must occur. In 1975, the U. S. Supreme Court in *Donaldson v. O'Connor* put states on notice that indefinite confinement of nondangerous persons, without treatment, was constitutionally unacceptable. Patients may have the burden of proving that they are eligible for release after the long-term period has expired, however, and re-commitments are not uncommon.

In 1979, the U. S. Supreme Court ruled in *Addington v. Texas* that a person's committability must be proven in an adversarial hearing at least by clear and convincing evidence; a mere preponderance of the evidence was not enough. The Court did not, however, articulate what the standard or criteria of committability must be (Wexler, 1981). In other words, the Court did not say the state had to prove the person dangerous.

In the same year, the Court took a very different stance toward the commitment of children. In *Parham v. J. R.* (1979), the Court rejected the argument that children should have the benefit of an adversarial hearing before being committed to mental institutions by their parents or caretakers, including state child-welfare officials. All that was needed, the majority said, was "some kind of inquiry" by a neutral factfinder soon after the commitment. The neutral factfinder could, the Court said, be a staff physician. The three Justices who dissented in the case argued that parental decisions to institutionalize their children may be unrelated to the child's mental condition, and that "even well-meaning parents lack the expertise necessary to evaluate the relative advantages and disadvantages of inpatient as opposed to outpatient psychiatric treatment" (442 U. S. at 632). The dissenters also cited a study which concluded that more than half of Georgia's institutionalized children did not need to be so confined. With respect to the "neutral factfinder," the dissenters noted:

> Even under the best of circumstances psychiatric diagnosis and therapy decisions are fraught with uncertainties.... . These uncertainties are aggravated when ... the psychiatrist interviews the child during a period of abnormal stress in connection with the commitment, and without adequate time or opportunity to become acquainted with the patient. These uncertainties may be further aggravated when economic and social class separate doctor and child, thereby frustrating the accurate diagnosis of pathology.

The uneasiness expressed by the dissenters in the Parham case reflects a theme running through many legislative and judicial decisions relating to civil commitment. The fallibility of diagnoses and questions about the effectiveness of various treatment approaches continue to haunt the civil commitment process today. On the other hand, it is important to recognize that restrictive criteria, even for emergency confinement, have created serious problems for the criminal justice system. Researchers have documented increases in the number of mentally disordered persons held in local jails (Steadman, McCarty & Morrissey, 1989), a problem second only to overcrowding (Ogloff et al., 1990). Researchers in some jurisdictions have found support for a **criminalization thesis**, which argues that otherwise noncriminal individuals are charged with minor crimes such as disorderly conduct or unlawful trespassing in order to justify detaining them in jail, arguably for their own protection. Other researchers have found little support for such a thesis, however (Arvanites, 1988) and believe that increases in the mentally disordered population in jail can be attributed to numerous social factors which cannot be linked directly with restrictive commitment statutes (Hiday, 1988). Whether a criminalization phenomenon actually occurs seems to depend upon local policies among law enforcement officers and the availability of community services for the mentally disordered.

Commitment Standards

Most states allow civil commitment if a person can be proven, at least by clear and convincing evidence, to be mentally ill and a danger to self or others. In addition, approximately thirty states allow involuntary commitment if a person is gravely disabled and unable to care for his or her own needs (Turkheimer & Parry, 1992). Recent research indicates that grave disability, rather than dangerousness, is the most frequent basis for civil commitment today (Turkheimer & Parry, 1992; Wexler, 1990a). Surprisingly, the gravely disabled are not generally elderly, but consist mostly of disturbed young persons, 21–35 years old (Wexler, 1990a, p. 173).

DANGEROUSNESS

Although dangerousness is not always precisely defined, some states have led the way in crafting clear criteria. North Carolina law, for example, defines dangerousness to others as follows:

> …within the recent past, the individual has inflicted or attempted to inflict or threatened to inflict serious bodily harm on another, or has acted in such a way as to create a substantial risk of serious bodily harm to another, or has engaged in extreme destruction of property; and that there is a reasonable probability that this conduct will be repeated (*N.C.G.S.* 122C-3 (11)b).

Recall from the preceding chapters that predictions of dangerousness in the criminal context, especially clinical as opposed to actuarial predictions, are often suspect. Researchers have demonstrated high numbers of "false positives," or overpredictions of dangerousness. In the civil commitment process, the concept is equally evasive. In fact, according to Alan Stone (1975), "neither objective actuarial tables nor psychiatric intuition, diagnosis, and psychological testing can claim predictive success when dealing with the traditional population of mental hospitals" (p. 33).

Referring to the three standards of proof in legal decisionmaking—preponderance of the evidence, clear and convincing evidence, and beyond a reasonable doubt—Stone asserts that mental health professionals have failed to prove their ability to predict violence by even the least demanding criterion, preponderance of the evidence (Monahan & Wexler, 1978).

Accepting Stone's quantification, Cocozza and Steadman (1976) conclude that any attempt to commit an individual solely on the basis of dangerousness would be futile if psychiatric testimony were subjected to any of these three standards of proof (p. 1101). They add that the research has demonstrated "clear and convincing evidence of the inability of psychiatrists or anyone else to predict dangerousness accurately" (p. 1109). Likewise, John Monahan (1976, p. 182), pointedly asks: "If, in the criminal law, we say that it is better that ten guilty men go free than one innocent man suffer, how can we reverse this ratio when it comes to mental health law?"

Recall that in Chapter 4 we discussed Monahan's (1981, 1984) research on risk assessment, or the prediction of violence, among mentally disordered offenders. According to Monahan, the best that could be achieved was a 1:2 ratio. In other words, for every three persons predicted to be violent, one would indeed be violent while two would not. With respect to the prediction of violence among *civil* patients, Monahan (1988) finds no better track record. While acknowledging that some research has been able to identify factors predicting violence in this group, he notes that the research is inconsistent. "For every study that reports increases in predictive accuracy there is another that finds clinical risk assessments no better than chance" (Monahan, 1988, p. 251).

The extensive research on the dangerousness standard has been hampered by a number of research design and definitional problems. More precisely, John Monahan and Henry Steadman (in press) argue that empirical research on the risk assessment of violence for the mentally disordered is plagued by four basic methodological problems. The first problem is impoverished predictor variables, which are analogous to the "independent variables" in experimental research. In psychology, a **predictor variable** is generally some measurable antecedent factor that aids in forecasting an outcome or a behavior. Monahan and Steadman point out that there are numerous antecedents to violence—including social, psychological, and biological —but much of risk assessment research has focused on only a very narrow range of "cues" or predictor variables (often only one). In addition to the multiple demographic, biological, or social, variables to consider in predictions of violence, environmental or situational factors have traditionally been neglected. For example, Monahan and Steadman note that Klassen and O'Connor (1985) found that the more friends a released mental patient had within the community, and the more time the patient spent with those friends, the more likely he or she was to commit a violent act. Surprisingly, it may be that friends—under some conditions—serve more as instigators of violence than as sources of social support (Monahan & Steadman, in press).

A second problem is the criterion variable (i.e., violent behavior) itself, because studies define violence in conflicting ways. Violence often means different things to different researchers. In addition, a large portion of violent behavior may go undetected. For example, many previously hospitalized mental patients who demonstrate violent behavior in the community are rehospitalized rather than formally arrested. If the criterion variable is defined as "official arrest for violent behavior," than the rehospitalized patients are likely to be overlooked.

A third difficulty relates to the design of research to test risk assessments. One of the major design problems, according to Monahan and Steadman, is the selection of the sample. Some studies restrict their sample to males within the hospital setting, whereas others sample males in a decidedly different context, the community. Some studies sample only those subjects who have a history of violent actions, whereas others use a mixed pool of subjects consisting of both already-violent individuals and potentially-violent individuals. Thus, the ecological validity of many of the studies is likely to be limited.

Finally, research efforts are rarely synchronized and rarely replicated. For example, Monahan and Steadman find that psychiatrists tend to favor one set of predictor variables, psychologists a second set, and sociologists a third. However, violence is a highly complex behavior that will require coordinated efforts across many disciplines. Thus, future research in risk assessment should be collaborative, enabling researchers to pool large sources of data and perform elaborate and meaningful statistical analyses.

Henry Steadman and his colleagues are directing an extensive study which attempts to overcome these methodological problems. The project is sponsored by the Research Network on Mental Health and Law of the John D. and Catherine T. MacArthur Foundation, and is called the MacArthur Risk Assessment Study. The project involves 1,000 patients discharged from mental institutions in three locations, Pittsburgh, Pennsylvania, Worcester, Massachusetts, and Kansas City, Missouri. The agencies involved are the Western Psychiatric Institute and Clinic at the University of Pittsburgh, the Worcester State Hospital, and the Western Missouri Mental Health Center. The MacArthur study is designed to study the relationship between violent behavior *against others* and mental disorders. It focuses on two closely related aspects of violent behavior by released mental patients: (1) risk assessment and (2) risk management. The ultimate goals of the project are threefold: (1) to improve the validity of clinical *risk assessment*, (2) to improve the effectiveness of clinical *risk management*, and (3) to provide useful information for reforming mental health law and policy. Results of the study should be available in 1995.

The requirement that dangerousness be proved by clear and convincing evidence, and in some states beyond a reasonable doubt, has had the effect of limiting the number of individuals hospitalized. This has raised the question of whether the public is being protected from potentially harmful individuals as well as whether the individuals themselves are getting the help they need. Additionally, because statutes limit the amount of time people can be held without continuing evidence of dangerousness, mental health practitioners have argued that patients are not institutionalized long enough to provide them with significant treatment (Hiday, 1988).

In an attempt to address some of these issues, Hiday (1990) followed, over a six-month-period, 727 individuals brought into civil commitment proceedings in North Carolina for mental illness and dangerousness. Psychiatrists had evaluated two-thirds of them as dangerous. In her follow-up study Hiday used arrest records, patient ward charts, psychiatric evaluations for readmission, civil commitment affidavits for re-commitment, and community mental health center patient records. Dangerousness was defined by objective criteria, such as actual injury to others and threats of physical injury.

Hiday found no reports of violent acts or threats for three-quarters of the 727 individuals. If we contrast the one-quarter for whom violent acts or threats were reported (182 individuals) with the two-thirds figure predicted by psychiatrists (484) we see the large number of false positives in the sample. Hiday suggests that the low level of violence during the six-month follow-up indicates that the civil commitment process works, because persons received the help they presumably required either in the hospital or the community. She is careful to note, though, that research from other jurisdictions is needed to see whether these results can be replicated. Another six-month follow-up study (Belcher, 1989) found involvement in criminal activity among a sample of 132 discharged patients but did not indicate the nature of the crimes. Belcher did find, however, that the discharged patients who were homeless were significantly more likely to commit crime.

A large body of research has explored the relationships among homelessness, mental disorder, and criminal activity from the perspective of criminal as opposed to civil commitments. The findings suggest that mentally disordered individuals are increasingly engaging in such activity, but the crimes seem to be nonviolent, petty, and/or victimless (e.g., loitering). Some recent research, however, (e.g., Martell, 1991) suggests that the subgroup of *seriously* mentally disordered persons who are homeless are at risk for committing violent crimes.

Additional recent research (Klassen & O'Connor, 1988, 1990; Monahan, 1992) finds that male mentally disordered patients who have a history of at least one violent incident have a high probability of being violent within a year after release from a mental hospital. Data collected by Swanson and colleagues (Swanson & Holzer, 1991; Swanson, Holzer, Ganju & Jono, 1990) suggest that *currently* mentally disordered patients are involved in violent behavior far more often than nondisordered members of the general population. This difference persists even when demographic and social factors are taken into account (Monahan, 1992).

Monahan stresses two things about the research showing a connection between mental disorders and violence. First, the relationship refers only to people *currently* experiencing a *serious* disorder (e.g., psychosis). People who have been seriously mentally disordered in the past and are not now showing symptoms are not prone to violence. Second, a great majority (over 90 percent) of currently mentally disordered individuals are not violent. In sum, then, the relationship between mental disorder and violence is strong for those currently, seriously mentally disordered individuals who have a history of violent behavior.

GRAVE DISABILITY

The dangerousness standard, while deserving continued research, should not overshadow the problems posed by the grave disability standard. Under grave disability, individuals are judged according to whether they are able to care for themselves and meet their own basic needs. In Arizona, for example, grave disability is defined as follows:

> a condition evidenced by behavior in which a person, as a result of a mental disorder, is likely to come to serious physical harm or serious illness because he is unable to provide for his basic physical needs such as food, clothing or shelter (*Ariz. Rev. Stat. Ann.* SS36-501(1) *Supp.* 1985).

Turkheimer and Parry (1992) note that, while studies of prediction of dangerousness abound in the literature, studies of predictions of the inability to care for self have not been undertaken. Yet, grave disability is being used more and more as a standard for commitment, and most particularly re-commitment. On the other hand, prediction of grave disability may not be as crucial as prediction of dangerousness, because grave disability statutes generally require proof of actual inability to care for oneself, not presumed or predicted inability (Wexler & Winick, 1991, p. 11).

Other aspects of grave disability commitments may be more troublesome than the prediction of behavior, however. Less restrictive alternatives to hospitalization, for example, seem especially warranted for individuals who are not committed under a dangerousness standard, yet this kind of consideration is often ignored. Wexler (1990a) also notes that grave disability statutes sometimes allow commitment for a longer period of time than dangerousness statutes.

Warren (1977) studied the cases of 100 persons committed to mental institutions in California under both grave disability and dangerousness standards. Although the grave disability statute required a demonstration that the individual was unable to care for him- or herself, Warren learned that individuals were committed without such demonstration. Instead, they were committed on the basis of medical conclusions that took into account refusal to take medicine, prior hospitalization record, a tendency to deny mental illness to the psychiatrist and fail to cooperate with mental health personnel, and the level of rejection expressed by the patient's family.

Many of the criteria used to arrive at grave disability were also used as a basis for dangerousness. In almost all the cases, there was a notable failure by the court and the medical experts to try to ascertain the imminence and seriousness of danger to others.

Research reveals that about one-quarter of the estimated 1.2 million civil commitments each year are *involuntary* commitments (Monahan & Shah, 1989). Although there are no clear national data on the standard by which patients are committed, Monahan, Ruggerio and Friedlander (1982) found, in California, that 70 percent of these patients were evaluated as dangerous to themselves, 29 percent as dangerous to others, and 43 percent as gravely disabled. One-third of these individuals met two or more of the standards during their commitment evaluation. In another California study, Segal et al. (1988) reported that 60 percent of the patients involuntarily committed were assessed as dangerous to themselves, 49 percent as dangerous to others, and 32 percent as gravely disabled. Again, many of the commitments satisfied as least two of the three standards. As noted earlier, however, there is research emerging from a number of jurisdictions showing that grave disability is the most frequent basis for civil commitment today (Turkheimer & Parry, 1992).

Warren (1977) also noted that in a majority of cases, the initial finding of dangerousness to others was replaced by grave disability for *continued* commitment. Turkheimer and Parry (1992) report that this is a common finding in the research on civil commitment proceedings. In other words, re-commitment hearings involve significantly less stringent requirements than initial hearings.

Hiday (1977) reported that courts in North Carolina were showing slightly less deference to psychiatrists in the implementation of the reformed statutes, although "we still find numerous instances of deference, and [of] commitment where a preponderance of evidence does not support imminent danger to self or others" (p. 655). The primary reason seems to be that judges and lawyers lack knowledge about psychiatry and mental illness which "allows psychiatrists to become the effective decision makers, often in absentia" (Hiday, 1977, p. 655).

Commitment Proceedings

Although the law requires an adversarial hearing for civil commitment, hearings are often informal and hinge on opinions of medical or psychiatric practitioners, who may or may not be cross-examined. Family members, social workers, employers or friends may also testify, but it is not uncommon for a judge to make a decision based solely on clinical testimony or written reports. In some jurisdictions, the affected person does not attend the hearing, under the rationale that his or her condition would be aggravated by observing and participating. In the Iowa study mentioned earlier, however (Stier & Stoebe, 1979), the researchers learned that individuals did not seem unduly upset by adversary proceedings. In general, despite conventional wisdom among mental health practitioners that hearings are countertherapeutic, there is no documentation to that effect. In fact, researchers are now beginning to explore the therapeutic benefits of civil commitment hearings (Ensminger & Liguori, 1990).

Despite the due-process safeguards introduced to the civil commitment process in the 1970s, statutory requirements for involuntary civil commitments continue to be circumvented by judges, lawyers, and mental health professionals alike, much as they were in the Wisconsin and Iowa studies cited earlier in the chapter. Although research in some jurisdictions suggests that the civil commitment process operates smoothly and with careful attention to due process, the experiences of observers and a fair body of data indicate that this is not the norm (Applebaum, 1992).

In a recent review of the literature on civil commitment proceedings, Turkheimer and Parry (1992) identified a litany of problems. Among them are the following: 1) attorneys are poorly prepared and often do not perform adversarial roles; 2) judges defer to mental health recommendations or discourage attorneys from questioning these witnesses; 3) least restrictive alternatives to hospitalization are not considered; 4) examinations are perfunctory or nonexistent; and 5) respondents are not advised of their rights, including the right to be represented by counsel.

After a similar review, however, Hiday (1988) took a more positive stance, concluding that the more flagrant abuses of the civil commitment process no longer occur systematically as they did before reform of civil commitment law. "While statutory definitions of dangerousness are not always explicit and often are vague, they do limit the number of candidates who are involuntarily hospitalized. And while the nonadversary nature and sometimes laxity of legal procedures may convey a sense of injustice, they do review petitioner allegations and hospital practice" (p. 37). She warns, however, that there are signs "the pendulum may be swinging away from protection of individual rights back to the old paternalism" (p. 37).

Parry and his colleagues (1991) found significant differences in procedures between initial or first-time commitments and re-commitments, and concluded that the law was circumvented, particularly in the latter cases. For example, there was no adversarial questioning in 19 percent of the re-commitments, compared to 4 percent of initial commitments. Attorneys did not confer with their clients in 80 percent of the re-commitment hearings, compared to 40 percent in initial hearings. This study found that re-commitment hearings averaged 8 minutes in length, initial commitment hearings 14 minutes. Earlier studies have reported commitment hearings lasting from an average of 1.9 minutes (Cohen, 1966) to 18.4 minutes (Hiday, 1977).

What explains this apparent lack of diligence in protecting the legal rights of persons facing involuntary commitment? Some scholars point to the twin failures of **deinstitutionalization** and community treatment. The social policy of deinstitutionalization (removing patients from the confines of traditional large institutions) is now widely regarded as having displaced the mentally disordered from mental hospitals to urban "psychiatric ghettos," shelters for the homeless, and (depending on the strength of the criminalization thesis) to jails. According to Turkheimer and Parry (1992, p. 649) "the desultory performance of participants in civil commitment hearings may be related to the absence of less restrictive treatment alternatives... ." They note that attorneys representing civil commitment candidates may be afraid their clients will not get the help they need if they are not civilly committed. Furthermore, they may not want to appear socially irresponsible in arguing for the release of persons they believe unable to function on their own. As one attorney whose practice frequently involves the representation of civil commitment candidates has remarked, "There isn't much satisfaction walking out the door arm in arm with your free, but crazy, client."

Applebaum (1992) adds other explanations. He notes that the advent of legal rules relating to a clinician's "duty to protect" has left mental-health practitioners in a quandary. Recall that mental health practitioners in some jurisdictions can be held liable for not protecting a potential victim from violence at the hands of their patients (e.g., *Tarasoff v. Board of Regents*, 1979). According to Applebaum, these requirements offer practitioners a strong incentive to seek to commit patients who present some risk of violence, even though they are not likely to benefit from hospitalization or do not meet commitment criteria.

Applebaum also suggests that many practitioners believe the deeply held value of the mental-health profession to provide treatment cannot give way to the goals of the justice system, which are to resolve disputes, impose punishments, protect public safety, and maintain procedural fairness. While recognizing that these are legitimate and important goals, Applebaum adds, "Conspicuous by its absence in this list…is any reference to affording treatment—at a minimum, hospitalization—to persons afflicted with severe mental illness" (p. 66).

He argues that neither the justice system nor the mental-health system is truly committed to the goals of civil commitment. He envisions, therefore, the creation of a third, independent system which would oversee the commitment process and assume all of the responsibilities now assigned to the mental-health and justice systems. It would include clinicians extensively trained not only in evaluation but also in the law, hearing officers with specialized training in clinical and legal aspects of mental disorder; and vigorous advocates for each side. The primary goal of all, however, would be the implementation of the civil commitment statute (p. 70).

FAMILIES AND CIVIL COMMITMENT

Some studies examining the civil commitment process have found that the inability or unwillingness of family members to take responsibility for disordered individuals has functioned as an implicit criterion for commitment. Warren (1977) found that the family, directly or indirectly, was the instigator of almost half of the commitments in her California sample. Stone (1975, p. 46) refers to the **convenience function**, the practice of warehousing family members considered bothersome. He notes that this factor has "seldom been explicitly acknowledged, rather it has been hidden behind a promise of technical treatment, although at some points during the past century it has been the only goal actually achieved" (p. 46). Stone adds that this convenience function is a "typical instance of the clandestine decisionmaking role of mental health practitioners which allows society to do what it does not want to admit to doing, i.e., confining unwanted persons cheaply."

Recent research, however, indicates that family members are increasingly serving as caregivers for the mentally disordered who remain in the community, and that these families should be given more support by the mental-health system (Petrila, 1992). Some recent evidence also shows that the "warehousing" function has all but disappeared (Hiday, 1988). Just as significantly, families and friends have been found to provide needed social support for individuals who have been involuntarily committed after their release back into the community (Hiday & Scheid-Cook, 1987). It is unfair to families of these individuals, therefore, to portray them as operating in collusion with coercive agents of government and against the interests of their mentally disordered relatives.

A distinct consideration, however, is the possibility of dysfunctional interaction between the person facing civil commitment and his or her family. Literature on mental disorder increasingly urges therapists to take the family system into consideration and recognize that positive change is less likely to occur when the individual is treated in isolation from her or his social system. Some persons faced with civil commitment may come from dysfunctional families. As Ensminger and Liguori (1990, p. 259) have noted, "the patient may just be the individual manifesting the most bizarre behavior of a maladaptation of the whole family unit." In a similar fashion, Wexler (1990a) notes that grave disability laws which require evidence of inability to care for oneself can be used by therapists to help a possibly dysfunctional family. The family members must "do something," create challenges for the individual and urge the individual to take steps toward improving his or her life. "The very process of gathering evidence of a person's committability under a libertarian law may operate therapeutically to render commitment unnecessary!" (p. 184).

Stone's reference to the "clandestine decisionmaking role of mental health practitioners" also must be addressed at this point. As indicated in the previous chapter, the literature is littered with assertions that practitioners are not making medical or scientific judgments when they diagnose and prescribe treatments, including institutional treatment. Rather, they are making moral and social judgments that reflect the values of the dominant class (Greenaway & Brickley, 1978). Shaffer (1973, p. 369), commenting on psychiatric testimony in involuntary civil commitment cases, states that "the commitment decision is a process of social definition, of rejection by society, of deviance from norms of behavior; there is nothing honestly scientific, let alone medical, about it." He notes that the poor and the powerless are at least twice as likely to be involuntarily committed as the rest of society. Finally, Shaffer concludes, "America has mental hospitals because it wants them."

A series of intriguing studies by Dorothea and Benjamin Braginsky provide strong support for the position that the diagnosis of mental illness can indeed be a value judgment (Mazer, 1978, pp. 98–100). The researchers were interested in whether a patient's political attitudes would affect a diagnosis. They videotaped two simulated interviews between actors posing as clinicians and mental patients. Each tape consisted of four segments: (1) presentation of the psychiatric complaints; (2) expression of the patient's political philosophy; (3) expression of the patient's views on political tactics for change; and (4) expression of the patient's attitude toward mental health professionals. The psychiatric complaints, which were identical in both interviews, depicted mildly neurotic problems (e.g., fatigue, irritability, listlessness). The second and third segments reflected, in one case, moderate and, in the other, radical views. In the fourth segment, both patients criticized mental-health professionals, but the radical patient called them "handmaidens of a repressive society," while the moderate accused them only of destroying traditional values and encouraging permissiveness.

Each videotape was played for different groups of trained and qualified psychiatrists and psychologists. The tape was stopped after each segment, and the clinicians were asked to rate the extent of the patient's mental illness.

After the first segment, both patients were rated as having mild problems. When subsequent segments were shown, however, the "radical" patient became progressively more deviant to the clinicians, whether they were psychologists or psychiatrists. The researchers wrote, "When the new left radical discusses his political philosophy, [and] has aired his political tactics, he is seen as being twice as disturbed as his moderate counterpart, whose rating stays the same as he voices his political attitudes" (Mazer, 1978, p. 99). When the patients criticized mental-health professionals, the mental illness ratings of both increased substantially. Both were suddenly seen as "severely and psychotically disturbed."

The Braginskys conducted a later study in which the "radical" patient had nothing but praise for mental-health professionals. New audiences rated the first three segments comparably to their colleagues in the first study. When the patient praised the professionals, however, estimations of his sickness were drastically reduced and he was seen as a sensible and rational individual. "If insults are the illness, then flattery is the cure," the researchers quipped (Mazer, 1978, p. 100).

Studies such as the above, accompanied by those discussed in the previous chapter which question reliability and validity of diagnoses, raise serious questions about the well-documented tendency of the courts to rely on the medical profession's diagnosis of mental illness. Although clinical recommendations are obviously needed, commitment decisions based *exclusively* on these recommendations—and most particularly on the recommendation of *one* clinician—are warranted.

Treatment In (and Outside) Hospitals

Historical accounts of treatment in mental institutions are replete with illustrations of neglect or inhumane practices. The egregious living conditions in many of these institutions have been liberally documented. It is generally acknowledged, also, that the dominant philosophy in mental institutions was historically based upon warehousing rather than treating the mentally disordered. Physical interventions, however, were not uncommon. During the eugenics movement of the 1920s and 1930s, for example, mentally disordered and defective individuals were often sterilized, a practice upheld by the U. S. Supreme Court (*Buck v. Bell*, 1929). Another not uncommon physical intervention was the involuntary frontal lobotomy, used to "cure" a range of mental disorders, from sexual deviancy to psychosis (Groves & Schlesinger, 1979). As more experience with this surgical procedure was gained, it became apparent that early reports of success were exaggerated and misleading. In many patients, the extensive destruction of the frontal lobes did not result in improvement, and in some patients with psychosis the condition was made worse (Freeman & Watts, 1942). Many disturbing side effects were noted several months after surgery, including substantial changes in personality and moods (Groves & Schlesinger, 1979). Later studies demonstrated that adequately matched lobotomized patients and control patients who had not had surgery showed no differences in improvement when rate of discharge from mental hospitals was used as a criterion (Robin & McDonald, 1975).

The gross psychosurgical techniques reported in the earlier years of psychiatry gave way to more refined methods of stereotaxic surgery, where minute electrodes could be placed into various parts of the brain with precision. Electrical current or chemicals could then be directed at different "centers" of the brain responsible for a wide assortment of behaviors. This form of surgery was hailed as an effective means of controlling a wide variety of thought processes, behaviors, and feelings (Mark & Ervin, 1970). Many claims were overstated (Valenstein, 1973), and stereotaxic surgery, widely regarded as a radical and unacceptable effort at thought control, did not survive in the U. S.

HOSPITALIZATION

Today, treatment in most mental institutions involves medication for a great majority of patients (Durham & La Fond, 1991). Julien (1992) notes that in 1955, over half a million persons in the United States were residing in state mental hospitals. By 1983, that figure had been reduced by about half, even though admissions to state hospitals had doubled. This shift reflects the quick turnover made possible by the use of psychoactive drugs which enabled hospital staffs to stabilize the mentally disordered and send them back into the community within a relatively short time. Treatment with psychoactive drugs is often characterized as callous and abusive, however. Brooks (1986) notes that not until the 1970s did psychiatry begin to acknowledge the seriousness of the side effects that often accompany them. We will leave this topic for the moment, but it will be reintroduced later in the chapter, when we discuss both outpatient treatment and the right to refuse treatment.

The adequacy and effectiveness of civil institutional treatment has traditionally been evaluated by one of three methods: (1) structural analysis, (2) process method, and (3) effectiveness method (Schwitzgebel, 1977). **Structural analysis** focuses upon the structure of the institution and uses criteria such as staff-to-patient ratios and per capita expenditure to determine the adequacy of treatment. The **process method** directly investigates the type and amount of treatment delivered to the patients. Patient records are examined to determine how often the patients were seen, by whom, and for what purposes. The **effectiveness method**, focuses on outcome and actual change in the patient's affect, thinking processes, and actions. Here, information is collected about the results or effects of the treatment provided.

Some courts have relied upon structural criteria for assessing and enforcing patient care and treatment, primarily because they are the easiest to document *en masse* (see, e.g., *Wyatt v. Stickney,* 1972). This is also the method most commonly used by social scientists in determining the effectiveness of treatment provided by both mental and correctional institutions (Quay, 1977). However, the structural method is the least useful for deciding whether treatment works and whether it justifies civil commitment. An adequate staff-to-patient ratio or sufficient funding does not ensure quality of staff performance or progress in implementing and achieving treatment goals.

The second method of evaluating treatment, the process approach, focuses upon how much and what type of treatment is actually received. The methodology usually entails an examination of treatment plans, detailed records of treatment, and periodic review of those records. The assessment is done strictly on the basis of what appears on the record. Thus, if a person received thirty minutes of therapy five days a week, it is presumed that he or she is receiving "more" treatment than a person receiving fifteen minutes, three days per week.

The third and probably most revealing method of evaluating treatment has been used very infrequently (Coleman, 1976; Ennis & Emery, 1978; Kittrie, 1971). It is the most adequate method of studying effectiveness, however, because it is primarily concerned with the outcome and results of therapy, an orientation the courts should have when referring persons for treatment (Schwitzgebel, 1974). Research using this third method to assess the treatment provided in mental institutions indicates that the recovery rates for groups who receive various regimens of drugs, psychotherapy, or nothing at all are about the same (Schwitzgebel, 1974; Katz, 1969; Ennis & Litwack, 1974; Chambers, 1972; May, 1968). However, it should be emphasized that when it comes to brief, intense episodes of biologically based mental disorders, such as bipolar depression or schizophrenia, certain psychoactive drugs have been found to be very effective at reducing the symptoms in a majority of cases (Lickey & Gordon, 1991).

Durham and La Fond (1990, p. 135) note that although "thousands of research studies" have examined treatment efficacy, "the scientific worth of the empirical evidence in this area is seriously flawed because it does not meet the standard criteria for empirical evidence." They also add, "Virtually no well designed studies have evaluated whether or not psychotherapy is effective in treating mentally ill patients confined against their wills to public psychiatric hospitals" (p. 148). Durham and La Fond (1991) add that even if psychotherapy were found effective, it is an impractical undertaking given the limited staff, time, and other resources available in mental institutions.

VOLUNTARY COMMITMENTS

Approximately 30 percent of patients in mental institutions have been placed there against their wills (Wexler, 1991). The remaining 70 percent may not be truly voluntary commitments (Carroll, 1991), however, because an unknown number have occurred under the threat of formal commitment proceedings. Furthermore, the issue of whether the mentally disordered are competent to make the decision to commit themselves voluntarily has now been raised as the result of a recent U. S. Supreme Court decision.

Zinermon v. Burch (1990) involved a diagnosed paranoid schizophrenic who had been found wandering along a highway, bloodied, bruised, and disoriented. Apparently still in a confused state, he signed forms consenting to admission and treatment in a short-term emergency facility, then to a state mental hospital. There was ample evidence in the record that he was disoriented, confused, and bizarre in both action and appearance during each form-signing episode. The Court ruled, in a 5-4 decision, that he had a substantive right to be competent before consenting to voluntary hospitalization and a consequent procedural right to a hearing to determine whether this competency existed. In other words, before being allowed to commit himself to a mental institution, he should have been given a hearing to determine whether he was able to make that decision.

According to Bruce Winick (1991b), the decision may have widespread, negative implications. If states interpret the Supreme Court's decision as requiring hearings in all voluntary commitments, the voluntary process would become nearly indistinguishable from the involuntary. "Not only would this impose high costs, but it also would undermine much of the presumed value of voluntary admission" (Winick, 1991b, p. 94). Furthermore, he argues that a broad reading of Zinermon v. Burch would, by extension, require a demeaning inquiry into the competency of mentally disordered individuals whenever they make significant decisions.

It remains to be seen whether the case will indeed have a significant effect on voluntary commitments. The issue of coercion associated with threat of forced confinement, as discussed by Carroll (1991), appears to be more problematic. Carroll attempts to reach a balance between forced hospitalization (or involuntary commitment) and voluntary commitments which are not truly voluntary. He argues that, rather than threatening some mentally disordered persons with commitment proceedings, officials should "persuade" them to seek treatment, allowing them to perceive that they are making their own decisions. From a therapeutic perspective, he suggests, such a decision is more likely to lead to positive change.

Outpatient Treatment Orders

An undetermined number of individuals who go through civil commitment proceedings are not institutionalized, but rather are "committed" to outpatient treatment, which represents a less restrictive alternative. Additionally, persons discharged from an institution may be "committed" to outpatient treatment as a transitional move. Psychotherapy provided in a community setting or on an outpatient basis, *when it is available*, has been found to be far more effective than that provided in a hospital or institutional setting (Ennis & Litwak, 1974, p. 718, note 80).

Studies demonstrate that persons treated in the community recover faster, have fewer relapses, deteriorate less from dependency fostered by hospitalization, maintain employment better, and cost the state about half as much money as similar patients treated in hospitals. As noted earlier, however, the concentrated effort in the 1970s to shift from an institutional to a community model has not been successful, often because community resources were not available. Furthermore, to achieve maximum effectiveness, outpatient programs should be longer in duration, spanning years rather than months (Durham & La Fond, 1990).

In some states, outpatient commitment orders are called **orders of nonhospitalization**. The treatment a person is ordered to take part in usually consists of drugs and counseling, both delivered at a local mental-health center (Lickey & Gordon, 1991). It may or may not include an alternate living arrangement such as placement in a group home.

To date, outpatient orders (as opposed to voluntary outpatient treatment) have received little empirical attention. One exception is research by Hiday and Scheid-Cook (1987, 1989), which is largely supportive of outpatient treatment orders, specifically for the chronic mentally ill who would otherwise be caught in the "revolving door" of hospitalization, release, and rehospitalization. Hiday and Scheid-Cook did an extensive six-month follow-up study of 1,266 adults who had gone through civil commitment hearings in North Carolina. Persons committed to outpatient treatment, compared to those who had been institutionalized and then released, were more likely to be working, to have maintained contact with community mental-health centers, and to have more social contacts at the end of the follow-up period.

Turkheimer and Parry (1992) believe that states should not only be required to investigate such less restrictive alternatives, but also to demonstrate their absence. Such documentations, they argue, would highlight the lack of effective community treatment outside the hospitalization setting, making it more difficult to ignore this problem. Development of more community treatment options may not per se solve the problems of mentally disordered individuals, however. Although outpatient treatment appears to be a better alternative than the traditional inpatient treatment, there are clearly problems associated with it. "In some states that have experimented with outpatient commitment, treatment has been imposed on unwilling patients in a more authoritarian and paternalistic manner than is allowed for hospital treatment" (Lickey & Gordon, 1991, p. 376).

A widely voiced criticism of outpatient treatment is its reliance on pharmacotherapy (Davis, 1975, 1976) which is often lauded by the psychiatric profession as the most effective way to deal with many mental disorders. Today, drugs are available for persons diagnosed with schizophrenia, anxiety, depression, panic disorders, phobias, and obsessive-compulsive disorders, to name but a few (Julien, 1992; Lickey & Gordon, 1991). Although institutionalized patients also routinely receive drug therapy, as noted earlier, they ironically have more right to refuse it than those in the community, whose freedom may be contingent upon their willingness to "take their meds."

Supporters of the medical model approach to treatment argue that, when used judiciously and for specified disorders, psychoactive drugs are remarkably successful and side effects can be minimized. Most importantly, they argue, the drugs relieve suffering. Durham and La Fond (1991), after reviewing research studies on the efficacy of various treatment modes, conclude that administering drugs to the mentally disordered as a group is better than doing nothing at all. They note that it has not been established, however, that drug treatment is effective for patients involuntarily hospitalized.

The other side of the coin is that the various forms of drug treatment for mental disorders have serious limitations (Groves & Schlesinger, 1979). In most cases they merely alleviate some of the symptoms, and drug withdrawal can result in relapses without significant changes in the disordered behavior. Continuous treatment with drugs can also produce numerous serious side effects (Groves & Schlesinger, 1979). Brooks (1986) describes a range of physical, emotional, cognitive, and social side effects associated with psychoactive medication. The worst is tardive dyskinesia, an irreversible condition for which there is no known cure. Tardive dyskinesia "is a physical disablement manifested by grotesque movements of the face, tongue, mouth, and limbs" (p. 250). It appears to be particularly a risk for long-term chronic patients on psychoactive drugs.

Moreover, even proponents of drug therapy warn that it should be accompanied by psychotherapy to teach cognitive and social skills and help individuals cope with problems of living (Lickey & Gordon, 1991). The extent to which such help is offered is unknown. In the absence of psychotherapy, however, drug treatment may well foster a lifelong dependency on medication without addressing other root causes of mental disorder.

167

RIGHTS,
FREEDOMS,
AND THE
NEED
FOR
MENTAL-HEALTH
SERVICES

Rights, Freedoms, and the Need for Mental-Health Services

I nvoluntary confinement of the mentally disordered has raised important questions about their rights to receive and to refuse treatment. The right to receive treatment represents the state's affirmative obligation to act to improve the individual's mental condition. It does not oblige the state to "cure," since the treatment provided may not be effective. As a federal court noted in *Rouse v. Cameron* (1966), all that is needed is a *bona fide* effort to provide patients with an individualized treatment program that includes periodic evaluation. The legal right to *refuse* treatment recognizes that involuntary medication violates the patient's autonomy and bodily integrity. Under the common-law doctrine of informed consent, which has since been recognized in numerous state statutes and integrated into constitutional law (*Cruzan v. Director*, 1990), a competent person has the right to refuse medication and life-sustaining artificial nutrition and hydration. As we noted in Chapter 1, however, in *Washington v. Harper* the Supreme Court recognized that there may be a governmental interest which supersedes that individual right.

Competency to refuse is a critical component of this issue, however. Are mentally disordered individuals competent to make decisions about treatment regimens deemed to be in their best interest? We will discuss both the right to receive and the right to refuse treatment separately.

RIGHT TO RECEIVE TREATMENT

It can be argued that if the state hospitalizes a mentally disordered person against his or her will, there should be a concomitant requirement to provide treatment. If the treatment that would produce an "adjusted" and "happy" person does not exist or is denied, confinement should not continue. On the other hand, if the individual is "dangerous" to self or others and/or gravely disabled, it could be argued that, even in the absence of treatment, continued confinement is justified. In the case of an individual dangerous to him- or herself but not to others, less restrictive alternative placements should be investigated.

A key case on the issue of right to treatment is a 1972 federal case, *Wyatt v. Stickney*. An Alabama statute permitted commitment to state institutions "for safekeeping." The court ruled that patients committed involuntarily to a state mental hospital had a constitutional right to a humane physical and psychological environment with adequate professional and nonprofessional staff, and to "receive such individual treatment as will give each of them a realistic opportunity to be cured or to improve his or her mental condition" *(Wyatt v. Stickney*, 1971, pp. 784–785). The court continued, "…[to] deprive any citizen of his or her liberty upon the altruistic theory that the confinement is for humane therapeutic reasons and then fail to provide adequate treatment violates the very fundamentals of due process." The court's decision was upheld by an appellate court, in *Wyatt v. Aderholt* (1975).

In the landmark U. S. Supreme Court case *O'Connor v. Donaldson* (1975), the Court retreated on the issue of a constitutional right to treatment, however. Instead, it emphasized that non-dangerous patients in a mental institution have a right to liberty if they are not receiving treatment. Donaldson had been diagnosed with paranoid schizophrenia and confined to a mental institution for care, maintenance, and treatment upon the recommendations of two nonpsychiatrist physicians and with the approval of his father. He had remained there for fifteen years, despite his frequent requests to be released. At no time was he considered a danger to himself or to others.

Donaldson apparently had received nothing but custodial care throughout those fifteen years. The superintendent of the institution described his treatment as "milieu therapy," but "witnesses from the hospital staff conceded that, in the context of this case, milieu therapy was a euphemism for confinement in the milieu of a mental hospital" (422 U. S. at 569).

The Supreme Court opinion emphasized that a finding of "mental illness" alone cannot justify involuntary custodial confinement of nondangerous individuals, nor can "mere public intolerance or animosity" constitutionally justify the deprivation of physical liberty. The Court ruled that, in light of the fact that no treatment was available to Donaldson, he should be released.

Nearly twenty years later, the efficacy of any one treatment approach has yet to be empirically demonstrated. This is particularly so with patients who resist being treated. Most therapists would agree that psychotherapy is destined to fail if it consistently compromises the person's sense of control and freedom. The hallmark of successful therapy, no matter what perspective or school of thought we are considering, is the reestablishment of the person's sense of control and the elimination of inhibiting dependency and rigid social restraints. When a mentally disordered individual is committed involuntarily, even with the best intentions or protective concerns, the fact remains that control and freedom have been removed from him. It is for this reason that Carroll (1991) favors intervening in such a way that an individual perceives she or he is making the decision.

Similarly, in their plea for a **therapeutic jurisprudence**, Wexler and Winick (1991) want to enable patients to become more involved in their own treatment. According to Winick (1991a), we must not assume that patients in mental institutions are incompetent to make any and all decisions, including those relating to their treatment. "Patient choice in favor of treatment appears to be an important determinant of treatment success. Treatment imposed over objections does not work as well" (p. 68). Winick also notes that even "normal" people occasionally lose contact with reality and lack ability to think straight and perform social tasks. Conversely, the mentally disordered function normally some of the time, even in the midst of a psychotic episode. Therefore, we should not assume it is unrealistic to allow them to have some say in their own treatment regimens.

RIGHT TO REFUSE TREATMENT

The issue of an individual's right to refuse treatment arises most often in the context of intrusive mental-health interventions such as psychoactive medications and electroconvulsive therapy (Winick, 1991a).

U. S. Supreme Court decisions dealing directly with the right to refuse antipsychotic medication have come from the criminal arena. As we have seen, for example, the Court ruled that prisoners have a liberty interest in being free from the administration of antipsychotic drugs (*Washington v. Harper*, 1990), but that such drugs may be administered if the state demonstrates in an administrative proceeding that the inmate is dangerous to self or others. Although the Harper case may appear to support strongly the right to refuse treatment, the fact that the Court did not require judicial oversight of the decision to administer drugs suggests otherwise. The Court did, however, support the right of a defendant pleading insanity to refuse antipsychotic drugs during his trial (*Riggins v. Nevada*, 1992). In still another case, *Perry v. Louisiana* (1991), the Court was asked whether a death-row prisoner had the constitutional right to refuse a strong, antipsychotic medication which would render him mentally competent to be executed. The case was remanded to the Louisiana Supreme Court, which then decided that the forced administration of psychoactive drugs in that context violated the *state* constitution.

Lower courts have supported the right to patients in mental institutions to refuse drug treatment (e.g., *Rogers v. Okin*, 1980; *Rennie v. Klein*, 1982). This refusal can be overridden if patients

169

RIGHTS,
FREEDOMS,
AND THE
NEED
FOR
MENTAL-HEALTH
SERVICES

are dangerous to themselves or others, in an emergency situation, and when patients are mentally incapable of making a rational treatment decision. A 1982 U. S. Supreme Court decision (*Youngblood v. Romeo*) which urged courts to defer to "professional judgment" in another context, however, makes the right to refuse very weak. "The right has become a right to object and to have one's treatment decision reviewed" (Brooks, 1986, p. 259). When patients in civil mental institutions do challenge the decision to forcibly medicate them, courts rarely rule in their favor (Brooks, 1986; Deland & Borenstein, 1990; Hoge et al., 1990).

Opponents of the right to refuse treatment, however, argue that it places patients in the classic situation of "rotting with their rights on" (Applebaum & Gutheil, 1979). Instead of being helped by medication, their conditions deteriorate progressively while their civil liberties remain intact. Opponents note also that courts which support a right to refuse treatment do not take into consideration the realities of many mental disorders, which are characterized by denial and ambivalence. According to Schwartz et al. (1990), autonomy as perceived by the legal system is drastically different from autonomy as perceived by the medical clinician. Mentally disordered individuals by definition cannot be considered autonomous while plagued by a "disease."

Schwartz and his colleagues studied twenty-five patients in an inpatient psychiatric unit who were involuntarily medicated. At discharge, seventeen of the twenty-five (called "retrospective compliers") reported that the decision to medicate them against their wills had been the correct one. There were seven "retrospective non-compliers," who still disagreed with the decision to medicate. One patient did not respond. When the patients about to be discharged were asked why they had refused medication, only five cited concerns about side effects. This minimal saliency of potential side effects has also been reported by Applebaum and Gutheil (1980). Schwartz et al. concluded that resistance to medication was not based on "principled objections," such as concern about autonomy, but rather on "psychotic perceptions, denial and negativism, struggles with staff or family, and other transient, situational factors" (pp. 196–197).

A comparison of the non-compliers with the compliers indicated that the former had had more past hospitalizations and poorer work histories. They were considered still ill at discharge and "continued to display grandiosity, suspiciousness, paranoia, hostility, conceptual disorganization, unusual thought content, and mannerisms and posturing" (p. 197).

Grisso and Applebaum (1991) explored the ability of mentally disordered patients to understand the implications of consenting to and refusing treatment. They compared fifty-one patients hospitalized in a state mental hospital with control groups of twenty-six hospitalized in a university medical hospital and twenty-five outpatients. The psychiatric patients had been diagnosed with major depression (N=26) or schizophrenia or schizoaffective disorder (N=25). The medical patients had ischemic heart disease (N=26) or were non-ill persons being seen at a primary care clinic (N=25).

The researchers had previously designed and tested an instrument to measure a patient's understanding of information disclosed in order to obtain consent for medication. The instrument describes the disorder, the medication, its benefits, its side effects, and alternative treatments along with their benefits and liabilities. Various methods of administering this instrument were tried, such as having the examiner read the complete form with the patient then having the patient paraphrase it; having the examiner present the paragraphs one at a time and having the patient paraphrase them; or reading paragraphs one at a time, then giving the patient new statements and asking which is similar to what had just been read.

Grisso and Applebaum learned that the schizophrenic patients as a group demonstrated significantly poorer understanding than the other three groups. Nonetheless, they exhibited a wide range of scores, indicating that some clearly understood better than others. The risk of poorer understanding was greater in those with severe symptoms and those who had experienced their first hospitalizations at adolescence or early adulthood. The depressed patients as a group did not display significantly poorer understanding. Those older at first mental-hospital admission and those with more severe depressive symptoms were at greater risk, however.

Applebaum and Grisso's study underscores the importance of examining the issue of informed consent closely and with recognition of the individual differences within the mentally disordered population as a whole. As they note, "...the recent trend in mental health law has been to treat mentally ill persons no differently than their non-mentally-ill counterparts.... . This trend has been evident especially with regard to decisions about treatment" (p. 378). Although this approach is a welcome change from the time when the mentally disordered were relegated to second-class status, it is critical that researchers continue in their efforts to differentiate the individuals whose decisionmaking competency has been abrogated by their disorder.

Even when a mentally disordered person cannot make a rational decision about medication, we should not assume that decisions to medicate should be made without oversight. Although psychoactive drug treatment today has made life more tolerable for many people, there are special concerns associated with administering it to individuals who are in an institution or whose freedom in the community is contingent upon taking it. Public mental institutions, primarily because their residents tend to come from disadvantaged and powerless groups in society, are especially likely to take the path of least resistance in treating patients (Brooks, 1986). Psychoactive medication, which makes patients easier to control, is just such a path. In community settings, the mentally disordered who experience adverse side effects find themselves in a no-win situation, because, by refusing to take the drugs, they risk reinstitutionalization. Cycles of taking and refusing to take drugs are not uncommon.

There is some indication that legal challenges to drug treatment have had a positive effect in some jurisdictions (Brooks, 1986). Specifically, hospitals and community mental-health centers have been alerted to the need to monitor carefully the side effects, make decisions on a case-by-case basis, and avoid policies which encourage blanket administration of psychoactive drugs to all patients. This is a step in the right direction, but it must be accompanied by continued skepticism about the use of medication as a panacea.

Summary and Conclusions

A historical overview of involuntary civil commitment in the United States suggests that the most outrageous abuses of the past have disappeared. No longer is it common for patients to be placed in public mental institutions without regard to their constitutional rights or to be kept there indefinitely under unsanitary, physically deteriorating conditions. Moreover, libertarian statutes requiring that candidates for civil commitment be proven dangerous to others or to themselves have replaced statutes based on a *parens patriae* approach, which required only that medical doctors certify mental illness. Gravely disabled statutes, which appear to be the predominant grounds for committing and re-committing persons today, are more likely to be based on a *parens patriae* philosophy. Even these laws, however, require some evidence that the person is both mentally disordered and a threat to his or her own safety.

Reviews of the civil commitment literature indicate, however, that the spirit of the more restrictive commitment statutes is being violated. Civil commitment proceedings in many jurisdictions are perfunctory and non-adversarial and continue to give deference to mental-health practitioners. Predictions of dangerousness are particularly troublesome. Empirical research demonstrates that the mentally disordered are rarely as dangerous as they are predicted to be (Hiday, 1988).

Cursory commitment proceedings will probably continue to be the norm, however. As Paul Applebaum (1992) has suggested, neither the law nor the mental-health system seems truly committed to a rights-oriented civil commitment process. Lawyers often believe commitment is in the best interest of their clients, and mental-health practitioners believe the law does not recognize the treatment needs of the mentally disordered. Furthermore, the lack of community alternatives encourage decisions to hospitalize, even for a shortened period of time.

The dominant way of treating the mentally disordered in both public mental institutions and the community is through medication, particularly psychoactive drugs. Proponents of such drug treatment assert it has shortened the length of hospital stays and has stabilized the behavior of the mentally disordered. Opponents assert the side effects of drug treatment are too often overlooked, and that such treatment is used as a panacea, without giving careful consideration to the root causes of mental disorder.

The law has assumed, and continues to assume, that many mentally disordered persons are not competent to make decisions in their own best interests. Thus, both hospitalization and unwanted medication may be foisted upon them. Whereas courts are increasingly sympathetic to the rights of *competent* individuals to refuse treatment, the mentally disordered tend to be omitted from this category. Additionally, the issue of questionable competency has even extended to voluntary civil commitment, as we saw in the Supreme Court's *Zinermon* decision.

The psychology of free will suggests that the perception that one has control over one's destiny is critical to the recovery process for those who are mentally disordered. The therapeutic jurisprudence model of mental-health law recognizes this by encouraging mental-health practitioners to strive to make the mentally disordered partners in their own treatment. Until such a perspective gains more favor among mental-health practitioners, it is unlikely that civil commitment will be an effective, long-term solution to the problems of the mentally disordered.

In a cogent analysis of mental-health law, John Petrila (1992) implores us to consider the possible relationships between need for mental health services and social problems such as the lack of employment opportunities and adequate housing. Virginia Hiday (1988) makes a similar point when she argues that libertarian civil commitment statutes cannot be blamed for the increase in mentally disordered individuals on the streets. Neither drug treatment nor psychotherapy should replace needed social changes which would preclude the onset of mental disorder altogether in a significant number of individuals.

Questions to Ponder

1. The *parens patriae* doctrine is applied in both civil commitment and juvenile proceedings. How, if at all, are mentally disordered adults similar to children and adolescents? Is *parens patriae* a humanistic concept? Can it coexist with due process?

2. How should society respond to the plight of mentally disordered individuals on our streets and in our jails?

3. Explain the difference between the "dangerousness" and "grave disability" standards in involuntary civil commitment. Is one more acceptable than the other?

4. Do you agree with Applebaum that neither the justice system nor the mental health system is truly committed to the goals of civil commitment? What *are* the goals of civil commitment?

5. How does the concept of therapeutic jurisprudence introduced in Chapter 1 apply to the material in this chapter?

THE PSYCHOLOGY OF THE JURY: PROCEDURAL CONSIDERATIONS

"T HERE IS NOTHING ELSE QUITE LIKE THEM IN OUR SOCIETY: A group of strangers brought together and required to sit in silence and listen to different versions of a story in which they have no personal interest, and who are locked inside a room where they must stay while they try to sort out what they believe to be the truth from all they have heard" (Guinther, 1988, p. xiii.) The jury is one of the most powerful components in the American system of justice, with authority to take away or bestow freedoms or to settle disputes and impose financial liability. It is one of the few channels through which ordinary citizens can impose on society their own standards or biases concerning moral or social behavior. Although judges are the final decisionmakers, only rarely will they overrule a jury's decision. The jury's responsibility is sobering, therefore, and there is good evidence that most citizen-jurors take their role in the judicial process seriously.

The Sixth Amendment to the U. S. Constitution guarantees the right to a jury trial in *criminal* cases whenever the potential penalty for the offense is greater than six months' imprisonment or a \$500 fine. The Sixth Amendment also guarantees that the accused shall have the right to a speedy public trial by an impartial jury in the jurisdiction where the alleged crime was committed. The Seventh Amendment guarantees a jury in all *civil* cases where monetary damages are sought, usually above \$500. Through the Fourteenth Amendment, individual states are required to honor the Sixth Amendment guarantee of a trial by jury. The Seventh Amendment has not been applied to the states, but most guarantee trial by jury in their own constitutions.

In both criminal and civil cases, defendants may waive the right to a trial by jury and take their chances with a judge, who serves both as a fact finder and determiner of the issues of law. A trial by a judge rather than jury is called a **bench trial**. Approximately one-third of all criminal trials are bench trials (U. S. Department of Justice, 1988).

Despite the constitutional guarantees for all defendants, participants in the judicial system are under social, political, and economic pressure to settle a case before it gets to the trial stage. Trials, especially by jury, are time consuming, expensive, and unpredictable, and their unpredictability often prompts even the most experienced attorneys to avoid them if possible. Thus, each case is submitted to a filtering process, replete with discretionary maneuvers which may include plea bargaining, dismissal of charges by the prosecutor or the court, and a mutually agreeable settlement by the parties in a civil suit. In jurisdictions where courts are especially overburdened, participants are encouraged to pursue alternative dispute resolution, or mediation, before approaching the court. The vast majority of criminal cases are disposed of through plea bargaining or plea negotiation, a procedure in which the defendant pleads guilty to a lesser charge, usually in exchange for a lighter sentence (Alschuler, 1979; Cole, 1992; Heumann, 1978). Most

174

CHAPTER
SEVEN:
THE
PSYCHOLOGY
OF THE
JURY:
PROCEDURAL
CONSIDERATIONS

civil cases today also are settled or dismissed before they make the tedious journey through the entire judicial sequence.

When cases do proceed to the trial stage, juries are used in about half of the criminal and civil cases in federal district courts and in fewer than 10 percent of cases in state trial courts (Vago, 1991). In general, criminal cases are the major producers of jury trials (Jacob, 1972), perhaps because there is a strong tradition in favor of being judged by a jury of one's peers when one is prosecuted for a criminal offense. The technical complexity inherent in many civil matters also accounts for some of the discrepancy, however. The judiciary discourages the use of juries in many civil cases because the litigation revolves around issues that are believed too complicated for the average person to comprehend (e.g., engineering patents, complex scientific data, or trade secrets). Sometimes, rather than asking jurors to decide for or against the defendant, a judge seeks a **special verdict**. The jury is asked to answer specific questions of fact, and the judge makes a final decision based on the jury's responses. With the exception of personal injury cases, however, civil cases are usually tried before a judge, if tried at all. More often, they are settled before the trial stage. For the above reasons, most of the discussion in this and the following chapter will relate to juries in criminal cases.

Psychology's interest in jury behavior centers around questions like these:

- Does the jury render verdicts based upon evidence presented in the courtroom, irrespective of the characteristics of the attorneys, the litigants, witnesses, or the jurors involved? Or do these extra-evidentiary factors play a significant role in the decisionmaking process?

- Are jury decisions based on whim, sympathy, or prejudice, or are they based on rational, logical foundations?

- Are there procedures or variables that help predict verdicts prior to the trial?

- Can jurors be significantly influenced by events prior to the trial, such as extensive pretrial publicity?

- How do members of the jury influence one another, both during the trial itself and during the deliberation process?

Answers to these questions are elusive, partly because empirical investigations of jury behavior are hampered by legal restrictions on access to jurors and the jury process. Deliberations are shrouded in secrecy, and the courts have traditionally resisted any infringement upon the jurors' privacy. Therefore, psychologists and other social and behavioral scientists have resorted to **simulation research**, where some segment of the jury selection or trial process is acted out in a way that approximates the real process, or where subjects read or listen to portions of trial transcripts or tapes. The groups of "jurors" in these studies, who are most often college students, are called **mock juries**. Findings from simulation research must be interpreted in a very guarded manner, however, as will be explained later in the chapter.

Experimentation through simulation is only one way psychology can help us understand jury behavior. Psychological theories and information on group decisionmaking, attitude change, attraction, and persuasion, although not directly related to legal matters, can shed light on events that transpire in the courtroom or in the privacy of the jury deliberation chamber. Applying psychological concepts in this manner is a good example of the psychology *and* law relationship. This chapter will first give attention to procedural and structural features of the jury and discuss what psychological research has uncovered about both. Then we will focus on juror comprehension of complex instructions. In the next chapter, the jury-decisionmaking process will be discussed.

Jury Selection

Jury composition is influenced at two stages of selection, **venire** and **voir dire**. In the first stage, the *venire* (which is part of a Latin phrase meaning "you should cause to come"), a pool of prospective jurors is drawn from an eligible population presumed to be representative of a local geographical area. Courts have consistently ruled that jury pools must represent a cross section of the community or general population. Usually, the prospective jurors are selected from voting or driver's license lists by a clerk of courts. In a few jurisdictions, a "key person" system is used: Outstanding or model citizens are asked to submit names of individuals they think would be good jurors. It has been suggested that all three of these ways of accomplishing the *venire*—voting lists, license lists, and the key person approach—are imperfect, if not plagued by biases and prejudices (Guinther, 1988). Furthermore, even when the system affords random representation, it has traditionally not been difficult to be excused from jury duty. Occupational groups such as teachers, police officers, attorneys, elected officials, firefighters, and sole proprietors of small businesses are exempted from jury duty in many jurisdictions. Increasingly, however, states are beginning to limit the exemptions.

Common sense would seem to suggest that the most impartial juries are those demographically representative of the community at large. This logic may be flawed, however. Gordon Bermant and John Shapard (1981, p. 89) indicate that "achieving demographical representativeness for any or all recognizable groups will not automatically, or even necessarily, move us closer to the major goal of eliminating bias." Moreover, a jury representative of the community may be different from, and perhaps more biased than, a jury of one's peers (Golash, 1992). In a 1990 case, *Holland v. Illinois*, the U. S. Supreme Court ruled that impartiality, rather than representation of a particular group, was the essential guarantee of the Sixth Amendment. Nonetheless, the Court has emphasized that jury composition should reflect the community, particularly in race, gender, and to a lesser extent economic status (Golash, 1992).

Persons on the *venire* are potential jurors for a given period and are eligible to be called into the next stage of jury selection, the *voir dire* (which is old French for "to speak the truth"). This process allows the judge and attorneys to question the prospective jurors and determine their fitness for duty. During *voir dire*, attorneys can apply their own common-sense hypotheses about people in an attempt to constitute a jury sympathetic to their clients. It is at this juncture also that findings from the psychological research are likely to be applied.

The prosecution and the defense (in civil cases, the plaintiff and the defendant) each have two options for challenging the impanelment of a prospective juror: **peremptory challenges** and **challenges for cause**. The peremptory option lets a lawyer request the removal of a prospective juror without giving reason. "The essential nature of the peremptory challenge is that it is one exercised without a reason stated, without inquiry and without the court's control.... The peremptory permits rejection for a real or imagined practicality that is less easily designated or demonstrable" (*Swain v. Alabama*, 1964, p. 220). It should be noted that appellate courts, including the U. S. Supreme Court, are often asked to rule on both peremptory challenges and challenges for cause. In *Batson v. Kentucky* (1986), for example, the Court ruled that prosecutors could not use the peremptory challenge to exclude blacks from juries trying black defendants without offering an explanation not based on race. *Defense* lawyers are also forbidden to exercise peremptories on racial grounds, however.

The number of peremptory challenges allowed an attorney is restricted by statute or by the presiding judge, who sets the rule in a pretrial conference. In some jurisdictions, the defense in a criminal trial may be allowed more peremptory challenges than the prosecution. For example,

176

CHAPTER
SEVEN:
THE
PSYCHOLOGY
OF THE
JURY:
PROCEDURAL
CONSIDERATIONS

in a federal criminal trial where the final jury size is twelve, the prosecution has six peremptories and the defense has ten. On the other hand, in a federal civil trial where the jury size is six, each side has three peremptories. The defense in a criminal trial is often allowed extra peremptories because it is recognized that defendants are at risk of losing their freedom.

A challenge for cause is exercised whenever it can be demonstrated that a would-be juror does not satisfy the statutory requirements for jury service (e.g., age, residence, occupational requirements), or when it can be shown that the prospective juror is so biased or prejudiced that he or she is not likely to render an impartial verdict based only on the law and on evidence presented at the trial. The presumed bias may be either for or against the defendant. Challenges for cause based on bias may be subdivided into those claiming a specific bias and those claiming nonspecific bias (Bermant & Shapard, 1981). A nonspecific bias may be expected due to the fact that a prospective juror is a member of some group or class similar to that of the plaintiff or defendant. If a writer is suing her publisher, for example, the publisher's attorney may want to exclude another writer from the jury. A specific bias may be assumed where the prospective juror has a blood relationship or a tie through marriage to one of the parties or has economic interests linked to the case.

The idealized purpose of *voir dire* is to eliminate jurors whose biases may interfere with a fair consideration of the evidence presented at the trial. Bermant and Shapard (1981) refer to this as the "probative purpose" of *voir dire*, probative in that the lawyer or the judge is searching for information about the prospective juror. However, lawyers also use *voir dire* to influence the jury, a strategy known as the "didactic purpose." There is some evidence that 80 percent of *voir dire* time is used to persuade the jury panel to be sympathetic to lawyers' clients (Broader, 1965), although a later study indicates that the percentage is closer to 40 (Balch, Griffiths, Hall & Winfree, 1976).

In 1977 the Federal Judicial Center gathered information about current *voir dire* practices as seen by federal district judges (Bermant, 1977). Completed questionnaires from 365 active federal judges and 55 senior judges were used in the analysis. Approximately 70 percent of the judges said they conducted the *voir dire* examinations themselves in both civil and criminal trials, although they would accept additional questions suggested by counsel. Between 1 and 2 percent said they conducted the *voir dire* completely by themselves, rarely seeking or accepting additional counsel from attorneys. Bermant (1977) concluded from earlier data that federal judges have increasingly taken over the *voir dire*, leaving little room for lawyer participation.

About 75 percent of the judges stated that insuring an impartial jury was the primary purpose of the examination. Eighty percent felt that there was considerable variation among lawyers in skill at conducting the *voir dire*. These data contrast with the opinions of judges about the skills of lawyers during trials. Judges have stated in other surveys that in about 75 percent of the cases they have heard, the lawyers were about equal in skill (Kalven & Zeisel, 1966; Partridge & Bermant, 1978). This difference is difficult to reconcile, but it does suggest that although judges believe lawyers vary widely in *voir dire* skills, they do not see such variety in the overall quality of advocacy during the trial process.

Another area of interest concerning *voir dire* centers around methods by which juror challenges are exercised and evaluated. There are two major protocols (Bermant & Shapard, 1981). One is the **struck jury method**, whereby the judge rules on all challenges for cause before the parties claim any peremptories. In a second method, called **sequential**, the lawyers exercise all challenges to a specific juror without knowing the characteristics of any subsequent juror to be interviewed. This method might allow a challenged juror to be replaced by someone even more objectionable. Preliminary research using mathematical models has shown that the struck jury method may be superior to the sequential method in eliminating bias (Bermant & Shapard, 1981), but much more research is needed before firm conclusions can be offered.

The iconoclastic Clarence Darrow swayed juries and stirred the imaginations of budding attorneys with his courtroom antics and his rousing summations. His modern television counterparts keep viewers and television jurors alike entertained with legal cunning and acerbic wit. One need only tune in to Court TV or to local news coverage of a criminal trial to understand that these legal models have few counterparts in American courtrooms. In fact, if the well-respected Kalven-Zeisel project (1966) accurately captures courtroom dynamics, the total impact lawyers have on the trial process is minimal.

Judges surveyed by Kalven and Zeisel believed that prosecution and defense lawyers were equivalent in both skill and impact in slightly more than three-quarters of the 3,567 criminal cases they had heard. Even superior performance by one or the other lawyer, however, did not necessarily seem to affect the jury's decision. In general, according to the judges, the nature of the case and the evidence presented, not the advocacy skills or personalities of the lawyers, accounted for the final verdict.

Nevertheless, it would be unwise to overlook the immense power held by attorneys in the courtroom, particularly when the evidence is ambiguous or of poor quality. Within broad limits, attorneys are able to direct and redirect testimony, making it appear credible or questionable. Furthermore, when two opposing lawyers *are* ill-matched in ability and/or personal charm, the effect of the stronger attorney on the jury is likely to be considerable. Even if lawyers have this kind of impact only within a narrow range of cases, their actions may still affect thousands of defendants.

Assuming a reasonable parity of skill and reasonably credible evidence, however, "hard sells" and strong persuasive appeals are likely to prove counterproductive. Not only does this approach damage the credibility of the communicator, it also may precipitate psychological **reactance** (Brehm, 1966, 1972). When individuals perceive that their freedom of choice is being threatened, or their decisions manipulated, they become "aroused," motivated to reassert their autonomy. Under these conditions, people often make decisions they perceive as contrary to the desires of the manipulator (Myers, 1993). A lawyer who implies, for example, that jurors have no choice other than to absolve his or her client may soon learn that the jurors do indeed have an alternative. Although the media reports anecdotal accounts of individual lawyers influencing jury decision-making by means of their dazzling arguments, research to support this happening on a widespread basis is not available.

And again, trials are often avenues of last resort, particularly in civil cases. They occur only when the attorneys have met an impasse in negotiations and the parties cannot agree on a settlement. Even in criminal cases a trial may be seen as the least desirable option. Unfortunately, even a defendant who is not guilty of the crime charged may prefer, or be persuaded, to plead guilty and avoid the expense and uncertainty of a trial. There is little doubt, therefore, that most of what attorneys do on behalf of their clients in both criminal and civil cases is bargain and negotiate. Their ability to persuade—even to persuade their own clients—is more likely to be tested in the pretrial arena than during the trial itself.

SCIENTIFIC JURY SELECTION

The possibility that individual juror personality, group status, or demographic characteristics might affect final verdicts has led some attorneys to experiment with new techniques for the *voir dire*. Lawyers have always used their assumptions about human nature to help them select juries, of course. For example, if one's client is a self-made businessperson with conservative values,

178

CHAPTER
SEVEN:
THE
PSYCHOLOGY
OF THE
JURY:
PROCEDURAL
CONSIDERATIONS

(even though he "slipped" and poisoned his business partner), one does not want left-leaning political activists on the jury. Sometimes, enterprising lawyers have used more than assumptions to choose jurors, however. At a 1981 meeting of the American Trial Lawyers Association, attorneys were advised to hang around the favorite bars of potential jurors, quizzing their friends whose tongues were loosened by liquor.

The traditional hunches, guesses, and amateur (sometimes professional) detective work are now being supplemented by the time-consuming and elaborate procedures of social scientists in the employ of attorneys. The process, alternately called **scientific jury selection** (Saks & Hastie, 1978) or **systematic jury selection** (Kairys, Schulman & Harring, 1975), was launched in the early 1970s, when the defense in the Harrisburg Seven conspiracy trial hired a group of psychologists and other social scientists to help them choose jurors who would be most sympathetic to their clients.

The defense reasoning was understandable. These defendants were antiwar activists who were accused of sabotaging a government installation. The conservative community in which the trial was being held, coupled with the money the state was funneling into the prosecution, made acquittal unlikely. The social scientists gathered background and demographic information on each potential juror, as well as measures of attitudes, interest patterns, and possible personality characteristics. All of the information was obtained indirectly, since the researchers could not contact members of the *venire* or the jury itself. After the trial, which acquitted the alleged co-conspirators, the defense publicly credited its victory in large part to the extensive help of the social scientists (Schulman et al., 1973). Psychologists were involved in the selection process of other juries during this time as well. In 1972, a group of five psychologists helped defense attorneys select a jury in the trial of Angela Davis, another political activist charged with murder, kidnapping, and conspiracy. She was acquitted. Joan Little, a jail detainee who killed a guard who had sexually assaulted her and who was threatening to do so again, was also helped by a scientific jury-selection process.

Since then, a growing number of sociologists and psychologists have been refining and expanding scientific jury selection techniques. Along with attitude and behavioral scales, elaborate statistical procedures and mathematical probability formulae are being applied to provide attorneys with an educated guess about whether a given individual will be the juror they want for their client. Sometimes, even after a jury is seated, the behavioral scientists continue to help attorneys by offering opinions regarding the nonverbal behavior of witnesses or jurors during the trial.

Do behavioral scientists belong in the courtroom in this advisory role? How helpful are their suggestions regarding the *voir dire* procedure? Opinions and findings regarding these questions vary (Suggs & Sales, 1978). Some critics call scientific jury selection little more than "social science jury stacking" (Penrod & Cutler, 1987). There is some evidence that scientific jury selection is slightly superior to random selection (Padawer-Singer, Singer & Singer, 1974) or even to the traditional selection methods used by attorneys (Zeisel & Diamond, 1978). Overall, however, we must remember that few juror characteristics have been found to predict with any consistency the outcome of the trial. One exception, to be discussed shortly, is in criminal cases in which the death penalty is at issue. In general, however, the persuasiveness and nature of the evidence strongly outweigh any personality or specific characteristics of individual jurors. When the evidence is ambiguous or poorly presented, however, the characteristics of the jurors might carry greater weight in the decisionmaking process, although it appears that group dynamics, rather than individual differences, plays the more significant role.

The weight that jurors give to evidence is not surprising if we remember that most people are not familiar with the judicial process and, in fact, are awed by it. Thus jurors tend to be more strongly influenced by the judicial context than by their own personality and attitudes. Within the judicial context, "jurors adopt a role of 'fairness' and 'objectivity' which may be as extreme as they ever have had or will have in their lives" (Saks & Hastie, 1978, p. 70). The jury box and the courtroom itself may exert powerful situational pressures that mitigate the individual differences of the jurors. In the death-penalty context, however, the situation seems to be quite different.

DEATH-QUALIFIED JURIES

Jury research on the death penalty has also proliferated since the 1970s. During that decade, the U. S. Supreme Court first declared the death penalty, as it was then being applied, cruel and unusual punishment in violation of the Eighth Amendment (*Furman v. Georgia*, 1972). Four years later, the Court approved the death penalty if state statutes were crafted to prevent arbitrary imposition (*Gregg v. Georgia*, 1976). Most death penalty states have responded to the Court's requirements by providing for a two-phase trial process: the guilt phase and the penalty phase. A jury first must decide whether the defendant is guilty beyond a reasonable doubt. Then, in a separate proceeding, careful deliberation must be given to whether the death penalty should be imposed. In a very few death penalty states, trial judges rather than juries set the penalty.

The process of deciding whether capital punishment should be imposed takes one of two forms (Costanzo & Costanzo, 1992). In the vast majority of states, jurors are instructed to consider and weigh **aggravating** and **mitigating circumstances** surrounding both crime and offender. An example of aggravating circumstances is a particularly heinous method of carrying out the crime, such as evidence that the victim was slowly tortured. Mitigating factors might include a childhood marred by extensive physical abuse or evidence of a mental disability which had not been sufficient to acquit the defendant.

The second and less common approach asks the jury to address specific questions. Texas, for example, requires that jurors ask: (1) whether the individual acted deliberately and with expectation that death would result; (2) whether there is a probability that the defendant will be a continual danger to society; and (3) whether the individual reacted in an unreasonable manner to the actions of the victim (in other words, whether the attack was unprovoked). In *Penry v. Lynaugh* (1989), the U. S. Supreme Court ruled that Texas's scheme did not encourage the jury to consider mitigating circumstances, and the Court emphasized that this must be done. Penry, convicted of murder, was a mentally retarded offender who had been denied the opportunity to introduce evidence of this retardation at sentencing. The Supreme Court overturned his death sentence and sent the case back to Texas for resentencing that took into consideration his retardation as a possible mitigating circumstances. The process did not help Penry, however, since he was resentenced to death.

It is important to note that the Supreme Court has allowed prosecutors and judges to remove during the *voir dire* jurors who are not "death-qualified." In the landmark case *Witherspoon v. Illinois* (1968), the Supreme Court ruled that prospective jurors could be eliminated if they made it unmistakably clear that, because of their philosophical opposition to the death penalty, they could not make an impartial decision as to a defendant's guilt (guilt nullifiers) or sentence an offender to death (penalty nullifiers). It is estimated that this death-qualification process excludes between 10 and 17 percent of eligible jurors (Fitzgerald & Ellsworth, 1984). Later, the Court broadened the pool of potential "excludables" by allowing trial judges the discretion to exclude a juror if the judge believed the juror's views would prevent or substantially impair the performance of the juror's duties (*Wainwright v. Witt*, 1985). In other words, even if a prospective juror says he or she is against the death penalty but could still find a defendant guilty in a capital case, a judge

180

CHAPTER
SEVEN:
THE
PSYCHOLOGY
OF THE
JURY:
PROCEDURAL
CONSIDERATIONS

may believe otherwise and the prospective juror could be excluded. In 1988, the Court gave *defense* lawyers the right to remove for cause a juror who would automatically vote for the death penalty upon conviction (*Ross v. Oklahoma*).

The nature of the death penalty suggests that any pertinent research should be extremely critical. As the Supreme Court has noted in numerous decisions, "…execution is the most irremediable and unfathomable of penalties;…death is different" (*Ford v. Wainwright*, 1985, p. 411). In this area of the law, however, the U. S. Supreme Court has been remarkably inattentive to research findings (Acker, 1990). Studies to date have been conducted in two broad areas: juror comprehension of instructions and the effects of the death-qualification process on the outcome of the case. Since juror comprehension issues will be covered in the jury dynamics section of this chapter, we turn our attention now to the death-qualification process.

Currently, the predominant line of jury research related to the death penalty focuses on **death-qualified jurors**. A number of studies have compared death-qualified jurors to excludable jurors and suggest that capital defendants may be at a disadvantage because of the death-qualification process (Bohm, 1991; Haney, 1984; Heilbrun, 1987). It is questionable, for example, whether death-qualified jurors are representative of the general population. Fitzgerald and Ellsworth (1984) found that the death-qualification process significantly excludes more blacks than whites, more females than males, more lower income people (below $15,000) than higher income people, and more Democrats than Republicans. Death-qualified jurors also have been found to favor the prosecution, be conviction prone (Thompson, Cowan & Ellsworth, 1984; Thompson, Cowan, Ellsworth & Harrington, 1984), and to be less receptive to mitigating circumstances than excludables (Luginbuhl & Middendorf, 1988). It should be noted, though, that a recent study challenges this evidence. Elliott and Robinson (1991) found that death penalty attitudes did not significantly affect verdicts.

Personality characteristics, such as authoritarianism (Middendorf & Luginbuhl, 1981; Moran & Comfort, 1986) and a just-world orientation (Lerner, 1980; Rubin & Peplau, 1975), also have been associated more with death-qualified jurors than with excludables. Finally, death-qualified jurors are apparently less trustful of psychological and psychiatric testimony (Williams & McShane, 1991) and less likely to consider mental disorder a mitigating factor (Ellsworth, Bukaty, Cowan & Thompson, 1984; Luginbuhl, 1988; Williams & McShane, 1991). In an interesting twist, Haney (1984) has demonstrated that the *voir dire* process itself biases the jury against the defendant, because jurors are asked to imagine the penalty phase long before the defendant has been convicted.

In *Lockhart v. McCree* (1986), the Supreme Court diminished the importance of much of the previously described research evidence, provoking extensive criticism from social scientists (Thompson, 1989). McCree had buttressed his claim that he had not received a fair trial with briefs citing research findings that death qualification systematically produces conviction-prone juries. The Court found that evidence unpersuasive, suggesting that McCree would have to show that the jury in his own case was biased. The Court took much the same approach in another death-penalty decision the following year (*McCleskey v. Kemp*, 1987), when it rejected the argument that the death penalty as applied in Georgia was administered in a racially biased manner. Like McCree, McCleskey had ample research data to support his claim; but like McCree, McCleskey was told he would have to prove discrimination in his own case.

In light of those decisions and the likelihood that both the death penalty itself and the death-qualification process will not soon disappear, some researchers propose alternative methods of evaluating prospective jurors in death-penalty cases. Cox and Tanford (1989), for example, offer **QUEST** (Qualification by Example Selection Test). QUEST is a questionnaire approach presumably more private, standardized, and objective than the traditional *voir dire* process. The juror being questioned is also less likely to be influenced by the answers of other prospective jurors or the tones of voice of lawyers.

Cox and Tanford believe that some jurors who are initially deemed excludable may be prompted to reconsider their position and, consequently, be allowed to serve. Such jurors, they argue, would ultimately be more representative and less biased than the death-qualified jurors obtained under the present *voir dire* system.

In the Cox and Tanford study, college students serving as subjects were first asked a "Witherspoon question" embedded in a general attitudinal questionnaire; they also were administered a variety of tests including Rotter's Internal/External Scale, a tolerance-for-ambiguity scale, and a crime-control/due-process scale. In a second session, the students were administered QUEST, which gives concrete descriptions of increasingly vivid, brutal crimes, and were again queried on death-penalty attitudes. By means of this process, Cox and Tanford uncovered "rehabilitated excludables." These were students who, after the session with QUEST, were willing to reconsider their original opinions against the death-penalty. The rehabilitated group were also less punitive, more tolerant of ambiguity, and less crime-control oriented than the original death-qualified group. Cox and Tanford acknowledge that more extensive research is needed on the effects of QUEST and whether it generalizes to older adult populations. Furthermore, the new system would require a radical change in the traditional jury selection process, something not easily accomplished in law.

Despite setbacks in the effective integration of death-penalty jury research with the law, continuing work in this area is critical. Costanza and Costanza (1992) offer an excellent research agenda for the future, replete with hypotheses in four areas: 1) the effects of guiding juror discretion; 2) comparisons of juries that vote for life with those that vote for death; 3) the relationship between guilt and penalty phases; and 4) models of decisionmaking in the penalty phase.

According to Costanza and Costanza (p. 188), however, jury simulation studies in the death-penalty context, particularly with respect to the penalty phase, are unlikely to be fruitful:

> …it is difficult to recreate the social psychological conditions of an actual penalty phase: the responsibility of the decision, the drama of the courtroom proceedings, the length of time actual proceedings require, and the dynamics already present in a group that has experienced both guilt and penalty proceedings as well as the guilt phase deliberation.

Jury Structure and Process

Whether by historical accident or some unknown logic, the traditional jury in Great Britain, the United States, and Canada has consisted of twelve persons who must come to an unanimous decision. Winick (1979) suggests that the English resistance to the decimal system and affinity for the number twelve (e.g., twelve pennies in a shilling) account for the system, which originated in fourteenth century England (Saks, 1977). In 1966, England began to require that only ten out of twelve jurors agree on a verdict (Saks, 1977), and soon after that, lawyers in the United States also began to challenge the traditional system. As a result, **decision rule,** which refers to the proportion of the total number of jurors required to reach a verdict, is no longer always unanimous, since some jurisdictions now allow agreement among fewer individuals (*majority* or *quorum* rule). Nor is the twelve-person jury now universal.

Beginning in the late 1960s and early 1970s, the U. S. Supreme Court permitted states and federal courts to experiment with both jury size and decision rules, in the interest of economy and efficiency.

182

CHAPTER
SEVEN:
THE
PSYCHOLOGY
OF THE
JURY:
PROCEDURAL
CONSIDERATIONS

Twelve-person juries are expensive and time consuming. The experimentation, however, has resulted in considerable controversy over the merits of changing the traditional jury structure and process.

JURY SIZE

In two landmark decisions, *Williams v. Florida* (1970), which dealt with state criminal trials, and *Colgrove v. Battin* (1973), dealing with federal civil trials, the Court claimed that reduction in jury size would not alter trial results significantly. In capital cases, however, twelve-person juries are required. Otherwise, a six-person jury does not violate a person's constitutional right as laid down by the Sixth Amendment, since that amendment mandates a jury "only of sufficient size to promote group deliberation, to insulate members from outside intimidation, and to provide a representative cross-section of the community" (*Williams v. Florida*, 1970, p. 100).

Although the Justices cited social and behavioral research to support their assertions, immediate responses decrying the logic of the two decisions erupted from some social and behavioral science representatives, who were concerned about the Court's misguided and inappropriate use of empirical data (e.g., Walbert, 1971; Zeisel, 1971, 1974; Saks, 1974, 1977). One statement in *Colgrove* was especially troublesome. The Court said that "four very recent studies have provided convincing empirical evidence of the correctness of the *Williams* conclusion that 'there is no discernible difference between the results reached by the two different sized juries'" (*Colgrove v. Battin*, 1973, fn. 15, p. 11). Most of the "experiments" cited by the Court were not experiments or empirical evidence at all, but the common-sense observations and opinions of individuals with experience in the judicial system. The experiments which the Justices relied upon were permeated with critical methodological flaws to the point of producing poor—or at best unconvincing—scientific evidence. In addition, Saks (1974) commented that some of the studies reported in *Colgrove* actually reported data *opposite* to the interpretation made by the Court.

In *Ballew v. Georgia* (1978), the Supreme Court once again broached the jury-size issue, this time drawing a line at the *minimum* number of jurors to be allowed. Georgia statutes permitted a five-person jury to decide a criminal case, and the petitioner, tried on an obscenity charge, claimed that this five-person-jury law deprived him of due-process rights. Since the Court had previously avoided establishing a constitutional minimum, the Justices apparently decided that a more specific ruling was necessary to prevent possible erosion of the jury system.

Arguing that a minimum jury size must be established, the opinion written by Justice Blackmun cited social and psychological research supporting the position that anything below six members violated the Sixth and Fourteenth Amendments. This time, the Court used the available research accurately and carefully, and the Justices somewhat improved their reputation in the eyes of the research community (see Box 7.1).

Common sense and information gleaned from the few empirical studies of jury size tell us that there are advantages and disadvantages to both small and large juries. Small groups allow more active participation from all members, because individuals have greater opportunity to speak, and because people are usually less inhibited in expressing their opinions in a small-group discussion. However, it has also been shown that small groups, because they place greater importance on group balance, sometimes inhibit expressions of disagreement among participants (Slater, 1958; Bales & Borgatta, 1955).

Larger groups have a number of advantages that are important to note if jury size is being considered. Large groups tend to provide the greater variety of skills and knowledge that may be necessary to arrive at a decision in a complex issue. Large juries appear to be better at remembering

■ 7.1: BALLEW v. GEORGIA

EIGHT YEARS BEFORE THE U.S. SUPREME COURT HEARD this case, in *Williams v. Florida*, it had been established that a jury of six members was not unconstitutional in non-capital cases. Two years later, in *Johnson v. Louisiana*, the Justices referred to a "slippery slope" of decreasing jury size but did not indicate when this slope would become too steep. Now, in *Ballew*, they were ready to be more specific. "We face now, however, the two-fold question whether a further reduction in the size of the state criminal trial jury does make the grade too dangerous, that is, whether it inhibits the functioning of the jury as an institution to a significant degree, and, if so, whether any state interest counterbalances and justifies the disruption so as to preserve its constitutionality."

The opinion written by Justice Blackmun made extensive use of empirical research to address and answer several concerns, including the following:

First, recent empirical data suggest that progressively smaller juries are less likely to foster effective group deliberation. At some point, this decline leads to inaccurate fact-finding and incorrect application of the common sense of the community to the facts. Generally, a positive correlation exists between group size and the quality of both group performance and group productivity....

Second, the data now raise doubts about the accuracy of the results achieved by smaller and smaller panels. Statistical studies suggest that the risk of convicting an innocent person (Type I error) rises as the size of the jury diminishes. Because the risk of not convicting a guilty person (Type II error) increases with the size of the panel, an optimal jury size can be selected as a function of the interaction between the two risks....

Third, the data suggest that the verdicts of jury deliberation in criminal cases will vary as juries become smaller, and that the variance amounts to an imbalance to the detriment of one side, the defense....

Fourth...the presence of minority viewpoint as juries decrease in size foretells problems not only for jury decisionmaking, but also for the representation of minority groups in the community. The Court repeatedly has held that meaningful community participation cannot be attained with the exclusion of minorities or other identifiable groups from jury service....

The Justices also referred to methodological problems in some studies that claimed no differences in the decisions of juries of varying sizes. Noting that there were a substantial number of individual cases which were significantly affected by jury size, Blackmun concluded that aggregate data, or averages, "masked significant case-by-case differences that must be considered when evaluating jury function and performance."

While we adhere to, and reaffirm our holding in *Williams v. Florida,* these studies, most of which have been made since *Williams* was decided in 1970, lead us to conclude that the purpose and functioning of the jury in a criminal trial is seriously impaired, and to a constitutional degree, by a reduction in size to below six members. We readily admit that we do not pretend to discern a clear line between six members and five. But the assembled data raise substantial doubt about the reliability and appropriate representation of panels smaller than six. Because of the fundamental importance of the jury trial to the American system of criminal justice, any further reduction that promotes inaccurate and possibly biased decisionmaking, that causes untoward differences in verdicts, and that prevents juries from truly representing their communities, attains constitutional significance. ■

---

testimony given during the trial, although small juries have been shown to be better at recalling the arguments presented (Saks, 1977). Also, as jury size increases, a more representative cross section of the community is obtained, thereby assuring minorities a better opportunity to be represented (Zeisel, 1974).

Larger juries also increase the probabilities of two kinds of minorities being represented: (1) racial, subcultural, or other demographic groups and (2) opinion minorities. This second type of minority, which refers to those persons within a decisionmaking group who resist or go against the majority, has significant implications. We will give this topic greater attention by referring to the research of Robert Roper (1980).

184

CHAPTER
SEVEN:
THE
PSYCHOLOGY
OF THE
JURY:
PROCEDURAL
CONSIDERATIONS

Roper tested a number of hypotheses, but only two directly concern us here. One predicted that juries with **viable minorities**, defined as at least two members not in agreement with the majority, will "hang" (fail to reach a verdict) more often than juries without viable minorities. Social psychological research initiated by Solomon Asch (1952) found that in group situations, if one minority member has one ally, he or she is much more likely to resist persuasion by the majority. On the other hand, one minority member, lacking an ally, is substantially less likely to resist the majority of three or more.

The second relevant hypothesis tested by Roper predicts that larger juries will hang significantly more often than smaller ones. This hypothesis is built upon the observation that viable minorities have a greater probability of occurring in larger juries, an observation for which Roper found convincing support in analyzing his own data.

Roper used a simulation design which strongly attempted to establish ecological validity. One hundred ten mock juries ranging from six to twelve members were selected from jury lists of Fayette County, Kentucky. A videotape of a trial was presented in a courtroom, and the juries were then permitted to deliberate for an unlimited amount of time to reach a verdict. The decision could take one of three forms: guilty verdict, not-guilty verdict, or hung jury. Juries that initially reported they were deadlocked were sent back twice to try to reach a decision. If they returned a third time without a verdict, a "mistrial" as the result of a hung jury was declared.

As predicted, juries with viable minorities were more likely to end up hung than juries with nonviable minorities. In addition, the larger the jury, the more likely it was that a viable minority would emerge—hence the more likely that the jury would be hung. The conclusions from the Roper study indicate that viable minorities are more successful at resisting conformity pressures exerted by the majority. Furthermore, larger juries over the long haul will result in significantly fewer convictions, a point which presents an interesting dilemma.

Juries always have the possibility of making either a **Type I** or **Type II judicial error**. A Type I error is made when an innocent person is convicted; a Type II error when a guilty person is released. Roper's results suggest that, if the judicial system and society wish to avoid making Type I judicial errors, they should endorse twelve-member juries. On the other hand, if Type II errors are to be avoided, six-member juries should be instituted. The dilemma, of course, is deciding which of the two we want least: the occasional conviction of innocent persons or the occasional acquittal of those who are in fact guilty.

One additional aspect concerning the viable minority issue needs to be mentioned. When jurors reach a deadlock and are close to mistrial, the judge in some jurisdictions (it is prohibited in some state and federal courts) has the option to use the **dynamite charge**—also known as the "shotgun instruction," the "third degree instruction," the "nitroglycerin charge" or the "hammer instruction" (Kassin, Smith & Tulloch, 1990). The dynamite charge refers to situations in which judges confronted with the possibility of a hung jury implore the jury to "...reexamine their own views and to seriously consider each other's arguments with a disposition to be convinced" (Kassin et al., 1990, p. 538). In other words, the judge attempts to "blast" the decisional logjam into a verdict. The charge may be used in either criminal or civil trials. In *Lowenfield v. Phelps* (1988), the U. S. Supreme Court held that the dynamite charge is not necessarily coercive and reaffirmed its use on a routine basis.

Kassin et al. (1990), in an exploratory study, found, however, that the dynamite charge did cause mock jurors in the minority to feel coerced by the majority to change their votes. Another serious drawback, as noted by the researchers, is that if jurors are uncertain of their right to declare a hung jury, the dynamite charge may lead them, mistakenly, to believe they cannot do this. The dynamite charge issue has not been examined to any great extent by psychologists, and much research needs to be done before we can assess its effect on various cases, jury compositions, and jury sizes.

Arguments about jury size are often tempered by the observation that a majority of criminal cases handled by the courts are clear-cut, i.e., cases in which any number of individuals would probably reach the same verdict. The sensational cases we encounter in the media, where juries deliberate for long periods, represent only a small percentage of all trials ushered through the courts. It has been estimated that small and large juries would disagree in no more than 14 percent of all verdicts (Lempert, 1975), but as a nationwide figure this represents many defendants. Moreover, policies and practices relating to constitutional issues should not be accepted or rejected on the basis of the number of individuals affected. And although it appears that the jury-size issue has been settled temporarily in view of the Court's ruling in *Ballew*, states would be well advised to examine the psychological evidence and to consider which judicial error they can least tolerate before deciding to opt for small juries. It should also not be assumed that hung juries occur only as a result of jury size. Factors such as quality of the evidence, the status of the defendant, and community sentiment with respect to the issue raised in a particular trial all may lead to a hung jury.

DECISION RULES

An issue closely related to that of jury size is the issue of the proportion of jurors needed to agree on a verdict before it may be rendered. In other words, is it constitutionally permissible to allow a less than unanimous decision to convict defendants or to resolve civil matters? It surprises many people to learn that unanimity is not always required.

Currently, forty-four states require unanimity in felony criminal verdicts, and twenty-seven states require it in misdemeanor verdicts. All states require unanimity in capital cases. Conversely, only eighteen states require unanimity in civil verdicts. The size of the majority differs from jurisdiction to jurisdiction. One may require a two-thirds majority in criminal verdicts, whereas another requires a five-sixths majority. U. S. Supreme Court cases relevant to this issue include *Johnson v. Louisiana* (1972) and *Apodaca, Cooper and Madden v. Oregon* (1972), in which the Court allowed nonunanimous verdicts, especially because such majority or quorum verdicts would presumably result in fewer hung juries. A six-person jury in a criminal case, however, must render a unanimous decision (*Burch v. Louisiana*, 1979).

Unfortunately, the research evidence examining the differences between majority and unanimous decisions is sparse. The few data available suggest that quorum juries demonstrate better recall of the arguments and display more communication among members (Saks, 1977). However, it has also been found that quorum juries often stop deliberating the moment they reach the requisite majority (Kalven & Zeisel, 1966; Saks, 1977), thus providing less opportunity for a minority member or dissenter to argue a position or even to be heard at all. Moreover, since the first vote of quorum juries generally becomes the final verdict (Saks, 1977), it appears that it is primarily in situations where unanimity is required that the minority can effectively alter the course set by the majority. On the other hand, unanimous juries also are more likely to block verdicts or to result in hung deliberation. In their classic work *The American Jury* (see Box 8.2), Kalven and Zeisel (1966) cite data that, in jurisdictions requiring unanimous verdicts, 5.6 percent of juries were hung. This figure compared to 3.1 percent in jurisdictions that required quorum verdicts.

The available research does not allow us to conclude whether the quorum or the unanimous jury is more advantageous. Regardless of which jury type is chosen, we lose some of the desirable

186

CHAPTER
SEVEN:
THE
PSYCHOLOGY
OF THE
JURY:
PROCEDURAL
CONSIDERATIONS

features of the unchosen. It appears, however, that concerns that quorum juries may deprive a defendant of due process are unjustified from the social-science perspective. Although unanimous juries, when convicting, seem more certain of a defendant's guilt, they apparently do not render verdicts significantly different from those rendered by quorum juries (Saks, 1977).

Jury Dynamics

During a trial, jurors are expected to remain *passive*, in the sense of having no direct involvement in the proceedings, but they are also expected to be *attentive*. They must listen to testimony and arguments, pay attention to demonstrations, scrutinize exhibits, and form their impressions. Much of the information must be acquired and retained through hearing and auditory memory, because jurors are generally prohibited from taking notes (see Box 7.2). "The jury is expected to absorb information and spew out a decision, much like an empty sponge can be filled with liquid and squeezed to obtain what it has absorbed" (Diamond, 1993, p. 425).

After the *voir dire*, the trial follows three phases: opening arguments, presentation of evidence, and closing arguments. The role of the presiding judge is to enforce rules of procedure in the courtroom by controlling the manner in which evidence is presented, by ruling on objections, and by choosing between the procedural arguments of attorneys the proper process to be followed. It is also the judge's prerogative to control the courtroom by threatening and imposing contempt citations for disturbances or other interference with courtroom procedure. A critical role of the judge is to instruct members of the jury as to their responsibilities.

JURY INSTRUCTIONS

In most jurisdictions, jury instructions are classified according to when they are given during the trial. Instructions given at the beginning of the trial, before opening arguments, are called **preliminary instructions**. Instructions given during or at the end of the trial process are called trial or **substantive law instructions**. In the preliminary instructions the judge explains the respective roles of judge and jury during the course of the trial. The preliminary instructions usually include comments about the

---

■ 7.2: JURY INSTRUCTIONS: NOTE-TAKING

THE FOLLOWING STATEMENT IS AN EXAMPLE of pattern instructions advocated by the Federal Judicial Center (1987) to be read by judges to the jury during criminal trials. These instruction were designed to be comprehensible to the average jury member. Earlier pattern jury instructions were widely criticized as too complex. We shall give additional examples of the instructions devised by the Federal Judicial Center in other boxes in this and the following chapter.

Note-Taking by Jurors
(Optional Addition to Preliminary Instructions)
You may not take notes during the course of the trial. There are several reasons for this. It is difficult to take notes and, at the same time,

pay attention to what a witness is saying. Furthermore, in a group the size of yours certain persons will take better notes than others and there is the risk that the jurors who do not take good notes will depend upon the jurors who do take good notes. The jury system depends upon all twelve jurors paying close attention and arriving at a unanimous decision. I believe that the jury system works better when the jurors do not take notes.

You will notice that we do have the official court reporter taking a record of the trial. However, we will not have typewritten transcripts of this record available for use in reaching your decision in the case. ■

jurors' conduct during the trial, their responsibility to avoid representatives of the media, their need for impartiality, and their duty not to discuss the case with other jurors or other persons during recess. At some point during the trial (usually at the end), the judge also gives instructions about the substantive law that should guide the jury in weighing the evidence and reaching a decision. These substantive law instructions include information about the law as it applies to the particular case.

Such instructions further outline the possible verdicts the jury can return, reexplain whether there must be a unanimous or a majority verdict, and explain what standard of proof is required. In criminal cases, jurors must be satisfied *beyond a reasonable doubt* that the defendant is guilty of every element of the offense before returning a conviction. In civil suits, the standard in most jurisdictions is a far less demanding one, *preponderance of the evidence*. An intermediate standard—clear and convincing evidence—is applied in rapidly developing areas such as mental health, educational, and family law. In proceedings involving temporary suspension of parental rights, for example, a state may require only that the parent's unfitness be proven by clear and convincing evidence. Some states require a tougher standard of proof in family and mental-health areas as well. For example, proof beyond a reasonable doubt that an individual is mentally disordered and dangerous may be required before he or she may be institutionalized.

Throughout the course of a trial, the judge also gives a number of warnings to the jury

188

CHAPTER
SEVEN:
THE
PSYCHOLOGY
OF THE
JURY:
PROCEDURAL
CONSIDERATIONS

not to consider some kinds of information in arriving at a verdict. Jurors are often told simply to disregard the testimony they have just heard, for example. In many jurisdictions, however, some of the substantive law instructions are included in the preliminary instructions and later repeated at the end of the trial. In some jurisdictions, the preliminary instructions are interspersed at various stages of the trial.

Classifying instructions according to when they are given, then, becomes confusing. For clarity, we will adopt J. Alexander Tanford's (1990) suggested classification scheme. Tanford recommends placing instructions into two main categories: (1) **charging instructions**; and (2) **admonitions**. "Charging instructions explain the jury's role, describe relevant procedural and substantive law, and provide suggestions on how to organize deliberations and evaluate evidence" (Tanford, 1990, p. 72). In short, they tell the jurors what their duties are. Members of the jury must listen, assess the credibility of witnesses, weigh the evidence, and render a decision. Charging instructions also contain the preliminary and substantive instructions described previously, including proper procedure to follow and the relevant substantive law pertinent to the case.

"Admonitions are given spontaneously in an effort to prevent jurors from misusing potentially prejudicial information" (Tanford, 1990, p. 95). In the legal literature, admonitions are often called **curative instructions** because they are presumed to correct or "cure" potential errors in the trial process. There are two basic types: admonitions that jurors must *completely disregard* information deemed by the court as being prejudicial; and (2) admonitions that jurors limit their use of certain kinds of evidence (termed *limiting* instructions). A judge may tell the jury to disregard a witness's comment that a civil defendant has offered to settle the case, or tell a jury to disregard improper remarks made by attorneys during the trial. These are examples of curative instructions to disregard. The classic illustration occurred during the trial of Charles Manson, charged with a highly publicized murder in California in 1969. Manson walked into the courtroom and held up a banner newspaper headline for the jurors to see. The headline was highly inflammatory, because it proclaimed that then President Richard M. Nixon had declared that Manson was guilty. The jury was told to disregard the incident. The judge was careful, however, to poll jurors individually in an effort to determine whether they were unduly influenced by the headline.

Limiting instructions warn jurors not to use evidence to evaluate or decide on a certain issue, although the evidence may appropriately be used for another issue (see Box 7.5). For example, the jury may be instructed not to use the defendant's criminal history to decide guilt or innocence in a particular case, "…but [it] may be used for the limited purpose of proving identity, low credibility, or a state of mind, such as intent, knowledge, notice, and absence of mistake" (Tanford, 1990, p. 78). Thus, when a defendant elects to testify on his own behalf, the judge may instruct the jury that his prior record should *not* be used as evidence of *present* guilt, but should be used *solely* to assess his credibility as a witness. Also, limiting instructions are frequently used when multiple defendants or multiple offenses are combined into a single trial, a trial referred to as **joined**. More specifically, the Federal Rules of Criminal Procedure, in the name of efficiency, allow criminal offenses to be joined for trial if they are similar in character or if they arise in the same incident. Consequently, in joined multiple-offender cases, evidence may be admissible against one defendant but inadmissible against the others; or, in joined cases of multiple offenses against one defendant, certain evidence may be used for proving one offense but not the others.

Two major questions arise in this context: Does the average juror really understand these apparent safeguards in the instructions and admonitions? Second, does the average juror—even if he or she understands and comprehends the instructions and admonitions—really do what is legally expected? That is, do typical jurors mentally disregard or separate one element of information from another? On the basis of jury research, we must answer both questions in the negative.

■ 7.5: LIMITING INSTRUCTIONS

THE FIRST STATEMENT—WHICH IS TO BE READ to the jury by the judge—is an example of a limiting instruction. The second statement is an example of a limiting instruction in a joined trial. The commentaries following the statements were written by the Federal Judicial Center Committee as further explanation of the statements.

Evidence Admitted for a Limited Purpose: Jury to Limit Its Consideration

Several times during the trial I told you that certain evidence was allowed into this trial for a particular and limited purpose. [Describe evidence]. When you consider that evidence, you must limit your consideration to that purpose.

Commentary: This instruction contemplates that the court gave limiting instructions when the evidence was received. The committee recommends that the jury be informed specifically which evidence was so admitted and what limitations were imposed.

Evidence Applicable to Only One Defendant: Jury to Limit Its Consideration

As you know, there are _____ defendants on trial here; [Give names]. They are being tried together because the government has charged that they worked together to commit the crime of [e.g.: importing heroin]. Nevertheless, each defendant is entitled to have his case decided just on the evidence which applies to him. Some of the evidence in this case was limited to one of the defendants and cannot be considered in the cases of the others. What that means is that you may consider this testimony in the case of _____, but you may not consider it in any way when you are deciding whether the government has proved, beyond a reasonable doubt, that the other defendants, [give names], committed the crime of _____.

Commentary: In even the most straightforward cases involving only two defendants, the problem which this instruction addresses can create great difficulties for both the court and the jury. The judge should make an effort to give this type of instruction each time limited evidence is admitted. ■

CHARGING INSTRUCTIONS

With regularity, research has found that jurors find jury instructions technical, full of ambiguity, and downright confusing (Elwork, Sales & Alfini, 1977; Forston, 1970; Jacob, 1972; Strawn & Buchanan, 1976). Investigators who have researched whether jurors understand charging instructions on the substantive law, evidence, and burdens of proof all reach the same conclusion: "typical pattern jury instructions, drafted by lawyers in an effort to be *legally* precise, are incomprehensible to jurors" (Tanford, 1990, p. 79). The term **pattern jury instructions** refers to a standard or uniform jury instruction that can be applied across *different* jurisdictions. In fact, the legal attempt to make the instructions uniform and legally precise has produced instructions so full of jargon and qualifying clauses that they are fundamentally incomprehensible to the average citizen. Sometimes, it is even difficult to find the verb. "Legalese" by itself is not the only problem, however. A number of grammatical constructions and discourse features (e.g., poor organization within paragraphs, redundancy) also contribute to a misunderstanding of the text (Levi, 1990). Therefore, many scholars and researchers believe that simplifying jury instructions will greatly improve comprehension. Still, even when jury instructions are rewritten to improve clarity, research shows that over half of the jurors have considerable difficulty understanding them (Charrow & Charrow, 1979). Furthermore, Elwork, Alfini and Sales (1987) raise some interesting questions concerning this issue. They ask: What percentage of jurors must understand the instructions in order to ensure a just and fair result? Should we require 100 percent comprehension by all the jurors? Or, more realistically, some fraction of that? Say 75 percent? In the Elwork, Alfini, and Sales research, a series of rewrites of jury instructions did improve comprehension in volunteer mock jurors but not to the researchers' standards of sufficient comprehension. The

190

CHAPTER
SEVEN:
THE
PSYCHOLOGY
OF THE
JURY:
PROCEDURAL
CONSIDERATIONS

researchers were trying to rewrite the instructions so that: (1) they would be understood by at least two-thirds of a twelve-member jury; and (2) this level of comprehension would be achieved by at least eight of ten juries. Even after rewriting the material a number of times, however, the researchers were unable to achieve their goals.

Tanford asserts, moreover, "Although rewriting and simplifying instructions would certainly be an improvement, its benefits are overstated" (p. 105). The abstract nature of the law creates its own problems. Legal concepts are often hard to understand—even for law students—because they are so abstract and so removed from any specific context or example. Thus, the judge should provide a context for them, refer to the actual evidence, and use numerous examples when communicating charge to the jury. Tanford posits, "Rewriting some instructions may be a pointless task because it is the law itself that is incomprehensible" (p. 102).

Many experts believe that providing charging instructions at the very end of the trial is a poor procedure for enhancing juror understanding of what is expected of them. Elwork, Sales, and Alfini (1977) and Kassin and Wrightsman (1979) report evidence that the jurors are far more likely to understand their charge and all its ramifications if instructions are communicated to them at the beginning of the trial as well as at the end. However, other researchers have not found these effects in other contexts. Greene and Loftus (1985) tested limiting instructions in joined criminal trials and found no difference in results, regardless of when the instructions were given.

A number of other strategies have been employed to enhance juror comprehension, but most have not been very successful. Note-taking has little effect on the memory of jurors for the judge's instructions. Both allowing jurors to take notes and providing jurors with *written* instructions have, for the most part, failed to improve comprehension (Penrod & Cutler, 1987). "A cautious review of instruction comprehension should start with the presumption that jurors cannot understand traditional pattern instructions. It should be emphasized that these difficulties are not the product of juror inadequacies but are a product of the instructions themselves" (Penrod & Cutler, 1987, p. 306). One thing that does appear sound from the research literature is that, at the very least, repeating the instructions two or more times aids comprehension and improves the likelihood that jurors will follow them.

Shari Seidman Diamond (1993) points out that a basic flaw in all charging instructions is the implicit assumption, by both trial courts and appellate courts, that the jury is passive and sponge-like, absorbing all the information dished out to them. They tend to "…treat the jury as a homogeneous, passive, and compliant decision producer" (Diamond, 1993, p. 425). She argues that the court must address the many biases, prejudices, and misinformation the jury members have. She writes, "…failing to address the erroneous beliefs that jurors *do* have does not make those beliefs go away, and it does not neutralize them. The schemas jurors bring with them about crime and punishment can have powerful effects on perception, attention, and recall" (Diamond, 1993, p. 425).

Death Penalty Cases

In death penalty cases, it is of course especially important that jurors understand the legal questions they are to address. A study of juror comprehension of instructions in North Carolina (Luginbuhl, 1992) comports with previous research suggesting that even highly conscientious jury members often miss the point in jury deliberations.

Luginbuhl showed a twenty-minute videotape of a judge reading instructions (pattern instructions) to eighteen groups of subjects (with an average of six subjects in each group). Nine groups heard old instructions previously used in North Carolina courts and nine heard new instructions designed to improve comprehension. The legal rules under the two sets of instructions were the same; only the instructions themselves were different. The new instructions emphasized that mitigating circumstances did not require a high standard of proof and that the jury need not be unanimous in finding mitigating circumstances. They also emphasized that mitigating circumstances must be considered together with aggravating circumstances in the final decision.

The subjects were then given an eight-item questionnaire designed to measure their understanding of the decision rules. For example, the jurors were asked:

Is the burden of proof for mitigating circumstances

a) a reasonable doubt or
b) simply to the jury's satisfaction?
  (Correct answer: b)

Does the finding of aggravating circumstances require

a) unanimity or
b) simply the agreement of one juror?
  (Correct answer: a)

There was no difference between the two groups on the three questions measuring their understanding of *aggravating* circumstances, but the "new instruction" groups were significantly better at understanding instructions regarding mitigation. Even so, only 53 percent of the new instruction group answered all eight questions correctly. Luginbuhl found no differences on demographic variables of race, gender, jury service, attitude toward the death penalty, age, or educational level. He did find a high educational level among his subject pool, however (only 14 of the 115 had no education beyond high school and 53 were college graduates), leading him to wonder how less well-educated groups would have fared. Luginbuhl also notes that defendants convicted under the old rules are beginning to appeal their death sentences, arguing that their sentencing juries might not have understood that mitigating circumstances need not be found unanimously. His research would provide support for this argument.

ADMONITIONS

Instructions to Disregard Totally

When jurors are told to do something—like disregard what they may consider critical or enlightening evidence—they are apt to do just the opposite. Moreover, telling jurors to disregard or to segment the evidence is likely to highlight the material in their minds even more. "The empirical research clearly demonstrates that instructions to disregard are ineffective in reducing the harm caused by inadmissible evidence and improper arguments" (Tanford, 1990, p. 95). In fact, instructions to disregard may make matters worse (Wolf & Montgomery, 1977). Yet the courts continue to think such instruction is effective and "fully protect the defendant's rights" (*People v. Brock*, 1988). The assumption that warnings to disregard are effective, or at least partially effective, on the thinking processes and prejudices of the jury is termed, in the legal literature, the **cured-error doctrine**.

Limiting Instructions

The courts also continue to believe that limiting instructions satisfy the cured-error doctrine. "…[M]ost courts hold 'unquestionably' that limiting instructions should be given, and once given, 'cure' any error" (Tanford, 1990, p. 98). Empirical studies have continually shown that limiting instructions are largely ineffective concerning prior criminal convictions (Wissler & Saks, 1985), evidentiary factors (Greene & Loftus, 1986; Tanford & Penrod, 1982, 1984), inadmissible evidence

192

CHAPTER
SEVEN:
THE
PSYCHOLOGY
OF THE
JURY:
PROCEDURAL
CONSIDERATIONS

(Sue, Smith & Caldwell, 1973), and prior convictions of perjury (Tanford & Cox, 1987, 1988).

Roselle Wissler and Michael Saks (1985) wanted to see whether limiting instructions neutralized the effects of prior criminal convictions on jury verdicts. The subjects, 160 adult men and women from the metropolitan Boston area, were asked to read a two-page case summary and answer some questions on a hypothetical case. Wissler and Saks found that these mock jurors were strongly influenced by prior criminal history of the hypothetical defendant, especially if the charged crime was similar to a prior conviction. The jurors were far more likely to convict an individual if he had a criminal history than if not, even after being told they could not incorporate that knowledge into their decision. In fact, subjects were willing to admit that the prior conviction evidence made a big difference in their decision and was the primary reason they found the defendant guilty—in spite of being told not to use that information for that purpose. They said it didn't make any difference what kind of warning they received; a prior record predisposed them to think "guilty."

The Wissler and Saks study used volunteers who were found in laundromats, supermarkets, airports, bus terminals, and homes. Had these individuals actually been serving on a real jury, they may have taken their responsibility to disregard prior record more seriously. Even in a more controlled mock juror setting, the results might have been very different. Nonetheless, the Wissler and Saks research does follow the same trend as other research on disregarding instructions.

Sarah Tanford and Michele Cox (1987) found that a defendant's prior perjury convictions in a civil trial increased the likelihood that the jury would find against the defendant, whereas evidence of honesty had little impact. They also found that limiting instructions did not remove the detrimental effect of character evidence of dishonesty on jury verdicts. "In summary, research demonstrates that impeachment evidence can be detrimental to a defendant in terms of verdicts, and limiting instructions do not remove this effect" (Tanford & Cox, 1988, p. 480).

Joined Trials

A majority of the courts, including the U. S. Supreme Court, approve of joined trials because of their time and financial economy, and continue to maintain that limiting instructions prevent prejudice to defendants (Tanford, 1990). Jurors' ratings of a defendant's guilt are higher when crimes are joined than when the offenses are tried separately, however (Horowitz, Borden & Feldman, 1980; Tanford & Penrod, 1982, 1984; Greene & Loftus, 1985).

Edith Greene and Elizabeth Loftus (1985) conducted two experiments in which mock jurors (college students) read evidence from actual criminal cases and decided on the guilt of the defendant. One defendant was either charged with murder *or* rape, and another defendant was charged with both. Greene and Loftus hypothesized that there would be a **spillover effect**, by virtue of which of the defendant's being charged with both offenses seems to spill over onto, and distort, the evidence presented on any single charge. Thus, the trial process is contaminated and the likelihood of a conviction is increased.

In experiment one, subjects were found more likely to convict the defendant accused of both offenses than the defendant charged with only one, thus confirming the spillover effect. The subjects also found the defendant accused of multiple offenses to be more dangerous, less likable, and less believable. Experiment two examined the effects of limiting instructions on joined criminal trials. The results were similar to those of experiment one. The defendant was judged more harshly if he or she was on trial for multiple offenses. It was clear, also, that limiting instructions had virtually no effect in neutralizing that bias. Defendants charged with multiple offenses were treated more harshly than those charged with only one offense, even when mock jurors had been told to disregard that information in delivering a verdict.

If attorneys do not object to a procedure or process that allegedly jeopardizes the right to a fair hearing *during* the trial, the individual they represent has implicitly waived the right to appeal on that issue. In other words, if an objection is not placed in the record during the trial, a person has lost the right to appeal to a higher court on the basis of that particular issue. In some jurisdictions, there is an additional requirement that the appellant must also have requested a remedy. The legal community refers to this as the **procedural default doctrine** (Tanford, 1986). However, there are dangerous pitfalls in this doctrine. Objections by a defendant's attorney may be misinterpreted by the jury as an attempt to hide or cover up something. Thus, it is possible that requesting an admonition in order to preserve an appeal may increase the likelihood that the jury will find the defendant guilty. On the other hand, remaining silent may also lead to a decision against the defendant, as well as preclude an appeal.

Summary and Conclusions

Wallace Loh (1979, p. 166) observes that the relationship between psychology and law is marked by recurrent cycles. "Initially, optimistic views regarding the contribution of psychology to law are presented. These are met with skeptical rejoinders from the academic legal community that dampen further interest. A period of silence and inaction follows. The lessons are soon forgotten and a new cycle of optimism-skepticism-silence is repeated."

At first glance, the behavioral science research on the jury seems to promote additional legal skepticism which may result in another period of silence. Certainly, a large segment of the jury research may lack ecological validity and some clearly can stand improvement. Other research, such as that on jury size and decisionmaking, is inconclusive. As we noted, there are good and questionable aspects of both larger and smaller juries. Still other research is much too new to gauge its implications. Research suggesting that the struck jury method of challenging jurors results in a less biased jury than the sequential method is a good example of this.

The quality of research during the past decade has improved substantially, however, and serious concerns about internal and ecological validity are being addressed. Psychologists and other researchers are also becoming much more sophisticated about the legal system. As a result, their contributions are more deserving of attention, because they are based on understanding of the processes involved and the role of participants. Furthermore, a good deal of the research in the jury area has now been replicated and clear trends are in evidence.

Research psychologists have revealed a number of significant problems in the way courts use jury instructions, for example. Despite this extensive research, the courts have made very few attempts to change the procedure. It is clear that juries have trouble understanding charging instructions. Additionally, admonitions to disregard testimony or to use it in a limited way are frequently misunderstood and well near impossible to heed. Depending upon how they are given, these admonitions also may provoke jurors into doing the opposite of what they are told. Social psychologists have long observed that people do not like to have their perceived freedom infringed upon. In order to reassert it, they do just the opposite of what is demanded. This well-known tendency was called reactance by Jack Brehm (1966). In light of this awareness, it may be wise for judges to appeal to reason and to explain, preferably as part of the charging instructions, why some testimony should be disregarded. Reactance is less likely to occur if jurors are told at the beginning of the trial that they may be asked to put some information out of their minds—and

Chapter
Seven:
The
Psychology
of the
Jury:
Procedural
Considerations

why this is necessary. The same information could be repeated in the judge's final charge to the jury.

The issue of the dynamite charge, where jurors are urged to reevaluate evidence against their own position, is more difficult to address. As we have seen, the dynamite charge is particularly problematic in the case of the lone holdout. In any case, the psychological pressure placed on dissenters to bend to the wishes of the majority would seem to militate against a fair verdict. At the very least, judges issuing a dynamite charge should make it clear that jurors still have the freedom not to reach a consensus.

Research on death-qualified juries and on instructions relating to the imposition of the death sentence also deserves the attention of the legal system. It seems quite clear that jurors who are considered qualified to sit in a capital case differ in attitudes and demographic characteristics from non-death-qualified individuals. This could change, however, now that defense lawyers are also allowed to remove jurors who would automatically vote for the death penalty upon a defendant's conviction. Additionally, there is evidence that instructions regarding the weighing of aggravating and mitigating circumstances in capital cases are not well understood. Although it is premature to draw conclusions about these instructions without further research, studies to date suggest that this issue should be watched very carefully.

Questions to Ponder

1. In light of the fact that courts are already overburdened, are criminal defendants and civil plaintiffs more likely to get justice by a) going to trial or b) plea bargaining or settling disputes without trial?

2. Although jurors tend to do their best and decide a case on the basis of the strength of the evidence, those who sit on a death penalty case seem to present special problems. Discuss.

3. Recall two or more situations in which you were part of a group which had to arrive at a decision. How did the size of the groups affect a) the opportunity for varying points of view to be aired and b) the amount of pressure placed on individuals to conform to a group consensus?

4. What are the pros and cons of allowing jurors to take notes during a criminal trial? Is there some way jurors could be allowed to take notes which would satisfactorily address the arguments against this practice?

5. Review the pattern instructions in Boxes 7.2 through 7.5. Are they comprehensible to the average adult citizen? If not, what are the problems? Write a clear set of instructions for non-sequestered jurors in a criminal trial which is about to recess from Friday afternoon to Monday morning.

The Psychology of the Jury: Decisionmaking Processes

A T THE END OF THE TRIAL, JURY MEMBERS ARE USHERED TO SPECIAL QUARTERS, where they are expected to deliberate in complete privacy until they reach a verdict or believe they are hopelessly deadlocked. No outside participants or information that might contaminate the deliberation are permitted in the jury room. An officer of the court—usually a sheriff's deputy or a U. S. Marshall—guards the door and, if necessary, delivers messages to and from the jury.

JURY DELIBERATIONS

When a jury begins its deliberation, one of its first decisions is to select one person to lead subsequent discussions and oversee the votes. Not surprisingly, early research showed that this leader (foreman) was most likely to be male, middle-aged, of high status in the community, and from a managerial or professional occupation (Strodtbeck, James & Hawkins, 1957; Strodtbeck & Mann, 1956). Although up-to-date information is not available, we know that women as well as men are now serving as jury leaders, although probably not proportionately to their representation on juries.

The place where a person chooses to sit at a rectangular table in the deliberation room seems to influence the possibility that he or she will be chosen; individuals who sit at the end of the table have a substantially higher probability of being picked than those persons who locate themselves along the sides (Strodtbeck & Hook, 1961; Nemeth & Wachtler, 1974). Of course, it is also expected that high-status males would be most likely to seat themselves at the head of the table as a matter of habit. The person who speaks first in the group is also more likely than others to be chosen to lead the group.

The elected jury leader is not necessarily the person who most influences jury deliberations, however. In fact, it appears that the influence of the jury leader on the jury's decisionmaking is minimal. He or she usually takes the position of moderator rather than advocate and tends to be more concerned with procedural rules than with any given position (Saks & Hastie, 1978).

Once settled in the deliberation chamber, jurors may only request clarification of legal questions from the judge or ask to look at items of evidence. In some cases, they have received permission to visit or revisit the scene of a crime or accident. If jurors have not returned a verdict by the end of their first day of deliberation, they may be given accommodations in a hotel and taken back to the deliberation chamber the following day. Judges may also send the jurors home at the end of a day of deliberations, after admonishing them not to discuss the case with anyone. Recalling the principle of reactance discussed in the previous chapter, we should note the importance of explaining carefully why this non-communication is necessary.

196

CHAPTER
EIGHT:
THE
PSYCHOLOGY
OF THE
JURY:
DECISIONMAKING
PROCESSES

In high-profile cases, juries may be sequestered for the length of the trial as well as the deliberation process. The purpose of sequestration is to protect the jury from the media and possible influences of their friends and family. Additionally, jurors may be contacted and even threatened by the public or contacts of the defendant or victim in a criminal case, or by either side in a civil suit.

The evidence suggests that most juries in criminal trials do not involve themselves in lengthy deliberations. Kalven and Zeisel (1966) found that, for trials lasting one or two days, 55 percent of the juries took one hour or less to reach a verdict, and 74 percent of the juries completed their deliberation in less than two hours. Most juries take a vote soon after settling into their deliberation chamber. The University of Chicago Jury Project (Broader, 1958; Kalven & Zeisel, 1966; see Box 8.2) found that in 30 percent of the cases jurors reached a unanimous decision after only one vote. In 90 percent of the cases, the majority on the first ballot usually won out, regardless of who sat on the jury or who constituted the majority and minority. Lengthier deliberations appear not so much to change a predominant opinion as to bring about consensus.

James (1959) examined the specific content of simulated jury deliberations and found that about 50 percent of the discussion was devoted to personal experiences and opinions. Another 25 percent was devoted to discussions of procedural issues, 15 percent to actual testimony, and 8 percent to the instructions provided by the judge. Another study found that the more highly educated they were, the more jurors emphasized procedure and instruction. Jurors with only a grade-school education were more likely to focus on opinions, testimony, and personal experiences (Gerbasi, Zuckerman & Reis, 1977).

As part of the extensive Chicago Jury Project, researchers sent questionnaires to judges throughout the country who had presided over a total of 3,567 criminal cases. The judges were asked to record general information about each case, the verdict of the jury, and what they would have decided in the absence of the jury. If they disagreed with the jury, they were asked why the jury probably decided as it did.

Judges agreed with juries in 75.4 percent of the cases, both believing that 13.4 percent of the defendants should be acquitted and that 62 percent of the defendants should be convicted. Although the judges disagreed with juries in about 25 percent of the cases, most of this disagreement occurred when a defendant had been acquitted. In fact, judges agreed with jurors in fewer than half the acquittals. Hence, juries appear to be more lenient than judges (a phenomenon called **leniency bias**). This suggests that a defendant has a slightly better chance of being acquitted if he or she elects a jury trial rather than a bench trial. Judges indicated the jurors were influenced by "sentiments" about law and about defendants, extralegal factors that did not enter into the judges' own decisions. Extralegal factors have received a great deal of attention from psychologists studying the jury process, and we will discuss many of them throughout the rest of this chapter.

More recently, some studies report on interviews with jurors in actual capital cases in an attempt to discover what transpired in their decisionmaking during the penalty phase of the trial. Recall that death-penalty cases routinely involve a two-stage process. In the first stage, jurors determine whether the defendant is guilty of the crime charged. In the second stage, they determine whether to impose the death sentence. Geimer and Amsterdam (1988) interviewed at least three jurors from each of ten capital trials in Florida. They learned that jurors had a presumption of death. That is, they wrongly believed they should impose the death sentence unless convinced otherwise. Under the law, they should have waited to be convinced to impose death. Costanza and Costanza (1989), interviewing jurors in one capital case, learned that the jurors did not weigh aggravating and mitigating circumstances and did not agree with attorneys on which

■ 8.1: *JURY DELIBERATION INSTRUCTIONS FROM THE FEDERAL JUDICIAL CENTER*

Jury's Duty to Deliberate

THE FEDERAL JUDICIAL CENTER (1987) RECOMMENDS that judges of criminal trials read the following instructions before the jury leaves to deliberate:

It is your duty, as jurors, to talk with one another and to deliberate in the jury room. You should try to reach an agreement if you can. Each of you must decide the case for yourself, but only after consideration of the evidence with the other members of the jury. While this is going on, do not hesitate to reexamine your own opinions and change your mind if you are convinced that you are wrong. But do not give up your honest beliefs solely because the others think differently, or merely to get the case over with. In a very real way you are judges, judges of the facts. Your only interest is to determine whether the government has proved the defendant is guilty beyond a reasonable doubt.

Commentary: At the discretion of the trial judge, this instruction can be given either as part of the charge or in response to a report of deadlock by a jury.

Jury Not to Consider Punishment

THE FOLLOWING STATEMENT IS RECOMMENDED by the Federal Judicial Center (1987) in those jurisdictions that do not allow jurors to determine punishment, only a guilty or not guilty verdict. The commentary, however, addresses state cases in which the juror *may* consider the punishment in criminal trials.

If you find the defendant guilty, it will then be my job to decide what punishment should be imposed. In considering the evidence and arguments that will be given during the trial, you should not guess about the punishment. It should not enter into your consideration or discussion at any time.

Commentary: In cases in which a punishment instruction will be given, it would normally be given at the end of the trial. Because of the possibility that in some serious cases the trial judge might wish to give the instruction twice, particularly in those jurisdictions in which jurors in state cases actually do consider punishment, the punishment instruction is included here with the preliminary instruction. ■

---

evidence was critical to imposing death. Instead, they made their decisions based on values and normative standards, asking themselves such questions as, "Does this person *deserve* to die?" In a study of the effects on jurors of imposing death, Kaplan (1985) found that four of sixteen jurors in capital cases appeared to suffer from Post-Traumatic Stress Disorder (PTSD) and that most of the others exhibited some symptoms of it (Costanza & Costanza, 1992).

A sobering documentary about a high-profile child sexual abuse case in North Carolina also sheds light on the jury deliberation process. Although the documentary—aired on public television in 1993—is not scientific evidence, it illustrates the dilemmas which may face good citizens trying to do their level best. Members of a jury which had convicted the owner of a day care center of multiple counts of sexual assault told of being intimidated by other jury members. One woman acknowledged she had discussed the case and her concerns with her son-in-law. During the deliberation process, a juror revealed that he had been sexually abused as a child, though he had denied this during the *voir dire*. Jurors also apparently consulted a popular magazine, against the judge's instructions, and "diagnosed" the defendant a pedophile. Three members of the jury admitted, after the fact, that they did not believe the defendant was guilty. They succumbed to group pressure, one man because he had a weak heart and found the stress intolerable.

HOW THE JURY PROCESS IS STUDIED

Nearly all psychological investigations of the jury have been conducted under simulated or *mock-jury* conditions. Although it would be helpful to carry out such research in the natural

198

CHAPTER
EIGHT:
THE
PSYCHOLOGY
OF THE
JURY:
DECISIONMAKING
PROCESSES

setting, ethical considerations, costs, and legal obstacles to obtaining permission to do so all preclude this.

Very few psychological investigations of the jury process were conducted prior to 1969 (Weiten & Diamond, 1979), but since then, simulation projects have increased dramatically. Although there are critical methodological flaws in many of the studies, the reader should become familiar with some of the frequently cited work to understand what has been attempted.

Anyone reviewing jury-simulation literature is confronted with a bewildering array of experiments, using a wide range of methods to investigate an assortment of jury variables. We will attempt to put some order in the disarray by presenting the studies and their findings by topic area and by trying to tie them together through a few theoretical themes. The failure to relate the data to some systematic theory enabling an organized summary of the results is one of the major problems of jury research. The topic areas covered in this section are those that research psychologists (usually social psychologists) have isolated. The following presentation by no means covers the constellation of possible variables that can be studied, nor does it describe all of the experiments in the areas discussed. The intent is to provide the reader with highlights and trends of the data, to foster appreciation of the problems faced by investigators, and to suggest future research directions.

Juror Perceptions of Defendant and Victim

Criminal defendants on trial, as well as litigants in civil suits, often look and act very differently than usual. A person who is unkempt or prefers casual clothing may appear in a suit or dress, with hair neatly brushed. Defense lawyers often coach their clients about proper courtroom demeanor, including posture and even facial expressions. They also may encourage family members to be prominently on display in the courtroom, where the jury can observe the emotional support the defendant is getting. There is good research evidence to suggest that such efforts and modifications are not in vain.

PHYSICAL ATTRACTIVENESS

According to research in social psychology, most people believe that good-looking people, compared to physically unattractive people, possess socially desirable traits and lead more successful and fulfilling lives (Dion, Berscheid & Walster, 1972). Moreover, transgressions or violations of the social code are more highly tolerated when they are committed by a physically attractive person (Dion, 1972; Efran, 1974). This may account in part for why convicted felons are appraised as being "uglier" than most people (Cavior & Howard, 1973). "Attractiveness," of course, is a subjective criterion that may be associated with background variables like health care, nutrition, and economic status. As society becomes increasingly aware of the broad range of criminal activity perpetrated by the economically advantaged, the connection between crime and attractiveness should become irrelevant.

When Michael Efran (1974) asked college-student subjects if they felt physical appearance should play a role in jury decisions, 93 percent said it should not. Efran then simulated a jury situation, drew different subjects from that same college-student population, and asked them to

■ 8.2: *THE CHICAGO JURY PROJECT*

THE UNIVERSITY OF CHICAGO JURY PROJECT, which officially began in September 1952, was financed through a $1.4 million grant provided by the Ford Foundation. The principal architect of the venture was legal scholar Edward H. Levi, Dean of the University of Chicago Law School, who later became Provost of the University. The project's broad goal was to further research in the law and the behavioral sciences by focusing upon the jury system, commercial arbitration, and income-tax law. The project leader was lawyer-academician Harry Kalven, Jr., who worked closely with Professor Hans Zeisel, former President of the American Statistical Society, and Professor Fred Strodtbeck, an expert on the behavior of small groups. Others associated with the project, whose names you will find cited throughout this text, included lawyer and professor Dale Broader, who did extensive interviewing research with jurors, and Rita James Simon, who investigated, among other things, the jury's handling of the insanity defense.

Numerous articles and several books resulted form the data collected during the seven-year project. Among the best known books are *The American Jury*, by Kalven and Zeisel (1966), *Delay in the Court*, by Zeisel, Kalven, and Buchholz (1959), and *The Jury and the Defense of Insanity*, by Rita James Simon (1967).

The project was plagued by numerous problems in the collection, analysis, and write-up of the data. Lawyers had trouble understanding social and behavioral scientists, and social and behavioral scientists had difficulty understanding lawyers (Broader, 1958).

At one point, the project's research approaches toward the jury resulted in a national scandal, complete with a Senate subcommittee investigation. Researchers had tape recorded jury deliberations in five civil cases in the federal district court in Wichita, Kansas, without the knowledge of jurors, but with the consent of the trial judge and counsel. This infringement upon the traditional privacy of the jury gener-

ated a public outcry, public censure by the United States Attorney General, hearings before the Subcommittee on Internal Security of the Senate Judiciary Committee, the enactment of statutes in some thirty-odd jurisdictions prohibiting jury-taping, and widespread editorial commentary and news coverage by the national press.

Among those leading the public charge was then Assistant Attorney General Warren E. Burger, who at a regional meeting of the American Bar Association stated he was "shocked" by the actions of the university researchers. He also claimed that the project had originally planned to include "surreptitious eavesdropping" on 500 to 1,000 federal juries *(New York Times*, Oct. 13, 1955). On October 12, 1955, Senate subcommittee counsel Julius Sourwine devoted most of his questioning to an attempt to link Dean Levi and Professor Kalven to subversive or communist causes, implying that the project was a communist plot designed to undermine the freedom of secret jury deliberation.

Dean Levi and Professor Kalven tried to defend the methodology of "eavesdropping" on the jury by arguing that the only way to improve the jury system was to collect data on the actual processes which occur within the secrecy of jury deliberation. This call to science did little to mitigate the furor that had been engendered. Impeachment of the federal judges who permitted the eavesdropping was entertained, though not carried through, and statutes prohibiting similar eavesdropping were adopted.

The data collected during the taping of the Wichita civil jury deliberations were never used by the Chicago Jury Project, but the data collected through other means (e.g., interviews and surveys of jurors and judges) resulted in one of the most extensive jury studies ever completed by social scientists. The material gained from the project is cited in the text. ■

evaluate the guilt or innocence of hypothetical students accused of cheating. The subjects also were asked to mete out punishment. Subjects were shown photographs of the "defendants." The physically attractive defendants were believed less guilty and deserving of less punishment than unattractive defendants accused of the same offense.

Several qualifiers must be attached to the Efran results. First, female subjects always evaluated male defendants and male subjects female defendants. This pairing of opposite gender probably accentuated a possible attractiveness variable. Second, the significant results occurred because male subjects responded favorably to female defendants. Female "jurors" were not as strongly influenced by the male attractiveness. Third, a juror's decision was not made after group

200

CHAPTER
EIGHT:
THE
PSYCHOLOGY
OF THE
JURY:
DECISIONMAKING
PROCESSES

discussion (deliberation), but individually and without any influence from others. We do not know whether group influence would have mitigated a possible attractiveness factor. Finally, the results may have been different if the subjects had been presented with a violation of the criminal code rather than a violation of the academic code.

A study by Sigall and Ostrove (1975) suggests that a defendant's physical attractiveness does not always lead to leniency by individual jurors; sometimes the nature of the crime overrides. Subjects (sixty male and sixty female undergraduates) were presented trial information about a female defendant accused of either burglary or a swindling scheme. Attractiveness was manipulated by showing the "jurors" photographs of the defendant. There was also a neutral-defendant condition, with no photographs shown. The burglary was a breaking and entering and grand larceny of $2,200 in cash and merchandise. In the swindle, the defendant allegedly induced a middle-aged man to invest $2,200 in a nonexistent corporation. The experimenters not only manipulated the attractiveness of the defendant, but also created a condition under which the defendant used that attractiveness to perpetrate her crime.

Attractive defendants in the swindle scheme received longer sentences than unattractive defendants for the same offense. On the other hand, attractive defendants in the burglary situation received substantially less severe punishment for the same offense. The results suggest, therefore, that good-looking criminals may be treated better, as long as they have not capitalized on their looks to commit their crime.

Physical attractiveness also emerged as a significant factor in a study using a simulated civil case involving personal damage suits. Stephen and Tully (1977) report that mock jurors were inclined to award larger amounts of money for damages when the plaintiffs were attractive. Also of interest was the finding that male mock jurors awarded the male plaintiff the largest amount of money and the female plaintiff the smallest amount. There was no difference in the awards given by female jurors on the basis of gender. In general, gender of defendants has not been found to influence mock jurors in criminal cases (Weiten & Diamond, 1979). Other demographic variables like socioeconomic status or race have been marginally important or not significant at all (Weiten & Diamond, 1979).

It should be noted, however, that research examining the effect of gender, socioeconomic status, and race on *actual* sentencing decisions suggests that these variables do indeed influence the outcome. Although this research falls out of the realm of psychological research, the reader should be aware of its existence. It has long been recognized that the criminal justice system is more punitive toward defendants of low socioeconomic status, not only at sentencing but at earlier stages of the process as well. With respect to gender, sentencing outcomes now appear more evenhanded (Steffensmeier, Kramer & Streifel, 1993). Race discrimination continues to haunt criminal justice decisions and outcomes, however, despite some claims that race is a less significant factor than socioeconomic status. Obviously, these conclusions do not do justice to the increasingly complex research on actual outcomes. It is interesting, though, that socioeconomic and race variables—at the least—do not enter strongly into the social psychological jury simulation research but do seem to affect actual decisions. In the great majority of criminal cases, verdicts and sentences are determined by judges, usually after a plea and sentence negotiation process. The simulation studies suggest that those who go to jury trial are less likely to experience discriminatory treatment on the basis of race or socioeconomic status. It is important to keep in mind, though, that simulation studies have a number of shortcomings, as we will discuss shortly.

In a Canadian study, Victoria Esses and Christopher Webster (1988) found that physical attractiveness may affect the decision to place offenders into a special classification, called the

Dangerous Offender Category, as spelled out in the Canadian Criminal Code. Specifically, physically unattractive sexual offenders were seen by special judicial boards and decisionmakers as more dangerous than average-looking or attractive sexual offenders. The judicial decisionmakers believed that the unattractive offenders were less likely to restrain themselves in the future. In the United States, Stewart (1980) reported that the less physically attractive the defendant, the more severe the sentences given by actual trial judges.

In summary, research results thus far suggest that physical attractiveness could be of considerable significance in the courtroom, especially in criminal cases. However, in light of group dynamics and the effects of evidence itself, we must remain extremely skeptical in making inferences about the total impact in a majority of cases. In other words, physical attractiveness is unlikely to be a major determinant of case outcomes.

SOCIAL ATTRACTIVENESS

Many of the investigations focusing on social attractiveness have weighted that variable heavily by manipulating several characteristics of a person at the same time. For example, marital status, work history, age, and occupational status have all been used to contribute to overall "social attractiveness." Therefore, it is difficult to know whether any one characteristic outweighed the others, or how combinations of them may have affected the total picture. Mock jurors are usually given descriptions of defendants that include several positive or several negative attributes. The crime is always identical, regardless of the defendant's description. The object of the experiment is to discover whether the socially unattractive defendant will be judged more harshly than the socially attractive one.

One of the earliest such empirical projects was a two-part study designed by Landy and Aronson (1969) examining both victim and defendant social attractiveness. In the first experiment, the hypothetical victim of a drunken driving accident with death resulting was presented as either of high or low social status, and there was no manipulation of the defendant's attractiveness. Jurors were harsher when defendants had killed the high-status victim. In the second experiment, the two levels of victim status were maintained, but the researchers introduced three levels of defendant status (high, neutral, low). Here, high- and neutral-status defendants were given less harsh sentences than those of low status, even though the offense was identical.

The Landy and Aronson experiments have been criticized on several fronts. The researchers have been accused of stacking the deck by making the victims or the defendants overly attractive and of examining too many variables. Age, past criminal record, occupational status, previous personal tragedies, and friendliness were all included as variables, thus making it difficult to determine precisely which variable or combination of variables affected sentencing. Davis, Bray, and Holt (1977) claimed that neither experiment, by itself, showed an effect for victim attractiveness; it was only after pooling scores across the two studies that an effect emerged. Davis and his colleagues argued that this method is of dubious validity, since the studies differed in samples and procedures.

The Landy and Aronson study stimulated a rash of additional research, because the suggestion that a relationship exists between social attractiveness and decisionmaking by juries was too provocative to ignore. Many of the subsequent studies have provided at least partial support for the hypothesis that defendants who are perceived as socially positive and as responsible members of society receive more lenient treatment than persons seen in a less positive light (Berg & Vidmar, 1975; Kaplan & Kemmerick, 1974; Reynolds & Sanders, 1973; Nemeth & Sosis, 1973; Friend & Vinson, 1974; Izzett & Fishman, 1976; Izzett & Leginski, 1974; Sigall & Landy, 1972;

201

JUROR
PERCEPTIONS
OF
DEFENDANT
AND
VICTIM

CHAPTER
EIGHT:
THE
PSYCHOLOGY
OF THE
JURY:
DECISIONMAKING
PROCESSES

Dowdle, Gillen & Miller, 1974; Kulka & Kessler, 1978; Solomon & Schopler, 1978). To date, studies regarding victim attractiveness have been less definitive.

ATTITUDINAL ATTRACTIVENESS

Is it any surprise that people tend to like those who agree with them better than those who disagree? We all view people who have many of the same attitudes as we do more positively than we view people whose attitudes are largely dissimilar to our own. The proportion of similar attitudes expressed by the other person is critical, however (Byrne & Nelson, 1965). If a person only agrees with us on twelve out of twenty-four topics, he or she is not liked as much as another who agrees with us on four out of six topics (Byrne, 1971). If jurors perceive a defendant (or any litigant) as having many of the same beliefs and attitudes they have, might they be more inclined to view the defendant favorably and to be more lenient in judging the person's behavior? Like physical and social attractiveness, attitudinal attractiveness has been subjected to empirical study under simulated conditions in an attempt to answer this question.

Griffitt and Jackson (1973) tested the attitude-similarity hypothesis and found that the more similar the defendant's attitudes were to the mock jury's attitudes, the less inclined they were to find him guilty. When they did find him guilty, jurors recommended that the attitudinally similar defendant be given a more lenient sentence.

Mitchell and Byrne (1973) also report some support for the attitude-similarity hypothesis. Their study looked at the relationship between juror-defendant attitude similarity and authoritarianism and how that relationship affected ratings of guilt and sentences. The results suggested that the personality of the juror may play an important role. Only jurors high in authoritarianism were significantly influenced by attitude similarity; they were more likely to consider a dissimilar defendant guilty than one who was like themselves. Furthermore, they recommended more severe sentences for defendants who were dissimilar to themselves. Jurors low on authoritarianism, however, were not influenced by attitude similarity.

As a whole, studies like these indicate that defendants who are physically and socially attractive or who are attitudinally similar to mock jurors will probably receive some degree of leniency. If these results were generalizable to actual courtroom situations, it would mean that defense attorneys could engender sympathy for their clients by emphasizing these attractiveness variables to the jury. On the other hand, some "unattractive" victims might be irremediably disadvantaged. However, we cannot say with assurance that the results can be applied so readily.

An experiment by Izzett and Leginski (1974) suggests that group deliberation reduces the tendency of individuals to give severe sentences to *unattractive* defendants, but that the effect of the group process on the sentencing of *attractive* defendants is negligible. Kaplan and Miller (1978) suggest that group deliberations tend to mitigate individual juror biases. On the other hand, Rumsey and Castore (1974) (cited by Davis, Bray & Holt, 1977) found that mock jurors were lenient toward an attractive defendant both before and after group discussion. At this point, we can only state that attitudinal attractiveness appears to play a significant role in influencing the judgments of individuals, but the effects of group deliberation remain equivocal.

Many of the studies on the relationship between attitudinal attractiveness and jury decision-making have been conducted by social psychologists testing Byrne's (1971) reinforcement theory of attraction, which predicts that the perception of similarity is rewarding and the perception of dissimilarity is nonrewarding, or even punishing. Byrne argues that similarity leads to liking, because it gives people independent evidence for the correctness of their own interpretation of social reality. While this theory has support (Clore & Byrne, 1974; Lott & Lott, 1974), it does not explain why jurors would respond favorably to physically or socially attractive defendants who may not be similar to the jurors themselves.

Juror Decisionmaking

The process of arriving at individual and group decisions involves numerous variables and complex cognitive processes, and considerable research has been directed at this topic. The most recent efforts have proposed new concepts and models to understand jury decisionmaking. Well-tested principles of social psychology can also be applied, however.

THE STORY MODEL

Nancy Pennington and Reid Hastie (1986) developed an interesting model of how jurors decide on guilt or innocence. Pennington and Hastie propose that, even before hearing all the evidence, jurors construct in their minds a story of how events—testified to at the trial—took place. In other words, jurors develop their own personal version of "what happened," and this conceptual structure allows them to incorporate the bits and pieces of trial evidence into it. Thus, the model tries to identify how jurors organize and make sense of the vast array of evidence that is presented during the trial process.

According to this **story model**, there is a central theme or character in the story jurors construct. For example, Vicki Smith (1991) found that prospective jurors have a pre-existing conceptual prototype of certain crimes and offenders. Prospective jurors in her study generally conceived of a kidnapping as being characterized by ransom demands, the victim being a child, the victim being taken away, and the motive being money. Moreover, jurors tended to persist with these conceptions or stereotypes, in spite of jury instructions on points of law. In fact, research has found that mock jurors actually have little correct information about the law (Smith, 1991). They do not enter the jury box "empty headed" waiting for their charge, however. Rather, they have a preconceived notion of the crime scenario and the type of person who would commit such a crime. These personal stories of the crime and their prototypes of crime categories can influence their perceptions of the trial evidence and their verdict decisions.

If the trial evidence matches this cognitive schema and the defendant follows the preconceived prototype, the juror is most likely to make a verdict decision along the lines of the developed story, regardless of the instructions or legal definitions. Smith found that the schema of laypersons concerning various types of crime were contrary to the way the categories are organized under the law. Smith (1991, p. 870) concludes: "These findings are consistent with research in other areas of social psychology demonstrating the potential dangers of prior knowledge of theories for accurate judgment and decision making."

HINDSIGHT BIAS

Another cognitive process that might contaminate jury decisionmaking is **hindsight bias**, which refers to biased judgments of past events after the outcome is known. It is "...a projection of new knowledge into the past accompanied by a *denial that the outcome information has influenced judgment*" (Hawkings & Hastie, 1990, p. 311). Thus, when people learn of an outcome they typically claim they "knew all along" what it would be. Said another way, "The hindsight bias is the tendency for people with outcome knowledge to believe falsely that they would have predicted the reported outcome of an event" (Hawkins & Hastie, 1990, p. 311). This bias

204

CHAPTER
EIGHT:
THE
PSYCHOLOGY
OF THE
JURY:
DECISIONMAKING
PROCESSES

potentially affects how jurors select, process, and integrate evidence for decisionmaking.

Researchers have found evidence of hindsight bias, particularly in medical malpractice or product liability suits. In these types of cases, jurors are supposed to base their judgments on the defendant's behavior *prior* to the occurrence of harm or damage. However, knowing that the defendant has curtailed his medical practice following the incident, jurors will find it extremely difficult not to blame him for the harm to the plaintiff. As another example, suppose police officers are charged with excessive force at arrest. The arrest, however, convinces an informant to come forward and help other officers solve a separate murder case. Knowledge that this occurred results in a tendency to excuse the original officers, even though they broke the law.

Casper, Benedict, and Perry (1989), in an effort to determine the power of hindsight bias in jury verdicts, used simulated case materials (on videotape) and mock juries composed of college students and other adults called for jury service. The researchers reasoned that in many legal disputes jurors are told a "story" that a particular outcome occurred, but they are instructed to ignore the outcome when deciding the important legal issues before them. The videotape showed two attorneys who gave the same general story, but shaded and interpreted the story in different ways. The central story was that two police officers received a tip from an informant that a man involved in a crime was at a particular address, an apartment building. The informant provided a general, vague description of the man. The officers proceeded to the address and knocked on the first door they saw. The door was answered by a man who fit the description given by the informant. When he refused to allow them in, the officers forced their way in, knocking him to the floor, causing a cut on his forehead. The officers proceeded to search the apartment, causing $600 in damages to the apartment.

The researchers set up three possible outcomes to the story. One-third of the mock jurors were told that the police search turned up evidence of illegal conduct, one-third were told the police found no evidence of illegality, and another third received no outcome information. The jurors were instructed by the mock judge to decide whether the police were liable for any compensatory and punitive damages. The judge's instructions indicated that their decisions should be based on the lawfulness of the police search.

The data indicated that the outcome knowledge (hindsight bias) had a significant effect on juror decisions. That is, jurors who had been told that something incriminating had been found during the illegal search of the apartment were less likely to award compensatory or punitive damages to a plaintiff. Hindsight bias, then, appears to be a complicated but important cognitive process in juror decisionmaking for cases where an outcome is already known.

JUST-WORLD HYPOTHESIS

Psychologists have observed that many people believe the world is a just place, where one gets what one deserves and deserves what one gets (Lerner, 1970). This simplistic belief may help to explain why juries sometimes make the decisions they do. In a just world, fate and a person's merit are closely aligned, "good" people are rewarded, and "bad" people are punished. Believers in a just world perceive a connection between what people do, are, or believe in and what happens to them. Over the past decade, these observations have been shaped into a hypothesis which is getting, and should continue to receive, considerable research attention.

According to the just-world hypothesis, for the sake of cognitive consistency, many people cannot believe in a world governed by a schedule of random reinforcements or events. The suffering of innocent or respectable people—those who have done nothing to bring about their own grief—would be too unacceptable and unjust (Lerner & Simmons, 1966). Thus, when tragedy strikes, believers in a just world tend to blame the victims, concluding that these victims must have deserved their fate in some way. Conversely, there is also a strong propensity to attribute good fortune and luck, like winning a lottery, to having done something good or positive (Rubin & Peplau, 1973). An important qualification, however, is that just-worlders tend to attribute causality or blame to the victim only as a last resort, preferring to blame another person or an obvious cause whenever possible.

Researchers examining the hypothesis have found that belief in a just world is positively related to belief in a higher being and religiosity (Staub, 1978; Zuckerman & Gerbasi, 1977); authoritarianism (Rubin & Peplau, 1973); political conservatism and adherence to traditional values (Lerner, 1977; Staub, 1978); trust (Rubin & Peplau, 1975); the "work ethic," by which it is assumed that hard work brings just rewards (Zuckerman & Gerbasi, 1977); and a tendency to admire and respect political leaders and powerful institutions (Rubin & Peplau, 1975). Believers in a just world are also presumed to be hostile and unsympathetic toward victims of social injustice, especially when their suffering cannot be easily alleviated (Lerner, 1970; Lerner & Simmons, 1966). Moreover, a just-world orientation encourages an adherence to the rules and laws that are intended to guide conduct and control the nature of a society as a whole (rather than a benevolent attitude toward individuals and their specific welfare).

Just-worlders use two dimensions to decide whether others deserve their fates—actions and attributes (Lerner, 1980). To just-worlders, acts displaying cruelty, unfriendliness, stinginess, hostility, or antisocial behavior deserve a range of negative consequences. However, attributes like physical attractiveness, intelligence, taste in dress, social status, or social power and influence also determine just-worlders' (as well as many other people's) impressions and judgments.

Attractiveness, whether physical or social, is assumed by many people to be deserved. That is, attractive people have earned their attractiveness by being good, positive persons. It follows the same logic as that proposed by Dion, Berscheid, and Walster (1972), that "what is beautiful or socially desirable must be good." Therefore, we would expect jurors who are just-worlders to consider attractive defendants as being basically good and deserving of lenient treatment.

The just-world hypothesis has been examined in relation to victims of criminal actions or accidents. Jones and Aronson (1973) investigated several hypotheses, including the prediction that a socially attractive victim of a crime is perceived as more at fault than a less socially attractive victim. Mock jurors were 234 college undergraduates who read a brief case account of either an actual rape or an attempted rape, involving victims presumed to differ in social "respectability" or social attractiveness: a married woman, an unmarried woman who had never had sex, and a divorced woman. The researchers had distributed a pretest questionnaire which indicated that married women and unmarried women who had not had sex were more highly regarded and respectable in society than divorced women. Subjects were presented with descriptions of the crime, the defendant, and the victim, and they were asked how many years the defendant should be imprisoned and how much the victim was at fault.

The first hypothesis predicted that more fault would be attributed to a respectable victim than to a less respectable one. This is in accordance with the just-world belief that something tragic does not happen to persons with good character; somehow, they must have done something to bring their fate upon themselves. A second hypothesis predicted that a defendant who injured a respectable person would be punished more severely. As a third hypothesis, Jones and Aronson predicted that an actual rape would be more severely punished than an attempted rape.

The results were generally in the direction of the predictions. Regardless of their own gender, subjects did feel that the women of high respectability were more at fault for the rape than the divorced woman. In assigning punishment to the defendant, the subjects gave more severe

206

Chapter
Eight:
The
Psychology
of the
Jury:
Decisionmaking
Processes

sentences when an actual rape had occurred. The second hypothesis was only partially confirmed, however. Although stiffer sentences were meted out when the victim of an actual rape was married, the jurors drew no distinction between the other two groups; similar punishments were given in both cases. For attempted rape, however, the offender received approximately the same sentence whether the victim was married or unmarried, and received substantially less punishment if the victim had been divorced. Interestingly, the severe punishment for the actual rape of a married compared to an unmarried woman may reflect a perspective that the woman's spouse was injured as well. Thus, though the married woman was considered at fault, the jurors may have been trying to compensate her husband by being especially punitive to the offender.

In general, the results of the Jones-Aronson study lend support to a just-world hypothesis where it concerns the evaluation of crime victims. Jurors persisted in attributing fault to women of high respectability who, because the world is just, somehow must have done something to bring the attack upon themselves. This attribution of fault did not affect the severity of punishment given the defendant, however.

There are many unanswered questions regarding the results of the above study, and had Jones and Aronson administered a just-world scale to their jurors, the results might have proved more intriguing. They are striking enough, however, to make a just-world interpretation worth pursuing. In light of changing social mores, results of that study would likely be different today, when society is more sensitive to the issue of rape, regardless of the marital status of the victim.

More research is needed to explore the just-world phenomenon in depth. Is it a near-universal attribute? If not, is it present in a significant percentage of the population? Have times changed so much that a just-world orientation is no longer discernible in a significant number of research subjects? These are questions worth placing on a social-psychology research agenda.

AUTHORITARIANISM

Authoritarianism is the term used to describe an ideology or an attitude system holding that one should unquestionably accept authority from recognized powerful people and institutions. Since authoritarianism is present in people in varying degrees, it is possible to speak of high or low authoritarians. The former conform strictly to conventional social norms and exhibit black-or-white thinking, rigid prejudice toward those who are different or do not embrace their points of view, and hostility toward those who deviate from established social norms. On jury panels, high authoritarians are hypothesized to be intolerant and to have a tendency to condemn, reject, and punish those who violate conventional wisdom and laws. Therefore, we would expect high authoritarians to convict frequently and to render severe punishments. On the other hand, it is hypothesized that authoritarians would be more accepting and lenient toward those individuals whom they perceive as sharing their own values.

Low authoritarians demonstrate opposite attitudes. Authority is not inherently respected, but must earn respect. Low authoritarians do not place great value on conventional norms, and they have more tolerance for those who deviate. Sometimes called egalitarians, people low in authoritarianism are believed to be more objective in making jury decisions.

A number of jury-simulation studies have examined the authoritarianism continuum and have contrasted persons at both poles. As expected, the research has reported that high-authoritarian jurors are more inclined to perceive guilt and give more severe punishments when the defendant is described as attitudinally dissimilar from themselves or as having a negative character (Berg & Vidmar, 1975; Mitchell & Byrne, 1973; Boehm, 1968). It has also been reported that authoritarians are more in favor of the death penalty than egalitarians are (Jurow, 1971) and are especially punitive toward low-status defendants (Berg & Vidmar, 1975). It will be recalled from Chapter 7 that authoritarianism was one of the characteristics distinguishing death-qualified jurors form non-death-qualified jurors.

Authoritarians seem to be more strongly influenced by the judge (Bandewehr & Novotny, 1976), but they are also more likely to ignore a judge when told to disregard testimony about a defendant's character. Egalitarians, presumably because they are open minded, recall more evidence about the crime (Berg & Vidmar, 1975). High authoritarians have also been found to be "source oriented" and nonauthoritarians to be "message oriented." That is, authoritarians pay comparatively little attention to arguments and testimony and base their responses more readily on the attributes of the sources (Johnson & Steiner, 1967).

Might group interaction limit the impact of an authoritarian personality? Several researchers have addressed this question. Boehm (1968) contended that authoritarians reach their minds early in a trial and resist changing their verdict in the face of new information. Egalitarians, on the other hand, presumably resist making early judgments until they are given all the information about a case. Other social-psychological research, however, has found that authoritarians are more susceptible to influence than egalitarians are (e.g., Kirscht & Dillehay, 1967; Bray & Noble, 1978).

In an attempt to obtain further information on the effects of group interaction on authoritarians, Bray and Noble (1978) conducted a simulation study in which forty-four six-person juries listened to a 30-minute audio recording of a murder trial based on an actual case. After hearing the tape, subjects entered into group discussion to simulate the jury-deliberation process. A verdict could be returned only if five of the six jurors agreed on a decision within 45 minutes; failure to do so resulted in a hung jury.

Prior to the experiment, the subjects were administered psychological scales to determine their level of authoritarianism. In addition, measures of the individual juror's judgments about guilt were made prior to and after the deliberation. The experimenters were interested in both individual juror decisions and in the six-member jury verdict.

The results revealed that authoritarian jurors and juries reached guilty verdicts more often and imposed more severe punishments than egalitarian juries did. The latter finding is consistent with other studies (e.g, Berg & Vidmar, 1975; Jurow, 1971; Mitchell & Byrne, 1973) and has some potential implications for trials involving capital punishment, as discussed earlier. Authoritarians were more likely than egalitarians to say they would convict when death was a potential penalty.

The data also showed that both authoritarians and egalitarians shifted their verdicts during deliberation, although authoritarians exhibited significantly more such shifts. This finding lends credence to the possibility that authoritarians are influenced substantially by group interaction. The direction of the shifts also differed for each group: Authoritarians gave more severe sentences after group deliberations, while egalitarians demonstrated a trend toward more lenience. These shifts reflected the choice initially favored by the jurors and provide support for the group-polarization effect to be discussed below.

Although we must be cautious about making generalizations from simulation to actual jury decisionmaking, it does appear that authoritarianism is an influential factor in the jury process. Ellison and Buckhout (1981) conclude that authoritarianism is common and very likely plays a significant role in the judgments made by juries. According to these researchers, mock jurors' scores on the authoritarian scale have been the best predictors of conviction they have encountered. Also, like Bray and Noble, Ellison and Buckhout found that authoritarians are consistently in favor of the death penalty and nonreceptive to consideration of mitigating factors.

This leads to an important issue, one that comes in the realm of the psychology *and* law

208

CHAPTER
EIGHT:
THE
PSYCHOLOGY
OF THE
JURY:
DECISIONMAKING
PROCESSES

relationship discussed in Chapter 1. Some researchers have suggested that authoritarians are undesirable as jurors and should as a matter of policy be eliminated in the *voir dire*. But law is a social and political enterprise developed from the moral fabric of society. If authoritarianism is a common ingredient of American culture and presumably of American juries, and if a democratic system is based on the attitudes of its citizens, shouldn't authoritarians be impaneled representatively? If attorneys are to reject prospective jurors on the basis of personality type, the rejections should be made via established judicial procedures of peremptory and for-cause challenges. A policy decision that would preclude authoritarians (or just-worlders or "neurotics") from being seated on a jury would be ill advised.

Group Processes

POLARIZATION

James Stoner (1961) discovered that when people got together in a group they were more daring or "risky" in their decisionmaking than when they made decisions as individuals. This phenomenon, eventually called the risky-shift effect, stimulated the interest of numerous investigators who generated a collection of studies to test it. As so often happens in psychological research, however, what appeared to be simple was discovered to be highly complex. "Risky shift" was a misnomer that did not portray accurately the effects of groups on individual decisions (Myers & Lamm, 1976). Subsequent research illustrated that group deliberation may produce more cautious, as well as more risky, decisions depending upon the context, and thus was born the group-polarization hypothesis.

The hypothesis states: "The average postgroup response will tend to be more extreme in the same direction as the average of the pregroup responses" (Myers & Lamm, 1976, p. 603). That rather complicated maxim simply means if individual members of a group are leaning toward a not-guilty verdict, the group interaction will increase their commitment to a not-guilty verdict. If, on the other hand, individual members tend to believe a defendant guilty, group discussion should encourage stronger commitment to a guilty verdict. In civil cases, an individual juror's belief that a plaintiff deserves a substantial award for damages might be reinforced in group discussion, and the ultimate group decision would award even higher damages. Thus, polarization refers to the shift toward the already preferred pole.

Myers and Kaplan (1976) presented subjects with case materials that clearly made defendants in eight hypothetical traffic felony cases appear either guilty or not guilty. If the subjects found the defendant guilty, they were also expected to recommend punishment. The guilty/not-guilty judgments were made on a scale ranging from 0 (definitely not guilty) to 20 (definitely guilty), and the punishment recommendation was given on a scale ranging from 1 (minimum punishment for the infraction) to 7 (maximum punishment).

Myers and Kaplan found that group deliberations polarized the initial response tendencies associated with a case. Mock jurors who leaned toward guilty verdicts and punishment became harsher following deliberations. Those with lenient initial judgments became more lenient after deliberations. When jury deliberations were not allowed, however, judgments did not change from the first to the final rating.

Walker and Main (1973) compared the civil liberties decisions of individual federal district court judges to the decisions of three-judge panels in the same cases. Initial individual views were mildly pro-civil-liberties, so it was anticipated that group interaction would magnify (polarize)

209

JURY
SIMULATION:
CRITIQUES
AND
CONCLUSIONS

these views. This hypothesis was supported, as the group condition engendered more pro-civil-liberties decisions than the single-judge condition (65 percent compared to 30 percent).

A number of other experiments using simulated jury conditions have demonstrated the shift from prediscussion tendency to postdiscussion certainty (Bray & Kerr, 1979; Kerr, Nerenz & Herrick, 1979; Bray et al., 1978; Kaplan, 1977). It appears that group discussion, at least under simulated conditions and with college students as mock jurors, does in fact polarize already existing opinions or beliefs.

LENIENCY BIAS

Harry Kalven and Hans Zeisel (1966) in their classic, *The American Jury*, reported that in criminal trials in which the judge disagreed with the jury's decisions, the jury was almost always more lenient toward the defendant than the judge. Overall, jury trials resulted in twice as many acquittals as might have occurred if the cases had been tried only by the judge. This phenomenon, seen primarily in criminal trials, has been called the **leniency bias**. The bias also refers to the frequent observation in *mock* criminal jury trials that people are prone to vote guilty on their own but are more likely to vote not guilty when in group deliberation. The group-deliberation process, for some unknown reason, seems to induce jurors to be more lenient.

Leniency bias appears to be especially prevalent in jury deliberations in which there is no clear, predominant preference for conviction or acquittal at the beginning (MacCoun & Kerr, 1988). It is also most likely to occur in situations requiring a dichotomous verdict (guilty or not guilty).

Jury Simulation:
Critiques and Conclusions

J ury simulation studies that attempt to understand both individual and group decisionmaking are being conducted at a steady pace, but doubts about their external or ecological validity persist. Can an experimental situation even approximate a real-life encounter? Studying the jury process is a formidable task. Even if researchers were allowed to observe or manipulate actual jury proceedings, there would be such an annoying myriad of independent variables that experimental control and precise measurement would be nearly impossible. More importantly, of course, such experimentation would impinge on the ethical, social, and legal issue of "justice."

THE LITANY OF COMPLAINTS

The simulation studies to date have had other problems, summarized bluntly by Neil Vidmar (1979). "It is argued that much jury simulation research, especially that involving investigation of the effects of defendant character on juror-jury decisions, can be fairly described as marked by (a) legal naivete, (b) sloppy scholarship, and (c) overgeneralization combined with inappropriate value judgments" (Vidmar, 1979, p. 96).

Vidmar's first criticism refers to the lack of legal sophistication and knowledge of the judicial system displayed by research psychologists. Thus, experimental designs have been flawed by the inclusion of unrealistic scenarios or instructions. For example, many studies have required subjects to determine the amount of punishment a defendant should receive, when in actual practice, except for capital cases, juries are rarely involved in sentencing. Some researchers have been known to confuse criminal and civil trials, as by presenting subjects with criminal trial materials and asking

210

CHAPTER
EIGHT:
THE
PSYCHOLOGY
OF THE
JURY:
DECISIONMAKING
PROCESSES

them both to determine guilt or innocence and award damages! More subtle gaffes have occurred when researchers have not been familiar with statutes, with what is permissible evidence, or with what are legally acceptable jury instructions. Sometimes, courtroom procedures have been presented out of sequence, or researchers have failed to provide subjects with clear definitions of the standards of proof for determining guilt.

Researchers also commonly ask subjects to determine degrees of guilt (as on scales from one to ten) rather than simply return a guilty or not-guilty verdict. In defense of this practice, we must note that simple guilty or not-guilty verdicts are difficult to analyze statistically. They result in a dichotomous variable—one that has only two possibilities. Researchers prefer a continuous variable denoted by different degrees, since such a variable is sensitive to differences and allows a more powerful computer analysis. In recent years, however, researchers have become more sophisticated and have largely overcome errors in methodology related to ignorance of law and procedure.

As an example of sloppy scholarship, Vidmar notes a frequent, unwarranted practice on the part of researchers to cite inaccurately the findings of Kalven and Zeisel's *The American Jury* and to align their own results with those of that classic study. In essence, Vidmar argues, many investigators are not justified in claiming similarity between their studies and the Kalven-Zeisel project, because their results simply do not correspond. The Kalven-Zeisel project was based on actual jury deliberations, whereas the vast majority of studies are based on mock juries. Some researchers are just as lax with respect to other studies, inaccurately citing results or misunderstanding the theoretical positions of other scholars. This builds pyramids of inaccuracy and misinformation into the research literature.

Vidmar's third criticism pertains to grandiose assertions by researchers that their studies will help solve the problems of the judicial system. "Researchers have tended to puff up the potential importance of their findings without taking into consideration all the other factors that might offset them in a real world trial" (Vidmar, 1979, p. 100).

It is debatable whether jury-simulation studies, as they have thus far been designed, can make significant contributions to understanding courtroom procedures, primarily because of the artificial and dissimilar conditions under which they are conducted. No matter how much the simulation approaches authenticity, subjects still realize they are playing a role devoid of all the stresses and anxieties that deciding the fate of another human being can generate.

Researchers also may overvalue the extralegal influences and biases of jurors. Although these factors can affect some of the proceedings, the strength of the evidence is a significant factor in the determination of guilt. On the other hand, as noted above, researchers studying the criminal-justice system have long been aware of disparities in the treatment of offenders at all stages of the process, based on extralegal factors. With respect to the trial itself, researchers in social psychology cannot forget that there are various legal procedural safeguards that reduce bias. Attorneys can mitigate prejudice during the *voir dire*, although the extent to which this is done varies widely with the competence of the attorneys.

Several other problems undermine the quality of the simulation research and limit its applicability to the judicial system. An often repeated criticism questions the use of college students as mock jurors. Students at research universities where the studies are generally conducted tend to be from the middle class, well educated, intelligent, young, and liberal in ideology—hardly representative of the population at large from which juries are typically drawn. It can also be argued that the lack of experiential learning by college students is a deficit. In any case, the student subjects are not representative of the population. With increases in continuing-education programs and the fact that a greater proportion of the public is college educated, this problem may be attenuated.

211

JURY
SIMULATION:
CRITIQUES
AND
CONCLUSIONS

Still another problem with jury-simulation research pertains to the presentation of materials. In over half of the studies on jury decisionmaking, subjects have been presented with written case materials that are often extremely brief and simplistic summaries of usually hypothetical cases (Bray & Kerr, 1979). In about a third of the experiments, audio presentation has been used, and it too was of short duration (thirty to ninety minutes). These time limits and modes of presentation in no way reflect the intricacies of courtroom trials. True jurors receive trial information at uneven, sometimes lengthy time-intervals—through all the sense modalities. By and large, the information is received through auditory channels. Jurors rarely read case materials while trials are in progress.

Another fundamental problem is that most jury-simulation research has focused on individual juror decisions rather than on collective jury decisions. Those projects that have included group discussion or group-derived verdicts have had unreasonable time restrictions (e.g., a verdict must be reached within thirty minutes) and have used an exceedingly small number of "jurors." Rarely have the subjects been asked to return a final group verdict; rather, individual verdicts after group discussion have been sought (Weiten & Diamond, 1979).

Some researchers believe that studying individual jurors is a valid approach. Citing the Kalven and Zeisel data, they argue that the first ballot in deliberation is a strong predictor of the final outcome, even without group discussion. Although the first vote often does predict the eventual verdict, some group interaction has occurred prior to the vote, sometimes pertaining to evidence, sometimes to opinions about a wide range of issues. By preventing some group interaction, some researchers have altered significantly the conditions they are trying to simulate.

Finally, the subjective values of the behavioral and social-science researcher have entered frequently into their studies' conclusions. As Vidmar notes (1979, p. 101), if it were up to psychologists, the jury "would be an elitist body composed primarily of liberal ('nonauthoritarian'), well educated persons.... Potential jurors who are conservative in their sociopolitical attitudes are assumed to be less competent as jurors." This position is hardly in keeping with the scientific objectivity espoused over the years by research psychologists. On the other hand, it is no less objectionable to exclude the "liberal" group of jurors, as appears to happen in the context of capital cases.

IS SIMULATION RESEARCH VALUABLE?

The problems discussed above are some of the major flaws making generalizations from laboratory to courtroom risky. While the foregoing may make one wonder if any of the research on jury simulation is of value, it is important to remember that one of the hallmarks of science is skepticism of interpretations and willingness to seek alternative explanations and approaches. The behavioral sciences move forward in a spiral fashion, becoming more sound both in theory and in method as the pioneer approaches are critiqued and improved. We must also keep in mind that a great majority of the jury-simulation studies have occurred only since 1970.

Some researchers argue that the simulated-jury approach still offers the best alternative to research testing real juries, which is seldom tolerated by the judicial system. Of course, it is possible to study the approach of the jury—the verdict—and to obtain demographic and personality characteristics of the jurors, as well as their personal accounts, after their decision has been rendered. The major problem with this approach is that the nearly endless list of possible contributors is difficult to disentangle. It is much more advantageous to investigate before and during the decisionmaking process.

In summary, the simulation research done so far hardly approximates the reality of the jury

212

CHAPTER
EIGHT:
THE
PSYCHOLOGY
OF THE
JURY:
DECISIONMAKING
PROCESSES

process. Theories developed from these studies have a high risk of being inadequate in accounting for jury decisionmaking. Although empirical psychology is self-corrective in the long run, a premature conclusion by researchers that they have discovered the psychological secrets of the jury process through simulation study may do more harm than good. Theories and hypotheses developed within the confines of the artificial atmosphere of the psychological laboratory must be tested against the actual natural event before conclusions can be advanced. This may require archival and case-by-case analysis of actual trials. In any event, results acquired from simulation research should be treated with great caution and skepticism.

Mathematical Models: Theory and Skepticism

One of the most recent trends in jury research is the development by psychologists of cognitive, behavioral, mathematical, and computer models of juror (and jury) decisionmaking. The models try to describe the operations human beings use to make decisions and judgments as they sort through both preconceived notions and information gained during the trial process. Some of these decisionmaking models are extremely elaborate and technical; those of the mathematical and computer variety, for example, often employ algebraic combinations, weights, constants, and intricate formulae. They are designed to take into consideration relevant quantifiable variables, to combine these variables by means of mathematical logic, and to produce an end result which should approximate decisions actually made by men and women.

The numerous models now being tested are too complicated and incomplete to present here. Considerable work remains to be done before they are ready to apply to the judicial process. The reader is referred to Penrod and Hastie (1979) and Pennington and Hastie (1981) for a complete assessment of the mathematical and computer models germane to juror and jury decisionmaking. For illustrative purposes, we will focus on one such model.

THE INFORMATION INTEGRATION MODEL

Martin Kaplan and his colleagues (see, generally, Kaplan & Schersching, 1980; 1981) have drawn connections between *information integration theory* and the jury deliberation process. The theory attempts to describe the way people combine information about an object or person in reaching a judgment. Each bit of information or impression about a judged object is assigned a *scale value*, which "refers to the quantitative expression of the belief on the judgment dimension" (Kaplan & Schersehing, 1981, p. 236). For example, if we are talking about a guilty/not-guilty dimension, and the defendant matches a witness's description, we would conclude that this bit of information has high scale value in determination of guilt. However, if other evidence indicates that the defendant may have been at another place at the time of the crime, the *descriptive* information would have lower scale value for establishing guilt.

If the **information integration model** is correct, a juror assigns cognitively an impression or scale value to each bit of information which relates to the judgment. These separate scale values must be integrated into a unified impression or judgment. Obviously, not all pieces of information will contribute equally to the judgment. For instance, discovering that a defendant had a good motive for committing the crime may not be as informative as finding out that the defendant was at the scene of the crime. The model, therefore, assumes that each belief has two quantifiable

213

MATHEMATICAL
MODELS:
THEORY
AND
SKEPTICISM

features: a scale value on the judgment continuum and a weight (or importance) for the judgment. These weighted scale values can then be integrated into an overall judgment concerning a defendant or other relevant object. This integration process is theorized to be analogous to (and representable by) an algebraic operation in each juror's head.

For illustrative purposes let us examine how the model might account for the polarization effects described above. Polarization effects, remember, are specific to group deliberations. If the model is to account for them, it must explain what transpires within the "cognitive algebraic processing" of each juror during the group deliberation. It is assumed that a preliminary judgment has already been made by each juror prior to deliberation. According to the polarization hypothesis, this preliminary judgment becomes more extreme after discussion. Kaplan makes the theoretical assumption that the preliminary or predeliberation judgment will not be as extreme in guilt-value as warranted by the evidence provided during the trial. This theoretical assumption can be supported by a weighted-averaging model: When a "neutral" initial impression possessed by most jurors is averaged in with the evidentiary information received during the trial, the predeliberation judgment will be less polarized than might be expected strictly from the evidence. In other words, the initial impression will tend to dampen the overall judgment, at least until the jury deliberates.

During the deliberation process, information received during the trial is exchanged among the jurors. While all the information that is exchanged was available to each juror during the course of the trial, each juror, due to individual attention and cognitive restraints, based her or his initial or predeliberation judgment only on a segment of the total information. Such information was also dampened (assuming neutrality) by that initial impression. During discussion with other jurors, a larger amount of trial information is acquired. The information integration model predicts that increasing the amount of non-neutral informational elements (trial information) relative to the more neutral initial impression will move the judgment closer to the information value. This process essentially represents the polarization effect.

The information integration model hypothesizes that other influences occur during deliberation, but these are tangential to our current discussion. However, it is important to note that Kaplan's model strongly supports the value of a twelve-person jury compared to a six-person jury, because of the information sharing which occurs. Even more important from a psychological perspective, however, is the considerable theoretical value the model has for integrating our knowledge about the jury process and for stimulating further research.

SHOULD MATHEMATICAL MODELS BE USED?

The mathematical and computer models do raise an issue which merits some consideration. Let us imagine that one of the mathematical models can accurately predict (99 percent of the time) the verdicts juries will deliver. The prediction track-record eventually becomes so impressive, in fact, that it generates the suggestion that the model should replace the jury. After all, it would probably be much more cost efficient. The question then becomes, *should it?*

In an influential *Harvard Law Review* article in 1971, law professor Laurence H. Tribe was extremely critical of the potential use of scientific mathematical techniques in place of the more "intuitive tools" traditionally brought to bear in the trial process. Specifically, he asserted that the use of mathematical analyses and models in legal decisionmaking should be banned. The trial process and juror decisionmaking should be based on intuition and humanity rather than on quantifiable variables, in keeping with the long tradition of Anglo-Saxon law. Legal "truth" can be garnered from the "soft quantifiable variables" inherent in the human reliance on values and

214

CHAPTER
EIGHT:
THE
PSYCHOLOGY
OF THE
JURY:
DECISIONMAKING
PROCESSES

justice, Tribe added. The institution of the jury and the human involvement it ensured should be preserved because of the social, political, and psychological benefits it affords society. Humans should be judged by other humans, he said, not by mathematics and computers.

But let's take our impressive model one step further and assume that not only does it predict jury decisions, it also produces its own decisions about guilt or innocence. Moreover, its decisions are accurate 98 percent of the time, while jury decisions are accurate 90 percent of the time. (We are postulating, of course, an acceptable definition of *accuracy*, which makes this discussion purely an intellectual exercise.) Nevertheless, given greater decisionmaking accuracy, *do we substitute our model for human jurors?* Should the symbolic function of the trial be more important than accurate fact-finding? The question is similar to that raised by differences in accuracy between clinical and actuarial predictions discussed in Chapters 1, 4, and 6.

Saks and Kidd maintain that mathematical models are more accurate in general decision-making than the information processing of humans. The models, they argue, apply "the same logic, while the human decision maker fluctuates, being over-influenced by fortuitous, attention-catching pieces of information that vary from time to time, and processing a too-limited set of variables. Unaided individuals tend to have great difficulty incorporating quantified variables, give excessive weight to bits and pieces that happen for whatever reason to be salient, base their decision on less information (often the less useful information) than do mathematical models, and apply their decision policies inconsistently" (Saks & Kidd, 1980–81, p. 147). However, as Saks and Kidd add, it is precisely because the models fail to capture the realistic cognitive functioning of human beings that they are considered undesirable. The judicial system, as Tribe argues, prefers the imperfect but human element.

Saks and Kidd do present an argument in favor of cognitive-behavioral models of human decisionmaking (such as the Kaplan information integration model covered earlier) in contrast to the mathematical models. However, regardless of whether a model is cognitive, behavioral, or mathematical, the bottom line is: to what extent does it provide answers about human decisionmaking and offer grist for theory development? The goal of mathematical models is not to predict jury decisionmaking with total accuracy and thus take the job of trying facts away from the citizenry. Rather, insofar as the model predicts the decisionmaking of each juror or of the group, it accounts for some of the processes operating in the jurors' minds. Understanding leads to prediction, and both lead to theoretical development, the ultimate goal of the science of psychology.

Summary and Conclusions

In the summary of the previous chapter, we referred to Wallace Loh's (1979) observation that the relationship between psychology and law is marked by recurrent cycles. Part of this is due to changing interests of psychologists studying the legal system. As a group, research psychologists like to be pioneers, exploring new areas and, perhaps, settling none. Mundane replication and synchronized research efforts tend to draw them away from the excitement of being on the cutting edge of knowledge.

Thus, during the 1970s, jury research in social psychology focused on the physical and social characteristics of defendants and plaintiffs, and how these features influence jury decisionmaking. The just-world hypothesis generated a good deal of research, as we have noted. There were also attempts to develop "models" of jury decisionmaking, which led to scientific jury selection. Jury size and decision rules, discussed in the previous chapter, were explored but abandoned abruptly for other areas of discovery.

In the 1980s and 1990s, research has taken a more cognitive approach, focusing first on the effects of curative instructions and admonitions on decisionmaking. Lately, the story model has emerged, showing great promise. Hindsight and similar cognitive biases should continue to draw more attention in the years ahead. In fact, the entire research area of cognitive constructs and schemata, beliefs and attitudes, appears to be the direction taken not only by jury research, but by research in psychology and law in general.

Questions to Ponder

1. Review the recent studies in which persons who actually sat on a death-penalty jury were interviewed. What is the significance of such research for both death-penalty and non-death-penalty criminal cases?

2. Would "common sense" suggest that jurors are most likely to be influenced by physical, social, or attitudinal attractiveness? Do the jury simulation studies support this? Discuss.

3. Assuming that a "story model" does indeed operate, what explains it?

4. After summarizing the findings on the authoritarian and egalitarian personalities, discuss how (or whether) this research should realistically be used to improve the judicial process.

5. Pretend you are an ardent fan of jury-simulation research. Recognizing that jury-simulation studies have numerous problems, how would you design one that comes as close as possible to being methodologically flawless?

THE PSYCHOLOGY OF EVIDENCE: EYEWITNESS TESTIMONY

THE TESTIMONY OF A WITNESS CAN BE the most influential parcel of evidence delivered in the courtroom, particularly if the witness claims to have personally *seen* the legally relevant event, object, or person. The impact of eyewitness testimony is especially great if other kinds of evidence (e.g., weapon or fingerprints) are sparse or unavailable. Loftus (1979) notes, however, that jurors have often been known to accept eyewitness testimony at face value, even when it is heavily contradicted by other evidence. People are more apt to believe someone who was at the scene of an incident, despite what experts may assert about the evidence. Even judges, attorneys, and law-enforcement officials are more apt to accept rather than reject the observations of witnesses.

Eyewitness evidence, in fact, often has even greater legal status than other kinds of evidence in the eyes of the law. Experienced trial attorneys have long known that visual identification is one of the most cogent forms of evidence they can present to jurors and judges. They also fully realize that the quality of eyewitness testimony often determines the outcome of a case, no matter how logically tight and persuasive the arguments presented to the jury are. In her excellent review of eyewitness research, Elizabeth Loftus (1979, p. 19) summarizes the impact of witnesses on the court when she states: "All the evidence points rather strikingly to the conclusion that there is almost nothing more convincing than a live human being who takes the stand, points a finger at the defendant, and says 'that's the one!'." A discredited eyewitness seems to have less impact on jurors than a creditable one, however (Kennedy & Haggard, 1992).

The strength of eyewitness testimony can be partially explained by the legal profession's traditional reliance on common-sense generalizations about human behavior. Paul Meehl (1971) refers to this legal proclivity as "fireside induction," which is "those commonsense empirical generalizations about human behavior which we accept on the culture's authority plus introspection plus anecdotal evidence from ordinary life. Roughly, the phrase 'fireside induction' designates …what everybody (except perhaps the skeptical social scientist) believes about human conduct, about how it is described, explained, predicted, and controlled" (Meehl, 1971, p. 66). Thus, "everybody knows" that an eyewitness's account is the best piece of evidence that can be found to assure justice in the courtroom. This is especially true if the person who recalls and identifies the legally relevant information does so with conviction and confidence. Hence, fireside-induction logic holds that the more confident the witness appears, the more accurate is the recall of the event. As we shall see, however, the scientific evidence does not necessarily support this.

Eyewitness testimony is also powerful because of a belief in the ultimate accuracy of observation and human memory. Throughout its long history, law has had to be highly dependent upon what people saw and what people said they saw. Re-creations of crime scenes were almost

CHAPTER
NINE:
THE
PSYCHOLOGY
OF
EVIDENCE:
EYEWITNESS
TESTIMONY

exclusively dependent upon human memory, which was considered to be occasionally fooled, sometimes purposely distorted, but basically accurate. Today, sophisticated technology that can re-create crime scenarios and provide forensic evidence to the smallest detail is being increasingly made available to the courts, but belief in the accuracy of human perception and memory persists.

How reliable is such eyewitness testimony? Most psychologists will answer, "It depends." Eyewitness testimony may be highly reliable under some conditions and extremely unreliable in other settings. However, the psychological research on perception and memory over the past 100 years underscores the discouraging fact that in most cases eyewitness testimony is at least partially unreliable and highly susceptible to numerous influences.

In this chapter we shall examine this psychological research and theory and discover how closely the findings approximate the numerous fireside inductions inherent in the law's reliance on eyewitness testimony. Like the jury-simulation research discussed in Chapter 7, a large segment of the research on eyewitness testimony lacks a well-integrated theoretical foundation. Yet, the general purpose of applied eyewitness-testimony research "is to generate scientific knowledge that will maximize the chances that a guilty defendant will be justly convicted while minimizing the chances that an innocent defendant will be mistakenly convicted" (Wells, 1978, p. 1546). Therefore, even though an all-encompassing theoretical framework has yet to be developed, there is enough research literature to begin closely questioning the law's reliance on the accuracy of eyewitnesses.

Other problems we encountered in the last chapter pertaining to the jury process will not reappear here, however. Simulation studies are better able to approximate real-life witnessing than real-life jury decisionmaking. In addition, eyewitness research has the benefit of methodologically sound data about human perception and memory which have been developed by empirical psychologists for nearly a century. These traditional works offer a solid foundation for the study of eyewitness observation. The contributions psychology can make in this area are substantial, and they warrant the careful attention of participants in the judicial process. It is important to note that the research in this chapter refers to *nonexpert* witness testimony, to be distinguished from *expert* witness testimony. A nonexpert witness testifies to personal knowledge of the facts, not to opinions and inferences. As we noted in Chapter 4, expert witnesses, because of their ability and knowledge, may both testify to facts and, if allowed by the court, render opinions or draw inferences (such as from information they obtained during interviews with a defendant or victim).

Human Perception and Memory

When a person recalls and identifies events, objects, and persons, two fundamental but exceedingly complicated mental processes are at work: **perception** and **memory**. In the first, sensory inputs (what one sees, hears, smells, touches, tastes) are transformed and organized into a meaningful experience for the individual. In the second process, the transformed inputs are stored in the brain, ready to be called up when needed. Let us examine each operation in more detail.

PERCEPTION

Perceptions are reports of what a person sees or senses at any particular moment. Note that seeing is only a part of the process of perceiving; in fact, what one *perceives* is not always what one sees. The eye does not relate to the brain like a camera operates on film. The eye communicates by electrochemical "blips" along neural pathways and eventually to processors in various sections of the brain, specifically in the cerebral cortex. Once these neural impulses reach the cortex, they may be further coded, reorganized, and interpreted, or they may be left undeveloped. Neurophysiological researchers have not yet discovered exactly what happens in the human brain when it receives incoming information, although there are many theories. It is clear, however, that the perception of stimuli and the person's reaction to them depend upon past experiences, especially with similar stimuli. If you were once the beneficiary of a very painful hornet sting, you perceive those insects in a far different way than a friend who has never had such an experience. Perception, then, is an interpretive process, and it appears that our senses are not only physical organs, but social ones as well (Buckhout, 1974).

There is ample evidence in the research literature that people are not consciously aware of the processes that determine their perceptions or the perceptual content of their sense experiences. Yet, these nonconscious processes are extremely important in the representation of events or objects and therefore are crucial determinants of what occurs on the witness stand. Researchers also know that the end products of these perceptual processes are often incomplete, inaccurate, and highly selective. Much external information is either not attended to, lost in the filtering and selection of information, or misinterpreted. Past experience or learning, expectations, and preferences all determine how this partial or incomplete information will be synthesized. Yarmey (1979) reminds us also that many individuals have sensory deficiencies, like visual defects of depth perception, color blindness, failures in adaptation to darkness, and lack of visual acuity. Even before the stimulus information is synthesized at the higher levels of perceptual interpretation, these individual defects may contaminate the information. Human sensory mechanisms are far from perfect, and this basic frailty should not be overlooked in the search for potential errors in eyewitness testimony.

MEMORY

Memory, the second fundamental process with which we are concerned, is usually studied in three stages: **acquisition**, **retention**, and **retrieval**. Acquisition, also called the encoding or input stage, is intimately involved with the perceptual process, and a clear demarcation between the two is difficult to make. The point at which perception registers in the various areas of the cortex is the point of acquisition. Retention (also called the storage stage) occurs when information becomes "resident in the memory" (Loftus, 1979). In the retrieval stage, the brain searches for the pertinent information, retrieves it, and communicates it. Any one of these three processes may not function properly, and the result, then, is a failure to remember (Klatzky, 1975).

Eyewitness research has continually found that memory is highly malleable and easily subject to change and distortion (Yuille, 1980). Apparently, humans continually alter and reconstruct their memory of past experiences in the light of present experiences, rather than store past events permanently and unchangingly in memory (Leippe, 1980; Yuille, 1980). That is, people rebuild past experiences to fit better their understanding of events. Memory, especially for complex or unusual events, involves the integration of perceptual information with pre-existing experiences, as well as with other subjective relevant information that may be introduced later. In this sense, memory is very much a reconstructive, integrative process, developing with the flow of new experiences and thoughts. This perspective is called the **reconstructive theory** of memory.

As is true for the perceptual processes, people are unaware of their memory processes. They are aware of the products or content of memory, but there is every reason to believe they are not aware of the transformations that have occurred during acquisition, retention, and retrieval. While eyewitnesses may remember an event or person, they are not conscious of the

220

CHAPTER
NINE:
THE
PSYCHOLOGY
OF
EVIDENCE:
EYEWITNESS
TESTIMONY

complex neurological encoding, decoding, organizing, storing, interpreting, and associating that preceded the final memory of that event or person. Moreover, there are ample opportunities for witnesses to encounter additional information after the event and then integrate it unknowingly into their original memories. Therefore, even the most well-intentioned eyewitnesses may err and unconsciously distort their recall and identification. In part, this explains the radically different accounts of the same event that are provided by witnesses who are "absolutely positive" about what they saw.

Human beings forget easily and quickly, and they especially forget visual information. Information becomes less available as the time interval increases between the first witnessing of an event and later attempts to retrieve it (Loftus & Loftus, 1980). Based on the available research, we can say that the unretrieved information is, in large part, lost forever, regardless of the method used to try to retrieve it. Claims that hypnosis brings back "forgotten" memories are unsubstantiated. Forgotten or partially remembered events become reconstructed and embellished as the person gains additional information. Imagination plays a part in this reconstruction, sometimes to the point of letting the person exaggerate aspects of initial events or perceptions. People are sometimes surprised when they return as adults to a childhood home, for example. The "large, almost majestic" house is actually a small, unpretentious structure, with very few of the stately features they "remembered."

Forgetting is also explained by **interference theory**. According to this theory, forgetting is caused by both interference from material learned previously (called by cognitive psychologists "proactive interference") and interference from material learned afterward ("retroactive interference") (Bourne, Dominowski & Loftus, 1979).

In the following sections, we will discuss characteristics of the situation, the witness, and the defendant which are believed to be influential in determining the accuracy of eyewitness testimony. Although this classification does not totally represent the interaction that occurs among the variables in determining eyewitness accuracy, it does promote a more organized presentation.

Situational Variables Affecting Eyewitness Testimony

Courts are most interested in learning details about events that are generally fast-moving, unusual, chaotic, and threatening to the observers. In most instances, the legally relevant incident produces a "stimulus overload"; too many things are happening too quickly and under less-than-ideal conditions for careful scrutiny. Thus far the study of situational variables as they relate directly to eyewitness accounts has been a relatively neglected area, but the research to date agrees with many common-sense observations about the effects of these variables.

TEMPORAL FACTORS

Not surprisingly, the less time a witness has to observe something, the less complete the perception and recall will be. Obviously, studying a topic for a long time will mean a better exam grade, provided the student was concentrating. There is abundant literature in the field of cognitive psychology and memory to demonstrate that the longer a subject is exposed to material, the more accurate the recall (e.g., Loftus, 1972; Loftus & Loftus, 1976; Klatzky, 1975). Some researchers have found that the longer subjects had to inspect slides of faces, the more accurate they later were at recognizing a given face from photographs (Laughery, Alexander & Lane, 1971). In addition,

Laughery and his colleagues found that the smaller the number of photographs the subjects had to search through, the more likely the subjects were to be accurate. The researchers suggested that law-enforcement agencies might keep this in mind when having witnesses look through photospreads ("mugshots") for criminal identification. Fewer photos might result in more accurate recognition.

Closely related to the duration of eyewitness exposure time is frequency of exposure. The more often a witness observes an event or person, the more accurate his or her description or recognition should be. Although there is substantial support for this in the experimental literature, dating as far back as Hermann Ebbinghaus's work in 1885, frequency of exposure has not been examined in studies of eyewitness testimony. Loftus (1979) suggests that perhaps the relationship is such a common-sensical one that it has failed to draw the attention of eyewitness researchers.

Another temporal factor that is likely to influence witness accuracy is the rate at which things happen. Fast-moving events are more difficult to process and thus to remember than slow-moving events, because of the limited processing capacity of human beings and their selective attention mechanisms. Therefore, incidents surrounded by complex activity tend to confuse, even when witnesses have a reasonably long opportunity to observe the occurrence.

It has repeatedly been found that witnesses frequently overestimate the time a criminal incident takes (Buckhout, 1974, 1977; Marshall, 1966; Johnson & Scott, 1976). While Ellison and Buckhout (1981) suggest that some witnesses may consciously lengthen time estimates to strengthen the validity of their descriptions, there is abundant laboratory evidence to indicate that humans generally think unpleasant events last longer than they really do (Loftus, 1979). It appears also that if people feel especially anxious or threatened during an incident, they tend to overestimate its duration even more (Sarason & Stoops, 1978). Therefore, in obtaining evidence from witnesses, it is important to try to determine how long and how often the person observed the incident and how much activity was present. It is important also to realize that the witness very probably is overestimating the event's duration.

Detail Significance: Weapon Focus

Not all details of a scene are equally remembered, because certain novel, complex, ambiguous, or arousing features draw more attention than others. Blood, masks, weapons, and aggressive actions are more likely to be noticed than clothing, hairstyle, height, facial features, or other background stimuli in a crime scene. A gun pointed at a person is likely to be studied more intently than other features impinging on that person's mind at that moment. People are quite certain about whether a gun or a knife was threatening them, but they are perhaps less certain of an assailant's clothes or facial characteristics. This phenomenon is known as weapon focus or "weapon effect." Specifically, **weapon focus** refers to the concentration of some victim's or witness's attention on a threatening weapon which forces him or her to pay less attention to other details and events of a crime. In short, it refers to a "tunneling of attention."

The primary theoretical underpinning for weapon focus is James Easterbrook's (1959) observation that under high arousal people tend to narrow their attention to the cues that are most threatening or relevant, and correspondingly reduce their attention to other cues in the immediate environment. Therefore, highly anxious or tense individuals will not scan their environments as broadly as less anxious individuals. Easterbrook's classic theory is known as **cue-utilization theory**. It is well known to psychologists, as illustrated in a poll conducted by Yarmey and Jones (1983). Ninety percent of the psychologists they surveyed subscribed to the view that a victim is more likely to focus on a gun, whereas lay people and jurors believed that victims would also get a good look at the offender's face.

221

SITUATIONAL
VARIABLES
AFFECTING
EYEWITNESS
TESTIMONY

222

CHAPTER
NINE:
THE
PSYCHOLOGY
OF
EVIDENCE:
EYEWITNESS
TESTIMONY

Weapon focus has received empirical support. The tendency to focus on some details to the exclusion of others is well illustrated by a study in which unsuspecting students sat in an anteroom waiting to participate in an experiment conducted by Johnson and Scott (1976). A no-weapon condition and a weapon condition were created. Subjects in the no-weapon condition overheard a conversation from the experimental room concerning equipment problems, after which an individual entered the waiting room, holding a pen in greasy hands. The individual, who was part of the experiment (a confederate), made a brief comment and then exited quickly. In the weapon condition, subjects overheard an angry confrontation, accompanied by sounds of bottles breaking and chairs crashing. The confederate bolted into the waiting room, holding a bloodied letter opener in blood-stained hands. As in the no-weapon condition, the confederate muttered something and then left.

Subjects were interviewed about the scenario either immediately or one week later. Nearly every subject in the weapon condition described a weapon, while very few of the no-weapon subjects could describe the pen. More importantly, the presence of a weapon (weapon focus compounded by emotional arousal) reduced the ability of the subjects to identify the confederate from a set of fifty photographs. Apparently, the witnesses focused their attention primarily on the weapon rather than on facial features. However, it should be emphasized that in both the weapon and no-weapon conditions, the confederate was only in the presence of the witnesses for about four seconds. A longer exposure time might have dissipated weapon focus.

There are other problems with the experiment as well. The two conditions (weapon or no-weapon) differed in a number of significant ways, preventing a firm conclusion as to what contributed to what. For example, one condition had an argument take place, accompanied by bottles breaking and chairs crashing, whereas the other condition did not. Also, the weapon condition had two highly arousing stimuli—a weapon *and* a bloody hand. The no-weapon condition had none. Even the statements uttered by the confederate in each condition were different. Furthermore, the subjects were uninvolved (passive observers) in the scenario.

Elizabeth Loftus and her colleagues (1987) tried to correct these shortcomings by setting up conditions where the sole differing condition was the presence of the weapon. College students viewed a series of slides in which a customer goes through the cafeteria line of a fast-food restaurant. In one condition the customer pointed a gun at the cashier and she gave him money. In a second condition, the customer handed the cashier a check and she gave him money. The researchers then had the students identify the customer from a twelve-person photo lineup. Students in the weapon condition were significantly less accurate than students in the check condition. There was an 8.5 percent probability of identifying the right customer by chance. Weapon-condition subjects correctly identified the customer only about 15 percent of the time compared to the check-condition subjects who were accurate 35 percent of the time. Weapon-condition students were also less accurate when asked details about the customer.

But how realistic is this situation? College students are sitting in the comfort of their environments passively watching slides in a situation which they know is a psychological experiment. And where is the stress or highly arousing event? At a minimum, Easterbrook's cue-utilization theory, premised on high anxiety, should have been tested.

Tooley, Brigham, Maass and Bothwell (1987) had college students observe slides of various individuals either holding a weapon or some other object in their hands. Subjects were randomly assigned to view the slides while experiencing white noise in the form of a constant, irritating hissing sound or threat of electric shock (high arousal) or without such conditions (low arousal). The researchers hypothesized that, of the two groups, high-arousal subjects would be better at distinguishing the faces of people without a weapon from those with a weapon. High-arousal

223

SITUATIONAL
VARIABLES
AFFECTING
EYEWITNESS
TESTIMONY

subjects would be better at recognizing faces than low-arousal because they would focus on the most interesting or attention-getting stimuli. In the case of the no-weapon condition, the prominent stimulus was the face. Recall that Easterbrook's cue-utilization theory predicts a focusing on prominent cues under high arousal. If the hypothesis is correct, highly aroused subjects would focus on the weapon to the exclusion of other cues—such as the face—and in the no-weapon condition, they would focus on the face more. The researchers did find the weapon effect. Subjects as a group were *better* at identifying the faces of individuals *not* holding a weapon than the face of those who were. However, when arousal was factored in, aroused subjects did better *overall* at recognizing faces than low-arousal subjects. They were not better (or worse) at distinguishing the faces of those individuals holding weapons from those holding non-weapon, however. Thus, this experiment did not support cue-utilization theory.

In a more realistic experiment, Maass and Kohnken (1989) tried to reexamine the arousal component of weapon focus by threatening college students participating in an experiment with a needle injection. Maass and Kohnken noted that none of the previous research actually threatened the subjects directly with a weapon. While it would be clearly unethical to approach subjects with a gun or knife, the researchers saw no such objections to approaching volunteers with a syringe. Almost everyone is at least somewhat fearful of an injection, usually stemming from childhood visits to the doctor's office. One-half of the subjects were approached by an experimenter holding a pen and the other half were approached by an experimenter holding a syringe. Furthermore, one-half of the subjects expected to have an injection, whereas the remaining half did not. Thus, there were four conditions in this experiment: (1) approached by experimenter with *syringe* with *expectation* to receive injection; (2) approached by experimenter with a *pen* with *expectation* to receive injection; (3) approached by experimenter with *syringe* with *no expectation* to receive any injection; and (4) approached by experimenter with *pen* with *no expectation* to receive any injection. The major dependent variables were based on two different forms of memory, **recognition** and **recall**. In the recognition task, subjects were required to identify the face of the experimenter from a seven-person photo lineup (although the experimenter was not actually in the lineup). In the recall task, subjects were required to answer specific questions about the experimenter's face as well as the hand which carried the pen or syringe.

The results showed that the syringe (the weapon) did arouse the subjects but the threat of an injection by itself did not. Furthermore, subjects exposed to the syringe, with or without expectations of receiving an injection, were more likely to make false identifications in the recognition tasks than the other groups. In addition, the results of the recall tasks demonstrated that the syringe groups were more accurate in recalling details about the *hand area* of the experimenter (i.e., length, color and diameter of the syringe) than the non-syringe groups. However, there were no clear trends in who could accurately recall *facial* cues. The researchers asserted: "At this point, one can only conclude—that contrary to what many jurors and judges believe—the presence of a weapon is in and of itself distracting as well as arousing" (p. 406).

The studies by Maass et al. (1989), Tooley et al. (1987), and Loftus et al. (1987) do highlight an important distinction with respect to weapon focus: the attention-getting properties of a weapon *and* its arousal effect. A weapon is usually novel or attention-getting in and of itself, independent of the arousal-inducing properties it has when one is threatened with it. Passive observers watching slides normally do not experience much arousal but the evidence does suggest the weapon distracts the audience temporarily from other environmental cues.

Kramer, Buckout, and Eugenio (1990) tested this weapon-distraction hypothesis by showing a series of slides to college students while controlling for arousal. The results supported the viewpoint that a salient weapon, regardless of arousal level, distracts attention substantially.

224

CHAPTER
NINE:
THE
PSYCHOLOGY
OF
EVIDENCE:
EYEWITNESS
TESTIMONY

SIGNIFICANCE OF THE EVENT ITSELF
(OR WHAT'S HAPPENING?)

Another aspect which may influence eyewitness accuracy is that persons in the midst of a crime do not always perceive that something significant is happening. People have often been present during the commission of a crime and have failed to realize it. Baron and Byrne (1977) cite the tragic sniper incident on the University of Texas campus in 1966 as an example. Disgruntled student and veteran Charles Whitman managed to gain access to the top of the 307-foot tower with an arsenal of weapons and begin firing at passersby below. Some heard the shots, noticed bodies falling, and immediately ran for cover. A surprising number of people simply continued along their way without perceiving the seriousness of the situation. Some individuals who survived later said they interpreted the event as a fraternity stunt and did not take it seriously.

Social psychologists (e.g., Darley & Latané, 1968) have studied the phenomenon of "bystander apathy," where people sometimes fail to come to the aid of an accident or assault victim. The researchers have found that, in many cases, the observers simply did not interpret the event as significant. (It is possible, of course, that the bystanders told the researchers this to save face.) Therefore, it would seem prudent for law-enforcement officers to learn how far the crime had progressed before a witness realized the incident was significant enough to warrant attention. Some witnesses may conclude that a crime is taking place only near the end of the sequence and may embellish their awareness of the beginning so as not to appear too foolish.

Perceiving the seriousness of an event is as important as perceiving its significance. Leippe, Wells, and Ostrom (1978) staged a theft in front of a group of students waiting to participate in an experiment. The item stolen in one condition was a $50 electronic calculator (high seriousness); in another it was a pack of cigarettes (low seriousness). In both conditions one of the waiting subjects (actually a confederate) grabbed the item, dropped it to assure that everyone present noticed the theft, and quickly left the room. There was no doubt that all the waiting subjects recognized that a theft had happened and knew the relative value of the stolen item.

After the theft, subjects were told individually that it had been planned as part of the experiment, and they were shown six photographs and asked to identify the thief. In the high-seriousness condition, 56 percent of the subjects made an accurate identification, whereas in the low-seriousness condition only 19 percent made accurate identification. These results suggest that the perceived seriousness of a crime may be a powerful determinant of accurate offender-identification.

The researchers in the above experiment suggested two possible hypotheses for the increased accuracy as a result of crime seriousness. First, perceived seriousness may prompt witnesses to make full use of selective attention and acquisition processes during the event. Second, the perceived seriousness may have motivated the witnesses to rehearse the event in their memories, which would have improved the retrieval of the information at a later time.

VIOLENCE LEVEL OF EVENT

Crimes differ in the amount of emotional arousal they generate in both victim and witnesses. Generally speaking, increases in violence produce a corresponding increase in arousal, probably to a peak point where further increases in extreme, terrifying violence no longer increase arousal because the observer chooses not to watch any longer. It has been suggested that the recall and recognition abilities of witnesses (and victims) reflect a negative relationship to that violence-arousal continuum (Clifford & Scott, 1978). That is, the higher the violence of the crime, and hence the higher the emotional reaction to the incident, the lower the accuracy and completeness of the

225

**WITNESS
VARIABLES:
PERCEPTUAL
AND
MEMORY
INFLUENCES**

testimony of witnesses and victims. Clifford and his colleagues have been the leading proponents of the high-violence-low-accuracy hypothesis; it is worthwhile to review two of their experiments designed to test it.

Clifford and Scott (1978) found that persons who watched violent events on videotape were significantly less able to recall the incidents than those who watched nonviolent versions. In the nonviolent scenario, two police officers searched for a suspect, found him, and entered into a verbal exchange with the man. The exchange culminated in some "weak restraining movements" by one of the officers. In the violent episode, the same situation escalated into a physical confrontation, with one of the officers delivering blows to the suspect.

In addition to the finding that witnesses demonstrated poorer recall of the violent incident, the study also discovered that female subjects were significantly less accurate than male subjects in their recall of the violent film. There were no significant gender differences in recall of the nonviolent version.

In another investigation of the effects of violence on eyewitness accuracy, Clifford and Hollin (1981) learned that accuracy depends not only on the level of violence observed, but also on the number of perpetrators. Violent incidents were less well remembered as the number of perpetrators increased, while nonviolent incidents yielded no such difference. The results suggest that, in violent events involving more than one offender, the accuracy of eyewitness testimony can be expected to be poorer than in violent events having only one perpetrator. In fact, the Clifford-Hollin data revealed that almost three-fourths of the witnesses observing the violent scenes were incorrect in their identification of the key perpetrator. Apparently, no significant gender differences emerged, since the researchers made no reference to this effect in their report. It seems, therefore, that the influence of violence on the recognition and recall ability of males and females remains equivocal. This is one area in obvious need of further investigation.

The results from the Clifford studies imply that the legal system must be especially careful in its reliance on the testimony of eyewitnesses to a violent episode, especially in cases in which violence is high and there are several perpetrators. At the very least, the data certainly counsel against any fireside induction that violence leads to accuracy in testimony.

The violence level of the crime also seems to influence jurors strongly. Saul Kassin and David Garfield (1991) found that videotapes depicting a high level of blood and gore at a crime scene had a significant impact on mock jurors. Jurors exposed to a videotape showing such a crime scene were more inclined to decide in favor of the prosecution and to set lower standards of proof for themselves in making that decision.

Witness Variables: Perceptual and Memory Influences

While situational factors may strongly affect the accuracy of eyewitness testimony, individual variables may be even more powerful influences. Obviously, not all witnesses are equally affected by violence, and some are better than others at recalling details of an event observed for even a brief moment. Researchers have begun to identify individual characteristics which are most likely to affect perceptions and ultimately the accuracy of eyewitness reports. Current psychological research also suggests that some features of the witness add credibility to her or his testimony.

226

CHAPTER
NINE:
THE
PSYCHOLOGY
OF
EVIDENCE:
EYEWITNESS
TESTIMONY

WITNESS AROUSAL AND STRESS

Most criminal incidents precipitate some continuum of stress and emotional arousal in both victims and other witnesses. However, the effects of this emotional arousal on eyewitness testimony have baffled the legal system for many years (Katz & Reid, 1977). Some jurists believe that stress increases the accuracy of witness observation and subsequent testimony. Others think stressful incidents generate so much nervousness that they promote unreliability in witnesses.

An example of the first position is a very old but often cited appellate court opinion quoted by Wall (1965). Two men were accused of torturing and killing a husband and wife, based on the oral dying declaration of the husband. In affirming the conviction and commenting about the victim's ability to identify the accused, the court stated that "every peculiarity of each of the murders...must have been literally burned into the memory" of both the husband and his wife (*Commonwealth v. Roddy*, 1898). In another case *(State v. Lanegan*, 1951), a man and his wife had been awakened by an intruder pointing a firearm in their faces and demanding money. The court found these to be "circumstances calculated to impress [the defendant's appearance] upon their minds." In still another example (*U. S. ex rel. Gonzalez v. Zelker*, 1973), the U. S. Court of Appeals defended the validity of a robbery victim's identification by asserting that "the robbery unquestionably made a deep impression on Mrs. D'Amora, who was obviously terrified by Gonzalez when he pointed the gun at her and announced the holdup." However, as Katz and Reid (1977) have observed, the court demonstrated its confusion about the effects of stress by also stating that the same victim should be excused for her inaccurate initial description since "she was understandably nervous at the time of the robbery."

Few court decisions have dealt with the effects of stress on eyewitness or victim accuracy, and any decisions handed down have left the issue vague, confused, and largely unresolved (Katz & Reid, 1977). If a position could be teased out of legal precedent up to this point, it would be the fireside induction that stress or fear increases witness and victim testimonial accuracy.

According to psychological research, does arousal strengthen or weaken memory? Not surprisingly, empirical investigations have found that it sometimes facilitates perception and memory and sometimes hinders these processes. In many instances, the relationship between arousal and performance can be best represented by an inverted **U**-shaped function: very low or very high levels of arousal reduce perceptions and inhibit memory, while moderate levels facilitate them.

This hypothesized relationship is known as the **Yerkes-Dodson Law**, first proposed in 1908. The relationship depends not only on the existing level of arousal, but also on the difficulty or complexity of the task. If the task is relatively simple, high arousal will improve the performance. If the task is complex, high levels of arousal will decrease performance and moderate levels will improve it. The relationship also holds for memory and perception. Intermediate levels of stress improve memory and perception.

The eyewitness's task in recalling events or persons is an extremely complex one, requiring perceptual and memory components. We can expect, therefore, that the high arousal which is presumably typical of witnesses' reactions to violent crimes causes a spectrum of inaccuracies and incomplete information in testimony. The Yerkes-Dodson Law does not hold for everyone, of course, nor will every study find it because of the complexity of researching human subjects, but the bulk of the research over the years finds it holds in general (Loftus, 1986).

Recall the experiment by Leippe and colleagues (1978) in which either a package of cigarettes or a $50 calculator was stolen. The calculator theft produced more accurate descriptions of the perpetrator, very likely because it generated more arousal than the cigarette theft. Moreover, the arousal generated would be moderate, rather than high— just right to improve performance or identification of the offender. On the other hand, the experiment conducted by Johnson and

Scott (1976), which involved a weapon condition (bloody letter opener) and a no-weapon condition (greasy pen), apparently produced such high levels of arousal in the weapon condition as to interfere with accurate recall and recognition of the perpetrator. The Yerkes-Dodson Law indicates that persons who are extremely frightened or emotionally upset during an incident are not the most dependable witnesses to that incident.

In summary, there is considerable evidence from the psychological laboratory that extreme arousal interferes with eyewitness accounts of violent scenes. In petty crimes, like shoplifting or even purse snatching, arousal is significantly lower and eyewitness accounts are probably more accurate. Rarely is the testimony of eyewitnesses needed in these petty situations, however, because they seldom come to trial. Finally, it is likely that eyewitnesses who were not themselves crime victims are less aroused than the victims and therefore more accurate in their recollection of events.

227

WITNESS
VARIABLES:
PERCEPTUAL
AND
MEMORY
INFLUENCES

EXPECTANCIES AND STEREOTYPES

A powerful determinant of what a person perceives is what he or she expects to perceive in any given situation. Every hunting season is replete with tales of hunters mistakenly shooting other hunters, cows, or horses in the belief that they are game. Hunters who shoot at these nongame targets typically have high expectations of seeing a deer (or pheasant, squirrel, or rabbit) at any moment. In addition, the hunt traditionally is at its best at dawn and early dusk, because these are times when wildlife move toward feeding areas. These are also times when visibility, particularly at long distances, is poor. Any movement in the meadow at this time can be quickly embellished with antlers (or feathers) by the tense and expectant hunter intent on finding prey.

Many sightings of unidentified flying objects, Loch Ness monsters, Bigfoot, and other unusual creatures may be explained by expectations of the observers. Psychologists have found that eyes do indeed play tricks. Expectancies shaped by previous experiences and learning (including tales and legends) form cognitive templates to which unusual experiences are compared. Any out-of-the-ordinary sight may be interpreted in such a way that it will fit these cognitive templates. Thus, unusual ripples in a lake at dusk can easily become a highly publicized, unexplained creature.

Incidents of crime, particularly violent ones, are highly unusual events to most persons and are especially susceptible to distortions consistent with expectations. If we have learned that robbers often carry .38 revolvers, we may see a .38 in an assailant's hand when it is actually a brick. However, while abundant collateral research clearly and convincingly demonstrates that expectancies negatively influence descriptive accuracy, none has tested the expectancy hypothesis in specific relation to eyewitness testimony in a simulated crime setting. The substantial body of research already available on related issues, though, would lead us to agree with Loftus (1979, p. 48) that "one thing is clear and accepted by all: expectations have an enormous impact on what a person claims to have seen."

Stereotypes—which are a form of expectancy—are cognitive shorthand devices that allow us to simplify and organize the vast array of social stimuli present in a complex society. We all use them to some extent, and as long as they do not promote social injustices, they tend to be effective and harmless psychological adaptations that help manage our implicit personality theories about others. However, stereotypes can distort our perceptions and subsequent identifications of others. There is evidence that some people may in fact incorporate their stereotype of "criminal" in their identification of suspects. Shoemaker, South, and Lowe (1973) asked subjects to select from a set of twelve facial photographs the individuals most likely and least likely to have engaged in murder, robbery, or treason. None of the persons in the photos had actually engaged in these

228

CHAPTER
NINE:
THE
PSYCHOLOGY
OF
EVIDENCE:
EYEWITNESS
TESTIMONY

behaviors. Subjects tended to categorize the photos into criminal-noncriminal stereotypes, and they also tended to match faces with specific types of behavior. The researchers discovered that males were more likely than females to use facial stereotypes in judging guilt or innocence. The study suggests that many people have in their minds stereotypes about the way criminals look. These stereotypes could influence an eyewitness's selection of a perpetrator, especially if that witness observed the incident under intense stress or other less-than-ideal conditions.

Arthur Lurigio and John Carroll (1985) found that experienced probation officers (POs) have well-developed, rich schemata of stereotypes: how certain offenders look, the nature of their interpersonal relationships, their prior criminal history, the reasons for their criminal activity, and their prognosis for rehabilitation. For example, experienced POs stereotype a burglar as typically a male in his early thirties, married, intelligent, with an extensive burglary record, and unlikely to change because he is very set in his lifestyle. Welfare fraud, according to the POs, is typically committed by a black woman in her twenties who is unmarried but involved with a male who controls her life. She is easily manipulated and feels forced to commit fraud through concern for her kids or her man. The prognosis for change is guarded to good, depending on whether she can break from the relationship.

Lurigio and Carroll found that experienced POs (more than three years' experience) had richer but fewer schemata than less-experienced POs (less than three years on the job). The caseloads of the POs were large. Thus, the more experienced ones seem to use these well-developed schemata as a form of cognitive economy so that decisions regarding counseling and referrals and frequency of probationer reporting could be made quickly and confidently. The inexperienced POs had more—but more ambiguous—schemata that were not developed sufficiently to enable them to make quick, efficient decisions about the many probationers on their caseloads. Experienced POs seem to have weeded out many useless stereotypes and enriched the few they retained. There is also some evidence to suggest that experienced police officers use schemata of certain environmental cues to identify suspicious activity (Ryan & Taylor, 1988). However, although these stereotypes afford cognitive efficiency to their users, they promote the ecological fallacy and produce decisions that are inequitable and simply in error for those individuals who do not fit the cognitive mold.

WITNESS MEMORY: RETENTION FACTORS

Witnesses, of course, generally must recall events weeks, months, or even years after they occur. Yet cognitive psychology has firmly established that people are less accurate and complete in their accounts of events after a long interval has elapsed between the event and the recall than after a short interval. Part of this inaccuracy stems from the higher probability that new information will be received and processed by the person during the longer interval.

Elizabeth Loftus has designed numerous experiments demonstrating that post-event experiences, such as exposure to additional information, can substantially affect a person's memory of the original event. She showed, for example, that the simple mention of an existing object in an interview significantly increased the probability that the object would be recalled by the witness later on (Loftus, 1975). For example, asking an eyewitness to a traffic accident, "How fast was the car going when it ran the stop sign?" will enhance the recall of the stop sign, even if the witness failed to notice it in the first place. Similarly, casually mentioning an object that did not actually exist in an accident scene increases the likelihood that a witness will later report having seen that nonexistent object (Loftus, Miller & Burns, 1978).

Loftus (1975, 1977) also found that witnesses compromised their memories when they learned of new information that conflicted with an initial observation. For example, if a witness

229

WITNESS
VARIABLES:
PERCEPTUAL
AND
MEMORY
INFLUENCES

thought he noticed a red car passing in the wrong lane and the investigating officer mentioned a green car, the witness would be likely to recall an off-colored green or blue-green car in a later report. If a witness thought a vehicle was traveling at eighty-five miles per hour, and the investigating officer mentions the speed of sixty-five, the witness would later report the speed to be somewhere between sixty-five and eighty-five, probably closer to sixty-five. The witness might be aware of the compromise, but it might also be an unconscious phenomenon attributable to perceptual and memory processes occurring outside awareness.

The above studies imply that police officers or attorneys can manipulate a witness's memory by feeding relevant information. However, there is evidence that this is more difficult to do with important or even noticeable factors than with less important details (Loftus, 1979). Furthermore, data also suggest that misleading information provided to witnesses sometime after the event and just before a recall test will have greater impact than misleading information given immediately after the incident (Loftus, Miller & Burns, 1978). On the other hand, interviewers wishing to maintain a consistent description of the initial incident would be wise to obtain the information from witnesses immediately after the incident and then reiterate the material before and as close as possible to the time of courtroom testimony.

WITNESS CONFIDENCE: RETRIEVAL FACTORS

Persons given to fireside inductions about eyewitness testimony believe that the more confident witnesses are about what they saw, the more accurate their observations and memories. As a result, testimony presented assertively and positively is generally treated with deference by the courts; it is believed to be accurate and truthful (Deffenbacher, 1980). For example, in *Neil v. Biggers* (1972), the U. S. Supreme Court ruled that eyewitness *confidence* is a valid criterion upon which to judge the trustworthiness of eyewitness testimony.

Studies indicate that the confidence-accuracy relationship assumed by many judges, attorneys, and jurors is far more complicated than they suppose, however. Yarmey (1979) concludes from his research on the identification of faces that the confidence-accuracy relationship in that area is exceedingly weak or virtually nonexistent. Leippe (1980) asserts that recognition accuracy has little to do with witness confidence, primarily because people are usually unaware of the inaccurate mental operations that lead to their conclusions. According to Leippe, the conditions under which witnesses observe an incident may affect recognition accuracy but not confidence. Thus, witnesses may be just as confident of what they see under poor observing conditions as they are of what they see under excellent observing conditions. Wells, Lindsay, and Ferguson (1979) found that the confidence of witnesses, whether measured by the witnesses themselves or through jurors' estimates, was unrelated to accuracy in identifying a thief from a six-person picture gallery. In other studies (Lindsay, Wells & Rumpel, 1981; Clifford & Hollin, 1981; Clifford & Scott, 1978) the confidence-accuracy relationship was also found wanting.

Any belief that accuracy can be assumed merely on the basis of the confidence expressed by eyewitnesses is untenable, given the present state of psychological knowledge. It is difficult to change these beliefs, however. Fox and Walters (1986) found that jurors continue to use eyewitness confidence as a guide in making their decisions, even after being warned several times by an expert that confidence does not necessarily translate into accuracy. Loftus (1986) described her own trials and tribulations in having the courts accept her expert testimony on eyewitness reliability. Furthermore, she found higher courts unsympathetic, noting that they routinely uphold convictions of defendants when the trial judge had refused to permit expert testimony. In recent years, though, some state supreme courts are beginning to allow expert testimony in the eyewitness area.

230

CHAPTER
NINE:
THE
PSYCHOLOGY
OF
EVIDENCE:
EYEWITNESS
TESTIMONY

Furthermore, while many psychologists themselves initially expressed doubts that eyewitness research was sufficiently developed to communicate it to the courts, this is no longer the case.

EFFECTS OF ALCOHOL AND OTHER DRUGS

Much of the research on eyewitness testimony deals with subjects who are not under the influence of alcohol or other drugs. Police officers interviewing witnesses at the scene report, though, that witnesses are often under the influence of some substance, usually alcohol. One of the few studies in this area was conducted by Yuille and Tollestrup (1990), who explored the effects of alcohol on the memories of male student volunteers who witnessed a staged theft. Three groups were used: an alcohol, a placebo, and a control group. The alcohol group consumed three drinks composed of a mixture of fruit juice (5 percent) and alcohol (95 percent). The placebo group was led to believe they had ingested alcohol, but actually consumed only three drinks of fruit juice with a thin layer of alcohol on the surface so that it tasted and smelled like alcohol. The control group did not consume any drinks. Half the subjects were interviewed immediately after the crime, and all subjects were interviewed one week later. All the subjects were also shown a photospread consisting of the thief and seven foils (subjects who looked much like the thief) after the second interview.

Alcohol blood levels in the alcohol group averaged .10 (a level that most jurisdictions consider legally intoxicated). The results suggested that even mild intoxication significantly affected eyewitness memory. Members of the control group recalled 20 percent more information than those in the alcohol group immediately after the crime, suggesting that the alcohol group had stored significantly less. Even after one week the control group continued to recall *more* information about the scene than did the alcohol group. However, the *accuracy* of the information was similar for both groups, and the alcohol did not interfere with the ability of the witnesses to identify correctly a picture of the culprit one week later.

The evidence indicates that alcohol reduces recall by interfering with the original perception and coding of the event. The finding of Yuille and Tollestrup is consistent with previous research on memory and alcohol that suggests that alcohol has a greater effect on the immediate storage of information than on its retrieval (Hastroudi et al., 1984).

TRIVIAL PERSUASION

Research suggests that jurors are more persuaded by testimony that is full of trivial details than by testimony that contains less detail (Bell & Loftus, 1988, 1989). For example, Brad Bell and Elizabeth Loftus (1988) had subjects read a summary of a court case in which a man was accused of murdering a store clerk during a robbery. Two eyewitnesses, one for the prosecution and one for the defense, described the shooting. The eyewitness for the prosecution was positive that the defendant shot the clerk, whereas the eyewitness for the defense was positive that the defendant had not, suggesting they were matched in level of confidence. The study involved a 2 × 2 design. In one summary the prosecution witness described the crime scene in considerable detail (defendant requested Kleenex, Tylenol and a six-pack of Pepsi prior to robbery); whereas in another summary given to a different group of subjects the witness did not provide much detail (defendant requested some store items). Two other groups of mock jurors read similar summaries (high detail, low detail) presented by the defense witness.

The results suggested that detail was significant in the prosecution-witness condition but not so significant for the defense-witness condition. Mock jurors who read highly detailed testimony by the prosecution witness were more likely to find the defendant guilty than those who read low-detailed testimony. Added detail did not influence the decision when the detail was presented by the defense witness. In another study, Bell and Loftus (1989) discovered that eyewitnesses who provide more detail, regardless of what side they represent, are perceived by mock jurors as being more credible and having better memory and attention. In summary, the available evidence suggests that witnesses whose testimony is replete with detail, even if the detail is not directly relevant to the case, may play a powerful role in encouraging jurors to believe the testimony. Bell and Loftus call this **trivial persuasion**.

Witness Age

No topic associated with eyewitness testimony has received more public attention in recent years than that of witness age, particularly when witnesses are children. High profile cases involving child victims of sexual assault have fueled this interest. Psychologists in private practice are increasingly specializing in work with child victims and consultation with attorneys and courts. Consequently, research exploring the effects of age has proliferated. While most has focused on the testimony of children, some research has explored the effect of advanced age on the accuracy of testimony.

CHILDREN

Participants in the judicial process have long believed that the information acquired through the questioning and testimony of children is far more distorted and inaccurate than that acquired from young and middle-aged adults (Cohen & Harnick, 1980; Marin et al., 1979; Yarmey & Kent, 1980; Yarmey, 1979). This perception is common among the general public as well (Ross et al., 1990). Survey research suggests that prospective jurors, criminal attorneys, and even psychologists tend to perceive young children as highly susceptible to suggestion and not very accurate in their testimony (Leippe & Romanczyk, 1989; Yarmey & Jones, 1983). According to one survey, defense and prosecuting attorneys view eyewitnesses aged five to nine as having poorer memories and being more suggestible than adults (Leippe et al., 1989). Defense attorneys were even stronger in that belief than prosecutors, a fact that is not surprising since children usually testify for the prosecution.

232

CHAPTER
NINE:
THE
PSYCHOLOGY
OF
EVIDENCE:
EYEWITNESS
TESTIMONY

The age at which children may testify as credible and competent eyewitnesses in criminal and civil proceedings has long been controversial. Many jurisdictions stipulate that fourteen is the minimum age for delivering competent testimony, with exceptions being made only after a judicial inquiry into the child's mental and emotional capacity. Other jurisdictions regularly allow ten-year-olds to qualify as competent witnesses. Many states, however, require that the competency of the child witness under twelve (or even fourteen) be evaluated prior to allowing his or her testimony as evidence. These "competency determinations" focus on whether the child knows the difference between telling the truth and lying, appreciates the obligation to tell the truth, and "whether the child is able to observe, remember, and communicate what happened and answer simple questions about the event" (Bulkley, 1989, p. 211).

In recent years numerous changes have been made in the law to make it easier and less traumatic for a child eyewitness to testify. For example, over half the states have adopted Rule 601 of the Federal Rules of Evidence (Bulkley, 1989), which establishes a rebuttable presumption of competency for children. Under Rule 601, the normal developmental differences in memory or narrative abilities between children and adults are no longer critical in determining a child's competency. In other words, the fact that a child cannot narrate an event does not preclude his or her testimony. However, a **minimum credibility standard** must still be met. Child testimony can be rejected "if a reasonable juror could believe that 'the witness is so bereft of his powers of observation, recordation, recollection, and recount as to be so untrustworthy as a witness as to make his testimony lack relevance'" (Bulkley, 1989, p. 212).

In Great Britain, prior to the British Criminal Justice Act of 1988, the uncorroborated evidence of any witness under the age of fourteen was not to be taken seriously, even if that witness was under oath (Mackay, 1990). In Scandinavian countries, there is currently no age limit for a child to give testimony, as long as it is clear the child has sufficient understanding and ability to express him- or herself (Andenaes, 1990). In Germany, there is also no formal age for competency as a witness, as long as "the child has reached a mental and cognitive stage to make evidential perceptions, to understand questions, and to give a comprehensible report of facts" (Frehsee, 1990, p. 32).

RESEARCH EVIDENCE

Psychological research on all facets of children's eyewitness testimony has exploded within the past two decades. Part of the impetus for this dramatic increase is a growing awareness that children are highly vulnerable and often the victims of crime—especially sexual abuse. This awareness also prompted a number of reforms during the 1980s to make the legal system more sensitive to child victims (Bulkley, 1989). "Numerous state legislatures and local jurisdictions have adopted innovative approaches to reduce trauma to children and improve prosecutions" (Bulkley, 1989, p. 210).

A fairly consistent collection of data emerging from psycholegal research by developmental psychologists on eyewitness testimony indicates that children generally recall less detail about an event than adults do (Goodman & Hahn, 1987). However, they are also less likely than adults to make errors about what they did see (Goodman & Reed, 1986).

One of the earliest systematic studies on children's testimony was a project by Marin and her colleagues (1979), which documented that, under certain circumstances, young children can be as accurate in eyewitness accounts as adults. The nature of the questioning and the type of memory retrieval required in order to answer seem to be critical variables, however. Marin's subjects were divided into four groups: kindergartners and first-graders, third- and fourth-graders, seventh- and eighth-graders, and college students. When recall memory was requested in an open-ended way ("What happened?"), older subjects were able to report more material than younger ones. The younger the subject, the less detail his or her description provided. Neverthe-less, the younger subjects were accurate in the incomplete information they reported. When Marin's tasks demanded recognition memory (identifying photographs or answering yes and no to a series of questions), younger subjects were just as accurate as those in the older groups. Furthermore, they were no more easily misled by leading questions.

Very young children, however, (e.g., three years of age) seem to provide less accurate information than older children across a variety of testimony tasks: free recall, answers to objective and suggestive questions, and eyewitness identifications (Goodman & Hahn, 1987). Gail Goodman and Rebecca Reed (1986) conducted a study in which children three and six years of age and adults interacted for five minutes with a man they did not know. Four or five days later, the subjects were asked questions about the incident and tried to identify the man from a photo lineup. Compared to the six-year-olds and the adults, the three-year-olds answered fewer questions correctly, recalled much less about what happened, and were able to identify the man less frequently. The six-year-olds did not differ from the adults in answering questions correctly or in identifying the man, but they did recall less about the event, a finding which is consistent with the Marin research discussed earlier. In addition to a list of objective (nonleading) questions, the researchers also used a list of suggestive questions designed to imply incorrect information to the subjects. Both the three-year-olds and the six-year-olds were more influ-enced by these suggestive questions than the adults, indicating that young children may be more suggestible when questioned by an adult. The results do indicate, however, that if six-year-old children are questioned in a nonsuggestive manner and provided with straightforward lineup, they are at least as accurate in their answers and identifications as adult witnesses.

Another area of research is concerned with **reality monitoring**, which refers to a child's ability to distinguish *actual* from *imagined* events (Dunning, 1989). Research to date suggests that children older than age eight can usually distinguish between what is fantasy and what is "real" (Dunning, 1989). Below age eight, however, the distinction between fantasy and the real world is blurred for the child (Foley & Johnson, 1985), and accuracy in testimony will probably be diminished.

Another central issue in psycholegal research is the question of how credible jurors *perceive* child witnesses to be, independent of how accurate they actually are. The low conviction rates in child sexual-abuse cases, for example, have been attributed to juror skepticism of a child's testimony (Harvard Law Review, 1985; Leippe & Romanczyk, 1989). In the 1980s the McMaster trial, which ended with the acquittal of day-care workers on charges of widespread sexual abuse, may be illustrative. It is widely believed that the children's account of their victimization strained the credulity of jurors in that case.

Some studies have tended to confirm the view that the public and prospective jurors do not credit the testimony of children (Goodman et al., 1987; Leippe & Romanczyk, 1987). A growing body of research, however, indicates that under certain conditions people may perceive children as *more* credible witnesses than adults (Ross et al., 1990; Goodman, Bottoms, Hersocvici & Shaver, 1989). The mixed findings in this area prompted David Ross and his colleagues (Ross et al., 1990, p. 18) to posit: "…we are led to conclude that witness age has no uniform influence on juror perceptions of credibility. Sometimes jurors view the child as less credible than an adult offering the same testimony; at other times they view the child as more credible."

Ross et al. (1990) offer two possible reasons for these contradictory findings. First, stereotypes may influence social judgment. That is, the public in general may believe that children are usually not confident when confronted with authority, are highly suggestible, and easily confused. The more the child's behavior fits the stereotype (confused, suggestible, compliant), the more convinced the juror is that the child's testimony is suspect. This is a process known as **assimilation**. The juror judges the individual child's statement by assimilating it into his or her favored stereotype about children's statements.

234

CHAPTER
NINE:
THE
PSYCHOLOGY
OF
EVIDENCE:
EYEWITNESS
TESTIMONY

If the child witness defies the stereotype, however, by being confident, forceful, and consistent, the juror perceives the seemingly atypical child witness as *more* credible. When stereotypes are violated, there is a tendency for human beings to perceive the individual as *more* dissimilar to the stereotype than he or she really is, a phenomenon known as **perceptual adaptation** or **contrast effects**. Because the child witness in the Ross et al. study violated the stereotype, jurors tended to perceive the child as unusually credible. A similar finding was reported by Leippe and Romanczyk (1989, p. 127) who concluded from their series of studies: "It seems that adults' negative preconceptions about children's memory will not dispose them to reject a child's memory message if the message's quality is sufficiently 'mature' to belie the stereotype." Nigro et al. (1989) also report that when a child witness speaks confidently and without hesitation (called in the research literature "powerful speech") jurors view him or her as more credible than an adult. Leippe, Manion, and Romanczyk (1992) report that the more *consistent* and confident the child witnesses appear to be, the more believable they are. These findings suggest that a confident child who does not become confused—and acts mature or adultlike—on the witness stand may become a highly credible witness in the eyes of the jury. This conclusion must be tempered a bit, however, by research reported by Gary Wells and his colleagues (1989). They argue that people on a jury rarely have heard or seen an actual child eyewitness testify. Therefore, their stereotypes are not built on actual experiences with child testimony, but are *imagined* stereotypes and biases, which almost invariably are very negative. Their cherished stereotypes may be violated, then, even by the *average* child witness. The actual child may rarely correspond to the imagined stereotype, virtually guaranteeing a process of perceptual adaptation rather than assimilation.

The second explanation offered by the Ross group for discrepant findings on perceptions of the credibility of children is also interesting. Ross et al. (1990) suggest that there is a difference between trials that require children to *remember* and those that require them to be honest. For example, if the testimony demands accurate recall of a complex crime scene, the jury is inclined to find a child witness less credible than an adult witness. Most adults believe children are less cognitively competent to put together or reconstruct a complex scenario that happened in the "adult world." Therefore, jurors, as a group, are less inclined to believe a child's testimony if it requires the *cognitive ability* to be precise, to remember, and to understand all the subtle nuances of what happened. On the other hand, jurors are more inclined to find a child witness credible if the trial demands *honesty*, such as truthful reports about whether she is encouraged to go to school or whether he has been asked to deliver drugs. Jurors apparently believe that adults often have ulterior motives for their testimony, whereas children are more straightforward and less likely to lie about things or fabricate events.

There are other important considerations about children's testimony, such as what happens to the child when under cross-examination compared to direct-examination. Research by Gary Wells and his associates (1989) sheds some light on this issue. The researchers exposed eight-and twelve-year-old children and college students to a staged criminal event (a videotaped abduction of a child from a playground). One day later the children and college students were subjected to direct questioning and cross-examination about the event. All age groups were equally accurate about the event during direct-examination, but under cross-examination, the eight-year-olds were much less accurate than the twelve-year-olds or the college students. During cross-examination, for example, questions were asked such as "You claimed before that the playground was fairly crowded, is that correct?" (when no such claim had been made), or "In which hand was the man carrying his wallet?" (a wallet was never visible in the scene). Eight year-olds were more influenced by these misleading questions than the older witnesses. Ceci, Ross, and Toglia (1987), using three- and twelve-year-olds, found similar results. To summarize, the susceptibility of young children to suggestion and misleading information appears to be influenced by the nature of the questions asked and the context in which those questions occur.

Another important but largely neglected factor associated with the credibility of child witnesses is **communication modality,** or the medium through which the child's testimony is presented (Ross, Dunning, Toglia, & Ceci, 1989). Courts are increasingly allowing alternate forms of testimony, particularly in civil cases. In criminal cases, the issue is more critical, because defendants have a constitutional right to confront their accusers. In 1990, however, the U. S. Supreme Court allowed the closed circuit testimony of children in a sexual assault case (*Maryland v. Craig*). Researchers are beginning to study whether written form (such as transcripts or a deposition), auditory format (an audiotape), or visual format (a videotape) make a difference with respect to perceived credibility. Some preliminary data from Ross et al. (1989) suggest that, regardless of a witness's age, he or she is seen as more credible when his or her testimony is videotaped than when it is written. Modality did not influence jurors' final ratings of guilt or innocence, however. In fact, the research at this point is not at all conclusive as to the impact of witness age on final verdict (Leippe & Romanczyk, 1987; Goodman, Golding et al., 1987). All we can tentatively say at this time is that witness age does not appear to influence directly how mock jurors feel about the guilt or innocence of a defendant.

We should be wary about making generalizations to real-life violent incidents, however. None of the simulation experiments with children involved terrifying depictions of violence or the stress of being a victim. In an effort to increase the ecological validity of research on witness studies, several projects have tested the effects of stress on the memories of children. Gail Goodman and her associates (Goodman, Hepps & Reed, 1986; Goodman, Aman & Hirschman, 1987) reasoned that venipuncture (blood drawing), inoculations, and going to the dentist are usually very frightening and stressful to children. Therefore, in some ways these situations resemble victimization. One project (Goodman, Hepps & Reed, 1986) studied children who were faced with a medically necessary venipuncture procedure to determine if their attention would become narrowly focused in a manner hypothesized by Easterbrook (1959). This experimental group was compared with a control group of children, who did not undergo venipuncture, but were matched for age, sex, race, and time in the venipuncture room. The results did not support Easterbrook's hypothesis that high levels of stress interfere with a victim's memory of peripheral aspects of a scene. There were no significant differences between the two groups in free recall (amount of information correctly recalled) or the proportion of correct answers to objective questions about the room in which they were sitting. Nor were there differences in responses to suggestive questions or photo identifications of people. In brief, the results did not support the hypothesis that stress interferes with a young victim's memory. Because the sample was too small to make sophisticated analyses or far-reaching conclusions, Goodman and colleagues (Goodman, Aman, & Hirschman, 1987) conducted a larger study. Here, they went to immunization clinics for more subjects (three-, four-, five-, and six-year-olds), and followed a similar experimental procedure, but apparently without a control group. Children had been prescheduled for an inoculation either as part of their normal medical care or as a requirement to attend school. Since some researchers have hypothesized that memory for arousal-producing events increases over time, the Goodman group required the children to recall the event and asked objective and subjective questions several days after the inoculation. The children also were asked a set of legal questions typically asked of children during child competence examinations (e.g., "Do you know the difference between the truth and a lie?" and "What happens if you tell a lie?").

Results showed no significant differences by age in the children's abilities to recall features of the event, nor did their ability decrease (or increase) over time. Age differences did appear in

236

CHAPTER
NINE:
THE
PSYCHOLOGY
OF
EVIDENCE:
EYEWITNESS
TESTIMONY

response to objective and suggestive questions, however. Older children (five- and six-year-olds) were better at answering objective questions after a delay of several days, and they showed greater resistance to the misleading information contained within the suggestive questions. All age groups were more accurate at recalling the central information (e.g., physical characteristics of the person who gave the shot, or the actions that took place) than peripheral information (e.g., features of the room). Overall, the projects reported by Goodman suggest that stress had no consistent effect on recall and recognition memory of a young child.

Peters (1987) took advantage of the stress usually experienced during a child's visit to the dentist. Subjects consisted of seventy-one children, ranging in ages from three to eight, who visited one of seven male dentists. The children were seen either within hours after their visit or after a period of several weeks. They were all given face- and voice-recognition tests for both the dentist and the dental assistant or hygienist who saw them. They were also given a recognition test to see if they could remember peripheral details of the visit. Children in the dental-visit condition were as accurate as controls on a battery of subsequent memory tests. Peters admits that the stress level induced by a visit to the dentist is highly unlikely to approximate what children would experience as a witness of a violent crime or a victim of assault or abuse. However, it would be unethical to create in an experimental situation a level of stress comparable to crime-based conditions. Like the Goodman research, the Peters study suggests that moderate levels of stress have little direct effect on recall or recognition memory.

OLDER WITNESSES

A vast majority of the psycholegal research examining the relationship between age and testimony has focused on the eyewitness testimony of children. Research focusing on the elderly and how the public perceives them as eyewitness has so far been underdeveloped. Interestingly, the available research suggests that there are similarities between older witnesses (ages sixty-five to ninety) and very young witnesses on the matter of accuracy. Advanced age appears to have little impact on the accuracy of recognition memory (Yarmey & Kent, 1980). Older subjects do appear to be less adept at free verbal recall of an incident, a finding also reported for children. Yarmey and Kent also noted that older witnesses were more cautious and less confident in their responses than younger subjects.

Similarities concerning the public's perceptions of child and elderly witnesses have been reported. Yarmey (1984) finds that elderly witnesses are commonly stereotyped as intellectually inferior and unable to recall events compared to younger witnesses. Ross et al. (1989) report that college students found an eight-year-old and a seventy-four-year-old less credible than a twenty-one-year-old with respect to accuracy of memory. The young and old witnesses were also perceived as more suggestible. The elderly witness was seen as the most *honest* of all the witnesses, however. Unfortunately, the memory accuracy and perceptions of the elderly witness have been seriously neglected in psycholegal study so far.

Identifying Characteristics of the Offender

THE FACE

Are witnesses who have observed a face once, perhaps only for a brief moment and often under conditions of stress or poor visibility, able to remember the face well enough to recognize it correctly sometime later? Since courts, particularly criminal courts, rely so heavily on such eyewitness

■ 9.2: PLACE THE FACE

ON A DECEMBER EVENING IN 1974, viewers of a New York City news program were "eyewitnesses" to a simulated purse-snatching incident. They saw a young woman confronted by a leather-jacket-clad man, who grabbed the woman's purse and knocked her down. The entire incident last twelve seconds, and for one or two seconds the perpetrator ran toward the camera. Immediately after the incident viewers saw a lineup of six men who resembled the assailant. They were told that the attacker might or might not be in the lineup, and they were asked to call in and indicate whether they recognized the assailant.

The real attacker was indeed in the lineup, but only 4.1 percent of the 2,000 viewer-witnesses who called in correctly identified the attacker. The data revealed the striking figure of 1,843 mistaken identifications (Buckhout, 1975). This is no better result than would be expected if the witnesses had been merely guessing; that is, according to probability theory, someone who had not even seen the incident would have one chance in six of picking the correct person. Men and women witnesses were equally inaccurate.

The above "experiment" illustrates a dilemma that the legal system cannot ignore. Witnesses who have observed a face once, perhaps for a brief moment and often under stressful conditions, usually cannot remember that face well enough to identify it correctly later. Yet, the law often encourages witnesses and victims to make such identifications. ■

recognition, it is important to consider whether this reliance is justified. An accumulation of studies demonstrates that the accurate recognition of a relatively unfamiliar face is an extremely complex and error-ridden task. Research by Memon et al. (1988) suggests that witnesses are more accurate if they have a full-face view of a person than a side view. The average person trying to identify a face seen once and for a short duration will be accurate about 70 percent of the time (Goldstein, 1977; Wells & Turtle, 1986). Rarely do studies report more than an 85 percent accuracy rate. Furthermore, it is highly probable that the research overestimates the accuracy rate. Subjects used in the research are college students whose age and general health may make them better witnesses than the general population (Yarmey, 1984). Additionally, they lack the stress levels characteristic of eyewitnesses to a "real" crime, though we should recall the stress-related research which indicates that moderate stress does not significantly influence recollection.

Psychological experiments examining face recognition usually follow a two-step paradigm. Subjects are first shown live people, films, photographs, or face illustrations and are then given either a recognition or recall task to test memory of the faces. Although the number of faces to study, the length of time allowed, and the time interval between study and test vary from experiment to experiment, the results have been surprisingly consistent.

In one of the earliest such experimental projects on face recognition, Howells (1938) discovered that faces were more difficult to recognize when the lower sections of the face area (middle of the nose down) were covered than when the upper sections were covered. In contradiction to this pioneering study, however, more recent experiments have reported with consistency that the upper portions of the face provide decidedly better recognition cues than the lower portions (Yarmey, 1979), although it is unclear which upper facial features are most important.

The current research also indicates that the relative importance of facial cues depends upon the particular face being evaluated. For reasons which are unknown, some faces are easier to discern and elicit more accurate identifications than others. Highly unique faces are better recognized than plain or average faces (Going & Read, 1974; Cohen & Carr, 1975). Faces high and low in attractiveness also are easier to recognize than faces judged to be of medium attractiveness (Shepherd & Ellis, 1973). There is some evidence to suggest that most people concentrate

238

CHAPTER
NINE:
THE
PSYCHOLOGY
OF
EVIDENCE:
EYEWITNESS
TESTIMONY

more on the right side than on the left when looking at a human face (Gilbert & Bakan, 1973; Liggett, 1974).

UNCONSCIOUS TRANSFERENCE

Some witnesses have mistakenly identified as offenders persons they have seen at some other time and place. This phenomenon, which Glanville Williams (1963) called **unconscious transference**, occurs when a person seen in one situation is confused with or recalled as a person seen in another situation. A witness may have had limited exposure to a face (e.g., on a subway) and, upon seeing the face at a later time, concluded that it is the offender's. Loftus (1979) theorizes that unconscious transference is another feature of the integrative, malleable nature of human memory, where earlier input becomes tangled up with later input. It should be recalled that perceptual and memory processes are unconscious and the mixtures produced by them often range widely on a continuum of transformation and potential distortion.

The phenomenon of unconscious transference illustrates that it is highly possible that a store clerk who is witness to a robbery might incorrectly identify as the perpetrator an occasional customer who may have some of the features of the actual culprit. However, for unconscious transference to take place, the previous encounters with the innocent face must have been brief. Continual, relatively prolonged encounters, even with nameless faces, would be unlikely to result in incorrect identification.

Unconscious transference may also come into play when witnesses are asked to glance through a series of "mug shots." The unconscious perceptual and memory processes may prime the witness to identify a suspect seen later on the basis of mug shot exposure rather than on the basis of observation at the scene of a crime (Laughery, Alexander & Lane, 1971; Laughery et al., 1974).

The pioneering Howells study (1938) suggested that subjects who were most accurate in the *recognition* test for faces were the least accurate in *verbally recalling* details of the faces. This hints that visual recognition of faces and their verbal descriptive recall may be two separate processes. More recent studies have supported the Howells data (Goldstein & Chance, 1970; Chance & Goldstein, 1976; Malpass, Lavigueur & Weldon, 1973). This indicates that accuracy of facial recognition is more dependent upon visual encoding than upon verbal processes of memory (Yarmey, 1979). These data also suggest that, as a group, witnesses are more accurate at recognition than recall. Law-enforcement officials who ask witnesses to describe the offender are tapping a very different and perhaps less accurate perceptual process than when they ask them to pick out an offender from a lineup or photospreads. One task calls for recall memory, the other demands recognition memory. A great wealth of information should not be expected if witnesses are asked to describe the perpetrator. It is a better tactic to pose questions jarring recognition memory, such as "Did he have a beard, a mustache, or was he clean-shaven?" This is especially true if young children or the elderly are witnesses.

As we discussed earlier in the chapter, recall demands a different kind of retrieval operation, requiring a reproduction of the initially seen object or event. Recognition is an operation which simply requires a subject to note whether he or she has seen an object before. An illustration from a typical campus nemesis—testing—will make the point. Multiple-choice exams tap recognition memory, while essay exams usually involve recall memory. Students often resist essay tests, claiming that they require too much memorization. The resistance is partly due to the fact that memorization is a more demanding task than recognition. Students find themselves resorting to cue words or mnemonic acronyms—each letter represents a key concept. By doing this, students are altering their task so that it will yield to a process more in line with the easier recognition operation. It will come as no surprise that a long series of experiments in cognitive psychology have confirmed the observation that people find recognition tasks far easier than recall tasks (Klatzky, 1975).

OTHER-RACE EFFECT

There is some evidence that people are better able to discriminate between faces of their own race than between faces of other races. Initially, the research focused on black or white subjects. More recently, it has been extended to include other racial groups. In one of the first laboratory studies of this type, Roy Malpass and Jerome Kravitz (1969) asked twenty black students and twenty white students to examine twenty slides of black or white faces for about two seconds each. The subjects were asked to identify the faces they had initially seen from eighty slides (sixty new faces, twenty old ones). The researchers discovered that white observers were more accurate with white faces than with black faces. Black observers gave equally correct responses for both white and black faces, however (Figure 9.1).

These results were later replicated by Cross, Cross, and Daly (1971), who found that whites were more accurate in recognizing faces of their own race (45 percent correct) than black faces (27 percent correct). However, again black subjects were about as accurate with white faces (40 percent correct) as they were with those of their own race (39 percent correct). Chance and colleagues (1975) reported that while whites recognize white faces best, they are even worse at recognizing Asian faces than black faces. Blacks, on the other hand, were more accurate in recognizing black faces, second best with white faces, and least accurate with Asian faces.

Stephanie Platz and Harmon Hosch (1988) asked eighty-six convenience store clerks to

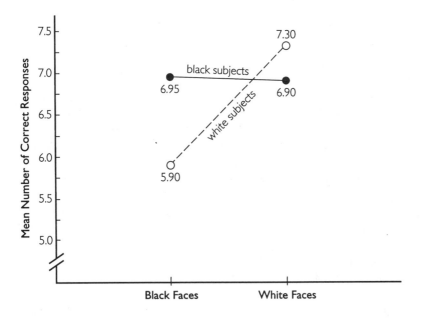

Figure 9.1 ■ The other-race effect. Relationship between the average number of correct responses to black or white faces by black or white subjects. [Figure developed from the data reported by Malpass and Kravitz (1969).]

240

CHAPTER
NINE:
THE
PSYCHOLOGY
OF
EVIDENCE:
EYEWITNESS
TESTIMONY

identify three customers who had visited their stores two hours earlier. The three customers were all confederates to the experiment: One was an African American, another was Chicano, and the third was a white American. The clerks were superior at identifying customers of their own racial or ethnic group and did not do as well at identifying customers of different racial or ethnic groups. A literature review and re-analysis of all available studies (Bothwell, Deffenbacher & Brigham, 1987) also confirmed that both white and black subjects are superior at identifying faces of their own race or ethnic group.

A similar pattern may exist for children (Yarmey, 1979; Feinman & Entwisle, 1976). White and black children are more adept at recognizing faces of their own race. Some evidence shows that recognition accuracy increases with age (Goldstein & Chance, 1964).

There are several possible explanations for this **other-race recognition** effect. One of the more popular, called the **differential experience hypothesis**, argues that individuals will naturally have greater familiarity or experience with members of their own race and will thus be better able to discern differences among its members. People are typically raised in social environments that require them to recognize own-race faces, beginning at a very early age.

Although some researchers (e.g., Loftus, 1979) dismiss the differential experience hypothesis as a valid explanation for the other-race recognition effect, much of the research supports the theory, at least as a partial explanation (Elliott, Wills & Goldstein, 1973; Yarmey, 1979). Yarmey suggests a clarification that may help the opposing parties reach a compromise. The experience presumed to be a significant factor in recognition must be distinguished from mere exposure, he says. Growing up in an integrated neighborhood does not necessarily allow one to discern other-race facial characteristics accurately. Rather, it is the frequency of meaningful and positive contacts with other races that engenders such perceptual skill. For example, having close friends of other races is more likely to promote facial discernment than having frequent but superficial exposure.

Additional support for the differential experience hypothesis is provided in studies showing that training in face familiarization dissipates the other-race effect (e.g., Elliott, Wills & Goldstein, 1973; Lavrakas, Burl & Mayzner, 1976). In the Elliot project, white observers' recognition of unfamiliar Asian faces significantly improved as a result of training in a learning task (paired associates) which increased their attention to identifying features of Asian faces. In another experiment (Ellis, Deregowski & Shepherd, 1975), white observers from Scotland were found to concentrate more on such features as hair color and texture and color of eyes when looking at white faces. Black observers from Rhodesia, looking at black faces, attended more to facial outline, hair style, eye size, whites of eyes, eyebrows, ears, and chin. These results suggest at least two possible explanations for differences in race identification. People may develop specific strategies based on certain distinguishing cues of the human face to identify same-race members. Or, in light of the Ellis data, blacks may process a greater number of useful facial cues than whites when discriminating own-race members.

If the strategies used by individuals in identifying same-race members can be delineated, it is possible that the discernment of eyewitnesses may be improved prior to any identification procedure. However, how crucial initial observations of suspects are and whether they might be improved by employing after-the-fact strategies remain unanswered questions.

A second possible explanation for the other-race effect pertains only to white observers, who seem to be the *least* able to identify other races. According to this hypothesis, there are differences between the races in the degree of homogeneity of facial features. White faces have more variability in hair, skin, and eye color than black faces and are therefore more inherently discernible. In a series of experiments designed to test this hypothesis, Goldstein and Chance (1976, 1978) found, however, that white subjects did not perceive Asian faces to be more homogeneous, or alike, than white faces. This outcome suggests that the source of the other-race effect lies not so much in the facial characteristics of the person being observed as it does in the observer.

In sum, the literature consistently concludes that people have difficulty recognizing unfamiliar persons of other races. This other-race effect is obviously a critical factor in the identification of suspects by eyewitnesses. The most valid explanation for the phenomenon at this point appears to be the differential experience hypothesis, which implies that substantial, meaningful interactions with members of a different race may promote the formation of strategies for facial discrimination.

Pretrial Identification Methods

The identification of suspects by witnesses begins as soon after the offense as possible. Police usually obtain verbal descriptions of the perpetrators from witnesses or show them photographs to obtain a preliminary identification. In some instances, the police will have witnesses scan photos of individuals with previous records, either to identify the specific offender or to obtain an approximation of the offender's appearance. Some police agencies routinely ask witnesses to examine a group of photographs (photoboards) fairly well matched to the physical characteristics described and including the person the police suspect to be the guilty party. Despite media portrayals, photo lineups are more common than live lineups. This is partly because suspects have a right to counsel at live lineups but not at photo lineups. The validity of these photo identification techniques has been addressed by the nation's highest court in a number of cases, however.

On February 27, 1964, two men entered a Chicago savings and loan association office. One man pointed a revolver at a teller and demanded that she place money into a sack. Soon afterward, the FBI apprehended two suspects, after tracing a motor vehicle described by one of the bank employees. The FBI then obtained group photographs—which included the suspects—from relatives of the suspects, and showed them to five bank employees. All five witnesses identified one of the suspects (Simmons); three identified the other.

After its route through the lower courts, the case was heard by the U. S. Supreme Court as *Simmons v. United States* (1968). Simmons asserted "that his pretrial identification by means of photographs was in the circumstances so unnecessarily suggestive and conducive to misidentification as to deny him due process of law" (*Simmons v. U. S.*, p. 381). The Court, however, felt otherwise. The Justices ruled that the photograph procedure used by the FBI was appropriate under the circumstances, and they elaborated: "Convictions based on eyewitness identification at trial following a pretrial identification by photograph will be set aside on that ground only if the photographic identification procedure was so impermissibly suggestive as to give rise to a very substantial likelihood of irreparable misidentification" (p. 384). An example of an "impermissibly suggestive" procedure would be one in which a black suspect is shown to eyewitnesses among five white persons, or one in which a perpetrator described as short is shown among tall foils known to be innocent persons.

Just prior to *Simmons*, the Supreme Court heard three cases dealing with pretrial identification abuses (*U. S. v. Wade*, 1967; *Gilbert v. California*, 1967; *Stovall v. Denno*, 1967). In *Wade* (see Box 9.3), the Court recognized the many problems inherent in pretrial identification, both showups (one person) and lineups, so it ruled that suspects who have been formally charged have the right to have counsel present to assure an unbiased procedure. (The Court later ruled, in *Kirby v. Illinois* (1972), that there is no right to counsel in identification procedures prior to the time a suspect is

242

CHAPTER
NINE:
THE
PSYCHOLOGY
OF
EVIDENCE:
EYEWITNESS
TESTIMONY

formally charged.) In *Gilbert*, the Court found the defendant was denied due process of law when he was identified in a large auditorium by 100 witnesses to several different robberies which he had allegedly committed. The Court was concerned about the possible effect of group suggestion on the identification of the defendant.

In *Stovall*, the defendant was brought to the hospital room of the victim, who had been stabbed eleven times. It was one day after major surgery to save the victim's life. The black defendant was handcuffed to one of the five escorting white police officers, who were also accompanied by two staff members of the District Attorney's office. This imposing contingent descended upon the hospital room for a showup to request victim identification. The badly injured victim identified Stovall as the offender.

The Supreme Court ruled that, under the unusual circumstances and because of the possible death of the sole witness, the procedure was *necessarily suggestive* and hence not improper. "The practice of showing suspects singly to persons for the purpose of identification, and not as part of a lineup, has been widely condemned. However, a claimed violation of due process of law in the conduct of a confrontation depends on the totality of the circumstances surrounding it, and the record in the present case reveals that the showing of Stovall to Mrs. Behrent in an immediate hospital confrontation was imperative" (Justice Brennan commenting, p. 292).

Interestingly, although the Court in *Stovall v. Denno* indicated that showups were more suggestive than lineups, recent research evidence questions this assumption. In fact, in a series of laboratory and field experiments, Gonzalez, Ellsworth, and Pembroke (1993) learned that the showup may produce fewer false positive identifications than the lineup. The researchers staged a theft in a college classroom and then assigned subjects to lineup and showup conditions, asking them whether the perpetrator was present. Subjects in the lineup condition were more likely to answer positively. In a second study, the subjects viewed a videotaped staged crime and again were asked to find the perpetrator in a lineup or showup procedure, this time using photographs. Again, the one-person showup did not increase the risk that an innocent person would be identified. In discussing the results of the two studies, the researchers noted that the "showup has a relatively high rate of misses, whereas the lineup has a relatively high rate of false positives" (p. 533).

The third study was a field test of the above two laboratory studies. A police detective was asked to keep track of all identifications he was involved in, both lineups and showups, until he reached 50 lineups. The process resulted in 50 lineups (all photo lineups) and 172 showups (almost all live). Witnesses were more likely to make positive identifications in lineups than in showups and were far more likely to assert the perpetrator was *not* there in showups than in lineups. These field results supported the findings of the laboratory research, though Gonzalez, Ellsworth, and Pembroke were careful not to base strong conclusions on this real-world identification procedure.

Taken together, the studies suggest that we should be cautious about assuming that showups are more suggestive than lineups. As the researchers noted, "People appear to approach showups more cautiously; they are more reluctant to say that the person they see is the perpetrator, even when he or she is" (p. 536).

IDENTIFICATION BIASES

Pretrial identification methods are especially susceptible to a wide spectrum of biases, running from very blatant practices to more subtle innuendo. A police investigator's suggestion to the witness that he look closely at "the third one from the right" is subtle innuendo when compared to other practices. Psychologists are beginning to examine more closely the psychology of the lineup and its ramifications for the criminal-justice system. Given that showups probably occur

■ 9.3: *WITNESS IDENTIFICATION CASES*

UNITED STATES V. WADE, GILBERT V. CALIFORNIA, and *Stovall v. Denno* form a trilogy of cases dealing with the effects of prejudicial lineups and witness identifications of accused persons. The following excerpts are from *Wade*, but they make reference to the critical aspects of the other two cases which relate to the manner in which witness identification was carried out by the police.

The Government characterizes the lineup as a mere preparatory step in the gathering of the prosecution's evidence, not different—for Sixth Amendment purposes—from various other preparatory steps, such as systematized or scientific analyzing of the accused's fingerprints, blood sample, clothing, hair, and the like. We think there are differences which preclude such stages being characterized as critical stages at which the accused has the right to the presence of his counsel....

But the confrontation compelled by the State between the accused and the victim or witnesses to a crime to elicit identification evidence is peculiarly riddled with innumerable dangers and variable factors which might seriously, even crucially, derogate from a fair trial. The vagaries of eyewitness identification are well-known; the annals of criminal law are rife with instances of mistaken identification....

A commentator has observed that "[t]he influence of improper suggestion upon identifying witnesses probably accounts for more miscarriages of justice than any other single factor. Perhaps it is responsible for more such errors than all other factors combined." ...Suggestion can be created intentionally or unintentionally in many subtle ways. And the dangers for the suspect are particularly grave when the witness' opportunity for observation was insubstantial, and thus his susceptibility to suggestion the greatest.

Moreover, "[i]t is a matter of common experience that, once a witness has picked out the accused at the line-up, he is not likely to go back on his word later on, so that in practice the issue of identity may (in the absence of other relevant evidence) for all practical purposes be determined there and then, before the trial."...

The lineup in *Gilbert*...was conducted in an auditorium in which some 100 witnesses to several alleged state and federal robberies charged to Gilbert made wholesale identifications of Gilbert as the robber in each other's presence, a procedure said to be fraught with dangers of suggestion. And the vise of suggestion created by the identification in *Stovall*... was the presentation to the witness of the suspect alone handcuffed to police officers. It is hard to imagine a situation more clearly conveying the suggestion to the witness that the one presented is believed guilty by the police....

Since it appears that there is grave potential for prejudice, intentional or not, in the pretrial lineup, which may not be capable of reconstruction at trial, and since presence of counsel itself can often avert prejudice and assure a meaningful confrontation at trial, there can be little doubt that for Wade the post-indictment lineup was a critical stage of the prosecution at which he was "as much entitled to such aid [of counsel]...as at the trial itself." ... Thus both Wade and his counsel should have been notified of the impending lineup, and counsel's presence should have been a requisite to conduct of the lineup. ■

---

more than lineups, however, additional research on showups is critical. With the exception of the Gonzalez et al. study discussed above, this area has been neglected.

Since the witness will look for a suspect in the live or photo lineup who fits the description he or she has given the police, the physical variety among members of the lineup is a crucial factor. Frequently, before appearing in a lineup, a suspect will change his or her appearance in order to mislead eyewitnesses, a tactic that is often successful (Cutler, Penrod & Martens, 1987). Each individual participant in the lineup should have as many of the relevant characteristics remembered by the witness as possible. Age, physical stature, race, hair style, and manner of dress—especially if described by the witness—should be approximately the same for all. If the witness remembered the offender as a six-foot-tall individual with blond, wavy hair and a moustache,

244

CHAPTER
NINE:
THE
PSYCHOLOGY
OF
EVIDENCE:
EYEWITNESS
TESTIMONY

the lineup is obviously biased if only one person in six follows that description. No matter how many foils are standing in the line, the test is effectively limited to the number of participants who resemble the suspect. We refer to this condition as **composition bias**.

Composition bias has been analyzed in a number of studies, but two which appear especially relevant are those of Wells, Leippe, and Ostrom (1979) and Doob and Kirshenbaum (1973). Using the previous work of Doob and Kirshenbaum, Gary Wells and his colleagues developed a concept they call the **functional size** of a lineup. This refers to the number of lineup members who resemble the suspect in physically relevant features. By contrast, **nominal size** refers to the actual number of members within the lineup, which theoretically may include some very dissimilar foils.

In a typical lineup of six persons, the functional size decreases as the number of physically dissimilar members of a lineup increases. For a lineup to be considered fair, its functional size should approximate the nominal size. If by employing various measures and statistical tests it is determined that all the members of a six-member lineup have equal probability of being selected on the basis of crucial characteristics, the functional size is six. If the actual suspect is included in the lineup and only three of the other members resemble the suspect, the functional size is four and the nominal size is six.

Obtaining theoretical and statistical indices of composition bias is an interesting academic exercise for researchers, but we also must consider the reality or ecological validity of this approach. In other words, how much real-world applicability does a particular finding have? Law-enforcement officials and prosecuting attorneys remind us that there are problems in composing a lineup of people who closely resemble the suspect. First, it is often difficult to find persons (outside of members of the police department) who are willing to participate *and* who resemble the suspect in salient features. A volunteer might be identified as the guilty party! This is particularly a problem for medium-sized-city or small-town police departments, where the subject pool is already limited. Second, law-enforcement officials worry about the possibility that a high level of similarity between lineup (or photoboard) members may confuse the witnesses and distract from the accurate identification of the primary suspect.

Another question spawned by the **similarity-to-suspect strategy** is, How similar should the foils be to the culprit? Do we try to match sex, race, height, weight, and age, and stop there, or do we match hair color, hair style, hair length, eye color, nose, eye shape and so forth? If all features matched, correct identification would become impossible, as lineup members would look *too much* alike (Luus & Wells, 1991). This strategy seems to recommend theoretically that we continue—if possible—until we obtain clonelike foils.

Elizabeth Luus and Gary Wells (1991) suggest a **match-to-description strategy**, where the selection of foils is based on the witness's description of the perpetrator. More specifically, Luus and Wells argue that the features shared by the foils should be based primarily on the eyewitness's free recall of the offender. Foils should be allowed to vary in characteristics not mentioned by the witness. The term "free recall" is critical here. It refers to the immediate description provided by the eyewitness without directed prompting (leading questions) or comparison stimuli (such as mug shots). This distinction is important because of the differences between recall memory and recognition memory. The match-to-description strategy utilizes both the free-recall description by the eyewitness and the recognition of the culprit in the lineup or photo display. However, this match-to-description strategy could produce lineups where the foils differ dramatically in physical characteristics, being matched only on a few salient characteristics recalled by the witness. The courts may have some difficulty with such lineups.

On the other side of the ledger, it can be argued that the quality of the evidence is enhanced when suspects are selected from lineups possessing high functional size. Lindsay and Wells (1980) provide evidence that high-similarity lineups reduce correct identification of suspects. Their research found low-similarity lineups produced correct identifications 71 percent of the time, whereas high-similarity lineups produced it 58 percent of the time. However, the researchers contend that the reduction in numbers of correct identification is compensated by the fact that the identifications under high-similarity conditions are stronger evidence in court and less open to counterargument.

A more subtle form of composition bias enters in with respect to who constructs the lineup. As we have learned, people have trouble discriminating the faces of other races, presumably because they do not attend properly to discerning features. If the suspect is black, the lineup constructor is white, and the witnesses are white, we have a situation with much potential bias. This possibility is suggested by John Brigham (1980), who bases his observations on accompanying research. To avoid bias, the constructor should be of the same race as the suspect.

Another area of pretrial identification which must be closely examined is **commitment bias**. Once a witness has identified a face, even an incorrect one, he or she will be more likely to choose that face again. This phenomenon is an offshoot of the "foot-in-the-door technique" long studied by social psychologists (Vander Zanden, 1977). It has been demonstrated in several simulation experiments on eyewitness testimony (Brown et al., 1977; Gorenstein & Ellsworth, 1980).

Commitment bias is most operative in conditions where witnesses want to please police investigators and also where they presume that the police have good evidence against someone in the identification proceedings. Because of commitment bias, a witness who initially identifies a suspect, but with some doubts, is more likely to identify the same suspect with greater conviction in subsequent exposures. Each subsequent identification promotes greater confidence because of the public and private commitment that he *is* the one.

Thus, a witness may begin the identification sequence by saying, "I think maybe he is the one." The police officer inquires, "Are you sure?" The witness replies, "Yes, I'm pretty sure." The police officer inquires further, "Pretty sure?" The witness affirms, "Yes, I'm sure."

Between the time of this identification procedure and the trial, the witness replays the scene in his or her mind, further strengthening the commitment. When the prosecuting attorney asks this key witness during the trial, "Are you sure this is the man?" the answer becomes, "Yes, I'm absolutely positive."

John Brigham and Donna Cairns (1988) discovered that commitment bias occurs even in the absence of strong external pressure. They had subjects view a videotape of a staged assault, following which some subjects (the experimental group) attempted to identify the assailant from a set of eighteen mugshots. They were told that the assailant might or might not be present in the mugshots. In order to magnify the effects of commitment bias, the researchers did not include the suspect in the photographs. Another group of subjects, who also viewed the videotape, simply rated the mugshots for attractiveness, without being asked to identify an offender. In this situation, since no choice was requested, no commitment bias should have been initiated. Two days later, all subjects were asked to identify the assailant from a six-person photo lineup that *did* contain the assailant. If the experimental subject had made a choice from the earlier mugshots (not all had), the researchers placed that mugshot into the photo lineup for that subject. Brigham and Cairns found that the experimental subjects demonstrated a strong commitment to their earlier misidentification or nonidentification. That is, they held to their previous inaccurate identification when viewing the photo lineup task that contained the real suspect. Experimental subjects who had not identified the attacker in the mugshots usually did not choose anyone from the subsequent lineup.

There are many other sources of bias inherent in pretrial identification procedures, but those delineated here have received the most attention from psychologists in recent years. One relatively unstudied source is **police bias**, which refers both to the use of police officers as foils

246

CHAPTER
NINE:
THE
PSYCHOLOGY
OF
EVIDENCE:
EYEWITNESS
TESTIMONY

and to the questioning techniques used by police investigators. The use of officers as foils in a lineup is a practice fraught with potential bias. Certain nonverbal cues, such as frequent glances in the direction of the suspect, could easily contaminate the witness's ability to make an independent judgment. Leading questions directed toward the witness and the quality of the questioning directed at lineup members by the police investigator can also skew the performance of a witness sensitive to police cues.

Summary and Conclusions

The material presented in this chapter illustrates that evidence obtained through traditional procedures of eyewitness questioning and testimony is replete with potential inaccuracies and misconceptions, regardless of the avowed certainty of the witness. Human perception and memory are like unexplored labyrinths where original input becomes altered, partially lost, and transformed into an arrangement that fits our expectancies, experiences, and sometimes the disguised needs of others. Situational, witness, and offender factors intermingle to produce an output which may barely resemble the incident as it "actually" occurred. Eyewitness research often contradicts common sense.

Nevertheless, eyewitness information has been, is, and will continue to be a principal source of evidence in both criminal and civil case law. The expanding research evidence suggests that the judicial system should carefully examine some of its assumptions about eyewitnesses and perhaps even entertain some small but critical changes in procedures. The "common-sense" view that a confident victim is most likely accurate is not supported in the research. A rapidly growing body of research evidence supports the accuracy of child testimony, particularly on *direct* examination and when not influenced by leading questions. While the research indicates that children generally recall less detail about an event than adults, what they do remember is reliable. The age of the child, however, is an important variable. For example, children under three years of age provide less accurate information than older children. Also, the accuracy of recall seems to show a drop if the child is under age eight. Surprisingly, moderate levels of stress and excitement do not seem to affect children's accuracy any more adversely than they do adults.

Gary Wells (1978) divides eyewitness research into examinations of two sets of variables— estimator variables and system variables. Estimator variables are those situational, witness, and offender cues present at the scene of a crime or incident, such as violence level, speed of events, the age of the witness, and the race of the perpetrator. No matter what strategy or procedure the law employs, it is unlikely to have major impact on this set of variables. Research on them, as presented in this chapter, can be used to estimate, *post hoc*, the likely accuracy of a witness. It can also be used to alter beliefs and attitudes about eyewitness testimony. It is likely to have little influence on legal strategy and procedure, however.

In contrast, system variables are under the direct control of the legal system and do lend themselves to changes in strategy and procedure. Examples of system variables include lineup procedures and guidelines, witness interview techniques, and, to some extent, the length of time between the initial event and subsequent testimony. Research data on system variables do apply to methods presently employed in the judicial system.

J. Alexander Tanford (1991) offers a helpful summary of conditions under which legal decisionmakers, including courts, are most likely to heed or not heed social-science research. Summarizing the evidence to date, Tanford notes (p. 156) that research will most likely be heeded if it is of high quality, understandable to lawyers, accessible, has "penetrated the culture of the educated elite," has been available for at least five years, will legitimate decisions reached on pragmatic grounds, and has been used by other lawmakers. Social science is less likely to be used if it is heavily statistical, contradicts faith or common sense, fails to support the policy predilections of lawmakers, would lead to major political disruption, demonstrates that something is ineffective without providing a better alternative, or reflects values incompatible with principles of law. Much of the eyewitness research discussed in this chapter has characteristics which make it most likely to be heeded.

Questions to Ponder

1. Watch a fifteen- to twenty-minute segment of a VCR high-drama movie. About half an hour later, write down as many verbal and visual details about the segment as you can recall. Play the tape once again and check yourself for accuracy. Discuss whether or not this exercise is relevant to studying the psychology of eyewitness testimony.

2. Summarize the information in this chapter which is the most helpful to a conscientious law-enforcement officer interviewing an adult eyewitness to a violent crime.

3. In light of what we have learned from the research on children's eyewitness testimony, is the presumption of competency for children's testimony a wise one? Why or why not?

4. Discuss the implications of the "other-race effect" for eyewitness identification. What does the existence of the other-race effect say about society?

5. What type of lineup is most likely to produce both the least composition bias and the most witness accuracy?

6. Do you agree with the final sentence in the summary section of this chapter? Explain your answer by discussing eyewitness research as it relates to each of Tanford's criteria for acceptance.

THE PSYCHOLOGY OF EVIDENCE: RELATED ISSUES

OW THAT THE SHORTCOMINGS AND UNRELIABILITY of some of the information obtained from eyewitnesses have been covered, it is time to give attention to information provided by accused persons themselves. The U. S. Constitution, of course, gives criminal defendants the right not to incriminate themselves. Courts have repeatedly reminded us that individuals may not be forced to testify against themselves, to confess, or otherwise provide testimonial evidence that may be damaging to their cases. These court warnings do not mean that defendants may not plead guilty or provide evidence. Neither do they mean that law enforcement officers cannot interrogate suspects and question witnesses to gather evidence. At issue are the psychological states of suspects, the methods of questioning, and the conditions under which interrogations are conducted.

We will begin this chapter with a look at psychological information relevant to interviewing and interrogating. We will evaluate some of the myths about nonverbal behavior and discuss various methods designed to detect lying, such as voice-stress analysis. Some material will be relevant to witnesses as well as to defendants, and to civil as well as criminal cases. For example, we will discuss extensively the polygraph and hypnosis and their legal status. We will briefly review the use of facial composites in identifying suspects. Later in the chapter we will redirect attention to the jury in an attempt to decide whether and to what extent jurors can be influenced by pretrial publicity and broadcast cameras in the courtroom.

Methods of Interrogation

Convictions based on "coerced" confessions have been overturned consistently by the U. S. Supreme Court and other appellate courts, although lively debate has surrounded the question of what conditions define coercion (Shapiro & Tresolini, 1979). Prior to the 1950s, courts accepted arguments that some methods employing physical restraints, prolonged physical discomfort, beatings, and a wide variety of physical abuses were, not surprisingly, coercive and not to be tolerated. In the landmark case *Brown v. Mississippi* (1936), the U. S. Supreme Court ruled that confessions obtained by brutality and torture violated due process rights. Criminal suspects in that case had been hanged from a tree, let down, whipped, laid over chairs, and beaten with a leather strap with a buckle on it. Gradually, courts also began to acknowledge the existence of more subtle forms of "psychological coercion."

In *Escobedo v. Illinois* (1964), the U. S. Supreme Court ruled that Escobedo's confession should not have been admitted as evidence because it was rendered only after he had repeatedly asked

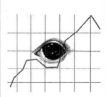

250

CHAPTER
TEN:
THE
PSYCHOLOGY
OF
EVIDENCE:
RELATED
ISSUES

for and been denied counsel. The Court also found that the interrogation methods used by police had so emotionally upset him that his capacity for rational judgement was impaired. As a result, his confession did not follow a valid waiver of his constitutional rights. The best way to prevent injustice of this sort, the Justices said, was to allow subjects to be interrogated in the presence of their attorneys. The Court held that once a police interviewing process shifts from an investigatory to an accusatory focus, or once its purpose is to elicit a confession, the individual must be permitted to have counsel present.

Two years later, in *Miranda v. Arizona* (1966), the Court said the shift to an accusatory focus occurred if the suspect was in custody or otherwise was significantly deprived of freedom. Commenting on the pressure tactics of custodial interrogation, the Court referred to the powerful effects of psychological coercion inherent in that process (see Box 10.1). "We stress that the modern practice of in-custody interrogation is psychologically rather than physically oriented. As we have stated before... 'this Court has recognized that coercion can be mental as well as physical, and that the blood of the accused is not the only hallmark of an unconstitutional inquisition' " (p. 448).

In light of this psychological pressure, the Court felt it was paramount that the accused be told beforehand of the right to remain silent, the implications of waiving that right, the right to have counsel present during custodial interrogation, and the right to have a lawyer be appointed if the suspect could not afford one. The Court did not *require* that counsel be present—only that suspects be informed of that right prior to questioning.

Since the *Miranda* decision, the U. S. Supreme Court has heard many cases which clarified that ruling, both supporting and—more often than not—eroding it. The Court has ruled, for example, that warnings are required for misdemeanors as well as felonies (*Berkemer v. McCarty*, 1984), and that once a suspect asserts the right to remain silent police cannot initiate questioning about a different crime (*Michigan v. Jackson*, 1986). The "functional equivalent" of custodial interrogation is also prohibited (*Brewer v. Williams*, 1977). (In that case, an officer transporting a religious criminal suspect discussed with him the importance of a Christian burial. The suspect's attorney had been told he would not be interrogated. The suspect revealed the location of the body.) On the other hand, the Court has allowed unwarned incriminatory statements when public safety was at issue (*N.Y. v. Quarles*, 1984), ruled that once a suspect has waived the right to remain silent he or she can be questioned about additional crimes (*Colorado v. Spring*, 1987), and ruled that a routine traffic stop does not qualify as custodial interrogation (*Berkemer v. McCarty*, 1984). The Court has refused to extend the requirements of the *Miranda* warning to the grand jury process (*U. S. v. Manduiano*, 1976), and has indicated that police officers have leeway in the language of the warning, as long as the substance is conveyed (*Duckworth v. Eagan*, 1989). The Court also did not accept the argument that a juvenile's request to see his probation officer required police to stop questioning him (*Fare v. Michael C.*, 1979).

The above are only illustrative of many self-incrimination cases heard by courts. Although *Miranda* has never been overturned, case law indicates that the courts have not been overwhelmingly sympathetic to defendants or unreasonably restrictive about police practices, including psychological strategies used in custodial interrogation. The interrogation process continues to be a powerful and commonly practiced method of securing evidence and obtaining confessions, though it would be a mistake to assume that many cases against suspects are built on confessions. Police classroom instruction and texts continue to advocate psychological tactics to obtain information, however. The words of Inbau and Reid (1967, pp. 213–14) are illustrative:

> Interrogations...must be conducted under conditions of privacy and for a reasonable period of time; and they frequently require the use of psychological tactics and techniques that could well be classified as "unethical," if we are to evaluate them in terms of ordinary, everyday social behavior.... We are opposed...to

■ 10.1: *EXCERPTS FROM MIRANDA v. ARIZONA*

WE DEALT WITH CERTAIN PHASES OF THIS problem [custodial police interrogation] recently in *Escobedo v. Illinois*, ...(1964). There, as in the four cases before us, law enforcement officials took the defendant into custody and interrogated him in a police station for the purpose of obtaining a confession. The police did not effectively advise him of his right to remain silent or of his right to consult with his attorney. Rather, they confronted him with an alleged accomplice who accused him of having perpetrated a murder. When the defendant denied the accusation and said "I didn't shoot Manuel, you did it," they handcuffed him and took him to an interrogation room. There, while handcuffed and standing, he was questioned for four hours until he confessed. During this interrogation, the police denied his request to speak to his attorney, and they prevented his retained attorney, who had come to the police station, from consulting with him. At his trial, the State, over his objection, introduced the confession against him. We held that the statements thus made were constitutionally inadmissible....

Our holding will be spelled out with some specificity in the pages which follow but briefly stated it is this: the prosecution may not use statements, whether exculpatory or inculpatory, stemming from custodial interrogation of the defendant unless it demonstrates the use of procedural safeguards effective to secure the privilege against self-incrimination. By custodial interrogation, we mean questioning initiated by law enforcement officers after a person has been taken into custody or otherwise deprived of his freedom of action in any significant way. As for the procedural safeguards to be employed, unless other fully effective means are devised to inform accused persons of their right of silence and to assure a continuous opportunity to exercise it, the following measures are required. Prior to any questioning, the person must be warned that he has a right to remain silent, that any statement he does make may be used as evidence against him, and that he has a right to the presence of an attorney, either retained or appointed. The defendant may waive effectuation of these rights, provided the waiver is made voluntarily, knowingly and intelligently. If, however, he indicates in any manner and at any stage of the process that he wishes to consult with an attorney before speaking there can be no questioning. Likewise, if the individual is alone and indicates in any manner that he does not wish to be interrogated, the police may not question him. The mere fact that he may have answered some questions or volunteered some statements on his own does not deprive him of the right to refrain from answering any further inquiries until he has consulted with an attorney and thereafter consents to be questioned....

Again we stress that the modern practice of in-custody interrogation is psychologically rather than physically oriented. ...this Court has recognized that coercion can be mental as well as physical, and that the blood of the accused is not the only hallmark of an unconstitutional inquisition. ■

the use of force, threats, or promises of lenience—all of which might well induce an innocent person to confess; but *we do approve of such psychological tactics and techniques as trickery and deceit that are not only helpful but frequently necessary in order to secure incriminating information from the guilty, or investigative leads from otherwise uncooperative witnesses or informants* [italics added].

SPECIFIC TACTICS

The reader should be aware of some psychological strategies for evidence-gathering used in custodial interrogation. Belief in the effectiveness of these strategies is based on procedural evidence and personal experience rather than any validating systematic research. Still, police employ the strategies whether or not the suspect is accompanied by counsel. Experienced interrogators make certain that the rights outlined in *Miranda* are read and understood by the suspect and that a signed waiver form is obtained. If a person requests a lawyer, questioning must

252

CHAPTER
TEN:
THE
PSYCHOLOGY
OF
EVIDENCE:
RELATED
ISSUES

stop. In order to be admissible in a criminal proceeding, a confession resulting from interrogation must be made knowingly and voluntarily. Proof of this is usually obtained by having the subject sign a brief, clearly written document attesting to that fact. However, a written document may not be enough because the courts often rely on the "totality of the circumstances" in deciding whether a confession was made voluntarily, including the duration and conditions of the detention, the manifest attitude of the police toward the suspect, his or her physical and mental states, and the nature of the pressure used to induce the confession (Abney, 1986).

The interrogative tactics to be sketched below have been culled from a variety of sources, mixed with one of the authors' personal experience in the application of these tactics in police-academy instruction programs. The most well-known source materials on interrogation are Inbau and Reid's *Criminal Interrogation and Confessions* (1962); Gerber and Schroeder's *Criminal Investigation and Interrogation* (1962); O'Hara's *Fundamentals of Criminal Investigation* (1970); and Aubry and Caputo's *Criminal Interrogation* (1965).

Interrogation as discussed here will be limited to those situations involving suspects in which an investigator seeks to obtain either an admission of guilt or clarification and elaboration of certain facts, under psychologically coercive—but not too coercive—conditions. Precisely what constitutes too much coercion is often unclear to police officials. Some legal scholars (e.g., Abney, 1986, p. 123) have concluded that the police may "…properly increase psychological stress and uncertainty by some artifices, tricks, and deceptions." However, no one has defined satisfactorily at what point psychological pressure becomes unlawful. Interviewing, in contrast to interrogation, is designed to obtain clarification and elaboration of relevant facts from witnesses, potential witnesses, victims, or informants. It involves different principles and approaches, which will not be discussed here.

Three general psychological principles are emphasized in most interrogation techniques. The first pertains to **psychological control**; the interrogator communicates to the subject that he or she has total control over both the subject and the interrogative situation. The second principle involves the use of methods designed to induce **tension** or guilt in the subject, with the assumption that this will break down the subject's defenses. The third principle is that the interrogator must appear confident and in command throughout the interrogation process.

Setting

Most outlined procedures for interrogations specify the most conducive setting. In general, a setting which ensures isolation from the psychological security and support of friends or familiar surroundings is advocated. The value of a special interrogation room which deprives the suspect of psychological advantages usually gained from familiar places is strongly emphasized. The setting should be private enough to guarantee no interruptions or distractions that would interfere with the flow of information or contaminate the control and tension-induction methods. This requires a room that is sparsely decorated, with no pictures or other items to encourage a breakdown in concentration or divided attention.

Conduct

The three psychological principles of control, tension-induction, and confidence can be reinforced by the personal conduct of the interrogator. Some sources recommend that the interrogator stand while the subject sits, a method intended to communicate control. A subject's request to smoke should sometimes be refused, not only to communicate control but also to preclude the tension-reduction gained from smoking behavior. When the subject is answering questions, it is suggested that the interrogator violate the subject's "personal space" by standing close to him or her so as to induce discomfort and tension.

Psychological control is also communicated through the calm, patient, and systematic approach exhibited by the interrogator throughout the process. Virtually all manuals and classroom instructors tell the interrogators that time is on their side and that extreme patience, combined with persistence and repetition, will eventually "break" most guilty subjects. Psychological control is also gained when the interrogator is fully informed of all known facts about the case and all possible motives. Inconsistencies and distortions are, of course, more likely to be detected by the carefully prepared, informed interrogator.

While control and tension-inducing procedures are being initiated, interrogators should simultaneously communicate sympathy for and understanding of the subject's predicament. Most manuals recommend that interrogators use only language that can be understood by the subject and that is permeated with the message, "We are only seeking the truth." Almost all manuals dictate that the subject should be treated with respect, regardless of the nature of his or her alleged offense. It is also recommended that paper and pencil be kept out of sight except to record names, dates and addresses, because extensive note-taking tends to inhibit "free" exchange. Today, interrogations are often audiotaped or videotaped.

The presence of weapons on the interrogator is discouraged, because these objects not only inhibit communication but also may instigate hostility. If the suspect is not "interrogation-wise," that is, if the suspect has not been questioned in the past, it is suggested that the interrogator sympathize by saying that others in similar situations might have done the same thing. In some instances, manuals suggest that it might be effective to reduce the suspect's guilt feelings temporarily by minimizing the moral seriousness of the offense.

Questioning

Certain general rules are offered to get the subject to talk about himself or herself. The interrogator is advised to open by asking background questions and general, nonthreatening questions that the subject can answer without having to deceive. Most instruction urges the interrogator to observe the mannerisms and behaviors of the subject while he or she is responding. Does the subject appear calm or nervous, intelligent and educated, arrogant, humble? These observations can provide information about what specific strategies to employ, although it is not wise to make conclusive judgments based on such nonverbal behavior, as we shall see later in the chapter.

Question content and form are given considerable attention in interrogation training. Questions should be directed at gaining specific information about details of an incident rather than at seeking a global confession. The interrogator should focus upon chipping away at the subject's resistance, since few persons are eager to incriminate themselves and since immediate confessions will not likely be forthcoming. Questions should be worded in relatively innocuous terms, so that they do not connote a specific offense like "rape," "kill," "shoot," or "molest."

Manuals warn interrogators against becoming personally involved to the point where they might get upset, angry, or otherwise demonstrate lack of control over the process. A subject will welcome the impression that the interrogator has lost confidence in the direction of the conversation.

Beyond these general points, specific strategies for dealing with certain types of offenders or kinds of offenses may be outlined. Inbau and Reid (1967) offer a dichotomy based upon the emotionality of offenders. They posit that emotional offenders typically commit crimes against persons, and because they often have strong feelings of remorse, are particularly responsive to the "sympathetic" approach. Nonemotional offenders are more likely to commit crimes for financial gain, are highly resistant to being detected and convicted, and more responsive to common-sense reasoning.

Inbau and Reid also make a division based on whether or not the suspect's guilt is quite

254

CHAPTER
TEN:
THE
PSYCHOLOGY
OF
EVIDENCE:
RELATED
ISSUES

certain or questionable. They suggest that, when he or she is certain of a suspect's guilt, the interrogator should make this belief known from the outset. However, the interrogator is warned not to ask questions which require the suspect to repeat a denial of guilt, since repetitive denials render the subject less likely to admit guilt later. The interrogator is told to ask direct questions of the "why" variety, rather than to ask "whether" the person committed the crime.

Cues

Interrogators should be alert to a number of physiological indicators of anxiety and stress. This is especially recommended in the case of emotional offenders who are strongly suspected. Sweating, blushing, dry mouth, shaking hands, elbows close to the body—all are nonverbal cues of tension that should be brought to the suspect's attention.

The interrogator is further instructed to be alert to deception indicators, such as avoidance of eye contact, frequent hand-to-face contact, or even frequent trips to the bathroom. Signs of deception are also claimed to be inherent in the way the suspect says things. For example, the interrogator should be suspicious of statements that are prefaced by "I swear to God I'm telling the truth" or "I'll swear on a stack of bibles." Suspicion is also drawn to the spotless-record-religious-man routine: "I've never done anything illegal in my life" or "I'm a deeply religious, churchgoing person." The interrogator is advised to be especially suspicious of the "not that I remember" comment, because it is often used by lying subjects. The implication is that deception cues help to establish the guilt or innocence of the interrogation subject. There is a danger in being too quick to adopt these suggestions, however, as we will discuss shortly in the section on deception.

Role Playing

The sympathetic approach frequently advocated combines tension-induction strategies with humanistic gestures. A pat on the shoulder, a grip on the hand, a proferred cigarette or soft drink or sandwich—all are intended as symbolic gestures of understanding and compassion. Experienced interrogators claim that this is an effective strategy to use with younger suspects or first-time offenders. Some police agencies use the unfriendly-friendly routine. Here, an interrogator plays the role of the gruff, insensitive cop who threatens and cajoles the subject. Then, a friendly, sensitive, compassionate officer arrives on the scene, advises his or her colleague to "take it easy," and speaks gently to the suspect. The effectiveness of this method is believed to stem primarily from the accent it places on the friendly officer, which ultimately emphasizes the sympathetic approach. Interestingly, in the *Miranda* decision, Chief Justice Warren spoke strongly against the use of this technique, asserting that it was unacceptable psychological coercion, but the state courts have been routinely supportive of the tactic when used in moderation (Abney, 1986).

Other Strategies

There is no dearth of suggested alternative strategies in the interrogation literature. Have the suspect tell his or her story a number of times, in backward sequence, then have the suspect explain the discrepancies that are likely to surface. Or propose a hypothetical situation: "It doesn't look as if you were involved in this crime, but if you had been, what would you have done? What techniques would you have used?" This presumably forces a suspect to propose a *modus operandi* that may give the interrogator clues to the crime under investigation. Another suggestion is directed at investigations of white-collar crimes. The interrogator is advised to enter the interrogating room armed with official-looking papers and to proceed to examine them periodically, sometimes frowning or shaking his or her head. This procedure assumes that white-collar offenders are impressed with the power of documents and are apt to become anxious in the face of possible evidence.

It is often recommended that investigators discover early in the process whether subjects are lying by asking questions to which answers are already known. Alternatively, the interrogator may present fabricated data about the case and notice how the subject deals with it. Any tactic that catches the subject in a lie not only will provide valuable information about the subject's integrity but also will give the interrogator the upper hand, once the subject realizes he or she has been caught fabricating.

Although we have outlined some of the commonly used methods of interrogation, the reader should realize that there are numerous other approaches which various agencies claim are highly effective. All, however, have the three basic ingredients of psychological control, tension induction, and confidence and persistence on the part of the interrogator. To what extent psychological manipulation and trickery should he allowed remains problematical. Police officers claim that any further limitations on interrogation procedures would hinder seriously any attempt to solve crimes. However, many civil libertarians are concerned about the infringement of individual rights and psychological dignity that occur when deceit, trickery, and psychological pressures are employed. From this perspective, the presence of a lawyer during the interrogation process is critical.

Detecting Deception

Deception is behavior that is intended to conceal, misrepresent, or distort truth or information for the purpose of misleading others. It is practiced, of course, by representatives of the law as well as by those who are alleged to have violated it. The detection of deception is most commonly found in the criminal-justice system when one or more individuals are suspected of having committed a crime or of having relevant information about a crime. Under these conditions, the goal of the system is to discover who, if anyone, is being deceptive. In business and industry, employers attempt to determine the veracity of prospective employees concerning their past experience, work behavior, and credentials, and try to assess the risks of hiring them. In intelligence and security settings, a continual surveillance and discovery process directed toward identifying individuals engaged in damaging or threatening behavior (espionage, terrorism) is based on various deception detection techniques. Three methods are commonly used to uncover such deception: interpretation of nonverbal behavior, the polygraph, and voice-stress analysis.

NONVERBAL INDICATORS

Our society is replete with folklore and procedural evidence concerning how to discern whether someone is lying. Interrogation procedures in particular often imply assumptions about nonverbal signs of deceit and guilt, as we have seen in the preceding section. Inbau and Reid, for example, assert: "When a subject fails to look the interrogator straight in the eye, or when he exhibits a restlessness by leg-swinging, foot-wiggling, hand-wringing, finger-tapping, the picking of fingernails, or the fumbling with objects such as a tie clasp or pencil, it is well for the interrogator to get the idea across that he is aware of such reactions and that he views them as manifestations of lying" (1967, p. 34). Other nonverbal behaviors believed to be indicative of guilt or lying include pulsation of the carotid artery in the neck, excessive activity of the Adam's apple, dryness of the mouth, and wiggling of the ears!

Over the past three decades many empirical studies have probed the relationship between nonverbal behavior and deception. Nonverbal cues like facial expressions, body postures, and

256

CHAPTER
TEN:
THE
PSYCHOLOGY
OF
EVIDENCE:
RELATED
ISSUES

movements of the legs and feet and arms have drawn the greatest attention. One general observation emerging from early scientific inquiry took researchers aback: Individuals who wish to deceive are also aware of the common folklore, and consequently they try to control the so-called indicators of lying. For example, people who are trying to deceive do *not* have more frequent eye shifts than truthful communicators (Mehrabian, 1971). Deceitful communicators also may smile more often than truthful communicators (Mehrabian & Williams, 1969), have longer eye contact (Mehrabian, 1971), or in some conditions maintain a more placid expression (McClintock & Hunt, 1975).

The above features all indicate an attempt, or even an over-attempt, to control the normal channels of nonverbal communications. Facial expressions and eye contact, normally used in communicating emotions and feelings, are held in check by the deceiving communicator. Thus, empirical study has found that deceit is not so much communicated through shifty eyes, decreased eye contact, or evasive facial expression, but rather through the absence of these indicators or the presence of their apparent opposites. These more covert nonverbal modalities are called **leaky channels** by researchers (Ekman & Friesen, 1969, 1974), because they "leak" information not intended by the communicator.

Placid expression, longer eye contact, and a tendency to smile can therefore be examples of leaky channels. In further attempts to control communication, deceitful individuals may speak at a slower rate, use fewer words, but produce more speech errors (Rosenfeld, 1966; Kasl & Mahl, 1965). Their posture often is rigid and stiff (Mehrabian, 1971), and they display very little head nodding (Rosenfeld, 1966). Hand gestures are kept to an unusually low level (Ekman, Friesen & Scherer, 1976), but there is considerable movement and shifting of feet and legs (Ekman & Friesen, 1969). There is also evidence that deceitful speakers make exceedingly few factual statements, but many sweeping statements (Knapp, Hart & Dennis, 1974).

A wide variety of communicative cues may accompany deception, but the fact is that they also may not, or may accompany truth instead. In addition, most studies have found that observers have difficulty distinguishing liars from truth-tellers; the accuracy rate of observers is slightly better than chance (Bauchner, Brandt & Miller, 1977; Littlepage & Pineault, 1978; Knapp, 1978; Ekman & Friesen, 1974). It is not wise, therefore, to make assumptions about truthfulness or deception strictly on the basis of nonverbal cues. It is especially foolhardy to accept the prevailing folklore in the area. If anything, the cues associated with deception may be better behavioral indicators of stress and anxiety than they are signs of lying.

Recently, Charles Bond and his colleagues (Bond, Omar, Pitre, Lashley, Skaggs & Kirk, 1992) have proposed an **expectancy-violation model** to account for what leads people to suspect lying in others. According to this model, people accept at face value nonverbal behaviors that are usual and expected under certain conditions. However, if these nonverbal behaviors are unusual or unexpected, perceivers begin to suspect deception. Specifically, "Perceivers infer deception from nonverbal norm violations when they have reason to question the actor's veracity and when innocent explanations for the unexpected behavior seem less credible" (Bond et al., 1992, p. 969). The expectancy-violation model asserts that deception may be inferred from any nonverbal behavior that violates the norm—in other words, any "weird" behavior is suspect. For example, if high levels of eye contact are expected, and the person avoids eye contact, this norm deviation may be interpreted as highlighting deception. Furthermore, the more frequently a person displays nonverbal behavior that violates the norm, the more dishonest or deceptive the person will appear. Recent research also suggests that people infer deceit when speech content contradicts facial expressions (Rotenberg, Simourd & Moore, 1989). The expectancy-violation model shows great promise in the deception literature and will generate more research in the years to come.

Witness credibility is a critical factor in courtroom trials. Jurors and judges not only consider the material presented in the courtroom but also evaluate its veracity. Regardless of the completeness or consistency of the testimony, if the decisionmakers perceive the source as less than honest, the value of the testimony is severely undermined. Veracity in the courtroom is largely judged on the manner in which the testimony is presented. More fundamentally, it is primarily determined by the conventional wisdom linked to certain nonverbal cues.

Gerald Miller and his colleagues conducted several experiments to replicate some previous findings reported in the deception-detection literature; at the same time, they tried to re-create critical aspects of the courtroom in an effort to improve ecological validity. The Miller studies were designed to examine the following three major questions:

1. In general, how accurate are jurors in detecting deception?

2. What effects do variations in the mode of presentation of a trial (live, televised, audio only, transcript only, and, in the televised case, color versus black and white) have on jurors' abilities to detect deception?

3. What sources of information facilitate a juror's ability to distinguish between deceitful and truthful testimony? (Miller et al., 1981, p. 149).

The basic experimental paradigm of the Miller studies was modeled after Ekman and Friesen (1974). In that project, motivated subjects were told to lie or to tell the truth about a stressful or nonstressful film they had just seen. The subjects' descriptions of the film were videotaped. Observer-subjects then viewed these videotapes and were asked to decide which narrators were telling the truth and which were lying. Results indicated that observer-subjects were not much better than chance at determining who was lying and who was not.

Two of the Miller studies deserve our close attention. In the first, a paradigm similar to the one described above was used. However, the videotaped subjects were not only asked to lie or to be truthful about the stimuli they had seen, they were also questioned about the facts of the events they had viewed. Therefore, both emotional and factual content were included in the design, allowing the experimenters to measure accuracy in depicting lying in both emotional and factual testimony. In addition to videotapes, audiotapes and transcripts of the interview were also made to determine the influence of verbal cues compared to visual cues in detection of deception. Furthermore, the individuals interviewed were videotaped in both color and black and white, with sound. Lastly, to determine what bodily, nonverbal cues might best communicate deception, camera shots included either (1) head only, (2) body only, or (3) head and body.

Nineteen male and four female criminal-justice undergraduates (seniors) served as the taped interviewees. To insure a reasonably high level of motivation, all the subjects—who were planning careers in law enforcement—were told that the School of Criminal Justice would receive information concerning their cooperation and performance in the experiment.

The observer-subjects who judged the videotapes were 719 undergraduate students enrolled in introductory communication classes and 193 adult residents of the local community. The primary dependent variable was the observer-subject's accuracy in identifying interviewee veracity. Each observer-subject was expected to make sixteen accuracy judgments, eight based upon identifying the veracity of statements by means of emotional content and eight by means of factual content.

The results revealed that people are no more accurate than chance in identifying deception. The results also indicated that judgments of witness veracity were not influenced by the use of color as opposed to black-and-white videotape. More surprisingly, the data suggest modification

258

CHAPTER
TEN:
THE
PSYCHOLOGY
OF
EVIDENCE:
RELATED
ISSUES

of Ekman and Friesen's (1969) leaky channel theory. It appears from the Miller study that leaky channels fall into two categories. Nonfacial cues are the most reliable cues to deception when lying involves the deceiver's *emotional* response to events or situations. However, facial cues seem to provide the best information for making judgments about factual veracity. It must be remembered, however, that regardless of the source or message content, people tend not to be accurate decipherers of deception.

Results from the transcript-only condition, the audio-only condition, and the visual-only condition also cast serious doubts on the assumption that detecting deception is enhanced by the presence of nonverbal behavioral cues. Observer-subjects in the transcript-only condition were as accurate as subjects in the audio-only condition when detecting deception dealing with factual information. Furthermore, audio-only and transcript-only subjects were more accurate than visual-only subjects, suggesting that nonverbal behavioral cues are less dependable sources for determining factual veracity than oral or verbal ones. Relative to detecting deception in expressing emotion, there were no significant differences in accuracy in visual, audio, or transcription sources.

Study II paralleled Study I in design except for four changes. First, in order to more closely approximate actual courtroom procedures, the interviewed subject in Study II was either seen or heard live by the observer-subjects. Second, an attempt was made to control for possible sex differences in deceptive behavior by having equal numbers of male and female interviewees. Third, the researchers tried to have the interviewees more ego-involved in their deception by offering monetary prizes. Fourth, while in Study I interviewees acted under both deceptive and truthful conditions, in Study II they were assigned to only one condition.

Observer-subjects saw or heard or read interviews, made a judgment as to whether the sources were lying, and specified the amount and type of information used in making their judgment. Those observer-subjects assigned to the live condition either watched the interview through a one-way mirror or listened to it through earphones, without seeing the subject.

Again, as in Study I, the results indicated that people are poor judges of the veracity of testimony and can detect deception no more often than by chance. Moreover, it does not seem to make any difference in the type and amount of information they receive; they still make poor judgments about veracity. Further, it makes little difference whether the information is live or videotaped. Although much still needs to be resolved, it does seem that the average juror is unable to distinguish between deceptive and truthful testimony, and it does not seem to matter whether the deception is based on factual issues or on feelings or emotions about stressful or exciting events.

VOICE ANALYSIS

Some law-enforcement agencies have been examining voice characteristics in an effort to identify suspects or to detect deception. In the identification procedure, it is assumed that each individual has a unique, personal style of speaking due to anatomical, structural differences in the speech mechanisms and the manner in which tongue, lips, and teeth are used. "Voiceprints" or voice exemplars are oscillographic representations of spoken sounds that identify these unique elements of vocalization.

Both the scientific community and the judicial system have guardedly accepted voiceprints as an adequate means of identification under certain conditions. In *U. S. v. Dionisio* (1973) the U. S. Supreme Court ruled that requiring criminal suspects to provide voice exemplars did not violate their Fifth Amendment protection against self-incrimination. Courts adjudicating several criminal cases have allowed voiceprints as evidence (*U. S. v. Franks*, 1975; *U. S. v. Baller*, 1975; *Commonwealth v. Lykus*, 1975; *State v. Andretta*, 1972). However, the courts have attached limitations. For example, courts have ruled that voiceprints could be used only as collaborative evidence, or in the absence of contradictory expert testimony, or to justify an arrest warrant (Schwitzgebel & Schwitzgebel, 1980).

The value of voiceprints as discriminators between deception and truth has yet to be accepted by science or law, however. Proponents argue that a deceptive speaker's voice changes under stress and that these stress-related changes are reflected through minute vibrations or microtremors. The physiological changes are recorded and analyzed by instruments specifically designed for this purpose.

A number of commercial firms have marketed various pieces of hardware claimed to detect stress, and ultimately lying, from live or recorded segments of speech. The level of sophistication and complexity in instrumentation differ widely from one piece of equipment to another. The most extensively marketed and researched instrument is the Psychological Stress Evaluator (PSE). In its marketing literature, the manufacturer claims that the PSE is 95- to 99-percent accurate in discriminating liars from truth-tellers. This claim has yet to be substantiated in the published scientific literature, and the manufacturer fails to support it with any cites of replicable research (Hollien, 1980; Yarmey, 1979). Research projects testing the PSE have consistently found that it does no better than chance at identifying deception through voice-stress analysis (Hollien, 1980; Podlesny & Raskin, 1977; Kubis, 1973; Yarmey, 1979). In fact, none of the voice analyzers to date have been able to distinguish deception from truthfulness in the scientific laboratory.

The basis of the PSE's discriminatory power supposedly rests on its sensitivity to slight tremblings (microtremors) that occur in the voice mechanism, apparently in the small laryngeal muscles. However, available research demonstrates that while microtremors do exist in the large muscles, especially in the extremities, they do not appear to exist in the small muscles of the larynx (Hollien, 1980; Bachrach, 1979). Miron (1980) has suggested that the microtremors detected by the PSE might be located in the network of the large, slow-acting muscles that support the laryngeal mechanisms. Considering the extremely high level of sensitivity required to measure even known microtremors in the large muscles using sophisticated laboratory equipment, it seems that the PSE may be based on some voice-stress principle other than microtremors.

In summary, there is little scientific evidence to support the reliability and validity of instruments that attempt to detect deception by means of voice analysis. In light of our present knowledge, reliance on this equipment by industry or by the judicial system is risky at best.

THE POLYGRAPH

Often called the "lie detector," the polygraph does not really detect lies or deception, but only the bodily responses that accompany emotions and stress. The assumption is that when one tries to deceive, there are telltale bodily or physiological reactions that can be measured with sophisticated equipment.

Variants of the modern polygraph have been used in the psychological laboratory for nearly a century, and much cruder versions or analogues existed as far back as 300 B.C. (Trovillo, 1939). The Bedouins of Arabia, for example, required the authors of conflicting statements to lick a hot iron; the one whose tongue was not burned was considered truthful (Smith, 1967). The ancient Chinese required people to put rice powder in their mouths and then spit it out (Smith, 1967). If the powder was dry, the individual was lying. The principle underlying these and other similar methods used throughout history is that the tense, nervous person (the one who is lying) has less saliva (dry mouth and tongue), and thus is more likely to burn the tongue, spit drier rice powder, or even be less able to swallow the "trial slice" of bread, as required centuries ago in England.

The Italian physician and anthropologist Cesare Lombroso is credited as the first to use an *instrument* to detect lies in 1881 (Barland, 1988). The device was designed to measure changes in

260

CHAPTER
TEN:
THE
PSYCHOLOGY
OF
EVIDENCE:
RELATED
ISSUES

blood volume in the arm, which were recorded on chart or graph. However, since the device had the capacity to record only blood volume, it would be more correct to call this early instrument a *monograph* (one measure) rather than a *polygraph* (many measures). Various other devices and refinements were largely developed in Europe (see Barland, 1988), but the idea of lie detection caught on rapidly in the United States. The development of the modern polygraph equipment and technique is generally credited to John Larson and Leonarde Keeler (Barland & Raskin, 1973). In 1920 Larson was asked by the chief of police in Berkeley, California to develop a "lie detector" to solve a case under investigation. This detector, according to Barland (1988, p. 75), became "the first true polygraph used for lie-detection purposes." A number of well-publicized successes by Larson and one of his students named Leonarde Keeler catapulted the instrument into the limelight. Eventually Keeler began to teach a two-week course for police and military examiners, which soon developed into a six-week course (Barland, 1988; Keeler, 1984). According to Barland (1988), the increasing demand for polygraph examiners resulted in the formation of at least thirty polygraph schools (both private and governmental) approved by the American Polygraph Association. Private schools normally require at least seven weeks of training, while the governmental programs last about fourteen weeks. In general, government training programs are more respected and considered more rigorous.

During its early beginnings, the polygraph was largely confined to criminal investigations and the equipment was almost exclusively the *field* polygraph. The field polygraph is a portable instrument that generally includes measures of respiration, skin conductance or electrodermal response (EDR), blood volume/blood pressure, and heart rate. Despite their simplicity in instrumentation and design, with proper calibration and maintenance, standard field polygraphs can measure, with reasonable accuracy, gross physiological activity.

Laboratory polygraphs are usually far more sophisticated and sensitive, and can record simultaneously a great number of physiological indices. Moreover, they are often linked to a computer system which allows monitoring, "hard copy," and technical or statistical analysis of the relevant physiological dimensions. Most of the laboratory research on the polygraph has used these more advanced instruments.

Today, the polygraph is primarily used in two major areas: investigation and personnel selection. It is estimated that several million such polygraphic exams are administered annually by about 10,000 professional examiners (Barland, 1988). Eighty to 90 percent of all polygraph examinations currently administered in America are employment-related (Barland, 1988), most commonly for preemployment screening (Lykken, 1988). The primary purpose of the preemployment polygraph test is to verify information provided by the job applicant. Employers are especially interested in the honesty of applicants in answering questions pertaining to past work history, drug and alcohol use, propensity toward theft, and credentials or qualifications. The examiners are usually licensed or certified after being trained at a school of polygraphy, but most do not have graduate psychological or research training. Although admissions to polygraph schools differ widely, the typical requirement is a bachelor's degree, a personal interview, and a polygraph test (Iacono & Patrick, 1987). America's fascination with the polygraph has made it, by far, the number one country in the world in the number of examinations given each year, as well as in the ratio of populations to examiners (Barland, 1988). The examiner-to-population ratio in the U. S. is 1:29,000, followed by Israel (1:95,000), and Canada (1:213,000).

Legal Status

Courts have traditionally not allowed polygraph results as evidence in a case. The precedent of inadmissibility of polygraph evidence was established by *U. S. v. Frye* in 1923. An appellate court in Washington, D.C. ruled that information acquired from polygraphic examination was unacceptable

■ 10.2: *FRYE AND DAUBERT: FROM GENERAL ACCEPTANCE TO RELIABILITY*

FOR SEVENTY YEARS, THE MOST FREQUENTLY cited case on expert testimony and the admissibility of novel scientific evidence was *Frye v. U. S.*, decided in 1923. Frye, a defendant charged with murder, appealed a lower court's decision not to allow polygraph evidence which supported his case.

Frye had taken and passed a "systolic blood pressure deception test." His attorney had asked that the scientist who conducted the test be allowed to testify to the results. That request was denied. The attorney then asked if the scientist could conduct the test in the jury's presence, a request which also was denied.

Quoting from the brief submitted by Frye's lawyer, the appeals court agreed that:

When the question involved does not lie within the range of common experience or common knowledge, but requires special experience or special knowledge, then the opinions of witnesses skilled in that particular science, art, or trade to which the question relates are admissible in evidence.

However, the court added the following requirement:

Just when a scientific principle or discovery crosses the line between the experimental and demonstrable stages is difficult to define. Somewhere in this twilight zone the evidential force of the principle must be recognized, and while courts will go a long way in admitting expert testimony deduced from a *well-recognized scientific principle or discovery, the thing from which the deduction is made must be sufficiently established to have gained general acceptance in the particular field in which it belongs* [italics added].

We think the systolic blood pressure deception test has not yet gained such standing and scientific recognition among physiological and psychological authorities as would justify the courts in admitting expert testimony deduced from the discovery, development, and experiments thus far made.

* * * * * * * *

Daubert v. Merrell Dow (1993), a civil case, was a direct challenge to the *Frye* standard. Two minor children and their parents sued Merrell Dow Pharmaceuticals, Inc., arguing that the children's serious birth defects were caused by the mother's ingestion of Bendectin, a prescription anti-nausea drug manufactured by the company. Merrell Dow submitted expert evidence that the drug had not been shown to be a risk factor for human birth defects. The plaintiffs, however, obtained the testimony of eight experts who had conducted new studies and reanalyzed previous research. A federal district court and a federal appeals court both rejected the new evidence, ruling that it did not meet the *Frye* standard of general acceptability. The U. S. Supreme Court, however, unanimously ruled that general acceptability was an austere standard which should no longer be applied in federal trials.

The merits of the *Frye* test have been much debated, and scholarship on its proper scope and application is legion. Petitioners' primary attack, however, is not on the content but on the continuing authority of the rule. They contend that the *Frye* test was superseded by the adoption of the Federal Rules of Evidence. We agree.

Noting that all relevant evidence is admissible, the Court continued, quoting the Federal Rules of Evidence:

"Relevant evidence" is defined as that which has "any tendency to make the existence of any fact that is of consequence to the determination of the action more probable or less probable than it would be without the evidence." ...The Rule's basic standard of relevance thus is a liberal one.

A majority of the Court then made it clear that trial judges nevertheless should screen evidence to assure that it was both relevant and reliable (meaning, to the Court, scientifically valid):

Proposed testimony must be supported by appropriate validation—i.e., "good grounds," based on what is known. In short, the requirement that an expert's testimony pertain to "scientific knowledge" establishes a standard of evidentiary reliability. ■

---

because the general scientific community did not endorse it (see Box 10.2). Since then, many courts have continued to reject the results of the polygraph, whether they have been submitted by the defense or the prosecution, as evidence of guilt or innocence (Schwitzgebel & Schwitzgebel, 1980). Many scholars have argued that the *Frye* test is not only unclear in its terminology, but excessively

CHAPTER
TEN:
THE
PSYCHOLOGY
OF
EVIDENCE:
RELATED
ISSUES

conservative and restrictive in what type of scientific evidence is admissible (Monahan & Walker, 1990). In fact, a U. S. Court of Military Appeals decision (*U. S. v. Gipson*, 1987) advocated that the test be replaced by the standards outlined in the Federal Rules of Evidence, a decision soon mimicked by at least one other federal court (Honts & Perry, 1992). Finally, as noted in Chapter 4, the U. S. Supreme Court itself rejected the rigid standard of *Frye* in favor of the more liberal standards of the Federal Rules of Evidence (see Box 10.2). The Rules encourage a "relevancy approach" which treats new, relevant scientific evidence in the same way as the courts treat all other types of evidence. For instance, polygraph data are considered in the same way as other forensic data acquired from physiological instruments, such as X-rays, DNA, and blood tests.

Currently, evidence gained from the use of the polygraph is inadmissible in twenty-eight of the fifty states (Honts & Perry, 1992; Morris, 1989). On the other hand, some state jurisdictions have admitted polygraphic data if the examinee has given full cooperation and if an established test procedure was used, but then only with a list of stipulations. There has also been some movement in the federal courts to allow some polygraph evidence (Honts & Perry, 1992). At the time of this writing, half of the federal court circuits and nineteen of the fifty states allow at least some polygraphic information to be entered into evidence (Honts & Perry, 1992). Many courts, however, continue to be wary of the powers of the polygraph.

While many courts continue to cite the precedent-setting *Frye* case as a basis for rejecting polygraph information, other reasons have also been given. Some courts have commented upon the lack of scientific recognition of the instrument and the paucity of qualified examiners (Langley, 1955). Others note the presence of too many variables that would cause excessive courtroom debate (e.g., *U. S. v. Urquidez*, 1973); undue influence upon the jury (*People v. Davis*, 1949; *People v. Sinclair*, 1942); an undermining of the credibility of witnesses (Richardson, 1961); the lack of soundness of polygraphic theory (*State v. Bohmer*, 1971); and infringement upon the freedom and privacy of the mind (Salving, 1956; Westin, 1967).

The resistance of the courts to accepting polygraph evidence as a general principle is baffling when we consider that courts generally do accept evidence gained through other "scientific" methods with low or questionable validity, e.g., psychological tests, psychiatric interviews and diagnoses, handwriting analyses, and eyewitness testimony. In fact, in one study, the polygraph was found to be the most accurate investigative tool, when compared with other such methods of identification as fingerprint analysis, handwriting analysis, and eyewitness testimony (Widacki & Horvath, 1978). Therefore, the criteria for admissibility do not appear to rest strictly on the empirical support for the polygraph's accuracy (Cavoukian & Heslegrave, 1980).

Resistance to accepting polygraph evidence against a defendant is more understandable. The polygraph is an information-gathering device that runs counter to legal philosophy about the legal process. Not only does it bring into the courtroom an aura of absolutes, but it also infringes upon the privacy of the mind. In essence, it forces people to testify against themselves. Their most hidden secrets and intimate transgressions may be exposed for public judgment, whether or not they have engaged in criminal conduct. Therefore, the polygraph may go too far by an invasion-of-privacy or self-incriminatory measure. It probes individual beliefs and desires and violates the sense of personal autonomy, without the individual being able to exert any control over this probing. In psychological tests and in the information provided to psychiatrists and psychologists, individuals still perceive that they have control over revelations and actions, regardless of the interpretations made by the clinical expert. The experts cannot prove that individuals lied or are guilty, no matter what level of the unconscious they feel they have tapped. However, the polygraph seems to offer "proof" of dishonesty, even though it may not be accurate.

In addition, the more reliable, valid, and accurate the polygraph becomes, the more it undermines the traditional judicial process and its adversarial nature. Awesome power may be given to the polygraphic examiner who becomes directly involved in decisions of guilt or innocence, a prerogative traditionally reserved for the judge or jury. Although Cavoukian and Heslegrave (1980) report simulation evidence that the impact of polygraphic testimony can be reduced if the examiner stresses the room for error in the report, its potential dangers still remain.

EVALUATING THE POLYGRAPH EXAMINATION

The field polygraph examination typically consists of four separate phases: data collection, pretest interview, test administration, and posttest interview (Abrams, 1989). In the data-collection stage, the examiner gathers all the relevant information concerning the area under investigation as well as known information about the subject. The pretest interview is intended to establish some rapport with the subject and to explain some of the questions and procedures that will be used during the examination. Often during the pretest interview, questions to be asked during the examination are devised with the cooperation of the subject, so that nothing will be surprising and ambiguities may be cleared.

Techniques

Several techniques are used by polygraphers to determine deception or truthfulness during the examination. In situations involving criminal suspects, the two most widely used methods are the control-of-question test and the guilty-knowledge test. In situations involving employment screening, the relevant-control test (RCT) test is most generally used.

The **control-of-question test** (CQT) is the procedure most preferred by professional polygraphers in cases requiring specific incident investigation, such as criminal acts (Iacono & Patrick, 1987; Abrams, 1989; Raskin, 1988). This approach, which usually requires at least two hours, uses a variety of questioning techniques based on three types of questions, (1) irrelevant or neutral questions, (2) relevant questions, and (3) control questions. Irrelevant questions are those posed about neutral topics, such as date of birth, name, age, height, and birthplace. They usually occur at the beginning and end of an examination, but they may be interspersed between other questions to bring the subject down to a normal physiological baseline following questions that generate stress.

The relevant question probes whether the subject committed the crime or behavior in question. For example, "On August 26 at approximately 9:00 P.M., did you break down the door at Mr. Brown's residence?" It is recommended that emotion-laden words not be used, since the subject may respond more to the word than to the question itself.

The control question is as important in determining deception or truthfulness as the relevant question. It is based upon either an assumed or a known lie. An assumed lie is denial of a behavior that most people would readily admit to. For example, "Did you ever steal anything when you were between the ages of five and fifteen? Did you ever take advantage of a friend? Have you ever lied to a person in a position of authority?"

If the physiological responses associated with relevant questions are higher than those for control questions, the person is assumed to be guilty or untruthful. If, on the other hand, physiological reactions are more pronounced for the control questions than the relevant ones, the examiner assumes innocence, or truthfulness on the relevant issue. One of the main problems with the CQT is the difficulty involved in constructing control questions that will elicit stronger physiological responses in the innocent than will relevant questions about the crime (Bull, 1988).

One critical phase in the CQT is to establish a "mind set" in the examinee. That is, the

264

CHAPTER
TEN:
THE
PSYCHOLOGY
OF
EVIDENCE:
RELATED
ISSUES

examiner attempts to convince the examinee that the polygraph is a very powerful detector of lies, and if you do lie, you are surely going to get caught. Truthfulness to all questions is emphasized. Various tactics are sometimes employed by examiners to reach this mind set. For example, to convince the examinee of the power of the instrument, the examiner may ask the examinee to pick a playing card from a deck. However, unknown to the examinee, the cards in the deck are all the same (e.g., jacks of clubs). The examinee is then asked not to reveal the card and to say no to each question asked by the examiner. Next, the examiner asks the examinee a series of questions about which card was picked (e.g., "Was it a nine of clubs? Was it a king of spades? Was it a jack of clubs?") while the examiner is watching the moving recording pens on the charts. The examiner then guesses the precise card, impressing the examinee with the mysterious accuracy of the instrument. This mind set may be one of the most important aspects of polygraph testing because it not only promotes honesty but also, on occasion, encourages confessions.

The **guilty-knowledge test** (GKT) has been strongly endorsed by psychologist and polygraph-expert David Lykken (1981) as the most powerful procedure for determining deception or truthfulness. Interestingly, while the CQT is the most frequently used method for investigative interrogation, the GKT is probably the most endorsed (Ben-Shakhar, Bar-Hillel & Lieblich, 1986). For the GKT, the examiner uses detailed, publicly unknown knowledge about a crime to construct questions that can be answered only by someone who was present at the scene. The answers are offered to the subject in a multiple-choice format. For example, in a case in which a robber dropped his hat, Lykken (1988, p. 121) provides an example of GKT as follows:

1. The robber in this case dropped something while escaping. If you are that robber, you will know what he dropped. Was it: a weapon? a face mask? a sack of money? his hat? his car keys?

2. Where did he drop his hat? Was it: in the bank? on the bank steps? on the sidewalk? in the parking lot? in an alley?

3. What colour was the hat? Was it: brown? red? black? green? blue?

Since the GKT assumes that the guilty subject will recognize the significant alternative, consistent physiological reactivity to this "correct" answer would indicate deception, regardless of the verbal content of the subject's answers. And since the questions are derived from information presumably not reported in the press and not generally known by the public, innocent subjects rarely give peak physiological reactions to "correct" items. The sensitivity of the GKT depends in part on whether the examiner can generate enough items pertaining to the crime scene which a suspect is likely to remember (Lykken, 1988). Raskin (1988) asserts that the GKT is rarely used in applied criminal cases because its practical utility is severely limited. For example, in a majority of criminal cases, very little inside, salient detail about the crime is known, and when it is known, such detail is often revealed to suspects by investigators, the media, and defense attorneys. Unfortunately, most training programs for polygraphers do not include the GKT (Bull, 1988).

The **relevant-irrelevant** (R-I) **technique** or relevant-control test (RCT) is the method of choice for a majority of examiners in preemployment and employee screening situations (Minor, 1989). The *traditional* R-I method was developed in 1917 by lawyer-psychologist William M. Marston primarily for criminal investigation. As a laboratory assistant in psychology at Radcliffe College, Marston discovered a significant positive correlation between systolic blood pressure and lying, a finding which formed the basis of the polygraph for many years. The original R-I method consisted of a list of relevant and irrelevant questions. Consistently strong physiological reactions to relevant questions over irrelevant ones were regarded as evidence of deception. However, polygraphers discovered that both truthful and deceptive persons can often show strong reactions to the relevant questions, masking any true differences between honest and dishonest subjects (Iacono & Patrick, 1987). Modern polygraphers rely more on a variant of the R-I method, sometimes referred to as the *relevant-relevant* (R-R) procedure.

David Raskin (1988) points out that the use of polygraph examinations in criminal investigations and judicial contexts differs substantially from commercial applications. Commercial screening tests try to assess suitability for employment by evaluating the prospective employee's honesty in reporting past behavior. Presumably, these tests will help the examiner predict a particular applicant's future integrity. According to Raskin, these commercial prescreening procedures may result in considerable social and personal damage to job applicants because they produce such a high rate of error. Raskin notes that these tests rarely incorporate control questions and are frequently conducted hurriedly, often by poorly trained examiners. Moreover, the psychological welfare of the applicant is rarely considered by either the examiner or the employer. A failed polygraph test is generally grounds for rejection for employment and often accompanied by some social and personal stigma. Furthermore, Raskin finds no acceptable research regarding commercial prescreening accuracy, prompting him to conclude: "[T]here seems to be little scientific support for such uses of polygraphs" (p. 109).

Statistical Accuracy

Historically, professional field polygraphers have claimed extraordinary accuracy rates: 92 percent (Bersh, 1969), 99 percent (Arther, 1965; MacNitt, 1942; MacLaughlin, 1953), and 100 percent (Kubis, 1950). The professional polygraph literature also reported with regularity that the trained polygrapher erred not more than 2 percent of the time, and often less than 1 percent (Barland & Raskin, 1973). Most psychophysiologists and research psychologists found these statistics hard to believe. Occasionally the high percentages were the consequence of arithmetical errors, but none of the published reports gave any details of methods and procedures, nor of criteria used to determine accuracy rates. David Lykken (1974) was so disbelieving of the many claims of the early professional polygraphers that he asserted: "Claims of 95%, 98%, and even, 100% validity are so implausible, they should be taken seriously only if accompanied by unusually clear, well-replicated empirical evidence. Such evidence is wholly lacking" (p. 738).

The accuracy of the polygraph in detecting who is telling the truth and who is deceptive is a complicated issue. A number of factors—such as the specific technique used, the nature of the population tested, the issues to be resolved, the context of the examination, whether one is trying to detect truth or deception, the training of the examiner, what cues the examiner considers besides the polygraphic data, or even whether one is examining the victim or the suspect—all must be carefully considered before any tentative conclusions can be advanced.

Base rates for the tested populations must be taken into consideration because they will affect the validity and/or significance of the polygraph results. Broadly, a base rate is the frequency with which a specific behavior occurs in a given population before any test or experiment is applied. For example, in a preemployment screening situation, let's assume that the employer, a police department, wants to reject all police-officer candidates who have used hard drugs on a regular basis within their lifetimes. The police department will wish to consider two base rates: (1) the percentage of the relevant population who have used hard drugs on a regular basis and (2) the percentage of *that* population who would lie about it.

Police candidates normally have very low base rates for hard drug use. Let's say, for illustrative purposes, that only 2 percent of the applicants have used hard drugs regularly during their lifetimes (base rate equals 2 percent). Let's further assume that 50 percent of these drug-using applicants will lie when asked about their drug use (second base rate equals 50 percent). In this

266

CHAPTER
TEN:
THE
PSYCHOLOGY
OF
EVIDENCE:
RELATED
ISSUES

example, the polygraph would have to identify the 1 percent who lie to be highly effective. But an examiner who knew nothing about the base rates would be 98-percent accurate if he proclaimed everyone clean, regardless of their polygraph results, and 99-percent accurate if he proclaimed everyone clean except those individuals who admitted to drug use during the interview! When base rates are this extreme it is very difficult for the polygraph to add anything new to what is already known about the relevant population.

On the other hand, if 50 percent of the police job applicants had used hard drugs on a regular basis, and all of *them* lied about it, then the polygraph would have a much better opportunity to produce a significant impact on the hiring decisions, by revealing information not available by simple deduction from the base rate. The question of how to interpret the results of the examinations and the ultimate question of how to judge whether an examiner is "accurate" in the determination of "truthful" or "deceptive" individuals would, however, also be significant in this scenario. Moreover, it is not always clear what the relevant base rates might be for a given population in a real-world situation, so that this method of analyzing validity—so useful in the laboratory—is often completely closed to the decisionmaker.

The experience and training of the examiner are important. Most studies have failed to sample adequately from the total examiner population (Barland, 1988). They often used one or two polygraphers without mentioning the nature of their training or qualifications or procedures. There is, of course, a broad range of examiner training, test techniques, and type of nonpolygraphic data included in the examiner's decision. None of these variables have been properly studied. As Blinkhorn (1988, p. 37) observes, "*Any* examination technique which involves live interaction between two people is potentially undermined by unwitting communication.... Yet the lie detector is treated as if it were simply a matter of the attachment of laboratory instruments, and the polygraph examiner himself is seen as a detector of signals rather than as engaged in a complex and highly loaded social relationship with the examinee." A reading of the research data suggests that original examiners do better when they take account of their observations of the behavior and demeanor of the subjects than when they score the charts blindly. Polygraph practitioners often admit that it is the whole process of examination that has validity, not strictly the charts (Abrams, 1989).

Another fundamental issue is whether the data are collected under controlled conditions, as found in the laboratory, or in the field, where the practical goal of uncovering deception brings with it all kinds of consequences, such as rejection from employment or becoming a criminal suspect. Obviously, the motivation and emotional tone are highly dissimilar between these two contexts. The typical experimental paradigm for the study of psychophysiological measures of deception has subjects (usually college students) engaging in mock crime, after which the polygrapher tries to discover deception in the subjects' responses. Consequently, they have questionable ecological validity. As David Lykken (1988) points out, most volunteer subjects regard an experiment on polygraph testing as kind of an interesting game. They are usually motivated to produce a "truthful" outcome simply by cash or other material reward. They really have no reason to fear the results because they will not be suspected, punished, or defamed if the test shows them "dishonest." Research that cultivates ecological validity and evaluates the reliability and validity of the polygraph within different contexts, given by different examiners, and with different objectives is desperately needed in the field of polygraph testing.

The specific technique used, of course, must also be a consideration in any discussion of accuracy rates. The CQT is currently the most extensively studied. Fourteen laboratory studies examining this procedure found that, on average, 88.6 percent of the guilty were correctly identified, while 82.6 percent of the innocent were correctly identified (Carroll, 1988). These results are based on chance-detection rates of 50 percent. However, these experiments demonstrate only a marginal resemblance to actual field lie-detection contexts (Carroll, 1988). For those experiments that closely resemble what actually takes place in the field, a slightly different picture emerges. In several studies reviewed by Douglas Carroll (1988), the average success rate of identifying the guilty was 85.4 percent, compared with an average success rate of 76.9 percent for detecting the innocent. Thus, CQT seems better at detecting the guilty than detecting the innocent, a situation that carries potentially serious ethical, social, and economic ramifications for those individuals falsely accused or suspected.

William Iacono and Christopher Patrick (1987) conducted an analogue field study of the CQT. An **analogue field study** is one in which the volunteers are genuinely concerned about the outcomes of their performance, and a clear criterion identifying who is guilty or innocent is available (Ekman, 1985). The Iacono-Patrick study involved forty-eight incarcerated criminals, half of whom committed a *mock* theft. Experienced polygraphers, using CQT procedures, were not told which inmates had committed the theft and were unaware of the base rate for guilt. Motivation to deceive was established by informing the inmates that consequences for the entire group were dependent on each person's performance. If no more than ten of the forty-eight volunteers failed the polygraph test, each inmate would receive $20 (a handsome sum by prison standards). Otherwise, no one would receive the bonus. Polygraphers, using only the physiological data recorded on the charts, were able to classify correctly 87 percent of the guilty subjects, but only 56 percent of the innocent subjects. These results suggest that innocent persons are in considerable danger of being misclassified when the CQT is used.

Field experiments on the CQT are difficult to conduct because *prima facie* evidence of innocence or guilt is extremely difficult to obtain (Iacono & Patrick, 1987). Relying strictly on the court's decisions on innocence or guilt is certainly unsatisfactory, since some people are wrongly convicted of crime and, for expedience, some people plead guilty to crimes they did not commit (Iacono & Patrick, 1987). Also, because defendants must be proven guilty beyond a reasonable doubt, some guilty defendants escape conviction. Relying on confessions is fraught with its own set of problems. Iacono and Patrick (1987, p. 475) conclude: "From our analysis…based on the field studies presently available, the validity of the CQT has not been established." While the CQT works much better than chance with guilty individuals, its effectiveness is considerably less impressive for identifying the innocent.

In addition, Ben-Shakhar and Furedy (1990) find fault with the CQT because the procedure depends heavily on subjective impressions of the examiner for its administration and scoring. Thus, objective data is difficult to find in field studies. Furthermore, Ben-Shakhar and Furedy affirm that the fundamental assumptions of the CQT are not only unsupported by scientific research, but the technique is not based on any testable theory.

The RCT, or R-I technique, in spite of its wide utilization in industry and preemployment screening, has yet to be studied with acceptable scientific methodology (Lykken, 1988; Iacono & Patrick, 1987). Therefore, summary statements about its accuracy must be made very cautiously. Iacono and Patrick (1987) report that, if anything, the extant literature suggests that the RCT is transparent and biased against the honest person, raising some important issues about the damage it may be doing to applicants. The RCT as an effective preemployment screening device simply needs to be validated. Otherwise, its use in government, business and industry is unjustified. Yet, this technique still plays a role in law enforcement and is taught as a basic technique to all federal polygraph examiner trainees (Honts & Perry, 1992).

Since the GKT is not used widely by professional polygraphers, it is not surprising that there are very few field studies examining its validity. Laboratory studies and researchers, however, as we discussed above, have been highly supportive of its validity (Ben-Shakhar & Furedy, 1990;

268

CHAPTER
TEN:
THE
PSYCHOLOGY
OF
EVIDENCE:
RELATED
ISSUES

Lykken, 1988; Iacono & Patrick, 1987). In summarizing mock-crime studies conducted between 1959 and 1984, for example, Iacono (1984) reports that the GKT was 100 percent accurate in identifying innocent subjects in five of the seven studies reviewed. Four of the studies reported a correct classification rate of at least 88 percent for guilty subjects. Lykken (1988) reviews eight laboratory studies in support of his claim for the accuracy of the GKT method. Overall, 97 percent of the 152 innocent subjects passed the test, and 88 percent of the 161 guilty subjects failed the test, for an overall accuracy rate of 93 percent.

In one of the few field studies exploring the validity of the GKT, Eitan Elaad (1990) examined ninety-eight actual GKT criminal polygraph records (fifty innocent and forty-eight guilty) taken from police investigations of the Israeli Police Scientific Interrogation Unit. The guilt or innocence of the examinees had been verified by the confession of the person who had committed the crime. Ninety-eight percent of the innocent and 42 percent of the guilty subjects were correctly classified. These results, together with the results from laboratory studies, strongly suggest that the strength of the GKT may be its power to protect innocent suspects from being falsely classified as guilty, and truthful job applicants from being eliminated from further consideration.

General Observations About Accuracy

Many professional polygraphers believe that the polygraph may be more accurate with criminal suspects than with victims (Barland, 1988). Many also believe that people who have committed property crimes (e.g., theft and burglary) are more difficult to detect than those who have committed crimes against persons, such as assault, robbery, or rape, primarily because the emotional baggage is usually higher for the latter than for the former (Horvath, 1977).

The polygraph is also believed to be more accurate when a suspect denies having physically committed a specific, illegal act (Barland, 1988, p. 83). It is probably less accurate when the suspect admits the act but denies criminal intent. ("It was an accident.") What the person was thinking at the time is more difficult to determine than what he or she actually did. If a criminal act is more mental than physical, such as a conspiratorial conversation that occurred months earlier, difficulties are magnified (Barland, 1988).

Countermeasures

Countermeasures are anything that an examinee might do to "fool" the polygraph and the examiner. Many types of countermeasures are possible, but the majority fall into the categories of physical, mental, hypnosis, biofeedback, or drugs. The most common physical countermeasures are either pain or muscle tension. For example, biting one's lip or tongue or jabbing oneself with a fingernail may induce enough pain to promote a physiological response that masks the actual response to control questions. Research suggests that even pressing one's toes to the floor may distort polygraph measures based on the CQT, and using a combination of physical methods, such as biting one's tongue and pressing toes to the floor, may be even more effective than any single physical technique (Gudjonsson, 1988).

Mental countermeasures include any deliberate attempt by an examinee to change his or her thought patterns during the polygraph test in order to distort the results. Examples would include counting backwards from ten, thinking of a sexually arousing scene, or thinking of a very peaceful scene (such as sailing on a calm lake on a sunny afternoon). Any thought that either minimizes the emotional impact of relevant questions or increases physiological arousal across all questions qualifies as a mental countermeasure. Research so far, however, indicates that mental countermeasures are less effective in deceiving the polygraph than physical ones, probably because physical techniques are easier to learn than mental techniques (Gudjonsson, 1988). There is very little evidence drugs can be used as an effective countermeasure to polygraph testing (Honts, 1987).

There is some unreplicated evidence (Waid, Orne, Cook & Orne, 1981) that a moderate dose of the tranquilizer meprobamate may have helped college students defeat a concealed-information procedure (Honts & Perry, 1992), but more research needs to be done before this finding can be substantiated. A recent study by Iacono, Cerri, Patrick, and Flemming (1992) raises serious doubt about the effectiveness of tranquilizers. They found that meprobamate and diazepam were not effective countermeasures.

Although alcohol does not seem to improve one's chances of "fooling" the polygraph either (Honts & Perry, 1992), Bradley and Ainsworth (1984) report that an individual mildly intoxicated while committing a crime *may* escape detection during a polygraph test. Hypnosis has also been tried as a countermeasure. The primary strategy in the use of hypnosis as a countermeasure is to induce a form of amnesia for the behavior in question. However, there is no evidence to date that hypnosis is an effective countermeasure (Gudjonsson, 1988).

Charles Honts and his research group (Honts, Hodes & Raskin, 1985; Honts, Raskin & Kircher, 1987) report that a significant proportion of highly motivated laboratory subjects can beat polygraph tests if they receive training in physical and mental countermeasures. On the other hand, individuals who lack specific training in techniques but try them on their own are generally not effective in defeating the polygraph. These results do suggest that polygraph tests can be defeated and raise troubling questions about the overall validity of the polygraph. The effectiveness of countermeasures is especially pertinent when the polygraph is used to detect espionage. Spies and intelligence agents are probably well-trained in the use of countermeasures for defeating polygraph tests.

One major drawback of a vast majority of the available research in the area of counter-measures is that the studies have not established ecological validity. That is, all the studies have been simulations, usually measuring the physiological responses in subjects who have been told to lie under laboratory conditions.

Conclusions

In summary, the few well-executed studies dealing with the accuracy of the polygraph show some commonality: lie detection based on the polygraph is wrong about one third of the time overall (Lykken, 1988). The CQT is effective at identifying the guilty, but apparently biased against the innocent or truthful subject. The GKT is good at identifying the innocent, but has practical problems and is not as good at classifying the guilty or deceptive person. The R-I technique does not seem to be effective at all. In reference to the R-I method, Honts and Perry (1992, p. 359) conclude: "Almost all of the scientists involved in detection of deception research reject the notion that the relevant-irrelevant test could be a useful discriminator of truth and deception." When used with naive subjects, the CQT and GKT are likely to produce results that are better than chance, sometimes significantly better than chance.

No matter what method is used, however, it appears that countermeasures can be intro-duced to defeat the polygraph. The overall effectiveness of a polygraph may lie more in its success at persuading individuals to admit the truth because they believe the test is infallible than in the test's actual power to discriminate truth from deception (Lloyd-Bostock, 1989).

Forensic Hypnosis

Hypnosis has long been used as entertainment, as a method of psychotherapy, as a procedure in several branches of medicine, and as a means of enhancing the memories of eyewit-nesses and victims in the criminal-justice system. For well over a century, the belief that hypnosis

270

CHAPTER
TEN:
THE
PSYCHOLOGY
OF
EVIDENCE:
RELATED
ISSUES

can exhume long-forgotten or buried memories has been widely held. This belief has frequently been bolstered by anecdotal or clinical claims describing cases in which previously inaccessible memories have been brought to light by the mysterious hypnotic trance. Enhancement or revival of memory through hypnosis is known as **hypnotic hypermnesia**. Enhancement or recovery of memory through nonhypnotic methods—free association, fantasy, recall techniques—are called **nonhypnotic hypermnesia**. It was the increased utilization of hypnosis in the courtroom during the 1960s that engendered considerable controversy and precipitated a wealth of research addressing the validity and application of hypnotic hypermnesia in forensic settings (Pettinati, 1988).

The ability to be hypnotized is an enduring and stable attribute which peaks during the life cycle in late childhood and declines gradually thereafter (Spiegel & Spiegel, 1987). The ability follows a normal distribution curve similar to intelligence. About 10 percent of the general population cannot be hypnotized, and 5 to 10 percent are highly suggestible (Hilgard, 1965). Most people fall somewhere between those two extremes. Therefore, almost everyone (90 percent) can experience at least some effects of hypnosis. Among the factors that are important in inducing hypnosis are: (1) the level of trust the subject places on the hypnotist; (2) the subject's motivation and desire to cooperate; (3) the kind of preconceived notions the subject has about hypnosis; and (4) the context and reasons for the hypnosis (e.g., entertainment or critical information gathering). Trust, motivation, a strong belief in its powers, and a serious context (such as a criminal investigation), allow most people to be hypnotized. Apparently, what distinguishes a true state of hypnosis from simple behavioral compliance is the person's ability to experience suggested alterations in perception, memory, and mood (Orne, Whitehouse, Dinges & Orne, 1988).

Relaxation and concentration are usually the primary goals of hypnosis. Subjects are sitting or lying down, and the hypnotist continually emphasizes quiet, calm, and drowsiness while subjects remain concentrated on a target (a candle, a button, a swinging object, or virtually any object that promotes sustained attention). The subject, asked to concentrate only on the target and the hypnotist's voice, is encouraged to drift off to sleep, all the while hearing what the hypnotist is saying. The hypnotist generally will suggest different behaviors, moods, or thoughts to the subject, and with each behavior or alteration, the subject falls deeper into a trance, or at least becomes increasingly convinced that hypnotism is in effect. Subjects are encouraged to involve themselves in various imaginative scenes, a process that adds to the positive aspects of hypnosis. In fact, "the subject's willingness to accept fantasy as reality during the hypnotic experience, together with the often dramatic vividness of recollections in hypnosis, may inspire great confidence that the recalled material is true to fact" (Orne et al., 1988, p. 25). This characteristic of hypnosis can be very troubling in forensic investigations concerned with recollections of witnesses or victims, as we shall see.

Despite its long history, hypnosis is still at a relatively young level of scientific development, and its application far outstrips our scientific knowledge of it. We still do not know precisely what hypnosis is. We have little knowledge of why one person is readily susceptible and another is not. We do know that hypnosis has no significant physiological effects other than general physical relaxation. We know also that hypnosis is not the same as sleep, nor is it the same state as that found during sleepwalking.

While hypnosis lacks scientific elucidation, there are two major theoretical explanations for its effects. The most widely accepted perspective, generally referred to as the **hypnotic trance theory**, assumes that hypnosis represents a special state of consciousness that promotes a high level of responsiveness to suggestion and changes in bodily sensation. In this special state of consciousness (some argue that it taps the unconscious), the subject may be able to regress to childhood and vividly remember or act out events that have been repressed, or at least put on the back burner of memory. While in the trance, subjects may be instructed to feel little or no pain, or to perform acts that they are unable to do when not hypnotized. Individuals can be instructed to sense, feel, smell, see, or hear things not normally possible outside of hypnosis; memory can be enhanced and even drastically improved in some situations. Generally speaking, the deeper the hypnotic trance, the more intense, detailed, and vivid a scene becomes to the subject. The chief spokesperson for this position has been Ernest Hilgard.

The second position advanced to explain hypnosis is the **cognitive behavioral viewpoint**, which maintains that the subject is not in a special state of consciousness when he or she appears hypnotized. Rather, it argues, hypnosis is a product of certain attitudes, motivations, and expectancies—not a mysterious alteration of consciousness. Specifically, people who have a positive attitude toward hypnosis are motivated to be hypnotized and expect to be hypnotized. They play the role suggested to them by the hypnotist; when the hypnotist asks them to relax, they will try and will probably feel relaxed.

Theodore X. Barber, chief advocate of the cognitive-behavioral perspective (Barber, Spanos & Chaves, 1974) has postulated that the good hypnotic subject is one who not only has the proper mixture of attitude, motivation, and expectancy, but also has the ability to think and imagine with the hypnotist. The good hypnotic subject is like the person who watches a motion picture and feels the emotions and experiences of characters on the screen. Intense and vivid experiences are suggested by the medium; Barber argues that hypnosis is, in most respects, a highly similar experience.

Martin Orne and his colleagues (1970, 1984, 1988) have hypothesized a viewpoint similar to the cognitive-behavioral theory, suggesting that role playing accounts for much of the so-called hypnotic phenomenon. That is, subjects act the way they think a truly hypnotized individual would act. Orne believes that a "prerequisite for hypnosis is the willingness to adopt the role of the 'hypnotic subject,' with its implicit social contract for uncritical acceptance of appropriate suggestions administered by the hypnotist" (Orne et al., 1988, p. 23). The hypnotic subject is willing temporarily to relinquish his or her sense of reality, hold any critical thinking in abeyance, and concentrate on what the hypnotist says. Orne has found in his research that the material described under so-called hypnotic trances is often inaccurate and embellished with many intervening events that occur between the initial incident and the hypnotic session. It appears that hypnotic subjects may be as susceptible to distortions, suggestions, and leading questions as the eyewitnesses described in the previous chapter. Particularly if the interrogator is a police officer convinced of the powers of hypnosis, he or she is apt inadvertently to suggest events or details that were not present at the crime scene. The hypnotized witness or victim, eager to please the interrogator, can easily imagine a scene decorated with subjective fantasies and thoughts in line with the suggestions of the questioner. Under these conditions, the hypnotized subject may begin to be convinced of the accuracy and power of hypnosis by the enthusiasm of the hypnotist. Furthermore, the subject also may become convinced of the accuracy of his or her account of the imagined scene.

When hypnosis is used as a tool to aid the recall of events that may be either several hours or several years old, the fundamental assumption is that human perception and memory functions like a videotape. All the events and details are stored accurately and simply must be located and brought to consciousness. We have seen, however, that this assumption is faulty. Human perception and memory are flawed and permeated with inaccuracies and distortions. The frailties of perception and memory, combined with the highly suggestive atmosphere of hypnosis, provide a situation in which critical inaccuracies have a high probability of occurring.

What does the research tell us about the reliability and validity of hypnosis in forensic

272

CHAPTER
TEN:
THE
PSYCHOLOGY
OF
EVIDENCE:
RELATED
ISSUES

settings? One way hypnosis is used by forensic investigators is to help individuals remember the details of events that happened in the past—a week, a month, or even years previously. In some instances, an investigation may require digging deep into the past for details of events that happened to a witness or victim at an early age. When hypnosis is used to help an individual relive an experience from his or her childhood, the procedure is known as **hypnotic age regression**. For example, in some instances, the victim or witness to a crime may become so emotionally or physically traumatized by the event that he or she has great difficulty remembering it or even identifying who was involved. This is especially the case if the criminal event happened a long time ago, such as we might find in cases involving sexual abuse during childhood. The hope is that, with the aid of hypnosis, a victim or witness can regress back to those early events and reconstruct them in some higher order of accuracy than is contained in nonhypnotic memories. However, the research does not seem to support the view that hypnosis enhances memory for events that happened during childhood. "On the basis of available data from properly controlled experiments and studies in which the researchers had access to biographical records, there is no support for the view that hypnotic age regression improves accurate recollection of childhood memories" (Orne et al., 1988, p. 36). In fact, there is reason to believe that memories acquired through hypnotic age regression are often far less accurate than nonhypnotic memories.

Hypnosis has the uncanny ability to instill a high degree of confidence in the things we remember under its spell. A highly hypnotizable subject might conclude, "I never realized that's the way it happened. I must have repressed it. It was so vivid when I was hypnotized. After experiencing it under hypnosis, I am convinced now that's the way it happened." However, the research is quite consistent in showing that a high degree of confidence in the veracity of hypnotic material is often a poor fit with the actual facts when independent evidence is available (Sanders & Simmons, 1983; Sheehan & Tilden, 1983, 1984). Unfortunately, this increased false confidence may permanently distort eyewitness testimony (Pettinati, 1988), or cement the subject's memory of the event to the extent that he or she believes it more credible than ordinary memory (Spiegel & Spiegel, 1987). Moreover, the inclination to confabulate and make up missing information seems to be greater under hypnosis (Orne et al., 1988; Stalnaker & Riddle, 1932). In effect, though hypnosis does increase the amount of information and number of peripheral details recalled, many of these may be incorrect or made up. Consequently, the information gathered from hypnosis is often a subtle mixture of fact and fantasy (Perry, Laurence, D'eon & Tallant, 1988).

Memory under hypnosis is highly malleable, especially in highly hypnotizable subjects (Laurence & Perry, 1983). Leading or suggestive questions or inadvertent responses to environmental cues can have a dramatic effect on posthypnotic recall. In practice, hypnosis seems to sensitize many subjects to subtle cues that are communicated—often inadvertently—by the hypnotist and others involved in the investigation. There is, therefore, a very high risk that counterfactual information will be incorporated into memory during the hypnotic process, especially among highly hypnotizable persons.

Hypnosis also fails to increase recognition accuracy beyond nonhypnotic performance (Sanders & Simmons, 1983; Wagstaff, 1982). Therefore, hypnosis is unlikely to improve identifications beyond what could be accomplished through standard investigative procedures.

Legal Status

Courts have been reluctant to admit testimony acquired through hypnosis as evidence (Schwitzgebel & Schwitzgebel, 1980), although the Supreme Court's decision in *Rock v. Arkansas* allows it (see Box 10.3). Considering the present scientific knowledge about hypnosis, particularly relative to the accuracy of memory under its influence, and the distortions apparently encouraged in the hypnotic

IN THIS CASE, A WOMAN NAMED VACUA LORENE ROCK was charged with shooting her husband. In order to refresh her memory as to the precise details of the shooting, she twice underwent hypnosis by a trained neuropsychologist. The hypnosis prompted her to remember details indicating that her gun was defective and had misfired, which was corroborated by an expert witness's testimony. The Arkansas Supreme Court, however, affirmed her conviction, ruling that hypnotically refreshed testimony was inadmissible because it is unreliable. The U. S. Supreme Court, with Justice Blackmun delivering the majority opinion, held that despite any unreliability hypnosis may introduce, the procedure has been credited as helpful in obtaining certain kinds of information. The Court noted:

> Hypnosis by trained physicians or psychologists has been recognized as a valid therapeutic technique since 1958, although there is no generally accepted theory to explain the phenomenon, or even a consensus on a single definition of hypnosis.... The use of hypnosis

in criminal investigations, however, is controversial, and the current medical and legal view of its appropriate role is unsettled.... The popular belief that hypnosis guarantees the accuracy of recall is as yet without established foundation and, in fact, hypnosis often has no effect at all on memory.... The most common response to hypnosis, however, appears to be an increase in both correct and incorrect recollections (p. 59).

The Court further stated:

> We are not now prepared to endorse without qualifications the use of hypnosis as an investigative tool; scientific understanding of the phenomenon and of the means to control the effects of hypnosis is still in its infancy.... [However, w]holesale inadmissibility of a defendant's testimony is an arbitrary restriction on the right to testify in the absence of clear evidence by the State repudiating the validity of all post-hypnosis recollections (p. 61). ■

situation, court resistance appears wise. Hypnosis has multiple effects, many of which contraindicate its use in the legal context (Orne et al., 1988). The research evidence is quite conclusive on the unreliability of hypnosis as a memory-restoring technique in forensic settings. According to Orne and his colleagues, current empirical studies "...compel the conclusion that hypnotically induced memories should *never* be permitted to form the basis for testimony by witnesses or victims in a court of law" (1988, p. 51). While *never* seems a bit strong, the statement does underscore the extreme caution that is necessary when applying hypnosis to gain information— whether in the courtroom or through the investigative process. Employing hypnosis to provide leads, especially those that can be corroborated by independent sources, is reasonable, however. And hypnosis can serve as an information facilitator for individuals who are fearful or embarrassed to report, or motivated by guilt to repress (Orne et al., 1988). But overall, standard forensic investigative techniques are substantially more fruitful than is the risky business of hypnosis.

Facial Composites

Composites are considered indispensable aids to criminal investigation by most police agencies. They are reconstructions of faces through memory, and are built either with the help of an artist's sketching skills or by using the various commercial kits available to law enforcement. The latter include an assortment of photographed or drawn facial features, which witnesses move about like pieces of a jigsaw puzzle to reconstruct a face.

Some law-enforcement agencies claim that face-memory reconstructions by artists based upon eyewitness verbal descriptions are superior to other composite reproductions, but few hard data to support these claims are available. As we learned in the previous chapter, accurate memory

274

CHAPTER
TEN:
THE
PSYCHOLOGY
OF
EVIDENCE:
RELATED
ISSUES

for faces is intrinsically difficult to achieve. Composites require one person to transform his or her perceptions and memories into verbal description, at which point another person continues the process, involving another set of perceptions, and finally, motor representation of the heavily processed "picture." The likelihood that some inaccuracy will be introduced during such reconstruction is very high.

Harmon (1973) asked an artist with experience in drawing police composites to describe verbally a facial image he had seen to another artist with similar police sketching experience. Only 50 percent of the subjects who knew the verbally described person were able to identify the person in the drawing. On the other hand, when an artist sketched faces from photographs, the subjects correctly identified the person in the drawing 93 percent of the time. These data suggest that artist sketches based upon verbal descriptions—a common way of creating composites—are subject to considerable distortion.

In the usual procedure, both the artist and the witness make repeated attempts at getting facial features "just right." It would appear, therefore, that closely examining a series of inaccurate constructions of the features in question could bias the witness's memory to the point where he or she could no longer discriminate between the reproductions created by the artist and his or her memory of the offender's face (Yarmey, 1979). We can also assume individual differences in the ability to describe facial features, in that some people have a knack for transforming visual perception and memory into precise descriptions displaying verbal precision while others lack this ability. In addition, it is likely that certain facial features draw more attention and therefore promote more accurate descriptions than others.

Many law-enforcement agencies, especially those in small cities and towns, rely on commercial composite kits to reconstruct pictures of faces from witness accounts, since skillful, experienced artists are not always readily available. The designers of composite kits assume that the world's faces can be reduced to manageable sets of commonalities. All chins, noses, and eyes, for example, can be represented by approximate types, which can then be combined to produce the vast majority of human faces. Most kit designers recognize that the facial reproductions will not be exact, but only close approximations.

All of the kits require witnesses to select individual features from groups of alternatives. Davis, Ellis, and Shepherd (1978) have reported data that the photographic type of kit is superior to systems using line drawings. There appears to be more information in photographs than in line transcriptions, no matter how much detail is provided in the drawings.

Research by Laughery and Fowler (1977, 1978) has indicated that composite kits using line drawings are inferior to photographs or even artist sketches. It appears, however, that neither composite kits of any type nor artist sketches can compare with the information and accuracy provided by actual photographs of the suspects. Law-enforcement agencies that use composite facial kits are advised to treat composites, and especially line drawings, with extreme caution as tools in the identification of suspects by witnesses. Even if composites are not used as evidence, their danger lies in the possibility that a witness will so painstakingly describe a face that the subsequent composite will replace the actual face in the witness's memory. This could lead to the misidentification of an innocent person who happens to resemble the composite.

Extraevidentiary Factors

The evidence obtained by law enforcement officers in the investigation of a case and later admitted into trial proceedings is not the only "evidence" a jury considers. Ideally, jurors should attend to testimony, exhibits, arguments, and the instructions of the judge, and they should resist influence from sources outside the courtroom, or in some cases, from within the courtroom as well. Jurors are warned not to allow prior information or prior sentiments to enter into their decisionmaking. They must decide cases solely on the evidence before them and on relevant law, as explained by the presiding judge. Realistically, as we learned in the jury chapters, a variety of factors can have an effect upon jurors, including their own biases (e.g., about race or political affiliation), the opinions of persons they respect, and community sentiments.

Although jury decisionmaking was introduced in previous chapters, the subject will not be closed until we consider two influences on jury deliberation that have received extensive attention of late, both from the judicial system and, ironically, from the media. They are the alleged influence of extensive pretrial publicity upon subsequent jury decisions and the so-called cameras-in-the-courtroom issue, the influence of electronic coverage on jury trials. The topics are introduced here because of their relevance to the psychology of evidence. Pretrial publicity allegedly bombards jurors with so much inadmissible evidence before the actual trial that they are rendered unable to make a fair decision. Cameras in the courtroom may interfere with the presentation of evidence to the jurors.

PRETRIAL PUBLICITY

Pretrial publicity can be divided into two central issues: (1) to what extent does extensive media coverage contaminate jury decisionmaking? and (2) can the judicial system neutralize the influence of the media on prospective and sitting jurors?

Adverse Effects of Media Coverage

Courts have often addressed the issue of extensive publicity and whether it prejudices the outcome of a trial. When especially flagrant, inflammatory publicity has been involved, courts, including the U. S. Supreme Court, have sometimes over-turned a conviction. Such was the case of Dr. Sam Sheppard, whom the media hounded mercilessly from the time his wife was murdered up to and during his trial. The *Sheppard* decision, *Sheppard v. Maxwell* (1966), focused on both the courtroom atmosphere during the trial, which the Supreme Court characterized as "bedlam," and on press reports of material that never was mentioned on the witness stand. The trial judge, however, bore the brunt of the Court's criticism. The Justices severely chastised him for not controlling his courtroom or enacting measures to insure fairness.

The case of *Irvin v. Dowd* (1961) also resulted in a reversal due to media coverage. Irvin, whom the press at one point called a "mad dog," was said to have confessed to six murders in a small Indiana community. Reporters and editors, aided by law-enforcement officials, made use of screaming headlines, streetcorner interviews ("He should be hanged"), and background stories revealing previous felony convictions. During the *voir dire*, two thirds of the jurors said they believed Irvin was guilty, although all also said they would be fair and would consider the evidence impartially. About this, the Supreme Court said, "No doubt each juror was sincere when he said he would be fair and impartial to petitioner, but the psychological impact requiring such a declaration before one's fellows is often its father. Where so many, so many times, admitted prejudice, such a statement of impartiality can be given little weight."

Flagrant media coverage by respectable publications is the exception today, at a time when many journalists are conscious of their obligations to the public. Still common, however, are extensive stories about a defendant's background, interviews with persons who knew him, reports of evidence taken during investigations, and even testimony during pretrial suppression hearings.

The free-press/fair-trial problem is troublesome because it represents an apparent clash between the First and Sixth amendments, the one guaranteeing press freedom and the other

276

CHAPTER
TEN:
THE
PSYCHOLOGY
OF
EVIDENCE:
RELATED
ISSUES

granting the right to a speedy and public trial by an impartial jury. Interestingly, in Great Britain, the effect of extensive press coverage on the defendant's rights to a fair trial became so alarming that it led to the passage of the British Contempt of Court Act of 1981. The Act restricts the amount of press coverage that may be reported on any ongoing British legal proceeding (Hans, 1990). In the U. S., the Supreme Court has carefully guarded the First Amendment right of the press not to be restrained in this manner, as will be noted below.

Defense attorneys have argued consistently that it is impossible for their clients to be judged by an impartial jury if those jurors have read extensive information prior to the trial, particularly if such coverage damns the defendant, is sensational, or includes information that may later be inadmissible as evidence during the trial. During the late 1960s and early 1970s, many judges agreed, and they enjoined the press from printing material about a case. Sometimes these injunctions were very general, restricting reporters from giving the public newsworthy information.

The U. S. Supreme Court severely restricted such "gag orders" in 1976, with its landmark *Nebraska Press Association v. Stuart* decision (see Box 10.4). Guessing that extensive prejudicial publicity doubtless had some effect on jurors, the Court said that press restraints were nevertheless the least tolerable infringement upon First Amendment rights. The Court stressed that it was the presiding judge's responsibility, in each case, to seek out and employ alternatives to gagging the press. Included among these alternatives were extensive *voir dire* questioning to determine whether the jurors had been influenced, changing the location of the trial, sequestering the jury, and postponing the trial.

A noteworthy, realistic research study was the interdisciplinary Fair Trial Project conducted by a group of sociologists, psychologists, lawyers, and journalists at Columbia University (Simon, 1980). The researchers chose subjects from an actual jury pool and conducted their project with cooperation of the judiciary, the bar, and the local media. Subjects listened to audiotapes of an actual jury trial, after having seen newspaper clippings that were either "neutral" or "prejudicial." Final results indicated that more jurors exposed to prejudicial publicity convicted than jurors not exposed to such publicity. Unanimous verdicts of not guilty were reached only by nonprejudiced juries. Of particular impact were newspaper stories which revealed that a defendant had a previous criminal record or had allegedly confessed and then retracted.

The researchers noted that much research is still needed to determine the relative effects of group influence during the decisionmaking process to other factors that might mitigate prejudicial publicity. They noted also that traditionally many defendants have been exposed to massive unfavorable publicity, but have nonetheless been found not guilty. "This leads one to speculate that different kinds of unfavorable publicity may have different outcomes, whether because of the political or nonpolitical nature of the cases or the national-versus-local type of publicity, among many other factors, and that methods of screening and instructing jurors to avoid prejudice do exist" (Padawer-Singer & Barton, 1975, p. 136).

Gary Moran and Brian Cutler (1991), in a two-part study, examined the effects of pretrial publicity on jury-eligible (*venire*) persons in the context of two criminal trials. In one study, 604 potential jurors were surveyed after one year of news coverage of the investigation, arrest, and indictment of defendants accused of distributing large quantities of marijuana. The second study dealt with the murder of a police officer involved in a drug sting. Moran and Cutler found that pretrial publicity prejudiced prospective jurors against the defendants in both cases, including those jurors who claimed that they were impartial in their judgments.

There is also some evidence to suggest that the pretrial publicity does not have to be directly related to the case to exert an influence on its outcome. **General pretrial publicity**—information that is prominently in the news but is *unrelated* to the particular case being tried—may strongly

■ 10.4: NEBRASKA PRESS ASSOCIATION v. STUART

AFTER A MULTIPLE MURDER IN A SMALL NEBRASKA town (population 850), Stuart, an appellate judge, acceded to the request of prosecuting and defense attorneys that he restrain all journalists, print and broadcast, from publishing information strongly implicative of the accused, one Erwin Charles Simants. The implicative information included a past criminal record, alleged confessions, statements made to other persons, and certain aspects of the medical testimony given at a preliminary hearing. Although the Nebraska Supreme Court modified Stuart's order, it remained in effect until the beginning of Simants's trial, at which point the jury was sequestered.

The Nebraska Press Association, through its attorneys, engaged in a spirited volley of appeals and counterappeals with the judicial system, including at one point the association's seeking and obtaining the direct intercession of U.S. Supreme Court Justice Harry Blackmun. Meanwhile, the case against Simants was readied and went to trial. Thus, by the time the Supreme Court heard the association's petition, the defendant's trial was over and he had been convicted. The Court nevertheless agreed to hear it because of the likelihood that the press/bar conflict would be repeated.

After commenting at length on the value of press freedom and the unconstitutionality of government interference with what the press published, the Court addressed, but very briefly, the effect of pervasive publicity. The relevant quotes are scant:

Our review of the pretrial record persuades us that the trial judge was justified in concluding that there would be intense and pervasive pretrial publicity concerning this case. He could also reasonably conclude, based on common human experience, that publicity might impair the defendant's right to a fair trial. He did not purport to say more, for he found only a "clear and present danger that pretrial publicity *could* impinge upon the defendant's right to a fair trial." (Emphasis added.) His conclusion as to the impact of such publicity on prospective jurors was of necessity speculative, dealing as he was with factors unknown and unknowable. (pp. 562–563)

Later, the Court added:

Reasonable minds can have few doubts about the gravity of the evil pretrial publicity can work, but the probability that it would do so here was not demonstrated with the degree of certainty our cases on prior restraint require. (p. 569)

The Court cited no studies to support its dicta that some pretrial publicity is bound to affect juror decisionmaking in a way that is unfair to the defendant. The Justices did not ask for empirical evidence, as they seemed to do in a later case (*Chandler v. Florida*). Rather, they relied on fireside induction to conclude that prejudice must result, in some cases. ■

---

affect jury decisionmaking also (Greene, 1990). For example, during the Gulf War with Iraq, or during the hostage crisis in Iran, there was considerable evidence that Arabs and/or Muslims living in the U.S. were treated shabbily and with prejudice across the spectrums of society. In another example, Edith Greene describes the case of Cathleen Crowell Webb who in April of 1985 recanted her 1977 testimony that she had been raped by Gary Dotson. Greene hypothesizes that it is entirely possible jurors in unrelated rape cases may have been affected by her well-publicized statements. Greene developed her hypothesis concerning the adverse influences of general pretrial publicity during a study involving eyewitness identification she was conducting (with Elizabeth Loftus) in Seattle. Halfway through the study, the local media ran a series of stories on the case of Steven Titus. Titus had been identified by a rape victim and was eventually convicted of sexual assault. However, another man later confessed to the crime. The local media elaborated on the many pitfalls and dangers of eyewitness testimony and how a completely innocent person can get tangled in the web of mistaken identity. Greene and Loftus serendipitously found that the news stories strongly influenced the thinking of the subjects in their study, a study completely unrelated to the Titus case. The mock jurors told the researchers that after hearing about the Titus case, they began to put little faith in the prosecution's eyewitness testimony during the second half of the study.

278

CHAPTER
TEN:
THE
PSYCHOLOGY
OF
EVIDENCE:
RELATED
ISSUES

Greene also elaborates on changes in public perception of the psychiatric profession after the case of John Hinckley, who tried to assassinate President Reagan. She writes (1990, p. 443): "Analysis of media coverage during and after the Hinckley case demonstrated that the psychiatrists who testified were often denigrated by the media and that their testimony was portrayed as having little merit." In a survey conducted in Delaware shortly after this publicity, over half the respondents said that if they had been Hinckley's jurors, they would have little confidence in the testimony of forensic psychiatrists who testified in the trial. Without knowing what the base rate is—what the Delaware population generally thinks of forensic psychiatric testimony—it is difficult to determine to what extent the news coverage influenced the Delaware survey. But Greene believes that general pretrial publicity—not simply pretrial publicity directly related to the case at hand—also has a strong influence on how jurors approach particular cases.

Until more information is obtained, our understanding of the effects of general news coverage on jurors remains fragmentary and largely inconclusive. This area seems destined to generate considerable interest and research in the near future.

Judicial Remedies

Currently, there is widespread faith within the judicial system in the variety of remedies available to the court to combat the presumed effects of pretrial publicity (Kramer, Kerr & Carroll, 1990; Hans, 1990; Carroll et al., 1986). These remedies include the *voir dire* (the most commonly used remedy), delaying the trial through continuance, moving the trial to a different venue or location, imposing a gag order on the attorneys, or simply admonishing the jury to disregard the pretrial information. There is also some belief that jury deliberation itself will neutralize the effects of pretrial publicity because the group members will point out to each other the inappropriateness of considering the publicity and consequently correct for external influences (Kramer, Kerr & Carroll, 1990). However, the empirical evidence does *not* support the view that these remedies are effective in neutralizing the contaminating influence of pretrial publicity.

In a well-designed study, Geoffrey Kramer, Norbert Kerr, and John Carroll (1990) examined the effects of three judicial remedies: (1) admonitions, (2) deliberation, and (3) continuance. Subjects viewed videotapes that included clips of television and newspaper stories relating to the upcoming mock trial. In these videos, two types of pretrial publicity were dramatized: (1) factual publicity (which contained true, damaging information about the defendant, such as the fact that he had a substantial prior criminal record) and (2) emotional publicity (which contained no explicitly incriminating evidence, but did contain material likely to arouse negative emotions). The emotional publicity content, for example, portrayed a seven-year-old girl who had been struck and seriously injured in a hit-and-run accident that occurred shortly after a robbery in which the defendant was a suspect. The description of the hit-and-run vehicle was highly similar to the one used in the robbery. The young girl, her family, and her health problems were described so as to personalize her difficulties.

The researchers found that admonitions from the judge to ignore all publicity had virtually no effect on jury verdicts, and that jury deliberation actually strengthened the preexisting bias promoted by the pretrial publicity. The results did, however, suggest, that a twelve-day continuance helped reduce bias created by factual publicity. The continuance did not have much effect on reducing the effects of emotionally biasing publicity. Kramer, Kerr, and Carroll speculated that jurors might forget factual material but be more apt to remember the emotionally tinged material. The study implies that continuance could be useful in reducing bias due to pretrial publicity that is factual in content, but not so effective when strong emotional content is involved.

Hedy Dexter, Brian Cutler, and Gary Moran (1992) examined the extent to which *voir dire* serves as a remedy for publicity-induced prejudice. Half the subjects (undergraduates) read news-paper articles containing information prejudicial to the defendant in a murder case. A week later, the subjects were subjected to either a minimal or extended *voir dire* by a judge and two attorneys in an actual courtroom. Minimal *voir dire* was based on the standard examination used by the Federal courts. It consists of ten rather superficial questions that are asked by the judge. The extended *voir dire* involved a one-hour information session describing legal reasons the news coverage should be ignored. Then they watched a two-hour videotape of the murder trial. Immediately after seeing the tape, the subjects were asked to give their verdicts on the guilt or innocence of the defendant. The results demonstrated that pretrial publicity increased perceptions of the defendant's guilt. Furthermore, an extended *voir dire* did little to dislodge this prejudicial perception.

As we found in the chapter dealing with jury instructions, the curative doctrine and legal remedies to neutralize prejudicial influence of extraevidentiary material are generally not sup-ported by the research literature. Social scientists are therefore compelled to help identify those strategies and procedures that reduce, mitigate, or even eliminate extraevidentiary influences on the cognitive processes of jurors.

ELECTRONIC COVERAGE OF TRIALS

The cameras-in-the-courtroom issue focuses on the effects of electronic coverage on all partici-pants in a trial, not the jury alone. It is often assumed that broadcast equipment will adversely affect the judicial process, that participants' conduct will be unnatural, and therefore the trial will not be fair. When broadcast technology was in its infancy, this argument was persuasive, so much so that it was accepted by the U. S. Supreme Court in the Billie Sol Estes case (*Estes v. Texas*, 1965). The Court ruled, in a 5-4 decision, that broadcasting was a punishment in itself, turning the courtroom into a "stadium setting." Furthermore, there was such a high probability of preju-dice—although no prejudice need be shown—that the defendant had certainly been deprived of due process. "The heightened public clamor resulting from radio and television coverage will inevitably result in prejudice. Trial by television is, therefore, foreign to our system." The Court added that "the distractions, intrusions into confidential attorney-client relationships and the temptation offered by television to play to the public audience might often have a direct effect not only upon the lawyers, but the judge, the jury and the witnesses."

Nearly twenty years later, a different Supreme Court again addressed the question of cameras in the courtroom, in *Chandler v. Florida* (1981), and this Court did an about-face. Noting the sophistication of broadcast technology today, the Justices remarked that there was no inherent prejudicial effect due to the presence of electronic equipment.

The petitioners in *Chandler* argued that television coverage of their robbery trial had deprived them of due-process safeguards. Florida, like numerous other states, had been experi-menting with allowing broadcasters to cover trials, even when the participants objected. (In general, state rules require broadcasters to notify the court prior to the trial that they are interested in covering it, and it is left to the court's discretion whether or not to grant the request.)

Noting that the court record revealed only "generalized allegations of prejudice" because of the cameras with no empirical evidence to support these charges, the Court said that the risk of juror prejudice in some cases did not justify an absolute ban on news coverage of trials. Nevertheless, "the general issue of psychological impact of broadcast coverage upon the partici-pants in a trial, and particularly upon the defendant, is still a subject of sharp debate."

The Court appears to be implicitly inviting researchers to study the effects of broadcast coverage upon trial participants. This issue raises a number of thought-provoking questions. It is

280

CHAPTER
TEN:
THE
PSYCHOLOGY
OF
EVIDENCE:
RELATED
ISSUES

unlikely that the relatively unobtrusive cameras of today will distract participants in the way that the wires, lights, and whirring noises which inevitably accompanied television crews in the 1950s and 1960s did. The closed circuit cameras often positioned in rooms where official proceedings take place testify to the omnipresence of today's media. Many judges will not allow cameras in their courtrooms unless they are stationary and unobtrusive, and they attach the stipulation that jurors may not be filmed.

Eugene Borgida, Kenneth DeBono and Lee Buckman (1990) examined some of the key psychological issues associated with electronic media coverage in courtroom trials. Subjects were undergraduate students who served as either witnesses or jurors in three types of mock trials. The investigators did find that electronic equipment has some *apparent* psychological effects on the witnesses in increasing their nervousness. In other words, the student witnesses did feel somewhat uncomfortable about being recorded. However, this witness nervousness did not adversely affect the jurors' perceptions of the quality of the witness testimony, nor did it impede the recall of facts, the flow of information, or the communication in the courtroom.

Nevertheless, questions remain. Will the knowledge that the trial is being televised force lawyers to "play" to cameras more than they now play to the print reporters? How will cameras affect the decisionmaking process of judges? It can be argued that the legal actors will do a better job in the face of such intense scrutiny, but there is no evidence to that effect as yet. Although most state guidelines allow the presiding judge to prevent reporters from televising the testimony of certain witnesses, this does not guarantee that the other witnesses are unaffected. Following the *Chandler* decision and with the increasing dominance of electronic journalism over print, it is very likely that judicial proceedings will be televised with more frequency. Psychological researchers must look for creative research designs to study this growing phenomenon.

Summary and Conclusions

We have continued our concentration upon evidence brought before the courts by discussing in this chapter the psychological research related to specific types of evidence gathering. Interrogation, the custodial questioning of criminal suspects or unwilling informants in an effort to persuade them to confess or to gain more information about a crime, is a process fraught with psychological implications and legal mine fields. Although students of psychology and law must be aware of what courts have allowed in relation to custodial interrogation, they must also know what methods are effective in eliciting information and what methods are still used by criminal investigators in interrogatory procedure. Information gathering in nonaggressive situations—such as interviewing witnesses of crimes or taking depositions in criminal and civil cases—was not covered in this chapter.

Another crucial evidence-gathering talent for criminal investigators to possess is the ability to detect deceptive responses. Here, law enforcement is sometimes aided by mechanical devices, such as the polygraph or voice-stress analyzer, but most often investigators look for nonverbal indicators that an individual is being less than truthful. As we have seen, there is no sure way to detect deception. Nonverbal behaviors can be misleading, especially if the investigator has swallowed the prevalent myths about shifty eyes, fumbling behavior, or restlessness. The expectancy-violation model offers considerable promise in explaining the myths and folklore surrounding deception and lying. The model predicts that any suspicious nonverbal behavior may lead to the conclusion that a person is deceitful.

Sophisticated suspects may well have learned to suppress the "dead giveaways." If the investigator is determined to use nonverbal indicators, he or she should pay attention to the so-called leaky channels, those not typically used to try to deceive. Even so, nonverbal indicators are by no means conclusive evidence of deception.

We warned about the use of the polygraph, hypnosis, voice-stress analyzers, and facial composites in gathering evidence. Manufacturers of stress analyzers have been able to offer no empirical evidence to support their claims, and the connection of voice stress with deception is a specious one. Facial composites, though they may give investigators clues as to the general description of a perpetrator, have the danger of imprinting the wrong face into a witness's memory.

The polygraph has been submitted to considerable empirical research during the past two decades. This research has shown with consistency that even the best trained polygrapher is wrong about one-third of the time in identifying deception. The three major methods used vary in their accuracy rates. The CQT seems best at identifying the guilty, but is inaccurate in identifying the innocent or truthful person. The GKT, on the other hand, seems to have a good track record at discerning the innocent, but is less than adequate when it comes to identifying the guilty or deceptive person. The R-I (or RCT) method appears inadequate for distinguishing either group. Furthermore, various countermeasures can be used to defeat the polygraph. These data suggest that considerable caution should be exercised when developing conclusions concerning the deceptiveness or truthfulness of a person based on polygraphic measures. The power of the polygraph seems to lie in myth and folklore. If subjects *believe* in the power of the polygraph to detect lying, they will be more willing to tell the truth when being examined.

Hypnosis is also beginning to draw much research interest. However, thus far the data have not been promising. To date, the research is quite conclusive that hypnosis is an unreliable technique to use in forensic settings. Human memory appears incomplete, fragile, reconstructive, and highly malleable. The hypnotic state seems to increase and promote these memory shortcomings. Thus, extreme caution is urged when applying hypnosis in the forensic setting in gathering information, whether in the courtroom or through the investigative process. Hypnosis may provide promising leads during an investigation, but reliable evidence does not appear to be its forté.

The chapter ended with some consideration of the effects of extraevidentiary factors on courtroom participants. Prejudicial publicity, which defense attorneys abhor and insist is detrimental to their clients, has received a good share of attention from researchers conducting simulation studies. Although evidence has indicated that jurors may be unfavorably disposed toward defendants who have received media attention, juror prejudice in such situations is not inevitable. Furthermore, it is impossible to control other sources of influence on a juror, such as his or her value system, comments from respected persons, community rumors, or even his or her attraction to the prosecutor. When pretrial publicity *does* bias a juror, however, simulation studies indicate that most efforts to dispel the bias are not successful. The effects of increasing broadcast coverage of criminal trials, and their extension to many other judicial proceedings, is an area demanding research attention.

Questions to Ponder

1. How would the presence of a defense lawyer during police questioning affect the interrogation techniques advocated by Inbau and Reed?

2. Research suggests that people are no more accurate than chance at detecting deception on

CHAPTER
TEN:
THE
PSYCHOLOGY
OF
EVIDENCE:
RELATED
ISSUES

the basis of nonverbal behavior. What are the dangers of trying to interpret the nonverbal behavior of those around us?

3. Discuss the causes of resistance to the admission of polygraph evidence. How is this similar to resistance to the admission of other implicative or exculpatory evidence, such as DNA evidence?

4. Discuss the pros and cons of allowing hypnotically-refreshed testimony from the victim of a crime. Should hypnotically-refreshed *exculpatory* testimony from the defendant be allowed? Discuss the similarities and differences between the polygraph and hypnosis.

5. Recall a recent high-profile case that has received extensive media attention. As a member of the jury hearing that case, would you be able to disregard the media coverage and make decisions only on the basis of the evidence you heard in court? As a member of the public, would you want the media to limit its coverage of the case?

PSYCHOLOGY AND FAMILY LAW

AMILY LAW CONCERNS STATUTES, COURT DECISIONS, AND PROVISIONS that relate to family relationships, rights, duties, and finances. It involves marriage, divorce, child custody, children's rights, and a wide range of matters influencing the welfare of children. Most experts in the field of psychology and law agree that a significant collection of psychological knowledge has direct relevance to many sectors of family law (Koocher, 1987). The primary purpose of this chapter is to offer a brief overview of that knowledge. A second goal is to provide basic information about concepts and procedures associated with family law.

It should be emphasized at the outset that the very definition of *family* is undergoing change. Although in most jurisdictions family remains limited to relationships by blood or marriage, legal decisions in a variety of contexts indicate a willingness to recognize that nontraditional domestic relationships, such as those of unmarried heterosexuals and homosexuals, can qualify as family. One court, for example, recently awarded custody of the minor child of a woman who had been killed in an automobile accident to her surviving female partner, with whom both mother and child had been living for a number of years. Although the child's grandparents had initially sought custody, they agreed with the final determination. We are also beginning to see court decisions supporting the rights of children to define their own family preference. The widely publicized Florida decision in 1992 involving the twelve-year-old boy who successfully "divorced" his mother in favor of foster parents is a case in point. Another is the 1993 case of the fourteen-year-old girl, switched at birth, who rejected attempts by her biological parents to reclaim her. The court allowed her to stay with the father who had raised her from birth. These and other similar decisions suggest that family law will be refined and perhaps even redefined for years to come.

The Abortion Issue: Competency, Consent, and Consequences

We will begin by reviewing how the legal system views the competence and decisionmaking capacity of minors (under age eighteen) on issues involving their welfare. We will focus on abortion, for which the key question is whether minors are psychologically competent to consent to an intrusive medical procedure. Issues involving competence also arise in the area of juveniles waiving their legal rights, including the right against self-incrimination and the right to a lawyer in the delinquency context. Delinquency-related competency issues will be discussed later in the chapter.

284

CHAPTER
ELEVEN:
PSYCHOLOGY
AND
FAMILY
LAW

In the eyes of the law, adults are presumed competent to make decisions in their own interest until proven incompetent in a court of law; children, by contrast, are presumed incompetent (Koocher, 1987). In most states, eighteen is the chronological age which signals adulthood; in some states, the age is sixteen or seventeen. Additionally, most states have an "emancipated minor" provision in their laws, allowing courts to recognize some children, on a case-by-case basis, as independent and eligible for adult status.

Despite the presumption of incompetence, there are several circumstances under which a child may be heard on his or her own behalf or may be treated as an adult (Koocher, 1987). For example, a juvenile offender charged with a major crime, such as murder or rape, may be tried as an adult in all states, although age limits and procedures vary widely. Many jurisdictions grant minors the right to seek medical treatment on their own authority under certain circumstances (Koocher, 1987), especially if treatment of the illness is deemed in the public interest. For example, if a minor has a sexually transmittable disease, it is in the best interest of both the child and society that this be treated, without parental consent if necessary.

The rights of a minor concerning abortion are among the most hotly debated issues in family law. In 1973, the U. S. Supreme Court held in *Roe v. Wade* that the "Constitutional right of privacy founded in the Fourteenth Amendment is broad enough to encompass a woman's decision whether or not to terminate her pregnancy" (p. 706). Since that time the Supreme Court has decided on at least eight different cases involving a minor's right to an abortion (Pliner & Yates, 1992). In general, the Court has held "...that while a minor female, like an adult female, does have the right to an abortion, the minor's right is more restricted." Further "the basis for the restrictions that have been imposed lies in the law's presumption that minors are immature and, therefore, not competent to give informed consent to undergo a medical procedure, such as an abortion" (Pliner & Yates, 1992, p. 204).

States vary widely in their approach to the abortion issue. In some, "restrictions are being proposed to narrow access to abortion, parental notification and/or consent for minors, husband notification and/or consent for married women, and limitations on information that family planning clinics can provide about abortion" (Russo, Horn & Schwartz, 1992, p. 184).

Although the courts have left the basic right to an abortion intact, they have issued a variety of decisions limiting that right. The U. S. Supreme Court, for example, in two separate decisions in 1992, upheld laws requiring a twenty-four-hour waiting period before an abortion could be obtained.

The Court struck down, however, a provision requiring married women to obtain the consent of their husbands. A federal appeals court recently declared unconstitutional a gag rule prohibiting federally funded family planning clinics from fully informing clients of their options, including the right to have an abortion. Also in 1992, the Freedom of Choice Act was introduced into Congress. If passed into law, this legislation could make it exceedingly difficult for states to restrict abortion rights.

PARENTAL NOTIFICATION

Several states have enacted statutory requirements for notification of parents before a minor obtains an abortion. The Supreme Court has upheld the constitutionality of such requirements, at least when applied to "immature" minors. Precisely what *immature* means remains open to debate and interpretation. The overall effects of such restrictions have yet to be evaluated. However, based on empirical work with child-parent relationships, these mandated restrictions are very unlikely to have notable positive effects on most minors. Indeed, the Interdivisional Committee on Adolescent Abortion (1987) of the American Psychological Association has identified three ways in which parental notification requirements may actually promote negative effects on pregnant adolescents.

First, research has shown that confidentiality is an important factor for adolescents in their decisions as to whether to seek services from family planning clinics. If clinics are required to notify parents, pregnant adolescents—particularly the younger ones—are likely to delay seeking professional help until late into pregnancy. This procrastination increases the psychological and physical risks of both abortion and bearing a fetus to term. The longer the delay, the more likely inducing labor will be necessary, and the greater the risk for adverse medical and psychological effects (Russo, 1992). More than 90 percent of all abortions are performed during the first trimester, and fewer than 1 percent take place after twenty weeks of pregnancy (Russo, 1992). Typically, abortions are performed in the third trimester only when the woman's life is in danger.

Second, there is little evidence that parent-child communication will improve simply because an agency notifies the parents about the pregnancy. Third, the committee asserts that "...it is...clear that there are circumstances in which parental consultation is likely to result in neither more reasoned decisionmaking nor diminished risk of psychological harm" (Interdivisional Committee, 1987, p. 74). In fact, for most adolescents who resist informing their parents, the forced communication promotes more psychological stress. In some cases, it threatens the physical well-being of the adolescent.

Approximately 1.6 million abortions take place in the United States every year (Russo, Horn & Schwartz, 1992). An examination of the nationwide statistics reveals that there are important variations in the life circumstances and motivations of women who seek abortions. In the case of minors, the physical, economic, psychological, and social outcomes of unwanted pregnancy are significantly different from those of adults (Russo, 1986).

About 12 percent of all legal abortions in the U. S. are obtained by minors (Russo, Horn & Schwartz, 1992). Most minors seeking abortions do not have dependent children and are white, enrolled in school, unmarried, and without prior abortions (Russo et al., 1992). On the other hand, more than 13 percent of these pregnant minors have had prior abortions, 9 percent already are mothers, and about 17 percent of the mothers already have two or more children. Moreover, this group of young mothers is generally economically disadvantaged and high in ethnic minority representation (nearly 80 percent).

Abortion plays an important role in delaying transition to parenthood for minors (Russo et al., 1992). Although reasons for seeking an abortion are multiple and complex, more than 75 percent of unmarried minors seeking abortion feel they are not mature enough to raise a child (Russo et al., 1992; Torres & Forrest, 1988).

Interestingly, adolescents who experience unwanted pregnancies tend to have a lower sense of self-esteem and to be more passive than adolescents who manage to avoid unwanted pregnancies (Russo, 1992). Adolescents who avoid unwanted pregnancies feel they have more personal control over what happens to them, and consequently they are more likely to use effective contraceptive protection (Adler, 1981). We should recognize, however, that contraceptives may not be available, that female adolescents are often pressured *not* to insist on condoms, and that many adolescent pregnancies may be the result of sexual assault.

ADOLESCENT COMPETENCE

Knowledge concerning the precise age at which children can make responsible judgments about their health and welfare is "...not sufficient enough to provide clear or convincing direction to a society ambivalent about children's self-determination rights." In short, a "comprehensive and

285

THE
ABORTION
ISSUE:
COMPETENCY,
CONSENT,
AND
CONSEQUENCES

286

CHAPTER
ELEVEN:
PSYCHOLOGY
AND
FAMILY
LAW

empirically validated design for the progressive development of the self-determination capacities of children does not exist" (Hart, 1991, p. 56). There is some evidence that adolescents by the age of fifteen can make health-care treatment decisions that demonstrate autonomous reasoning (Melton, 1983; Hart, 1991; Carter & Lawrence, 1985).

The U. S. Supreme Court has made two discernible but misinformed assumptions concerning adolescent competence to make decisions about abortions and the potential for psychological harm in those decisions (Interdivisional Committee, 1987; Melton & Russo, 1987). First, the Court has assumed that an adolescent is less likely than an adult to make a sound decision when she is faced with an unintended pregnancy. Second, the Court has also assumed that an adolescent is especially vulnerable to serious psychological harm as a result of having an abortion. The Court apparently believes that these risks are substantially greater than the psychological risks that arise in the decisions required when a minor carries a fetus to full term.

According to Melton and Russo (1987), the Court's neglect of social-science research has apparently resulted in the majority of the Justices relying on personal and social convictions that adolescents are vulnerable, dependent, and incompetent creatures. When the Court has cited scientific evidence in support of its decision, "it typically was from a medical rather than a social-scientific journal, perhaps reflecting the fact that clinical approaches rather than probabilistic approaches have greater credibility in the legal system" (p. 70). The social science empirical research on health care decisionmaking generally indicates that adolescents are as able to conceptualize and reason about treatment alternatives as adults are (Interdivisional Committee, 1987).

In reference to the second assumption of the Court, the research shows that, although "adolescents' reactions to abortions may be somewhat more negative on the average than adults, the magnitude of the age differences is small. Moreover, when negative reactions occur, they are almost always mild and transitory" (Interdivisional Committee, 1987, p. 74). In fact, the most common reaction to abortion among both minors and adults seems to be relief. The psychological damage which opponents of choice attribute to having an abortion seems to be a direct result of negative reactions from others, not from the decision itself.

In summary, there is no research evidence to support either of the Supreme Court's assumptions concerning the decisionmaking immaturity and vulnerability of adolescents. In fact, the empirical research suggests the adolescents are more mature and psychologically strong than the Court assumes.

PSYCHOLOGICAL CONSEQUENCES OF ABORTIONS FOR ADULT WOMEN

During the 1980s, about 45 percent of U. S. women experienced at least one unintended pregnancy (Russo, 1992). An unintended pregnancy is one that is not wanted at the time of conception. However, once pregnant, many women decide to have the child, so that although the pregnancy was initially unintended, the birth is wanted. Therefore, an unintended pregnancy is to be distinguished from an unwanted birth. An estimated 54 percent of unintended pregnancies are terminated through legal abortion (Russo, 1992). The reasons for terminating an unintended pregnancy are multiple. In one study, 93 percent of the women gave more than one reason, with the average being four reasons (Torres & Forrest, 1988). There are also wide variations in opportunities, resources, and responsibilities among adult women who seek abortions, often depending on whether they are married or unmarried, mothers or nonmothers.

In reference to the alternative of keeping an unwanted child, Nancy Felipe Russo (1992, p. 594) notes that "...unwanted childbearing has a host of negative physical, psychological and social risks that will vary with the health, age and personality of the mother, her marital status, her relationship with others and her socioeconomic circumstances, among other factors." Russo further finds that the "few available studies of women denied abortion suggest unwanted childbearing can have a profound and long lasting psychological impact" (1992, p. 594). The few well-designed studies that have been done suggest that at least one-third of the women who have an unwanted child still resented the child several years after birth. Moreover, the research indicates that unwanted children are at a much higher risk for psychological and social problems than other children (Russo, 1992).

There has been considerable research examining the emotional and psychological reactions after an abortion, for both minors and adults. Much of it is plagued by methodological shortcomings, but teams of experts (e.g., National Academy of Sciences, 1975, and the Interdivisional Committee of the APA, 1987) who have examined the research have concluded that the great majority of women who have a legal abortion do not suffer any long-lasting, adverse psychological or emotional effects from the abortion, especially if the abortion is done during the first trimester of pregnancy. As noted above in our discussion of the reactions of minors, the "predominant response to a legal abortion, particularly in the first trimester, is relief" (Russo, 1992, p. 613). Distress levels that do occur drop immediately after the abortion for most women and continue to do so for several months (Russo, 1992). In fact, the highest stress levels generally occur before the abortion. The lingering negative reactions that do occur after the abortion are usually mild and transitory. In addition, there is little evidence for a "postabortion syndrome," a variant of post-traumatic stress disorder.

In conclusion, Russo writes:

> The inaccurate portrayal of abortion as having widespread severe negative psychological effects could also subvert women's mental health by undermining the positive coping expectancies that are associated with beneficial mental health outcomes after abortion. Social ostracism and harassment of women seeking abortion could also have harmful mental health effects through inducing negative socially-biased emotions, undermining social support and encouraging unwanted childbearing (1992, pp. 618–19).

Adoption

Over the past two or three decades, the nature of adoption has changed dramatically. In the past, adopting parents were married, white, middle-class, infertile couples who were seeking white infants, preferably newborns. The adoptive landscape now consists of a wider range of adults: fertile couples (with or without biological children of their own), single adults, gay couples, and minority couples. And, although most adoptions in the U. S. are still closed, secretive, and designed to protect everyone's anonymity, there is a growing trend toward greater openness between the biological parent or parents and the adoptive parent or parents (Baran & Pannor, 1990). Marianne Berry (1991), for example, reports that, based on a survey of 1,396 newly adoptive parents in California, a majority of the adoptions were "open" in some form. An **open adoption** is one in which the biological parents and adoptive parents meet and exchange information. In some instances, the biological parents may retain the right to have contact and access to knowledge about the child. Currently, there is very little research evaluating the practice of open adoptive placements (Baran & Pannor, 1990). There is some evidence that adolescents who relinquish their children in an open adoption procedure are generally more satisfied with their decision than

288

CHAPTER
ELEVEN:
PSYCHOLOGY
AND
FAMILY
LAW

adolescent mothers who bear and keep their babies (Russo, 1992). **Transracial** and **transethnic adoption**—particularly of foreign-born children from Asia and Latin America, and of African-American children by white parents—are also becoming more common. All the issues described above are creating greater pressures on the courts to evaluate the appropriateness and soundness of each adoption, and often require the services of psychologists for assessments of the parents and child. Furthermore, a growing number of adoptees have, as adults, started a search for their biological parents, a process laden with all kinds of legal problems as well as potentially explosive psychological ramifications. A majority of the adoptee searchers are women in young adulthood (Schechter & Bertocci, 1990). Most statutes give the courts the power to open sealed court and agency records containing the identity of biological parents if it can be established that revealing the information is for a "good cause." While it is difficult to define precisely what is meant by *good cause*, the term has generally been restricted to situations that pose a serious threat to the physical or emotional well-being of the adoptee (Cole & Donley, 1990).

Searchers also include biological mothers (and sometimes biological fathers) who relinquish the child in the first place. Available research indicates that a large number of these biological parents have considerable difficulty adjusting to their decision many years afterward (Deykin, Campbell & Patti, 1984; Russo, 1992). This distress is especially apparent in mothers who were compelled to relinquish the child through external social pressure. Furthermore, this distress seems to increase rather than decrease over time (Russo, 1992). Russo (p. 622) also notes, "…it appears that if coercion is used to encourage women to use adoption as an alternative to abortion, the risk for the psychological distress after abortion may increase" (p. 622).

The legal process of adoption and the appropriate court (Family Court, Juvenile Court, Probate Court) for its confirmation vary from state to state. However, the powers of the various courts remain essentially the same: They all have the power to permit or deny the adoption (Cole & Donley, 1990). Normally, the agency or the family retains an attorney, then submits a variety of required and relevant documents to the court. The court then sets a date. The judge "…reviews the materials and, based on the validity of the documents and the judge's evaluation in the matter, a legal completion of the adoption is accomplished" (Cole & Conley, 1990, p. 291). The legal completion of the adoption is sometimes referred to as the *finalization*. Most state statutes stipulate a probationary period of about one year from the child's placement with the family before finalization is granted (Cole & Conley, 1990). In some cases, the adoptive family will request a delay in finalization because of their own doubts about the adoption.

The adoption process is fraught with potential psychological or emotional problems for the child, the adoptive parents, and the biological parents, all of which must be carefully considered before and after finalization. Recent research, spearheaded by David Brodzinsky (1987, 1990), has found that adopted children appear to be more vulnerable to psychological problems than nonadoptees. Adopted children make up approximately 2 percent of the total population of the children in the United States (Brodzinsky, 1990). However, they are overrepresented in the portion of the population who are being referred for psychological or behavioral problems. For example, between 4 and 5 percent of the children referred to outpatient mental-health clinics are adopted children, and between 10 and 15 percent of the children in residential care facilities are adoptees (Brodzinsky, 1990). Adoptees are also more likely to display conduct or acting out problems (aggression, stealing, lying, running away) than nonadopted children (Brodzinsky, 1990; Goldberg & Wolkind, 1992). Adoptees are also overrepresented in academic problems (Russo, 1992). The high incidence of psychological problems exists in both children adopted as infants and children adopted at a later age. According to Brodzinsky, the increased psychological and academic risks in children adopted as infants gradually begins to emerge during the elementary school years. It is during the early elementary years that the child begins to understand the meaning and implications of having been adopted. Prior to that time, children lack the cognitive sophistication or the social awareness to appreciate what adoption means, even if it has been explained to them. It is also interesting to note that infertile adoptive parents tend to have more difficulty disclosing the adoptive status to the child than other adoptive parents (Russo, 1992).

Brodzinsky argues that it is a sense of loss that significantly affects the child's psychological well-being: "Simply put, adopted children, once they come to realize the implications of being adopted, not only experience a loss of their biological parents and origins, but also a loss of stability in the relationship of their adoptive parents" (Brodzinsky, 1990, p. 7). Brodzinsky contends that it is a combined loss of self, genealogical continuity, and status associated with being different that often leaves the adoptee feeling incomplete, alienated, disconnected, abandoned, and unwanted. Furthermore, this sense of loss is likely to lead to an emotional and behavioral pattern similar to the grief process. Sants (1964) has coined the term "genealogical bewilderment" to describe the loss and incompleteness experienced by young adolescents trying to connect with their biological pasts.

The research into the psychology of adoption is still in its infancy, but with the growing policy issues surrounding adoption, there will be a great need for psychological research, expert testimony, and services well into the twenty-first century. Other related topics that have been underresearched to date include the psychological effects of surrogate motherhood and fertility techniques, both of which increasingly involve psychologists as expert witnesses.

Divorce and Child Custody

Today, about half of all marriages end in divorce or separation, and approximately two out of every five children grow up in divorced families (Ewing, 1991). If this pattern continues, about 50 percent of the children born in the 1980s will experience their parents' divorce and will spend, on average, about five years in a single-parent home before their custodial parent remarries (Hetherington, Stanley-Hagan & Anderson, 1989). There is also evidence that future divorce rates may be even higher (Martin & Bumpass, 1989; Glenn, 1991).

About 75 percent of divorced mothers and 80 percent of divorced fathers remarry; the divorce rate for remarriages, however, is even higher than for first marriages (Hetherington et al., 1989). Available data also indicate that approximately 2 percent of the population age sixteen and over who have been married at all have been married three or more times (Brody, Neubaum & Forehand, 1988). Therefore, children are at risk not only to suffer the emotional upheaval of family discord associated with the initial divorce, but many also experience a series of marital transitions and household breakups in subsequent divorces. Since mental-health professionals are frequently involved in court decisions regarding divorce and child custody, this is an important topic to cover.

In a divorce, four major areas of potential dispute must be settled: (1) property division; (2) spousal support; and, if there are children, (3) child support; and (4) custody and visitation. Psychological research in the area has focused almost exclusively on issues surrounding custody and visitation, an area we shall emphasize in this chapter. Psychology has gained much knowledge about the psychosocial development and adjustment of children, but not everyone agrees that this knowledge is directly relevant to determining standards and guidelines for legal custody following a separation, divorce, or remarriage (Melton et al., 1987). Mental-health professionals believe they can

290

CHAPTER
ELEVEN:
PSYCHOLOGY
AND
FAMILY
LAW

make valuable contributions to the courts in the area of child custody, primarily due to the extensive research in the area of developmental psychology and the study of family dynamics (Melton et al., 1987); however, mental-health professionals are involved in only a small fraction of custody cases. Approximately 90 percent of custody disputes are settled between the divorcing spouses themselves (Melton et al., 1987), and, in those cases that reach the court, mental-health professionals are involved in only a small number, primarily because many judges and other legal professionals feel that the testimony of clinicians is only occasionally helpful (Melton et al., 1987).

CUSTODIAL ARRANGEMENTS

In most states there are four basic custodial arrangements: sole custody, divided custody, joint custody, and split custody. In addition, these four arrangements are based on two fundamental categories of parental decisionmaking authority: legal and physical. **Legal parental authority** refers to decisionmaking concerning the child's long-term welfare, education, medical care, religious upbringing, and other issues significantly affecting the child's life. **Physical authority** involves decisions affecting only the child's daily activities, such as deciding whether the child can stay overnight at a friend's house, attend a party, or have access to the parent's car. In some situations, however, the dividing line between legal and physical authority is blurred, as when a fifteen-year-old wants to work twenty hours a week to earn extra spending money. It could be argued that although this seems to relate to the child's day-to-day life, the decision may have long-term implications if school work suffers as a result.

The most common arrangement is **sole custody**; one parent receives both legal and physical custody of the child and the other parent does not, although the noncustodial parent usually retains visitation rights. In most sole-custody decisions (85 to 90 percent), the mother becomes the custodial parent and the father the noncustodial parent (Glick, 1988). Another arrangement is **divided custody**; each parent is afforded legal and physical decisionmaking powers, but on an alternating basis. That is, the parental decisionmaking authority shifts (usually on a six-month basis), depending on which parent the child is living with as well as the location of the child's school district. If the parents live close to each other within the child's district, the "shift" may be as often as every five days or weekly. At the time the child is with one parent, that parent makes both the legal and physical decisions for the child. **Joint custody** is an arrangement in which both parents share legal authority but the children live with one parent, who will have the physical authority to make the day-to-day decisions. Deciding upon physical authority, however, is often troublesome in joint-custody arrangements, resulting in conflict and disagreement between the parents. One resolution of this problem is an arrangement called **limited joint custody** in which both parents share legal authority but one parent is given exclusive physical authority and the other parent is awarded liberal visitation rights. **Split custody** is a custodial arrangement in which the legal and physical authority of one or more children is awarded to one parent and the legal and physical authority of the remaining children to the other. Normally, each parent is given reciprocal visitation rights. Although there may be variants of any of the above arrangements, one of the four is generally observed.

JUDICIAL DECISIONMAKING DOCTRINES

Courts usually make decisions based on two doctrines: (1) the tender-years doctrine; and (2) the best-interests-of-the-child doctrine. The **tender-years doctrine** is derived from the traditional belief that the mother is the parent ideally and inherently suited to care for children of a "tender age" (Santilli & Roberts, 1990). Specifically, it means that if the courts must make a decision on custody of the child or children, then the mother is presumably the parent who can provide the best care, unless she be proven unfit. The tender-years doctrine was articulated as follows by an Illinois Appellate Court in 1899, in *People v. Hickey*: "In awarding care and custody of children of divorced persons, an infant of tender years will generally be left with the mother, where no objection is shown to exist as to her, even if the father be without blame, *because of the father's inability to bestow on it that tender care which nature requires, and which it is the peculiar province of the mother to supply*; and this rule will apply with much force in case of female children of a more advanced age" (quoted in Einhorn, 1986, p. 128).

Over the past three decades, the tender-years doctrine has been abolished or abandoned in a growing number of states, largely on the basis of three challenges (Santilli & Roberts, 1990). First, it has been argued that the tender-years doctrine is a violation of the equal protection provided under the Fourteenth Amendment (Radcliff, 1977). Second, the doctrine is also in violation of equal-rights amendments found in many state constitutions. Third, it makes a number of psychological assumptions about parenting which may or may not be valid. Whether the courts will actually abandon this doctrine remains to be seen. Current data suggest that maternal sole custody is still the pervasively dominant type of custody agreed upon by parents and confirmed by the courts under the best-interests-of-the-child standard (Lowery, 1986). In addition, Hellman (cited in Bolocofsky, 1989) reports that older judges are more apt to rely on the tender-years doctrine, even when the evidence indicates the father may be the better parent. Other writers have reported that the tender-years doctrine is still subscribed to by many of the courts (Bolocofsky, 1989; Santilli & Roberts, 1990).

The **best interests of the child** has become the standard in most courts when rendering custody decisions. According to this doctrine, the parents' legal rights should be secondary to what is best for the child. During the 1970s, the standard rapidly became popular and was strongly advocated as a replacement for the tender-years doctrine. However, the best interest standard has been criticized for being overly vague and leaving too much discretion to the judge. For example, what precisely constitutes effective or better parenting?

Because it is often extremely difficult to choose between two fit parents, joint custody is becoming increasingly favored by the courts. However, unless the court appoints a *guardian ad litem,* or the judge (in a contested custody case) interviews the children, very little attention is paid to the children's preferences. Split custody and divided custody are generally not seen as arrangements that are conducive to proper child development (and thus in the best interests of the child) because they involve shifting and shuttling the children back and forth. Thus, split and divided custody are rarely awarded.

By the early 1990s, thirty-three states had adopted joint-custody legislation (Crosbie-Burnett, 1991). Even among states that do not have joint-custody legislation, courts seem to prefer to use the **friendly parent rule** (Melton et al., 1987). Here, sole custody is granted to the parent most likely to facilitate the noncustodial parent's involvement with the child, as it is presumed that frequent contact with both parents is in the best interest of the child.

PSYCHOLOGICAL EFFECTS OF DIVORCE AND CUSTODY DECISIONS

The psychological effects of divorce and custody decisions must be looked at separately, because they represent two discernible sequences in the life of the child. The psychological effects of divorce can be divided into three central issues: (1) the effects of parental absence on the child; (2) the effects of economic disadvantage as a result of the divorce; and (3) the effects of family conflict on the development of the child (Amato & Keith, 1991).

292

CHAPTER
ELEVEN:
PSYCHOLOGY
AND
FAMILY
LAW

Divorce

The most heavily cited empirical studies on the effects of divorce are the Virginia Longitudinal Study of Divorce conducted by E. Mavis Hetherington, M. Cox, and R. Cox, and the Judith S. Wallerstein ongoing studies of sixty divorced families in Northern California. The Virginia project was a quasi-experimental study of seventy-two white, middle-class four- and five-year-old children and their divorced parents. The researchers learned that marital discord and divorce often result in an increase in behavioral problems, and that the nature of these problems is largely dependent on the age of the child (Hetherington, 1979). Furthermore, these behavioral problems were generally more pervasive and longer-lasting for boys than girls (Hetherington, 1979). Emotional disturbances and social-adjustment problems in girls largely disappeared within two years after the divorce. Moreover, the period of adjustment for children seems to be longer in remarriages than in divorce, especially for older children (Hetherington et al., 1989).

The Wallerstein project (Wallerstein & Kelly, 1980; Wallerstein, 1988, 1989) is an extensive clinical investigation of 131 children and their parents from sixty predominately white, middle-class families. Wallerstein found that children's initial responses to divorce depended on, among other things, the individual differences in the children's perception of the divorce, developmental factors, and their adaptive capacities. Each age group had different reactions to the divorce, ranging from anger to regression.

James Bray (1990, 1991), in his work on the effects of divorce, also emphasizes that children's reactions to parental separation, divorce, and remarriage differ significantly as a function of age. Bray posits that these events are not necessarily worse for children of certain ages, only that children of various ages have different reactions and, in some cases, different behavior disorders. He notes that there is yet no direct evidence on the effects of custodial or visitation arrangements for infants (birth to six months), although research on the effects of daycare on infants may provide helpful information for making custody decisions.

The daycare research suggests that very young children can adapt to short and regular separations from custodial parents. During the preschool ages (three to five years), children may experience separation anxiety (fear of leaving parent) if their parents also become particularly tense and upset about the parent-child separation. As Bray notes, children are generally highly susceptible to the feelings of parents at this age and react, sometimes strongly, to any conflict between parents. During the school age and preadolescent period, children have developed clear preferences for one or both parents and are very sensitive to subtle pressures and loyalty conflicts between parents (Bray, 1991). Further, Bray finds that children at this age are usually not able to understand divorce fully or to separate themselves psychologically from parental influence. However, during adolescence, children are usually able to understand the divorce process and tend not to be overly influenced by parental wishes or reactions.

In their review of the literature, Amato and Keith (1991) conclude that children of divorce have lower levels of well-being than do children who experience parental death. This finding, Amato and Keith note, suggests that there must be something else operating in divorced family dynamics than simple parental loss. Amato and Keith also find that children living with a stepparent exhibit significantly more problems than do children living with both biological parents.

As noted previously, divorce often leads to a decline in the standard of living, particularly in mother-headed families. Furthermore, the conflict between the parents before and after the divorce is assumed to impose stress on children. However, the research shows that the economic effects of divorce are only modestly associated with the well-being of the children. On the other hand, the negative effect of family conflict on the emotional well-being of children is commonly reported in the literature. In fact, the evidence suggests that children of divorced families appear to have a higher level of well-being than do children of high-conflict intact families. Postdivorce conflict between parents is also associated with a low level of well-being among children.

Research on the *long-term* effects of divorce suggests that a majority of children adjust well to divorce (Grych & Fincham, 1992). Children seem to be more competent, resilient, and adaptive than adults assume. In fact, many parents have more difficulty adjusting to divorce than the children. But there is some evidence that, at least over the *short term*, some children do have difficulty adjusting. According to Grych and Fincham, most of the child behavioral problems reported in divorced families are **externalizing problems** (behavior directed against the social environment). That is, aggression and conduct problems are more prevalent in children from divorced families than in children from intact families (Camara & Resnick, 1988). This seems especially the case for boys. The literature also reports a number of **internalizing problems** (such as depression, anxiety, and social withdrawal) in children who have experienced divorce, particularly during the first two years after the divorce (Grych & Fincham, 1992). Whether the psychological reactions and behavioral problems demonstrated by children of divorced parents are directly due to the divorce or other factors is unclear. Some research, for example, reports that child behavioral problems, assumed to be caused by divorce, may have existed long before the divorce proceedings began, while the family was still intact (Block, Block & Gjerde, 1986).

Custody Arrangements

Solid, systematic study of the psychological effects on children of custody disputes and decisions remains a rarity, and the few empirical studies that have been done generally focus on variables other than psychological impact (Wolman & Taylor, 1991). Two early reviews of the research on joint custody concluded that the available research offers little conclusive evidence about the positives and negatives of joint custody on the development of children (Clingempeel & Reppucci, 1982; Scott & Derdeyn, 1984). In their review, Clingempeel and Reppucci assert: "The available studies [on joint custody] are egregiously inadequate, and for the most part the debates have been nourished solely by opposing ideologies" (1982, p. 124). A large portion of the few studies conducted on joint custody have been primarily based on subjective clinical impressions. At this point, the evidence gathered so far suggests that, in most instances, joint-custody arrangements appear to be psychologically more healthy for the children involved than sole custody (Kelly, 1988). However, the available research also indicates that the overall effects of joint-custody may be only slightly more positive than other forms of custody arrangements (Grych & Finchman, 1992). It seems more likely that the type of custody arrangement may be less important in influencing the child's adjustment than the quality of the family relationships after the divorce.

One recent empirical study by Margaret Crosbie-Burnett (1991) examined the effects of joint-custody and sole-custody arrangements on white adolescents living in remarried families. Seventy-eight families living in a small midwestern city volunteered for the project. The Revised Children's Manifest Anxiety Scale and Step-family Adjustment Scale were administered in each family's home and used as measures of adjustment. The results support the hypothesis that adolescents in joint-custody arrangements are better adjusted than those of sole-custody arrangements. Some significant gender differences also emerged. The adolescent girls seemed to benefit more from joint custody than the boys, but the reasons for this difference remain unclear.

In summary, conclusions concerning the psychological effects of divorce or custodial arrangements are difficult to make because much of the research is (1) inconclusive, (2) of limited generalizability, and (3) flawed by serious methodological problems (Grych & Fincham, 1992; Barber & Eccles, 1992). Very few longitudinal studies have been conducted, making it nearly impossible to untangle preexisting differences in values, behavior patterns, and personality from

294

CHAPTER
ELEVEN:
PSYCHOLOGY
AND
FAMILY
LAW

differences that are directly a result of divorce (Block, Block & Gjerde, 1986).

Although the research on the psychological effects of custodial arrangements on children remains inconclusive, there are trends in the data. What little evidence we have suggests that a child's adjustment to various arrangements depends on many factors, including the age and gender of the child, the length of time the process takes place, family economic resources, parental conflict before and after the divorce, and the personality differences of the child (Barber & Eccles, 1992). There is some evidence that joint custody may be slightly better for the child from a psychological perspective, but these effects may be due to the quality of the postdivorce relationship between the custodial parents rather than the arrangement itself.

DIVORCE MEDIATION

Divorce mediation is the process of trying to resolve divorce disputes with the help of a professional mediator. A primary objective of the process is to reduce the adversarial relations between the divorcing parties. Adversarial maneuvering by the parties often prolongs court involvement and affects minor children in a negative way. Adversary court proceedings, particularly relative to custody determinations, often further strain fragile relationships between the divorcing parents and their children.

"In divorce mediation, the marital partners meet together with an impartial third party in order to identify, discuss, and ultimately resolve their disputes" (Emery & Wyer, 1987a, p. 472). The goal is not reconciliation but negotiation of a fair agreement between the parties. Traditionally, divorce settlements have been reached either through litigation or out-of-court negotiations between the parties' lawyers. Divorce mediation differs from these traditional and often bruising strategies in three ways: (1) the communication takes place with a single professional mediator; (2) the mediation is based on the assumption that the parties will cooperate; and (3) the parties make their own decisions (Emery & Wyer, 1987a). The third feature also distinguishes mediation from arbitration (Emery & Wyer, 1987a), because mediators have no authority to impose decisions on the parties; rather, they act as neutral agents who provide opinions and guidance in the search for a settlement. Professional mediators who are members of the Family Mediation and Association must have a minimum of forty hours' training. They frequently are trained psychologists, social workers, or sometimes attorneys.

Robert Emery and Melissa Wyer identify two major reasons why divorce mediation has become so popular during the past two decades. One is the enactment of "no-fault" divorce laws by all fifty states, a development that renders mediation a reasonable alternative to adversary proceedings. The second involves changes in the guidelines for awarding custody: "The rapid increase in no-fault divorce and elimination of the tender-years presumption leave the judiciary with no strong guidelines for making custody determinations as the best-interests standard is a vague directive open to many alternative interpretations" (Emery & Wyer, 1987a, p. 473). The best solution in many instances, therefore, rests with divorce mediation, through which a voluntary settlement and custody arrangement can be reached.

Mediation keeps a significant number of families out of court, and custody agreements reached through this process take half the time of in-court litigation (Emery, Matthews & Wyer, 1991; Emery & Wyer, 1987a). Between one-half and three-quarters of couples who go through mediation are believed to reach mutually satisfactory agreements. Available data also suggest that court mediators work primarily with divorcing partners who have attempted but failed to reach a settlement out of court (Emery & Wyer, 1987a). Joint custody is the most common mediation agreement. Mediation also appears to reduce substantially the amount of relitigation (going back

■ **11.1: MEDIATION: NEW KID ON THE BLOCK**

ALTERNATIVE DISPUTE RESOLUTION (ADR), sometimes called simply *mediation*, is catching fire nationwide, even in the legal profession. In both civil and criminal arenas, it is being hailed as the perfect solution to unclogging court dockets, obtaining satisfactory settlements, and solving problems in a rational manner.

Mediation services have become popular in the corporate world. In its March 22, 1993 edition, the *Wall Street Journal* reported that in 1992 alone, more than 40,000 civil cases that once would have been handled in the courts were resolved by four major mediation firms. Companies engaging in mediation save themselves legal fees, costs of expert witnesses, and the toll of pursuing a case in the courts.

ADR is increasingly used in citizen-to-citizen disputes, family courts, and the criminal-justice system as well. People who use mediation services in civil cases are reported to be more satisfied with the outcome. This is because mediation is quicker than going through the courts, and the parties are all involved in crafting a solution, rather than having a solution imposed upon them. On the other hand, critics of mediation urge caution, because it can easily become "second-class justice" for individuals who are unable to afford the cost of a lawyer.

In the criminal context, ADR is used thus far primarily in misdemeanor cases. In a simple assault case involving two neighbors, for example, the conviction of one will not solve the underlying problem that exists. Mediation, on the other hand, focuses on trying to do just that.

With respect to mediation in the domestic violence context, however, the concerns expressed by Rifkin (1989) cannot be overstated. When two parties go into mediation with unequal power, there is danger that the less powerful party will be at a major disadvantage. This dissymmetry could be overcome with the help of skillful, knowledgeable, and compassionate mediators. Unless they are available, however, we should guard against embracing mediation as a panacea to the complex issues associated with domestic violence. ■

---

to court) on custody arrangements. Despite these findings, mediation is not necessarily the best alternative in divorce situations, as we will note below.

Psychological Effects of Mediation

Data on the broad psychological impact of mediation and litigation on all parties concerned are virtually nonexistent (Emery & Wyer, 1987a). Preliminary data suggest, however, that divorcing parties are generally more satisfied with mediation than with adversary procedures (Emery & Wyer, 1987a). However, Emery and his colleagues caution that, when couples have children, there may be some differences between mothers and fathers in satisfaction with the mediation (Emery & Wyer, 1987a; Emery, Matthews & Wyer, 1991). Men reported considerably greater satisfaction with the mediation process than women. Specifically, men were positive about its impact on them personally as well as on their relationships with their former spouses. Women, on the other hand, felt positive about its effect on the children, but felt that they personally won less and lost more than did women who had gone through litigation. Women who experienced mediation also reported more depression than women who went through litigation for custody determination (Emery, Matthews & Wyer, 1991).

One explanation for these negative aspects of mediation could be the residual effects of the long-standing tender-years presumption, which had traditionally favored awarding custody to the mother. Thus, within that legal tradition, mediation may be seen as a loss for mothers and gain for fathers. Several writers have argued that the reasons for these discrepancies lie in a culturally-developed power imbalance between men and women (Emery & Wyer, 1987a; Grych & Fincham, 1992; Rifkin, 1989). Men have traditionally been employed in occupations that require negotiation, bargaining, financial, and management skills. Thus, many women who have not acquired such expertise through employment may be at a strong disadvantage in mediation. Furthermore, women often have less power in the marital relationship. Therefore, although the

296

CHAPTER
ELEVEN:
PSYCHOLOGY
AND
FAMILY
LAW

mediation process assumes the parties are on equal footing, this is often not the case. Rifkin (1989) adds that mediators themselves may not be well trained to understand the dynamics of such unequal circumstances. When gender imbalances cannot be recognized and accounted for, mediation should not be undertaken.

Domestic Violence

During the 1970s and 1980s, family violence came to the forefront of public attention, and research in that area has proliferated. Although the field originally focused on parental assault of children and spousal abuse, it has since expanded to encompass sibling violence and abuse of elderly parents by their adult children. However, because of difficulties in arriving at a definition of "family," many researchers prefer the term **domestic violence**, to refer to behavior among residents of a household. Thus, nonmarried couples with or without children, adults caring for unrelated children or elderly persons, and long-term roommates would all come under the rubric. Although there is research in all of the above areas, we will concentrate on child and wife abuse, the two areas which have received the most attention.

CHILD ABUSE AND NEGLECT

The modern era of domestic violence research began in 1962 when a Denver pediatrician, C. Henry Kempe, and four of his medical colleagues published a paper entitled "The Battered Child Syndrome" in the *Journal of the American Medical Association*. The article documented evidence of repeated multiple bone fractures in children suspected of being abused. The paper certainly was not the only precipitating factor in prompting interests and research in child abuse. During the 1960s, an influential child welfare movement, intent on drawing public and political attention to the plight of abused and neglected children, was also a strong factor.

It was not until the last three or four decades that society began to realize that child abuse is a serious matter, worthy of state scrutiny. Even in 1970, national polls reported that only 10 percent of the general population considered child abuse a serious problem. In 1983, however, over 90 percent of the population considered it a serious problem (Wolfe, 1985).

State governments and the courts have traditionally claimed that family relationships require or deserve special immunity from the law and have given parents broad authority in the rearing of their children. Included in this traditional perspective is the contention that parents have the right to discipline children as they see fit, even if it involves physical punishment. This view has been energetically challenged during the past three decades by various interest groups attempting not only to acquaint the public with the problem but also to activate lawmakers toward more stringent and social sanctions. While the U. S. Supreme Court apparently prefers not to address the issue of parental authority directly, the states have continued to develop broad international powers under child protection laws (Bulkley, 1988).

The **doctrine of family privacy** is at the heart of the legal and legislative debate about acceptable governmental intervention into family life. According to that doctrine, what goes on within the intact family unit is of concern only to the family itself, as long as there is no serious threat to any member or members of the family. Thus, "the taking of life, parental incest, and the imminent threat to the life or health of a minor child all trigger the law's willingness to penetrate the privacy of family life because the family privacy considerations are outweighed by other important public goals" (Zimring, 1989, pp. 552–53). Otherwise, the privacy of the family has been traditionally held sacred.

Zimring (1989) uses the case of *McGuire v. McGuire* (1953) to illustrate the seeming contradictions in the law when courts deal with the family context. Mrs. McGuire, age 66, sued her 79-year-old husband to enforce a marital duty to allow her to purchase furniture and other household necessities, including a kitchen sink, indoor bathing facilities, and an indoor toilet. The couple could easily have afforded these luxuries. However, the Nebraska court rejected the woman's request, ruling that it could not intervene so long as they lived as husband and wife. The court said "the living standards of the family are a matter of concern to the household, and not for the courts to determine, even though the husband's attitude toward the wife, according to his [sic] wealth and circumstances, leaves little to be said on his behalf" (quoted in Zimring, 1989, p. 550). The court asserted that, if Mrs. McGuire left home, she would be entitled to support from her husband in a style that was in accordance with his income.

The implications of cases like the above take on a sobering tone when considered in the context of assault. The law traditionally has not accepted that behavior which is illegal outside the family should also be illegal within it. Because children and women were historically considered the property of the adult male figure, the law was reluctant to step in. Consider these words, from *Joyner v. Joyner*, an 1862 North Carolina case:

> The wife must be subject to her husband. Every man must govern his household, and if by reason of an unruly temper, or an unbridled tongue, the wife persistently treats her husband with disrespect, and he submits to it, he not only loses all sense of self-respect, but loses the respect of the other members of his family.... [T]here may be circumstances which will mitigate, excuse, and so far justify the husband in striking the wife with a horse-whip on one occasion and with a switch on another, leaving several bruises on the person.... .

Despite modern reforms, family privacy continues to play a substantial role in the development and enactment of family law (Zimring, 1989). Thus, the physical discipline of children is usually not for legal review unless it represents a gross threat to the child; however, the manner in which each parent disciplines the child can become an issue in divorce cases where custody is contested: "[The] spanking parent may, for example, be immune from tort liability [or criminal prosecution], yet the same inappropriate physical discipline may deprive him or her the custody of a child after divorce" (Zimring, 1989, p. 554). The family's right to privacy dissipates when the family dissolves.

In recent years the label *battered-child syndrome* has given way to terms like child abuse, child abuse and neglect, and child maltreatment. The existence of child sexual abuse syndrome (CSAS) has also been proposed, and has received considerable attention. We will discuss CSAS in more detail later in the chapter. The most common term, *child abuse*, which Kempe had restricted to physical violence, has become increasingly broad, encompassing a wide assortment of behaviors and misbehaviors by parents and caretakers. Currently, research on child abuse is the most advanced, sophisticated, and extensive in the field of domestic violence (Finkelhor & Lewis, 1988).

The National Incidence Study (NIS), sponsored by the National Center on Child Abuse and Neglect, estimated that 625,000 American children were neglected or abused during 1980 (U. S. Department of Health and Human Services, 1982). Approximately 208,000 of this total were physically assaulted, with fatal injuries occurring in about 1,000 cases and serious injury occurring in another 137,000 cases. In 1986, a second National Incidence Study (NIS-2) was done. Both the 1980 and 1988 studies obtained abuse and neglect information from public schools, children's hospitals, police and sheriff's departments, mental-health agencies, probation departments, and county health departments. NIS-2 discovered that between 1980 and 1986 the number of child-abuse

298

CHAPTER
ELEVEN:
PSYCHOLOGY
AND
FAMILY
LAW

or neglect cases increased substantially. In 1986, 1,584,700 children were reported abused or neglected, an increase of nearly a million children over the 1980 figure. Of this total, 675,000 were classified as abused children, including 358,300 classified as physically abused, 155,900 sexually abused, and 211,100 emotionally abused. An *emotionally abused* child is one who receives at least one of three kinds of maltreatment: close confinement, frequent verbal or emotional assaults, or deprivation of the basic necessities of life (food, water, shelter, or sleep) for extended periods. Close confinement refers to cases in which the child was tied, bound, or confined in a closet or very small enclosure for extended periods of time. Verbal or emotional assault describes cases where the child was constantly belittled, denigrated, or threatened with sexual or physical abuse. Like the 1980 NIS report, NIS-2 found that approximately 1,100 children died of injuries suffered during physical abuse.

According to experts, the dramatic increase in child-abuse cases is not necessarily due to any explosion in maltreatment of children. Rather, it probably reflects a combination of better recording procedures and more awareness on the part of social agencies, the public, and medical professionals, leading to increased reporting.

The American Humane Association (AHA) (1987) also collects data from child-protective service agencies in all fifty states, the District of Columbia, Puerto Rico, the U. S. Virgin Islands, Guam, and the Mariana Islands. The AHA defines **abuse** as a report of intentional, nonaccidental injury, harm, or sexual assault inflicted on a child. **Neglect** is defined as failure of a caretaker to provide essential care to a child, such as food, clothing, shelter, medical attention, education, or supervision. The AHA reported that in 1986 (the same year as reported in NIS-2), 2,086,112 children were abused or neglected in the United States and its territories. Thus, according to the AHA data, the prevalence of child abuse and neglect is 32 out of every 1,000 American children compared to the NIS-2 rate of 24 per 1,000. The discrepancy between the NIS-2 and the AHA data is due to a number of factors. Agencies define abuse differently, collect data from different sources, and vary significantly in procedures and methodology. For example, the AHA includes both unsubstantiated and substantiated complaints in its survey, whereas NIS-2 includes only substantiated or documented cases.

About 10 to 12 percent of all reports of child abuse involve sexual abuse (Levine & Battistoni, 1991). The incidence rate for child sexual victims in the United States is about 21 per 10,000 children under age eighteen (Knudsen, 1991). Child sexual abuse victims are more likely to be females at all age levels, with the overall ratio being about four girls to every one boy (Knudsen, 1991). Most sexually abused children (about two-thirds) are victimized only once (Risin & Koss, 1987; Dube & Hebert, 1988; Knudsen, 1991). It is important to add that these data represent *known* victimization, not abuse which is not brought to the attention of authorities.

LEGAL PROCESS IN CHILD-ABUSE CASES

By 1967, child-abuse reporting laws were in effect in all fifty states. Criminal penalties for willful failure to report suspected cases have been established in forty-five states (Finlayson & Koocher, 1991). These laws require specified professionals who are likely to come in contact with children (e.g., pediatricians, social workers, nurses, teachers, psychologists, family counselors, psychiatrists) to report suspected abuse and neglect to all child-protective agencies (Zellman, 1990). However, exactly what behaviors or indicators prompt a professional to report a suspected case of child abuse is not at all clear. Moreover, there is some evidence that female professionals are more likely to report child sexual abuse than male professionals (Attias & Goodwin, 1985; Finlayson & Koocher, 1991).

■ 11.2: ANATOMICALLY CORRECT DOLLS

THE USE OF ANATOMICALLY CORRECT DOLLS as aids in obtaining information from children who have allegedly been sexually abused is a controversial practice. Anatomically correct dolls have breasts (if female), genitalia, and pubic hair. They are used primarily with children under age six in discussions with psychologists, psychiatrists, or social workers. Critics of this practice maintain that these dolls heighten the child's suggestibility and stimulate sexual fantasies, thereby throwing into question the validity of the child's reports. Those who support their use, however, say the dolls facilitate a meaningful exchange between the interviewer and the child.

The research to date indicates that the dolls do not lead children who have not been abused to make false reports of abuse (e.g., Goodman and Aman, 1990). However, the dolls are not a failsafe method for obtaining information, and should be used only by trained examiners.

Boat and Everson (1988) provide helpful suggestions for examiners who wish to use anatomically correct dolls:

- Use commercially manufactured dolls, which have been carefully tested and are less likely to be flawed.
- Use four dolls: an adult male, adult female, child female, and child male. More dolls may be added if it is believed the child has been victimized by more than one individual.
- Initially, dolls should be presented with their clothes on.
- Match dolls to the race of the child; if the suspected perpetrator is of a different race, the child should be allowed to choose dolls.
- Interview the child in a comfortable room with a one-way mirror to avoid needlessly subjecting the child to multiple interviews with other individuals.
- If law-enforcement officers are in the vicinity of the interview, they should be wearing civilian clothes and not have weapons in sight.
- Interview the child alone, unless the child cannot separate from the caretaker or needs an interpreter.
- Plan on two or three interviews, each lasting about thirty minutes.
- Siblings should always be interviewed separately.

Boat and Everson include an excellent structured doll interview format, suggesting specific wording for questions and directions. Examples include: "Does this doll look like a boy or a girl?" "Let's take off the doll's shirt." "Has anyone touched your——?" (using the word the child has used for genitalia).

They remind examiners, though, that the sexual abuse investigation process itself can be a traumatic event for the child, arousing fears of harm and separation from family members. Many children also need to hear assurances that the alleged incident was not their fault. Nevertheless, the examiner must avoid making promises that she or he may not be able to keep, such as promises that the abuse will never happen again. ■

Child-abuse cases may be litigated through a confusing array of legal proceedings: criminal prosecution, dependency proceedings, child custody and visitation litigation, proceedings to terminate parental rights, civil proceedings initiated by victims for monetary damages, and even civil litigation against child-welfare agencies (Sagatun, 1991). Most commonly, however, two basic forms of legal intervention occur in child-abuse or neglect cases: criminal prosecution against the offender, and/or child protection intervention and civil action in juvenile or family court (Bulkley, 1988). Either one or both interventions may take place. It should be mentioned that many victims of child abuse (sexual or otherwise) refuse to testify against their abusers not only because they fear the abuser, but also because they fear being moved away from the only home they know.

Bulkley notes that sexual abuse of a child by an adult typically results in criminal prosecution, whereas parental physical abuse or neglect usually results in child-protection intervention, unless the child is permanently or severely injured or dies. In recent years, however, victims of child sexual abuse—some of which occurred years ago—are filing more civil lawsuits seeking monetary damage awards, either against individuals or institutions such as schools, daycare centers, and churches (Bulkley, 1988). Moreover, American society has seen a discernible shift

300

CHAPTER
ELEVEN:
PSYCHOLOGY
AND
FAMILY
LAW

away from a therapeutic approach and toward a more punitive approach to abusive parents. During the 1980s legislatures enacted harsher penalties for child abuse of all kinds and increased the emphasis on criminal prosecution (Myers, 1985, 1986). One of the consequences of this legislative action is the demand for testimony from children.

No national statistics are available on the number of child sexual-abuse victims who are required to testify in criminal prosecutions. Prosecutors report, however, that children in the United States are more likely to testify in sexual-abuse cases than in any other kind of criminal case (Goodman et al., 1992).

Aspects of the criminal adversary process may have a negative impact upon the child's emotional well-being. These include facing the defendant, the jury, and the public throughout a trial; subjection to insensitive gynecological exams and polygraph tests; and long delays in the legal process (Bulkley, 1988). Recognizing the stress involved in testifying in a criminal proceeding, the U. S. Supreme Court ruled in 1990 (*Craig v. Maryland*) that the closed-circuit testimony of a child witness in a sexual assault case did not deprive the defendant of his Sixth Amendment right to confront witnesses against him.

From a legal point of view, child abuse, especially sexual abuse, is often difficult to prove. Corroborative testimony from more than one person is generally a critical feature in normal court cases, particularly those involving sexual assault or abuse. In response to the Women's Movement, many states have amended their rape laws to remove corroboration requirements (Levine & Battistoni, 1991). In recognition that the victim is often the only witness, these protections were later extended to child victims of sexual abuse. However, despite expanding procedural reform, empirical research on the immediate or long-term psychological reaction of children to court involvement and testimony is scarce and mostly limited to anecdotal data (Goodman et al., 1992).

Child protective cases, where decisions must be made to remove custody from parents on a temporary or permanent basis, are heard in family or juvenile courts. The family-court judge is given considerable discretion and may adjust the rules of evidence to protect child victims of abuse (Levine & Basttistoni, 1991). For example, if the judge feels it may be psychologically damaging for the child to testify in court, the child may be excused from doing so. Evidence of the alleged abuse, therefore, may be introduced in the form of a child's testimony gathered out of court. Expert testimony (by psychologists, social workers, and psychiatrists) becomes especially essential in these cases, because the expert provides "validation testimony."

The juvenile-court system, which is separate in some states from the family court, also plays a significant role in the legal response to child abuse. A request for juvenile court action is usually initiated either by law-enforcement or child-protective services, and the decision to continue with the petition rests with the county or prosecuting attorney (Myers, 1985, 1986).

Guardian ad Litem

Courts have relied increasingly on independent child advocates as part of the child-protection proceedings when abuse or neglect is alleged, as well as for a wide range of other situations, including delinquency proceedings. Duquette defines *guardian ad litem* as "a broad legal term referring to an individual officially appointed by the court to provide a range of types of representation in court proceedings. The term can apply to those appointed to represent the interests of individuals who are in some way incapacitated (for example, by old age, mental condition, or youth)" (1990, p. 21).

The *guardians ad litem* (literally "guardians for this litigation") serve a different function when children are involved than they serve in other forms of civil litigation, however, because the interests of the child are primarily psychological rather than monetary (Duquette, 1990). In much civil litigation, the protection is focused on financial and property matters. On the other hand, psychological interests may well enter other situations, as when guardians protect the interest of a person at risk of involuntary civil commitment to a mental institution.

In 1974, Congress enacted the Child Abuse and Neglect Prevention and Treatment Act, which requires the appointment of a *guardian ad litem* to represent the child in child-abuse or neglect cases that result in a judicial proceeding. The *guardian ad litem* does not have to be an attorney and very often is not. Currently, however, most state statutes also authorize the courts to appoint special legal representation for the child in custody or child-protection proceedings (Horowitz & Davidson, 1984). In delinquency proceedings, children have a constitutional right to a lawyer, although this right is very often waived, as we will see later in the chapter. In the 1988 reauthorization of the act, Congress continued to require the appointment of *guardians ad litem* to represent children in child-protection proceedings but remained silent on their specific duties.

PSYCHOLOGICAL EFFECTS OF CHILD SEXUAL ABUSE

The overwhelming evidence from both clinical and empirical studies is that most victims of sexual abuse are negatively affected by their experiences (Haugaard & Reppucci, 1988). However, the long-term effects of child sexual abuse are unclear and appear to differ significantly from individual to individual. Some victims apparently suffer no negative long-term consequences. On the other hand, many studies with adults confirm the long-term effects of sexual abuse mentioned in the clinical literature for a majority of the victims (Browne & Finkelhor, 1986). For example, adult women who were sexually victimized as children are more likely to manifest depression, self-destructive behavior, anxiety, feelings of isolation and stigma, poor self-esteem, and substance abuse. A history of childhood sexual abuse is also associated with greater risk for mental health and adjustment problems in adulthood. Children seem to suffer the immediate effects of abuse as well; one-fifth to two-fifths of sexually abused children who are seen in mental-health clinics manifest some type of psychological disturbance (Tufts, 1984).

Studies also indicate that sexual abuse by fathers or stepfathers has a more negative impact than abuse by perpetrators outside the home. Moreover, presence of force or physical coercion seems to result in more trauma for the victim (Browne & Finkelhor, 1986). Not surprisingly, experiences involving intercourse or attempted intercourse and genital contact by mouth seem to be more troubling than acts involving touching of unclothed breasts or genitals. Penetration is especially traumatic for the victim.

It must be emphasized that studies reporting these findings are often plagued by sample, design, and measurement problems that may undermine the validity of their findings. For example, results are often based on either adult women seeking treatment or children whose molestation has been reported (Browne & Finkelhor, 1986). These samples are very self-selected, because many victims never seek counsel. Some of the studies suggesting long-term trauma associated with child sexual abuse are actually reports of the prevalence of trauma among specialized populations, such as prostitutes or psychiatric patients. This by no means diminishes the seriousness of child sexual abuse. It merely emphasizes that research in the area must be improved, by such means as obtaining random samples from the general population.

The **child sexual abuse syndrome** (CSAS), also called the **child sexual abuse accommodation syndrome** (CSAAS), originally proposed by Summit (1983), has received considerable attention in the literature in recent years. The syndrome is reserved to describe a cluster of behaviors that occur in children who have been victims of sexual abuse by a family member or an adult with whom the child has a trusting relationship. According to Summit, children do not necessarily have an innate sense that sexual activity between an adult and a child is wrong. However, their privacy

302

CHAPTER
ELEVEN:
PSYCHOLOGY
AND
FAMILY
LAW

is violated and they are placed in fear because the adult usually pressures or threatens the child to prevent others from knowing about the activity. Often, the abuser presents these threats and pressures in such a way that the child is led to believe something terrible will happen (perhaps to a family member) if this "private" knowledge is shared. Hence, the child is placed in the position of being responsible for the welfare of the family. The child also feels helpless to stop the activity. Thus, the child must *accommodate* these secrets into his or her daily living pattern.

The behavioral indicators of CSAS may be seen in all ages, alone, or in combinations of two or more (Koszuth, 1991). The child may become overly compliant and unable to make decisions. The child may also present a facade of mature behavior because she or he is now called on to take more responsibility for the safety and care of the family. According to Koszuth (1991), the list of behavior indicators of sexual abuse also includes persistent and inappropriate sexual play (including sexual aggressiveness) with peers or toys; detailed and age-inappropriate understanding of sexual behavior; arriving early at school and leaving late, combined with few absences; extraordinary fear of adult males; running away from home; poor peer relationships or inability to make friends; depression; expression of suicidal feelings; and sleep disturbances. It is also usual for the child to delay reporting or talking about the sexual abuse, and some refuse to talk about it at all.

Since the gathering of physical or medical evidence is extremely difficult, CSAS is sometimes used by the courts to supplement a victim's testimony. Several courts have allowed the evidence to be admitted (e.g., *Keri v. State*, 1986; *People v. Gray*, 1986; *People v. Luna*, 1988; *People v. Payan*, 1985), but others have not (e.g., *Johnson v. State*, 1987; *Lantrip v. Commonwealth*, 1986; *People v. Bowker*, 1988; *People v. Roscoe*, 1985; *State v. Haseltine*, 1984). See Sagatun (1991) for more detail on these cases and Box 11.3 for another example. Sagatun posits that CSAS has been admitted in criminal cases primarily as rebuttal to the notion that the child's behavior does not reflect sexual abuse. On the other hand, courts have rejected expert opinion that utilizes CSAS as evidence that sexual abuse did occur.

However, there is still question whether the child sexual abuse syndrome actually exists. Haugaard & Reppucci, for example, write: "The principal flaw with the notion of a specific syndrome is that no evidence indicates that it can discriminate between sexually abused children and those who have experienced other trauma. Because the task of a court is to make such discriminations, this flaw is fatal" (1989, pp. 177–78). According to Haugaard and Reppucci, a syndrome must have **discriminant ability**. This means that a group of behaviors must occur regularly in a group of children who have had certain experiences, and they must not occur in children who have not had that experience. The behaviors listed by Summit may occur in a child who has experienced others types of trauma beside sexual abuse: "As a result, one cannot reliably say that a child exhibiting a certain combination of behaviors has been sexually abused rather than, for instance, physically abused, neglected, or brought up by psychotic or antisocial parents" (Haugaard & Reppucci, 1988, p. 178).

WIFE ABUSE

In the early 1970s, the Women's Movement was highly influential in the rediscovery of wife abuse and became instrumental shortly thereafter in drawing social and legal attention to marital rape. Women fought for and achieved legislation to increase or establish penalties for wife abuse, to strengthen civil remedies, and to make it easier for female victims to file criminal charges against their assailants, including their husbands (Pleck, 1989). However, despite these formal changes, the legal system has been slow and resistant to recognizing this abuse as a serious or widespread problem. There seems to be a strong and long-standing tendency in society (and in the courtroom) to blame women for their abuse and to deny or trivialize the violence involved (Mahoney, 1991).

■ 11.3: ADMISSIBILITY OF CHILD SEXUAL ABUSE ACCOMMODATION SYNDROME

IN STATE V. J. Q. (NEW JERSEY, 1993), a defendant was indicted for multiple acts of criminal sexual abuse of his two children. During the trial, Dr. Madeline Milchman, a developmental psychologist, testified for the prosecution as an expert witness on child sexual abuse. Dr. Milchman testified that based on her assessment of the two children, who lived with the defendant, it was her expert opinion that they had been sexually abused because they demonstrated the behavioral features of child sexual abuse accommodation syndrome (CSAAS) as described by Summit (1983). Based in part on Dr. Milchman's testimony, the defendant was convicted. However, the convictions were reversed by the New Jersey Supreme court on the grounds that the trial court committed plain error by permitting the use of the CSAAS testimony. The court noted that, while CSAAS was an accepted syndrome within the scientific community, the syndrome was not without its critics. The court pointed out, for example, that the same behavioral patterns found in CSAAS may also appear in other disorders. Thus, the existence of certain symptoms does not invariably prove abuse. The court reasoned that, in this case, CSAAS was being asked (by the state) to perform a task it could not accomplish. The court concluded that the presence of CSAAS is not enough, by itself, to prove sexual abuse. ■

It should be noted that the terms *women abuse, spouse abuse,* and *wife abuse* are sometimes used interchangeably. The subtle differences between the terms should be noted, however. **Spouse abuse** is generic, recognizing that both women and men are subjected to abuse by their partners. Because the overwhelming majority of victims are women, however, wife abuse is often the preferred term. On the other hand, because victims are usually women, and because women who are victimized are not necessarily married to their abusers, some researchers prefer the term women abuse. That covers non-domestic situations, such as dating relationships, as well as abuse by acquaintances or strangers. Because most of the literature reviewed below is based on abuse of women in marital situations, we will use the term wife abuse and differentiate when spouse or women abuse is the particular focus of a given study.

Studies estimating the prevalence and incidence of wife abuse differ significantly in their figures. The most conservative estimates suggest that women are physically abused in 12 percent of all marriages. Some scholars project that as many as 50 percent or more of all women will be battering victims at some point in their lives (Mahoney, 1991). Steinmetz (1977) estimates that 3.3 million wives and .25 million husbands out of a total population of 47 million married couples are subjected to severe beatings by their spouses. In one of the early national surveys on this issue conducted in 1975 at the Family Research Laboratory at the University of New Hampshire, 28 percent of the married persons interviewed said they had experienced marital violence at some point in the marriage (Straus, Gelles & Steinmetz, 1980). Sixteen percent reported some kind of physical violence between spouses during the year of the survey. In another nationwide survey conducted in 1985, the incidence of spouse physical abuse actually decreased 27 percent from the 1975 figure (Strauss & Gelles, 1986). These data contrast sharply with claims of an epidemic of abuse during the 1970s and 1980s. Regardless of this apparent reduction, which may be attributed to a variety of factors ranging from more empowerment of women to more fear in reporting, wife abuse remains a very serious issue. Approximately 1,700 women die each year as a direct result of abuse (Strube, 1988). It is not clear whether this figure includes deaths of women who were not married to their abusers.

The 1985 data of the Family Research Laboratory did reveal the very significant fact that wife abuse often does not begin during marriage, but rather before it. In another research study,

304

CHAPTER
ELEVEN:
PSYCHOLOGY
AND
FAMILY
LAW

over one-third of women about to be married reported having been the victims of physical violence from their fiancés (O'Leary & Curley, 1986). Furthermore, a substantial number of battered women continue to live with their assailants (Strube, 1988). Unfortunately, women are often reluctant to seek aid for their abuse and often do so only when it becomes life threatening. "Why doesn't she leave?" is the question continually asked, and it tends to be asked much more often than "Why doesn't he stop?" For a variety of reasons, including lack of community support, fear of retaliation, and hope that things will improve, women who are battered may believe themselves unable to leave a battering relationship. Recall that this issue was discussed earlier, in Chapter 5.

PSYCHOLOGICAL PROFILES OF ABUSERS

Despite several attempts to develop psychological categories for the wife or child abuser (e.g., Megargee, 1982), there does not seem to be any evidence for "typical" psychological profiles for either wife batterers or child abusers. The search for typical demographic characteristics of abusers has been equally unsuccessful (Weis, 1989; Hotaling & Straus, 1989). Wife and child abuse appear to cut across all socioeconomic, religious, and ethnic lines. Alcohol and other drug abuse does seem to play an exacerbating role, but it is a mistake to call them *causes* of the violence. Abusive men with severe alcohol or drug problems are apt to abuse their wives both when drunk and when sober. However, abusive men who drink heavily are violent more frequently, and they inflict more serious injuries on their wives and children than do abusive men who do not have a history of alcohol or drug problems (Frieze & Browne, 1989). Abusive men generally use alcohol or other drugs as an excusing agent that allows them to escape culpability for their antisocial or violent actions as well as to avoid the full impact of legal sanctions. It should be noted, however, that the drug marijuana has not been shown to be connected to violent behavior, whether in the domestic context or any other.

Once the abuse has occurred, it tends to be repeated (Frieze & Browne, 1989). Over time, wife abuse, if not skillfully dealt with, may also become more severe and more frequent. Recall the discussion of the cycle of violence identified by Lenore Walker (1989) in her description of battered-woman syndrome. Being violently victimized by a spouse over an extended period of time may result in emotional reactions and psychological scars decidedly different from those seen in victims of violent crime perpetrated by strangers.

Additionally, initiating a motivation to change in a wife abuser or child abuser is a formidable task. It requires establishing a series of events which demonstrate that the psychological and material costs for the abuse outweigh its psychological benefits. Usually, abusers have had a lifelong learning experience within their subculture in developing belief systems about the power men should have over family members. They also probably have had considerable reinforcement for their aggressive actions. Thus, it is not easy to break this behavioral cycle. Legal sanctions should have an effect, but often the abuser realizes that these sanctions are weak.

Serious, concentrated efforts by the legal system to put some bite into punishment for abusive behavior may be effective over the long haul. One arrest, fine, or lecture is unlikely to have much effect. It is more likely that a string of aversive and costly events, such as strong legal consequences combined with community sanctions (e.g., public disclosure, frequent visits by a social welfare agency) and clear emotional messages from the victim (e.g., reporting abuse regularly to the authorities, leaving the home, separating, and initiating divorce proceedings) will wear down the abuser to a point where a change in the abuse cycle becomes necessary. Fundamentally, however, a change in the cycle of violence requires a society-wide attack on the social conditions that promote it.

Juvenile Justice

Juvenile justice was officially launched in the United States on the last day of the 1899 session of the Illinois legislature when that body passed the **Juvenile Court Act**. The Act created a juvenile court in Illinois and gave that court jurisdiction over delinquent, dependent, or neglected children. Although other states had adopted various procedures and regulations to deal with youth, the Illinois Juvenile Court Act represented the first comprehensive attempt at codification. The Act did *not* create a new or separate court system in Illinois but established a special division within the existing system. The first entirely separate juvenile court was established in Indiana in 1903.

Because issues associated with dependent and neglected children were discussed earlier in the chapter, we will focus here on juveniles considered "at risk" for committing adult crimes, specifically those brought before juvenile courts for delinquency proceedings. Additionally, we will discuss only briefly the issue of status jurisdiction over juveniles. When juveniles exhibit behavior that is problematic only because of their age, such as running away from home, being "incorrigible," or skipping school, we say they are committing **status offenses**. Until the 1970s, status offenses were routinely treated as delinquency. Today, distinctions are drawn between violations of criminal law, such as committing a burglary, and status offenses. The latter behavior may still land the juvenile in juvenile court, but the disposition of the case will be different. A chronic status offender, for example, will not be adjudicated as a delinquent, but as a child or juvenile in need of supervision. The consequences of this approach will be discussed below.

The Illinois Court Act was directly relevant to juvenile justice in four ways: (1) it refined the definition of juvenile delinquency (a term which included status offending); (2) it removed the jurisdiction of juvenile cases from the adult criminal court; (3) it authorized the placement of juveniles in separate facilities away from adult offenders; and (4) it provided for a system of probation, allowing the state to supervise the child outside a facility or institution.

The Illinois Court Act quickly became the model for juvenile justice throughout the country. By 1911, twenty-two states had adopted similar measures, and by 1925, all but two states (Maine and Wyoming) had established juvenile courts (Tappan, 1947). The first juvenile court within the federal court system was created in 1906 in the District of Columbia, with jurisdiction over delinquent, dependent, incorrigible, and truant children. By 1938, the federal system had developed a national model for a juvenile court under federal jurisdiction. Today, the lower federal courts deal primarily with juveniles tried as adults on serious federal charges. The **Comprehensive Crime Control Act** passed by Congress in 1984 encourages federal prosecutors to leave the prosecution of juveniles to the states. In situations in which the federal courts hold sole jurisdiction, such as in the District of Columbia and American Indian reservations, this is not possible.

Juvenile courts were allowed wide discretion in decisionmaking during their first fifty years (Grisso, Tomkins & Casey, 1988). In the 1960s, however, the U. S. Supreme Court began to recognize that juveniles had constitutional rights, and in a series of decisions, it set procedural requirements for the handling of delinquency cases. In 1974, Congress passed landmark legislation designed to assure justice for juveniles, the **Juvenile Justice and Delinquency Prevention Act**. Included in that law was a provision encouraging states to decriminalize status offenders by removing them from institutions as well as from the definition of delinquency. There remains considerable debate, however, about whether the changes mandated by the Court and Congress have had the desired effect. Each of these developments is discussed below.

From the beginnings of the juvenile court, it was argued or implied that children below a

306

CHAPTER
ELEVEN:
PSYCHOLOGY
AND
FAMILY
LAW

certain age have different constitutional rights than adults. These differences were justified on the assumption that children do not have the emotional or mental maturity to make important decisions for themselves and exercise those rights. Thus the doctrine of *parens patriae*, giving the state authority to intercede in the best interest of the child, was a critical component in the philosophy of the juvenile court.

Children also were assumed to be more "rehabilitatable" than adults. Therefore, the early juvenile courts were encouraged to operate in a paternalistic manner, obtain extensive background information, and encourage children to "open up" and confess their illegal behavior. Judges, often at the recommendation of mental-health representatives and social workers, had widespread authority to order children to institutions or to be removed from their homes and placed in foster homes, even when their transgressions were minor. David Rothman (1980) has well documented the abuses associated with institutions for juveniles in the twentieth century.

Although lawyers were allowed in juvenile courts, they were not considered a necessity. In fact, they were more likely to be considered a hindrance to the rehabilitative process. Judges also had the power to remove the "hopeless" juvenile from the jurisdiction of the juvenile court and transfer the case to criminal court.

Such a transfer was the subject of the first landmark U. S. Supreme Court decision dealing directly with a juvenile offender, *Kent v. U. S.* (1966). Morris Kent, Jr. was a sixteen-year-old charged with housebreaking, robbery, and rape while on probation under the jurisdiction of the District of Columbia Juvenile Court. When arrested, the teenager admitted committing the offenses and was placed in a receiving home for children. The juvenile court transferred the boy's case to adult criminal court over the strong objections of his lawyer, who argued that the boy had rehabilitative potential that should be developed in a juvenile home. The lawyer also requested that he be allowed to review Kent's social service records, a request the juvenile court denied. In criminal court, the boy was found not guilty of the rape charge by reason of insanity, but guilty of housebreaking and robbery. He was sentenced to thirty to ninety years and transferred to St. Elizabeth's Hospital for the mentally ill in Washington, D. C. Kent appealed the original decision to transfer him to criminal court.

In reviewing Kent's appeal, the U. S. Supreme Court first recognized that there was no constitutional requirement for a separate juvenile court system. When there is a separate court system, that court may not waive jurisdiction and transfer the juvenile to criminal court without a hearing and accompanying safeguards: "There is no place in our legal system for reaching a verdict of such serious consequences without a hearing, without effective assistance of counsel, and without the statement of the reasons" (p. 554). The Court also ruled that Kent's lawyer should have been given access to the boy's social service records.

The opinion, written by Justice Abe Fortas, strongly criticized the operations of the juvenile court and the unchecked discretionary power it wielded over the lives of juveniles. The Kent case signaled radical changes in the procedures through which juveniles would be processed. A year later, in *In re Gault* (1967), the Court extended broad procedural safeguards to juveniles charged with criminal conduct, making a profound impact on the structure of juvenile courts.

In re Gault involved a fifteen-year-old Arizona boy, Gerald Gault, who was accused of making an obscene phone call to a neighbor. The Supreme Court called his comments "of the irritatingly offensive, adolescent sex variety." Shortly after the call, which was reported to police by the neighbor, the boy was taken into police custody without his parents' knowledge and placed in a children's detention home. When Gault's mother arrived home from work, she asked her older son to find Gerald. Upon learning that he was confined in a detention home, they went to see him and were abruptly told that a hearing was scheduled for the following afternoon. Gerald, his mother, and his older brother, along with two probation officers, appeared before the juvenile court judge in chambers. The father was working out of town and could not attend.

What transpired in the judge's chambers was not recorded, and a disagreement resulted about exactly what was said. A week later another hearing was held. Gerald was not represented by counsel. The neighbor never appeared to testify against him and be submitted to cross-examination. Gerald was pronounced a "delinquent" and was committed to the State Industrial School until he reached the age of twenty-one (recall that he was fifteen at the time). Making lewd or obscene phone calls qualified as a misdemeanor in the state of Arizona at that time. Had Gerald been an adult, his maximum penalty would have been $50 or two months in jail.

The Supreme Court used the Gault case as an opportunity to criticize the juvenile court process. In the majority opinion, Justice Fortas wrote that the court was run like a "kangaroo court [and that] neither the Fourteenth Amendment nor the Bill of Rights is for adults alone" (p. 13). The Court held that juveniles appearing before a juvenile court in a delinquency proceeding have the following constitutional rights: (1) adequate written notice of the charges against them in order to afford a reasonable opportunity to prepare a defense; (2) the assistance of counsel, and if indigent, the assistance of appointed counsel; (3) the ability to invoke the privilege against self-incrimination; and (4) the ability to confront and cross-examine witnesses.

The *Gault* decision was both heralded as a just and sensible decision that was long overdue and condemned as a decision which would gut the juvenile system. Opponents feared that the due-process guarantees were not in the best interests of delinquent youths, whose best hope for change was to be taken under the paternalistic wing of the juvenile court. Those who supported the decision, however, pointed to the widespread, documented abuses that had been allowed to develop.

Interestingly, although the decision clearly changed procedures in the juvenile courts, its impact is still questionable. Although states have complied with the Court's mandate to offer constitutional protections, the rights are often waived. Barry Feld, who has conducted extensive research on the issue, notes that "juveniles in most states never see a lawyer, waive their right to counsel without consulting with or appreciating the consequences of relinquishing counsel, and confront the power of the state alone and unaided" (1992, p. 80).

In the 1970s, the Supreme Court decided several other landmark cases relating to juveniles. Some extended juvenile rights, while others were more cautious. In the case of *In re Winship* (1970) the Court held that before juveniles can be adjudicated delinquent, there must be proof beyond reasonable doubt of every fact necessary to constitute the offense with which they have been charged. Until *Winship*, juvenile courts routinely adjudicated youths delinquent on the basis of less stringent standards, such as a preponderance of the evidence and clear and convincing evidence. In *Breed v. Jones* (1975) the Court announced its constitutional ban on double jeopardy, ruling that a child could not be tried in a criminal court after receiving a disposition in the juvenile court.

In *McKeiver v. Pennsylvania* (1971), however, the Court ruled that juveniles did not have a constitutional right to a jury trial. Noting that it did not wish to make juvenile proceedings identical to those in criminal courts, the Court indicated it wished to retain an element of informality and recognize the juvenile court's emphasis on treatment rather than punishment. Nevertheless, nothing prevents a state from allowing trial by jury in juvenile proceedings. It should also be noted that juveniles tried in criminal courts have the same constitutional rights to a jury trial as adults.

COMPETENCY TO WAIVE CONSTITUTIONAL RIGHTS

A major issue arising in the juvenile delinquency context deals with the ability of juveniles to knowingly, intelligently, and voluntarily waive their rights. Recall that most juveniles are not

308

CHAPTER
ELEVEN:
PSYCHOLOGY
AND
FAMILY
LAW

represented by lawyers (Feld, 1992), a fact which suggests that many have waived that right. An alternate explanation is that they were not informed of it. Remember that *Miranda v. Arizona* (1966) established the constitutional requirement that persons accused of crimes must be informed of their rights to an attorney and to avoid self-incrimination prior to being subjected to custodial interrogation by law-enforcement officers. Upon indication by the person in custody that he or she wishes an attorney, interrogation must stop. Self-incriminating evidence gained after the *Miranda* warning is given is admissible only if the person has given a knowing, intelligent, and clearly voluntary waiver of these rights. The central terms of the *Miranda* decision—*knowing*, *intelligent*, and *voluntary*—constitute a critical issue for both psychology and law. Where juveniles are concerned, this issue is particularly problematic. At what age can the average juvenile meet these standards? For that matter, can even the average adult understand and competently exercise his or her rights within the *Miranda* context?

In *Fare v. Michael C.* (1979), the Supreme Court considered the question of whether a sixteen-year-old boy's request to speak to his probation officer before police interrogation was equivalent to a wish to speak with an attorney. Michael C., described as immature, distraught, and poorly educated, asked to see his probation officer instead of an attorney, and was told his probation officer would be contacted after he spoke to police. He apparently interpreted the *Miranda* warning as a police ruse. "How I know you guys won't pull no police officer in and tell me he's an attorney?" (p. 711). The Court (by a 5 to 4 vote) rejected the argument that the boy's request to see his probation officer should have been granted before questioning continued. The majority held that a probation officer is in no position to represent the interests of a juvenile, as intended by *Miranda*, because the probation officer is essentially a representative of the state.

The Court expressed concern, however, as to whether juveniles really have the capacity to understand the warnings given to them, the nature of their constitutional rights, or the consequences of waiving them. Thus, *Fare* warned judges to consider the circumstances (or the social context) of the interrogation as well as the subject's age, experience, education, background, and intelligence in deciding whether a waiver was valid.

Indeed, there is empirical evidence suggesting that juveniles cannot understand their constitutional rights. Grisso (1981) has examined the ability of juveniles to understand the *Miranda* warnings and to comprehend their function and significance within the context of interrogation and subsequent court proceedings. The Grisso research found that most juveniles age fourteen and younger neither really understand the meaning of *Miranda* warnings nor their implications. Therefore, it is highly questionable whether they can meaningfully waive their rights to an attorney during questioning or interrogation, or even waive their rights to remain silent. Furthermore, juveniles between the ages of fifteen and sixteen with below-average intelligence also are unable to comprehend the meaning of *Miranda* in a manner that meets the knowing, intelligent standard set forth in the *Miranda* ruling.

On the other hand, fifteen- and sixteen-year-old juveniles of at least average intelligence did as well in their understanding of *Miranda* as the adults—who, as a group, did not do particularly well either. Grisso discovered that at least one-quarter of the adult groups failed to meet the absolute standard for adequately understanding *Miranda* and its implications. Surprisingly, many juveniles and adults were convinced that refusal to talk about one's illegal involvements when questioned by a judge would amount to perjury. Many also believed that the right to remain silent can be given or taken away by the judge at his or her discretion. Grisso concluded, "using adults as the standard, then, our results indicate that juveniles' competence to waive their rights to silence and counsel is seriously diminished by their inferior understanding of the function and significance of those rights" (1981, p. 128). The one exception to this conclusion applied to the juvenile with a great deal of experience with court processes (those referred for felony charges three or more times in the past).

Some research has examined the attitudes and expectancies of juveniles about lawyers, with early studies suggesting that they are generally quite negative (Rafkey & Sealey, 1975). Grisso (1981) discovered that one-third of the juveniles with little court experience believed that defense attorneys defend the interests of the innocent but not the guilty. More research is needed before conclusions can be drawn about how juveniles view lawyers and other legal authorities.

Because the law gives little guidance to judges in how to assess the ability of juveniles to waive their rights, juvenile courts often turn to information provided by mental-health professionals, especially in the evaluations they submit to the court (Grisso, Tomkins & Casey, 1988). However, the laws also do not provide guidance on what kinds of information clinicians are supposed to present to the court. Grisso recommends that "...a psychologist or lawyer may use a juvenile's age, IQ, and other characteristics to provide an estimate of his or her degree of understanding of the *Miranda* rights" (1983, p. 141). In addition to individual differences in what juveniles understand, there might also be differences in how they go about the process of deciding how to respond under the circumstances of an arrest, a police accusation, and a potential interrogation.

TRANSFERRING JUVENILES BETWEEN JUVENILE AND CRIMINAL COURTS

The decision to transfer a juvenile from juvenile to criminal court, or from criminal to juvenile court, has major implications. Recall that the U. S. Supreme Court recognized this in *Kent v. U. S.*, and required procedural safeguards before a judge could waive his or her authority over a juvenile. A juvenile tried in criminal court has the same constitutional rights as an adult, but also is subject to punishment, including capital punishment. A juvenile whose case is heard in juvenile court may be held by the state only until the age of adulthood, which has been extended to twenty-one in some states. The perception that serious juvenile offenders do not get punished enough in the juvenile system has led to a nationwide trend to treat them more punitively by dealing with their cases in criminal courts.

A number of researchers have concluded that the waiver decision is arbitrary, discriminatory, and does not accomplish what it is assumed to accomplish (e.g., Champion, 1989; Feld, 1992; Hamparian et al., 1982). Ironically, juveniles transferred to the criminal court and treated as adults get less harsh sentences than adults. This may reflect a reluctance on the part of judges to sentence them to prison, where it is assumed they will be preyed upon. Indeed, as Champion (1989) reports, when juveniles are sentenced to prison, they present special problems for prison administrators. They are more likely than adults to need protection, more disruptive, and less likely to earn good-time credits and qualify for rehabilitative programs.

States vary widely in their statutory requirements on the waiver issue. The child's age and seriousness of the crime, however, are the two factors that dictate where the case will initially be brought. Nevertheless, in most states, judges have ultimate authority to transfer the case. It is important to note that they are not always transferring juveniles accused of violent crimes. Dean Champion (1992), summarizing the research in this area, has pointed out that "in many jurisdictions...transferred juveniles consist primarily of property offenders or those charged with non-violent, petty crimes."

Before such transfer decisions are made, judges are required to hold hearings, often called **waiver** or **bindover hearings**. At these hearings, the expertise of mental-health professionals will

310

CHAPTER
ELEVEN:
PSYCHOLOGY
AND
FAMILY
LAW

be sought, if rehabilitative potential is at issue. Therefore, a lawyer representing a juvenile will argue, as did Morris Kent's attorney, that her or his client has potential for change which will not be met in an adult prison context. Alternately, the attorney might refer to the juvenile's immaturity and inability to understand the consequences of his or her actions. To support these claims, mental-health professionals will testify as to the results of their assessments.

JUVENILE REHABILITATION

The existence of a separate system to deal with the troublesome behavior of juveniles is based on assumptions that: (1) they are not as responsible for their illegal behavior as adults and (2) they are more rehabilitatable than adults. If we assume that they can be rehabilitated, we must have available programs which do indeed change their behavior. Unfortunately, this is not necessarily the case. The juvenile-justice system is replete with programs geared to the goal of changing the attitudes and character of juveniles. They range from highly structured programs, in which every moment of the day is accounted for, to community-based group or individual therapy programs. Decisionmaking programs, juvenile diversion, youth wilderness programs, boot camps, anger management, meditation, sex offender treatment programs, probation camps, intensive supervision—all illustrate the diversity of approaches. Note that the programs may be educational, therapeutic, or vocational, or a combination of the three.

The "get tough" approach illustrated by the trend to deal with juveniles in criminal court is partly based on the assumption that programs such as the above have not been effective. Rehabilitation programs within an institutional setting, or secure custody, have been especially questionable. The victimization of vulnerable juveniles within these settings is well documented. Indeed, many observers would agree with Barry Feld that the "juvenile court's rhetorical commitment to rehabilitation has been contradicted since its inception by the reality of custodial institutions" (1992, p. 75).

The majority of successful rehabilitation programs, for both juveniles and adults, are community-based (Gendreau & Ross, 1984). Nonetheless, some positive results have been obtained with rehabilitation in an institutional setting. The critical factors appear to be the size of the institution, a high staff-to-juvenile ratio, and the careful selection of juveniles matched to available programs. Even so, we cannot assume that rehabilitation of even a majority of youths will be accomplished.

A recently published report of an ongoing experiment involving delinquent youths randomly assigned to Paint Creek Youth Center in Ohio is illustrative. Paint Creek is a privately-operated facility which offers a wide variety of psychological, educational, and social services for up to 34 males between the ages of fifteen and eighteen. Its director is Dr. Vicki Agee, a psychologist with many years' experience working with juveniles. Greenwood and Turner (1993) compared the post-release arrest records and self-reported crimes of Paint Creek youths to those of youths held in two state juvenile facilities. Over a one-year period, 75 percent of the Paint Creek youths had committed at least one serious delinquent act, compared to 62 percent of the controls. (The difference was not statistically significant, however.) The research serves as a reminder that behavioral change can be a very elusive goal, even in a program which seems to have many indicators of success.

The question for juvenile justice is not, does rehabilitation work, but which programs work with which offenders? In a review of rehabilitation programs in corrections, Gendreau and Ross (1984) identified factors associated with successful and unsuccessful efforts. No one approach, however, was associated with success; rather, a multifaceted approach toward rehabilitation was needed. Successful programs, they found, were based on a social-learning model of criminal behavior, in which it is assumed that the offender's cognitive and social skills need to be developed. Successful programs often involved family therapy, problem-solving training, vocational and social-skills training, role playing, modeling, reinforcement, and contingency contracting. The careful spelling out of rules is important, as well as the use of community resources.

Unsuccessful rehabilitation programs included those based on the medical model, wherein it is assumed that the individual has a biological or psychological deficit that must be cured. Behavior-modification programs have had little success unless they included a cognitive component, involved the individual meaningfully in his or her progress, neutralized the effect of the peer group, and dealt with behavior that could be generalized to the social context. Programs based on total acceptance of the youth without making him or her responsible for conduct have had very little positive effect. Finally, deterrence-type programs, wherein efforts are made to "scare" the youth into behaving, do not have long-lasting effects. Boot camps, on the other hand, where juveniles are subjected to a military regime for up to 180 days, may have some rehabilitative value if treatment programs—such as substance abuse or anger management—are also included. At this stage, however, boot camps are too new on the correctional scene to be assessed for their long-term impact, and there are many problems associated with their use (Sechrest, 1989).

Advocates for youth very often argue that treating children fairly, rather than emphasizing traditional rehabilitation, should be the goal of the juvenile-justice system. The "leave the child alone" view suggests that the problems for most juveniles lie not with the juveniles themselves, but with their social situations. Alternately, if "rehabilitation" focuses on education, job training, and social-skills training, this is acceptable.

Summary and Conclusions

The broad field of family law has developed rapidly over the last decade, perhaps more than any other area involving interface between law and psychology. Psychologists are becoming increasingly involved—through both research and practice—in the adoption process, custodial arrangement, and parental suitability in divorce proceedings. They are also more involved in the psychological aspects of abortion, particularly the mental and emotional competence of adolescents who must make decisions regarding the termination of unwanted pregnancies.

Although we have covered highlights of what may seem to be disparate topics, three themes dominate the chapter. First, more recognition is being given to the rights and needs of children. This has encouraged a reevaluation of the doctrine of *parens patriae*, whereby the best interest of the child was presumed but often not achieved. Thus, questions of a child's competence to make autonomous decisions and emphasis on the interests of the child in custody decisions occur frequently in the literature. Second, there is increasing recognition of domestic violence, the "dark side" of the family. The rights and needs of victims of abuse, including sexual abuse, are finding their way into both research and practice. Third, the role of the psychologist in the family-law context has been altered. In the history of the juvenile court, for example, mental-health practitioners worked in collusion with the court to obtain extensive information about the social and psychological backgrounds of the child. Today, rather than working in direct consultation with the courts, psychologists are more likely to be conducting research in such

312

CHAPTER
ELEVEN:
PSYCHOLOGY
AND
FAMILY
LAW

areas as the capacity of juveniles to consent or the effects of joint custody on children at different ages. Their courtroom testimony is sought on special occasions, such as when juvenile waivers are being contemplated or a child is believed to suffer from CSAS. Most custody decisions, however, do not directly involve mental-health practitioners (Melton, et al., 1987).

The role of psychologists working in juvenile corrections has also changed, due to both the emphasis on "getting tough" and the belief that traditional rehabilitation methods have not been widely successful. Psychologists are much less likely to be involved in one-to-one or small-group therapy than to be administering routine batteries of tests and, perhaps, teaching decisionmaking skills. However, therapy with a select number of juveniles (e.g., chronically violent juveniles or sex offenders) is still needed and accomplished. On the other hand, we cannot be too sanguine about the outcome of such therapy, particularly in an institutional setting.

The work of research psychologists in the areas of juveniles' competence to consent to treatment and competence to waive constitutional rights is progressing rapidly. The consent-to-treatment issue has been studied primarily in the context of a minor making a decision regarding abortion. Courts have assumed that juveniles are less likely to make an informed decision and are especially vulnerable to psychological harm as a result of having an abortion. Research has not borne this out. In fact, the more likely reaction among girls, as among adult women, is relief.

Inability to understand the implication of waiving the right against self-incrimination has been documented, however. Research indicates that juveniles do not knowingly and intelligently waive their *Miranda* rights, a finding that has led some observers (e.g., Schwartz, 1992) to recommend that they not be allowed the waiver—in other words, that attorneys *always* be present.

Domestic violence, a phenomenon which came to public attention in the 1970s, challenges the resolve of the legal system as well as of mental-health practitioners. The legal system is still divided on the best policy approach to take on this highly troubling issue. When not ignored, cases of child or wife abuse, for example, are often handled by family or juvenile courts, rather than treated as criminal offenses. Alternately, domestic partners may be referred to mediation, which has been called "a paradox for women" (Rifkin, 1989), both in the divorce and domestic-abuse context.

For the mental-health practitioner, domestic violence presents formidable ethical questions, particularly for those testifying about syndromes associated with it. The child sexual abuse syndrome (CSAS), though it seems quite logical, has not been documented as a separate syndrome elicited only by sexual victimization. The battered-woman syndrome, discussed previously in Chapter 5, must be carefully articulated so as not to turn the victim into a mentally disordered individual. Furthermore, the emphasis on studying the adult victim in domestic violence draws attention away from needed research on the batterer. Thus far, we know only that batterers exist across social classes and occupational groups. Why do they do it and how can they change? are broad research questions that need to be more adequately addressed.

Questions to Ponder

1. What are the various custodial options available in divorce cases involving minor children? How do the tender-years and best-interests-of-the-child doctrines affect the choice of custodial options? Propose a research study which would provide helpful information to courts making custody decisions.

2. Studies of the effect of divorce mediation suggest that men are often more satisfied by the mediation process than women. Why might that be?

3. What type of person would make an ideal *guardian ad litem*?

4. What are the pros and cons of identifying a "syndrome" such as CSAS and using this information in the legal process?

5. Review the legal rights of juveniles mentioned in this chapter. Some people argue that juveniles cannot be helped and rehabilitated if these rights are in place. Discuss. How is the best interest of the child served when a juvenile retains these rights?

THE PSYCHOLOGY OF CRIMINAL BEHAVIOR

RIMINOLOGY, THE MULTIDISCIPLINARY STUDY OF CRIME, CAN BE psychological, sociological, anthropological, biological, political, psychiatric, or even economic in emphasis. To a large extent, however, criminology has been dominated over the years by three disciplines: sociology, psychology, and psychiatry. Recently, a more active interest in **criminal anthropology** has begun to emerge (Rafter, 1992).

Sociological criminology traditionally has emphasized the effects on crime of variables such as age, race, gender, social group, interpersonal relationships, and social class. This approach allows us to conclude, for example, that young, African-American males from the low socioeconomic class are disproportionately more likely to be both perpetrators and victims of homicide. The sociological approach also probes the situational factors most conducive to criminal action, such as the time, place, and circumstances surrounding crime, or the kinds of weapons used. Homicides, for instance, often occur after considerable alcohol has been ingested by either the offender or the victim; the weapon most often used is a firearm; and in most cases, the offender and victim have known one another, frequently as relatives or friends. In addition to providing information about correlates of crime, however, the sociological perspective encourages us to explore underlying social conditions which may precipitate criminal activity, such as inequities in educational and employment opportunity or differential treatment by agents of the criminal justice system.

Psychological criminology, which is emphasized in this text, is the science which studies the behavior and mental processes of antisocial individuals. While sociological criminology focuses on group variables and society in general, psychological criminology concentrates on individual antisocial behavior—how it is acquired, evoked, maintained, and modified. Both environmental and personality influences on antisocial behavior are considered, along with the mental processes that mediate that behavior. In this context, personality refers to all the traits and biological and cognitive qualities of the human being that psychology has identified as important in the mediation and control of behavior. In recent years, psychological criminology has shifted noticeably to an emphasis on cognitive aspects.

Psychological criminology is often confused with **psychiatric criminology**, which dominated the study of crime at the turn of the twentieth century and continues to attract strong support. The confusion between the two approaches is understandable because sharp demarcations between psychology and psychiatry are often difficult to make. It is perhaps more meaningful to distinguish psychiatric and psychological criminology on the basis of their primary perspectives of human nature and their approaches to the study of human behavior.

Much of the traditional psychiatric-criminology literature follows the Freudian, psychoanalytic,

316

CHAPTER
TWELVE:
THE
PSYCHOLOGY
OF
CRIMINAL
BEHAVIOR

or psychodynamic perspective, and views human nature as *innately* antisocial. In some circles of psychiatric criminology, overt behavior is believed to reveal symbolic distortions of underlying unconscious structures which make up the personality (e.g., Sadoff, 1975; MacDonald, 1976; Abrahamsen, 1960). Criminal behavior, therefore, is said to spring from unconscious urges and conflicts that are basically animalistic, unruly, and antisocial in nature. According to this perspective, society is the mechanism that holds innate, biological, animalistic urges in check. Without an organized society with rules and laws, humans would attack, steal, and even kill at will.

While the traditional psychiatric criminology views human nature as innately unruly, it would be unfair to classify contemporary psychiatric criminology this way. It is much more diverse, offering a rich fountain of knowledge, and is considerably less steeped in the belief that criminals are acting out their animalistic, deep-seated urges. In addition, we should make the distinction between psychiatric criminology and **forensic psychiatry**. Forensic psychiatry is "...a subspeciality of psychiatry in which scientific and clinical expertise is applied to legal issues in legal contexts embracing civil, criminal, correctional, or legislative matters..." (Rosner, 1989, p. 323). Thus, psychiatric criminology is concerned with the study of criminal behavior, whereas forensic psychiatry is much broader.

Psychiatric criminology has developed on the basis of clinical experience, observation, and anecdotal data. It places heavy emphasis on clinical material as a reliable source for systematically understanding the universal dynamics of human nature. The psychiatric perspective uses clinical data (procedural evidence) to develop theories of crime. The psychological viewpoint, in contrast, relies heavily on empirical investigation (validating evidence). The price paid for relying on validating evidence is that it becomes extremely difficult to offer all-encompassing theories of criminality or empirically sound proposals for the reduction of antisocial behavior. Science requires patience and a high tolerance for conflicting, contradictory data that are highly susceptible to multiple interpretations. Scientific knowledge is gained slowly and often cannot provide glib answers or easy solutions, even when answers are demanded by political, economic, and social forces. We will now take a closer look at sociological and psychological criminology.

Sociological Criminology

Before proceeding with a summary of representative sociological theories, it must be emphasized that this is but a cursory introduction. Each of the positions outlined below is described in far more detail in criminological literature approached with a sociological focus. Sociological theories are most commonly divided into three groups: structural, process, and conflict theories. **Structural theories** explain crime by referring to the structure or organization of society, with particular attention given to social stratification, or division into socioeconomic classes. **Process theories**, which focus on small groups and individuals rather than the structure of society, examine the process through which people engage in criminal behavior or are defined as criminal. Interactions between individuals and social systems, such as schools and the criminal justice system, are important to process theorists. **Conflict theories** highlight power differentials between groups in society and an unfair distribution of wealth as major explanations for crime. We will briefly discuss representative theories below.

STRAIN THEORY

The chief spokesperson of strain theory, one of the structure theories, is sociologist Robert K. Merton. According to Merton (and the strain theorists who followed him), American society communicates to its citizens that the accumulation of wealth and status is paramount—designer clothes, expensive cars, beautiful homes, and manicured neighborhoods. Although these goals are supposedly desired by all, the means for achieving them are not equally available to all. Those in the lower socioeconomic classes, for example, are denied access to the goals because they lack the means to get there, such as education, a social network, personal contacts, and family influences.

Strain theorists contend that crime and delinquency occur when there is a perceived discrepancy between the materialistic values and goals cherished and highly esteemed by a society and the availability of legitimate means to reach these goals. Under these conditions, a strain develops: "I'd like to have this American dream of wealth, but the ways and means for getting it are not available to me." Groups and individuals experiencing a high level of this strain must decide whether to violate laws to acquire some of this sought-after wealth, give up on the American dream and go through the motions, withdraw, or rebel. These alternative ways of adapting to strain form the basis of Merton's theory.

Strain theory has developed over the years to account for criminal activity among youth gangs as well as the middle class, who would not generally be acknowledged as lacking opportunities to achieve materialistic goals. More recent adaptations of strain theory recognize the pressure placed on individuals in the corporate world to maintain the high standard of living they believe is necessary in order to succeed.

DIFFERENTIAL ASSOCIATION THEORY

Edwin Sutherland's differential association theory is a major representative of the process group of sociological theories. According to Sutherland (1939; Sutherland & Cressey, 1974), small intimate groups, nestled within a larger society, teach their members the ways of crime. Criminal behavior, like all social behavior, is learned through interactions with other people. It is not the result of emotional disturbance, mental illness, or innate qualities of "goodness" or "badness." Most importantly, criminal behavior is not limited to the lower socioeconomic class. In fact, Sutherland's theory was developed after he had done extensive research on the law-violating behavior of business and professional people, whom he called "white-collar criminals" (Sutherland, 1940).

Sutherland maintained that people learn criminal behavior from the messages they get from others and from society as a whole. He noted that an excess of messages favorable to law violation over messages unfavorable to law violation promotes criminal activity. The conventional wisdom that bad company promotes bad behavior finds validity in differential association theory. We must be careful to note, though, that in Sutherland's theory individuals may get subtle messages that violating the law is acceptable even from noncriminal individuals. Moreover, persons who are criminals may "teach" others that criminal behavior is not acceptable. Simple association, therefore, is not the key to learning criminal behavior.

SOCIAL-CONTROL THEORY

Another process theory, **social-control** or **bonding** theory, contends that crime and delinquency occur when an individual's ties to the conventional order or normative standards are weak or largely nonexistent. It can be argued that this position actually perceives human beings as fundamentally "bad" or "antisocial," an innate tendency that must be held in check.

The chief spokesperson for social-control theory is Travis Hirschi, whose position was outlined in his classic book, *Causes of Delinquency*, published in 1969. Hirschi identified four basic elements that are necessary to prevent youths from committing crime: (1) **attachment** to parents, teachers, and peers; (2) **commitment** to conventional lines of activity, evidenced by educational

318

Chapter
Twelve:
The
Psychology
of
Criminal
Behavior

and occupational aspirations; (3) **involvement** in that conventional activity; and (4) **belief** in the legitimacy and morality of society's rules and laws.

Hirschi believed that these elements did not work in isolation but had a cumulative effect: the more attachment, commitment, involvement, and belief a youth had, the less likely it was that he or she would engage in delinquent activity. In other words, the more "bonded" the individual was to society, the more likely it was that he or she would abide by its standards and beliefs. As should be apparent, Hirschi's theory emphasizes strongly the role of the family and the school in preventing delinquent behavior.

Conflict Theory

As a group, conflict theorists consider divisions and conflicts among groups and participants as a natural course of events. These divisions engender multiple patterns of conflicting interests and values. Nevertheless, when the group in power insulates itself from punishment, problems arise. Conflict criminologists focus attention on the selective criminalization of drug-related behavior, for example, or the selective enforcement of laws against prostitution or vagrancy. Like Sutherland, conflict criminologists also point to the great harm done to society by individuals and corporations whose actions may violate civil or administrative, but not criminal, laws. Examples of such laws are violations of health and safety standards in the workplace, sexual harassment, and other forms of discrimination. Whereas Sutherland theorized about how such behavior was learned, however (process), conflict theorists emphasize how differential power promotes and maintains it.

The unequal distribution of power, then, is the basic explanation for crime. Those without power commit crimes out of necessity or frustration; those with power commit crimes which will help them maintain their status. Political crimes (such as bribe-taking), medical-insurance fraud, and violations of environmental laws fall into this latter category. Furthermore, those with power have the resources to keep themselves immune from prosecution and conviction. A subgroup of conflict theorists, referred to as radical criminologists, see capitalism as the main culprit producing the division between the powerful and powerless (Reiman, 1979). Still another subgroup, feminist criminologists, focus on gender inequity to explain criminal behavior and the creation and enforcement of criminal laws (Daly & Chesney-Lind, 1988; Simpson, 1989). Feminist criminologists also point out, however, that traditional theories of criminology, whether sociological or psychological, do not address adequately the issue of crime, particularly crime against and by women and girls (Klein, 1973; Leonard, 1982; Simpson, 1989).

There are several other sociological theories of crime, each either an offshoot or a variant of the major perspectives just described. Although sociological perspectives are not the focus of this book, they have dominated the history of criminology over the twentieth century and continue to hold a prominent place in the explanation of crime.

Psychological Criminology

As defined earlier, psychological criminology is the science of determining how criminal behavior is acquired, evoked, maintained, and modified. It assumes that various criminal behaviors are acquired by daily living experiences, in accordance with the principles of learning, and are perceived, coded, processed, and stored in memory in a unique fashion by each individual. Criminal behaviors depend on how each individual perceives and interprets a situation and what he or she expects to gain by acting in a certain fashion. An analysis of a given criminal behavior requires inquiry into the perpetrator's learning history and expectancies and the way these interact with the situation and the social environment.

Psychological criminology concentrates on the individual as its subject, but it emphasizes the cognitive and social context of behavior as well. Mainstream psychology, since the turn of the century, has viewed humans as neutral creatures malleable to the cultural and social environment surrounding them. The traditional psychologies, such as behaviorism and trait theory, believe genetics and biological predispositions do place certain restrictions on human behavior (and perhaps play other significant roles), but the major force in molding human nature is thought to be social environmental. This position is very similar to the sociological learning theory discussed earlier.

Contemporary psychological criminology, however, stresses that three factors are critical in explaining criminal behavior: (1) the **reciprocal interaction** between the individual and the social environment; (2) the enormous power of *arousal* (e.g., anger, fear, sexual excitement); and (3) the *cognitive processes* of the individual (each person's version of the world). Reciprocal interaction refers to the continual process by which the person, through behavior and beliefs, influences the social environment, and the environment in turn influences the person. For example, while parents affect the development of the child, the child also impacts the development and growth of the parents, including their marital relationship, relationships with friends, and even their level of job satisfaction. Even the newborn stimulates certain types of parental behavior, as the parent elicits certain behaviors in the newborn. A fussy, irritable baby may try the patience of most parents, and a parent ill equipped to deal with such an infant may treat the baby harshly or fail to provide emotional comfort. Eventually, this reciprocal cycle is apt to result in serious problems between the child and parent and may even promote delinquent behavior.

Another illustration of the importance of reciprocal interaction is the case of the former offender who has served his time, but whom society persists in regarding as a criminal. Despite his efforts to secure gainful employment, he is shunned by the community but accepted by a peer group which is continually engaged in crime. It is not a simple task for the former offender to reach out to others in the hope that, eventually, someone will reciprocate in kind.

Physiological arousal, the second element critical to explaining criminal behavior, is generally prominent when humans engage in violence and destruction. The widely respected psychologist Donald Hebb (1955) once noted that arousal "is an energizer, but not a guide, an engine but not a steering gear" (p. 249). Very high levels of arousal interfere with cognitive processes that mediate our judgment, common sense, and operation of our internal codes of conduct. People often do things when highly aroused that they wish they had not done. When very angry, for instance, a person may say cruel things, kick the dog, or push the stereo system to the floor in rage. Highly aroused people in the midst of an escalating quarrel may reach for a handgun, a scenario that sometimes ends with the shooting death of a family member. Arousal can be the irrational demon of human conduct. It disengages us from our normal way of behaving and from our internal (cognitive) standards and beliefs. One cardinal rule followed by law-enforcement officers in domestic disturbances, for example, is to utilize strategies that quickly reduce the escalating arousal of the individuals involved. Otherwise, arousal may lead to unpredictability, impulsiveness, and more harm.

There is little evidence that human beings are simply driven by animal instincts, genetic programming, chromosomal anomalies, hormonal imbalances, or primitive biological urges from their evolutionary past. Rather, the contemporary contention is that cognitive processes can override the biology of human nature. Humans are thinking, active agents with dreams, goals, and unique (sometimes bizarre) versions of the world. Repetitively violent and chronically antisocial

320

CHAPTER
TWELVE:
THE
PSYCHOLOGY
OF
CRIMINAL
BEHAVIOR

individuals may be those who are essentially trapped in an isolated, socially closed-off, and self-constructed cognitive system that relies on simple, straightforward aggressive solutions for survival (Bartol, 1991a). Physical aggression is, after all, a very straightforward, simplistic solution to problems, compared to the more complicated processes of discussion, negotiation, and compromise. Mass murderers and serial murderers, for example, appear to be those who have fallen out of mainstream society, in part because they see the world differently. Isolation, especially in the case of mass murderers, further propels their already deviant cognitive system to become more narrow and restrictive, enabling them to make decisions to kill other human beings.

THE EYSENCKIAN THEORY OF CRIMINALITY

The German-born British psychologist Hans J. Eysenck (1977) has proposed an **interactionist theory of criminality**, in which criminal behavior is the result of environmental conditions and inherited personality traits. Eysenck argues that we must explore the biological makeup and socialization history of the individual in order to develop a comprehensive and useful theory of criminality.

Eysenck does not suggest that individuals are born criminal in the Lombrosian tradition. Rather, he proposes that some individuals are born with nervous-system characteristics that are significantly different from those of the general population and that affect their ability to respond to social expectations and rules. Armed with an impressive body of research support, Eysenck has conceptually isolated certain features of the central and peripheral systems to account for a substantial portion of the differences found in personality. He finds that particular functions in the reactivity, sensitivity, and excitability of these two subdivisions of the nervous system account not only for differences in behavior, but also for predispositions to antisocial behavior.

Eysenck has built his theory of criminality on three basic concepts: **cortical excitation**, **conditionability**, and **drive**. Cortical excitation refers to hypothesized properties of the cerebral cortex, that part of the brain responsible for a majority of human cognitive functions such as memory, association, and thinking. The cerebral cortex is the core of the central nervous system. Eysenck theorizes that everyone seeks an optimal level of cortical excitation, and this search for a just-right level explains, in part, human behavior. Furthermore, cortical excitation is a function of the amount of stimulation input we receive from our environment.

According to Eysenck, some of us find that our cortical arousal level is too high (e.g., too much stimulation or commotion), and we avoid environmental stimulation by taking time away from others, reading a book by the fireplace, or taking a nap. Other persons are often at a low level of cortical arousal, so they actively seek excitement from the environment, such as by frequenting loud parties or places of amusement. Most of the population falls somewhere between needing constant avoidance and constant seeking of stimulation.

Eysenck labels these behavioral patterns along a continuum called **extraversion-introversion**. Stimulation seekers who are frequently cortically underaroused are labeled—for research convenience—**extraverts**; stimulation avoiders who are frequently cortically overaroused are called **introverts**. The majority of the population, falling between these two polar extremes, are called **ambiverts**.

Why are there individual differences in cortical excitation or arousal? The explanation appears to rest ultimately with the functioning of a complicated neurological structure located within the brain stem known as the reticular activating system (RAS). The hypothesized properties of the RAS are believed to be inherited. This means that part of everyday behavior can be traced back to the inherited neurophysiological substrata of the central nervous system, most particularly the RAS.

Eysenck posits that criminal behavior is partly determined by two properties of the RAS which affect the functioning of the nervous system. First, those individuals who are chronically seeking stimulation or excitement are more apt to run afoul of the law. That is, they are more likely to be impulsive, out looking for a good time, and involved in risk-taking behaviors. In essence, they are trying to increase their cortical arousal to the optimal level.

Second, and related to Eysenck's second major concept in his theory of criminality, extraverts condition less readily than either introverts or ambiverts (Eysenck, 1967). Conditioning is one of the three primary processes of learning as proposed by researchers. The other two are instrumental or operant learning and cognitive-social or observational learning.

The reader with a background in introductory psychology will recall the Russian physiologist Ivan Pavlov and his famous experiments with dogs that learned to salivate at the sound of a bell. Pavlov discovered that pairing a naturally neutral stimulus (in this case, a bell) with a significant stimulus (for example, food) resulted in the dogs' eventually learning to associate the sound of the bell with food. The response which indicates that the association has been acquired is the dog's salivation, a response normally associated with food and not with bells. The process of learning to respond to a formerly neutral stimulus (bell), which has been paired with another stimulus (food) that already elicits a response (salivation), is known as classical or Pavlovian conditioning. When the dog begins to salivate to the bell even when food is not forthcoming, classical conditioning has been established.

A more personal example is the rapid conditioning involving alcohol and nausea. Too much scotch during an evening party, followed by a memorable bout with nausea, will render even the most devout of scotch drinkers reeling with uncomfortable associations (the conditioning) between the taste and smell of scotch and nausea. Similarly, if we happen to become miserable with a case of flu within hours after eating our favorite food (e.g., lobster), that dish may never again appear on our list of favorites. Although in that case the two experiences are causally unrelated, the taste and sight of lobster quickly becomes associated with the nauseating experience of the flu. It should be emphasized that conditioning is basically a term which describes learning through paired experiences; it is not an explanation of the way learning takes place.

Introverts, and to a lesser extent ambiverts, condition more easily than extraverts. Eysenck (1977) presents a compelling argument, well grounded in the research literature on conditioning, that the fundamental reason why more people do not engage in criminal activity has to do with individual differences in conditionability. Through the long and sometimes tumultuous process of childhood socialization, people generally acquire, in an uneven way, the association between "bad" or inappropriate conduct and some form of punishment. Pavlov was able to condition his dogs to connect bells with punishment. That is, when a bell was closely followed by an aversive stimulus, such as an electrical shock to the left front paw, the dog quickly learned to associate the bell with pain and began lifting its paw at the sound of the bell, even if the electrical shock did not always follow. Eysenck contends that the socialization process that discourages antisocial conduct operates essentially in the same manner. The child who immediately receives a hand slap for inappropriate behavior will eventually associate that particular behavior with aversive events (contiguity without reinforcement). Therefore, Eysenck believes that conscience, pangs of guilt, and even the superego are all results of classical conditioning.

Because extraverts condition less readily than introverts or ambiverts, they are less likely to develop a constantly haunting conscience or fear the consequences of antisocial or illegal behavior. Extraverts, therefore, would be more likely to be involved in criminal actions, not only because of their higher level of risk-taking and general neurophysiological needs for stimulation, but also because of their less developed conscience and lack of concern for anticipated consequences of their actions.

Extensive psychological research has found that neurophysiological activity and reactivity "propel" the individual to demonstrate certain behaviors. Eysenck has called this cluster of

322

CHAPTER
TWELVE:
THE
PSYCHOLOGY
OF
CRIMINAL
BEHAVIOR

behaviors **neuroticism** or **emotionality**. He postulates that they spring from the reactivity and sensitivity of the peripheral nervous system, specifically its sympathetic subdivision. This is also an innate or inherited characteristic of the human neurological mechanism.

Like extraversion-introversion, neuroticism is hypothesized to represent a continuum, with most persons falling at the midpoint. Individuals who demonstrate most of the characteristic behaviors of this trait are called, again for research purposes, *neurotics*, while persons displaying few of the relevant behaviors are referred to as *stables*. Persons exhibiting neurotic behaviors overreact to stress and take an unusually long time to recover from stressful events. In many ways, neuroticism is similar to the clinical concept of "anxiety" and the research concept of "arousal."

Neuroticism measures two things: the amount of drive and the amount of reactivity or arousal a person typically experiences under stress and pressure. Drive reflects the amount of pressure or push toward some activity a person demonstrates. Suppose a neurotic extravert has not been properly conditioned to avoid stealing. Because of the rewards that stealing often brings, it becomes a well-learned habit, and neuroticism is likely to be the impelling force encouraging (or driving) the individual to steal.

But arousal plays a role also, especially in violent crimes. As we discussed early, arousal has the property of disengaging individuals from their cognitive processing, rendering them more susceptible to doing things they normally would not do. Thus, under highly arousing conditions, a person prone to violence (especially one with a history of it) and high in neuroticism is more apt to engage in violent actions than a person low in neuroticism. Thus, neuroticism measures both drive and arousal. According to Eysenckian theory, therefore, a large percentage of violent criminal activity is committed by persons who demonstrate extraverted behaviors and also are highly emotional or easily upset.

No neurophysiological mechanism has yet been proposed by Eysenck to account for psychoticism, his most recently formulated dimension. Behaviorally, **psychoticism** is characterized by cold cruelty, social insensitivity, unemotionality, high risk-taking, troublesome behavior, dislike of others, and an attraction to the unusual. Psychotic individuals are hostile toward others and enjoy duping or ridiculing them.

Psychoticism has not yet received the research attention that extraversion and neuroticism have. However, Eysenck hypothesizes that, like extraversion and neuroticism, psychoticism is closely related to criminal behavior. He suggests that psychoticism will be especially prominent in hardcore, habitual offenders convicted of crimes of violence (Eysenck, 1983). Moreover, the behavioral pattern is apparent even in young children.

RESEARCH TESTING EYSENCK'S THEORY

The research designed to test Eysenck's theory has produced mixed results (Passingham, 1972; Allsopp, 1976; Feldman, 1977; Bartol, 1991a). The trend supports some aspects of the theory, but as a general explanation of criminality, the theory needs considerable refinement. For example, while the theory appears to hold for European males convicted of property crimes, it has not been supported for a U. S. group of African-American male inmates convicted of violent offenses (Bartol & Holanchock, 1979). Also, the theory is not sensitive enough to take into account the differences in motives and situational forces demonstrated by various offender groups. For example, individuals who commit a once-in-a-lifetime homicide possess very different expectations and socialization processes than those who pursue a lifetime of lucrative burglaries.

Moreover, it does not explain the phenomenon of corporate and other white-collar crime, in which calculated risk-taking is more likely to be apparent. In fact, Eysenck's theory is far more persuasive for spontaneous crimes than for those requiring a carefully planned approach.

Despite these problems, Eysenck's theory of criminality does offer the promising possibility of a testable theory of criminal behavior based on the interactions of biological factors and learning processes. Perhaps its major weakness lies in its heavy reliance upon conditioning as the primary learning process. Other forms of learning—operant and observational, for instance—also appear to be interwoven in the development of antisocial or criminal behavior.

THE PSYCHOPATH

One of the most interesting ongoing discoveries in criminal behavior is the phenomenon of psychopaths, the clinical or diagnostic group of individuals who offer the most promise as a support base for Eysenck's theory. While it is always wise to be cautious in cataloging humans into neat diagnostic packages, the clinical entity called the *psychopath* does have some validity as a distinct behavioral pattern.

Psychopaths should not be confused with **sociopaths** or people with **antisocial personality disorders** (APD). In common usage, sociopath and APD refer to a person who is *repetitively* in conflict with the law, with an apparently limited capacity to learn from past experiences. The psychopath, on the other hand, although he or she also seems to have little capacity to learn, may or may not demonstrate antisocial or criminal behavior. However, he or she does exhibit certain behavioral, interpersonal, and emotional patterns that appear to be fundamental to the disorder.

The characteristic behavior patterns of the psychopath are most ably described by Hervey Cleckley (1976) in his classic, *The Mask of Sanity.* Two main features are superficial charm and average to above-average intelligence, both of which are especially apparent during initial contacts. Psychopaths seem to be friendly, sociable, outgoing, likeable, and alert. They often appear well educated, knowledgeable, and interested in a wide variety of things.

Although some psychopaths may participate in socially deviant behavior, they generally do not exhibit behaviors that would qualify as clinically descriptive of neurosis or psychosis. Under even the most stressful conditions, psychopaths are likely to remain cool and calm, manifesting few of the typical indicators of anxiety. They appear emotionally flat, with few mood swings, and display few signs of a genuine sense of humor.

In many ways, the psychopath is unreliable, irresponsible, and unpredictable, regardless of the importance of the occasion or the consequences of impulsive actions. This pattern is cyclical, however. For extended periods, the psychopath may appear responsible and may have outstanding achievements. Then, without warning, the psychopath will do something that jeopardizes his or her status. For example, the person may open a window and scream obscenities at the crowd below a third-floor executive suite, go on a drunken spree, steal a car, or impulsively drive off into the sunset. Because of this cyclical pattern, psychopaths rarely pursue consistent, successful criminal careers. Rather, they are more likely to participate in capers or hastily planned crimes that offer immediate satisfaction.

Other typical behaviors include extreme selfishness and an inability to love or give affection to others. Psychopaths are unable to learn from past mistakes and become vulgar, domineering, loud, and boisterous under the influence of alcohol. The cardinal trait of psychopaths appears to be an unusually high need for stimulation. Most of their behavior seems to be a result of attempts to satisfy their insatiable requirement for excitement and outside stimulation. In this way, they are very similar to the extremely extraverted individuals described by Eysenck.

People who display a large number of the behaviors described above also possess neurophysiological functions that generally reflect underarousal (Hare & Schalling, 1978). Extensive research has revealed notable differences in peripheral and central nervous-system functioning

324

CHAPTER
TWELVE:
THE
PSYCHOLOGY
OF
CRIMINAL
BEHAVIOR

between individuals who fit the behavioral description of the psychopath and those who do not (e.g., Hare, 1970; Lykken, 1957, 1978; Hare & Schalling, 1978; Bartol, 1991a). Although additional investigation is needed, the data do suggest that neurophysiological factors may predispose certain individuals to antisocial or criminal behavior.

It is important that we underscore that it is only a predisposition. Whether someone who is neurophysiologically predisposed ultimately engages in criminal behavior depends upon the person's learning history, cognitive expectancies, and the situation at hand. Theoretically, if the person has learned to meet needs for excitement and stimulation in ways that run counter to society's rules, and if socialization (conditioning) has done little to generate anxiety when codes are violated, then antisocial behavior is likely to result.

Currently, the best instrument to measure psychopathy is the twenty-two-item Psychopathy Checklist (PCL) (Hare, 1980) and its twenty-item revision (PCL-R) (Hare, 1991). The available research indicates that the PCL and the PCL-R have high reliability and validity (Hare, Forth & Strachan, 1992). Cut-off scores of 30 on the PCL-R and 34 on the PCL have been found to be useful diagnostic indicators of psychopathy. The checklists include many of the same psychopathic behaviors described earlier. Interestingly, although a large percentage of criminal offenders are diagnosed with antisocial personality disorder (about 80 percent), only about 15 percent to 25 percent of them meet the PCL-R criteria for psychopathy (Hare et al., 1992).

Inmates who meet the PCL-R criteria are more likely to have been convicted for violent offenses, to have used weapons, and to have threatened others with violence than nonpsychopathic offenders (Serin, 1991). Once in prison, psychopathic inmates engage in more institutional violence and aggression than other inmates (Hare & McPherson, 1984). Moreover, psychopathic inmates commit a much greater variety of offenses than nonpsychopathic inmates (Kosson, Smith & Newman, 1990). Female criminal psychopaths, although rare, are believed to follow similar patterns (Hare et al., 1992).

Research by Robert Hare and his colleagues also indicates that criminal psychopaths begin their antisocial activities early, at least by age fifteen or sixteen (Hare, 1991). In addition, while a dysfunctional family background appears to be associated with the development of antisocial activity in nonpsychopaths, it does *not* seem to be related to the development of criminal psychopathy (Devita, Forth, Hare & McPherson, 1991). Criminal psychopaths continue to offend and cause social and emotional distress to others throughout their lifetimes. As a group, they seem to continue to commit both violent and nonviolent crimes, even after age sixty (Harris, Rice & Cormier, 1991). However, there is also some evidence that criminal psychopaths reduce their level of violent offending as they get older, especially as they approach forty, although their nonviolent offenses remain frequent throughout their lives (Hare et al., 1992). The reasons for this intriguing pattern remain unknown.

Psychosocial Factors in Criminal Behavior

As mentioned earlier, one weakness of Eysenck's theory of criminality is his failure to account for possible effects of operant or instrumental and observational learning. He relies instead almost exclusively on classical conditioning. However, behavior that enables us to obtain rewards or avoid punishing circumstances is likely to be repeated when similar conditions recur. This process illustrates instrumental learning. The rewards may be physical (e.g., money, material goods), psychological (e.g., feelings of control over one's life), or social (e.g., improved status).

Even behaviors that are considered antisocial or criminal may bring rewards that are worth the psychological risks and costs.

In psychological parlance, rewards are termed reinforcements. The acquisition of physical, psychological, or social rewards as a consequence of behavior is called **positive reinforcement**. The successful avoidance of negative or aversive events as a result of behavior is called **negative reinforcement**. Avoiding a painfully boring meeting by malingering provides negative reinforcement and is likely to be repeated if the ploy is successful.

Instrumental learning, the process we have been illustrating, offers the most easily grasped explanation of criminality from a psychological perspective. People who commit crimes are seeking to gain or avoid something. A person may wish to terminate the pain caused by an abusive spouse (negative reinforcement) or yearn for the new boat which can be obtained by embezzling company profits. The reinforcements may seem fairly straightforward, but they can also be deceptively complex. Some antisocial behavior may be directed at gaining the social approval of a significant subgroup, such as a youth gang, or the psychological feeling of personal control over one's situation, and it may be independent of the obvious material gain promised by the successful completion of the crime. The behavior also may be intended to gain reward in more than one area. Consider the crime of perjury, as when a law-enforcement officer lies under oath in order to see a defendant convicted. Although there are no material gains, the solidarity of the law-enforcement subgroup and the feeling of personal control over the outcome of the case which the officer may feel as a result of the perjury are reinforcement enough.

If the eventual reinforcement makes the investment worthwhile, the behavior is likely to be repeated. Therefore, criminal behavior will continue to be practiced if it is materially, socially, or psychologically profitable. But this is only part of the story, because criminal behavior can also occur as a result of observational learning, or more broadly, cognitive-social learning.

COGNITIVE-SOCIAL LEARNING THEORY

Julian Rotter (1954, 1966, 1972) is a major contributor to cognitive-social learning theory because of his emphasis on the cognitive, mediating aspects of human learning. Cognition refers to structures and processes within the brain which produce mental activity, including thinking, planning, deciding, wishing, organizing, reconciling, and mental transformation. Cognitive psychology, the study of these processes, is the dominant force in the field today.

Cognitive psychology emphasizes the internal or "mind" representations of the external world. Generally it sees behavior as a function of the subjective world transformed and represented in the person's mind. That is, people behave in accordance with their thoughts and interpretations about the world rather than in reaction to the way the outside world objectively or "really" is.

The traditional theories of classical conditioning and instrumental learning fail to take into careful consideration what goes on between the time the organism perceives a stimulus and responds or reacts to it. Cognitive-social learning theory posits that this classical view is too simple and too general to allow complete understanding of human behavior.

Rotter stresses the importance of the individual's cognitive expectations about the consequences of behavior and the rewards that will be gained from it. In other words, before responding to a given set of circumstances, an individual evaluates: "What has happened to me before in this situation, and what will I gain if I do this?" This self-questioning process may occur very rapidly or take place after much deliberation. According to Rotter, the probability of a specific behavior occurring depends upon the individual's expectations about the outcomes of the behavior and the subjectively perceived gain that will result. Therefore, behavior is a function of the person's

326

CHAPTER
TWELVE:
THE
PSYCHOLOGY
OF
CRIMINAL
BEHAVIOR

relevant expectancies, acquired from past experiences, and the perceived importance of the rewards to be gained. Over the long haul of daily living, the person will develop **generalized expectancies** which tend to be stable and consistent across relatively similar circumstances (Mischel, 1976).

With reference to criminal events, we can posit that the individual expects or anticipates the action to be effective in the acquisition of status, power, affection, material goods, or generally positive living conditions. The specific behavior chosen (and its concomitant expectancies) need not have been directly reinforced previously, however. An individual may obtain the cognitive imagery of a particular behavior simply by observing another person performing the action. This is known as **observational learning** or **modeling** (Bandura, 1973, 1986). Consider, for example, the use of a gun. Although many individuals have never directly fired a gun, almost everyone knows how to do so. Although there are technical aspects of the firearm, like the safety catch and loading mechanisms, the overall general operating procedure is familiar to most of us: point the barrel and pull the trigger. How do we learn this? By *observing* others using firearms.

Albert Bandura (1973) postulates that much of our behavior is acquired initially by watching others, who are known as **models**. The more significant and meaningful these models are to us, the greater the likelihood that the observed behavior will be imitated. Models may be parents, teachers, siblings, friends, peers, and even symbolic figures like television or film characters or the protagonist in a favorite novel.

The observed behavior may be copied immediately or at a future time deemed most appropriate by the observer. Once tried, its continuance depends substantially upon its consequences. If the new behavior delivers gain or reinforcement, it will probably be used again. If not, it is likely to drop out of our behavioral repertoire. Therefore, although initial cognitive activity patterns may be acquired through observation, their maintenance usually depends upon the nature of the rewards.

Although we have outlined cognitive-social learning theory in relatively simple terms, it would be a mistake to assume that the observer simply mimics the behavior of the model. The observer also notes if, how, and when the model is rewarded, disregarded, or punished. Adults in particular also evaluate the consequences in relation to their own position and capacities. Hence, the observer assesses self-evaluative components as well as external outcomes. "People do not indiscriminately absorb the influences that impinge upon them" (Bandura, 1974, p. 862). They weigh and consider, and once they have decided to behave a certain way, they expect something.

Criminal behavior is intended to gain something that is subjectively useful or meaningful to the agent. In this sense, criminal behavior may be perceived as *subjectively adaptive* rather than simply deviant or emotionally sick. It may be antisocial or deviant in reference to society's rules and values, but for that particular person, at that particular time, in a particular psychological state, the conduct is perceived as the best choice possible.

Thus far, we have discussed neurophysiological predispositions to classical conditioning, instrumental learning, and cognitive-social learning as psychological factors that help explain crime. The reader may be wondering at this point, "Which is the culprit?" Criminal behavior appears to be due to a varying composite of all of these factors. People who engage in crime, however defined, do so for a variety of subjective reasons, stemming from their learning histories, their neurophysiological predispositions, and their cognitive styles and competencies. Therefore, antisocial or criminal behavior can best be regarded as subjectively adaptive, even if socially deviant.

RECIPROCAL DETERMINISM

Thus far, however, we have emphasized the individual and neglected the situation. Cognitive-social learning theory tries to accommodate both personal (or dispositional) and situational factors. It analyzes behavior in relation to reciprocal interaction or determinism (Bandura, 1974, 1977). *Determinism* in this context signifies "the production of effects by events, rather than in the doctrinal sense that actions are completely determined by a prior sequence of causes independent of the individual" (Bandura, 1978, p. 345). Reciprocal determinism refers to the hypothesis that behavior is influenced by the environment, but also that the environment is partly of a person's own making. By their own actions, people create their social milieu; the social milieu, in turn, affects their actions. Therefore, from a cognitive-social learning perspective, criminal behavior is a result of a continuous reciprocal interplay between behavioral, cognitive, and environmental influences.

Reciprocal determinism needs further elaboration before the reader can obtain a clear understanding of the way people and the environment interact. According to Bandura (1978), *interaction* has been used in three fundamentally different ways—as unidirectional, partially bidirectional, and reciprocal.

In **unidirectional interaction**, the person and the situation are seen as independent entities that combine to produce behavior. The person finds himself or herself faced with a set of circumstances, remembers previous, similar circumstances, and responds accordingly. Therefore, neither the person nor the situation affect one another.

In the **partial-bidirectional** conception, the person and the situation are considered interdependent causes of behavior. The person's behavior influences the situation, and the situation in turn influences the behavior.

What is missing from both of these interpretations is cognition, an element which Bandura's third type of interaction—**reciprocal determinism**, takes into account. In psychological activity, cognitions influence both behavior and the situation, and these, in turn, influence cognitions.

Any complete understanding of criminal behavior from a psychological perspective requires an analysis of the reciprocal interaction which occurs. A vivid illustration can be found in the literature on **deindividuation**, a process whereby a group can activate behaviors, including antisocial and brutal ones, in individuals not normally so inclined (Festinger, Pepitone & Newcomb, 1952). Crowd violence, looting, vandalism, gang rapes, and crowd panic are all examples of this phenomenon.

Deindividuation is dependent upon an interplay between each individual's perceptions of himself or herself (cognitions), his or her behavior (individual conduct), and the actions of the crowd (situation). The process usually follows a sequence. First, the presence of many other people prompts one to begin to feel part of a group, or at least personally diffused in the group, so that he or she cannot be singled out or easily identified. In this phase, the behavior of others influences a person's cognitions and self-awareness, and the person's behavior reciprocally begins to influence the actions of others in the group. During the second phase, the behavior of the group is imitated, usually cautiously and tentatively. In news footage of crowd violence, for example, one often can observe individuals who are looking at the illegal activity around them (e.g., brick throwing), seemingly hesitant about whether to join in.

Once begun, the antisocial or violent behavior is found rewarding and pleasurable, bringing physiological arousal into play. The behavior provides the cognitive component of the triad with feedback, and the cognitive component interacts with the behavioral one, "urging it on." Meanwhile, of course, the person is still receiving and providing behavioral and cognitive cues (attitudes and values about the activity) from and to the crowd.

In the third and final deindividuation phase, the behavior of the individuals and the collective crowd reaches a crescendo of violence, brutality, and destruction. All three components are involved in reciprocal interaction. Once the group action has reached this stage, very little can be

328

CHAPTER
TWELVE:
THE
PSYCHOLOGY
OF
CRIMINAL
BEHAVIOR

done to terminate it, including measures to dispel the crowd, until there is a change in the state of the group (e.g., people become fatigued or injured), a change in the state of the victims (e.g., they lose consciousness or die), or a change in the weapons used (e.g., bullets rather than bricks). Because the crowd has reached the final stage of deindividuation, and because individuals are melded into the group, appeals to reason are unlikely to be effective.

Escalation is another psychological process which illustrates triadic reciprocal determinism. In escalation, one offended or humiliated person resorts to salvaging self-esteem by "going one better" and insulting his or her humiliator. Thus, two people are caught up in an escalating conflict, and exchanges of barbs will continue until one of them decides to quit or must stop. Verbal insults become pushes, pushes become punches, and ultimately, lethal weapons may be used. However, during each step of the escalation, each individual is continually appraising the conflict, the other person's behavior, the situation, his or her own behavior, the antecedents, and the consequences. At the beginning of the scenario, neither party may have wished for the final outcome. The nature of the conflict, the context, and the cognitive appraisals of the actors at each progressive step determine the ultimate effect. Many homicides and aggravated assaults follow this escalating pattern.

Prediction of Criminal Behavior

Since person-situation reciprocity indicates that the factors involved in crime are dynamic, ever changing, and complex, can we make predictions about the likelihood of anyone engaging in criminal behavior? Can we even talk about criminal "personalities" with any degree of confidence? Cognitive-social learning theory certainly casts doubt upon the validity of the long-standing search to determine the personality of the murderer, the person engaged in securities fraud, or the child abuser. However, examining a particular individual's response pattern under certain conditions gives us some predictive power. Past behavior is perhaps one of the best predictors of future behavior we have available. A repeat offender who has engaged in a string of burglaries is predictable to some degree. But any predictive equation will have to examine the individual's competencies, expectancies, and other relevant behavioral patterns, as well as the specific conditions which activate the burglary behavior. Even after careful study, the predictive equation will likely result in only a rough estimation of behavior within a certain time frame.

The concepts of cross-situational and temporal consistency should also help in any analysis of criminal behavior. As the reader will recall, cross-situational consistency refers to the degree to which behaviors or traits generalize from one situation to another, dissimilar situation. Temporal consistency refers to the degree to which behaviors are consistent over time in similar situations. Research has found that individuals in general reflect greater temporal than cross-situational consistency. Therefore, criminal behavior that has been reinforced in a particular context is more apt to recur in a similar context than across a wide variety of situations. For example, a person who has engaged in a lifetime of burglary is more likely to burglarize again if surrounded by familiar situations. On the other hand, if his or her environment has changed substantially (e.g., a longtime partner in crime has died; the former burglar is now living in Lubec, Maine, instead of Boston, Massachusetts), it is less likely that the criminal activity will continue.

Psychologists have often remarked that their discipline helps them to predict some of the people some of the time (Bem & Allen, 1974). Actually we can be more optimistic and say that we should be able to predict most people's behavior much of the time if we apply the principles covered in this chapter. It is also important to take note of a "discovery" brought to light by several psychologists (Kenrick & Stringfield, 1980; Mischel, 1973, 1976). A valuable resource in helping psychologists improve their predictive power is the information people provide about themselves. The best clues to understanding people are the traits and behaviors they say they have, and people are surprisingly willing to reveal such information. Rather than dismiss reports because they are self-serving, psychologists are listening more carefully and applying these comments to their evaluations. A person who admits he is often hostile, loses his temper, feels like physically abusing others, and who has a history of assault convictions, would probably merit careful monitoring. On the other hand, without these self-reported behaviors, predictive power becomes less convincing.

In sum, full consideration of criminal behavior requires analysis of the triadic reciprocal system, the situation, and "personality" (expectancies, learning history, competencies, subjective values, cognitive structures, and self-regulatory systems and plans). We make no pretense that this is a simple task. It is often more appealing to advance dogmatic, simplified generalizations that are cognitively easier than to tackle the immense problem of understanding, predicting, and changing criminal behavior.

PROFILING REVISITED

Criminal profiling (also called **psychological profiling** or **criminal personality profiling**) refers to the process of identifying personality traits, behavioral tendencies, and demographic variables of an offender, based on characteristics of the crime. To a large extent, the profiling process is dictated by a database collected on previous offenders who have committed similar offenses. Experienced profilers assert that profiling is most successful when the offender demonstrates some form of psychopathology at the crime scene, such as sadistic torture, evisceration, postmortem slashings and cuttings, and other mutilations (Pinizzotto, 1984). Profiling appears to be particularly useful in sexual offenses, such as serial rape and serial sexual homicides (Pinizzotto & Finkel, 1990), because we have a more extensive research base on sexual offenses than we do on homicides. On the other hand, profiling is largely ineffective in identifying offenders involved in fraud, burglary, robbery, political incidents, theft, and drug-induced crimes because of the limited research base.

Although psychological profiling was used by the Office of Strategic Services (OSS) during World War II (Ault & Reese, 1980), the technique has only become popular since being adopted by the Federal Bureau of Investigation in 1971 (Pinizzotto & Finkel, 1990). The behavioral science unit of the bureau receives numerous requests for profiles from various law-enforcement agencies, primarily in cases involving homicide (65 percent), rape (35 percent), or kidnapping (8 percent) (Pinizzotto, 1984). An example of the information gathered in a homicide case includes: (1) color photos of the crime scene; (2) the nature of the neighborhood (economic and social data); (3) the medical examiner's report; (4) a map of the victim's travels prior to the death; (5) a complete investigative report of the incident; and (6) complete background of the victim, including habits and lifestyle.

Computer-based models of offender profiles based on extensive statistical data collected on similar offenses hold considerable promise. However, professional profilers often claim—like experienced clinicians—that accurate profiling must rely heavily on common sense, logic, intuition, and experience (Pinizzotto, 1984). It is "...an art developed through experience" (McCann, 1992, p. 479). Profiling based on anything but a strong database, however, is likely to be plagued by many of the same biases, cognitive distortions, and inaccuracies so characteristic of clinical judgment when predicting dangerousness. To date, there is very little research on the utility,

330

CHAPTER
TWELVE:
THE
PSYCHOLOGY
OF
CRIMINAL
BEHAVIOR

reliability, and validity of criminal profiling. Much needs to be done in this area before even tentative conclusions can be advanced.

More recently, a similar attempt at reconstructing the personality profile and cognitive features (especially intentions) of deceased individuals has gained some popularity. This postmortem psychological analysis is called **reconstructive psychological evaluation** (RPE) or **equivocal death analysis** (Poythress, Otto, Darkes & Starr, 1993) The analysis is also known as a **psychological autopsy** (Brent, 1989; Ebert, 1987; Selkin, 1987), although this technique is often reserved for suicide cases. The psychological autopsy is frequently done to determine the reasons for the suicide and ultimately to establish some legal culpability by other persons or organizations. For example, in a civil suit for damages, the plaintiff (e.g., the victim's spouse) may wish to establish that the suicide was directly caused by some company policy or procedure.

The RPE differs from criminal profiling in two important ways: the profile is constructed on a dead person and the identity of the person is already known. However, the reliability and validity of the RPE and its variants (psychological autopsies) has yet to be demonstrated. Norman Poythress et al. (1993) warn that "…persons who conduct reconstructive psychological evaluations should not assert categorical conclusions about the precise mental state or actions suspected of the actor at the time of his or her demise. The conclusions and inferences drawn in psychological reconstructions are, at best, informed speculations or theoretical formulations and should be labeled as such" (p. 12).

Defining and Recording Crime

Crime is commonly defined as "an intentional act in violation of the criminal law committed without defense or excuse, and penalized by the state as a felony or misdemeanor" (Tappan, 1947, p. 100). Criminal behavior, therefore, refers to the broad span of actions which violate the criminal code. This expansive definition does not suit our purpose, because it is not specific enough. If we were to abide strictly by Tappan's definition, we could describe most of the U. S. population as, in some sense, "criminal." Have you, the reader, never engaged in some action regarded as criminal according to the above definition? Have you ever behaved in a way that could justifiably be considered a misdemeanor or felony and carried with it a possible jail or prison sentence? Illegal drug use, willfully damaging property, shoplifting, stealing from one's employer, and punching another individual all qualify. Driving while intoxicated is another example of behavior in violation of criminal codes.

In a dated but relevant self-report survey of criminal conduct (Wallerstein & Wyle, 1947), approximately seventeen hundred persons were asked to indicate on a list of forty-nine criminal offenses which, if any, they had committed. The list excluded traffic violations but included both felonies and misdemeanors. Fully 91 percent of the respondents admitted they had committed one or more offenses for which they might have received jail or prison sentences.

Therefore, unless we plan to include a conservative 90 percent of the population in our criminal sample, we should give our definition more specific limits. Other proposed definitions may be just as troublesome, however. For example, for research purposes a criminal is typically defined as one who has been both arrested and convicted. However, legal determinations are dependent upon what society, at some point in time, considers socially harmful or, in some cases, morally wrong. Societies differ in their criteria for criminal behavior; even states differ; and the same society or the same state, over time, may change the criminal code and its perceptions of what constitutes illegal or criminal conduct.

■ 12.1: *FUNDING VIOLENCE RESEARCH*

RESEARCH ON VIOLENCE, PARTICULARLY that funded by the federal government, is under considerable scrutiny. Controversy has erupted over projects sponsored by the Public Health Service (PHS) and the National Institutes of Health (NIH) which imply there is a biological link between race and violence. In 1992, for example, NIH agreed to sponsor a conference at the University of Maryland titled "Genetic Factors in Crime." Many of the papers scheduled to be read suggested a genetic predisposition to violent criminal behavior.

NIH eventually withdrew its support, and the conference was canceled. In announcing the restriction of funds, NIH representatives said conference literature diverged radically from norms acceptable by peer review (APA, 1992). Many observers believed, however, that the uproar that ensued among scientists and other concerned citizens had prompted NIH to remove its funding.

Criminologist C. Ray Jeffery (1993), who opposed the cancellation of the Maryland conference, believes it is irresponsible to close our minds to the possibility that biological predisposition may be a factor in violent crime. As an interdisciplinary science, criminology should be receptive to research from many perspectives, including the biological one, argues Jeffery. The results of genetically based research, in his view, might ultimately allow us to intervene early in the lives of children who are at risk of becoming violent offenders.

That is precisely what concerns the opponents of such research. They note that violence researchers seldom use assaultive, middle-class white men as subjects. Instead, racial minorities and economically disadvantaged groups have traditionally been the targets of the research; they also would likely be subjected to the intervention. Furthermore, the prevention of violence in those who are supposedly biologically predisposed may well take the form of physical manipulation, including drug therapy.

There are numerous other reasons for opposing public funding of biologically based violence research. Many believe that public money is better spent dealing with the social conditions frequently associated with street crime, including inferior education, unemployment, and discrimination. NIH and PHS, in the opinion of community activists, would serve the public better by ensuring adequate health care, substance-abuse treatment, and AIDS education and treatment than by funding projects which suggest that minority groups and the poor somehow are genetically defective.

In the scientific community, however, suppression of research remains a key issue. The announcement that the Maryland conference had been canceled produced a wave of renewed protest. The possibility of a biological predisposition to violence apparently is appealing enough to some members of the scientific community that they will continue to conduct research on that topic, with or without government support. ■

Restricting ourselves to convicted persons to help us define crime is also troublesome because of the discriminatory practices of each culture. Each judicial system perceives and processes alleged violators of the criminal code with some discrimination, so that offender background, social status, personality, motivation, age, sex, race, and even choice of lawyer may affect the judicial process, along with the circumstances surrounding the crime itself. Accepting the legal description, therefore, means that our definition of criminal behavior would be contaminated with the biases and discriminatory practices inherent in the system.

Finally, there is a host of behaviors that are technically not criminal, but still illegal. They involve the violation of administrative law that carries civil penalties, including fines or an order to cease and desist a certain activity. Examples of such behavior are an employer's failure to abide by government-established safety regulations and a corporation's violation of rules of the Federal Trade Commission. Sociologist Edwin Sutherland (1949), in his classic book, *White Collar Crime*, argued that such behavior should be regarded as criminal in our society because of its widespread harmful effect. Although many criminologists today agree, there continues to be a double standard in favor of corporations; corporate law-breaking activities are not usually regarded as criminal (Mokhiber, 1988).

Defining criminal behavior, therefore, is no easy task. Precise operational definitions often

332

CHAPTER
TWELVE:
THE
PSYCHOLOGY
OF
CRIMINAL
BEHAVIOR

fail to include all possible violations or relevant behavior. Even by conservative estimates, thirty-six to forty million Americans—16 to 18 percent of the total U. S. population—have arrest records for nontraffic offenses (U. S. Department of Justice, 1988). Since almost all the available data on crime are based on arrest or conviction records and self-reports, this chapter's research content will be directed at these populations. The theoretical discussion, however, can be expanded to include criminal behavior broadly defined, or any behavior that violates prevailing codes of conduct and for which criminal or civil penalties may be imposed.

CRIME STATISTICS

Official Numbers

Official crime statistics kept by law-enforcement agencies, such as those found in the annual FBI *Uniform Crime Reports* (UCR), are strongly influenced by the social, economic, and political climate at the time they are reported. Generally, however, official law-enforcement reports underestimate the total number of actual crimes committed—a total known as the **dark figure**. The UCR, compiled since 1930, is the most-cited source of U. S. crime statistics. It contains arrest information received on a voluntary basis from approximately ten thousand law-enforcement agencies throughout the United States. Arrests are classified as to whether they are for serious crimes presumably of most concern to society (**index crimes**) or for the "less serious" ones (**nonindex crimes**). The index crimes are murder and nonnegligent manslaughter, forcible rape, robbery, aggravated assault, burglary, larceny/theft, motor-vehicle theft, and arson. Nonindex crimes include a wide range of offenses, among them embezzlement, fraud, vandalism, carrying illegal weapons, a variety of drug-offending behaviors, and buying, receiving, or possessing stolen property.

UCR data have continually indicated that arrest rates for serious property crimes peak at around age seventeen or eighteen, the age at which many courts routinely begin prosecuting offenders as adults. After age eighteen, arrest rates for property crime decline dramatically. The pattern for violent crime is quite different. These arrests gradually peak at around age seventeen, level off until about age twenty-three, and then show a gradual decrease.

In response to perpetual criticism, the FBI has revised its methods of gathering data to more accurately reflect the prevalence and incidence of crime. Still, it is important to recognize that the UCR data which are currently available must be approached guardedly.

Self-Report Surveys

Many researchers are convinced that the **self-report** (SR) **method** offers a more reliable estimate of actual offending than UCR statistics, even though some individuals may inflate or deflate personal reports on their criminal activity. The longitudinal **National Youth Survey** (NYS) (Elliott & Huizinga, 1983; Elliott & Ageton, 1980) is one of the most comprehensive SR studies undertaken to date. The NYS is based on a compilation of both SR and official data collected on 1,725 youths who were between the ages of eleven and seventeen when the project began in 1977. The survey involves a **panel design** in which the same youths are sampled repeatedly over several years. The NYS has addressed many of the major criticisms leveled at traditional SR measures of delinquency. Specifically critics often complain that SR questionnaires ask about status or trivial offenses, such as frequency of running away from home, violation of sexual mores, acting out in school, occasional drinking of alcohol, or disobeying parents. Others complain that the questions are ambiguous or that the choices are unclear or inappropriate.

Self-report surveys have been administered primarily to youths, although some researchers have recognized a need to use this method of data gathering with adults as well. Whether administered to youths or to adults, self-report surveys have confirmed what has long been suspected, namely that involvement in crime cuts across socioeconomic class, race, and family background.

Victimization Surveys

In recent years, victimization surveys have shed further light on crime statistics. Based on a representative sampling of households, these surveys provide information about the victim's experiences with crimes, both those which were reported to the police and those which were not. Information obtained from victims yields data about the details of the criminal events, the circumstances under which they occurred, and the effects on the victims. The surveys tap crimes that for a variety of reasons were never reported to police and therefore provide information as to why certain criminal acts go unreported.

One of the more ambitious surveys in recent years, the **National Crime Survey** (NCS) is conducted by the Bureau of the Census. The NCS reports the results of contacts with a large national sample of households (approximately 49,000) representing 101,000 persons over the age of twelve. A member of the household is first asked whether anyone has experienced a crime during the previous six months. If the answer is yes, the victim is interviewed more extensively. The NCS is currently designed to measure the extent to which households and individuals are victims of rape, robbery, assault, burglary, motor-vehicle theft, and larceny. Murder and kidnapping are not covered, because these serious criminal offenses are almost always reported to the authorities. The most recent revision of the NCS asks those victims who reported crime how law-enforcement officials responded. A **victimization rate**, expressed by the number of victimizations per thousand potential victims or households, is obtained and reported to the public.

The NCS is most useful in estimating crimes against victims who understand what happened to them, how it happened, and are willing to report what they know. Note that we often do not know when we have been victimized, especially by some types of white-collar crime. Patients are generally not aware when a physician submits them to unnecessary surgery or files false medicare claims on their behalf, for example (Pontell et al., 1984). Like other forms of obtaining crime data, the victimization survey is far from perfect. However, it is an extremely useful supplement to the UCR and self-report surveys. Some criminologists, as a matter of fact, consider victimization surveys the most valid instruments available for measuring the extent of crime in our society.

The data collected through the NCS are extensive. For illustration, we will consider the highlights of a recent report, especially those characteristics relating to violent personal crimes. The intention here is not to present definitive statistics, but rather to give the reader an idea of the type of information derived from the NCS. The interested reader is encouraged to examine the original source for additional information.

DEMOGRAPHICS OF CRIME VICTIMS

The statistics on personal crimes of violence are highest among males, the young (ages sixteen to nineteen), African-Americans, Hispanics, the divorced or separated, the poor, and the unemployed. African-Americans are more likely to be victims of household burglary or motor-vehicle theft, but not household larceny. The poor are the most likely to experience burglary, but the least likely victims of household larceny or motor-vehicle theft.

Overall, males are far more likely to be victims of personal robbery (8.7 per 1,000) and assault (37.5) than females (4.0 and 16.9, respectively). With regard to personal larceny (e.g., purse

334

CHAPTER
TWELVE:
THE
PSYCHOLOGY
OF
CRIMINAL
BEHAVIOR

snatching, pocket picking), males also are more likely to be victimized (107.9 versus 87.5 per 1,000).

According to the NCS, about two women in every thousand are raped. This statistic is extremely questionable, as are the assault statistics. A woman who has been raped may be no more willing to report this to an interviewer than to police. We will return to this issue shortly, when we discuss some of the research specifically associated with this particular crime.

NCS data suggest that the most likely woman to be raped is one who is separated or divorced (2.8 per 1,000), followed by victims who have never been married (1.7), those married (0.3), and those widowed (0.6). The age group most frequently raped is between sixteen and nineteen (5.3); the least-frequently raped group is between fifty and sixty-four (0.1). Of the three violent personal crimes, rape is the most likely to have happened inside victims' homes. Furthermore, approximately as many rapes occur inside or near victims' residences as in outdoor areas away from them.

For personal crimes of violence and personal crimes of theft, the NCS indicates that the age bracket of twelve to fourteen has the highest victimization rate, and the elderly (sixty-five and over) have the lowest. Actually, persons under twenty-five have a violent crime victimization rate three times higher than that for persons aged twenty-five and older, and the rate difference between these two age groups for crimes of theft is approximately 2 to 1. These patterns are especially true for young males.

Minorities (African-Americans and Hispanics) report the highest victimization rate when it comes to violent crime. This has been a consistent finding in the sociological literature, especially in regard to African-Americans. For example, in his classic investigation of 588 homicides in Philadelphia between 1948 and 1952, Marvin Wolfgang (1958, 1961) found that about 73 percent of the offenders and 75 percent of the victims were African-American. In almost all the reported cases (about 94 percent), violence was intraracial, not interracial.

Stranger-to-stranger offenses comprised 63 percent of all personal crimes of violence, ranging from 59 percent for assaults to 75 percent for personal robberies. In terms of victimization rates, 21.4 per 1,000 incidents were a result of stranger-to-stranger contact, compared to 12.6 per 1,000 which resulted from interaction with acquaintances, friends, or relatives. In addition, approximately one-half of all personal robberies were carried out by two or more offenders. Also, multiple offenders were more likely to engage in more serious (aggravated) assaults than in simple assaults.

The NCS found that the extent to which a crime was reported to the police depended on the type or seriousness of victimization, and there was a good deal of consistency in the reasons given by victims for not notifying the police. Altogether only 30 percent of all personal crimes were reported, compared to 38 percent for household crimes. This implies that about two out of every three crimes go unreported. The highest report rate was associated with motor-vehicle theft (88.6 percent), while the lowest pertained to household larcenies in which the loss amounted to less than $50 (14.4 percent).

Although serious crimes tended to be reported, only slightly more than half of the rapes had been filed (58.4 percent), along with two-thirds of the robberies with injury. Only about a quarter of the personal larcenies had been reported, varying, of course, with the amount stolen.

The two most common reasons victims gave for not reporting crimes were: (1) nothing could have been done; and (2) the offense was not important enough to warrant police attention. Inconvenience and fear of reprisal were rarely mentioned as reasons. It is important to note that both rape and assault victims were more likely than robbery victims to view their victimizations as a private or personal matter. This was especially true when the offender was an acquaintance, friend, or relative.

The Crime of Rape

There would be little value in attempting to examine each type of criminal offense at this time, since only cursory treatment would be possible. Instead, we will focus upon one offense, examine the statistics, and consider the psychological theory and research surrounding it. Rape has been chosen because it is a crime associated with misconceptions and myths, has engendered considerable statutory reform and legal attention, and has been the subject of psychological research directed at both the offender and the victim. Also, rape is an offense that is particularly sensitive to the moral, social, and political climate of a society. Therefore, there are interesting trends that emerge from law-enforcement statistics in comparison to victimization studies. Overall, the study of rape exemplifies many of the points we have stressed concerning the interface between psychology and law.

DEFINITIONS OF RAPE

Definitions of rape vary widely from state to state. In a majority of states the term *sexual assault* has replaced *rape* in the criminal statutes. Additionally, it is an offense which can be perpetrated against males as well as females. According to the U. S. Department of Justice, rape is "unlawful sexual intercourse...by force or without legal or factual consent" (1988, p. 2).

The FBI *Uniform Crime Reports* defines rape somewhat differently, distinguishing forcible from statutory rape or rape by fraud, and focusing on the female victim. According to the UCR, **forcible rape** is "the carnal knowledge of a female, forcibly and against her will" and includes rape by force, assault to rape, and attempted rape. Forcible rape is to be contrasted with **statutory rape**, where the age of the female is the crucial distinction, regardless of whether she gives her consent to engage in sexual intercourse or not. The age limit appears to be an arbitrary legal cut-off considered to be the point at which the person has the cognitive and emotional maturity to give her meaningful consent and understand the consequences. Although age limits vary from state to state, most are set at sixteen or eighteen. Therefore, if it can be determined to the satisfaction of the court that an adult male has engaged in sexual relations with a female who was under the legal age at the time, he can be convicted of statutory rape.

Rape by fraud refers to the act of having sexual relations with a consenting adult female under fraudulent conditions, such as when a physician or psychotherapist has sexual intercourse with a patient under the guise of "effective treatment." The legal scope of forcible rape has traditionally been confined to imposed sexual contact or assault of adolescent and adult females who are not related to the offender. However, today the definition of rape is being expanded, despite some opposition,to include sexual assault of a wife by her husband.

Still, many people (including the victims themselves) do not define sexual attacks as rape unless the assailant is a stranger. Thus, if the victim is sexually assaulted by a husband, a boyfriend, or a date, she is unlikely to report the incident. Criminal-justice officials and the general public frequently feel that marital or date rape is less significant because they believe that it is not as psychologically traumatic to the victim and more difficult to prove. Prosecutors, for example, admit they are reluctant to prosecute marital or date-rape cases because it is hard to convince juries that husbands or boyfriends could be sexual assailants (Kilpatrick et al., 1988). However, available data suggest that over 40 percent of the total number of rapes that occur may be committed by husbands or male friends (Kilpatrick et al., 1988).

PREVALENCE AND INCIDENCE OF RAPE

Based on available data, the United States has the highest rape rate in the world. During the past decade, official (based on the FBI *Uniform Crime Reports*) incidents of reported rape numbered

336

Chapter
Twelve:
The
Psychology
of
Criminal
Behavior

between 65 and 75 for every 100,000 women. These figures probably greatly underestimate the actual incidence, however, because data suggest that only 55 percent of rape victims report the crime in the U. S., and only 38 percent of them report it in Canada (Roberts & Gebotys, 1992).

Individual victimization self-report studies provide an even more disconcerting picture. As we noted above, even these figures may be low, of course, because of reluctance to admit that one did not report a rape. Russell (1983) interviewed 930 women living in the San Francisco Bay Area and found that 19 percent said that they had been the victim of at least one completed extramarital rape. Another 13 percent said they had been the victim of at least one attempted extramarital rape. Only 8 percent of all victims of completed or attempted rape had reported the incident to the police. Koss and her colleagues (Koss, Gidycz & Wisniewski, 1987) discovered that 28 percent of the college women surveyed in a national study involving thirty-two U. S. colleges and universities had been victims of rape or attempted rape. More surprising, however, was the fact that virtually none of the incidents had been reported to the police and therefore were not included in the official crime statistics. Based on her data, Koss estimates the victimization rate for women to be 3,800 per 100,000, a rate drastically different from the official rates of 65 to 75 per 100,000.

Additional victimization data suggest that there is approximately a one-in-five chance a woman will be raped at some time during her life (Furby, Weinrott & Blackshaw, 1989). If attempted rapes were included in the statistics, the chances approach one-in-three. A startling number of women are sexually victimized while on a date. Approximately 22 percent of women surveyed said they had been subjected to a coercive sexual encounter (e.g., fondling, oral sex, or intercourse) by a date at some point in their lives (Yegidis, 1986; Dull & Giacopassi, 1987).

The rape victim is frequently twice victimized: by the sexual assailant and by exposure to the judicial process (Borgida, 1980). Rape cases require thorough investigation and attention to detail, which demand keen recall and the description of intimate, stressful sexual events. Victims are also required to undergo a medical examination to establish physical evidence of penetration and use of physical force.

If the victim is able to withstand these stressful conditions, which are often exacerbated by negative reactions from parents, husband, and friends, and sometimes by threats from the assailant, the next step requires the preparation and successful prosecution of the case in court. Ninety-two percent of the prosecutors surveyed by the Law Enforcement Assistance Administration (LEAA) (1977b) asserted that the credibility of the victim was one of the most important elements in convincing juries to convict for forcible rape. Therefore, the defense often has concentrated upon the victim's prior sexual history to destroy credibility and portray her as promiscuous.

The procedure of derogating the victim by using her sexual history has come under attack in recent years, and all fifty states have revised their rape laws in an effort to abolish this tactic (Marsh, 1988). Most states have enacted **rape shield** reform statutes which restrict, to varying degrees, the admissibility of the victim's sexual history into the courtroom (Borgida, 1980).

In addition to impeaching the victim's credibility via her sexual history, some defense attorneys can invoke **corroboration rules**, which require evidence other than the victim's testimony before a person can be charged with rape. In recent years, many states have relaxed the type of evidence required to verify the victim's testimony, while others have abolished the requirement altogether.

A third practice peculiar to rape law is the judge's cautionary instructions to the jury, which stress that a rape charge can be easily brought by a woman and is often difficult to prove. Therefore, the jury is told that the victim's testimony should be viewed with caution.

All three of the above practices center on the credibility of the victim and exist in varying degrees in different jurisdictions. In addition, and closely aligned to victim credibility, the absence of victim consent must be established in deciding what level of guilt, if any, is to be ascribed to the defendant. These determinations of credibility and consent of the victim are among the peculiar and unique aspects of rape law.

There are three major concerns involved in any revision of forcible-rape law: (1) the legal definition of rape; (2) rules of evidence, especially concerning the admissibility of sexual history and corroboration that the crime occurred; and (3) a penalty structure (Marsh, 1988; Loh, 1980). **Comprehensive reforms** of the rape law deal with all three aspects, while limited reforms generally focus on evidence rules, especially admissibility of sexual history (Marsh, 1988). Moreover, the new provisions in forcible-rape legislation show a notable shift in the definition of the crime. Specifically, rape-law reforms transfer the cause of the crime from the victim to the offender and redefine rape as a violation of a personal right (a woman's right to choose to engage in sexual activity) rather than an infringement of a property right (Marsh, 1988).

Very few studies have examined the effects of rape-law reform on the judicial process. Jeanne Marsh (1988), in her review of the extant research, finds that comprehensive reforms in the states of Michigan and Washington have increased the number of convictions for rape. Criminal-justice officials in these states report that two particular aspects of these comprehensive reform statutes have had the greatest influence on improving conviction rates: (1) better definitions of rape; and (2) clarified evidentiary requirements, such as restrictions on sexual-history evidence and changed standards in establishing resistance or consent. However, although these comprehensive reforms did alter formal evidentiary requirements and increased the conviction rates for rape, they did not change the factors considered by police and prosecutors when assessing convictability. Law-enforcement officials and prosecutors continued to use their traditional ways of determining whether an arrest should be made and whether they should proceed with the prosecution. Similar findings are reported in Canada by Roberts and Gebotys (1992) on the judicial effects of nationwide, comprehensive, rape reform legislation passed in 1983.

Eugene Borgida and his colleagues (1980) tested the validity of rape-law reforms in relation to juror interpretations of two elements: (1) the amount of consent given, or implied, by the victim; and (2) the perceived guilt of the defendant. Borgida divided state rape laws into three categories, depending upon the amount of judicial discretion allowed and the statutory restrictions on the admissibility of prior sexual activity. It is worthwhile to consider Borgida's research in detail, because it is a good example of the relationship between psychology and law.

Statutes permitting comparatively unlimited sexual-history evidence, when focused on the issue of the victim's consent, were labeled **common-law rules**. A second category consisted of the **moderate-reform exclusionary rules**. These state statutes permitted a partial limitation on the admissibility of sexual history. While these reform rules allowed trial judges considerable discretion in deciding whether sexual-history evidence could be admitted, they required that: (1) any history allowed be directly relevant to a fact at issue; and (2) the history would not induce unreasonable prejudicial effects on the jury.

A third division, comprising the **radical-reform exclusionary rules**, included statutes which required total exclusion of information on prior sexual activity as related to the issue of consent. However, a qualifier was added. The rules pertain only to sexual history involving third parties and not necessarily to the victim's past sexual conduct with the defendant. The primary purpose of the radical-reform rules was to relieve the trial judge of discretionary power in decisions involving sexual behavior with third parties. The admissibility of evidence about sexual behavior with the defendant was left to the judge's discretion.

Borgida and his colleagues were interested in the effects of these three types of evidentiary

338

CHAPTER
TWELVE:
THE
PSYCHOLOGY
OF
CRIMINAL
BEHAVIOR

rules on the amount of victim consent perceived by jurors. The overriding hypothesis was that the more extensive a woman's sexual history, the greater the likelihood that jurors would believe she had given, or implied, her consent to sexual activity with the defendant. This would result in jurors finding the defendant not guilty of forcible rape.

Over a three-month period, Borgida and his group administered questionnaires to 180 male and female jurors serving their last day of jury duty in a state district court. The questionnaires included the condensed case facts of a hypothetical rape trial involving a consent defense. The jurors were asked to render a personal verdict on the guilt or innocence of the defendant, as well as to rate the degree of victim consent (dependent variables).

The independent variables comprised a 3 × 3 experimental design. Since there were nine conditions in all, twenty jurors were assigned to each condition. The rape-trial description given to each juror was governed by the evidentiary rules found in either common-law, reform, or radical reform categories. That is, depending upon the situation the juror was assigned, he or she would receive considerable, partial, or no sexual history. In addition, again depending upon which situation the subject was assigned, each would read case material conveying a low probability, an ambiguous probability, or a high probability of victim consent.

Borgida hypothesized that the jurors in the common-law category would be more likely to acquit the defendant than the jurors in the radical-reform one. Verdicts in the moderate reform category were expected to be somewhat between. Presumably, the juror who learned the victim had a sexual history would be more likely to believe she had given her consent to the assault than the juror who had no such information. Borgida expected similar findings for those situations in which jurors were given high probability of victim consent compared to those where they were given low probability. Raped women who gave some indication of consent had brought on the assault, the jurors were hypothesized to believe, and thus the defendant was less likely to be convicted.

Exclusionary rules were expected to interact with probability-of-consent conditions. High probability of consent interacting with common law (unlimited sexual history) would most likely lead to an acquittal for the defendant.

The results showed that under a radical-reform rule the likelihood of conviction was increased. As expected, likelihood of conviction also increased when the probability of the victim's consent was low. On the other hand, the lowest conviction rate was obtained under the common-law rule when the case description conveyed a high probability of consent. Under the moderate-reform rule, however, the results were not quite so clear-cut. Overall, the moderate-reform rule elicited the same conviction rate as the common-law rule. More specifically, in both the common-law and moderate-reform situations, twenty jurors found the defendant guilty and forty found him not guilty. Under the radical-reform rule (no sexual history), thirty-two jurors found the defendant guilty and twenty-eight found him not guilty.

The above patterns exist only when we do not take into account the probability of consent, however. Under low probability of consent, jurors in the moderate-reform category were no more likely to find the defendant guilty than jurors in the radical-reform one. The overall differences reported above emerged for both moderate-reform and common-law rules compared to radical-reform ones, but only when the probability of consent was high or ambiguous.

The second dependent measurement—degree of perceived victim consent—proved to be more straightforward. There were no significant differences in the juror's perception of consent under common-law and moderate-reform rules. The major differences were found in relation to radical-reform rules. Specifically, significantly less consent by the victim was believed to have taken place in the sexual assault when jurors did not receive prior sexual history.

Altogether, these simulation-based results suggest that third-party evidence of the victim's sexual history will have a prejudicial effect on the outcome of a rape trial. Jurors tend to be overly influenced by such evidence; they appear more willing to base their verdicts on judgments about the victim's past than on facts concerning the case in question. Furthermore, it also appears that the radical reform exclusionary rules will have the greatest impact in limiting this prejudicial trend.

THE
CRIME
OF
RAPE

SITUATIONAL FACTORS

According to the National Crime Survey (NCS), victims reported offenders used weapons in nearly one-third of all rape incidents; this was especially true when the offender was a stranger. The most commonly used weapon was a knife (45.6 percent), followed by a firearm (34.8 percent), and then by "other." Victims who reported the rapes stated that in over two-thirds of the incidents, the offenders threatened or used force against them. About one-fourth of the victims sustained injuries serious enough to warrant medical treatment or hospitalization (LEAA, 1979c).

Treatment or hospitalization is subject to varying interpretations. The NCS found that 27 percent of the rape victims sustained injuries serious enough to incur expenses in excess of $250. Another 60 percent required medical expenses ranging from $50 to $249, suggesting that physical injury of some sort is extremely common for rape victims. Recent research suggests that rape victims commonly undergo more physical and emotional trauma when their assaulters are spouses or men with whom they have an intimate relationship than when they are strangers (Kilpatrick et al., 1988). Moreover, the psychological trauma seems to be longer lasting and more damaging, resulting in severe depression, intense apprehension, and serious problems in sexual adjustment.

Victims' surveys indicate that the most frequently used method of coercion during date rapes is verbal persuasion, commonly combined with encouragement to use alcohol or other drugs (Kanin, 1984). While weapons are not normally used, brute physical strength in overpowering the victim is very common (Kanin, 1984). In addition, most date rapes apparently occur in the male's apartment or room, and less frequently in the female's residence.

Research on stranger rape reveals that a majority of women resisted the sexual assault, either through verbal or physical means or both (LEAA, 1978b). Initial resistance was usually verbal and fell into one of three strategies. In the first, the victim said things she thought would make herself unattractive to the assailant, such as telling him she was pregnant, sick, had a sexually transmitted disease, was a virgin, or was menstruating. A second strategy consisted of threats that the victim would report the incident to authorities or seek retaliation with the help of family or friends if the assailant continued. A third type of verbal resistance was to feign consent, with the stipulation that the victim be given the opportunity to use a rest room, change clothes, or call a friend. Overall, however, verbal resistance alone was an ineffective method for thwarting sexual assaults, as was crying.

The survey disclosed that the most effective method of thwarting a sexual assault was by screaming or using some noise device, such as a whistle, to attract attention. In some cases, however, this form of resistance caused offenders to become more violent, as we will see below. Physical resistance—struggling, biting, hitting, scratching, kicking—seldom terminated the attack, although some victims were able to escape by using these tactics.

THE RAPIST

Sociological Correlates

Fewer than 5 percent of rape complaints ultimately result in forcible-rape convictions (LEAA, 1978b). Therefore, over 95 percent of the potential offenders are never arrested, never charged, or never convicted of rape, and thus are often not the subjects of research on sexual assaults.

340

CHAPTER
TWELVE:
THE
PSYCHOLOGY
OF
CRIMINAL
BEHAVIOR

Whether the small sample of offenders covered by the conviction statistics is representative of all rapists is debatable. Like those convicted of other crimes, and with the exception of "celebrity" cases, those convicted of rape are more likely to be the powerless, or at least the less powerful, members of society.

Both official and victimization statistics continually show that offenders are young, most between the ages of eighteen and twenty-five. Davis and Leitenberg (1987) found that when both arrest statistics and victim surveys are combined, about 20 percent of all rapes and about 30 to 50 percent of all cases of child sexual abuse can be attributed to adolescent offenders. Abel, Mittelman, and Becker (1985) report that 50 percent of all sex offenders admit their first sexual assault occurred during early adolescence.

Arrested and convicted offenders have frequently been in conflict with the law prior to the rape incident. About one-fourth of those arrested for forcible rape have raped previously, and about one-third have a prior arrest history of violent offenses other than rape (LEAA, 1977b). In a sample of 114 convicted rapists surveyed by Scully and Marolla (1984), for example, 12 percent had previous convictions for rape or attempted rape, 39 percent had for burglary and robbery, 12 percent for abduction, 25 percent for sodomy, and 11 percent for first- or second-degree murder.

One-half of the people arrested for rape apparently come from the blue-collar working class (about 50 percent) and another sizeable portion (approximately 30 percent) are unemployed (LEAA, 1977b). Few persons from the professional and other white-collar fields are arrested for rape. In the Scully and Marolla (1984) study, only 20 percent of all convicted rapists had a high school education or better. In a study conducted in England, 75 percent of those arrested for rape were in the unskilled working class, and only 2 percent were classified as professional or managerial (Wright, 1980). Not surprisingly, statistics show that when professional people are accused in the U. S. of rape or sexual assault, their numbers drop precipitously when the case gets to the prosecutor's office, while other occupational groups remain about the same. These data suggest that the more affluent or privileged offender is more likely to be filtered out early in the criminal process, in contrast to the less privileged, less powerful one.

About two-thirds of the victims report their assailants were strangers. In addition, as mentioned earlier, strangers were much more likely to use weapons than nonstrangers. Eighty percent of the rapes were committed by a single assailant. In most instances (about 75 percent), the offender released the victim immediately after the assault. Some (22 percent) engaged the victim in a conversation for an hour or more after the assault, and the remainder drove the victim to a less accessible spot before letting her go.

One-third of a sample of convicted rapists said they would rape the same woman twice if given the opportunity (LEAA, 1978b). These assailants based their reasons for return on the following (in order of importance): the victim responded well, they were invited back, a good relationship was established, they had a desire to humiliate the woman even more, and the woman agreed not to report the rape to the police.

When they were asked how a woman could best prevent a rape, the above sample of convicted assailants sounded like law-enforcement officers. They advised women not to go out alone (32 percent), not to hitchhike (36 percent), to learn self-defense (16 percent), to buy a dog (8 percent), to carry weapons (6 percent), to dress conservatively (6 percent), and not to drink alone (2 percent). Some of these suggestions, of course, represent gross infringements on the basic freedoms of women, and also wrongfully imply that the victims brought the attacks upon themselves.

Psychological Correlates

Several attempts have been made to classify rapists into groups. Such classification systems, either based on personality traits or behavioral patterns of individuals, are called **typologies**, and have been moderately successful in their ability to add to our understanding of criminal behavior. A group of researchers at the Massachusetts Treatment Center (MTC) (Cohen, Seghorn & Calmas, 1969; Cohen et al., 1971; Knight & Prentky, 1987; Prentky & Knight, 1986) have developed a useful typology based on the behavioral patterns of convicted rapists, including the appearance of aggressive and sexual patterns in the assaults. The MTC has identified four major categories of rapists: (1) displaced aggressive; (2) compensatory; (3) sexual aggressive; and (4) impulsive.

The **displaced-aggressive rapist**, also called displaced-anger or anger-retaliation type in other classifications systems, demonstrated a predominance of violent and aggressive behaviors with a minimum or total absence of sexual feeling in his attacks. It appears that these men used the act of rape to harm, humiliate, and degrade women. The victims were brutally assaulted and subjected to sadistic acts such as biting, cutting, or tearing of breasts, genitals, or other parts of the body. In most instances, the victims were complete strangers and only served as the best available objects for the rapists' aggression. The assaults were not usually sexually arousing for the assailants. From the information gained about these rapists' behavior during the assaults, it appears that physical resistance only made them more violent.

Although many of these rapists were married, their relationships with women were often characterized by periodic irritation and violence, and they probably qualified as wife abusers. These men generally perceived women as demanding, hostile, and unfaithful. They sometimes selected their victim because they perceived something in her behavior or appearance which communicated assertiveness, independence, and professional competence. The attacks typically followed some incident which made them angry about women and their behavior.

This rapist is labeled displaced aggressive because the victim's identity is incidental to the attack. The offender's major focus is aggression and anger toward women in general. His occupational history is usually stable and often reveals some level of success. More often than not, his occupation is a "masculine" one, such as truck driver, carpenter, mechanic, or plumber. According to Knight and Prentky (1987), an offender must demonstrate the following characteristics during the attack to be classified as displaced aggressive: (1) the presence of a high degree of nonsexualized aggression or rage expressed either through verbal and/or physical assault that clearly exceeds what is necessary to gain the compliance of the victim; (2) clear evidence, in verbal form or behavior, of the intent to demean, degrade, or humiliate the victim; (3) no evidence that the aggressive behavior is eroticized or that sexual pleasure is derived from the injurious acts; and (4) the injurious acts do not have to be focused on parts of the body that have sexual significance.

Compensatory offenders rape, or attempt to rape, because of an intense sexual arousal prompted by specific stimuli in the environment. Although rape is, by definition, clearly a violent act, supplemental aggression is not a significant feature in the attack. Rather, the fundamental motivation is the desire to prove sexual prowess and adequacy. Behaviorally these men tend to be unusually passive, withdrawn, and lacking in social skills. They live in a world of fantasy, oriented around the idea that victims will yield eagerly under attack, submit to pleasurable intercourse, and find their skill and performance so outstanding that they will want them to return. These rapists fantasize that they will at last be able to prove their masculinity and sexual competence.

Acquaintances often describe these men as quiet, shy, submissive, and lonely. Although they are dependable workers, their poor social skills and resulting low self-esteem prevent them from succeeding at occupational advancement. Because their sexual attacks are an effort to compensate for overwhelming feelings of inadequacy, these offenders are called compensatory.

The victim of such a rapist is most often a stranger, but the rapist has probably watched and followed her for some time. Certain things about her have drawn his attention and excited him. For instance, he may be attracted to wealthy college women who normally would pay him

342

CHAPTER
TWELVE:
THE
PSYCHOLOGY
OF
CRIMINAL
BEHAVIOR

little attention. If the victim physically resists this offender, he is likely to flee the scene. During the attack, there are few additional indicators of violence. Moreover, this sexually excited, passive assailant will often ejaculate spontaneously, even upon mere physical contact with the victim. Generally, he confines his illegal activity to sexual assault and is not involved in other forms of antisocial behavior.

The **sexual aggressive rapist** exhibits both sexual and aggressive elements in his assault. Victim pain is a prerequisite for sexual excitement. He believes women enjoy being abused, forcefully raped, aggressively dominated, and controlled by men. Therefore, this type of rapist interprets the victim's resistance and struggle as a game, and the more the victim resists, the more excited and aggressive he becomes. As a result, there is often a direct relationship between physical and verbal resistance by the victim and the amount of injury she sustains.

These offenders are frequently married, but show little commitment to a relationship. Their backgrounds often are replete with antisocial behavior, beginning during adolescence or before and ranging from truancy to rape-murder. They have often had severe behavior problems in school, and throughout their lifetimes, they have displayed poor behavior control and a low frustration tolerance. On occasion, this type of rapist engages in sexual sadism much like the displaced-aggression rapist; in the extreme, the woman is viciously violated and murdered. In order to qualify as a sexual aggressive rapist, the offender must demonstrate: (1) a level of aggression or violence that clearly exceeds what is necessary to force compliance of the victim; and (2) the explicit, unambiguous evidence that aggression is sexually exciting and arousing to him.

The **impulsive** or **exploitative rapist** engages in sexual assault simply because the opportunity to rape presents itself. The rape usually occurs within the context of some other antisocial act, such as a robbery or burglary, and a victim happens to be available. To be classified into this group, the offender must show: (1) callous indifference to the welfare and comfort of the victim; and (2) the presence of more force than is necessary to force the compliance. Although human beings rarely fit neatly into typologies, the MTC profile is useful in understanding rape. It takes into consideration behavioral patterns, rather than simply personality traits, as well as the context within which the behavior patterns operate. Furthermore, the typologies are helpful in understanding why some sex offenders respond better to therapy than others, a topic we will return to in Chapter 13. In sum, Cohen's categories represent an interactionist more than a trait or situationist approach, and they provide a good beginning framework for theory development.

Etiology

Sexual socialization and social learning play very critical roles in the development of those who choose to sexually assault. Sexual behavior and attitudes toward women are acquired through day-to-day contacts with peers, others, and media. Koss and Dinero (1988) found that sexually aggressive men express greater hostility toward women, frequently use alcohol, often view violent and degrading pornography, and are closely connected to peer groups that reinforce highly sexualized and dominating views of women. These same men are more likely to believe that force and coercion are legitimate ways to gain compliance in sexual relationships. Koss and Dinero conclude: "In short, the results provided support for the developmental sequence for sexual aggression in which early experiences and psychological characteristics establish conditions for sexual violence" (p. 144).

Research by Abel and his associates (1977, 1978) found that rapists became equally sexually aroused by audiotaped portrayals of rape and consenting sexual acts. The researchers also learned that convicted rapists were highly sexually excited by rape depictions in which the victim experienced terror and pain rather than sexual pleasure. Nonsexually aggressive men, on the other hand, demonstrated sexual excitement while watching pleasurable depictions but not assaultive ones. And some convicted rapists became sexually aroused by witnessing even nonsexual assaults of women.

Research reveals that a majority of sexually aggressive men subscribe to attitudes and ideology that encourage them to be dominant, controlling, and powerful, whereas women are expected to be submissive, permissive, and compliant. Such an orientation seems to have a particularly strong disinhibitory effect on sexually aggressive men, encouraging them to interpret the ambiguous behaviors of females as come-ons, to believe that women are not really offended by coercive sexual behaviors, and to perceive rape victims as desiring and deriving gratification from sexual assault (Lipton, McDonel & McFall, 1987). Some sexually aggressive men believe that women must be kept in their place—even if it means humiliating them—and the best way to achieve this world order is to assault them physically and sexually.

More disturbing is the evidence that male beliefs and fantasies about the pleasurable aspects of denigrating women may be more widespread than commonly believed. For example, in a survey conducted by Malamuth (1981), 35 percent of male college students on several campuses felt there was some likelihood that they would sexually assault if they could be sure of getting away with it. In another study, 60 percent of a group of 352 male undergraduates indicated that they might rape or force a female to perform sexual acts against her will if given the opportunity (Briere, Malamuth & Ceniti, 1981).

This section of the chapter has described one type of criminal behavior, outlining statistical, sociological, and psychological data available on both the victim and the offender. A solid, testable theory of criminal behavior will require careful analysis and integration of each element partially described here. Theoretical integration of statistical data or frequencies requires a keen understanding of the limitations and pitfalls that accompany tabulation. Criminal-behavior theory building also requires careful consideration of the knowledge available from several disciplines, especially sociology and psychology.

Summary and Conclusions

The position taken in this chapter is that criminal behavior defies easy explanations or pat solutions. Crime cannot be explained solely by external factors like poverty, low socioeconomic status, racism, or unemployment compounded by poor job training and education. Nor can crime be explained solely by internal factors like psychological deficiencies in the superego, a lack of emotional maturity or mental balance, or criminal personalities.

Criminal behavior must be perceived as unique and as a result of each individual's conditioning, instrumental learning, and cognitive-social learning processes in reciprocal relation to the situation. Each crime must be seen as subjectively adaptive for each individual in a particular set of circumstances. Understanding criminal behavior, therefore, will require at the very least an individualized appraisal of how the antisocial individual perceives his or her predicament. Assessment, theories, and empirical studies which fail to take into consideration the cognitive, subjective value of the acts for the individual are destined to provide fragmentary perspectives. Moreover, the reciprocal nature of crime renders predictions of dangerousness and future criminal behavior exceedingly difficult and prone to inaccuracy.

Unfortunately, this approach does not play well with those who argue that either the sociological or the psychological perspective—but certainly not both—must be adopted. Nor is it easily applied to the prevention of crime. In fact, it is likely to be labeled too complex to be of value in developing policies in that regard. People have argued that criminal behavior may be

344

CHAPTER
TWELVE:
THE
PSYCHOLOGY
OF
CRIMINAL
BEHAVIOR

reduced by ensuring economic opportunity, changing the socialization process of children, reducing the amount of aggressive and violent models available throughout society, and substantially minimizing the reinforcement value and personal gain to be achieved. These are obviously goals worth pursuing. However, criminal behavior is too deeply interwoven into the fabric of our society to be eradicated by these measures, short of establishing a powerful dictatorship that will require massive "experimental" changes in child-rearing practices, censorship of the media, elimination of firearms, and radical changes in the democratic process.

A more realistic, attainable goal is the development of a rational, consistent, economical, and comprehensible criminal-justice system, including the juvenile-justice level. We must strive for a system with considerable sophistication in its understanding of criminal behavior, one which handles each case with sensitivity about the uniqueness of individual behavior, devoid of dogmatic, simplistic generalizations. In many respects, this, too, is an idealistic proposal, but it is critical if we are to take control of the crime problem.

One place to begin is to urge courts to avoid seeking psychiatric or psychological opinions about criminal behavior which are not tempered with empirical caution, and to view all opinions with skepticism. Many psychiatric or psychological statements about criminal behavior are philosophical, theoretical, or moral opinions not based upon scientific information. Often, these statements may have no more validity than a layperson's opinions and speculations. If the judicial system intends to use the behavioral sciences, it appears crucial for it to understand their methods and develop a good understanding of scientific philosophy.

Likewise, law-enforcement agents should not be too quick to embrace criminal profiling; they are better advised to take seriously their responsibility to serve as law-abiding models for society's youth. In fact, society as a whole must learn to value its children. Psychological research has consistently indicated that offering children love and acceptance, treating them fairly, meeting their basic physical needs, and educating them well provide the best hope for their future.

From this book's perspective, the most effective approach toward reducing and partially controlling criminal behavior is first understanding it. This understanding can emerge not only from continued psychological research directed at the learning, maintenance, and extinction processes of criminal behavior, but also at theoretical development, which ultimately could translate into realistic policies and procedures to be implemented by the law. Therefore, in the spirit of the psychology *and* law relationship, it behooves the science of psychology to pursue empirical investigations that may help lead to the formulation of legal policies that ensure the safety of the members of society, without massively curtailing their freedom.

Questions to Ponder

1. Does criminal profiling have a successful future in law enforcement? Why or why not?

2. When members of the public think of a rapist, they usually have a single image in mind. Why do you think this is so?

3. Pretend you are an expert on crime, and a newspaper reporter asks you, "What are the causes of violent crime?" What would you say?

4. Of all the theories discussed in the chapter, which one seems most feasible to you in explaining the greatest amount of crime?

5. Why is it so difficult to get an accurate account of the prevalence and incidence of crime in the United States?

THE PSYCHOLOGY OF CORRECTIONS

 N THE UNITED STATES AT THE END OF THE 1980S, about one in fifty-two adults over the age of eighteen were under some form of correctional supervision (U. S. Department of Justice, 1988). By the middle of 1992, that figure had apparently risen to one in forty-three (Bureau of Justice Statistics, 1992). Correctional supervision includes incarceration in prisons and jails as well as a wide range of community-based alternatives, such as probation, parole, and their many variants (see Figure 13.1). In this chapter we will focus only on the psychological aspects of institutional confinement. Although some reference will be made to short-term confinement in jails, the material focuses primarily on long-term prison confinement.

Persons detained, accused, and convicted are housed in three types of facilities when not allowed to remain in their own homes: jails, prisons, and community-based facilities. **Jails** are operated by local governments to hold persons temporarily detained, awaiting trial, or sentenced to confinement after having been convicted of a misdemeanor. Sentences are usually for no more than one year, but, in some states, misdemeanors carry a penalty of up to two years. Jails also may house a wide variety of individuals awaiting transfer, such as to prison, to a mental institution, to another state, to a juvenile facility, or to a military detention facility. Thus, they hold a collection of persons at various stages of criminal, civil, or military justice processing. The vast majority of jail inmates (over 80 percent) are at various stages of criminal justice processing (U. S. Department of Justice, 1988). Moreover, about 50 percent of the jail population have been charged, not convicted of crime. Overall, about one-third of the U. S. inmate population is housed in jails.

Prisons are operated by state and federal governments to hold persons sentenced under state or federal laws, generally for terms of more than one year. Prisons are classified partly by the level of security maintained over the inmates: maximum, medium, and minimum. They may also hold special categories of offenders, such as those who are mentally disordered. Most recently, some states have begun to build "supermax" facilities to hold their most violent, troublesome prisoners. Maximum- or close-security prisons are typically surrounded by a double fence or wall (usually eighteen to twenty-five feet high) guarded by armed correctional officers in observation towers. Approximately 36 percent of all prison inmates are housed in maximum-security facilities in this country (Bureau of Justice Statistics, 1992). Medium-security prisons are usually enclosed within double fences topped with barbed or razor wire. Roughly 50 percent of the prison population is confined in medium-security facilities. Minimum-security prisons usually do not have armed guards at the perimeters and may or may not have fences surrounding the buildings. Different custody levels are also found within facilities. For example, an inmate may be kept in close custody in a medium-security prison for disciplinary reasons, or an inmate in a maximum-security prison

346

CHAPTER
THIRTEEN:
THE
PSYCHOLOGY
OF
CORRECTIONS

may have attained "trustee" status, requiring minimal custody. Prisons are often brutal, demeaning places which promote isolation, helplessness, and subservience through the imposition of overwhelming power and often, fear. This is especially true of maximum-security facilities.

Because the nomenclature of corrections has changed rapidly over the years, it is not always possible to tell from the name of an institution whether it is a jail or a prison. For example, detention centers may be used to hold those awaiting trial. Prisons may be called *institutes, correctional centers, facilities,* or *penitentiaries.* In six states, a combined jail-prison system exists, meaning that persons accused of crime, convicted of misdemeanors, and convicted of felonies can be housed in the same facility.

Currently, there are 1,395 state and 67 federal prisons, and 3,042 jails in the U. S. (plus 18 in the District of Columbia) (American Correctional Association, 1991). In addition, there are 1,678 juvenile facilities nationwide. These figures do not include correctional facilities operated by the private sector for state and federal governments. "Privatization," while still the exceptional approach, is a controversial area in criminal justice policy making.

The number of prisoners held in federal and state correctional facilities in the U. S. by midyear 1992 reached a record high of 855,958 (Bureau of Justice Statistics, 1993). The rate of growth in prison populations within the decade 1982–92 is shown in Figure 13.2. It is expected that by 1994, the prisoner population will reach at least a million (American Correctional Association, 1991). The U. S. has, by far, the highest incarceration rate in the world (Smith, 1991).

Community-based facilities are operated by state or federal governments or by private organizations under governmental contract. The private sector is far more likely to be involved in community-based corrections than institutional corrections. Community-based facilities hold individuals for less than twenty-four hours of each day to allow them limited opportunity to work, attend school, or participate in other community activities. The goal of the facilities is to provide an alternative to jail or prison confinement, both because the nation's prisons and jails are overcrowded and because the majority of persons convicted of crimes neither need nor benefit from incarceration.

Overall, community-based facilities house about 4 percent of all those confined in the correctional system. The term *community-based corrections* also includes situations in which persons convicted of crime remain in their own homes. They may be on standard probation or parole, or under house arrest, intensive supervision, electronic monitoring, or a combination of these.

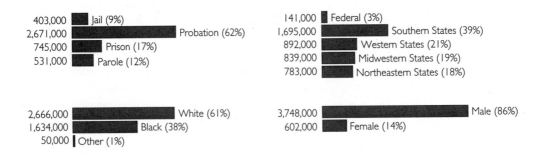

Figure 13.1 ■ *Demographic breakdown of U. S. adult population under correctional supervision. Total: 2.35% of U. S. adult population (4,350,000). Source: Bureau of Justice Statistics, 1992.*

Probation and parole are by far the most common forms of correctional supervision; three of every four persons under correctional supervision are on probation or parole (Bureau of Justice Statistics, 1992).

This chapter will focus on the psychological effects of prisons on human behavior, although, as noted above, some research on jails will be included. We will pay particular attention to special aspects of the confinement, such as overcrowding, solitary confinement, and prisonization. We will also examine the philosophies of the correctional system from a psychological perspective, particularly in relation to rehabilitation and deterrence. First, we begin with a discussion of the typical responsibilities of the correctional psychologist in an institutional setting.

Correctional Psychology

In a nationwide survey of American correctional psychologists, we (Bartol, Griffin & Clark, 1993) found that the services most commonly provided by psychologists working full-time in the correctional system are counseling or treatment (14.1 percent) and psychological assessment (12.9 percent) (see Figure 13.3). During the 1970s, similar findings were reported by Clingempeel, Mulvey, and Reppucci (1980). Psychological assessment has the longest history, beginning with intellectual assessment of offenders for placement in appropriate educational and vocational programs. Later, psychological assessment was expanded to include personality and behavioral appraisal, especially evaluations of dangerousness to self and others.

ASSESSMENT

Assessment is warranted at a minimum of four points in an inmate's career: (1) when he or she enters the correctional system; (2) when decisions are to be made concerning the offender's exit into the community; (3) at times of psychological crisis; and (4) in death-penalty cases, when competency to be executed is considered. Ideally, reassessments should occur on a periodic basis, because of a growing awareness that the needs of mentally disordered inmates in prisons and jails are often not recognized (Steadman et al., 1989; Toch, 1982; Toch & Adams, 1989a).

As a matter of institutional or systemwide policy, correctional facilities often require **entry-level**

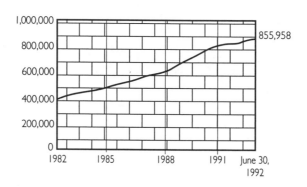

Figure 13.2 ■ *Growth of prison populations in U.S. (1982-92). From the beginning of 1982 to midyear 1992, the state and federal prison populations increased by almost 487,000 prisoners. Source: Bureau of Justice Statistics, 1993.*

348

CHAPTER
THIRTEEN:
THE
PSYCHOLOGY
OF
CORRECTIONS

assessments so that inmates can be psychologically "processed" and "classified." In many states, an offender is initially sent to a classification or reception center, which may or may not be part of the correctional institution to which the offender is eventually sent. The inmate may spend several days or even many weeks in this assessment center, until assigned to a facility or wing, and to specific programs, within the prison system. The classification process addresses both security and treatment.

The reception unit usually consists of psychologists, psychiatrists, social workers, and other professionals, who are expected to make diagnostic conclusions and treatment recommendations. They might recommend, for example, that an inmate receive substance-abuse treatment and be taught to read, and that contacts with her or his children be facilitated. The chief concern of many correctional systems, however, is to use the classification process for management purposes. Classification for custody, rather than classification for treatment, becomes the dominant goal. Therefore, estimates of dangerousness and potential escape risks become very important.

The reports of the classifiers typically are submitted to administrative authorities, who may

---

■ 13.1: *WHAT CORRECTIONAL PSYCHOLOGISTS DO, WHERE THEY WORK, AND WHAT THEY EARN*

What Correctional Psychologists Do

	Percentage of Time Spent
Administration	14.3%
Counseling, Treatment	14.1%
Psychological Assessment	12.9%
Consulting with Correctional Staff	9.1%
Supervision of Other Psychologists	8.8%
Crisis Intervention	8.8%
Teaching (Usually as an Adjunct)	6.3%
Psychological Testing	6.0%
Research	4.5%
Training Correctional Staff	3.2%
Other or Undefined	11.1%

Where Correctional Psychologists Work

In a nationwide survey, full-time correctional psychologists were asked to specify the type of correctional setting in which they worked. The following percentages show the distribution.

Type of Facility	
Federal	6.2%
State	64.2%
Private	1.8%
County	7.1%
Municipal	2.7%
Other	0.9%
Not Specified	17.1%

Salaries of Correctional Psychologists

In a nationwide survey of correctional psychologists, 67 percent indicated they had doctorate degrees in psychology, with a majority holding a Ph.D. in Clinical Psychology. Twenty-seven percent of the respondents were women. The data listed below give an idea of the current salaries in the field.

	Mean	Median	Range
Overall	$50,920	$50,000	$25,000 to $175,000
Doctorate	$55,310	$51,000	$30,000 to $175,000
Master's	$43,771	$47,000	$25,000 to $62,000
Men Ph.D.s	$57,201	$54,000	$25,000 to $175,000
Women Ph.D.s	$49,500	$48,000	$34,000 to $80,000
Men Master's	$45,380	$48,000	$25,000 to $62,000
Women Master's	$39,750	$38,000	$25,000 to $56,000
Federal	$59,900	$60,500	$55,000 to $65,000
State	$53,085	$50,000	$30,000 to $175,000

Source: Bartol, Griffin, & Clark (1993). Nationwide Survey of American Correctional Psychologists.

continued page 351

or may not follow the recommendations or even read the reports. Even if high-quality and conscientious assessments are provided, the recommendations may not be followed because the reports do not link up adequately with ongoing or available programs. In some cases, administrators do not know how to apply the results or know what they want from classification programs, because they have not clarified their own goals or the goals of the institution (Bartollas, 1981).

Psychological assessments for **exit decisions** are most likely to occur in state systems with **indeterminate sentencing**, by which parole boards exercise discretion as to whether to release prisoners to serve the rest of their sentences in the community. In the federal system, and in approximately ten states, the authority for such decisions no longer resides with parole boards. The U. S. Sentencing Reform Act of 1984 abolished the procedure of routinely releasing inmates in federal prison to parole. Instead, the federal system has adopted **determinate sentencing**, by which judges use strict guidelines to impose prison sentences that are served in full, except when reduced for good behavior.

Assessments for exit decisions are usually prepared at the request of state parole boards (Brodsky, 1980). They often ask specific questions about the value of continued imprisonment, the extent to which the inmate will be a risk to the community, and the probability of recidivism. As we have seen in previous chapters, it is highly debatable whether psychology can satisfactorily answer these questions. We should note, also, that decisions may be made without any psychological input at all, by means of risk-assessment instruments specifically designed for that purpose.

The third area which requires the assessment skills of correctional psychologists is **crisis intervention**. Suicide attempts, emotional agitation, psychotic behaviors, and refusal to eat or to participate in programs may precipitate a request for psychological assessment and consultation. Our survey found that crisis-intervention incidents accounted for nearly 9 percent of correctional psychologists' time. Prison officials are interested in obtaining from the psychologist both immediate

---

■ **13.1** *CONTINUED*

Future Opportunities for Correctional Psychologists

The top part of the chart at right summarizes results of our survey asking currently employed correctional psychologists how they see the future for job opportunities in their field. They were asked to predict job opportunities in correctional psychology for the next five years, as well as for the next ten years. "Excellent" meant they foresaw many more positions than qualified psychologists; "very good" denoted a balance between available positions and qualified psychologists; "good" described slightly more qualified psychologists than available positions; "fair" referred to far more qualified psychologists than available positions; and "poor" meant substantially more qualified psychologists than available positions. Respondents were classified by highest degree attained and by gender.

The chart at lower right displays responses to a question aimed at measuring career satisfaction.

	Excellent	Very Good	Good	Fair	Poor
		In Five Years			
Doctorate	27.8%	50.0%	12.5%	6.9%	2.8%
Master's	23.7%	39.5%	21.1%	15.8%	0.0%
Men	24.7%	45.7%	17.3%	9.9%	2.4%
Women	31.0%	48.3%	10.3%	10.3%	0.0%
		In Ten Years			
Doctorate	33.3%	46.4%	15.9%	1.4%	3.0%
Master's	21.6%	40.5%	27.0%	8.1%	2.8%
Men	28.2%	43.6%	21.8%	3.8%	3.8%
Women	32.1%	46.4%	14.3%	3.6%	3.6%

Would You Choose This Line of Work Again?

	Yes	No	Don't Know
Doctorate	83.6%	14.9%	1.5%
Master's	83.3%	16.7%	0.0%
Men	78.9%	19.7%	1.3%
Women	96.3%	3.7%	0.0%

Source: Bartol, Griffin, & Clark (1993).   ■

350

Chapter
Thirteen:
The
Psychology
of
Corrections

solutions to the crisis and long-range solutions which will help avoid a similar problem in the future.

There is strong indication that crisis intervention may be needed even more in jails than in prisons. Ironically, however, jails are much less likely than prisons to have well-developed mental-health services available to inmates (Steadman et al., 1989). Although most jail detentions last just a few days, arrest and subsequent incarceration is a traumatic event for many detainees. In a confusing, noisy, often crowded, and unclean environment, detainees may experience "entry shock." Suicide is the leading cause of death in jails (U. S. Department of Justice, 1990).

The fourth area demanding the assessment skills of correctional psychologists revolves around the death penalty. Because this is an extremely controversial area, we give special attention to the topic.

In 1986, in *Ford v. Wainwright*, the U. S. Supreme Court ruled that it is a violation of due process to carry out a death sentence if an offender is so mentally disordered that he or she is unable to comprehend what is happening. Executing an incompetent defendant, the Court said, offended humanity, had no retributive value, and violated the dignity of both the prisoner and the law. Although most states recognized this prohibition long before the Supreme Court gave it constitutional status, the decision reopened philosophical debate on the critical role of mental-health professionals with respect to offenders sentenced to die (e.g., Bonnie, 1990; Brodsky, 1990; Ewing, 1987; Mossman, 1987; Radelet & Barnard, 1986).

Furthermore, the Supreme Court left many unanswered questions after its decision, including what standards should be applied in deciding whether the offender is competent, who should conduct the evaluation, whether the examiner's testimony is needed at a subsequent hearing, and what are the appropriate consent requirements (Mossman, 1987). Not surprisingly, there is little consistency among states (Heilbrun, 1987) and very little research on how evaluations of competency are being conducted. Both the American Psychological Association and the American Psychiatric Association, however, say that the ultimate decision as to whether the offender is competent to be executed should be made by the court, and that adversarial expert witnesses are essential in this context. In other words, the psychologist or psychiatrist conducting the evaluation should neither be the sole examiner nor the decisionmaker in that determination.

Mossmann (1987) summarizes the ethical objections to evaluating competency as follows. First, evaluating an offender's competency to be executed appears to conflict with the basic ethical principles to avoid harm, relieve suffering, and preserve life (called the **principle of nonmali-ficence**). Second, the issue of informed consent is clouded in this area, because an offender who truly understands the purpose of the evaluation may not cooperate with the examiner. Third, by participating in the death-penalty process, the psychologist is implicitly lending consent to the death penalty, a social policy which remains extremely controversial.

Mossman and others (e.g., Bonnie, 1990), nevertheless believe that mental-health experts should be involved in this process. They maintain that the arguments against participation can be satisfactorily addressed. The psychologist can help relieve the suffering of the death-row inmate and help him or her prepare for impending death. This in itself is consistent with the principle of nonmalificence. They note also that psychologists involve themselves in numerous other situations in which consent is a cloudy issue, including assessments of sanity and competency to stand trial.

In the final analysis, it is left to individual psychologists to decide for themselves whether to participate as examiners of a person's competency to be executed. Approaches to such a decision vary widely, however. In a questionnaire mailed to 335 forensic psychiatrists and psychologists (with an impressive 74 percent response rate), Deitchman, Kennedy, and Beckham (1992) discovered significant attitudinal differences between those who were willing to conduct evaluations and those who were not. Clinicians who were philosophically opposed to the death penalty were least likely to participate in evaluations and tended to attribute responsibility more to environmental factors than to individuals. Deitchman and her colleagues note that this could suggest bias in the outcome of evaluations. Even so, there was considerable overlap in opposing views. For example, a large number of willing examiners did not favor capital punishment and a large number of unwilling examiners did favor it.

Although most of the literature deals with the ethical implications of involvement in the death-penalty process, mental-health practitioners are beginning to publish articles on the evaluation process itself. Heilbrun (1987), for example, discusses a variety of issues to be considered when evaluating death-row prisoners, ranging from the selection of appropriate examiners to the production of reports clearly outlining clinical data pertinent to the relevant legal criteria. Small and Otto (1991) have addressed the issue of how competency-for-execution evaluations should be conducted. Noting that these evaluations will be scrutinized by courts, they highlight the importance of informing the prisoner of the purpose of the evaluation, describing its procedure, and explaining the implications of the findings as well as who will get the results. Additionally, they recommend videotaping the assessment.

They note that traditional psychological tests, while they may not be helpful at the assessment stage, would be useful at the treatment stage, when the clinician is providing services to help the convicted person adjust to impending death. "Central to the evaluation is the clinical interview," they say (p. 154), which should be an effort to determine whether the prisoner understands that he or she has been convicted and is about to be executed. In some states, they note, the ability to assist one's attorney remains a critical criterion for competency to be executed, because an attorney presumably is continuing the appeals process. In other words, if a person is so disordered that he or she cannot help an attorney, competency to be executed becomes questionable.

TREATMENT

After assessment, the next major function of the psychologist in the correctional system is to provide psychological *treatment*, a term that encompasses a wide spectrum of strategies, techniques, and goals. Among the most common treatments that are used within correctional institutions today are person-centered therapy, cognitive therapy, behavior therapy, group and milieu therapy, transactional analysis, reality therapy, and responsibility therapy (Kratcoski, 1989; Lester, Braswell & Van Voorhis, 1992). As in the mental institutions discussed in Chapter 6, treatment with psychoactive drugs is also very common and is usually not supplemented with any of the therapies listed above—although it should be. The method of treatment used depends largely on the professional training and orientation of the psychologists (or psychiatrists) at each institution, the nature of the inmate population, the overall mission of the correctional facility, and the learning capacity and offense history of the offender. In correctional settings, where the professional staff is limited and overwhelmed by the number of inmates requesting or being placed in treatment programs, group therapy is often the norm. In the typical group session, inmates talk about their concerns, experiences, and anxieties, while the psychologist directs and controls the topic flow.

During the 1970s and early 1980s, behavior therapy was popular both because it was an empirically solid procedure for changing specific behaviors, and because it aided facility management for prison authorities. However, the widespread use of behavior therapy raised a number of troubling questions regarding prisoner rights. Some behavior therapies, for example, involved depriving the offender of basic necessities like a mattress or a blanket until the offender earned them through good behavior. Behavior therapy's general effectiveness once an offender left the institution also was questioned. Widespread misunderstanding about what behavior therapy is, abuses of the therapy by some practitioners, and failure to support its use empirically resulted in

352

CHAPTER
THIRTEEN:
THE
PSYCHOLOGY
OF
CORRECTIONS

loss of its popularity. However, more recent research has shown that cognitive-behavior therapy may be highly effective in treatment, especially of sex offenders, a topic we will return to below.

Although we do not have the space here to detail and evaluate the many therapies, we will examine the general effectiveness of treatment and rehabilitation. The reader should also understand that the realities of prison life today too often militate against successful psychological treatment. There is far more hope for various forms of treatment provided in conjunction with community-based corrections.

Goals of Prison Confinement

Four fundamental goals or rationales are usually involved in the sentencing of offenders: incapacitation, retribution, rehabilitation, and deterrence. Because we focus on imprisonment, we will examine, from a psychological perspective, each of these as they operate in a prison setting. It is very important to note, however, that these goals may be reached in community-based settings as well as through incarceration. In fact, for some offenders, these goals are met far more easily when the offenders are not incarcerated.

INCAPACITATION

Focusing on protecting society from the individual, **incapacitation**, is the most straightforward justification for prison confinement. If an offender is dangerous to society, it is obvious that, while incarcerated, he or she is unable to harm society. Incarceration does prevent further infractions of the criminal code unless the individual still can operate behind prison walls through cohorts on the outside. Additionally, prisoners may display violent behavior toward other prisoners or staff, such as assault, rape, or murder. Despite these possibilities, incapacitation may be touted as the most effective method of containing crime.

The problem is, of course, that it is neither possible nor desirable to incapacitate all persons convicted of crime. This has led to calls for **selective incapacitation**. This term refers to the imprisonment of offenders, such as "career criminals," who are believed to pose the greatest threat to society. However, selective incapacitation raises the same questions about dangerousness as we have encountered throughout the text. *Dangerousness* is a vague term, its use is highly imprecise, and it can be molded to dovetail into almost any social or political purpose. Predictions of dangerousness simply cannot identify a broad collection of offenders who will continue to perpetrate substantial injury or loss to society. There are exceptions, of course, like the offender who promises to get back at persons or at society, and who perhaps already has a violent or long criminal record. Generally speaking, however, "the concept of dangerousness for sentencing purposes is an equivocal principle that leads to gross injustice" (Morris, 1974, p. 63). Sentences and prolongations of confinement by parole boards on the basis of presumed dangerousness are largely unwarranted and without predictive validity. Selective incapacitation is also philosophically questionable, because offenders are being punished not only for what they did but also for what they might do.

RETRIBUTION

The second rationale for confinement, **retribution**, embodies the principle that a wrongful act must be "repaid" by a punishment that is as severe as the wrongful act. Therefore, the offender should receive what he or she rightfully deserves, no more, no less. The retributive philosophy, therefore, is incompatible with the concept of selective incapacitation.

When the effectiveness of rehabilitation was being seriously questioned, the just-deserts model—a variant of retribution—received the endorsement of a Task Force on the Role of Psychology in the Criminal Justice System (American Psychological Association, 1978). The APA-commissioned group concluded that retribution is the correctional model most conducive to the ethical use of psychologists in corrections. Noting that this approach was not without its conceptual difficulties, the task force decided that it was more acceptable than the rehabilitative approach, because of the demonstrated ineffectiveness of rehabilitative treatment methods tried during the 1970s. Rehabilitation was closely aligned with the concept of the indeterminate sentence. According to the task force:

> While it [just-deserts approach] will not ameliorate the horrendous human degrada-tion that is part of many prisons—and nothing an offender has done could "deserve" the physical and sexual violence rampant in American "correctional" institutions—it has the important virtue of placing an upper limit on the power of the state to expose persons to such conditions... .
>
> Even in the unlikely event that substantial improvements in the prediction of criminal behavior were documented, there would still be reason to question the ethical appropriateness of extending an offender's confinement beyond the limits of what he or she morally "deserves" in order to achieve a utilitarian gain in public safety (Task Force, 1978, pp. 1109-1110).

Were the task force to meet again today, it *may* have second thoughts about endorsing so strongly the just-deserts model. If it were truly possible to allocate a just sentence for each criminal offense, just deserts would have considerable appeal. However, we must remember that sentences are first set by legislatures, then allocated by judges. In the rehabilitation or indeterminate model, legislatures give judges a range from which to choose. In the retribution model, associated with determinate sentencing, the legislative body carefully circumscribes the appropriate sentence, leaving little discretion to judges. We have learned that when elected representatives control the sentencing scheme, they set harsher penalties, often more than the offenders really deserve. The move to determinate sentencing in the federal government, and in some states, has contributed to the overcrowding of prisons.

The third and fourth rationales of imprisonment—rehabilitation and deterrence—are of major concern here since the one may involve psychotherapy and presumed psychological change, and the other centers on the effects of punishment—threatened or applied—on behavior.

REHABILITATION

Rehabilitation is an ambiguous concept surrounded by controversy and misunderstanding. As we discuss it here, rehabilitation refers to psychological interventions intended to bring about change in behavior patterns. Other forms of rehabilitation, such as education or job training, are not considered here. The debate about the effectiveness of rehabilitation became particularly heated when R. M. Martinson (1974), who reviewed studies assessing both psychological and nonpsychological methods of rehabilitation, concluded that "with few and isolated exceptions, the rehabilitative efforts that have been reported so far have had no appreciable effect on recidi-vism" (p. 25). His literature review, published in the journal *Public Interest*, has become one of "the most frequently quoted and least frequently read in the criminal-justice rehabilitation literature" (Gendreau & Ross, 1987, p. 349). In later articles, Martinson tempered his views, asserting that he was wrong in his wholesale condemnation of rehabilitation and that there were, indeed, many studies that demonstrate successful rehabilitation (1979; Martinson & Wilks, 1977). Before the success or failure of any rehabilitation program is evaluated, however, some key issues need to be addressed.

354

CHAPTER
THIRTEEN:
THE
PSYCHOLOGY
OF
CORRECTIONS

Evaluation of Treatment

It is impossible to evaluate properly the effectiveness of treatment in the correctional environment unless the researcher carefully delineates the *type of treatment* and assures that the therapists being studied are using the same methods. This is necessary because therapy comes in so many varieties in the correctional system. Many studies have neglected to include these preliminary steps (Quay, 1977).

Studies evaluating effectiveness also have not explored the *integrity* of treatment programs, neglecting to ask whether the services outlined in the programs were actually delivered. Far too often, a written treatment plan cannot be carried out for a range of reasons, including lack of resources or the inmates' own unwillingness to participate. In reality, the program being offered to inmates may be fragmented and may show little resemblance to the one that exists "on paper." Another factor in a program's integrity has to do with whether inmates actually attend the treatment sessions or any part of them. Even when inmates themselves want to attend, they may be prevented from doing so by correctional officers or by any of the many unpredictable realities of prison life. A cell block may be locked down for a day, for example, while prison officials conduct cell searches or investigate a suspected plot. Evaluation studies often fail to address the question of whether inmates actually attend the treatment sessions.

A judgment about any program's integrity must also consider the *specific goals* of the therapy. Was it designed to alter some specific habit pattern (e.g., fear of small spaces), or was it intended to change the individual's lifestyle (e.g., criminal behavior in general)? The narrowly focused goal will probably have minimal effect on posttreatment criteria (recidivism rate, for example) while, the broader goal, although far more difficult to achieve, could produce notable changes in the inmate's approach to life situations.

The *training* and *supervision* of those operating the program are also important considerations. Untrained, unsupervised paraprofessional staffs are likely to provide a different quality of treatment than highly trained staff members who have access to competent supervision and consultation. State correctional systems differ widely in this respect, which must be considered in any treatment-evaluation project. Other crucial components of treatment in the correctional setting include the *duration* (two years or six months?) and the *intensity* (fifty minutes of directionless talk or fifty minutes of purposeful conversation and therapy?).

Treatment evaluation studies often struggle with the *criteria* to be used to determine effectiveness. Many researchers favor a recidivism index as the most sensitive measure of effectiveness. However, they fail to agree upon whether it is more useful to measure the proportion of pre- to postincarceration arrests or simply the incidence of postincarceration arrest and conviction. Furthermore, even when the criteria of recidivism are agreed upon, the time limit remains an important consideration. A rehabilitation program followed by a year of successful postrelease behavior is far less impressive than one followed by five years of such behavior.

Regardless of the methodology or the results of evaluation studies, however, the problem remains that, under the present correctional system in American society, psychological rehabilitation continues to produce discouraging results, particularly if one measures success by the recidivism yardstick. This ill fate can be attributed to four factors.

Coercion

First, institutional treatment often suffers from the faulty logic that psychological change can be coerced. Traditional forms of psychological treatment have been successful only when subjects were *willing* and *motivated* to participate. This basic principle applies regardless of whether the person is living in the community or within the walls of an institution which has overwhelming power over the lives of its inmates. Ironically, coercive treatment which involves temporary or permanent alterations of the nervous system, such as occurs with the administration of psychoactive drugs, is a different story. Coerced or not, these modes of treatment do effect psychological change, although it is not clear whether they produce change primarily through punishment principles or through modifications of the neurological mechanisms responsible for certain cognitive and emotional processes. Psychoactive drugs can, for example, stabilize the behavior of a person who displays violence toward others. Nevertheless, as we discussed earlier in the text, the drugs may be accompanied by a range of negative side effects; furthermore, the underlying problem contributing to the person's behavior is not resolved. The Supreme Court has ruled that although inmates have a right to refuse such treatment, the interests of the prison in keeping them stable may outweigh this right to refuse (*Washington v. Harper*, 1990).

When individuals are forced to engage in psychotherapy for the expressed purpose of ameliorating their criminal behavior, the therapy is highly unlikely to succeed. Furthermore, if early release is inexorably dependent upon the prisoner's apparent commitment to a treatment program, the prisoner may enter into a perpetual game with those who can open the doors to freedom. Part of the rationale behind indeterminate sentencing is to elicit cooperation from inmates in the rehabilitation process, but sentences based on the dictum that a person "should remain in custody until cured" not only perpetuate the coercive power of the institution, they also promote the inmates' behavioral confidence game.

This is not to say that treatment and rehabilitation programs should not be offered in the prison system. As Norval Morris (1974) argues, treatment programs not only should be offered, but expanded and improved for those inmates who voluntarily seek them. Additionally, as Toch (1982) has observed, we cannot ignore the mental-health needs of disturbed and/or disruptive inmates who are so seriously disordered that they pose a threat to themselves or others. Disruptive inmates in particular, he notes, are submitted to "bus therapy," involving frequent transfers back and forth between prisons and mental institutions. Crisis management is the modal approach to these inmates, but it is obviously an unsatisfactory one. Overall, though, we can expect coerced treatment to have, at best, minimal effects on the long-term behavioral patterns of inmates.

Motivation

A second reason for the limited success of rehabilitation in most prison settings is closely allied with the first. Many prisoners do not want to be changed in accordance with societal standards. They want only to serve their time and move on. Many, however, do want to be more gainfully employed, have better social relationships with family and friends when they get out, and eliminate some troubling habits or emotional problems. Meaningful services should be provided for those inmates. It is important to recognize that such services need not be psychological. Job training, followed by prerelease services to help the inmates prepare for reentry into society, may be much more meaningful for a given inmate than individual psychotherapy.

The belief that prisoners want to change derives from the medical model that criminal behavior is "sick" behavior that needs to be cured. As we learned in Chapter 12, it might be better to conceive of much criminal behavior as adaptive though deviant from society's norms, rather than as evidence of illness. From the offenders' perspectives, their behavior has provided them with the most adaptive responses under their circumstances, and until something better comes along, they may feel it is wise to continue their current behavior patterns.

Environment

The third stumbling block to rehabilitation is the unusual nature of the prison environment itself.

356

CHAPTER
THIRTEEN:
THE
PSYCHOLOGY
OF
CORRECTIONS

The physical surroundings of most prisons simply are not conducive to effective treatment. The list of negative features ranges from overcrowding, violence, and victimization by both other prisoners and staff to isolation from families and feelings of a lack of control over one's life. Acknowledgment of this problem led to the establishment of *milieu therapy* or "therapeutic communities" in corrections in the late 1950s and 1960s. These were (and still are, in some correctional facilities) specialized living quarters where inmates, on a voluntary basis, would be housed separately from the rest of the prison population. They would be involved in decisionmaking, group therapy, and operating their own community within the broader prison setting. Followup research indicated that inmates who had participated in these special programs did not have significantly better recidivism rates than inmates who had not (Gendreau & Ross, 1984). Nevertheless, supporters of the therapeutic-community concept note that prison life was made more tolerable and that both staff and inmates benefitted from a safer, more humane environment while they were incarcerated.

The System

The fourth factor contributing to the poor record of rehabilitation is the purposes and goals in the criminal-justice system, an often rudderless bureaucracy whose deeply entrenched political forces continually obstruct change. Scholars and practitioners agree that the system is imperfect, but disagree about what should be done. The crippling effect of overcrowding in the 1980s overshadowed a host of other problems which demanded the attention of correctional institutions, including how to respond to the AIDS crisis, the increasing numbers of offenders with mental disorders, special problems of women inmates, and budgetary constraints, to name a few. Under these conditions, rehabilitation and treatment often took a secondary role in the institution's day-to-day operations.

Positive Programs

Nevertheless, champions of rehabilitation as a meritorious goal of imprisonment have not given in. The task ahead is to hone the many programs competing for funds and carefully select those which have the most promise. Recall from Chapter 11 that Gendreau and Ross (1984) have summarized features held in common by those programs which have shown positive results. They include programs based on social-learning theory, in which inmates are expected to take responsibility for their actions, and in which decisionmaking and social skills are developed.

One such program involves cognitive-behavior therapy with sex offenders, who, as a group, are highly resistant to changing their deviant behavior patterns (Bartol, 1991). After an extensive review of the research and clinical literature on the subject, Furby, Weinroth, and Blackshaw (1989, p. 27) were forced to conclude, "there is as yet no evidence that clinical treatment reduces rates of sex reoffenses in general and no appropriate data for assessing whether it may be differentially effective for different types of offenders." The Furby et al. review included all variants of therapeutic approaches.

Despite this pessimistic appraisal, cognitive-behavior approaches currently offer the most effective method in the temporary cessation of deviant sexual behavior in motivated individuals. The cognitive-behavior approach contends that maladaptive sexual behaviors are learned according to the same principles as normal sexual behaviors and are largely the result of attitudes and beliefs. Cognitive-behavior therapy, compared to traditional verbal, insight-oriented therapy, has demonstrated short-term effectiveness in eliminating exhibitionism and fetishism (Kilmann et al., 1982), some forms of pedophilia (Marshall & Barbaree, 1988), and sexual violence and aggression (Quinsey & Marshall, 1983).

The key words are *temporary cessation* and *motivated individuals*. The problem of cognitive-behavior—and all therapies for that matter—is not in getting the motivated offender to stop the deviant sexual patterns, but in preventing relapse across time and varying situations. In this respect, it is analogous to dieting. Although most dieting regimens are effective in getting the motivated individual to lose weight initially, the real problem is the eventual relapse into old eating patterns.

A treatment approach demonstrating much promise in the treatment of sex offenders is called **Relapse Prevention** (RP): "RP is a self-control program designed to teach individuals who are trying to change their behavior how to anticipate and cope with the problem of relapse" (George & Marlatt, 1989, p. 2). The program emphasizes self-management; clients are considered responsible for the solution of their problems. Relapse prevention is a very recent development, and its long-term success has yet to be established. However, it is a refreshing new cognitive-behavioral approach that has considerable promise for the elimination of deviant behavior in offenders motivated to change.

In sum, under the present conditions of the prison setting, effective rehabilitation and psychological treatment will have limited success. Thus, it should come as no surprise that the track record of psychological change for confined offenders has been less than impressive. Nevertheless, attempts to bring about change cannot be abandoned. As we have seen, extensive efforts to rehabilitate one type of offender have yielded some positive results, but the success of any rehabilitative program in the prison setting will still depend upon the level of coercion and commitment exerted and the extent to which evaluation studies consider the crucial variables outlined above.

Even more important, however, is the fact that, upon release, offenders return to a society which is too often not ready to accept them. They are confronted with many of the same survival problems they encountered before their convictions, and often return to the same social situations, where crime may be a way of life. Despite efforts by correctional authorities to reintegrate former offenders into the community by such means as parole supervision and gradual release, the available resources are severely taxed.

DETERRENCE

Any discussion of the precise meaning of **deterrence** as a rationale for imprisonment leads to a jungle of heavy conceptual foliage. It is sometimes wise to divide the concept into two categories, as Andenaes (1968) suggests: general deterrence and specific deterrence.

General deterrence refers to the threat of punishment or, more broadly, the threat of law. Presumably, the anticipation of unpleasant consequences for specified behavior will discourage or deter the general public from engaging in that behavior. Many people are prevented from cheating on their income-tax returns by the threat of social embarrassment or even imprisonment. In fact, the Internal Revenue Service is probably the government agency that utilizes general deterrence to its fullest impact.

Special deterrence is a term reserved for the actual experience of punishment, which presumably will deter the punished individual from engaging in future transgressions. In evaluating the effectiveness of special deterrence, we ask, do certain forms of punishment reduce or suppress certain behaviors? Much of the psychological research relevant to deterrence has concentrated upon this question, with the result that broad principles of punishment have been developed. Unfortunately but understandably, psychology has developed the principles primarily after studying the behavior of nonhuman creatures, such as rats, dogs, pigeons, or monkeys. The critical drawback to such research is that it cannot take into account the powerful features of

358

CHAPTER
THIRTEEN:
THE
PSYCHOLOGY
OF
CORRECTIONS

human cognitive processes. Humans have attitudes, expectancies, values, and experiential histories which do not approximate the cognitive equations found in animals. We will discuss these and other aspects at the end of this section, but first let us return to the topic of general deterrence.

GENERAL DETERRENCE

This type of deterrence is concerned not with the effect of punishment on the person being punished, but rather with the overall symbolic impact punishment has on the population as a whole. One way of determining the effectiveness of general deterrence is to study the behavior of large aggregates of people after statutes or policies have been changed. Statutory changes might include the abolition (or establishment) of capital punishment, or the adoption of mandatory penalties, like a one-year sentence added to the usual sentence if a crime is committed with a gun. Legal policy changes might include increased active detection of and arrests for certain offenses, such as road-blocks to apprehend drunk drivers or mandatory arrests in domestic-violence situations.

It makes good sense to assume that the threat of punishment has an effect on certain sectors of the population and on certain crimes, but the question remains: how great is effect, and on what sectors? Interestingly, threats of informal punishment from one's community and circle of family and friends may have more of a deterrent effect than punishment from the state. With regard to public punishment, the elementary data we have gathered thus far do not provide clear answers. Some trends suggest that crime rates decrease as certainty of imprisonment increases. However, the relationship between sentence severity and crime rates remains equivocal (Siegel, 1992).

Two lines of empirical inquiry emerging from the psychological laboratory are pertinent here. One line of research focuses on the effects of vicarious punishment on subsequent behavior, the other on threats of punishment on subsequent behavior.

Vicarious Punishment

Research examining vicarious punishment generally has involved a modeling situation, where subjects first observe the punishment of another person (a model) and are then observed to see if they engage in similar behavior under tempting or permissive conditions. The research in this area has relied almost exclusively on children as subjects.

An exemplary study was that conducted by Walters and Parke (1964), who used six-year-old boys as subjects. Each child was shown some toys and warned by an adult: "Now these toys have been arranged for someone else, so you'd better not touch them." Each subject was then assigned to one of four experimental conditions. In one, the boys saw a three-minute film depicting a female adult, presumably a mother, who warned the child that he should not play with the toys placed on the table. The mother then sat the child down at the table, handed him a book, and left the room. After the mother left the room, the boy in the film put down the book and began to play with the toys for about two minutes. When the mother returned to the room, she snatched the toys from the child, shook him, and sat him down once more in the chair with the book. This sequence was referred to as the *model-punished condition*. In another experimental condition, boys saw the same sequence, but here the mother returned, handed the child some toys, and played with him in an affectionate manner—the *model-rewarded condition*. In a third condition, the *no-consequence condition*, the three-minute film was shortened to two minutes, and the mother did not return. A *control* group, in which the children saw no film, constituted condition four.

In each condition, after the subject had seen the film, the adult researcher gave the boy a book to read, made an excuse, and left the room. The child was then observed for fifteen minutes. Boys in the model-punished condition played with the toys less quickly, less often, and for shorter periods of time than the boys in the model-rewarded and no-consequence conditions. However, subjects in the model-punished situation did not play with the toys any less quickly, less often, or for shorter periods than the subjects in the control group, who did not see the film at all. When compared to the model-rewarded condition, the model-punished condition "got the message across" to its subjects, which would indicate that vicarious punishment is an effective method for reducing wrongdoing. However, the acid test was whether vicarious punishment made a difference in the behavior of subjects who had seen the film when compared with subjects who had not. If vicarious punishment is an effective procedure, we would predict that the children who observed the model punished for transgressions would play with the toys significantly less than the children who did not see the film at all. This was not the case in the Walters-Parke study. It would be more accurate to conclude, therefore, that vicarious reinforcement encourages subsequent behavior, but vicarious punishment does not appear to discourage it.

Another study by Bandura, Ross, and Ross (1963) showed nursery-school children films depicting an adult model using considerable physical and verbal aggression against another adult. In one condition the aggressive model received severe punishment for his behavior, while in the other the model was rewarded for the behavior. The study had two control conditions: one in which the children saw a film where the models engaged in vigorous but nonaggressive play, and another in which there was no model. The children in the model-punished condition did not demonstrate less aggressive behavior than the children in the two control conditions.

Bandura (1965) also conducted a frequently cited study in which an adult model behaved aggressively toward an inflated rubber doll. In one film sequence, the adult was punished for the behavior; in another, he was rewarded; in a third, there were no consequences for the behavior. Results revealed that children who saw the model punished for aggression showed less aggressive behavior in a later test condition than children in both the rewarded and no-consequence conditions. However, this experiment is not really a test case for the effects of vicarious punishment, because it had no control group which did not observe an aggressive model at all. While the experiment does demonstrate the power of modeling and vicarious reinforcement on the acquisition of behavior, it does not show the effects of vicarious punishment on behavior.

The numerous limitations of these studies (e.g., using children as subjects) make questionable their conclusions about the effects of vicarious punishment and its relationship to general deterrence. However, they continue to be among the very few studies on humans available. Some researchers and commentators have tentatively concluded that watching models being punished does not deter observers from engaging in the punished behavior at a later time, particularly if the behavior was in the observer's behavioral repertoire prior to watching the model (Hoffman, 1970; Rosenkoetter, 1973; Walters & Grusec, 1977). The preliminary data available to us suggest that media portrayals of models being punished do not deter a majority of the population from engaging in that particular conduct at a later date.

Threats of Punishment

The second line of empirical study has dealt with the effects of threats of punishment, without the subject's direct observation of some ill-fated model. The threat of punishment corresponds closely to Andenaes's (1974) "threat of law" concept, since it involves an explicit or implicit, clear or ambiguous threat of what might happen if one transgresses. Preliminary evidence indicates that threatened punishment may deter antisocial or illegal behavior, but only under specific, restricted conditions. Most of the research on this topic has focused on aggressive or violent behavior, again often with children as subjects.

In an extensive review of the research literature, Robert Baron (1977) has identified four specific conditions which significantly influence the effects of punitive threats on aggressive

360

CHAPTER
THIRTEEN:
THE
PSYCHOLOGY
OF
CORRECTIONS

behavior. The first condition involves the level of emotional arousal (e.g., anger) the aggressor is experiencing. Under relatively low levels of emotional arousal, the impact of threatened punishment remains at full strength. The individual apparently continues to think rationally of the consequences of his or her behavior. However, as the arousal level increases, the power of threatened punishment diminishes. A person extremely provoked and emotionally agitated is apt to think less rationally about the consequences of behavior and engage in the antisocial, aggressive, or prohibited behavior, regardless of the consequences.

A second condition identified by Baron is the apparent probability or perceived certainty that the threatened punishment will actually be delivered. Threats that are perceived as having little chance of being enacted have minimal effects as deterrents. If the public realizes that there is a law on the books, but also realizes that the law is rarely enforced or punishment rarely delivered, the deterrent influence of that law will be small or virtually nonexistent.

A third condition centers on the magnitude of the punishment expected. Psychological experiments on human aggressive behavior have found that threatened punitive measures, if severe, have greater impact than threatened mild reprimands. While this relationship is clear-cut in the experimental setting, it has not been reported with consistency outside the laboratory. As reported above, increasing the sentences for certain offenses does not generally have the effect of reducing the crime rates. It may be that the relationship between the intensity of threatened punishment and prohibited behavior is curvilinear. That is, allusions to punishment severity may have a diminishing effect after a certain point. Many violations of criminal law are already severely punished by years of imprisonment; adding a few years is likely to have limited effect.

A fourth condition concerns the amount of gain a person expects from prohibited behavior. If the perceived gain is substantial, it is possible that regardless of the magnitude or certainty of threatened sanction, the person will be willing to take the risks involved.

Baron correctly observes that "together, these apparent limitations on the influence of threatened punishment seem to offer unsettling implications for our present system of criminal justice. In particular, they suggest that existing conditions, under which the probability of being both apprehended and convicted of a single violent crime is exceedingly low, may be operating largely to nullify the potential influence of the penalties established for such crimes" (1977, p. 234).

In summary, the limited psychological literature does not support the concept of general deterrence as having a powerful influence on illegal behavior except under very restricted conditions, and rarely are these conditions met by the criminal-justice system. Neither the symbolism of vicarious punishment nor the presumed fear generated by threatened punishment have any significant impact on subjects except under the conditions outlined above. However, the data are in a preliminary stage of theoretical development, and the few experiments that have studied vicarious or threatened punishment do not generalize to adults in relation to criminal law and its sanctions.

The Death Penalty

The Eighth Amendment to the Constitution states: "Excessive bail shall not be required, nor excessive fines imposed, nor cruel and unusual punishment inflicted. As John Monahan and Laurens Walker (1990 p. 226) point out, social-science research has been used to address both the *cruel* and the *unusual* prongs of the Eighth Amendment. Monahan and Walker find that the cruelty issue arises when social science considers whether the death penalty acts as a general deterrent to crime. The issue of whether punishment is "unusual" is used by those who contend that the death penalty is applied in a discriminatory manner. In this context, we will only consider the issue of the deterrent effect of the death penalty.

Supporters of the death penalty often make the argument that it will deter people from committing heinous crimes. Empirical research on this question began with Theodore Sellin (1959), who found no support for a deterrent effect. Since that time, a large majority of the research has yielded similar results (Bandura, 1986; Decker & Kohfeld, 1990; Berkowitz, 1993). There have been some notable exceptions (e.g., Ehrlich, 1975, 1977; Layson, 1985; Yunger, 1976), but due to methodological shortcomings they have not been convincing. In sum, there is very little empirical evidence that the death penalty deters people from committing murder.

Yet, the American public still clamors for the death penalty as a way to stop crime. Public support fluctuates as a function of the amount of fear of crime and the number of heinous crimes that occur within a certain amount of time. However, since 1966 public support for the death penalty has increased and the number of advocates seems to be climbing still (Vidmar & Ellsworth, 1974; Skovron, Scott & Cullen, 1989). Today, public-opinion favoring it is at its highest since public opinion polls were introduced (Bohm, 1991). It is estimated that over 80 percent of the American population as a group supports its use. The strongest support is found among whites, the wealthy, males, Republicans, and Westerners (Bohm, 1987). As Bohm notes, however, "a fundamental problem with all death penalty opinion research is uncertainty about what death penalty support or opposition actually means...what little we know about American death penalty opinion is based on responses of people who know very little about it" (1991, p. 136).

Bohm contends that a majority of Americans might reject capital punishment if they knew that it does not deter violent crime more effectively than an alternative such as life imprisonment. Additionally, if the public knew that innocent persons are executed, that the death penalty is administered in a discriminatory manner, and that it costs much more than life imprisonment, support for this form of punishment would go down.

The U. S. is increasingly isolated in its use of capital punishment (Berkowitz, 1993), and it also remains one of the very few countries in the world that allows the death penalty for juveniles. However, in contrast to public sentiment about adult offenders, a majority (two-thirds) of the American public do not support the death penalty for juveniles (Skovron et al., 1989).

One explanation for the ineffectiveness of capital punishment as a deterrent is that the arousal level of the offender is usually high in times of violence. In fact, as we discussed in Chapter 12, extremely high arousal disengages us from our normal and logical ways of thinking. Thus, it is unlikely that a highly aroused offender is thinking about the negative consequences of the behavior at the time of the crime. In addition, persons planning their crimes seldom think they will be caught, much less get the death penalty (Berkowitz, 1993).

There is some evidence (e.g., Bowers & Pierce, 1980) that executions may actually increase the rate of murder rather than reduce it. This phenomenon is called the **brutalizing effect:** Execution legitimizes violent behavior in others. At the very least, it devalues human life: "When society executes offenders, it conveys a dual message condemning murder but also morally sanctioning violence by modeling the very abhorrent behavior it wishes to discourage in others" (Bandura, 1986, p. 333). According to this perspective, by modeling violence, a state-sanctioned killing merely serves to heighten human cruelty.

SPECIAL DETERRENCE

The empirical data on the psychology of special deterrence, or the effects of actual punishment on subsequent behavior, is far more extensive than that on general deterrence, but it too has its limitations. Empirical studies on general deterrence have been few and most were conducted with children as subjects. Psychological investigations of the effects of punishment, by contrast, have been largely confined to animals. Therefore, generalizations to society and the criminal-justice system must be applied only with caution. However, certain principles have been gained

362

CHAPTER
THIRTEEN:
THE
PSYCHOLOGY
OF
CORRECTIONS

from the research and can be related to human behavior in institutional settings as well as outside prison walls.

Although studies have been conducted with regularity over the years, prior to the late 1950s psychological research on the effects of punishment was dormant. The psychologists Edward Lee Thorndike, B. F. Skinner, and William Estes postulated that punishment was, for the most part, an ineffective procedure for the suppression of undesirable behavior. Instead, they believed, rewarding desirable behavior and not rewarding undesirable behavior would be far more effective in producing desired results. Many psychologists subscribed to this position, and punishment had very few proponents.

However, during the late 1950s N. H. Azrin and his colleagues reexamined the concept of punishment under a wide range of experimental conditions (Azrin & Holtz, 1966). They discovered that the application of punishment was not only a highly complicated process, but also that it could be an effective method of behavioral suppression under certain conditions. Azrin's experiments stimulated further research by numerous other investigators, and the experimental literature on punishment began to build on a more solid, scientific platform.

Punishment is generally defined in one of two ways: (1) presentation of an aversive or painful stimulus when a certain behavior occurs and (2) presentation of any event that reduces the probability of responding (Walters & Grusec, 1977). The administration of a verbal reprimand, a shock, or a slap are obvious examples of the first definition. Therefore, there is no distinction made as to whether the punishment is physical, psychological (withdrawal of love), or social (embarrassment). The second definition is more functional, in that it refers to any situation or event which reduces the occurrence of a behavior. The research literature has favored the former definition, and most designs have employed some form of aversive or painful stimulus, physical or psychological.

Psychological experiments have delineated three major principles with relation to the effectiveness of punishment: magnitude, consistency, and immediacy. The *magnitude*, or the *intensity*, of punishment has been found to affect substantially the occurrence of behavior in both humans and animals. The level of punishment delivered to humans, however, has been relatively mild, for obvious ethical and humane reasons. Generally speaking, the more severe the punishment, the greater its impact on behavioral suppression, at least with experimental animals. The situation is not this clear-cut with humans, however, because of the cognitive variables which radically distinguish human subjects from animals, and because "intense" punishments for humans are relatively mild compared to those administered to animals.

A second principle developed in the laboratory is the *consistency* of the punitive delivery. Punishment that is administered regularly, rather than occasionally or haphazardly, is highly effective in suppressing targeted behavior. For example, punishment delivered only periodically or at whim communicates to the person that the punishment is not contingent upon anything that he or she is doing, but rather is due to chance or fate. On the other hand, if the person receives immediate, consistent punishment contingent upon the performance of a specified act, the act will be quickly suppressed, or at least an association between the act and an aversive event will be established. In general, the research with both animals and humans indicates that we may have considerably more faith in the consistency principle than the intensity principle.

Studies have reported that parents of delinquents often administer erratic discipline, characterized by a random combination of punitiveness and permissiveness (Bartol & Bartol, 1989). Our present system of criminal justice, in which adult offenders are punished by the courts, continues this pattern. Inconsistent applications of law and apparently random sentencing procedures mean that links between behavior and consequences are not clearly established.

The third principle that must be considered in discussing the effectiveness of punishment is *immediacy*, which refers to the time interval between an act and its punishment. Overall, it appears that the shorter the time between the behavior and the contingent punishment, the more effective the suppression of the targeted behavior. While there are exceptions, this immediacy principle has been supported across a variety of situations, in many animal studies (Mowrer, 1960). However, the results are far less clear when human subjects are involved.

The cognitive mediation between act and anticipated punishment in human subjects accounts for the discrepancy in findings. Consider the effect on a child of the familiar statement, "Just wait till your father gets home!" The child becomes highly vulnerable to the emotional effects produced by the anticipation of punishment, which actually may be temporally removed from the transgression. In fact, the anxious anticipation may be far worse than the eventual punishment. One often hears the argument that legal punishment is ineffective because of the time lag, which is almost inevitable, between detection and adjudication. The anxiety generated between the time of arrest and the final disposition may be immediate punishment in itself. In fact, this can become a due-process concern. The person who has not been convicted does not deserve interim punishment. Thus, extensive delays in seeing a case through the system are undesirable, but not for the reasons so often advanced. It is not that passage of time ameliorates the effect of eventual punishment; it is that the very passage of time becomes punishment, often unjustifiably.

As a whole, the psychological studies applied to questions about the effectiveness of general or specific deterrence have not provided many clear answers. In fairness to the researchers who conducted them, however, it should be noted that they were not intended to do so. Almost all the studies were designed to examine the effects of direct or vicarious punishment on child development, or to develop theories of punishment *vis-à-vis* theories of learning. We have taken the data out of context and tried to relate them to an applied setting of enormous magnitude—the criminal justice system. Although we have been able to suggest possible connections between punishment and behavior, the area continues to be underresearched and needs much more attention before additional conclusions can be drawn.

Psychological Effects of Imprisonment

Craig Haney, Curt Banks, and Philip Zimbardo (1973) conducted an experiment to try to understand what it means psychologically to be a prisoner or a guard. The researchers created their own prison in the basement of the Stanford University Psychology Department. Small rooms were arranged to simulate six-by-nine-foot cells, a small "yard" was provided, and the researchers even added a solitary confinement "hole" (actually a closet). The "prison" had all the physical and psychological markings of an actual maximum-security institution: bars, prison drab, identification numbers, uniformed guards, and other features which not only closely approximated a prison environment but also encouraged "identity slippage": a loss of personal identity, known as **deindividuation**. In deindividuation, persons lose a sense of who they are or what they stand for.

The participants in the mock prison were young, male, largely middle-class, white students who responded to a newspaper ad for volunteers for a psychological experiment. In all, seventy-five volunteers answered the ad, but through careful screening, twenty-four were selected because of their maturity, emotional stability, and other indicators of normalcy. None had criminal records.

364

CHAPTER
THIRTEEN:
THE
PSYCHOLOGY
OF
CORRECTIONS

The experiment required two roles, guard and prisoner. Each subject was arbitrarily designated one or the other by a flip of a coin. Guards were allowed to develop their own formal rules for maintaining law, order, and respect, and they were relatively free to improvise new rules during their eight-hour, three-man shifts. Prisoners were unexpectedly picked up at their homes by police, were spread-eagled and frisked, handcuffed, taken to a police station, and booked. They were then led blindfolded to the mock prison, where they were stripped, sprayed with a delousing preparation (a deodorant spray), and made to stand alone and naked for a while in the cell yard. They were then issued a uniform and an identification number, and placed into a cell where they were to live with two other prisoners for the next two weeks. All subjects understood ahead of time what the experiment would entail; they were paid fifteen dollars a day.

The uniformed guards carried various symbols of power: a nightstick, keys to cells, whistles, and handcuffs. Prisoners were required to obtain permission from the guards to do even routine things like writing letters or smoking cigarettes. Prisoners were referred to only by number, their toilet visits were supervised, and they were lined up three times a day for a count. In addition, they were required to do pushups, clean toilets, and memorize sixteen rules and recite them on demand.

The events that occurred in the prison were observed and recorded on videotape, and the guards and prisoners were interviewed at various points throughout the project. Although the study was intended to continue for two weeks, it had to be terminated within six days because the behavior of the college men degenerated so rapidly. Zimbardo writes:

> In less than a week the experience of imprisonment undid (temporarily) a lifetime of learning; human values were suspended, self-concepts were challenged and the ugliest, most base, pathological side of human nature surfaced. We were horrified because we saw some boys (guards) treat others as if they were despicable animals, taking pleasure in cruelty, while other boys (prisoners) became servile, dehumanized robots who thought only of escape, of their own individual survival and of their mounting hatred for the guards (1973, p. 163).

During the early stages of the experiment, prisoners were rebellious and even attempted to take over the prison. The uprising was thwarted by the guards, however, and prisoners began to display increasing passivity and depression. Five prisoners had to be released during the first days because of extreme emotional depression, crying, rage, and acute anxiety. Many others begged to be paroled, and most were willing to forfeit all the money earned if released. However, when the prisoners' requests for parole were denied, they had absorbed their prisoner roles so well that they returned docilely to their cells. During the later stages, prisoners began to adopt a personal, self-centered philosophy of "each man for himself." Some of the guards, on the other hand, were becoming increasingly brutal and sadistic, enjoying their control over the prisoners. Some of the guards performed their role with toughness and fairness, a few were even friendly, but none interfered with commands issued by one of the most brutal, demeaning guards. In summary, the simulated "prison" became a real prison with "prisoners" acting like prisoners and "guards" acting like guards. For obvious reasons, no attempts have been made to replicate the Stanford study.

The Stanford Prison Experiment does reveal vividly the power and pervasiveness of prison situations over individual behavior. It demonstrates what confinement, monitored and controlled by persons who have been given awesome power over the behavior of those confined, can do to the psychological functioning of both prisoners and guards. A valid critique of the study is that the subjects might have been merely playing roles they thought they should be playing, so that although situational properties may have had considerable impact on behavior, expectancies were also involved. On the other hand, we can assume that expectancies also play a part in the behavior of the participants in the real prison system. The most frequent critique of the study, however, is that it lacked external validity concerning whether its findings can be generalized to "real" prisoners and guards (Johnson, 1987, Monahan & Walker, 1990).

In addition to the Stanford Prison study, a number of case studies on the effects of prison life have indicated that imprisonment can be brutal, demeaning, and generally psychologically devastating for many individuals (Zamble & Porporino, 1988; Bartollas, 1981). These studies often describe a variety of psychological symptoms believed to be directly caused by imprisonment, including psychosis, severe depression, inhibiting anxiety, and complete social withdrawal. There are many other stressors, such as fear of contagious diseases (e.g., TB or incurable viruses). The threat of AIDS is growing within prison walls as it is in the general population. In 1985, for instance, there were only 433 reported cases in state prisons; by 1989, the number had grown to 3,456 reported cases (Moini & Hammett, 1990).

Overall, the results indicate that each individual who experiences confinement reacts to the situation in an idiosyncratic manner. Some find the experience of incarceration extremely stressful, while others who are dependent, passive, and generally incompetent may find that the structure of the prison offers a positive experience.

Much of the literature on the psychological effects of prison life neglects the important variable of offense conviction. In most correctional facilities, there exists a social hierarchy determined by individual criminal histories and types of crimes committed. For example, prisoners often despise fellow inmates who were convicted of certain sexual crimes, such as child rape or molestation. These offenders not only are placed at the bottom of the prisoner hierarchy, but they are also harassed to the point where they must seek protection from other inmates. Material acquisition offenses (e.g., robbery and burglary) are high-status offenses, particularly if performed ingeniously. Therefore, the nature of one's offense can either add to one's confinement woes or make them lighter.

A growing body of research (e.g., Toch & Adams, 1989a, 1989b; Zamble & Porporino, 1988) raises serious questions about the extent and nature of psychological damage that is directly caused by imprisonment. Zamble and Proporino (1988) studied the coping strategies of inmates in several Canadian penitentiaries. They found that emotional disruption and adjustment were clearly problems for most inmates during the early segments of their sentences. Deleterious reactions resulted from the dramatic disruptions in customary behavior created by the many restrictions, deprivations, and constraints inherent in prison life. However, these initial reactions soon dissipated for most inmates, and, as the inmates became accustomed to prison routine, no lasting emotional problems were discernible.

Toch and Adams (1989b) reported a similar pattern of adjustment in their research on American prisoners. These researchers found not only that emotional distress was highest among inmates during the early beginnings of their sentences but also that these same inmates were the most troublesome and disruptive with regard to prison rules and regulations. In addition, the Toch-Adams data supported the frequent observation that age is a strong correlate of prison violations, with the younger inmates being much more prone to engage in prison misconduct than older inmates. In fact, Richard McCorkle (1992) reports that younger inmates assume a more aggressive, violent stance toward all individuals within the prison walls compared to their older counterparts, and thus are more likely to be the targets of violent victimization. Older inmates, on the other hand, assume more passive avoidance techniques in adapting to the expectations of the prison environment.

If we follow psychological reactions across the entire timespan of an inmate's sentence, we

366

CHAPTER
THIRTEEN:
THE
PSYCHOLOGY
OF
CORRECTIONS

will often find a curvilinear or **U**-shaped pattern, with the strongest emotional stress reactions occurring at the beginning of the sentence, and at the end, as the time to be released approaches (Bukstel & Kilmann, 1980). During the middle segments, anxiety is usually quite low and some resignation sets in. The pattern of increased stress reactions at the end of an inmate's sentence—such as high anxiety, restlessness, sleeplessness, and other indicators of distress—is often referred to as the "short-timer's syndrome." These reactions probably reflect an uncomfortable anticipation and feeling of uncertainty about one's ability to adjust again to the outside world after adjusting to prison life. Total adjustment to prison life is sometimes called "instutionalization" or "jailing." It refers specifically to a process in which the inmate loses interest in the outside world, views the prison as home, loses the ability to make independent decisions, and, in general, defines him- or herself totally within the institutional context (MacKenzie & Goodstein, 1985).

Zamble and Porporino concluded from their research "that prisons do not produce permanent harm to the psychological well-being of inmates" (p. 149). In another context, Zamble summarizes:

> We included a wide variety of measures of behavior, cognitions, and emotional experience, and examined these changes over a 1½-year period in prison. These measures failed to show a generalized pattern of emotional damage from imprisonment, and, except for a reduction in dysphoria and a loss of apparent motivation for change, psychological functioning was remarkably stable over time in prison (1992, p. 410).

On the other hand, they could not conclude that there were positive psychological effects of imprisonment either: "Our data show very little positive behavioral change in prison, just as earlier we could see little evidence for generalized negative effects" (p. 151). However, when the researchers expanded the period of time to seven years, they were able to conclude: "When we follow a group of men over time, we find much more evidence of improvement than of deterioration" (p. 421).

Zamble and his associates found that changes in adaptation occurred particularly in the areas of socialization. That is, the majority of the long-term inmates withdraw from the prison social networks and spend much of their discretionary time in their cells, or with one or two close friends. Long-termers seem to be living within a world of their own, physically inside the prison, but cognitively outside: "They avoided the entanglements that result from involvement with other inmates, and they began to monitor, analyze, and control their own behavior better" (p. 422).

Toch and Adams (1989b) also assert that prison experiences provide positive effects for some inmates, particularly the younger inmates under twenty-five: "Young inmates, who are presumably more rambunctious and less mature than older inmates, appear to derive some benefit from this forced environment…it is encouraging to find that prison inmates who are initially most resistant to restrictions on their personal liberty demonstrate increasing levels of conformity over time" (pp. 19–20). Precisely why these effects happen remains largely a mystery, although Toch and Adams suggest that the maturation process facilitated by humane prison environments plays a critical role. The researchers contend that inmate behavior is likely to improve when inmates learn the association between behavior and its positive or negative consequences within the institution, and when they have psychological support, as well as the opportunity to participate in conventional activities, to form attachment bonds, and to build relationships.

In summary, as Adams (1992) notes in a review of prison adjustment literature, a vast majority of inmates do not exhibit long-standing psychological impairment or problems as a direct result of imprisonment. However, there are certain prison conditions under which this conclusion may not hold, namely, crowding and isolation.

CROWDING

The issue of crowding is becoming increasingly important as correctional institutions are forced to house far more inmates than they were designed to hold. Prison officials estimate that the United States is at least 11 percent short in bed space in state prisons, a situation likely to get worse (Patrick, 1988). During the 1980s, state and federal prison populations in the U. S. increased by 76 percent, with the federal prison system growing at a faster rate than the state prison systems (Pelissier, 1991). The prisons that are the most overcrowded tend to be the older, maximum-security facilities containing more than 1,000 male inmates (Ruback & Innes, 1988). While the United States has the highest proportion of crowding in its prison population, the problem exists worldwide (Patrick, 1988). Prison populations everywhere are increasing.

Not only does crowding reduce the personal, physical, and psychological space available, it also means that the already marginally adequate work and activity programs are offered to fewer inmates or for shorter time periods, thereby increasing inmate confinement and time spent with nothing to do. Crowding brings increases in noise pollution, and it reduces the opportunity for inmates to remove themselves from constant view and surveillance. The problem of crowding is particularly relevant in the dormitory arrangements now common in many prisons, where as many as sixty prisoners may be jammed into one large room, spending twenty or more hours together. It is no wonder that prisoners prefer nine-by-six-foot cells, which provide some privacy and considerable protection (Clements, 1979).

Crowding can be measured physically or psychologically. Psychologically, crowding is a subjective condition based on a person's perception of discomfort as the number of people increases. Crowding can also be defined objectively as the number of square feet per inmate, a measurement referred to as "physical density." In addition, three major categories of dependent

368

CHAPTER
THIRTEEN:
THE
PSYCHOLOGY
OF
CORRECTIONS

variables are used as indices of the effects of crowding: (1) physiological, (2) psychological, and (3) behavioral. (The most common physiological reaction to stress is blood pressure.) Behavioral measures include the number of infractions of prison rules or other forms of misconduct. Psychological measures encompass self-reports of anxiety, depression, hostility, feelings of helplessness, and other indicators of emotional discomfort.

Research suggests that prison and jail overcrowding is associated with higher incidences of physical illness, socially disruptive behavior, and emotional distress (Bukstel & Kilmann, 1980; Cox, Paulus & McCain, 1984; Ruback & Innes, 1988). Some researchers have further suggested that disruptive behavior and violence in correctional facilities increases directly as the available living space decreases (Megargee, 1976; Nacci, Prather & Tetelbaum, 1977; Gaes & McGuire, 1984). This relationship seems to be particularly prevalent in juvenile institutions (Megargee, 1976), and among women prison inmates (Ruback & Carr, 1984), who normally display little violent behavior.

The available evidence implies that crowding generates stress, which further instigates behavior of coping by any available means. Carl Clements (1979) observes that in a New Mexico state penitentiary of two thousand inmates, three hundred were fortunate enough to earn solitary confinement for twenty-three hours per day, foregoing programs and many other privileges. Clements found that these single cells were a sought-after premium, despite the fact that inmates confined to them would be the subjects of disciplinary reports sent to parole boards.

In a fifteen-year study on prison crowding, Paulus (1988) discovered that increasing the number of residents in correctional facilities significantly increased the negative psychological (e.g., tension, anxiety, depression) and physiological reactions (e.g., headaches, high blood pressure, cardiovascular problems) in inmates. The critical factor appeared to be the number of residents sharing a particular space rather than simply the footage of space available. For example, providing at least some privacy and limiting the visual and physical contact with other inmates, by providing cubicles instead of open dormitories, for example, reduces the negative impact of living there.

Paulus also ascertained that socioeconomic level, education level, and prior prison or jail confinements were related to inmate reactions to crowded conditions. That is, the higher the socioeconomic and education level, the more difficult the adjustment to and the lower the tolerance for crowded conditions. One explanation for this finding is that many people with lower socioeconomic status are accustomed to living under crowded conditions. Therefore, they are more tolerant of invasions of privacy and other factors involved in crowded environments. Surprisingly, prior confinement in a correctional facility interfered with adjustment to crowded conditions. Specifically, inmates who had some history of prior incarceration exhibited more problems in adjustment than those without prior time. Paulus suggests that individuals with extensive prison histories probably spent at least part of their sentences in single cells or under less crowded conditions and thus were not accustomed to the present-day crowded conditions. Paulus did not find significant gender, race, or ethnic differences in how individuals react to variations in social density in correctional institutions.

Paulus hypothesizes that three factors may be at work in causing the adverse effects of crowded prison environments. First, crowded conditions reduce one's sense of control over the social environment since other inmates are unpredictable, and the more of them there are, the less predictable the social environment becomes. This same observation has also been made by Ruback and his associates (Ruback & Carr, 1984; Ruback, Carr & Hopper, 1986). Second, crowded conditions also interfere with one's daily habits, destroying freedom from intrusions, a sense of privacy, and time for carrying out daily activities. Third, crowded conditions instigate much more activity, noise, unwanted interactions, smells, violations of personal space, and generally excessive environmental stimulation.

Overcrowding also taxes the correctional staff to the point where it is safest for all if inmates are kept in cells and dormitories as much as possible, except for meal calls. There are fewer constructive jobs for inmates, little exercise, and less access to therapeutic programs, all of which generates inactivity and boredom and, consequently, stress. The forced idleness also lowers self-esteem and engenders feelings of incompetence, hardly conducive to any form of rehabilitation or self-improvement.

In summary, the available research does indicate that prison crowding is associated with negative psychological and health reactions. The U. S. Supreme Court, however, has rejected the argument that overcrowding *per se* constitutes cruel and unusual punishment and violates the Eighth Amendment (*Rhodes v. Chapman*, 1981). Relegating the social-science findings on the issue to footnotes, the Court said that the "totality of the conditions" should be looked at on a case-by-case basis to determine whether overcrowding represents cruel and unusual punishment.

Some scholars (e.g., Gaes, 1985) also argue that a direct causal link between crowding and negative effects has yet to be convincingly established. For instance, some of the problems associated with overcrowding may be the result of bad management, either in a particular prison or throughout the entire prison system. Administrative changes can reduce the negative effects of high social density in prisons. For example, Bernadette Pelissier (1991) studied the effects of a rapid doubling (less than six months) of an inmate population at a federal correctional facility. Random samples of both staff and prisoners were interviewed before and after the dramatic inmate population expansion. Results showed no overall increase in rule-infraction or illness-complaint rates associated with the doubling of the prison population. Pelissier attributed the findings to the prison staff and administration's preparedness for the increase. Correctional personnel made certain that prison programs and services were not adversely affected by the rapid growth. Effective management seemed to neutralize any major negative effects of crowding for a majority of both the inmates and the prison staff.

Individuals react differently to crowded conditions, some demonstrating much better (or much worse) adjustment than others. There are many variables that must be considered as well, such as the type of institution (e.g., jails versus prisons, maximum security versus minimum security), the institution's orientation and mission, the type of social milieu, the racial and ethnic composition of the institution, the degree of crowding, and the phase an individual has reached in her or his sentence.

ISOLATION

Inmates in prison may be physically isolated from each other for many different reasons and under a wide variety of conditions. Isolation, solitary confinement, and restrictive housing are broad terms used to cover this separation of inmates from the general prison population. More specifically, **disciplinary segregation** (or punitive isolation) is imposed as punishment for infractions or violations of prison rules and regulations. While prison authorities are investigating an incident, the inmate may be placed in **administrative segregation**. Another form of isolation, sometimes considered a category of administrative segregation, is **protective custody**, by which the inmate is separated to protect him or her from possible harm. The threat of harm may come from the inmate him- or herself, as with suicide, or it may come from other inmates, as with revenge or sexual assault.

The threat of harm continues to be a serious problem in corrections. In 1990, seventy-six prison homicides were reported in state and federal facilities, and there were close to ten thousand inmate-on-inmate assaults that required medical attention that same year (McCorkle, 1992; Camp

370

CHAPTER
THIRTEEN:
THE
PSYCHOLOGY
OF
CORRECTIONS

& Camp, 1991). Victims of sexual assault frequently resort to self-imposed solitary, spending most of their time in their cells and away from areas where they may be attacked again (McCorkle, 1992). Many inmates, fearful of physical attack, sexual or otherwise, request protective custody, preferring to be locked up twenty-four hours per day rather than risk attack. Those inmates who do venture into common areas of the institution often carry crude weapons constructed from raw materials gathered from their cells or work stations (McCorkle, 1992).

Unfortunately, much of what we know about the psychological effects of isolation has come from research using college-student volunteers, who submit to social isolation for varying periods of time, usually in cells similar to those used in correctional settings. Generally, the methodology has been sound, and some relevant, but very tentative, conclusions can be drawn (Bukstel & Kilmann, 1980). The ecological validity of this research remains questionable, however, primarily because the conditions used in the research rarely simulate those in prison settings. Furthermore, there is a wide range of conditions under which prison inmates are isolated. In one prison, prisoners may be able to see and even communicate with other inmates similarly isolated; in another, the cells may be covered with plexiglass, allowing them to see but not throw things at correctional officers; in still another, a small, barred opening in the cell door may be their only way of seeing out.

It comes as no great surprise that the research with volunteers has found that individuals respond differently to solitude; some are glad to be away from the noise and activity of everyday living, while others demonstrate behavioral indicators of stress and frustration. Solitary confinement of a week or less does not appear to produce significant changes in motor behavior or perceptual or cognitive functioning (Walters, Callagan & Newman, 1963; Weinberg, 1967). Additional data suggest that, for most persons, solitary confinement does not generate more stress than would be expected in normal prison life (Ecclestone et al., 1974; Gendreau et al., 1972). These data are based on situations in which the primary focus was on social isolation for brief periods of time, and not on sensory deprivation or the deprivation of necessities of life. The introduction of additional deprivations, like cutting off food supplies or any sounds, is known to produce substantial changes in a number of psychological functions (Zubek, 1969).

The very few studies examining the effects of involuntary solitary confinement in correctional facilities have found that there do not seem to be any deleterious effects on inmates over the short haul (less than seven days) (Suedfeld, Ramirez, Deaton & Baker-Brown, 1982), but there might be for those inmates placed in solitary confinement for up to a year (Grassian, 1983). Taken as a whole, the research on voluntary and involuntary solitary confinement does not show long-lasting deleterious effects, and the negative effects that are reported may depend more on how the inmate is treated while in solitary: "When inmates are dealt with capriciously by management or individual custodial officers, psychological stress can be created even in the most humane of prison environments" (Bonta & Gendreau, 1990, p. 361). It is important to note, however, that courts have found some conditions of isolation so bad that they violated the Eighth Amendment prohibition against cruel and unusual punishment. In addition, the U. S. Supreme Court has allowed lower courts to set a limit on how long inmates can be kept under conditions of disciplinary segregation (*Hutto v. Finney*, 1978).

GENDER DIFFERENCES

Most of the research dealing with prison adjustment has been done on male inmates. Part of the explanation for the neglect of female inmates is that they make up only about 6 percent of those incarcerated in state and federal prisons. Presently, only 71 of the 1,037 prisons (4 percent) are for women only, and another 77 (7 percent) house both sexes (Bureau of Justice Statistics, 1992). Because of research neglect, women inmates, especially those serving long sentences, are sometimes referred to as the "forgotten offenders" (Unger & Buchanan, 1985). Research on women long-term offenders is almost nonexistent (MacKenzie, Robinson & Campbell, 1989).

Some scholars argue that many of the problems faced by female prisoners are unlike those faced by male prisoners. For example, due to the small numbers of women in prison, there are far fewer correctional facilities available, thus severely restricting opportunities for inmates to be near their families or to have occupational, educational, or social activities while incarcerated. More importantly, their relationships with their children are often severely hampered, more than typically found for the male inmate parent (MacKenzie, et al., 1989). This parent-child deprivation is especially severe for long-term women inmates, who may lose their major source of identity when they lose their parental role (Weisheit & Mahan, 1988). Weisheit and Mahan note that, on average, women inmates have two children and often are the heads of their households. Moreover, they are likely to be poor, poorly educated, and members of racial or ethnic minorities.

Doris Layton MacKenzie and her colleagues (1989) studied the characteristics, adjustment, and coping of women serving three types of prison sentences in Louisiana's only prison for adult women. These researchers found that inmates serving short sentences were more likely to be members of "play families" than those inmates serving longer sentences. Play families are organized voluntarily by mutual agreement among inmates, and may or may not include homosexual relationships. Family members are given titles, such as mother, child, uncle, aunt, father, or sister. These families seem to provide a coping and protective structure for women inmates new to the prison environment. Women serving long-term sentences were less likely to belong to play families but also reported more situational problems such as boredom, nostalgia for amenities, and lack of opportunities for education, job training, and treatment. The researchers concluded that these situational problems were not due to an inability to cope as much as a realistic appraisal of the accumulative limitations of the prison environment.

PRISON SUICIDE

Suicide rates reflect the fact that prison life is stressful to many individuals. Jails, however, have a higher suicide rate than prisons (Lester & Danto, 1993). Suicide in custody is usually committed by young, unmarried white males during the early stages of confinement, and the usual method is hanging. Other inmates try to mutilate themselves with razor blades, fragments of metal, glass, or wire, or even eating utensils. An analysis of suicides in Australian prisons indicated that those inmates who committed or attempted suicide were more likely to have a history of self-inflicted injury or attempted suicide prior to being incarcerated (Hatty & Walker, 1986). This suggests that suicide is not necessarily caused by the stresses of prison life.

Bartollas (1981) notes that prison suicides can be roughly grouped into several categories. One includes those offenders who are embarrassed by the disgrace they have brought upon themselves and their families and find their guilt and debased self-esteem intolerable. A second group is represented by those inmates who find that the sense of helplessness and lack of control over their lives is intolerable. A third group uses suicidal behavior to manipulate others. Although the inmates in this third group usually select methods that insure their survival or detection, they sometimes die accidentally.

DEATH ROW

Some researchers have also probed the psychological effects of death row. As of January, 1993, there were 2,482 prisoners sentenced death in American prisons (Bureau of Justice Statistics, 1993).

372

CHAPTER
THIRTEEN:
THE
PSYCHOLOGY
OF
CORRECTIONS

How to deal with inmates awaiting capital punishment is becoming an important humanitarian concern. Also, the courts do ask clinicians to assess the death-row inmate's appreciation of the appeal process and competency for execution, as discussed earlier.

So far we know very little about how death-row inmates adjust to their fate. In one of the earlier studies, Bluestone and McGahee (1962) interviewed eighteen men and one woman on death row at Sing Sing. They did not find intense depressive or anxious reactions. Johnson (1982) interviewed thirty-five men awaiting execution and found them concerned over their powerlessness, fearful of their surroundings, and feeling emotionally drained. These observations were especially characteristic of the younger inmates. In a more extended study of death-row conditions, Johnson (1990) described negative psychological reactions in both inmates guards. Smith and Felix (1986) conducted unstructured psychiatric interviews of thirty-four death-row inmates. Most of their sample exhibited well-developed defenses regarding their alleged guilt. Debro, Murty, Roebuck, and McCann (1987) interviewed twenty-five death-row inmates and found that all slept well and felt relatively good about themselves. None requested or received tranquilizers.

PRISONIZATION

In 1940, Clemmer defined **prisonization** as "the taking on in greater or less degree of the folkways, mores, customs, and general culture of the penitentiary" (p. 299). Prisonization means that inmates adopt and internalize the prisoner subculture within any particular institution. It is hypothesized that the longer one is incarcerated, the more deeply ingrained the attitudes and behavioral patterns endorsed by this subculture become. The inmate who rejects the protective subculture is left physically and psychologically vulnerable. The process by which an inmate leaves or detaches from the subculture is often called "resocialization," and it appears to occur with some regularity near the end of the confinement period and just before the inmate is about to return to the community.

Wheeler (1961) recommended conformity to staff expectations as a barometer of prisonization—the lower the conformity, the higher the prisonization. Wheeler also hypothesized that the prisonization process would change according to which segment of the sentence was being served by the inmate. An inmate beginning a sentence would embrace the prison subculture somewhat differently than he or she would at the midpoint or end of the sentence.

Research examining the validity of the prisonization concept has been contradictory and inconclusive (Bukstel & Kilmann, 1980). The findings suggest that some mixture of personality differences, postprison expectations, and the nature of the institution operates in the prisonization process. In other words, prisonization is not a unitary concept that can be applied across all prisoner populations. Rather, it appears more likely that "prisoner clubs" vary from institution to institution. The extent to which an inmate incorporates the subculture values, codes, and social hierarchies will depend not only on the orientation of the particular prison but also on individual needs and expectancies.

Institutions for juvenile and young offenders tend to be somewhat less regimented than adult facilities. In three studies designed to examine the effects of institutionalization (prisonization) on the behavior of delinquents, similar results emerged (Buehler, Patterson & Furness, 1966; Duncan, 1974; Furness, 1964). Delinquent peers strongly reinforced one another for such behaviors as rule breaking, criticizing adults, aggressive actions, and other anti-institutional maneuvers. On the other hand, actions that deviated from the delinquent subculture were met with peer disapproval. These findings suggest the existence of a fairly generalizable delinquent subgroup, although it may be restricted to anti-authority behavioral patterns rather than to an all-encompassing subcultural code of conduct or value system.

Simha Landau (1978) cites some interesting data on prisonization among young offenders (ages 17.5 to 21) serving time in an Israeli prison (Tel-Mond). Wheeler (1961) had hypothesized a **U**-shaped trend for prisonization, meaning that at the beginning and at the end of imprisonment, inmates are less influenced by, or less in need of, a prison subculture. Landau found a similar phenomenon among inmates he studied.

It appears from the research that the beginning and end of incarceration serve as crucial temporal guideposts for prisoners, a finding that has been reported with consistency in the research literature (Bukstel & Kilmann, 1980). The middle of a sentence, by contrast, becomes a cognitive fog in which the average offender tries to make the best of a negative situation.

Early during his imprisonment, the prisoner is still close to the outside world, thinks about it regularly, and does not display a high degree of involvement in the prisoner subculture. As the inmate approaches the midpoint of his or her sentence, however, fellow inmates become the main social support and reference group. As release approaches, the inmate again begins to think about the outside world and gradually becomes detached from the prisoner subculture, which no longer fulfills the supportive and protective functions it did during the middle phase of incarceration.

Summary and Conclusions

The late John Conrad, an expert in corrections, has written that the prison will exist for the foreseeable future and will inevitably be an authoritarian community: "Intelligently managed, it can be a benevolent despotism at best; stupidly managed, it will belie our national claim to magnanimity, becoming either a dangerous anarchy or the worse of tyrannies" (1982, p. 328). An intelligently managed prison, Conrad argued, was safe and secure for both inmates and staff, and was industrious, lawful, and hopeful. The first three of Conrad's ideal features, important as they are, are peripheral to this text. The fourth—hope—implies that inmates be given reasonable opportunities to improve their lives, something we may argue is best achieved with continuing attention to rehabilitative needs.

Psychologists working in institutional corrections can play a significant role in providing hope. We have focused in this chapter on their two primary functions—to assess and to treat. Through their involvement in the classification process, psychologists can recommend programs which will best match offenders to their needs. These might include substance-abuse treatment programs, development of reading and writing skills, decisionmaking, anger control, meaningful job training, contact with families, or sex-offender treatment. Psychologists also can be alert to signs of impending serious mental disorder and recommend preventive measures. In their treatment role, they may offer individual or group therapy to inmates on a voluntary basis, with a minimum goal of helping them to cope with the realities of prison life.

Most offenders adjust to their confinement and manage to survive, with the earliest and latest stages of the sentence appearing to be critical periods. As we have seen, however, special adjustment problems affect certain categories of offenders, including those in solitary confinement, women offenders, young offenders, and the mentally disordered. Additionally, studies indicate that jail detainees and inmates require at least as much psychological attention as prison inmates. Although we have not discussed them here, other categories of offenders such as elderly inmates and those with AIDS or other physically debilitating illnesses also need special attention. Overcrowding, the number-one problem for correctional institutions in the 1980s, has had a significant psychological effect on prison inmates, as most of the research in that area demonstrates.

374

CHAPTER
THIRTEEN:
THE
PSYCHOLOGY
OF
CORRECTIONS

We have examined the goals or rationales of imprisonment from a psychological perspective. Incapacitation, as we noted, has little justification if it is based on predictions of dangerousness, as selective incapacitation tends to be. Retribution, which seems to be a noble goal, is seldom truly achieved. Furthermore, retributive sentencing, which is often unusually harsh, has contributed to the overcrowding problem, and has not reduced disparity in sentencing. There is some indication that general deterrence works for specific offenders and specific crimes. However, much more research in this area is needed before we can say with confidence that there is psychological support for this rationale. With respect to crimes which carry the death penalty, however, general deterrence is not supported. In fact, there is some evidence that capital punishment has a brutalizing effect on society.

Psychology has directed a good deal of attention toward the merits of rehabilitation in the prison setting. The research to date is not impressive. Martinson's (1974) conclusions, although overstated, still apply to many rehabilitative programs offered by prisons today when rehabilitation is measured by the recidivism yardstick. Nevertheless, some psychological approaches, particularly those based on bringing about cognitive-behavioral change, show promise. As with all therapeutic measures, psychological rehabilitation in the prison setting is most likely to occur if the offenders are not coerced, if the treatment is voluntary, and if the "system" does not place obstacles in its way. Society must recognize, however, that it cannot continue to incarcerate its offenders at the present rate. Both prevention of crime and development of suitable community-based alternatives are the wisest policy alternatives to pursue.

Questions to Ponder

1. Your sister, who originally wanted to be a psychologist working closely with the courts, now wants to be a correctional psychologist. Discuss with her the satisfactions and frustrations of this profession.

2. What personal conflicts are likely to be experienced by psychologists working with death-row inmates?

3. How would you incorporate John Conrad's advice in a program to make prisons safe, industrious, lawful, and hopeful?

4. As defined in this chapter, rehabilitation refers to psychological intervention with offenders. What other types of rehabilitation programs are available to prison inmates? Are they more likely to succeed?

5. Most inmates adjust to prison life. To what extent should society lessen the pain of those who do not? Would you find it easier to adjust to overcrowding or isolation, and why?

GLOSSARY

A priori method. Method for eliminating doubt about one's world through logic and systematic reason from self-evident propositions.

Acquisition (also called the **encoding** or **input stage**). The first stage of memory, in which perception registers in the various areas of the cortex and is initially stored.

Actuarial method of prediction. A prediction method that employs statistics to identify certain facts about a person's background and known behavior that can be related to the behavior being predicted, based on how *groups* of individuals with similar characteristics have acted in the past.

Administrative law. Law created and enforced by representatives of the numerous administrative agencies of national, state, or local governments.

Admonitions or curative instructions. Warnings or instructions given by a trial judge in an effort to prevent jurors from misusing potentially prejudicial information or which are presumed to correct or "cure" possible errors in the trial process.

Adversarial process. A process of argument and counterargument adopted by the judicial system as the most effective way to arrive at the truth in legal disputes or controversies.

Aggravating circumstances. Circumstances surrounding a crime which heighten its seriousness for purposes of sentencing. An example would be a particularly heinous or cruel method of carrying out a crime, such as a torture murder.

Aggressive cynicism. Niederhoffer's third stage of police cynicism (e.g., "I hate civilians and society") which gradually builds until it becomes most prevalent during the tenth year of service.

Alarm stage. Violanti's first stage of career development in police work where the new officer experiences "reality shock."

ALI Rule. A standard for judging the insanity defense based on the Model Penal Code formulated by the American Law Institute. The ALI Rule suggests that a person may be absolved of criminal responsibility if he or she lacks the capacity to appreciate the wrongfulness of conduct or to conform that conduct to the law. The ALI Rule forms the basis of the **Brawner Rule**. *See also* **Caveat paragraph**.

Amicus curiae (Latin for "friend of the court"). An *amicus curiae* brief is a document submitted to an appellate court by an outside party to call attention to some matter that might otherwise escape its attention.

Amnesia. Complete or partial memory loss of an incident, series of incidents, or some segment of life's experiences. *See also* various types, such as **chronic organic amnesia** and **anterograde amnesia**.

Analogue field study. A study in which the volunteers are genuinely concerned about the outcome of their performance.

Anamnestic prediction. Prediction based on how a *particular* person acted in the past in similar situations.

Anomie. A term developed by the French sociologist Emile Durkheim and later refined by the American sociologist Robert Merton, it describes a state of normlessness or alienation from one's society and traditional culture.

Anterograde amnesia. Memory loss confined to the acquisition and retention of new material.

Anxiety. An unpleasant emotional state marked by worry, fear, anger, apprehension, and muscular tension, and manifested in various kinds of behavior. Also called **stress reaction**.

Archival method. A method of data collection in which the researcher relies on previously recorded information, such as court documents.

Arousal. A neurophysiological state that temporarily disengages a person from his or her normal way of thinking. It is generally prominent when humans engage in violence and destruction.

Arraignment. The court proceeding during which a defendant is formally charged with an offense, informed of their rights, and asked to enter a plea.

Assimilation. The process by which a person, using existing knowledge, stereotypes, or schemas, takes in and makes sense of new information about the environment.

Attachment. One of the four elements of the social bond from Hirschi's Social Control Theory. It refers to the degree of bonding a child has to her or his parents, teachers, and peers.

Authoritarianism. The term used to describe an ideology or an attitude system holding that one should unquestioningly accept authority from recognized powerful people and institutions.

Base rate. The frequency or probability of an occurrence within a given population during a given period of time. In testing, base rate refers to the proportion of persons expected to succeed on a criterion before any test is administered.

Battered-woman syndrome. A cluster of behavioral and psychological characteristics believed common to women victimized in abusive relationships. **Battered-child syndrome** is a cluster of behavioral and psychological characteristics believed common to abused children. Compare to **Child sexual abuse syndrome**.

Belief. In Hirschi's Social Control Theory, the internalization of the legitimacy and morality of society's rules and laws.

Bench trial. A civil or criminal trial in which the judge, rather than a jury, is the finder of fact, responsible for reviewing the evidence and rendering a verdict.

Best interests of the child. The legal doctrine that the parents' legal rights should be secondary to what is best for the child.

Brawner Rule. A standard for evaluating the insanity defense which recognizes that the defendant must suffer from a condition which *substantially* (a) affects mental or emotional processes or (b) impairs behavioral controls. Expands on the **ALI Rule**.

Brutalizing effect. The postulated effect of state-sponsored executions on criminal behavior which holds that because executions are themselves violent, they may actually serve to increase violence rather than deter it.

Case law or **"judge-made" law**. Law based on judicial precedent rather than on legislative enactments or statutes.

Caveat paragraph of the ALI Rule. This section of the rule excludes abnormality manifested only by repeated criminal or antisocial conduct. It was intended to disallow the insanity defense for psychopaths.

Certiorari. Certification by the U. S. Supreme Court that it will hear a case. When the Court agrees to hear an appeal, it issues a *writ of certiorari*.

Challenge for cause. Exercised by an attorney or judge whenever it can be demonstrated that a would-be juror does not satisfy the statutory requirements for jury duty.

Charging instructions. Instructions given by the judge to the jury explaining the jury's role, describing the relevant procedural and substantive law, and providing suggestions on how to organize deliberations and evaluate evidence.

Child abuse. Intentional, nonaccidental injury or harm inflicted on a child. Sexual abuse may be included in the term, although it is increasingly regarded as a separate category of abuse. Emotional abuse without physical injury is more likely to be called **child neglect**.

Child sexual abuse syndrome (CSAS), (or **child sexual abuse accommodation syndrome**) (CSAAS). Originally proposed by Summit (1983), it is a term reserved for a cluster of behaviors that occur in children who have been victims of sexual abuse by a family member or an adult with whom the child has a trusting relationship.

Chronic organic amnesia. Describes a wide range of neurological damage due to physical head trauma (such as from a car accident), a disease (such as Alzheimer's), or organic dysfunction (such as results from a stroke).

Civil law. That part of the law concerned with noncriminal matters pertaining to the rights and duties of citizens.

Clinical or **experience prediction**. Prediction of human behavior based on experience dealing with past patients or situations.

Clinical psychologist. Usually a doctorate-level psychologist trained and specializing in the study, diagnosis, and treatment of psychological disorders.

Cognitive behavioral viewpoint on hypnosis. A perspective which maintains that a hypnotized person is not in a special state of consciousness, but instead that hypnosis is a product of certain attitudes, motivations, and expectancies toward the "hypnotic state."

Cognitive miser model. The model argues that humans are fundamentally stingy with mental work and will avoid it when possible.

Cognitive processes. The internal processes that enable humans to imagine, to gain knowledge, to reason, and to evaluate. Each person has his or her own cognitive version of the world.

Cognitive psychology. The study of the internal or "mind" representations of the external world.

Commitment. A component of Hirschi's Social Control Theory that represents the extent to which a youth is emotionally invested in conventional lines of activity, including educational and occupational aspirations.

Commitment bias. The phenomenon that once a witness commits to a certain viewpoint, such as identification of a face, the witness is less likely to change her or his mind.

Common law. The body of law which constitutes the basis of the English legal system and of most of U. S. law, it developed primarily from judicial decisions based on custom or precedent, unwritten in code or statute.

Community-based facilities. Supervisory facilities that hold individuals for less than twenty-four hours of each day to allow them opportunity to work, attend school, receive treatment, or participate in other community activities.

Compensatory offenders. A classification of rapists that categorizes those men who rape, or attempt to rape, because of an intense sexual arousal prompted by specific stimuli in the environment.

Competency to stand trial. The legal requirement that a criminal defendant must have sufficient present ability to understand the charges and legal proceedings and to help his or her attorney in the preparation and carrying out of a defense. Related competencies include: competency to waive the Fifth Amendments right against self-incrimination, competency to waive the Sixth Amendment right to an attorney, and competency to plead guilty.

Competency to be executed. The legal requirement that a person convicted of a capital crime and sentenced to death must be emotionally stable enough to be put to death. The Supreme Court has ruled it is cruel and unusual punishment to execute someone who is so mentally disordered that he or she cannot understand what is happening.

Composition bias. The use of foils in a lineup which might contaminate the identification of a suspect (e.g., witness has described an overweight perpetrator, foils are noticeably thinner than the suspect).

Comprehensive Crime Control Act of 1984. Passed by Congress in 1984 as a far-reaching revision of Federal Criminal Law, it included major changes in the insanity defense, sentencing, and drug laws, among others.

Compulsion. An action a person feels compelled by internal thoughts to take, even though it is irrational.

Concurrent validity. In psychological testing, such validity is measured by comparing one test with another, already established, one.

Conditionability. The speed with which a person is susceptible to making an association between two stimuli.

Conflict theory. A theoretical perspective that views conflict between groups as a naturally occurring phenomenon of pluralistic societies, but holds that the group (or groups) in power creates and enforces laws to support its own interests.

Confounding variable. An extraneous variable that interferes with or clouds research findings.

Constitutional law. Law based on that contained in the U. S. Constitution and the constitutions of individual states. It provides the guidelines for the organization of national, state, and local government, and places limits on the exercise of government power (e.g., through a Bill of Rights).

Construct validity. Answers the question "to what extent does the test or experiment measure a theory or theoretical construct?"

Content validity. A measure of a test's content to determine whether it covers a representative sample of the behavior domain it purports to measure or identify.

Control (experimental). The systematic attempts by the researcher to account for all potentially influential variables on the relationship being investigated.

Control-of-question test (CQT). The most preferred procedure by professional polygraphers in cases requiring specific incident investigation, such as criminal acts. The technique uses a variety of questioning protocols based on three types of questions, (1) irrelevant or neutral questions, (2) relevant questions, and (3) control questions.

Convenience function. The warehousing in a mental institution or similar facility of one or more family members considered bothersome. Changes in law recognizing the due-process rights of persons at risk of being institutionalized have placed limits on this function.

Correctional psychologist. Psychologists who are employed by prisons, jails, and other correctional facilities.

Correlation coefficient. A mathematical index of the relationship between two variables.

Corroboration rule. The requirement in some jurisdictions that evidence other than the victim's testimony be available before a person will be charged with a crime.

Counseling psychologist. A mental health professional with a doctorate in counseling psychology specializing in the research of and treatment for adjustments to daily living.

Cortical excitation. Refers to hypothesized arousal properties of the cerebral cortex, that part of the brain responsible for a majority of human cognitive functions such as memory, association, and thinking.

Criminal anthropology. Study of crime from a comparative-culture perspective.

Criminal law. Law concerned with crime and its punishments.

Criminal profiling (also called **psychological profiling** or **criminal personality profiling**). The process of identifying personality traits, behavioral tendencies, and demographic variables of an offender based on characteristics of the crime.

Criminal responsibility. The extent to which a person is held responsible for a criminal act he or she committed.

Criminalization thesis. Argues that mentally disordered but otherwise noncriminal individuals are charged with minor crimes such as disorderly conduct or unlawful trespassing in order to justify detaining them in jail, arguably for their own protection.

Crisis intervention. The intervention of mental health practitioners into emergency or crisis situations, such as suicide attempts, emotional agitation, psychotic behaviors, and refusal to eat or to participate in programs.

Criterion-related validity. Validity based on the power of a measure to predict an individual's performance in specified activities.

Cross-situational or **trans-situational consistency**. The extent a person's behavior remains the same across different or similar situations.

Cue-utilization theory. The hypothesis that highly anxious or tense individuals will not scan their environments as broadly as less anxious individuals.

Curative instructions. *See* **admonitions**.

Cured-error doctrine. Judicial assumption that warnings to disregard are effective, or at least partially effective, on the thinking processes and prejudices of the jury.

Curvilinear hunch. In law-enforcement research, the hypothesis that a curvilinear relationship exists between stress and experience.

Cynicism. A pattern of thought among some individuals, usually developed with increasing experience, and characterized by diffuse feelings of mistrust, envy, and impotent hostility toward others. Defined in three stages by Niederhoffer relative to law enforcement officers. *See also* **aggressive cynicism**.

Dark figure. The number of crimes that go unreported in official crime data reports.

Darwinism. In psychology, a belief that humans should be placed on a *single* continuum along with all creatures in the animal kingdom.

Death-qualified jurors. Jurors who are not so opposed to the death penalty that they are believed unable to render a guilty verdict in a capital case and recommend the death sentence.

Decision rule. The proportion of the total number of jurors required to reach a verdict.

Deindividuation. Process wherein individuals feel they cannot be identified, are aroused, and are inclined to commit actions, including antisocial, bizarre, or brutal ones, which they would not commit under normal conditions.

Deinstitutionalization. Refers to having individuals supervised, cared for and/or treated outside the confines of traditional large institutions.

Dependent variable. The variable that is measured to see how it is changed by manipulations in the independent variable.

Determinate sentencing (as contrasted with **indeterminate sentencing**). Sentencing to a specifically defined term which allows an offender to know his or her date of release, barring conviction of another crime while incarcerated. Offenders given a determinate sentence may be released earlier, as for good behavior.

Deterrence. One of the four goals or purposes of punishment, it refers to the use of punishment to dissuade individuals from committing crime in the future. **General deterrence** refers to the overall symbolic impact punishment has on the population as a whole. **Specific deterrence** is based on the actual experience of punishment, which presumably will deter the punished individual from engaging in future transgressions.

Differential association theory. The theory formulated by Edwin Sutherland which argues that criminal behavior is learned, as is all social behavior, through *social interactions* with others.

Differential experience hypothesis. The argument that the frequency of meaningful and positive contacts one has with other races or ethnic groups engenders perceptual skill in accurate facial discrimination.

Diminished capacity or **diminished responsibility**. The lack of capacity to achieve a state of mind requisite to be held completely responsible for the commission of crime. Though the impairment does not qualify as insanity under the prevailing test, evidence of diminished capacity allows the court to reduce the severity of the offense and the punishment.

Discovery process. The legal pretrial procedure by which one party in a civil or criminal case discloses to the other party infromation vital for his or her defense.

Discriminant ability. A research requirement that a group of behaviors must occur regularly in a group who have certain experiences, and that they must not occur in those who have not had that experience.

Disenchantment. Violanti's second stage of career development in policing that sets in and continues until mid-career (twelve to fourteen years). During this stage, bitter disappointment develops when a mid-career officer realizes that pressures and demands of law-enforcement work far outweigh his or her ability to respond effectively.

Displaced-aggressive rapist (also called **displaced-anger** or **anger-retaliation rapist**). A rapist who demonstrates a predominance of violent and aggressive behaviors with a minimum or total absence of sexual feeling in his attacks.

Disposition. The resolution of a legal matter. In criminal law, an example would be the sentence a defendant receives. In civil law, the disposition of a case may be a judgement in favor of the plaintiff.

Divided custody. Court decision affording each parent legal and physical decisionmaking powers, but on an alternating basis.

Divorce mediation. The attempt to have respective parties in a divorce suit reach a mutually satisfying settlement, usually with the assistance of a trained mediator.

Doctrine of family privacy. The doctrine that what goes on within the intact family unit is of concern only to the family itself, as long as there is no serious threat to any member or members of the family.

Drive. A motivating state resulting from some physiological deficit or tension.

Dual-purpose evaluation (in pretrial psychological or psychiatric assessments). A simultaneous evaluation of both the defendant's competency to stand trial and mental state at the time of the offense.

Durham Rule (also known as the **product rule**). A legal standard of insanity by which the accused is not held criminally responsible if his or her unlawful act was the product of a mental disease or mental defect.

Dynamite charge (also known as the shotgun instruction, the third degree instruction, the nitroglycerin charge, or the hammer instruction). Refers to instructions of judges who, confronted with the possibility of a hung jury, request that jury members reconsider carefully their positions in a renewed attempt to render a verdict.

Ecological validity (also called **external validity**). The degree of practical or useful application of a theory or idea to the "real world."

Effectiveness method. An evaluation of psychotherapy methods that focuses on outcome and actual change in the patient's affect, thinking processes, and actions.

Emergency detention. In the civil commitment context, temporary confinement intended to protect individuals from imminent serious harm to themselves or to prevent injury to others.

Endogenous depression (also known as **bipolar disorder**). Refers to depression believed to be precipitated by biochemical or physiological imbalance.

Entry-level assessments. Psychological assessments in correctional facilities conducted at the time an inmate such a facility.

Equivocal death analysis (EDA). *See* **reconstructive psychological investigation**.

Escalation. A process whereby each party in a conflict increases the magnitude or intensity of a response in reaction to the increased response received from the other party.

Exit decision. Most likely to occur in indeterminate sentencing states, where parole boards exercise discretion as to whether to release prisoners to serve the rest of their sentence in the community.

Expectancy-violation model. The theory that any suspicious nonverbal behavior may lead to the conclusion that a person is deceitful.

Experimental or **treatment group**. In a controlled experiment, the group that is subjected to a change in the independent variable.

Experimental method. A research method that requires careful control and measurement of the phenomena being studied.

External stressors. In the work setting, stressors that are outside one's daily tasks. In the law enforcement context, they include frustration with the courts, the prosecutor's office, the criminal process, the correctional system, the media, and public attitudes.

External validity.   *See* **ecological validity**.

Externalizing problems. Describes the process of dealing with inner conflicts by creating behavior patterns which stimulate conflict with other people and, more generally, with the social environment.

Extravert. In Eysenck's theory, a person who seeks stimulation due to characteristics of his or her nervous system.

False negative. A prediction that someone will not do something, which he or she, in fact, does. Contrast **true negative**.

False positive. A prediction that someone will do something, which he or she, in fact, does not do. Contrast **true positive**.

Feminine style. Wexler's term for a policing style believed to be used by some women in law enforcement. Being attractive at work is important to its practitioners.

Feminist criminology. The perspective that gender inequities in society must be taken into account in explaining crime, the treatment of suspects and defendants, and the punishment given to convicted offenders.

Forensic neuropsychology. The psychological assessment of brain injury and nervous system functioning for the legal system.

Forensic psychiatrist. A medical doctor (M.D.) who specializes in assessment and treatment of legally relevant behavioral disorders.

Forensic psychologist. A psychologist who works within the judicial system, particularly as a consultant to courts or to attorneys.

Friendly parent rule. The judicial doctrine which encourages sole custody to be granted to the parent most likely to facilitate the noncustodial parent's involvement with the children.

Functional retrograde amnesia. Refers to memory loss due to severe psychological or emotional trauma, such as being the victim of a violent crime.

Functional size. The number of lineup members who resemble the suspect in physically relevant features.

Fundamental attribution error. A tendency to underestimate the importance of situational determinants and to overestimate the importance of personality or dispositional determinants.

General pretrial publicity. Information that is prominently in the news but is *unrelated* to the particular case being tried.

Generalized expectancies. Expectations about the consequences of one's behavior that tend to be stable and consistent across relatively similar circumstances.

Grand jury. A body of citizens (usually twenty-three in number) that is directed by the prosecutor to weigh evidence and decide whether there is enough to charge a person with a criminal offense.

Grave disability statutes. In the civil commitment context, laws that allow the commitment of a individuals who are not dangerous to society but who are so gravely disabled, usually from mental disorder, that they are unable to care for themselves.

Group cognitive ability tests. Usually paper-and-pencil instruments devised to be administered to small or large *groups* of people.

Guardian ad litem (Latin for "guardian for this action"). A broad legal term referring to an individual officially appointed by the court to provide a range of types of representation, usually for impaired or very young people, in court proceedings.

Guilty But Mentally Ill (GBMI). An option intended to be an alternative to, not a substitute for, the verdict NGRI. It allows jurors a "middle-ground" verdict in cases of allegedly insane defendants.

Guilty-knowledge test (GKT). A method of polygraphy requiring knowledge about a crime or incident not known by the public.

***Habeas corpus* petition**. A procedure for obtaining a judicial determination of the legality of an individual's custody or confinement.

Hard determinism. Asserts that all behavior is determined by antecedent stimuli or events and that all human behavior, therefore, is theoretically predictable. Contrast **soft determinism**.

Hindsight bias. Biased judgments of past events after the outcome is known.

Hypnotic age regression. A hypnotic process in which the hypnotized individual is asked to relive an experience from his or her childhood.

Hypnotic hypermnesia. The enhancement or revival of memory through hypnosis.

Hypnotic trance theory. The perspective that hypnosis represents a special state of consciousness that promotes a high level of responsiveness to suggestion and changes in bodily feelings. Contrast with the **cognitive behavioral viewpoint**.

Hypothesis. A speculative explanation of behavior, a tentative assumption advanced in order to expose and test its logical or empirical consequences.

Idiographic approach. Emphasizes the intensive study of one individual.

Impotent hostility. In Niederhoffer's delineation of law enforcement officers' psychology, this refers to feelings of powerlessness to express hostility.

Impulsive or **exploitative rapist**. Engages in sexual assault simply because the opportunity to rape is available.

***In pauperis* petition**. A request from an individual unable to afford legal representation that an appeals court hear his or her case.

Incapacitation. One of the four goals or purposes of punishment. Isolation of the individual from society so that he or she cannot commit more crime. *See also* **selective incapacitation**.

Incompetent to stand trial. A judicial determination that a defendant lacks sufficient present ability to understand the legal process against him or her and to assist a lawyer in the preparation of a defense.

Independent variable. The measure whose effect is being studied, and, in most scientific investigations, is manipulated by the experimenter in a controlled fashion.

Index crimes. The crimes that are of most concern, as defined in the FBI's Uniform Crime Reports, and are used to indicate the seriousness of the crime problem. The eight index crimes are murder and nonnegligent manslaughter, aggravated assault, robbery, rape, burglary, larceny-theft, arson, and motor-vehicle theft.

Indictment. A grand jury's formal written statement of the reasons for an individual to be charged with an offense.

Individual cognitive ability tests. Designed to be administered to one examinee at a time by a highly trained examiner.

Industrial and/or organizational psychologist. A psychologist routinely involved in personnel selection, human factors in machine and equipment design, executive development, consumer research, organizational working conditions, and retirement counseling.

Information integration model. A theory concerned with how people combine information about an object or person in reaching a judgment.

Injunction. A judicial remedy awarded to one party for the purpose of requiring another party to refrain from doing a particular act or activity.

Insanity. In the legal context, this term describes a judicial determination that an individual's degree or quantity of mental disorder relieves him or her of criminal responsibility for illegal actions.

Insanity Defense Reform Act of 1984. A law passed by Congress that is designed to make it more difficult for defendants using the insanity defense in the federal courts to be acquitted.

Interactionist theory of criminality. The perspective that criminal behavior is the result of environmental conditions and personality factors.

Interference theory. According to this theory, forgetting is caused by both interference from material learned previously (called by cognitive psychologists proactive interference) and interference from material learned afterward (retroactive interference).

Inter-judge reliability. The degree to which a test produces the same results when scored or interpreted by different clinicians or examiners.

Internal consistency. The extent to which different parts of a psychological test yield the same results.

Internal validity. A measure of the level of confidence we can place in the results obtained in a particular study due to its methodology and design.

Internalizing problems. Describes the process of dealing with inner conflicts by turning them against oneself, or further inward, producing such symptoms as depression, anxiety, and social withdrawal.

Introspective stage. A career stage identified by Violanti in which a law enforcement officer looks back on earlier years as the good old days and becomes secure and settled in the job.

Introvert. In Eysenck's theory, a person who avoids stimulation due to characteristics of the nervous system.

Involvement. An element in Hirschi's Social Control Theory that represents the amount of participation in conventional activities.

Irresistible-impulse test. A standard of the Brawner Rule which recognizes that, in some instances, an impulse or desire can be uncontrollable.

Jail. Operated by local governments to hold persons temporarily detained, awaiting trial, or sentenced to confinement, after having been convicted of a misdemeanor.

John Wayne syndrome. Normally takes hold early in the career of a law enforcement officer and lasts for three to four years. A behavior pattern characterized by coldness toward others and emotional withdrawal, authoritarian attitudes, cynicism, overseriousness, and a black-or-white, inflexible approach to daily problem solving.

Joined trial. The combining of multiple defendants or multiple offenses into a single trial.

Joint custody. An arrangement by which both parents share legal authority, but the children live with one parent who will have the authority to make the day-to-day decisions.

Jurisdiction. The geographic area, subject matter, or persons over which a court can exercise authority.

Just-world hypothesis. A belief that one gets what one deserves and deserves what one gets.

Juvenile Court Act. Passed by the Illinois legislature in 1899, the Act created a juvenile court in Illinois and gave that court jurisdiction over delinquent, dependent, or neglected children.

Juvenile Justice and Delinquency Prevention Act of 1974. Wide-ranging federal legislation which encouraged states to reform laws relating to juveniles.

Leaky channels. Nonverbal communication channels that "leak" information not intended by the communicator.

Least restrictive alternative. A standard that requires decisionmakers to consider living arrangements that offer the least confinement or restriction of an inmate or patient, yet still provide protection of society and the individual.

Legal parental authority. Refers to the decisionmaking authority regarding a child's long-term welfare, education, medical care, religious upbringing, and other issues significantly affecting the child's life.

Legal system. An umbrella term meant to encompass the courts, both civil and criminal, law-enforcement agencies, corrections, and a wide array of administrative agencies.

Leniency bias. A tendency for juries to be more lenient than judges in rendering verdicts.

Limited amnesia. A pathological inability to remember a specific episode, or small number of episodes, from the recent past.

Limited joint custody. An arrangement by which both parents share legal authority, but one parent is given exclusive physical authority and the other is awarded liberal visitation rights.

Limiting instructions. Judicial instructions that warn jurors not to use evidence to evaluate or decide on a certain issue, although the evidence may be used for another issue.

Match-to-description strategy. Basing the selection of foils in a lineup on the witness's description of the perpetrator. Compare **similarity-to-suspect strategy**.

Medical model. The view that every abnormal behavior has a specific organic cause corresponding to a specific set of symptoms.

Memory. The retention of information over time.

Method of authority. A method for eliminating doubt and gaining knowledge that relies on the information provided by experts in the field.

Method of tenacity. A method for eliminating doubt that relies heavily on adherence to stereotypes and prejudices.

Minimum credibility standard. Assumes that any child testimony (or adult testimony) can be rejected if it can be established that he or she lacks the necessary powers of observation, recordation, and recollection to narrate effectively.

Mitigating circumstances. Conditions which, while not completely exonerating a defendant, might at least reduce the punishment if he or she is convicted. An example would be evidence of a childhood marred by extensive physical or sexual abuse.

Mixed style. One of the styles identified by Wexler for female officers, it is characterized by utilization of several strategies, with no one of them necessarily predominant.

M'Naghten Rule. An insanity standard that is based on the conclusion that if a defendant has a defect of reason, or a disease of the mind, so as not to know the nature and quality of his or her actions, then he or she cannot be held criminally responsible. Also called the right-from-wrong test.

Mock juries. Experimental or simulated juries used by researchers to study the structure and dynamics of actual juries. Also refers to "artificial" or training juries with which lawyers or prospective lawyers practice.

Moderate reform exclusionary rules. With respect to rape reform laws, state statutes that permit a partial limitation on the admissibility of sexual history in a rape trial.

Multiple personality amnesia. Memory deficits specifically observed in individuals with MPD.

Multiple personality disorder (MPD). A mental disorder characterized by the existence within an individual of two or more distinct personalities, each of which may be dominant at any given time.

National Crime Survey (NCS). A survey conducted by the Bureau of Census for the Department of Justice that involves contacts with a large national sample of households to learn the extent of criminal victimization.

National Youth Survey (NYS). A self-report survey and official data collected from a large sample of youths to determine the prevalence of illegal behavior among them. The project began in 1977 with 1,725 youths between the ages of eleven and seventeen.

Negative linear hunch. In law enforcement research, the hypothesis that predicts that as job experiences increases, job stress will decrease.

Negative reinforcement. Successful avoidance of negative or aversive events connected with behavior.

Neglected child. A child who, as a result of the behavior of a caretaker, lacks essential care, such as food, clothing, shelter, medical attention, education, or supervision.

Neuroticism or **emotionality scale**. A self-report scale designed to measure the amount of physiological reactivity in the peripheral nervous system.

Neutral-impersonal style. One of the policing styles identified by Wexler used by some women, it is characterized by a business-like attitude toward male colleagues.

Nominal size. The actual number of members within the lineup, which theoretically may include some very dissimilar foils.

Nomothetic. A research approach that concentrates on general principles, relationships, and patterns that transcend the single individual.

Nonhypnotic hypermnesia. Enhancement or recovery of memory through nonhypnotic methods, such as free association, fantasy, recall techniques.

Objective test. Basically, a test is objective to the extent that scorers can apply a scoring key and agree about the result.

Observational learning or **modeling**. The hypothesis that individuals may learn a particular behavior simply by observing another person performing the action.

Open adoption. An adoptive arrangement by which the biological parents and adoptive parents meet and exchange information.

Orders of nonhospitalization. Outpatient commitment orders which require a person to take part in some form of treatment, such as drug therapy and counseling, delivered at a local mental-health center as a condition for remaining in the community.

Organizational stressors. Stressors confined to the policies and practices of the job itself. In the law-enforcement context, they may include poor pay, excessive paperwork, insufficient training, inadequate equipment, weekend duty, shift work, limited promotional opportunities, poor supervision and administrative support, and poor relationships with supervisors or colleagues.

Other-race effect. The finding that people are better able to discriminate between faces of their own race than other races.

Panel design. A survey method where the same respondents are sampled at specified intervals over time.

Parens patriae (Latin for "parent of the country"). The doctrine in law which establishes the right of the state to substitute its presumably benevolent decisionmaking for that of individuals who are thought to be unable or unwilling to make their own decisions.

Partial-bidirectional interaction. A perspective in which the person and the situation are considered interdependent causes of behavior. Contrast **unidirectional interaction**.

Pattern jury instructions. A standard or uniform jury instruction that can be applied across *different* jurisdictions.

Perception. A process by which sensory inputs (what one sees, hears, smells, touches, tastes) are transformed and organized into a meaningful experience for the individual.

Perceptual adaptation or **contrast effects**. When an individual violates stereotypes, the tendency is for other human beings to perceive that individual as *more* dissimilar to the stereotype than he or she really is.

Peremptory challenge. A rule that allows a lawyer to request the removal of a prospective juror without giving reason.

Personal stressors. Stressors that involve marital relationships, health problems, addictions, peer group pressures, feelings of helplessness and depression, and lack of achievement.

Personalization stage. A stage identified by Violanti that occurs during the mid-career of law enforcement officers, in which they focus more on personal goals before retirement and pay less attention to the goals of the agency.

Physical authority. A judicial determination that allows a parent to make decisions affecting only the child's daily activities, such as whether the child can stay overnight at a friend's house, attend a party, or have access to the parent's car.

Plaintiff. The person or party who initially brings a legal suit.

Police bias. Bias introduced either in the use of police officers as foils in a lineup or in the questioning techniques used by the police investigator.

Police power. The obligation and responsibility of the state to protect the public from harm to persons or to property. It encompasses the state's power to make laws and regulations for the protection of public health, safety, welfare, and morals.

Police psychologist. Psychologist specializing in working in law enforcement.

Positive law. Sometimes referred to as "the law on the books," it refers to the primary sources of law, such as constitutions, statutes, case decisions, and the rules of administrative agencies.

Positive linear hunch. In law-enforcement research, the hypothesis that as law-enforcement experience increases, stress will correspondingly increase.

Positive reinforcement. The acquisition of physical, psychological or social rewards as a consequence of behavior.

Post-Traumatic Stress Disorder (PTSD). A cluster of behavioral patterns that result from a psychologically distressing event that is outside the usual range of human experience.

Predictive validity. The degree to which a test predicts a person's subsequent performance on the dimensions and tasks the test is supposed to measure.

Predictor variable. A term analogous to the term "independent variable" in experimental research. In psychology, a predictor variable generally refers to some measurable factor (an antecedent) that aids in forecasting an outcome or a behavior.

Preliminary instructions. Instructions given at the beginning of the trial, before opening arguments. The judge instructs the jury about the respective roles of judge and jury during the course of the trial.

Premenstrual syndrome (PMS). The cluster of behavioral patterns and psychological changes that sometimes accompany the cyclic physiological changes that occur prior to (four to seven days before) to the onset of menstruation. The prevalence of PMS is widely disputed.

Principle of nonmalificence. The ethical requirement and understanding among the medical profession that its members do no harm. Evaluations of competency to be executed are believed by some to violate this principle.

Prisonization. The process by which inmates adopt and internalize the prisoner subculture within any particular institution.

Prisons. Correctional facilities operated by state and federal governments to hold persons convicted of felonies and sentenced generally to terms of more than one year.

Procedural default doctrine. The rule that if an objection is not placed on the record during the trial, a person has lost the right to appeal to a higher court on the basis of that particular issue. In some jurisdictions, there is an additional requirement that the appellant must have also requested a remedy.

Procedural evidence. Clinical information and hunches that clinicians suspect to be correct based on their personal observations, assessments, and interpretations.

Procedural law. Law that outlines the rules for the administration, enforcement, and modification of substantive law in the mediation of disputes.

Process method. A research method that directly investigates the type and amount of treatment delivered to the patients in a mental-health setting. Patient records are examined to determine how often the patients were seen, by whom, and for what purposes. Contrast **structural analysis**.

Projective tests. Psychological tests designed under the assumption that personality attributes are best revealed when a person responds to ambiguous stimuli. The most famous example is the Rorschach test.

Protective custody or **protective seclusion**. Isolation or confinement in a special area for the primary purpose of protecting inmates from possible harm from themselves or other inmates.

Pseudo-cynicism. One of Niederhoffer's stages of police cynicism that is most recognizable among recruits at the police academy. The recruits try to act cynical (like some of their instructors), but cognitively they remain idealistic about helping humankind.

Psychiatric criminology (also called **forensic psychiatry**). The field of psychiatry, working within the legal system and represented by the Freudian, psychoanalytic, or psychodynamic perspectives, that traditionally views human nature as innately antisocial.

Psychoactive drugs. Drugs that exert their primary effects on the brain, thus altering mood or behavior.

Psychological assessment. Refers to *all* the techniques used to measure and evaluate an individual's past, present, or future psychological status. It usually includes interviews, observations, and various measuring procedures which may or may not include psychological tests.

Psychological control. An important principle in successful interrogation, according to which the interrogator communicates (verbally and nonverbally) to the subject that he or she has total control over both the subject and the interrogative situation.

Psychological criminology. The science of the behavior and mental processes of antisocial individuals. Psychological criminology emphasizes individual factors, such as personality, learning experiences, or cognitive processes, as explanations for criminal behavior.

Psychological tests. Measuring devices that include measures of intelligence, aptitude, attitudes, interest, and personality. Psychological testing, when employed, is but one component of psychological assessment. Compare **psychological assessment**.

Psychological theory. *See* **theory**.

Psychoticism. A personality dimension characterized by cold cruelty, social insensitivity, unemotionality, high risk-taking, troublesome behavior, dislike of others, and an attraction to the unusual.

Quasi-experimental designs. Designs that allow researchers to study subjects outside their direct control under already existing conditions.

QUEST (Qualification by Example Selection Test). A questionnaire approach suggested for use with potential death-penalty jurors.

Radical conflict perspective. A perspective of criminology that believes crime is fundamentally caused by the social order and the long-standing struggle between the "haves" (the rich, powerful capitalists of the ruling class) and the "have nots" (the working class).

Radical-reform exclusionary rules. In the rape context, these are statutes that require total exclusion of prior sexual activity when offered on the issue of consent.

Rape by fraud. The act of having sexual relations with a supposedly consenting adult female under fraudulent conditions, such as when a physician or psychotherapist has sexual intercourse with a patient under the guise of "effective treatment."

Rape-shield reform statutes. Statutes which restrict, to varying degrees, the admissibility of the victim's sexual history into the courtroom.

Reactance. The unpleasant psychological arousal experienced when an individual perceives that his or her freedom of choice is threatened.

Reactive depression. Depression resulting from a traumatic event or a series of negative events.

Reality monitoring. In the context of child victimizations, this refers to the child's ability to distinguish actual from imagined events.

Recall. The task of remembering by retrieving information from long-term memory. Compare **recognition**.

Reciprocal determinism. The perspective which holds that cognitions influence both behavior and the situation, and these, in turn, influence cognitions.

Reciprocal interaction. The continual process by which the person, through behavior and beliefs, influences the social environment, and the environment in turn influences the person.

Recognition. The task of remembering by matching information with that stored in long-term memory.

Reconstructive memory theory. The belief that memory is a reconstructive, integrative process, developing with the flow of new experiences and thoughts.

Reconstructive psychological evaluation (RPE) or **equivocal death analysis** (EDA), also called **psychological autopsy**. A technique designed to develop a psychological image of a dead person (his or her personality, habits, intentions, dreams, motivations, lifestyle) when alive. The FBI prefers the term EDA.

Rehabilitation. Any attempt intended to bring about change in behavior patterns.

Reinforcement. Anything that increases response rate.

Relapse Prevention (RP). A self-control program designed to teach individuals who are trying to change their behavior how to anticipate and cope with temptations to revert to earlier behavior.

Relevant-irrelevant technique. A polygraph technique developed in 1917 by the lawyer-psychologist, William M. Marston, primarily for criminal investigation. It is now the method of choice in employment and preemployment screening situations in which the polygraph is used.

Reliability. Consistency of measurement. A test is reliable if it yields the same results over and over again.

Replicability. The requirement that the descriptions of the variables studied and the procedures used to study them be precise and objective enough so that any researcher can do the experiment again.

Resigned cynicism. One of Niederhoffer's police cynicism stages that occurs during the last few years of a police career.

Retention (also called the **storage stage**). The second stage of memory, when information becomes "resident" in the memory.

Retribution. One of the purposes or goals of punishment, it is the principle that society must exact just the right amount of punishment, as severe as (although not identical to) the wrongful act. Also referred to as "just deserts."

Retrieval stage. A stage of memory processes where the brain searches for pertinent information, retrieves it, and communicates it to the conscious mind.

Retrograde amnesia. Memory loss involving past or old material.

Right-from-wrong test. *See* **M'Naghten Rule**.

Risk assessment. Prediction of dangerousness and risk to the community based on psychological assessment of an offender or suspect. **Objective risk assessment** refers to the use of specified criteria which are not necessarily psychological to predict dangerousness. Examples of such criteria include age, prior record, ties to the community, employment, and behavior in prison.

Romantic cynicism. One of Niederhoffer's police cynicism stages that is reached during the first five years of the police career. *See also* **pseudo-cynicism**.

Rorschach. A projective test administered by a trained examiner who presents the examinee with a series of ten bilaterally symmetrical inkblots and asks the person to describe what each inkblot resembles or suggests.

Scientific jury selection. An attorney's use of social-science consultants, data, and techniques to choose jurors presumed most favorable to her or his side.

Secondary variable. Extraneous variable that may influence the results of an experiment, such as intelligence, time of day, gender, age, or even room temperature. *See also* **confounding variable**.

Security stress. Law enforcement stress that centers around the extreme sense of isolation experienced by officers confronting incidents in the field.

Segregation (also called **solitary confinement**). In corrections, this refers to the complete social isolation of an individual for disciplinary, protective, or administrative reasons. Physical conditions of segregation vary widely. *See also* **protective custody**.

Selective incapacitation. The imprisonment, for longer terms, of offenders who are believed to pose the greatest threat to society. This is a controversial policy often suggested for use with "career criminals."

Self-report method. A method of research that expects people to report various aspects about themselves.

Self-serving bias. A tendency to attribute positive things that happen to us to our abilities and personalities, and to attribute negative events to something outside ourselves or beyond our control.

Semimasculine style. One of Wexler's policing styles, it is believed to be used by policewomen who tend to be professional and to do the job well, while believing that they will not be totally accepted as equals.

Sequential jury-selection method. A rule that requires lawyers to exercise their challenges without knowing the characteristics of the next juror to be interviewed.

Sexual-aggressive rapist. This type of rapist exhibits both sexual and aggressive elements in his assault. Victim pain is a prerequisite for sexual excitement. He believes women enjoy being abused, forcefully raped, aggressively dominated, and controlled by men.

Similarity-to-suspect strategy. An attempt to create lineups where all members of a lineup look very much alike. Compare **match-to-description strategy**.

Simulation research. Research conducted in a laboratory that is designed to mimic as closely as possible the "real world." Used often used in jury research.

Situational tests. Assessment techniques where an applicant's behavior is observed under simulated conditions, intended to mimic real-world situations, such as that of a job environment.

Social control or **bonding theory.** Contends that crime and delinquency occur when an individual's ties to the conventional order or normative standards are weak or largely nonexistent.

Social stressors. In law enforcement, refers to the feeling of social isolation from those outside of law enforcement.

Sociological criminology. The perspective that emphasizes the impact of social factors, such as class structure, social and group processes, and differential power on crime.

Sociopath. A person who is *repetitively* in conflict with the law, with apparently limited capacity to learn from past experiences.

Soft determinism. A perspective that some degree of determinism plays a substantial role in human behavior, but is not the full explanation. Contrast **hard determinism**.

Sole custody. A judicial ruling in which one parent receives both legal and physical custody of the child, although the noncustodial parent usually retains visitation rights.

Special verdict. One rendered on specific facts which the jury has been directed to answer. More likely to be found in complex civil cases.

Spillover effect. A situation where knowledge that a defendant has several charges pending, psychologically "spills" onto the evidence presented on any single charge.

Split custody. A custodial arrangement where the legal and physical authority of one or more children is awarded to one parent, and the legal and physical authority of the remaining children to the other.

Standard error of measurement (SEM). (Also called the standard error of a score). A mathematical index of how much variation we can expect in a test score each time a person takes that same test.

Standardization or **normative group.** A representative sample of the population for which that test is designed.

Stare decisis et non quieta movere (Latin for "stay with the decision and do not disturb that which is settled"). A doctrine that encourages appellate courts to build on past decisions and be cautious about interfering with principles announced in the past.

State anxiety. An emotional reaction to a specific situation or context.

Status offenses. Offenses by juveniles that would not be offenses if committed by adults, such as running away from home, violating curfew, or skipping school.

Statutory law. Written rules drafted and approved by a federal, state, or local lawmaking body.

Statutory rape. Rape for which the age of the victim is the crucial distinction, on the premise that a victim below a certain age (usually 16) cannot validly consent to sexual intercourse with an adult.

Story model. The theory that, in their minds, jurors construct a story of how events related in testimony at the trial took place, even before hearing all the evidence.

Strain theory. A prominent sociological explanation for crime, it is based on Merton's theory that crime and delinquency occur when there is a *perceived* discrepancy between the materialistic values and goals cherished and held in high esteem by a society and the availability of the legitimate means for reaching these goals.

Stressors. Stress factors that may be external to the organism (*exogenous*) or within the organism (*endogenous*).

Struck jury method. A rule whereby the judge decides all challenges for cause before the parties claim any peremptories.

Structural analysis. In research examining the adequacy or effectiveness of treatment, this method focuses on the structure of the institution and uses criteria such as staff-to-patient ratios and per capita expenditure.

Structured interview. An interview in which the questions are standardized and the responses are recorded in a systematic manner.

Substantive law. Law that defines the rights and responsibilities of members of a given society.

Substantive law instructions. Instructions given during or at the end of the trial process on aspects of the law as applied to a particular case.

Survey research. Involves obtaining information about people by asking them well-prepared questions, usually in written form.

Syndrome. A collection of thoughts, feelings, and behaviors that are believed to be held in common by individuals who have experienced or are experiencing a given situation.

Task-related stressors. Stressors related to the nature of work itself. In a law-enforcement context, for example, these include the possibility of being killed in the line of duty.

Temporal consistency. The degree of consistency of any given behavior over time.

Tender-years doctrine. A legal assumption, derived from the traditional belief, that the mother is the parent ideally and inherently suited to care for children of a "tender age."

Tension induction. A principle of interrogation that creating tension in an individual will eventually break down the subject's defenses.

Test-retest reliability. A measure of whether the same test yields the same results when administered to the same person at two different times.

Thematic Apperception Test (TAT). A projective test consisting of twenty-nine pictures on separate cards and one blank card designed to measure common human needs.

Theory. A set of interrelated constructs (concepts), definitions, and propositions that present a systematic view of some phenomena by specifying relations among variables, with the purpose of explanation and prediction. A **psychological theory** then is an explanation which systematically connects many different behaviors.

Therapeutic jurisprudence. A position by Wexler and Winick that attempts to reconcile the goals and principles of due process and therapeutic intervention.

Trait anxiety. Anxiety as a result of a personality trait, such as neuroticism.

Trait psychology. Assumes that stable personality traits or personality structures determine behavior.

Trait Syndrome I. Law-enforcement behavioral clusters including social isolation and secrecy, defensiveness and suspicion, and cynicism.

Trait Syndrome II. Law-enforcement behavioral clusters which encompass behaviors generally carrying the label "dogmatic" or "authoritarian."

Transracial and **transethnic adoption.** Adoption in which adoptive parents are of a different race or ethnic group than the child.

Trivial persuasion. The phenomenon of jurors being more inclined to believe witnesses whose testimony is replete with detail, even if that detail is not directly relevant to the case. The evidence suggests jurors are persuaded by trivial detail.

True negative. A prediction that something will not happen which, in fact, does not happen. Contrast **false negative.**

True positives. A prediction that something will happen which, in fact, does happen. Contrast **false positive.**

Type I judicial error. Made when an innocent person is convicted.

Type II judicial error. Made when a guilty person is released.

Typology. In psychology, a classification system, either based on personality traits or behavioral patterns of individuals.

Unconscious transference. Occurs when a person seen in one situation is confused with or recalled as a person seen in another situation.

Unidirectional interaction. A perspective in which the person and the situation are conceptualized as independent entities that combine to produce behavior. Contrast **partial-bidirectional interaction.**

Validating evidence. Evidence or knowledge gained through careful, controlled research.

Validity. The psychological standard that a test should measure what it claims to be measuring.

Venire (Latin for "to come"). The pool of prospective jurors drawn from an eligible population presumed to be representative of a local geographical area.

Viable minorities. In the jury context, defined as at least two members not in agreement with the majority.

Vicarious punishment. The concept that when people observe the punishment of another person for some act, they feel the effects and are less to act in that same way at a later time. Similar to **general deterrence.**

Victimization rate. Expressed as the ratio of the number of actual victims over the number of potential victims.

Voir dire. A process that allows the judge and attorneys to question the prospective jurors and possibly disqualify them from jury duty.

Volitional prong. This part of the insanity defense requires acceptance of the possibility that a defendant could not control his or her behavior to conform to the requirements of the law. Compare **irresistible-impulse** test.

Waiver or **bindover hearings**. Adversary court proceeding during which evidence is heard as to whether a juvenile case should be transferred to criminal court from juvenile court. A reverse waiver hearing considers whether the case should be transferred from criminal to juvenile court.

Weapon focus. The concentration of some victim's or witness's attention on a threatening weapon, so that he or she pays less attention to other details and events of a crime, resulting in poor recall of some important details.

Yerkes-Dodson Law. First proposed in 1908, it refers to the observation that moderate levels of arousal produce optimal performance on a variety of tasks.

List of Cases

Addington v. Texas, 99 S.Ct. 1804 (1979).

Ake v. Oklahoma, 470 U. S. 68 (1985).

Albermarle v. Moody, 95 S.Ct. 2362 (1975).

Apodaca, Cooper, and Madden v. Oregon, 406 U. S. 404 (1972).

Ballew v. Georgia, 435 U. S. 223 (1978).

Barefoot v. Estelle, 463 U. S. 880 (1983).

Batson v. Kentucky, 476 U. S. 79 (1986).

Berkemer v. McCarty, 468 U. S. 420 (1984).

Breed v. Jones, 421 U. S. 519 (1975).

Brewer v. Williams, 430 U. S. 387 (1977).

Brown v. Board of Education of Topeka, 347 U. S. 483 (1954).

Brown v. Mississippi, 297 U. S. 278 (1936).

Buck v. Bell, 274 U. S. 200 (1927).

Carter v. U. S., 252 F.2d 608 (D.C. Cir. 1957).

Chandler v. Florida, 101 S.Ct. 802 (1981).

Colgrove v. Battin, 413 U. S. 149 (1973).

Colorado v. Spring, 479 U. S. 564 (1987).

Commonwealth v. Lykus, 327 N.E.2d 671 (Mass. Sup. Jud. Ct. 1975).

Coy v. Iowa, 108 S.Ct. 2798 (1988).

Cruzan v. Director, 497 U. S. 261 (1990).

Daubert v. Merrell Dow, 53 Cr.L. 2210 (1993).

Director of Patuxent Institute v. Daniels, 243 Md 16, 221 A.2d 397, 385 U. S. 940 (1966) *(cert. denied)*.

Drope v. Missouri, 420 U. S. 162 (1975).

Duckworth v. Eagan, 109 S.Ct. 2875 (1989).

Durham v. U. S., 214 F.2d 862 (D.C. Cir. 1954).

Dusky v. U. S., 363 U. S. 402 (1960).

Escobedo v. Illinois, 378 U. S. 478 (1964).

Estelle v. Gamble, 429 U. S. 97 (1976).

Estes v. Texas, 381 U. S. 532 (1965).

Fare v. Michael C., 442 U. S. 707 (1979).

Ford v. Wainwright, 477 U. S. 399 (1986).

Foucha v. Louisiana, 51 Cr.L. 2084 (1992).

Frye v. U. S., 293 Fed. 1013 (D.C. Cir. 1923).

Furman v. Georgia, 408 U. S. 238 (1972).

Gilbert v. California, 388 U. S. 263 (1967).

Gregg v. Georgia, 428 U. S. 153 (1976).

Griggs v. Duke Power Co., 401 U. S. 424 (1971).

Harris v. New York, 401 U. S. 222 (1971).

Hobson v. Hansen, 269 F. Supp. 401 (D.C. Cir. 1967).

Holland v. Illinois, 110 S.Ct. 803 (1990).

Hutto v. Finney, 437 U. S. 678 (1978).

In re Gault, 387 U. S. 1 (1967).

In re Oakes, Monthy Law Reporter (Mass.) 1845, 8, 122-129.

In re Winship, 397 U. S. 358 (1970).

Irvin v. Dowd, 366 U. S. 717 (1961).

Jackson v. Indiana, 406 U. S. 715 (1972).

Jenkins v. U. S., 307 F.2d 637 (D.C. Cir. 1962, *en banc*).

Johnson v. Louisiana, 406 U. S. 356 (1972).

Johnson v. State, 292 Ark. 632, 732 S.W.2d 817 (1987).

Jones v. U. S., 463 U. S. 354 (1983).

Joyner v. Joyner, 59 N.C. 322 (1862).

Kent v. U. S., 383 U. S. 541 (1966).

Keri v. State, 179 Ga. App. 664, 347 S.E.2d 236 (1986).

Kirby v. Illinois, 406 U. S. 682 (1972).

Lantrip v. Commonwealth, 713 S.W.2d 816 (Ky. 1986).

Larry P. v. Riles, 343 F. Supp. 1306 (N.D. Cal. 1972) (order granting preliminary injunction), *aff'd*, 502 F.2d 963 (9th Cir. 1974), 495 F. Supp. 926 (N.D. Cal. 1979) (decision on the merits), *aff'd* (9th Cir. Jan 23, 1984).

Lessard v. Schmidt, 349 F. Supp. 1078 (E.D. Wisc. 1972), *vac and remanded on other grounds*, 94 S.Ct. 713 (1974), *reinstated* 413 F. Supp. 1318 (E.D. Wisc. 1976).

Lockhart v. McCree, 476 U. S. 162 (1986).

Lowenfield v. Phelps, 108 S.Ct. 546 (1988).

McCleskey v. Kemp, 481 U. S. 279 (1987).

McGuire v. McGuire, 157 Neb. 226, 59 N.W.2d 336 (1953).

McKeiver v. Pennsylvania, 403 U. S. 538 (1971).

M'Naghten, 10 Clark & Fin.200, 210, 8 Eng.Rep. 718 (1843).

Maryland v. Craig, 497 U. S. 836 (1990).

Merriken v. Cressman, 364 F. Supp. 913 (E.D. Pa. 1973)

Michigan v. Tucker, 417 U. S. 433 (1974).

Miranda v. Arizona, 384 U. S. 436 (1966).

Nebraska Press Assoc. v. Stuart, 427 U. S. 539 (1976).

Neil v. Biggers, 409 U. S. 188 (1972).

New York v. Quarles, 467 U. S. 649 (1984).

O'Connor v. Donaldson, 422 U. S. 563 (1975).

Ohio Dept. of Mental Health v. Milligan, 38 Ohio St. 3d 178, (1988).

Parham v. J.R., 442 U. S. 584 (1979).

PASE v. Hannon, 506 F. Supp. 831 (N.D. Ill. 1980).

Pate v. Robinson, 383 U. S. 375 (1966).

Penry v. Lynaugh, 492 U. S. 302 (1989).

People v. Bowker, 203 Cal. App.3d, 231 Cal. Rptr. 886 (1988).

People v. Brock, 143 A.D.2d 678 N.Y.S.2d 903 (1988).

People v. Davis, 151 Neb. 368, 37 N.W. 2d. 593 (1949).

People v. Gray, 187 Cal. App.3d, 231 Cal. Rptr. 658 (1986).

People v. Hickey, 86 Ill. App. 20 (1989).

People v. Luna, 204 Cal. App.3d 776, 250 Cal. Rptr. 878 (1988).

People v. McQuillan, 392 Mich. 511, 221 N.W.2d 596 (1974).

People v. Payan, 173 Cal.App.3d 27, 220 Cal. Rptr. 126 (1985).

People v. Rosco, 168 Cal. App.3d 1093, 215 Cal. Rptr. 45 (1985).

People v. Sinclair, 300 Mich. 562, 2N.W. 2d 503 (1942).

Perry v. Louisiana, 111 S.Ct. 449 (1990).

Regina v. Oxford, 175 Eng. Rep. 941 (1840).

Rennie v. Klein, 720 F.2d 266 (3d Cir. 1983).

Rhodes v. Chapman, 452 U. S. 337 (1981).

Richmond Newspapers, Inc. v. Commonwealth of Virginia, 448 U. S. 555 (1980).

Riggins v. Nevada, 504 U. S. ___ (1992).

Rivers v. Katz, 495 NE.2d 337 (NY 1986).

Rock v. Arkansas, 483 U. S. 44 (1986).

Roe v. Wade, 410 U. S. 113 (1973).

Rogers v. Okin, 634 F.2d 650 (1st Cir. 1980).

Rouse v. Cameron, 373 F.2d 451 (D.C. Cir. 1966).

Schall v. Martin, 467 U. S. 253 (1984).

Sheppard v. Maxwell, 384 U. S. 333 (1966).

Simmons v. U. S., 390 U. S. 377 (1968).

State v. Andretta, 269 A.2d 644 (N.J. 1972).

State v. Bianchi, appeal filed No. 79-10116 (Wash. Sup. Ct. October 19, 1979).

State v. Bohmer, Va. Sup. Ct. (1971).

State v. Haseltine, 120 Wis.2d 92, 352 N.W.2d 673 (1984).

State ex rel Hawks v. Lazaro, 202 S.E.2d 109 (W.Va. 1974).

State v. J.Q., 52 Cr.L. 1398 (1993).

Stovall v. Denno, 388 U. S. 293 (1967).

Swain v. Alabama, 380 U. S. 202 (1965).

Tarasoff v. Regents of the Univ. of Cal., 529 P.2d 553 (Cal. 1974), *vac., reheard en banc, & aff'd* 131 Cal.Rptr. 14, 551 P.2d 334 (1976).

Tran Van Khiem v. U. S., 51 Cr.L. 1061 (D.C. Cir. 1992).

U. S. v. Baller, 519 F.2d 463 (4th Cir. 1975).

U. S. v. Brawner, 471 F.2d 969 (D.C. Cir. 1972).

U. S. v. Charters, 863 F.2d 302 (4th Cir. 1988).

U. S. v. Franks, 511 F.2d 25 (6th Cir. 1975).

U. S. v. Gipson, 24 M.J. 246 (C.M.A. 1987).

U. S. v. Manduiano, 425 U. S. 564 (1976).

U. S. v. Piccinonna, 885 F.2d 1529 (11th Cir. 1989).

U. S. v. Urquidez, 356 F. Supp. 1363 (S.D. Cal. 1973).

U. S. v. Wade, 388 U. S. 218 (1967).

Vitek v. Jones, 445 U. S. 480 (1980).

Wainwright v. Witt, 105 S.Ct. 844 (1985).

Ward's Cove Packing Co., Inc. et al. v. Atonio, 490 U. S. 642 (1989).

Washington v. Davis, 426 U. S. 229 (1976).

Washington v. Harper, 494 U. S 210 (1990).

Westbrook v. Arizona, 384 U. S. 150 (1966).

Williams v. Florida, 399 U. S. 78 (1970).

Witherspoon v. Illinois, 391 U. S. 510 (1968).

Wyatt v. Aderholt, 503 F.2d 1305 (5th Cir. 1974).

Wyatt v. Stickney, 325 F. Supp. 781 (S.D. Ala. 1971), *enfrc'd in* 334 F. Supp. 1341 (S.D. Ala. 1971), 344 F. Supp. 373, 379 (S.D. Ala. 1972).

Youngblood v. Romeo, 457 U. S. 307 (1982).

Zinermon v. Burch, 110 S.Ct. 975 (1990).

REFERENCES

Abel, G. G., Barlow, D. H., Blanchard, E. B., & Gould, D. (1977). The components of rapists' sexual arousal. *Archives of General Psychiatry, 34,* 895–903.

Abel, G. G., Becker, J. V., Blanchard, E. B., & Djenderedjian, A. (1978). Differentiating sexual aggressives with penile measures. *Criminal Justice and Behavior, 5,* 313–332.

Abel, G. G., Mittelman, M. S., & Becker, J. V. (1985). Sexual offenders: Results of assessment and recommendations for treatment. In H. H. Ben-Aron, S. I. Hucker, & C. D. Webster (Eds.), *Clinical criminology.* Toronto: MM Graphics.

Abney, D. (1986). Mutt and Jeff meet the Constitution: The propriety of good guy/bad guy interrogation. *Criminal Law Bulletin, 22,* 118–130.

Abadinsky, H. (1991). *Law and Justice.* Chicago: Nelson-Hall.

Abplanap, J. M. (1985). Premenstrual syndrome. *Behavioral Sciences and the Law, 3,* 103–115.

Abrahamsen, D. (1960). *The psychology of crime.* New York: Columbia University Press.

Abramovitch, R., Freedman, J. L., Thoden, K., & Nikolich, C. (1991). Children's capacity to consent to participation in psychological research: Empirical findings. *Child Development, 62,* 1100–1109.

Abrams, S. (1989). *The complete polygraph handbook.* Lexington, MA: Lexington Books.

Acker, J. R. (1990a). Social science in Supreme Court criminal cases and briefs: The actual and potential contribution of social scientists as amici curiae. *Law and Human Behavior, 14,* 25–43.

Acker, J. R. (1990b). Finding the law: A criminal justice guide to basic legal research techniques. *Journal of Criminal Justice Education, 1,* 215–244.

Acker, J. R. (1991). Social science in Supreme Court death penalty cases: Citation practices and their implications. *Justice Quarterly, 8,* 421–446.

Adler, N. E. (1981). Sex roles and unwanted pregnancy in adolescents and adults. *Professional Psychology, 12,* 56–66.

Adler, N. E., & Dolcini, P. (1986). Psychological issues in abortion for adolescents. In G. B. Melton (Ed.), *Adolescent abortion: Psychological and legal issues.* Lincoln: University of Nebraska Press.

Adler, T. (1990, January). PMS diagnosis draws fire from researchers. *APA Monitor,* p. 12.

Adorno, J., Frenkel-Brunswik, E., Levinson, D., & Sanford, R. (1950). *The authoritarian personality.* New York: Harper & Row.

Allsopp, J. F. (1976). Criminality and delinquency. In J. J. Eysenck & G. D. Wilson (Eds.), *A textbook of human psychology.* Baltimore: University Park Press.

Alschuler, A. W. (1979). Plea bargaining and its history. *Law and Society Review, 13,* 211–245.

Amato, P. R., & Keith, B. (1991). Parental divorce and the well-being of children: A meta-analysis. *Psychological Bulletin, 110,* 26–46.

American Correctional Association. (1991). *Vital statistics in corrections.* Laurel, MD: ACA.

American Psychiatric Association Task Force. (1992). *The use of psychiatric diagnosis in the legal process.* Washington, DC: APA. American Psychological Association. (1978). Report of the

task force on the role of psychology in the criminal justice system. *American Psychologist, 33,* 1099–1113.

Anastasi, A. (1988). *Psychological testing* (4th ed.). New York: Macmillan.

Andenaes, J. (1968). Does punishment deter crime? *The Criminal Law Quarterly, 11,* 76–93.

Andenaes, J. (1974). *Punishment and deterrence.* Ann Arbor, MI: University of Michigan Press.

Andenaes, J. (1990). The Scandinavian countries. In J. R. Spencer, G. Nicholson, R. Flin, & R. Bull (Eds.), *Children's evidence in legal proceedings: An international perspective* University of Cambridge, England: Faculty of Law.

Anson, R. H., Mann, J. D., & Sherman, D. (1986). Niederhoffer's cynicism scale: Reliability and beyond. *Journal of Criminal Justice, 14,* 295–305.

Applebaum, P. S. (1985). Empirical assessment and innovation in the law of civil commitment: A critique. *Law, Medicine and Health Care, 13,* 304–309.

Applebaum, P. S. (1992). Civil commitment from a systems perspective. *Law and Human Behavior, 16,* 61–74.

Applebaum, P. S., & Grisso, T. (1988). Assessing patients' capacities to consent to treatment. *New England Journal of Medicine, 319,* 1635–1638.

Applebaum, P. S., & Gutheil, T. G. (1979). "Rotting with their rights on": Constitutional theory and clinical reality in drug refusal by psychiatric patients. *Bulletin of the American Academy of Psychiatry and Law, 7,* 306–315.

Appley, M. H., & Trumbull, R. (1967). *Psychological stress.* New York: Appleton-Century-Crofts.

Arther, R. 0. (1965). *The scientific investigator.* Springfield, IL: C. C. Thomas.

Arvanites, T. M. (1988). The impact of state mental hospital deinstitutionalization on commitments for incompetency to stand trial, *Criminology, 26,* 307–320.

Asch, S. E. (1952). *Social psychology.* Englewood Cliffs, NJ: Prentice-Hall.

Attias, R., & Goodwin, J. (1985). Knowledge and management strategies in incest cases: A survey of physicians, psychologists, and family counselors. *Child Abuse and Neglect, 9,* 527–533.

Aubry, A. S., & Caputo, R. R. (1965). *Criminal interrogation.* Springfield, IL: C. C. Thomas.

Ault, R., & Reese, J. T. (1980). A psychological assessment of criminal profiling. *F.B.I. Law Enforcement Bulletin, 49,* 22–25.

Ayd, F. J. (1975). The depot fluephenazines: A reappraisal after 10 years' clinical experience. *American Journal of Psychiatry, 132,* 491–500.

Azen, S., Snibbe, H., & Montgomery, H. K. (1973). A longitudinal predictive study of success and performance of law enforcement officers. *Journal of Applied Psychology, 57,* 190–192.

Azrin, N. H., & Holtz, W. C. (1966). Punishment. In W. K. Honig (Ed.), *Operant behavior: Areas of research and application.* New York: Appleton-Century-Crofts.

Bachrach, A. J. (1979). Speech and its potential for stress monitoring. In C. E. C. Lundgren (Ed.), *Proceedings, workshop on monitoring vital signs in the diver.* Bethesda, MD: Undersea Medical Society and Office of Naval Research.

Bakal, D. A. (1975). Headache: A biopsychological perspective. *Psychological Bulletin, 82,* 369–382.

Balch, R. W, Griffiths, L. T, Hall, E. O., & Winfree, L. T. (1976). The socialization of jurors: The voir dire as a rite of passage. *Journal of Criminal Justice, 4,* 271–283.

Bales, R. F., & Borgatta, E. F. (1955). Size of group as a factor in the interaction profile. In A. P. Hare, E. F. Borgatta & R. F. Bales (Eds.), *Small groups.* New York: Knopf.

Balkin, J. (1988). Why policemen don't like policewomen. *Journal of Police Science and Administration, 16,* 29–37.

Bandewehr, L. J., & Novotny, R. (1976). Juror authoritarianism and trial judge partiality: An experiment in jury decision making. *Journal of Experimental Study in Politics, 5,* 28–33.

Bandura, A. (1965). Influence of models' reinforcement contingencies in the acquisition of imitative responses. *Journal of Personality and Social Psychology, 1,* 589–595.

Bandura, A. (1973). *Aggression: A social learning analysis.* Englewood Cliffs, NJ: Prentice-Hall.

Bandura, A. (1974). Behavior theory and the models of man. *American Psychologist, 29,* 859–869.

Bandura, A. (1977). *Social learning theory.* Englewood Cliffs, NJ: Prentice-Hall.

Bandura, A. (1978). The self system in reciprocal determinism. *American Psychologist, 33,* 344–358.

Bandura, A. (1986). *Social foundations of thought and action: A social cognitive theory.* Englewood Cliffs, NJ: Prentice-Hall.

Bandura, A. (1989). Human agency in social cognitive theory. *American Psychologist, 44*, 1175–1184.

Bandura, A., Ross, D., & Ross, S. A. (1963). Vicarious reinforcement and imitative learning. *Journal of Abnormal and Social Psychology, 67*, 601–607.

Baran, A., & Pannor, R. (1990). Open adoption. In D. M. Brodzinsky and M. D. Schechter (Eds.), *The psychology of adoption*. New York: Oxford University Press.

Barber, B. L., & Eccles, J. S. (1992). Long term influence values, behaviors, and aspirations. *Psychological Bulletin, 111*, 108–126.

Barber, T. X., Spanos, N. R., & Chaves, J. F. (1974). *Hypnosis, imagination, and human potentialities*. New York: Pergamon Press.

Barland, G. H., & Raskin, D. C. (1973). Detection of deception. In W. F. Prokasy & D. C. Raskin (Eds.), *Electrodermal activity in psychological research*. New York: Academic Press.

Barland, G. H. (1988). The polygraph use in the USA and elsewhere. In A. Gale (Ed.), *The polygraph test: Lies, truth and science*. London: Sage.

Baron, R. A. (1977). *Human aggression*. New York: Plenum.

Baron, R. A., & Byrne, D. (1981). *Social psychology: Understanding human interaction* (3rd ed.). Boston: Allyn & Bacon.

Bartol, C. R. (1980). *Criminal behavior: A psychosocial approach*. Englewood Cliffs, NJ: Prentice-Hall.

Bartol, C. R. (1991a). *Criminal behavior: A psychosocial approach* (3rd ed.). Englewood Cliffs, NJ: Prentice-Hall.

Bartol, C. R. (1991b). Predictive validation of the MMPI for small-town police officers who fail. *Professional Psychology: Research and Practice, 22*, 127–132.

Bartol, C. R., & Bartol, A. M. (1989). *Juvenile delinquency: A systems approach*. Englewood Cliffs, NJ: Prentice-Hall.

Bartol, C. R., & Bergen, G. T. (1992). Police psychology and its future. *Criminal Justice and Behavior, 19*, 236–239.

Bartol, C. R., Bergen, G. T., Volckens, J. S., & Knoras, K. M. (1992). Women in small-town policing: Job performance and stress. *Criminal Justice and Behavior, 19*, 240–259.

Bartol, C. R., Griffin, R., & Clark, M. (1993, July). *Nationwide survey of American correctional psychologists*. Unpublished manuscript.

Bartol, C. R., & Holanchock, H. (1979). A test of Eysenck's theory on an American prison population. *Criminal Justice and Behavior, 6*, 245–249.

Bartollas, C. (1981). *Introduction to corrections*. New York: Harper & Row.

Bauchner, J. E., Brandt, D. R., & Miller, G. R. (1977). The truth/deception attribution: Effects of varying levels of information availability. In B. D. Ruben (Ed.), *Communication yearbook (Vol. 1)*. New Brunswick, NJ: International Communication Association.

Bazelon, D. L. (1991). Psychology and correctional treatment. Address delivered at the American Association of Correctional Psychologists' Conference, 1972. In K. C. Haas & G. P. Alpert (Eds.), *Dilemmas of corrections*. Prospect Heights, IL: Waveland Press.

Bedrosian, R. C., & Beck, A. J. (1979). Cognitive aspects of suicidal behavior. *Suicide and Life-Threatening Behavior, 9*, 87–96.

Belcher, J. R. (1989). On becoming homeless: A study of chronically mentally ill persons. *Journal of Community Psychology, 17*, 173–185.

Bell, B. E., & Loftus, E. F. (1988). Degree of detail of eyewitness and mock juror judgments. *Journal of Applied Social Psychology, 18*, 1171–1192.

Bell, B. E., & Loftus, E. F. (1989). Trivial persuasion in the courtroom: The power of (a few) minor details. *Journal of Personality and Social Psychology, 56*, 669–679.

Bell, D. J. (1982). Policewomen: Myths and reality. *Journal of Police Science and Administration, 10*, 112–120.

Bem, D. J. (1967). Self-perception: An alternative interpretation of cognitive dissonance phenomena. *Psychological Review, 74*, 183–200.

Bem, D. J. (1972). Self-perception theory. In L. Berkowitz (Ed.), *Advances in experimental social psychology* (Vol. 6). New York: Academic Press.

Bem, D. J., & Allen, A. (1974). On predicting some of the people some of the time: The search for cross-situational consistencies in behavior. *Psychological Review, 81*, 506–520.

Bennett-Sandler, G., Frazier, R. L., Torres, D. A., & Waldron, R. J. (1979). *Law enforcement and criminal justice: An introduction.* Boston: Houghton Mifflin.

Ben-Shakhar, G., Bar-Hillel, M., & Lieblich, I. (1986). Trial by polygraph: Scientific and juridical issues in lie detection. *Behavioral Sciences and the Law, 4,* 459–479.

Ben-Shakhar, G., & Furedy, J. J. (1990). *Theories and applications in the detection of deception: A psychophysiological and international perspective.* New York: Springer-Verlag.

Berg, B. L., & Budnick, K. L. (1986). Defeminization of women in law enforcement: A new twist in the traditional police personality. *Journal of Police Science and Administration, 10,* 180–185.

Berg, K. S., & Vidmar, N. (1975). Authoritarianism and recall of evidence about criminal behavior. *Journal of Research in Personality, 9,* 147–157.

Bergen, G. T., Aceto, R. T., & Chadziewicz, M. M. (1992). Job satisfaction of police psychologists. *Criminal Justice and Behavior, 19,* 314–329.

Berk, S. F., & Loseke, D. R. (1980–81). "Handling" family violence: Situational determinants of police arrest in domestic disturbances. *Law and Society Review, 15,* 315–346.

Berkowitz, L. (1993). *Aggression: Its causes, consequences, and control.* New York: McGraw-Hill.

Bermant, G. (1977). *Conduct of the voir dire examination: Practices and opinions of federal district judges.* Washington, DC: Federal Judicial Center.

Bermant, G., & Shapard, J. (1981). The voir dire examination, juror challenges, and adversary advocacy. In B. D. Sales (Ed.), *Perspectives in law and psychology: Vol. 2. The trial process.* New York: Plenum.

Berry, M. (1991). The practice of open adoption: Findings from a study of 1,396 adoptive families. *Children and Youth Services Review, 13,* 379–395.

Bersh, P. J. (1969). A validation of polygraph examiner judgments. *Journal of Applied Psychology, 53,* 399–403.

Bersoff, D. N. (1979). Regarding psychologists testily: Legal regulation of psychological assessment in the public school. *Maryland Law Review, 39,* 27–120.

Bersoff, D. N. (1981). Testing and the law. *American Psychologist, 36,* 1047–1056.

Bersoff, D. N. & Ogden, D. W. (1991). APA amicus curiae briefs: Furthering lesbian and gay male civil rights. *American Psychologist, 46,* 950–956.

Beutler, L. E., Nussbaum, P. D., & Meredith, K. E. (1988). Changing personality patterns of police officers. *Professional Psychology: Research and Practice, 19,* 303–307.

Beutler, L. E., Storm, A., Kirksih, P., Scogini, F., & Gaines, J. A. (1985). Parameters in the prediction of police officer performance. *Professional Psychology: Research and Practice, 16,* 324–335.

Bezanson, R. P. (1975). Involuntary treatment of the mentally ill in Iowa: The 1975 legislation. *Iowa Law Review, 61,* 261–396.

Black, D. (1971). The social organization of arrest. *Stanford Law Review, 23,* 1087–1111.

Blackmore, J. (1978, July). Are police allowed to have problems of their own? *Police Magazine,* pp. 47–55.

Blinkhorn, S. (1988). Lie detection as a psychometric procedure. In A. Gale (Ed.), *The polygraph test: Lies, truth and science.* London: Sage.

Block, R. (1977). *Violent crime.* Lexington, MA: Lexington Books.

Bluestone, H., & McGahee, C. L. (1962). Reaction to extreme stress: Impending death by execution. *American Journal of Psychiatry, 119,* 393–396.

Block, J. H., Block, J., & Gjerde, P. F. (1986). The personality of children prior to divorce: A prospective study. *Child Development, 57,* 827–840.

Blum, R. H. (1964). *Police selection.* Springfield, IL: C. C. Thomas.

Blunk, R., & Sales, B. D. (1977). Persuasion during the voir dire. In B. D. Sales (Ed.), *Psychology in the legal process.* New York: Spectrum.

Boat, B. W., & Everson, M. D. (1988). Interviewing young children with anatomical dolls. *Child Welfare, 27,* 337–353.

Boehnert, C. E. (1989). Characteristics of successful and unsuccessful insanity pleas. *Law and Human Behavior, 13,* 31–39.

Boehm, V. (1968). Mr. prejudice, Miss sympathy, and the authoritarian personality: An application of psychological measuring techniques to the problems of jury bias. *Wisconsin Law Review, 12,* 734–750.

Bohm, R. M. (1991). *The death penalty in America: Current research.* Cincinnati, OH: Anderson Publishing.

Bolocofsky, D. N. (1989). Use and abuse of mental health experts in child custody determinations. *Behavioral Sciences and the Law, 7*, 197–213.

Bond, C. F., Omar, A., Pitre, U., Lashley, B. R., Skaggs, L. M., & Kirk, C. T. (1992) Fishy-looking liars: Deception judgment from expectancy violation. *Journal of Personality and Social Psychology, 63*, 969–977.

Bonnie, R. J. (1990). Dilemmas in administering the death penalty: Conscientious abstentions, professional ethics, and the needs of the legal system. *Law and Human Behavior, 14*, 67–90.

Bonta, J., & Gendreau, P. (1990). Reexamining the cruel and unusual punishment of prison life. *Law and Human Behavior, 14*, 347–372.

Borgida, E. (1980). Evidentiary reform of rape laws: A Psycholegal approach. In P. D. Lipsitt & B. D. Sales (Eds.), *New directions in psycholegal research*. New York: Van Nostrand-Reinhold.

Borgida, E., DeBono, K. G., & Buckman, L. A. (1990). Cameras in the courtroom: The effects of media coverage on witness testimony and juror perceptions. *Law and Human Behavior, 14*, 489–510.

Bork, R. H. (1977). Testimony given in hearings before the Subcommittee on Courts, Civil Liberties, and the Administration of Justice of the Committee on the Judiciary, House of Representatives. In *State of the judiciary and access to justice*. Washington, DC: USGPO.

Bothwell, R. K., Deffenbacher, K. A., & Brigham, J. C. (1987). Correlation of eyewitness accuracy and confidence: The optimality hypothesis revisited. *Journal of Applied Psychology, 72*, 691–695.

Bourne, L. E., Dominowski, R. L., & Lotus, E. F. (1979). *Cognitive processes*. Englewood Cliffs, NJ: Prentice-Hall.

Bowers, K. (1973). Situationalism in psychology: An analysis and a critique. *Psychological Review, 80*, 307–336.

Bowers, W. J., & Pierce, G. L. (1980). Deterence or brutalization: What is the effect of executions? *Crime and Delinquency, 26*, 453–484.

Bradley, M. T., & Ainsworth, D. (1984). Alcohol and the psychophysiological detection of deception. *Psychophysiology, 21*, 63–71.

Brandreth, D. (1978). Stress and the policeman's wife. *Police Stress, 1*, 41–42.

Bray, J. H. (1988). Children's development during early remarriage. In E. M. Hetherington & J. Arasteh (Eds.), *The impact of divorce, single-parenting and step-parenting on children*. Hillsdale, NJ: Lawrence Erlbaum Associates.

Bray, J. H. (1990). Impact of divorce on the family. In R. E. Rakel (Ed.), *Textbook of family practice* (4th ed.). Philadelphia: W. B. Saunders.

Bray, J. H. (1991). Psychosocial factors affecting custodial and visitation arrangements. *Behavioral Sciences and the Law, 9*, 419–437.

Bray, R. M., & Kerr, N. L. (1979). Use of simulation method in the study of jury behavior: Some methodological considerations. *Law and Human Behavior, 3*, 107–120.

Bray, R. M., & Noble, A. M. (1978). Authoritarianism and decisions of mock juries: Evidence of jury bias and group polarization. *Journal of Personality and Social Psychology, 36*, 1424–1430.

Brehm, J. W. (1966). *A theory of psychological reactance*. New York: Academic Press.

Brehm, S., & Brehm, J. W. (1981). *Psychological reactance: A theory of freedom and control*. New York: Academic Press.

Brent, D. A. (1989). The psychological autopsy: Methodological issues for the study of adolescent suicide. *Suicide and Life-Threating Behavior, 19*, 43–57.

Briere, J., Malamuth, N., & Ceniti, J. (1981). Self-assessed rape proclivity: Attitudinal and sexual correlates. *Paper presented at APA Meeting*, Los Angeles.

Brigham, J. C. (1980). Perspectives on the impact of lineup composition, race, and witness confidence on identification accuracy. *Law and Human Behavior, 4*, 315–321.

Brigham, J. C., & Cairns, D. L. (1988). The effect of mugshot inspections on eyewitness identification accuracy. *Journal of Applied Social Psychology, 18*, 1394–1410.

Brodsky, S. L. (1972). *Psychologists in the criminal justice system*. Urbana, IL: University of Illinois Press.

Brodsky, S. L. (1977). The mental health professional on the witness stand: A survival guide. In B. D. Sales (Ed.), *Psychology in the legal process*. New York: Spectrum Publications.

Brodsky, S. L. (1980). Ethical issues for psychologists in corrections. In J. Monahan (Ed.), *Who is the client? The ethics of Psychological intervention in the criminal justice system*. Washington, DC: American Psychological Association.

Brodsky, S. L. (1990). Professional ethics and professional morality in the assessment of competence for executions: Response to Bonnie. *Law and Human Behavior, 14*, 91–97.

Brodsky, S. L. (1991). *Testifying in court: Guidelines and maxims for the expert witness*. Washington, DC: American Psychological Association.

Brody, G. H., Neubaum, E., & Forehand, R. (1988). Serial marriage: A heuristic analysis of an emerging family form. *Psychological Bulletin, 103*, 211–222.

Brodzinsky, D. M. (1987). Adjustment in adoption: A psychosocial perspective. *Clinical Psychology Review, 7*, 25–47.

Brodzinsky, D. M. (1990). A stress and coping model for adoptive adjustment. In D. M. Brodzinsky and M. D. Schechter (Eds.), *The psychology of adoption*. New York: Oxford University Press.

Brooks, A. D. (1974). *Law, psychiatry and the mental health system*. Boston: Little, Brown.

Broughton, R. S. (1991). *Parapsychology: The controversial science*. New York: Ballatine Books.

Brown, E., Deffenbacher, K., & Sturgill, W. (1977). Memory for faces and the circumstances of encounter. *Journal of Applied Psychology, 62*, 311–318.

Browne, A. (1987). *When battered women kill*. New York: Free Press.

Browne, A., & Finkelhor, D. (1986). Impact of child sexual abuse: A review of the research. *Psychological Bulletin, 99*, 66–77.

Buckhout, R. (1974). Eyewitness testimony. *Scientific American, 321*, 23–31.

Buckhout, R. (1977). Eyewitness identification and psychology in the courtroom. *Criminal Defense, 4*, 5–10.

Buehler, R. E., Patterson, G. R., & Furniss, J. M. (1966). The reinforcement of behaviour in institutional settings. *Behaviour Research and Therapy, 4*, 157–167.

Bukstel, L. H., & Kilmann, P. R. (1980). Psychological effects of imprisonment on confined individuals. *Psychological Bulletin, 88*, 469–493.

Bulkley, J. (1988). Legal proceedings, reforms, and emerging issues in child sexual abuse cases. *Behavioral Sciences and the Law, 6*, 153–180.

Bulkley, J. A. (1989). The impact of new child witness research on sexual abuse prosecutions. In S. J. Ceci, D. F. Ross, & M. P. Toglia (Eds.), *Perspectives on children's testimony* New York: Springer-Verlag.

Bull, R. H. (1988). What is the lie-detection test? In A. Gale (Ed.), *The polygraph test: Lies, truth and science*. Newbury Park, CA: Sage.

Bureau of Justice Statistics. (1992, July). *National update*. Washington, DC: USGPO.

Bureau of Justice Statistics. (1993, January). *National update*. Washington, DC: USGPO.

Buwalda, I. W. (1945). The policewoman—yesterday, today and tomorrow. *Journal of Social Hygiene, 31*, 290–293.

Byrne, D. (1971). *The attraction paradigm*. New York: Academic Press.

Byrne, D. (1974). *An introduction to personality* (2nd ed.). Englewood Cliffs, NJ: Prentice-Hall.

Byrne, D., & Nelson, D. (1965). Attraction as a linear function of proportion of positive reinforcement. *Journal of Personality and Social Psychology, 1*, 659–663.

Callahan, L. A., Steadman, H. J., McGreevy, M. A., & Robbins, P. C. (1991). The volume and characteristics of insanity defense pleas: An eight-state study. *Bulletin of Psychiatry and the Law, 19*, 331–338.

Callahan, L. A., McGreevy, M. A., Cirincione, C., & Steadman, H. J. (1992). Measuring the effects of the guilty but mentally ill (GBMI) verdict: Georgia's 1982 GBMI reform. *Law and Human Behavior, 16*, 447–462.

Camara, K. A., & Resnick, G. (1988). Interparental conflict and cooperation: Factors moderating children's post-divorce adjustment. In E. M. Hetherington & J. Aratesh (Eds.), *Impact of divorce, singleparenting, and stepparenting on children*. Hillsdale, NJ: Erlbaum.

Camp, G. M., & Camp, C. G. (1991). *Corrections yearbook*. South Salem, NY: Criminal Justice Institute.

Caplan, R. D., Cobb, S., French, J. R. P., Harrison, R. V., & Pinneau, S. R. (1975). *Job demands and worker health*. Washington, DC: U. S. Department of Health, Education, & Welfare.

Carney, R. M., & Williams, B. C. (1983). Premenstrual syndrome: A criminal defense. *Notre Dame Law Review, 59*, 253–269.

Carroll, D. (1988). How accurate is polygraph lie detection. In A. Gale (Ed.), *The polygraph test: Lies, truth and science*. Newbury Park, CA: Sage.

Carroll, J. S. (1980). Judgments of recidivism risk: The use of base-rate information in parole decisions. In P. D. Lipsitt & B. Sales (eds.), *New directions in psycholegal research*. New York: Van Nostrand-Reinhold.

Carroll, J. S., Kerr, N. L., Alfini, J.J., Weaver, F. M., MacCoun, R. J., & Feldman, V. (1986). Free press and fair trial: The role of behavioral research. *Law and Human Behavior, 10*, 187–201.

Carter, L. H. (1979). *Reason in law*. Boston: Little, Brown.

Carter, P. I., & Lawrence, J. S. (1985). Adolescents' competency to make informed birth control and pregnancy decisions: An interface for psychology and the law. *Behavioral Sciences and the Law, 3*, 309–319.

Casper, J. D., Benedict, K., & Perry, J. L. (1989). Juror decision making, attitudes, and the hindsight bias. *Law and Human Behavior, 13*, 291–310.

Cavior, N., & Howard, L. R. (1973). Facial attractiveness and juvenile delinquency among black offenders and white offenders. *Journal of Abnormal Child Psychology, 1*, 202–213.

Cavoukian, A., & Heslegrave, R. J. (1980). The admissibility of polygraph evidence in court: Some empirical findings. *Law and Human Behavior, 4*, 117–131.

Ceci, S. J., Ross, D. F., & Toglia, M. P. (1987). Age differences in suggestibility: Narrowing the uncertainties. In S. J. Ceci, M. P. Toglia, & D. F. Ross (Eds.), *Children's eyewitness memory*. New York: Springer-Verlag.

Chaudhuri, M., & Daly, K. (1992). Do restraining orders help? Battered women's experience with male violence and legal process. In E. S. Buzawa & C. G. Buzawa (Eds.), *Domestic violence*. Westport, CT: Auburn House.

Chambers, C. C. (1972). Alternative to civil commitment: Practical guides and constitutional imperatives. *Michigan Law Review, 70*, 1108–1152.

Champion, D. J. (1989). Teenage felons and waiver hearings: Some recent trends, 1980–1988. *Crime and Delinquency, 35*, 577–585.

Champion, D. J., & Mays, G. L. (1991). *Transferring juveniles to criminal courts*. New York: Praeger.

Chance, J., & Goldstein, A. G. (1976). Recognition of faces and verbal labels. *Bulletin of the Psychonomic Society, 7*, 384–386.

Chance, J., Goldstein, A. G., & McBride, L. (1975). Differential experience and recognition memory for faces. *Journal of Social Psychology, 97*, 243–253.

Chandler, E. V, & Jones, C. S. (1979). Cynicism: An inevitability of police work? *Journal of Police Science and Administration, 7*, 65–71.

Chappell, D., & Meyer, J. C. (1975). Cross-cultural differences in police attitudes: An exploration in comparative research. *Australian and New Zealand Journal of Criminology, 8*, 5–13.

Chenoweth, J. H. (1961). Situational tests: A new attempt at assessing police candidates. *The Journal of Criminal Law, Criminology, and Police Science, 52*, 232–238.

Charrow, R. P., & Charrow, V. R. (1979). Making legal language understandable: A psycholinguistic study of jury instructions. *Columbia Law Review, 79*, 1306–1374.

Clear, T. R., & Cole, G. F. (1990). *American corrections* (2nd ed.). Pacific Grove, CA: Brooks/Cole.

Cleckley, H. (1976). *The mask of sanity* (5th ed.). St. Louis: Mosby.

Clements, C. B. (1979). Crowded prisons: A review of psychological and environmental effects. *Law and Human Behavior, 3*, 217–225.

Clemmer, D. (1940). *The prison community*. Boston: Christopher.

Clifford, B. R., & Hollin, C. R. (1981). Effects of the type of incident and the number of perpetrators on eyewitness memory. *Journal of Applied Psychology, 66*, 365–370.

Clifford, B. R., & Scott, J. (1978). Individual and situational factors in eyewitness testimony. *Journal of Applied Psychology, 63*, 352–359.

Clingempeel, W. G., Mulvey, E., & Reppucci, N. D. (1980). A national study of ethical dilemmas of psychologists in the criminal justice system. In J. Monahan (Ed.), *Who is the client? The ethics of psychological intervention in the criminal justice system*. Washington, DC: American Psychological Association.

Clingempeel, W. G., & Reppucci, N. D. (1982). Joint custody after divorce: Major issues and goals for research. *Psychological Bulletin, 91*, 102–127.

Clore, G. L., & Byrne, D. (1974). A reinforcement-affect model of attraction. In T. L. Huston (Ed.), *Foundations of interpersonal attraction*. New York: Academic Press.

Cocozza, J., & Steadman, H. (1976). The failure of psychiatric prediction of dangerousness: Clear and convincing evidence. *Rutgers Law Review, 29*, 1084–1101.

Cogan, N. H. (1970). Juvenile law before and after the entrance of "parens patriae." *South Carolina Law Review, 22*, 147–181.

Cohen, I. (1966). The function of the attorney and the commitment of the mentally ill. *Texas Law Review, 44*, 424–459.

Cohen, M. (1985). *Legal research in a nutshell* (4th ed.). St. Paul, MN: West.

Cohen, M. E., & Carr, W. J. (1975). Facial recognition and the von Restorff effect. *Bulletin of the Psychonomic Society, 6*, 383–384.

Cohen, M. L., Garafalo, R., Boucher, R., & Seghorn, T. (1971). The psychology of rapists. *Seminars in Psychiatry, 3*, 307–327.

Cohen, M. L., Seghorn, T., & Calmas, W. (1969). Sociometric study of the sex offender. *Journal of Abnormal Psychology, 74*, 249–255.

Cohen, R. L., & Harnick, M. A. (1980). The susceptibility of child witnesses to suggestions: An empirical study. *Law and Human Behavior, 4*, 201–210.

Colarelli, J. J., & Siegel, M. (1964). A method of police personnel selection. *Journal of Criminal Law, Criminology and Police Sciences, 55*, 287–289.

Cole, E. S., & Donley, K. S. (1990). History, values and placement policy issues in adoption. In D. M. Brodzinsky & M. D. Schechter (Eds.), *The Psychology of adoption*. New York: Oxford University Press.

Cole, G. F. (1992). *The American system of criminal justice* (6th ed.). Pacific Grove, CA: Brooks/Cole.

Coleman, J. C. (1976). *Abnormal psychology and modern life* (5th ed.). Glenview, IL: Scott, Foresman.

Comer, R. J. (1992). *Abnormal psychology*. New York: Freeman.

Comment. (1972). *Police power in Illinois: The regulation of private conduct*. Champaign, IL: University of Illinois Law Forum.

Conrad, J. (1982). What do the undeserving deserve? In R. Johnson & H. Toch (Eds.), *The pains of imprisonment*. Prospect Heights, IL: Waveland.

Constantini, E., & King, J. (1980/81). The partial juror: Correlates and causes of prejudgment. *Law and Society Review, 15*, 9–40.

Cooper, C. L., & Marshall, J. (1976). Occupational sources of stress: A review of the literature relating to coronary heart disease and mental ill health. *Journal of Occupational Psychology, 49*, 11–28.

Cooper, R. P., & Werner, P. D. (1990). Predicting violence in newly admitted inmates: A lens model analysis of staff decisions. *Criminal Justice and Behavior, 17*, 431–447.

Costanzo, S., & Costanzo, M. (1989). Penalty phase decision making: A case study. *Paper presented at the Annual Meeting of the Law and Society Association*, Madison, WI.

Costanzo, M., & Costanzo, S. (1992). Jury decision making in the capital penalty phase: Legal assumptions, empirical findings, and a research agenda. *Law and Human Behavior, 16*, 185–201.

Cowan, C. L., Thompson, W. C., & Ellsworth, P. C. (1984). The effects of death qualification on jurors' predisposiiton to convict and on the quality of the deliberation. *Law and Human Behavior, 8*, 53–79.

Cox, M., & Tanford, S. (1989). An alternative method of capital jury selection. *Law and Human Behavior, 13*, 167–183.

Cox, V. C., Paulus, P. B., & McCain, G. (1984). Prison crowding research: The relevance for prison housing standards and general approach regarding crowding phenomena. *American Psychologist, 39*, 1148–1160.

Crank, J. P., & Caldero, M. (1991). The production of occupational stress in medium-sized police agencies: A survey of line officers in eight municipal departments. *Journal of Criminal Justice, 19*, 339–349.

Crosbie-Burnett, M. (1991). Impact of joint versus sole custody and quality of co-parental relationship on adjustment of adolescents in remarried families. *Behavioral Sciences and the Law, 9*, 439–449.

Cross, J. F., Cross, J., & Daly, J. (1971). Sex, race, age and beauty as factors in recognition of faces. *Perception and Psychophysics, 10*, 393–396.

Cutler, B. L., Penrod, S. D., & Martens, T. K. (1987). Improving the reliability of eyewitness identification: Putting content with context. *Journal of Applied Psychology, 72,* 629–637.

Dahlstrom, W. C. (1972). Whither the MMPI? In J. N. Butcher (Ed.), *Objective personality assessment.* New York: Academic Press.

Dale, M. W. (1976). Barriers to the rehabilitation of ex-offenders. *Crime and Delinquency, 22,* 322–337.

Dalessio, D. J. (1972). *Wolff's headache and other head pain.* New York: Oxford University Press.

Dalton, K. (1961). Menstruation and crime. *British Medical Journal, 2,* 1752–1753.

Daly, K., & Chesney-Lind, M. (1988). Feminism and criminology. *Justice Quarterly, 5,* 497–535.

Danto, B. L. (1976). Police suicide. *Paper presented at the American Association of Suicidology,* Los Angeles.

Darley, J. M., & Latane, B. (1968). Bystander intervention in emergencies: Diffusion of responsibility. *Journal of Personality and Social Psychology, 8,* 377–383.

Dash, J., & Reiser, M. (1978). Suicide among police in urban law enforcement agencies. *Journal of Police Science and Administration, 6,* 18–21.

Davidson, G. C., & Neale, J. M. (1982). *Abnormal psychology: An experimental clinical approach.* New York: Wiley.

Davis, G., Ellis, H., & Shepherd, J. (1978). Face recognition accuracy as a function of mode of representation. *Journal of Applied Psychology, 63,* 180–187.

Davis, G., & Leitenberg, H. (1987). Adolescent sex offenders. *Psychological Bulletin, 101,* 417–427.

Davis, J. H., Bray, R. M., & Holt, R. W. (1977). The empirical study of decision processes in juries: A critical review. In J. L. Tapp & F. J. Levine (Eds.), *Law, justice, and the individual in society: Psychological and legal issues.* New York: Holt, Rinehart & Winston.

Davis, J. H., Kerr, N. L., Atkin, R. S., Holt, R., & Meek, D. (1975). The decision processes of 6– and 12–person mock juries assigned unanimous and two-thirds majority rules. *Journal of Personality and Social Psychology, 32,* 1–14.

Davis, J. M. (1976). Overview: Maintenance therapy in psychiatry: II. Affective disorders. *American Journal of Psychiatry, 133,* 1–13.

Davis, S. (1991). Violence by psychiatric inpatients: A review. *Hospital and Community Psychiatry, 42,* 585–590.

Dawes, R. M. (1989). Experience and validity of clinical judgment: The illusory correlation. *Behavioral Sciences and the Law, 7,* 455–467.

Dawes, R. M., Faust, D., & Meehl, P. E. (1989). Clinical vs. actuarial judgment. *Science, 243,* 1668–1674.

Debro, J., Murty, K., Roebuck, J., & McCann, C. (1987). Death row inmates: A comparison of Georgia and Florida profiles. *Criminal Justice Review, 12,* 41–46.

Decker, S. H., & Kohfeld, C. W. (1990). The deterrent effect of capital punishment in the five most active execution states: A times series analysis. *Criminal Justice Review, 15,* 173–191.

Deffenbacher, K. A. (1980). Eyewitness accuracy and confidence. Can we infer anything about their relationship? *Law and Human Behavior, 4,* 243–260.

Deland, F. H., & Borenstein, N. M. (1990). Medicine court, II: Rivers in practice. *American Journal of Psychiatry, 147,* 38–43.

Dershowitz, A. M. (1974). The origins of preventive confinement in Anglo-American law. Part 2, The American experience. *University of Cincinnati Law Review, 43,* 781–846.

Deutsch, A. (1949). *The mentally ill in America.* New York: Columbia University Press.

Dexter, H. D., Cutler, B. L., & Moran, G. (1992). A test of voir dire as a remedy for the prejudicial effect of pretrial publicity. *Journal of Applied Social Psychology, 22,* 819–832.

Deykin, E. V., Campbell, L., & Patti, P. (1984). The postadoption experience of surrending parents. *American Journal of Orthopsychiatry, 54,* 271–280.

Diamond, S. S. (1993). Instructing on death: Psychologists, juries, and judges. *American Psychologist, 48,* 423–434.

Dickey, W. (1980). Incompetency and the nondangerous mentally ill client. *Criminal Law Bulletin, 16,* 25–40.

Diliman, E. C. (1963). Role-playing as a technique in police selection. *Public Personnel Review, 24,* 116–118.

Dion, K. (1972). Physical attractiveness and evaluations of children's transgressions. *Journal of Personality and Social Psychology, 24,* 207–213.

Dion, K. K., Berscheid, E., & Waister, E. (1972). What is beautiful is good. *Journal of Personality and Social Psychology, 24,* 285–290.

Dobash, R. E., & Dobash, R. (1979). *Violence against wives.* New York: Free Press.

Doerr, H. O., & Carlin, A. S. (Eds.), (1991). *Forensic neuropsychology: Legal and scientific bases.* New York: Guilford Press.

Doob, A. N., & Kirshenbaum, H. M. (1973). Bias in police lineups—Partial remembering. *Journal of Police Science and Administration, 1,* 287–293.

Dowdle, M., Gillen, H., & Miller, A. (1974). Integration and attribution theories as predictors of sentencing by a simulated jury. *Personality and Social Psychology Bulletin, 1,* 270–272.

Dreher, G. G., Ash, R. A., & Hancock, P. (1988). The role of the traditional research design in underestimating the validity of the employment interview. *Personnel Psychology, 41,* 315–327.

Dube, R., & Hebert, M. (1988). Sexual abuse of children 12 years of age: A review of 511 cases. *Child Abuse and Neglect, 12,* 321–330.

Dubois, P. H., & Watson, R. I. (1950). The selection of patrolmen. *Journal of Applied Psychology, 34,* 90–95.

Dull, R. T., & Giacopassi, D. J. (1987). Demographic correlates of sexual and dating attitudes: A study of date rape. *Criminal Justice and Behavior, 14,* 175–193.

Duncan, D. F. (1974). Verbal behavior in a detention home. *Corrective and Social Psychiatry and Journal of Behavior Technological Methods and Therapy, 20,* 38–42.

Dunford, F. W., Huizinga, D., & Elliott, D. S. (1990). The role of arrest in domestic assault: The Omaha police experiment. *Criminology, 28,* 183–206.

Dunn, G. E. (1992). Multiple personality disorder: A new challenge for psychology. *Professional Psychology: Research and Practice, 23,* 18–23.

Dunning, D. (1989). Research on children's eyewitness testimony: Perspectives on its past and future. In S. J. Ceci, D. F. Ross, & M. P. Toglia (Eds.), *Perspectives on children's testimony.* New York: Springer-Verlag.

Duquette, D. N. (1990). *Advocating for the child in protection proceedings.* Lexington, MA: Lexington Books.

Durham, M. L., & La Fond, J. Q. (1991). A search for the missing premise of involuntary therapeutic commitment: Effective treatment of the mentally ill. In D. B. Wexler (Ed.), *Therapeutic jurisprudence.* Durham, NC: Carolina Academic Press.

Easterbrook, J. A. (1959). The effect of emotion on cue utilization and the organization of behavior. *Psychological Review, 66,* 181–201.

Easterbrook, J. A. (1978). *The determinants of free will: A psychological analysis of responsible, adjustive behavior.* New York: Academic Press.

Ebert, B. W. (1987). Guide to conducting a psychological autopsy. *Professional Psychology: Research and Practice, 18,* 52–56.

Ecclestone, J. E. J., Gendreau, P., & Knox, C. (1974). Solitary confinement of prisoners: An assessment of its effects on inmates personal constructs and cortical activity. *Canadian Journal of Behavioral Science, 6,* 178–191.

Efran, M. C. (1974). The effect of physical appearance on the judgment of guilt, interpersonal attraction, and severity of recommended punishment in a simulated jury task. *Journal of Research in Personality, 8,* 45–54.

Ehrlich, I. (1975). The deterrent effect of capital punishment: A question of life and death. *American Economic Review, 65,* 379–394.

Ehrlich, I. (1977). Capital punishment and deterrence: Some further thoughts and additional evidence. *Journal of Political Economy, 85,* 741–788.

Einhorn, J. (1986). Child custody in historical perspective: A study of changing social perceptions of divorce and child custody in Anglo-American law. *Behavioral Sciences and the Law, 4,* 119–135.

Eisenberg, T. (1975). Labor-management relations and psychological stress: View from the bottom. *The Police Chief, 42,* 54–58.

Ekman, P. (1985). *Telling lies: Clues to deceit in the marketplace, politics, and marriage.* New York: Norton.

Ekman, P., & Friesen, W. (1969). Nonverbal leakage and clues to deception. *Psychiatry, 32,* 88–106.

Ekman, P., & Friesen, W. (1974). Detecting deception from the body and face. *Journal of Personality and Social Psychology, 29,* 288–298.

Ekman, P., Friesen, W. V., & Scherer, K. R. (1976). Body movement and voice pitch in deceptive interaction. *Semiotica, 16,* 23–27.

Elaad, E. (1990). Detection of guilty knowledge in real-life criminal investigations. *Journal of Applied Psychology, 75,* 521–529.

Ellis, H. D., Deregowski, J. B., & Shepherd, J. W (1975). Descriptions of white and black faces by white and black subjects. *International Journal of Psychology, 10,* 119–123.

Elliot, E. S., Wills, E. J., & Goldstein, A. G. (1973). The effects of discrimination training on the recognition of white and oriental faces. *Bulletin of the Psychonomic Society, 2,* 71–73.

Elliott, D. S. (1989). Criminal justice procedures in family violence crimes. In L. Ohlin & M. Tonry (Eds.), *Family violence* (Vol. 11). Chicago: University of Chicago Press.

Elliott, D. S., & Ageton, S. S. (1980). Reconciling race and class differences in self-reported and official estimates of delinquency. *American Sociological Review, 45,* 95–110.

Elliott, D. S., & Huizinga, D. (1983). Social class and delinquent behavior in a national youth panel. *Criminology, 21,* 149–177.

Elliott, R. (1987). *Litigating intelligence: IQ tests, special education, and social science in the courtroom.* Dover, MA: Auburn House.

Elliott, R., & Robinson, R. J. (1991). Death penalty attitudes and the tendency to convict or acquit. Some data. *Law and Human Behavior, 15,* 389–404.

Ellison, K. W., & Buckhout, R. (1981). *Psychology and criminal justice.* New York: Harper & Row.

Ellsworth, P. C. (1984). Due process versus crime control. *Law and Human Behavior, 8,* 31–51.

Ellsworth, P. C., Butkaty, R. M., Cowan, C. L., & Thompson, W. C. (1984). The death qualified jury and the defense of insanity. *Law and Human Behavior, 8,* 81–93.

Elwork, A. (1992). Psycholegal treatment and intervention: The next challenge. *Law and Human Behavior, 16,* 175–183.

Elwork, A., Alfini, J. J., & Sales, B. D. (1987). Toward understandable jury instructions. In L. S. Wrightsman, S. M. Kassin, & C. E. Willis (Eds.), *In the jury box: Controversies in the courtroom.* Newbury Park, CA: Sage.

Elwork, A., Sales, B. D., & Alfini, J. J. (1977). Juridic decisions: In ignorance of the law or in light of it? *Law and Human Behavior, 1,* 163–189.

Emery, R. E. (1988). *Marriage, divorce, and children's adjustment.* Newbury Park, CA: Sage.

Emery, R. E., & Wyer, M. M. (1987a). Divorce mediation. *American Psychologist, 42,* 472–480.

Emery, R. E., & Wyer, M. M. (1987b). Child custody mediation and litigation: An experimental evaluation of the experience of parents. *Journal of Consulting and Clinical Psychology, 2,* 179–186.

Ensminger, J. J., & Liguori, T. D. (1990). The therapeutic significance of the civil commitment hearing: An unexplored potential. In D. B. Wexler (Ed.), *Therapeutic jurisprudence.* Durham, NC: Carolina Academic Press.

Esses, V. M., & Webster, C. D. (1988). Physical attractiveness, dangerousness, and the Canadian Criminal Code. *Journal of Applied Social Psychology, 18,* 1017–1031.

Ewing, C. P. (1987). *Battered women who kill: Psychological selfdefense as legal justification.* Lexington, MA: Heath.

Ewing, C. P. (1990). Psychological self-defense: A proposed justification for battered women who kill. *Law and Human Behavior, 14,* 579–594.

Ewing, C. P. (1991). Introduction to divorce and child custody. *Behavioral Sciences and the Law, 9,* 373.

Eysenck, H. J. (1967). *The biological basis of personality.* Springfield, IL: C. C. Thomas.

Eysenck, H. J. (1977). *Crime and personality.* London: Routledge & Kegan Paul.

Eysenck, H. J. (1983). Personality, conditioning, and antisocial behavior. In W. S. Laufer & J. M. Day (Eds.), *Personality theory, moral development, and criminal behavior.* Lexington, MA: Lexington Books.

Eysenck, H. J., & Gudjonsson, G. H. (1989). *The causes and cures of criminality.* New York: Plenum.

Farr, J. L., & Landy, F. J. (1979). The development and use of supervisory and peer scales for police performance appraisal. In C. D. Spielberger (Ed.), *Police selection and evaluation: Issues and techniques*. Washington, DC: Hemisphere.

Faust, D., & Ziskin, J. (1988). The expert witness in psychology and psychiatry. *Science, 241*, 31–35.

Feinman, C. (1986). *Women in the criminal justice system* (2nd Ed.). New York: Praeger.

Feinman, S., & Entwisle, D. R. (1976). Children's ability to recognize other children's faces. *Child Development, 47*, 506–510.

Feld, B. C. (1988). In re Gault revised: A cross-state comparison of the right to counsel in juvenile court. *Crime and Delinquency, 34*, 393–424.

Feld, B. C. (1992). Criminalizing the juvenile court: A research agenda for the 1990s. In I. M. Schwartz (Ed.), *Juvenile justice and public policy*. New York: Praeger.

Feldman, M. P. (1977). *Criminal behaviour: A psychological analysis*. London: John Wiley.

Felner, R. D., & Terre, L. (1987). Child custody dispositions and children's adaption following divorce. In L. A. Weithorn (Ed.), *Psychology and child custody determination: Knowledge, roles and expertise*. Lincoln: University of Nebraska Press.

Fenster, C. A., Wiedemann, C. F., & Locke, B. (1977). Police personality: Social science folklore and psychological measurement. In B. D. Sales (Ed.), *Psychology in the legal process*. New York: Spectrum.

Festinger, L., Pepitone, A., & Newcomb, T. (1952). Some consequences of deindividuation in a group. *Journal of Abnormal and Social Psychology, 47*, 382–389.

Finckenauer, J. O. (1988). Public support for the death penalty: Retribution as just deserts or retribution as revenge. *Justice Quarterly, 5*, 81–100.

Finkel, N. J. (1988). *Insanity on trial*. New York: Plenum.

Finkel, N. J., Meister, K. H., & Lightfoot, D. M. (1991). The self-defense defense community sentiment. *Law and Human Behavior, 15*, 585–602.

Finkelhor, D., & Lewis, I. A. (1988). An epidemiologic approach to the study of child molestation. In R. A. Prentky & V. I. Quinsey (Eds.), *Human sexual aggression: Current perspectives*. New York: New York Academy of Sciences.

Finlayson, L. M., & Koocher, G. P. (1991). Professional judgment and child abuse reporting in sexual abuse cases. *Professional Psychology: Research and Practice, 22*, 464–472.

Frieze, I. H., & Browne, A. (1989). Violence in marriage. In L. Ohlin & M. Tonry (Eds.), *Family violence* (Vol. 11). Chicago: University of Chicago Press.

Fisher, J., Epstein, L., & Harris, M. (1967). Validity of the psychiatric interview: Predicting the effectiveness of the first Peace Corps volunteers in Ghana. *Archives of General Psychiatry, 17*, 744–750.

Fitzgerald, R., & Foley, M. A., & Johnson, M. K. (1985). Confusions between memories for performed and imagined actions: A developmental comparison. *Child Development, 56*, 1145–1155.

Flanagan, T. J., & Maguire, K. (Eds.) (1991). *Sourcebook of criminal justice statistics*. Washington, DC: USGPO.

Fong, G. T., Lurigio, A. J., & Stalans, L. J. (1990). Improving probation decisions through statistical training. *Criminal Justice and Behavior, 17*, 370–388.

Forston, R. F. (1970). Judges' instructions: A quantitative analysis of jurors' listening comprehension. *Today's Speech, 18*, 34–38.

Fox, S. G., & Walters, H. A. (1986). The impact of general versus specific expert testimony and eyewitness confidence upon mock juror judgment. *Law and Human Behavior, 10*, 215–228.

Frank, J. (1949). *Courts on trial: Myth and reality in American justice*. Princeton, NJ: Princeton University Press.

Frazier, P. A., & Borgida, E. (1992). Rape trauma syndrome: A review of case law and psychological research. *Law and Human Behavior, 16*, 293–311.

Frehsee. D. (1990). Children's evidence within the German legal system. In J. R. Spencer, G. Nicholson, R. Flin, & R. Bull (Eds.), *Children's evidence in legal proceedings: An international perspective*. University of Cambridge, England: Faculty of Law.

Freeman, W., & Watts, J. W. (1942). *Psychosurgery*. Springfield, IL: C. C. Thomas.

Freudenberger, H. (1974). Staff burnout. *Journal of Social Issues, 30*, 159–165.

Friedman, A. F., Webb, J. T., & Lewak, R. (1989). *Psychological assessment with the MMPI*. Hillsdale, NJ: Lawrence Erlbaum.

Friedman, M., & Rosenman, R. H. (1974). *Type A behavior and your heart*. New York: Knopf.

Friedman, P. (1967). Suicide among police. In E. Schneidman (Ed.), *Essays in self-destruction*. New York: Science House.

Friend, R. M., & Vinson, M. (1974). Leaning over backwards: Jurors' responses to defendants' attractiveness. *Journal of Communication, 24*, 124–129.

Furby, L., Weinrott, M. R., & Blackshaw, L. (1989). Sex offender recidivism: A review. *Psychological Bulletin, 105*, 3–30.

Furniss, J. M. (1964). *Peer reinforcement of behavior in a institution for delinquent girls*. Unpublished master's thesis. Oregon State University.

Gaes, G. G. (1985). The effects of overcrowding in prison. In M. Tonry & N. Morris (Eds.), *Crime and justice: An annual review of research* (Vol. 6). Chicago: University of Chicago Press.

Gaes, G. G., McGuire, W. J. (1984). Prison violence: The contribution of crowding versus other determinates of prison assault rates. *Journal of Research in Crime and Delinquency, 22*, 41–65.

Gallagher, T. (1979). Discretion in police enforcement. In L. E. Abt & I. R. Stuart (Eds.), *Social psychology and discretionary law*. New York: Van Nostrand-Reinhold.

Garb, H. N. (1989). Clinical judgment, clinical training, and professional experience. *Psychological Bulletin, 105*, 387–396.

Gearing, M. L. (1979). The MMPI as a primary differentiator and predictor of behavior in prison: A methodological critique and review of the recent literature. *Psychological Bulletin, 86*, 929–963.

Gendreau, P., Freedman, N., Wilde, G. T. S., & Scott, G. D. (1972). Changes in EEG alpha frequency and evoked response latency during solitary confinement. *Journal of Abnormal Psychology, 79*, 54–59.

Gendreau, P., & Ross, R. R. (1984). Correctional treatment: Some recommendations for effective intervention. *Juvenile and Family Court Journal, 34*, 31–39.

Gendreau, P., & Ross, R. R. (1987). Revivification of rehabilitation: Evidence from the 1980s. *Justice Quarterly, 4*, 349–407.

Gendreau, P., & Ross, R. R. (1991). Correctional treatment: Some recommendations for effective intervention. In K. C. Haas & G. O. Alpert (Eds.), *The dilemmas of corrections*. Prospect Heights, IL: Waveland Press.

Gentry, W. D., Shows, W. D., & Thomas, M. (1974). Chronic low back pain: A psychological profile. *Psychosomatics, 15*, 174–177.

George, W. H., & Marlatt, G. A. (1989). Introduction. In D. R. Laws (Ed.), *Relapse prevention with sex offenders*. New York: Guilford Press.

Gerbasi, K. D., Zuckerman, M., & Reis, H. (1977). Justice needs a new blindfold: A review of mock jury research. *Psychological Bulletin, 84*, 323–345.

Gerber, S. R., Schroeder, O. (1962). *Criminal investigation and interrogation*. Cincinnati, OH: W. H. Anderson.

Gettman, L. R. (1978). Aerobics and police fitness. *Police Stress, 1*, 22–25.

Gilbert, C., & Bakan, P. (1973). Visual asymmetry in perception of faces. *Neuropsychologia, 11*, 355–362.

Gilbert, S. (1988). *Hard-core delinquents: Reaching out through Miami experiment*. University, AL: University of Alabama Press.

Gillespie, C. K. (1989). *Justifiable homicide*. Columbus: Ohio State University Press.

Glaser, D. (1954). A reconsideration of some parole prediction factors. *American Sociological Review, 19*, 335–341.

Glaser, D. (1962). Prediction tables as accounting devices for judges and parole boards. *Crime and Delinquency, 8*, 239–258.

Glaser, D. (1964). *The effectiveness of a prison and parole system*. Indianapolis, IN: Bobbs-Merrill.

Glaser, D. (1987). Classification for risk. In D. M. Gottfredson & M. Tonry (Eds.), *Prediction and classification* (Vol. 9). Chicago: University of Chicago Press.

Glass, D. C. (1977). *Behavior patterns, stress, and coronary disease*. Hillsdale, NJ: Erlbaum.

Glass, L. S. (1991). The legal base in forensic neuropsychology. In H. O. Doerr & A. S. Carlin (Eds.) *Forensic neuropsychology: Legal and scientific bases*. New York: Guilford Press.

Glenn, N. D. (1991). The recent trend in marital success in the United States. *Journal of Marriage and the Family, 53*, 261–270.

Glick, P. C. (1988). The role of divorce in the changing family structure: Trends and variations. In S. A. Wolchik & P. Karoly (Eds.), *Children of divorce: Empirical perspective on adjustment*. New York: Gardner Press.

Going, M., & Read, J. D. (1974). Effects of uniqueness, sex of subject, and sex of photograph on facial recognition. *Perceptual and Motor Skills, 39*, 109–110.

Golash, D. (1992). Race, fairness, and jury selection. *Behavioral Sciences and the Law, 10*, 155–177.

Goldberg, D., & Wolkind, S. N. (1992). Patterns of psychiatric disorder in adopted girls: A research note. *Journal of Child Psychology and Psychiatry, 33*, 935–940.

Goldberg, L. R. (1968). Simple models or simple processes? Some research on clinical judgments. *American Psychologist, 23*, 483–496.

Goldberg, L. R. (1970). Man vs. model of man: A rationale, plus some evidence for a method of improving on clinical inferences. *Psychological Bulletin, 73*, 422–432.

Goldberg, L. R., & Werts, C. E. (1966). The reliability of clinician's judgments: A multitrait-multimethod approach. *Journal of Consulting Psychology, 30*, 199–206.

Golden, M. (1964). Some effects of combining psychological tests on clinical inferences. *Journal of Consulting Psychology, 28*, 440–446.

Golding, S. L., & Roesch, R. (1987) The assessment of criminal responsibility: A historical approach to a current controversy. In I. B. Weiner & A. K. Hess (Eds.), *Handbook of forensic psychology*. New York: Wiley.

Golding, S. L., Roesch, R., & Schreiber, J. (1984). Assessment and conceptualization of competency to stand trial: Preliminary data on the Interdisciplinary Fitness Interview. *Law and Human Behavior, 8*, 321–334.

Goldstein, A. G. (1977). The fallibility of the eyewitness: Psychological evidence. In B. D. Sales (Ed.), *Psychology in the legal process*. New York: Spectrum.

Goldstein, A. G., & Chance, J. E. (1964). Recognition of children's faces. *Child Development, 35*, 129–136.

Goldstein, A. G., & Chance, J. E. (1970). Visual recognition memory for complex configurations. *Perception and Psychophysics, 9*, 237–241.

Goldstein, A. G., & Chance, J. (1976). Measuring psychological similarity of faces. *Bulletin of the Psychonomic Society, 7*, 407–408.

Goldstein, A. C., & Chance, J. (1978). Judging face similarity in own and other races. *Journal of Psychology, 98*, 185–193.

Goldstein, B. (1975). *Screening for emotional and psychological fitness in correctional officer hiring*. Resource Center on Correctional Law and Legal Services.

Gonzalez, R., Ellsworth, P. C., & Pembroke, M. (1993). Response biases in lineups and showups. *Journal of Personality and Social Psychology, 64*, 525–537.

Goodman, G. S., Aman, C., & Hirschman, J. (1987). Child sexual and physical abuse: Children's testimony. In S. J. Ceci, M. P. Toglia, & D. F. Ross (Eds.), *Children's eyewitness memory*. New York: Springer-Verlag.

Goodman, G. S., & Aman, C. (1990). Children's use of anatomically detailed dolls to recount an event. *Child Development, 61*, 1859–1871.

Goodman, G. S., Bottoms, B. L., Hersocvici, B. B., & Shaver, P. (1989). In S. J. Ceci, D. F. Ross, & M. P. Toglia (Eds.), *Perspectives on the child witness*. New York: Springer-Verlag.

Goodman, G. S., Golding, J. M., Helgeson, V., Haith, M., & Michelli, J. (1987). When a child takes the stand: Jurors' perception of children's eyewitness testimony. *Law and Human Behavior, 11*, 27–40.

Goodman, G. S., & Hahn, A. (1987). Evaluating eyewitness testimony. In I. B. Weiner & A. K. Hess (Eds.), *Handbook of forensic psychology*. New York: Wiley.

Goodman, G. S., Hepps, D., & Reed, R. S. (1986). The child victim's testimony. In A. Haralambie (Ed.), *New issues for child advocates*. Phoenix, AZ: Arizona Associates of Council for Children.

Goodman, G. S., & Reed, R. S. (1986). Age differences in eyewitness testimony. *Law and Human Behavior, 10*, 317–332.

Goodman, G. S., Taub, E. P., Jones, D. P. H., England, P., Port, L. K., Rudy, L., & Prado, L. (1992). Testifying in criminal court. *Monograph of the Society for Research in Child Development, 57* (Serial No. 229).

Gordon, C. C. (1969). *Perspectives on law enforcement. I. Characteristics of Police applicants*. Princeton, NJ: Educational Testing Service.

Gorenstein, G. W., & Ellsworth, P. C. (1980). Effect of choosing an incorrect photograph on a later identification by an eyewitness. *Journal of Applied Psychology, 65,* 616–622.

Gorer, G. (1955). Modification of national character: The role of the police in England. *Journal of Social Issues, 11,* 24–32.

Gottesman, J. (1975). *The utility of the MMPI in assessing the personality Patterns of urban police applicants.* Hoboken, NJ: Stevens Institute of Technology.

Gottfredson, D. M., and Tonry, M., (Eds.). (1987). *Prediction and classification: Criminal justice decision making.* Chicago: The University of Chicago Press.

Gottfredson, M. R., & Gottfredson, D. M. (1980). *Decisionmaking in criminal justice: Toward the rational exercise of discretion.* Cambridge, MA: Ballinger.

Gottfredson, M. R., & Gottfredson, D. M. (1988). *Decisionmaking in criminal justice: Toward the rational exercise of discretion* (2nd ed.). New York: Plenum.

Gough, H. G. (1969). A leadership index on the California Psychological Inventory. *Journal of Counseling Psychology, 16,* 283–289.

Grassian, S. (1983). Psychopathological effects of solitary confinement. *American Journal of Psychiatry, 140,* 1450–1454.

Greenaway, W. K. & Brickley, S. L. (Eds.). (1978). *Law and social control in Canada.* Scarborough, Ont.: Prentice-Hall of Canada.

Greene, E., & Loftus, E. F. (1985). When crimes are joined at trial. *Law and Human Behavior, 9,* 193–207.

Greene, E. (1990). Media effects on jurors. *Law and Human Behavior, 14,* 439–450.

Greenwood, P. W., & Turner, S. (1993). Evaluation of the Paint Creek Youth Center: A residential program for serious delinquents. *Criminology, 31,* 263–280.

Grenick, J. M. (1973, June). *The psychological fitness of deputies assigned to the patrol functions and its relationship to the formulation of entrance standards for law enforcement officers.* Law Enforcement Assistance Administration Grant, Final Report, Washington, DC.

Griffitt, W., & Jackson, T. (1973). Simulated jury decisions: The influence of jury-defendant attitude similarity-dissimilarity. *Social Behavior and Personality, 1,* 1–7.

Grisso, T. (1981). *Juveniles' waiver of rights: Legal and psychological competence.* New York: Plenum.

Grisso, T. (1983). Juveniles' consent in delinquency proceedings. In G. B. Melton, G.P. Koocher, & M. J. Saks (Eds.), *Children's competence to consent.* New York: Plenum.

Grisso, T. (1986). *Evaluating competencies: Forensic assessments and instruments.* New York: Plenum

Grisso, T. (1988). *Competency to stand trial evaluations: A manual for practice.* Sarasota, FL: Professional Resource Exchange.

Grisso, T., & Applebaum, P. S. (1991). Mentally ill and non-mentally-ill patients' abilities to understand informed consent disclosures for medication: Preliminary data. *Law and Human Behavior, 15,* 377–388.

Grisso, T., & Saks, M. J. (1991). Psychology's influence on constitutional interpretation. *Law and Human Behavior, 15,* 205–211.

Grisso, T., Tomkins, A., & Casey, P. (1988). Psychosocial concepts in juvenile law. *Law and Human Behavior, 12,* 403–437.

Groves, P., & Schlesinger, K. (1979). *Introduction to biological psychology.* Dubuque, IA: Wm. C. Brown.

Grych, J. H., & Fincham, F. D. (1992). Interventions for children of divorce: Toward a greater integration of research and action. *Psychological Bulletin, 111,* 434–454.

Gudjonsson, G. H. (1988). How to defeat the polygraph tests. In A. Gale (Ed.), *The polygraph test: Lies, truth and science.* London: Sage.

Guilmette, T. J., & Faust, D. (1987, October). A survey of U. S. clinical neuropsychologists. *Presentation at the Annual Convention of the National Academy of Neuropsychologists,* Chicago, IL.

Guinther, J. (1988). *The jury in America.* New York: Roscoe Pound Foundation.

Guion, R. M. (1977). Content validity: Three years of talk—What's the action? *Public Personnel Management, 6,* 407–414.

Gusfield, J. (1980). *Illusions of authority.* Chicago: University of Chicago Press.

Haas, K. (1979). *Abnormal psychology.* New York: D. Van Nostrand.

Hafemeister, T. L., & Melton, G. B. (1987). The impact of social science research on the judiciary. In G. B. Melton (Ed.), *Reforming the law: Impact of child development research*. New York: Guilford.

Hafemeister, T. L., Ogloff, R. R. P., & Small, M.A. (1990). Training and Careers in Law and Psychology: The perspective of dual degree programs. *Behavioral Sciences and the Law, 8*, 263–283.

Hageman, M. J. C. (1978). Occupational stress and marital relationships. *Journal of Police Science and Administration, 6*, 402–409.

Hagerty, T. J. (1976). Police union studies job stress. *Wisconsin Law Enforcement Journal, 16*, 35.

Halleck, S. (1980). *Law in the practice of psychiatry*. Washington, DC: National Institute of Mental Health.

Halpern, A. L. (1974). Use and misuse of psychiatry incompetency examination of criminal defendants. *Psychiatric Annals, 8*, 3–17.

Hamparian, D. M., Estep, L. K., Muntean, S. M., Priestino, R. R., Swisher, R. G., Wallace, P. L., & White, J. L. (1982). *Youth in adult courts: Between two worlds*. Washington, DC: USGPO.

Haney, C. (1980). Psychology and legal change: On the limits of a factual jurisprudence. *Law and Human Behavior, 4*, 147–200.

Haney, C. (1984). Examining death qualification: Further analysis of the process effect. *Law and Human Behavior, 8*, 133–151.

Haney, C., Banks, W, Jaffe, D., & Zimbardo, P. (1973). Interpersonal dynamics in a simulated prison. *International Journal of Criminology, 1*, 69–97.

Hans, V. P. (1990). Law and the media: An overview and introduction. *Law and Human Behavior, 14*, 399–408.

Hargrave, G. E., & Hiatt, D. (1988). F+4+9+Cn: An MMPI measure of aggression in law enforcement officers and applicants. *Journal of Police Science and Administration, 16*, 268–273.

Hardisty, J. H. (1973). Mental illness: A legal fiction. *Washington Law Review, 48*, 735–762.

Hare, R. D. (1970). *Psychopathy: Theory and research*. New York: Wiley.

Hare, R. D. (1980). A research scale for the assessment of psychopathy in criminal populations. *Personality and Individual Differences, 1*, 111–119.

Hare, R. D. (1985). Comparison of procedures for the assessment of psychopathy. *Journal of Consulting and Clinical Psychology, 53*, 7–16.

Hare, R. D. (1991). *The Hare Psychopathy Checklist, Revised*. Toronto: Multi-Health Systems.

Hare, R. D., Forth, A. E., & Strachan, K. E. (1992). Psychopathy and crime across the life span. In R. D. Peters, R. J. McMahan, & V. L. Quinsey (Eds.), *Aggression and violence throughout the life span*. Newbury Park, CA: Sage.

Hare, R. D., & McPherson, L. M. (1984). Violent and aggressive behavior by criminal psychopaths. *International Journal of Law and Psychiatry, 7*, 35–50.

Hare, R. D., McPherson, L. M., & Forth, A. E. (1988). Male psychopaths and their criminal careers. *Journal of Consulting and Clinical Psychology, 56*, 710–714.

Hare, R. D., & Schalling, D. (Eds.). (1978). *Psychopathic behaviour: Approaches to research*. Chichester, England: Wiley.

Hargrave, G. E., & Hiatt, D. (1987). Law enforcement selection with the interview, MMPI, and CPI. *Journal of Police Science and Administration, 15*, 110–117.

Harmon, L. D. (1973, November). The recognition of faces. *Scientific American*, pp. 71–82.

Harris, G. T., Rice, M. E., & Cormier, C. A. (1991). Psychopathy and violent recidivism. *Law and Human Behavior, 15*, 625–637.

Harry, B., & Balcer, C. M. (1987). Menstruation and crime: A critical review of the literature from a clinical criminology perspective. *Behavioral Sciences and the Law, 5*, 307–321.

Hart, S. D., Kropp, P. R., & Hare, R. D. (1988). Psychopathy and conditional release from prison. *Journal of Consulting and Clinical Psychology, 56*, 227–232.

Hart, S. W. (1991). From property to person status: Historical perspective on children's rights. *American Psychologist, 46*, 53–59.

Harvard Law Review. (1985). The testimony of child victims in sex abuse prosecutions: Two legislative innovations. *Harvard Law Review, 98*, 806–827.

Harvey, J. H., & Smith, W. P. (1977). *Social psychology: An attribution approach*. St. Louis: C. V. Mosby.

Hastroudi, S., Parker, E. S., DeLisi, L. E., Wyatt, R. J., & Mutter, S. A. (1984). Intact retention in acute alcohol amnesia. *Journal of Experimental Psychology: Learning, Memory, and Cognition, 10*, 156–163.

Hatty, S. E., & Walker, J. R. (1986). *A national study of deaths in Australian prisons*. Camberra: Austrialian Institute of Criminology.

Haugaard, J. J., & Reppucci, N. D. (1988). *The sexual abuse of children*. San Francisco: Jossey-Bass.

Hawkins, S. A., & Hastie, R. (1990). Hindsight: Biased judgments of past events after the outcomes are known. *Psychological Bulletin, 107*, 311–327.

Hebb, D. O. (1955). Drives and the C.N.S. (Conceptual Nervous System). *Psychological Review, 62*, 243–254.

Heiman, M. F. (1975). Police suicides revisited. *Suicide, 5*, 5–20.

Heilbrun, K. S. (1987). The assessment of competency for execution: An overview. *Behavioral Sciences and the Law, 5*, 383–396.

Heilbrun, K. S. (1992). The role of psychological testing in forensic assessment. *Law and Human Behavior, 16*, 257–272.

Henderson, N. D. (1979). Criterion-related validity of personality and aptitude scales. In C. D. Spielberger (Ed.), *Police selection and evaluation: Issues and techniques*. Washington, DC: Hemisphere Publishing.

Hess, J. H., & Thomas, H. E. (1963). Incompetency to stand trial: Procedures, results and problems. *American Journal of Psychiatry, 119*, 713–720.

Hess, L.R. (1973). Police entry tests and their predictability of score in police academy and subsequent job performance. *Dissertation Abstracts International, 33-B*, 5552.

Hetherington, E. M. (1979). Divorce: A child's perspective. *American Psychologist, 34*, 851–858.

Hetherington, E. M., Stanley-Hagan, M., & Anderson, E. R. (1989). Martial transitions: A child's perspective. *American Psychologist, 44*, 303–312.

Heumann, M. (1978). *Plea bargaining: The experiences of prosecutors, judges, and defense attorneys*. Chicago: University of Chicago Press.

Hiatt, D., & Hargrave, G. E. (1988a). MMPI profiles of problem peace officers. *Journal of Personality Assessment, 52*, 722–731.

Hiatt, D., & Hargrave, G. E. (1988b). Predicting job performance problems with psychological screening. *Journal of Police Science and Administration, 16*, 122–125.

Hibbard, W., & Worring, R. (1982). *Psychic criminology*. Springield, IL: C. C. Thomas.

Hiday, V. A. (1977). Reformed commitment procedures: An empirical study in the courtroom. *Law and Society Review, 11*, 651–666.

Hiday, V. A. (1988). Civil commitment: A review of empirical research. *Behavioral Sciences and the Law, 6*, 15–44.

Hiday, V. A. (1990). Dangerousness of civil commitment candidates. *Law and Human Behavior, 14*, 551–567.

Hiday, V. A., & Scheid-Cook, T. L. (1987). The North Carolina experience with outpatient commitment: A critical appraisal. *International Journal of Law and Psychiatry, 10*, 215–232.

Hiday, V. A., & Scheid-Cook, T. L. (1989). A follow-up of chronic patients committed to outpatient treatment. *Hospital and Community Psychiatry, 40*, 52–58.

Higgins, L. L. (1961). *Policewoman's manual*. Springfield, IL: C. C. Thomas.

Hilgard, E. R. (1965). *Hypnotic susceptibility*. New York: Harcourt Brace Javanovich.

Hilton, J. (1973). Psychology and police work. In J. C. Anderson & P. J. Stead (Eds.), *The police we deserve*. London: Wolfe Publishers.

Hirschi, T. (1969). *Causes of delinquency*. Berkeley, CA: University of California Press.

Hoffman, M. L. (1970). Moral development. In H. Mussen (Ed.), *Carmichael's manual of child psychology* (Vol. 2). New York: Wiley.

Hogan, R. (1971). Personality characteristics of highly rated policemen. *Personnel Psychology, 24*, 679–686.

Hoge, S. K., Applebaum, P. S., Lawlor, T., Beck, J. C., Litman, R., Greer, A., Gutheil, T. G., & Kaplan, E. (1990). A prospective, multi-center study of patients' refusal of antipsychotic medication. *Archives of General Psychiatry, 47*, 949–956.

Hollien, H. (1980). Vocal indicators of psychological stress. In F. Wright, C. Bahn, & R. W. Rieber (Eds.), *Forensic psychology and psychiatry: Annals of the New York Academy of Sciences* (Vol. 347). New York: Academy of Sciences.

Holmes, T. H., & Masuda, M. (1974). Life change and illness susceptibility. In B. S. Dohrenwend & B. P. Dohrenwend (Eds.), *Stressful life events: Their nature and effects*. New York: Wiley.

Holmes, T. H., & Rahe, R. H. (1967). The social readjustment rating scale. *Journal of Psychosomatic Research, 11*, 213–218.

Holt, R. R. (1958). Clinical and statistical prediction: A reformulation and some new data. *Journal of Abnormal and Social Psychology, 56*, 1–12.

Honts, C. R. (1987). Interpreting research on polygraph countermeasures. *Journal of Police Science and Administration, 15*, 204–209.

Honts, C. R., Hodes, R. L., & Raskin, D. C. (1985). Effects of physical countermeasures on the physiological detection of deception. *Journal of Applied Psychology, 70*, 177–187.

Honts, C. R., & Perry, M. V. (1992). Polygraph admissibility: Changes and challenges. *Law and Human Behavior, 16*, 357–379.

Honts, C. R., Raskin, D. C., & Kircher, J. C. (1987). Effects of physical countermeasures and their electromyographic detection during polygraph tests for deception. *Journal of Psychophysiology, 1*, 241–247.

Hooke, J. F., & Krauss, H. H. (1971). Personality characteristics of successful police sergeant candidates. *Journal of Criminal Law, Criminology and Police Science, 62*, 104–106.

Horowitz, I. A., Bordens, K. S., & Feldman, M. S. (1980). A comparison of verdicts obtained in severed and joined criminal trials. *Journal of Applied Social Psychology, 10*, 444–456.

Horne, P. (1975). *Women in law enforcement*. Springfield, IL: C. C. Thomas.

Horney, J. (1978). Menstrual cycles and criminal responsibility. *Law and Human Behavior, 2*, 25–36.

Hotaling, G. T., & Straus, M. A. (1989). Intrafamily violence, and crime and violence outside the family. In L. Ohlin & M. Tonry (Eds.), *Family violence* (Vol. 11). Chicago: University of Chicago Press.

Horvath, F. S. (1977). The effect of selected variables on interpretation of polygraph records. *Journal of Applied Psychology, 62*, 127–136.

Howells, T. H. (1938). A study of ability to recognize faces. *Journal of Abnormal and Social Psychology, 33*, 124–127.

Hunt, Y. C., Jr. (1971). *Minority recruiting in the New York City Police Department: Part 1. The attraction of candidates*. New York: Rand Institute.

Iacono, W. G. (1984, May). Research on the guilty knowledge test. In D. T. Lykken (Chair), The detection of deception in 1984. *Symposium conducted at the meeting of the American Association for the Advancement of Science*, New York.

Iacono, W. G., & Patrick, C. J. (1987). What psychologists should know about lie detection. In I. B. Weiner & A. K. Hess (Eds.), *Handbook of forensic psychology*. New York: Wiley.

Iacono, W. G., Cerri, A. M., Patrick, C. J., & Fleming, J. A. E. (1992). Use of antianxiety drugs as countermeasures in the detection of guilty knowledge. *Journal of Applied Psychology, 77*, 60–64.

Inbau, F. E., & Reid, J. E. (1967). *Criminal interrogation and confessions*. Baltimore: Williams & Wilkins.

Interdivisional Committee on Adolescent Abortion. (1987). Adolescent abortion. *American Psychologist, 42*, 73–78.

Inwald, R., & Kenny, D. J. (1989). Psychological testing of police candidates. In D. J. Kenny (Ed.), *Police and policing: Contemporary issues*. New York: Praeger.

Inwald, R. E., Levitt, D. B., & Knatz, H. F (1980). Preemployment psychological evaluation as a predictor of correction officer job performance. *Paper presented at Meetings of the American Psychological Association*, Montreal.

Izzett, R., & Fishman, L. (1976). Defendant sentences as a function of attractiveness and justification for actions. *Journal of Social Psychology, 100*, 285–290.

Izzett, R., & Leginski, W. (1974). Group discussion and the influence of defendant characteristics in a simulated jury setting. *Journal of Social Psychology, 93*, 271–279.

Jacob, H. (1972). *Justice in America: Courts, lawyers, and the judicial process* (2nd ed.). Boston: Little, Brown.

Jacobi, H. (1975). Reducing police stress: A psychiatrist's point of view. In W. H. Kroes & J. Hurrell (Eds.), *Job stress and the police officer*. Washington, DC: U. S. Department of Health, Education, and Welfare.

James, F., Jr. (1965). *Civil procedure*. Boston: Little, Brown.

James, R. (1959). Status and competence of jurors. *American Journal of Sociology, 64*, 563–570.

James, W. (1962). *Essays on faith and morals.* New York: New American Library.

Jirak, M. (1975). Alienation among members of the New York City Police Department of Staten Island. *Journal of Police Science and Administration, 3,* 149–161.

Johnson, C., & Scott, B. (1976). Eyewitness testimony and suspect identification as a function of arousal, sex of witness, and scheduling of interrogation. *Paper presented at meeting of the American Psychological Association,* Washington, DC.

Johnson, H., & Steiner, I. (1967). Some effects of discrepancy level on relationships between authoritarianism and conformity. *Journal of Social Psychology, 9,* 179–183.

Johnson, L. B. (1991). Job strain among police officers: Gender comparisons. *Police Studies, 14,* 12–16.

Johnson, R. (1982). Life under the sentence of death. In R. Johnson & H. Toch (Eds.), *The pains of imprisonment.* Beverly Hills, CA: Sage.

Johnson, R. (1987). *Hard time: Understanding and reforming the prison.* Monterey, CA: Brooks/Cole.

Jones, R. A. (1977). *Self-fulfilling prophecies: Social, psychological, and physiological effects of expectancies.* Hillsdale, NJ: Erlbaum.

Julien, R. M. (1992). *A primer of drug action* (6th ed.). New York: W. H. Freeman.

Jurow, G. L. (1971). New data on the effect of a "death-qualified" jury on the guilt determination process. *Harvard Law Review, 84,* 567–611.

Kahneman, D., & Tversky, A. (1973). On the psychology of prediction. *Psychological Review, 80,* 237–251.

Kairys, D., Schulman, J., & Harring, S. (1975). *The jury system: New methods for reducing prejudice.* Philadelphia: National jury Project and National Lawyers Guild.

Kalven, H. Jr., & Zeisel, H. (1966). *The American jury.* Boston: Little, Brown.

Kanin, E. J. (1984). Date rape: Unofficial criminals and victims. *Victimology, 9,* 95–108.

Kaplan, M. F. (1977). Discussion polarization effects in a modified jury decision paradigm: Informational influences. *Sociometry, 40,* 262–271.

Kaplan, M. F., & Kemmerick, G. D. (1974). Juror judgments as information integration: Combining evidential and nonevidential information. *Journal of Personality and Social Psychology, 30,* 493–499.

Kaplan, M. F., & Miller, L. E. (1978). Reducing the effects of juror bias. *Journal of Personality and Social Psychology, 36,* 1443–1455.

Kaplan, M. F, & Schersching, C. (1981). Juror deliberation: An informational integration analysis. In B. D. Sales (Ed.), *Perspectives in law and psychology: Vol. 2. The trial process.* New York: Plenum.

Kaplan, S. (1985, July). Death, so say you all. *Psychology Today,* pp. 48–53.

Kasl, Q. V., & Mahl, G. F. (1965). The relationship of disturbances and hesitations in spontaneous speech to anxiety. *Journal of Personality and Social Psychology, 1,* 425–433.

Kassin, S. M., & Garfield, D. A. (1991). Blood and guts: General and trial-specific effects of videotaped crime scenes on mock jurors. *Journal of Applied Social Psychology, 21,* 1459–1472.

Kassin, S. M., Smith, V. L., & Tulloch, W. F. (1990). The dynamic charge: Effects on the perceptions and deliberation behavior of mock jurors. *Law and Human Behavior, 14,* 537–550.

Kassin, S. M., & Wrightsman, L. S. (1979). On the requirements of proof: The timing of judicial instruction and mock juror verdicts. *Journal of Personality and Social Psychology, 37,* 1877–1887

Katz, J. (1969). The right to treatment—An enchanting legal fiction. *University of Chicago Law Review, 36,* 755–788.

Katz, L. S., & Reid, J. F. (1977). Expert testimony on the fallibility of eyewitness identification. *Criminal Justice Journal, 1,* 177–206.

Keeler, E. (1984). *Lie detector man.* Boston: Telshare Publishing.

Keith-Spiegel, P. (1983). Children and consent to participate in research. In G. B. Melton, G. P. Koocher, and M. J. Saks (Eds.), *Children's competence to consent.* New York: Plenum.

Kelly, J. B. (1988). Longer-term adjustment in children of divorce: Converging findings and implications for practice. *Journal of Family Psychology, 2,* 119–140.

Kelman, H. C., & Hamilton, V. L. (1989). *Crimes of obedience.* New Haven, CT: Yale University Press.

Kennedy, T. D., & Haygood, R. C. (1992). The discrediting effect in eyewitness testimony. *Journal of Applied Social Psychology, 22*, 70–82.

Kenner, W. D. (1986). Competency on death row. *International Journal of Law and Psychiatry, 8*, 253–255.

Kenrick, D. T., & Stringfield, D. O. (1980). Personality traits and the eye of the beholder: Crossing some traditional philosophical boundaries in the search for consistency in all of the people. *Psychological Review, 87*, 88–104.

Kent, D. A., & Eisenberg, T. (1972, August). The selection and promotion of police officers: A selected review of recent literature. *The Police Chief*, pp. 20–29.

Kerlinger, F. N. (1973). *Foundations of behavioral research* (2nd ed.). New York: Holt, Rinehart & Winston.

Kerr, N. L., Nerenz, D., & Herrick, D. (1979). Role playing and the study of jury behavior. *Sociological Methods and Research, 7*, 337–355.

Kilmann, P. R., Sabalis, R. F., Gearing, M. L., Bukstel, L. H., & Scovern, A. W. (1982). The treatment of sexual paraphilias: A review of the outcome research. *Journal of Sex Research, 18*, 193–252.

Kilpatrick, D. G., Best, C. L., Saunders, B. E., & Veronen, L. J. (1988). Rape in marriage and in dating relationships: How bad is it for mental health. In R. A. Prentky & V. L. Quinsey (Eds.), *Human sexual aggression: Current perspectives*. New York: New York Academy of Sciences.

Kirscht, J. P., & Dillehay, R. C. (1967). *Dimensions of authoritarianism: A review of research and theory.* Lexington: University of Kentucky Press.

Kittrie, N. N. (1971). *The right to be different: Deviance and enforced therapy.* Baltimore: Johns Hopkins University Press.

Klassen, D., & O'Connor, W. (1985). Predicting violence among ex-mental patients: Preliminary research results. *Paper presented at the Annual Meeting of the American Society of Criminology*, Chicago.

Klassen, D., & O'Connor, W. (1988). Crime, inpatient admissions, and violence among male mental patients. *International Journal of Law and Psychiatry, 11*, 305–312.

Klassen, D., & O'Connor, W. (1990). Assessing the risk of violence in released mental patients: A cross-validation study. *Psychological Assessment: A Journal of Consulting and Clinical Psychology, 1*, 75–81.

Klatzky, R. L. (1975). *Human memory: Structures and processes.* San Francisco: W. H. Freeman & Co..

Klein, D. (1973). The etiology of female crime: A review of the literature. *Issues in Criminology, 8*, 3–30.

Knapp, M. L. (1978). *Nonverbal communication in human interaction* (2nd ed.). New York: Holt, Rinehart & Winston.

Knapp, M. L., Hart, R. P., & Dennis, H. S. (1974). An exploration of deception as a communication construct. *Human Communication Research, 1*, 15–29.

Knight, R. A., & Prentky, R. A. (1987). The development antecedents and adult adaptations of rapist subtypes. *Criminal Justice and Behavior, 14*, 403–426.

Knudsen, D. D. (1991). Child sexual coercion. In E. Grauerholz & M. A. Koralewski (Eds.), *Sexual coercion: A sourcebook on its nature, causes, and prevention.* Lexington, MA: Lexington Books.

Konecni, V. J., & Ebbesen, E. B. (1986). Courtroom testimony by psychologists on eyewitness identification issues: Critical notes and reflections. *Law and Human Behavior, 10*, 117–126.

Koocher, G. P. (1987). Children under law: The paradigm of consent. In G. B. Melton (Ed.), *Reforming the law: Impact of child development research.* New York: Guilford Press.

Koss, M. P., & Dinero, T. E. (1988). Predictors of sexual aggression among a national sample of male college students. In R. A. Prentky & V. L. Quinsey (Eds.), *Human sexual aggression: Current perspectives.* New York: New York Academy of Sciences.

Koss, M. P., Gidycz, C. A., & Wisniewski, N. (1987). The scope of rape: Incidence and prevalence of sexual aggression and victimization in a national sample of higher education students. *Journal of Consulting and Clinical Psychology, 55*, 162–170.

Kosson, D. S., Smith, S. S., & Newman, J. P. (1990). Evaluating the construct validity of psychopathy on Black and White male inmates: Three preliminary studies. *Journal of Abnormal Psychology, 99*, 250–259.

Kostlan, A. (1954). A method for the empirical study of psychodiagnosis. *Journal of Consulting Psychology, 18*, 83–88.

Koszuth, A. M. (1991). Sexually abused child syndrome: Res Ipsa Loquitur and shifting the burden of proof. *Law and Psychology Review, 15*, 277–297.

Kozol, H. L., Boucher, R. L., & Garofalo, R. F. (1972). The diagnosis and treatment of dangerousness. *Crime and Delinquency, 8,* 371–392.

Kramer, G. P., Kerr, N. L., & Carroll, J. S. (1990). Pretrial publicity, judicial remedies, and jury bias. *Law and Human Behavior, 14,* 409–438.

Kramer, T. H., Buckhout, R., & Eugenio, P. (1990). Weapon focus, arousal, and eyewitness memory: Attention must be paid. *Law and Human Behavior, 14,* 167–184.

Kratcoski, P. C. (1989). *Correctional counseling and treatment* (2nd ed.). Prospect Heights, IL: Waveland Press.

Kroes, W. H. (1976). *Society's victim—the policeman: An analysis of job stress in policing.* Springfield, IL: C. C. Thomas.

Kroes, W. H., Hurrell, J.J., & Margolis, B. (1974). Job stress in Police administrators. *Journal of Police Science and Administration, 2,* 381–387.

Kroes, W. H., Margolis, B. L., & Hurrell, J. J. (1974). Job stress in policemen. *Journal of Police Science and Administration, 2,* 145–155.

Kubis, J. (1973). *Comparison of voice analysis and polygraph as lie detection Procedures.* Aberdeen Proving Ground, MD: U. S. Army Land Warfare Laboratory.

Kubis, J. F. (1950). Experimental and statistical factors in the diagnosis of consciously suppressed affective experience. *Journal of Clinical Psychology, 6,* 12–16.

Kuhn, T. S. (1970). *The structure of scientific revolutions* (2nd ed.). Chicago: University of Chicago Press.

Kulka, R. A., & Kessler, J. B. (1978). Is justice really blind?—The influence of litigant physical attractiveness on juridical judgment. *Journal of Applied Social Psychology, 8,* 366–381.

Kulka, R.A., Schlenger, W. E., Fairbank, J. A., Hough, R. L., Jordan, B. K., Marmar, C. R., & Weiss, D. S. (1990). *Trauma and the Vietnam War generation: Report of findings from the National Vietnam Veterans Readjustment Study.* New York: Brunner/Mazel.

Kulka, R. A., Schlenger, W. E., Fairbank, J. A., Jordan, B. K., Hough, R. L., Marmar, C. R., & Weiss, D. S. (1991). Assessment of post-traumatic stress disorder in the community: Prospects and pitfalls from recent studies of Vietnam veterans. *Psychological Assessment: A Journal of Consulting and Clinical Psychology, 4,* 547–560.

Labovitz, S., & Hagedorn, R. (1971). An analysis of suicide rates among occupational categories. *Sociological Inquiry, 41,* 67–72.

Landau, S. F. (1978). Thought content of delinquent and nondelinquent young adults: The effect of institutionalization. *Criminal Justice and Behavior, 5,* 195–210.

Landy, D., & Aronson, E. (1969). The influence of the character of the criminal and his victim on the decisions of simulated jurors. *Journal of Experimental Social Psychology, 5,* 141–152.

Landy, F. J. (1976). The validity of the interview in police officer selection. *Journal of Applied Psychology, 61,* 193–198.

Langworthy, R. H. (1987). Police cynicism: What we know from the Niederhoffer scale. *Journal of Criminal Justice, 15,* 17–35.

Laughery, K. R., Alexander, J. E., & Lane, A. B. (1971). Recognition of human faces: Effects of target exposure time, target position, pose position, and type of photograph. *Journal of Applied Psychology, 55,* 477–483.

Laughery, K. R., Fessler, P K., Lenorovit, D. R., & Yoblick, D. A. (1974). Time delay and similarity effects in facial recognition. *Journal of Applied Psychology, 59,* 490–496.

Laughery, K. R., Duval, G. C., & Fowler, R. H. (1977). *Factors affecting facial recognition* (Rep. No. UHMUG-3). Houston: University of Houston, Mug File Project.

Laughery, K. R., & Fowler, R. H. (1978). Analysis of procedures for generating facial images. *Paper presented at the annual meeting of the American Psychological Association,* Toronto.

Laurence, J. R., & Perry, C. (1983). Hypnotically created memory among highly hypnotizable subjects. *Science, 222,* 523–524.

Lavrakas, P. J., Burl, J. R., & Mayzner, M. S. (1976). A perspective on the recognition of other-race faces. *Perception and Psychophysics, 20,* 475–481.

Law Enforcement Assistance Administration. (1977a). *Forcible rape: A national survey of the response by police.* Washington, DC: USGPO.

Law Enforcement Assistance Administration. (1977b). *Forcible rape: A national survey of the response by prosecutors.* Washington, DC: USGPO.

Law Enforcement Assistance Administration. (1978a). *Forcible rape: An analysis of legal issues.* Washington, DC: USGPO.

Law Enforcement Assistance Administration. (1978b). *Forcible rape: Final project report.* Washington, DC: USGPO.

Law Enforcement Assistance Administrator's State Court Caseload *Statistics: Annual Report, 1975.* (1979a). Washington, DC: USGPO.

Law Enforcement Assistance Administration. (1979b). *Prisoners in state and federal institutions on December 31, 1977.* Washington, DC: USGPO.

Law Enforcement Assistance Administration. (1979c). *Criminal victimization in the United States, 1977.* Washington, DC: USGPO.

Layson, S. (1985). Homicide and deterrence: A reexamination of the United States time series evidence. *Southern Economic Journal, 52,* 68–89.

Lazarus, R. S. (1966). *Psychological stress and the coping process.* New York: McGraw-Hill.

Leary, M. R. (1991). *Introduction to behavioral research methods.* Belmont, CA: Wadsworth.

Leestma, J. E. (1991). Neuropathology and pathophysiology of trauma and toxicity. In H. O. Doerr & A. S. Carlin (Eds.), *Forensic neuropsychology: Legal and scientific bases.* New York: Guilford Press.

Lefcourt, H. M. (1973). The function of the illusions of control and freedom. *American Psychologist, 28,* 417–425.

Lefkowitz, J. (1975). Psychological attributes of policemen: A review of research and opinion. *Journal of Social Issues, 31,* 3–26.

Lefkowitz, J. (1977). Industrial-organizational psychology and the police. *American Psychologist, 5,* 346–364.

Leifer, R. (1964). The psychiatrist and tests of criminal responsibility. *American Psychologist, 19,* 825–830.

Leippe, M. R. (1980). Effects of integrative memorial and cognitive processes on the correspondence of eyewitness accuracy and confidence. *Law and Human Behavior, 4,* 261–274.

Leippe, M. R., & Romanczyk, A. (1987). Children on the witness stand: A communication/persuasion analysis of jurors' reactions to child witness. In S. J. Ceci, M. P. Toglia, & D. F. Ross (Eds.), *Children's eyewitness memory.* New York: Springer-Verlag.

Leippe, M. R., Brigham, J. C., Cousins, C., & Romanczyk, A. (1989). The opinions and practices of criminal attorneys regarding child witnesses: A survey. In S. J. Ceci, D. F. Ross, & M. P. Toglia (Eds.), *Perspectives on children's testimony.* New York: Springer-Verlag.

Leippe, M. R., Manion, A. P., & Romanczyk, A. (1992). Eyewitness persuasion: How and how well fact finders judge the accuracy of adults' and children's memory reports. *Journal of Personality and Social Psychology, 63,* 181–197.

Leippe, M. R., & Romanczyk, A. (1989). Reactions to child (versus adult) eyewitnesses: The influence of jurors' preconceptions and witness behavior. *Law and Human Behavior, 13,* 103–132.

Leippe, M. R., Wells, G. L., & Ostrom, T. M. (1978). Crime seriousness as a determinant of accuracy in eyewitness identification. *Journal of Applied Psychology, 63,* 345–351.

Lempert, R. D. (1975). Uncovering "nondiscernible" differences: Empirical research and the jury-size cases. *Michigan Law Review, 73,* 643–708.

Lerner, M. J. (1970). The desire for justice and reactions to victims. In J. Macaulay, & L. Berkowitz (Eds.), *Altruism and helping behavior.* New York: Academic Press.

Lerner, M. J. (1977). The justice motive: Some hypotheses as to its origins and forms. *Journal of Personality, 45,* 1–52.

Lerner, M. J. (1980). *The belief in a just world: A fundamental delusion.* New York: Plenum.

Lerner, M. J., & Simmons, C. H. (1966). Observer's reaction to the "innocent victim": Compassion or rejection? *Journal of Personality and Social Psychology, 4,* 203–210.

Lester, D. (1992). Suicide in police officers. *Police Studies, 15,* 146–147.

Lester, D., Braswell, M., & Van Voorhis, P. (1992). *Correctional Counseling* (2nd ed.), Cincinnati, OH: Anderson Publishing.

Lester, D., & Danto, B. L. (1993). *Suicide behind bars: Prediction and prevention.* Philadelphia: The Charles Press.

Levi, J. (1990). The study of language in the judicial process. In J. Levi & A. G. Walker (Eds.), *Language in the judicial process.* New York: Plenum.

Levine, M., & Battistoni, L. (1991). The corroboration requirement in child sex abuse cases. *Behavioral Sciences and the Law, 9*, 3–20.

Lickey, M. E., & Gordon, B. (1991). *Medicine and mental illness.* New York: W. H. Freeman.

Liggett, J. (1974). *The human face.* London: Constable.

Lindsay, R. C. L., & Wells, C. L. (1980). What price justice? Exploring the relationship of lineup fairness to identification accuracy. *Law and Human Behavior, 4*, 303–313.

Lindsay, R. C. L., Wells, C. L., & Rumpel, C. M. (1981). Can people detect eyewitness identification within and across situations? *Journal of Applied Psychology, 66*, 79–89.

Lipton, D. N., McDonel, E. C., & McFall, R. M. (1987). Heterosocial perception in rapist. *Journal of Consulting and Clinical Psychology, 55*, 17–21.

Little, K. B., & Schneidman, E. S. (1959). Congruencies among interpretations of psychological test and anamnestic data. *Psychological Monographs, 73*(6, Whole No. 47).

Littlepage, G., & Pineault, T. (1978). Verbal, facial, and paralinguistic cues to the detection of truth and lying. *Personality and Social Psychology Bulletin, 4*, 461–464.

Litwack, T. R., & Schlesinger, L. B. (1987). Assessing and predicting violence: Research, law, and applications. In I. B. Weiner & A. K. Hess (Eds.), *Handbook of forensic psychology.* New York: Wiley.

Lloyd-Bostock, S. (1989). *Law in practice: Application of psychology to legal decision making and legal skills.* Chicago: Lyceum.

Loftus, E. F. (1975). Leading questions and the eyewitness report. *Cognitive Psychology, 7*, 560–572.

Loftus, E. F (1977). Shifting human color memory. *Memory and Cognition, 5*, 696–699.

Loftus, E. F. (1979). *Eyewitness testimony.* Cambridge, MA: Harvard University Press.

Loftus, E. F. (1980). Impact of expert psychology testimony on the unreliability of eyewitness identification. *Journal of Applied Psychology, 65*, 9–15.

Loftus, E. F. (1986). Ten years in the life of an expert witness. *Law and Human Behavior, 10*, 241–263.

Loftus, E. F., & Loftus, G. R. (1980). On the permanence of stored information in the human brain. *American Psychologist, 35*, 409–420.

Loftus, E. F., Loftus, G. R., & Messo, J. (1987). Some facts about "weapon focus." *Law and Human Behavior, 11*, 55–62.

Loftus, E. F., Miller, D. G., & Burns, H. J. (1978). Semantic integration of verbal information into a visual memory. *Journal of Experimental Psychology: Human Learning and Memory, 4*, 19–31.

Loftus, G R. (1972). Eye fixations and recognition memory. *Cognitive Psychology, 3*, 525–557.

Loftus, G. R., & Loftus, E. F. (1976). *Human memory: The processing of information.* Hillsdale, NJ: Erlbaum.

Loh, W. D. (1979). Psychology and law: A coming of age. *Contemporary Psychology, 24*, 164–166.

Loh, W. (1980). The impact of common law and reform rape statutes on prosecution: An empirical study. *Washington Law Review, 55*, 543–652.

Lott, A. J., & Lott, B. E. (1974). The role of reward in the formation of positive interpersonal attitudes. In T. Huston (Ed.), *Foundations of interpersonal attraction.* New York: Academic Press.

Lotz, R., & Regoli, R. M. (1977). Police cynicism and professionalism. *Human Relations, 30*, 176–186.

Lowery, C. R. (1984). The wisdom of Solomon: Criteria for child custody from the legal and clinical points of view. *Law and Human Behavior, 8*, 371–380.

Lowery, C. R. (1986). Maternal and joint custody: Differences in the decision process. *Law and Human Behavior, 10*, 303–316.

Luginbuhl, J., & Middendorf, K. (1988). Death penalty beliefs and jurors' responses to aggravating and mitigating circumstances in capital trials. *Law and Human Behavior, 12*, 263–281.

Luginbuhl, J. (1992). Comprehension of judges' instructions in the penalty phase of a capital trial. *Law and Human Behavior, 16*, 203–218.

Lurigio, A. J., & Carroll, J. S. (1985). Probation officers' schemata of offenders: Content, development, and impact on treatment decisions. *Journal of Personality and Social Psychology, 48*, 1112–1126.

Luus, C. A. E., & Wells, G. (1991). Eyewitness identification and the selection of distracters for lineups. *Law and Human Behavior, 15*, 43–57.

Lykken, D. T. (1957). A study of anxiety in the sociopathic personality. *Journal of Abnormal and Social Psychology, 55*, 6–10.

Lykken, D. T. (1974). Psychology and the lie detector industry. *American Psychologist, 29*, 725–739.

Lykken, D. T. (1978). The psychopath and the lie detector. *Psychophysiology, 15*, 137–142.

Lykken, D. T. (1981). *Tremor in the blood: Uses and abuses of the lie detector.* New York: McGraw-Hill.

Lykken, D. T. (1988). The case against polygraph testing. In A. Gale (Ed.), *The polygraph test: Lies, truth and science.* London: Sage.

Lyons, A., & Truzzi, M. (1991). *The blue sense: Psychic detectives and crime.* New York: Mysterious Press.

MacCoun, R. J., & Kerr, N. L. (1988). Asymmetric influences in mock jury deliberation: Jurors' bias for leniency. *Journal of Personality and Social Psychology, 54*, 21–33.

MacDonald, J. M. (1976). *Psychiatry and the criminal* (3rd ed.). Springfield, IL: C. C. Thomas.

MacKay, Lord of Clashfern. (1990). Introduction. In J. R. Spencer, G. Nicholson, R. Flin, & R. Bull (Eds.), *Children's evidence in legal proceedings: An international perspective.* University of Cambridge, England: Faculty of Law.

MacKenzie, D. L., & Goodstein, L. (1985). Long-term incarceration impacts and characteristics of long-term offenders: An empirical analysis. *Criminal Justice and Behavior, 12*, 395–414.

MacKenzie, D. L., Robinson, J. W., & Campbell, C. S. (1989). Long-term incarceration of female offenders: Prison adjustment and coping. *Criminal Justice and Behavior, 16*, 223–238.

MacLaughlin, G. H. (1953). The lie detector as an aid in arson and criminal investigation. *Journal of Criminal Law and Criminology, 43*, 693–694.

MacNitt, R. D. (1942). In defense of the electrodermal response and cardiac amplitude as measures of deception. *Journal of Criminal Law and Criminology, 33*, 266–275.

McCann, J. T. (1992). Criminal personality profiling in the investigation of violent crime: Recent advances and future direction. *Behavioral Sciences and the Law, 10*, 475–481.

McClintock, C. G., & Hunt, R. C. (1975). Nonverbal indicators of affect and deception in an interview setting. *Journal of Applied Social Psychology, 5*, 54–67.

McCloskey, M., Egeth, H., & McKenna, J. (1986). The experimental psychologist in court: The ethics of expert testimony. *Law and Human Behavior, 10*, 1–13.

McCorkle, R. C. (1992). Personal precautions to violence in prison. *Criminal Justice and Behavior, 19*, 160–173.

McDonough, L. B., & Monahan, J. (1975). The quality control of community caretakers: A study of mental health screening in a sheriffs department. *Community Mental Health Journal, 11*, 33–44.

McDowell, J. (1992, February 17). Are women better cops? *Time,* pp. 70–72.

McGarry, A. L. (1971). The fate of psychiatric offenders returned for trial. *American Journal of Psychiatry, 127*, 1181–1184.

McGinley, H., & Pasewark, R. A. (1989). National survey of the frequency and success of the insanity plea and alternate pleas. *Journal of Psychiatry and Law, 17*, 205–221.

McIntosh, J. L. (1991). Epidemiology of suicide in the U. S. In A. A. Leenaars (Ed.), *Life span perspectives of suicide.* New York: Plenum.

McKinney, T. S. (1973). *The criterion-related validity of entry level police officer selection procedures.* Phoenix, AZ: City of Phoenix Personnel Department.

McLean, P D. (1976). Depression as a specific response to stress. In I. G. Sarasuri & C. D. Spielberger (Eds.), *Stress and anxiety* (Vol. 3). Washington, DC: Hemisphere Publishing.

Maass, A., & Kohnken, G. (1989). Eyewitness identification: Simulating the "weapon effect." *Law and Human Behavior, 13*, 397–408.

Malamuth, N. M. (1981). Rape proclivity among males. *Journal of Social Issues, 37*, 138–157.

Mahoney, M. R. (1991). Legal images of battered women: Redefining the use of separation. *Michigan Law Review, 90*, 1–94.

Malloy, T. E., & Mays, G. L. (1984). The police stress hypothesis: A critical evaluation. *Criminal Justice and Behavior, 11*, 197–223.

Maloney, M. P., & Ward, M. P. (1976). *Psychological assessment: A conceptual approach.* New York: Oxford University Press.

Malpass, R. S., Lavigueur, H., & Weldon, D. E. (1973). Verbal and visual training in face recognition. *Perception and Psychophysics, 14*, 285–292.

Margolis, B. L. (1973). Stress is a work hazard too. *Industrial Medicine, Occupational Health and Surgery, 42*, 20–23.

Marin, B. V, Holmes, D. L., Guth, M., & Kovac, P. (1979). The potential of children as eyewitnesses: A comparison of children and adults on eyewitness tasks. *Law and Human Behavior, 3*, 295–306.

Mark, V. H., & Ervin, F. R. (1970). *Violence and the brain*. Hagerstown, MD: Harper & Row.

Marin, S. E. (1980). *Breaking and entering: Policewomen on patrol*. Berkeley, CA: University of California Press.

Marsh, J.C. (1988). What we have learned about legislative remedies for rape? In R. A. Prentky & V. L. Quinsey (Eds.), *Human sexual aggression: Current perspectives*. New York: New York Academy of Sciences.

Marsh, S. H. (1962). Validating the selection of deputy sheriffs. *Public Personnel Review, 23*, 41–44.

Marshall, J. (1966). *Law and psychology in conflict*. New York: Bobbs-Merrill.

Marshall, J. (1968). *Intention in law and society*. New York: Minerva Press.

Marshall, J. (1972). Trial, testimony and truth. In S. S. Nagel (Ed.), *The rights of the accused* (Vol. l). Beverly Hills, CA: Sage.

Marshall, W. L., & Barbaree, H. E. (1988). An outpatient treatment program for child molesters. In R. A. Prentky & V. L. Quinsey (Eds.), *Human sexual aggression: Current perspectives*. New York: New York Academy of Sciences.

Martell, D. A. (1991). Homeless mentally disordered offenders and violent crime. *Law and Human Behavior, 15*, 333–347.

Martell, D. A. (1992). Forensic neuropsychology and the criminal law. *Law and Human Behavior, 16*, 313–336.

Martin, M. J. (1972). Muscle-contraction headache. *Psychosomatics, 13*, 16–19.

Martin, S. E. (1980). *Breaking and entering: Policewomen on patrol*. Berkeley: University of California Press.

Martin, S. E. (1989). Women on the move?: A report on the status of women in policing. *Women and Criminal Justice, 1*, 21–40.

Martin, S. E. (1992). The effectiveness of affirmative action: The case of women in policing. *Justice Quarterly, 8*, 489–504.

Martin, T. C., & Bumpass, L. L. (1989). Recent trends in marital description. *Demography, 26*, 37–51.

Martinson, R. M. (1974). What works—questions and answers about prison reform. *Public Interest, 35*, 22–54.

Martinson, R. M. (1979). New findings, new views: A note of caution regarding sentencing reform. *Hofstra Law Review, 7*, 242–258.

Martinson, R. M., & Wilks, J. (1977). Save parole supervision. *Federal Probation, 41*, 23–27.

Maslach, C., & Jackson, S. E. (1981). The measurement of experienced burnout. *Journal of Occupational Behaviour, 2*, 99–113.

Matarazzo, J. D. (1990). Psychological assessment versus psychological testing. *American Psychologist, 45*, 999–1017.

Matarazzo, J. D., Allen, B. V, Saslow, G., & Wiens, A. (1964). Characteristics of successful policemen and firemen applicants. *Journal of Applied Psychology, 48*, 123–133.

May, P. R. (1968). *Treatment of schizophrenia: A comparison study of five treatment methods*. New York: Science House.

Mazer, D. (1978). Mental illness and the law. In W. K. Greenaway & S. L. Brickley (Eds.), *Law and social control in Canada*. Scarborough, Ont.: Prentice-Hall of Canada, 94–104.

Mears, F., & Gatchel, R. J. (1979). *Fundamentals of abnormal psychology*. Chicago: Rand McNally.

Meehl, P. E. (1954). *Clinical versus statistical prediction*. Minneapolis: University of Minnesota.

Meehl, P E. (1959). Some ruminations on the validation of clinical procedures. *Canadian Journal of Psychology, 13*, 102–128.

Meehl, P. E. (1965). Seer over sign: The first good example. *Journal of Experimental Research in Personalty, 1*, 27–32.

Meehl, P. E. (1971). Law and the fireside inductions: Some reflections of a clinical psychologist. *Journal of Social Issues, 27,* 65–100.

Meehl, P. E. (1986). Causes and effects of my disturbing little book. *Journal of Personality Assessment, 50,* 370–375.

Megargee, E. I. (1976). Population density and disruptive behavior in a prison setting. In A. K. Cohen, F. G. Cole, & R. G. Bailey (Eds.), *Prison violence.* Lexington, MA: Lexington Books.

Megargee, E. I. (1982). Psychological determinants and correlates of criminal violence. In M. E. Wolfgang & N. A. Wiender (Eds.), *Criminal violence.* Beverly Hills, CA: Sage.

Mehrabian, A. (1971). Nonverbal betrayal of feeling. *Journal of Experimental Research in Personality, 5,* 64–73.

Mehrabian, A., & Williams, M. (1969). Nonverbal concomitants of perceived and intended persuasiveness. *Journal of Personality and Social Psychology, 13,* 37–58.

Melton, G. B. (1983). Toward "personhood" for adolescents: Autonomy and privacy as values in public policy. *American Psychologist, 38,* 99–103.

Melton, G. B. (1987). Bringing psychology to the legal system: Opportunities, obstacles, and efficacy. *American Psychologist, 42,* 488–495.

Melton, G. B. (1990). Realism in psychology and humanism in law: Psycholegal studies in Nebraska. *Nebraska Law Review, 69,* 251–277.

Melton, G. B. (1992). The law is a good thing (psychology is, too): Human rights in psychological jurisprudence. *Law and Human Behavior, 16,* 381–398.

Melton, G. B., Petrila, J., Poythress, N. G., & Slobogin, C. (1987). *Psychological evaluations for the courts.* New York: Guilford Press.

Melton, G. B., & Russo, N. F. (1987). Adolescent abortion: Psychological perspectives on public policy. *American Psychologist, 42,* 69–72.

Melton, G. B., Weithorn, L., & Slobogin, C. (1985). *Community mental health center and the courts: An evaluation of community based forensic services.* Lincoln: University of Nebraska Press.

Memon, A., Dionne, R., Short, L., Maralani, S., MacKinnon, D., & Geiselman, R. E. (1988). Psychological factors in the use of photospreads. *Journal of Police Science and Administration, 16,* 62–69.

Menzies, R. J. (1989). *Survival of the sanest: Order and disorder in a pre-trial psychiatric clinic.* Toronto: University of Toronto Press.

Messick, S. (1980). Test validity and the ethics of assessment. *American Psychologist, 35,* 1012–1027.

Middendorf, K., & Luiginbuhl, J. (1981). Personality and the death penalty. *Paper presented at the Annual Meeting of the Southeastern Psychological Association,* Atlanta.

Miller, G. R., Bauchner, J. E., Hocking, J. E., Fontes, N. E., Kaminski, E. P., & Brandt, D. R. (1981). "…and nothing but the truth." How well can observers detect deceptive testimony? In B. D. Sales (Ed.), *Perspectives in law and psychology: Vol. 2. The trial process.* New York: Plenum.

Mills, C. J., & Bohannon, W. E. (1980). Personality characteristics of effective state police officers. *Journal of Applied Psychology, 65,* 680–684.

Mills, J. (1966). Opinion change as a function of the communicator's desire to influence and liking for the audience. *Journal of Experimental Social Psychology, 2,* 152–159.

Mills, J., & Jellison, J. (1967). Effect on opinion change of how desirable the communication is to the audience the communicator addressed. *Journal of Personality and Social Psychology, 6,* 98–101.

Mills, R. B. (1969). Use of diagnostic small groups in police recruit selection and training. *Journal of Criminal Law, Criminology, and Police Science, 60,* 238–241.

Mills, R. B. (1976). Simulated stress in police recruit selection. *Journal of Police Science and Administration, 4,* 179–186.

Mills, R. B., McDevitt, R. J., & Tonkin, S. (1966). Situational tests in metropolitan police recruit selection. *Journal of Criminal Law, Criminology, and Police Science, 57,* 99–104.

Miner, J. B. (1992). *Industrial-organizational psychology.* New York: McGraw-Hill.

Minor, P. L. (1989). The relevant-irrelevant technique. In S. Abrams (Ed.), *The complete polygraph handbook.* Lexington, MA: Lexington Books.

Miron, M. S. (1980). Issues of psychological evidence: Discussion. In F. Wright, C. Bahn, & R. W. Rieber (Eds.), *Forensic psychology and psychiatry: Vol. 347. Annals of the New York Academy of Sciences.* New York: New York Academy of Sciences.

Mischel, W. (1968). *Personality and assessment*. New York: Wiley.

Mischel, W. (1973). Toward a cognitive social learning reconceptualization of personality. *Psychological Review, 80*, 252–283.

Mischel, W. (1976). *Introduction to personality* (2nd ed.). New York: Holt, Rinehart & Winston.

Mischel, W. (1979). On the interface of cognition and personality: Beyond the person-situation debate. *American Psychologist, 34*, 740–754.

Mischel, W. (1981). *Introduction to personality* (3rd ed.). New York: Holt, Rinehart & Winston.

Mischel, W., & Mischel, H. N. (1977). *Essentials of psychology*. New York: Random House.

Mitchell, H. E., & Byrne, D. (1973). The defendant's dilemma: Effects of jurors' attitudes and authoritarianism on judicial decisions. *Journal of Personality and Social Psychology, 25*, 123–129.

Moini, S., & Hammett, T. M. (1990). *1989 update: AIDS in correctional facilities*. U. S. Department of Justice, Washington, DC: USGPO.

Mokhiber, R. (1988). *Corporate crime and violence*. San Francisco: Sierra Club Books.

Monahan, J. (1973). Abolish the insanity defense? Not yet. *Rutgers Law Review, 26*, 719–740.

Monahan, J. (1976). Violence prediction. *Virginia Law Review, 27*, 179–183.

Monahan, J. (1977). Social accountability: Preface to an integrated theory of criminal and mental health sanctions. In B. D. Sales (Ed.), *Perspectives in law and psychology: Vol. 1. The criminal justice system*. New York: Plenum.

Monahan, J. (1978). The prediction of violent criminal behavior: A methodological critique and prospectus. In A. Blumstein, (Ed.), *Deterrence and incapacitation: Estimating the effects of criminal sanctions on crime rates*. Washington, DC: National Academy of Sciences.

Monahan, J. (Ed.). (1980). *Who is the client? The ethics of Psychological intervention in the criminal justice system*. Washington, DC: American Psychological Association.

Monahan, J. (1981). *Predicting violent behavior: An assessment of clinical techniques*. Beverly Hills, CA: Sage.

Monahan, J. (1984). The prediction of violent behavior: Toward a second generation of theory and policy. *American Journal of Psychiatry, 141*, 10–15.

Monahan, J. (1992a). Risk assessment of violence: The MacArthur research. *The Correctional Psychologist, 24*, 1, 3.

Monahan, J. (1992b). Mental disorder and violent behavior: Perceptions and evidence. *American Psychologist, 47*, 511–521.

Monahan, J. (1993). Limiting therapist exposure to *Tarasoff* liability: Guidelines for risk containment. *American Psychologist, 48*, 242–250.

Monahan, J., Ruggiero, M., & Friedlander, H. (1982). The Stone-Roth model of civil commitment and the California dangerousness standard: An operational comparison. *Archives of General Psychiatry, 39*, 1267–1271.

Monahan, J., & Shah, S. A. (1989). Dangerousness and commitment of the mentally disordered in the United States. *Schizophrenia Bulletin, 15*, 541–553.

Monahan, J., & Steadman, H. J. (in press). Toward a rejuvenation of risk assessment research. In J. Monahan & H. J. Steadman (Eds.), *Violence and mental disorder: Developments in risk assessment*. Chicago: University of Chicago Press.

Monahan, J., & Walker, L. (1988). Social science research in law: A New paradigm. *American Psychologist, 43*, 465–472.

Monahan, J., & Walker, L. (1990). *Social science and law: Cases and materials* (2nd ed.). Westbury, NY: The Foundation Press.

Monahan, J., & Wexler, D. B. (1978). A definite maybe: Proof and probability in civil commitment. *Law and Human Behavior, 2*, 37–42.

Monson, T. C., & Snyder, M. (1977). Actors, observers, and the attribution process: Toward a reconceptualization. *Journal of Experimental Social Psychology, 13*, 89–111.

Moran, G., & Comfort, J. (1986). Neither "tentative" nor "fragmentary": Verdict preference of impaneled felony jurors as function of attitudes toward capital punishment. *Journal of Applied Psychology, 71*, 146–155.

Moran, G., & Cutler, B. L. (1991). The prejudicial impact of pretrial publicity. *Journal of Applied Social Psychology, 21*, 345–367.

More, H. W. (1992). *Special topics in policing*. Cincinnati, OH: Anderson Publishing.

Morris, N. (1974). *The future of imprisonment*. Chicago: The University of Chicago Press.

Morris, N., & Miller, M. (1985). Prediction of dangerousness. In M. Tonry & N. Morris (Eds.), *Crime and justice: An annual review of research (Vol. 7)*. Chicago: University of Chicago Press.

Morris, R. A. (1989). The admissibility of evidence derived from hypnosis and polygraphy. In D. C. Raskin (Ed.), *Psychological methods in criminal investigation and evidence*. New York: Springer-Verlag.

Morse, S. J. (1978a). Crazy behavior, morals, and science: An analysis of mental health law. *Southern California Law Review, 51*, 527–654.

Morse, S. J. (1978b). Law and mental health professionals: The limits of expertise. *Professional Psychology, 9*, 389–399.

Morse, S. J. (1985). Excusing the crazy: The insanity defense reconsidered. *Southern California Law Review, 58*, 777–836.

Morse, S. J. (1986). Why amnesia and the law is *not* a useful topic. *Behavioral Sciences and the Law, 4*, 99–102.

Mossman, D. (1987). Assessing and restoring competency to be executed: Should psychologists participate? *Behavioral Sciences and the Law, 5*, 397–409.

Mowrer, O. H. (1960). *Learning theory and behavior*. New York: Wiley.

Mullineaux, J. E. (1955). An evaluation of the predictors used to select patrolmen. *Public Personnel Review, 16*, 84–86.

Murphy, J. J. (1972). Current practices in the use of psychological testing by police agencies. *The Journal of Criminal Law, Criminology and Police Science, 63*, 570–576.

Murray, H., et al. (1948). *Assessment of men: Selection of personnel for the Office of Strategic Services*. New York: Rinehart.

Myers, D. G. (1993). *Social psychology* (4th ed.). New York: McGraw-Hill.

Myers, D. G., & Kaplan, M. F. (1976). Group-induced polarization in simulated juries. *Personality and Social Psychology Bulletin, 2*, 63–66.

Myers, D. G., & Lamm, H. (1976). The group polarization phenomenon. *Psychological Bulletin, 83*, 602–627.

Myers, J. E. B. (1985–86). The legal response to child abuse: In the best interests of children? *Journal of Family Law, 24*, 149–244.

Nacci, P. L., Teitelbaum, H. E., & Prather, J. (1977). Population density and inmate misconduct rates in the federal prison system. *Federal Probation, 41*, 26–31.

Narrol, H. G., & Levitt, E. E. (1963). Formal assessment procedures in police selection. *Psychological Reports, 12*, 691–694.

Nemeth, C., & Sosis, R. M. (1973). A simulated jury: Characteristics of the defendant and the jurors. *Journal of Social Psychology, 90*, 221–229.

Nicholson, R. A., Briggs, S. R., & Robertson, H. C. (1988a). Instruments for assessing competency to stand trial: How do they work? *Professional Psychology: Research and Practice, 19*, 383–394.

Nicholson, R. A., & Kugler, K. E. (1991). Competent and incompetent criminal defendants: A quantitative review of comparative research. *Psychological Bulletin, 109*, 355–370.

Nicholson, R. A., Robertson, H. C., Johnson, W. G., & Jensen, G. (1988b). A comparison of instruments for assessing competency to stand trial. *Law and Human Behavior, 12*, 313–321.

Niederhoffer, A. (1967). *Behind the shield: The police in urban society*. New York: Doubleday.

Nigro, G. N., Buckley, M. A., Hill, D. E., & Neslon, J. (1989). When juries "hear" children testify: The effects of eyewitness age and speech style on jurors' perceptions of testimony. In S. J. Ceci, D. F. Ross, & M. P. Toglia (Eds.), *Perspectives on children's testimony*. New York: Springer-Verlag.

Nimmer, R. T. (1977). The system impact of criminal justice. In J. L. Tapp & F. J. Levine (Eds.), *Law, justice, and the individual in society*. New York: Holt, Rinehart & Winston.

Nisbett, R. E., & Borgida, E. (1975). Attribution and the psychology of prediction. *Journal of Personality and Social Psychology, 32*, 932–943.

Nisbett, R. E., Borgida, E., Crandall, R., & Reed, H. (1976). Popular induction: Information is not necessarily informative. In J. S. Carroll & J. W. Payne (Eds.), *Cognition and social behavior*. Hillsdale, NJ: Erlbaum.

Nixon, M. (1990). Professional training in psychology: Quest for international standards. *American Psychologist, 45*, 1257–1262.

Nowicki, S. (1966). A study of the personality characteristics of successful policemen. *Police, 11*, 39–41.

O'Brien, M. D. (1971). Cerebral blood change in migraine. *Headache, 10,* 139–143.

O'Brien, M. D. (1973). The hemodynamics of migraine—A review. *Headache, 12,* 160–162.

O'Hara, C. E. (1970). *Fundamentals of criminal investigation.* Springfield, IL: C. C. Thomas.

O'Leary, K. D., & Curley, A. D. (1986). Assertion and family violence: Correlates of spouse abuse. *Journal of Marital and Family Therapy, 12,* 281–289.

Olson, B. T. (1973). Police opinions of work: An exploratory study. In J. R. Snibbe & H. M. Snibbe (Eds.), *The urban policeman in transition.* Springfield, IL: C. C. Thomas.

Ondrovik, J., & Hamilton, D. (1991). Credibility of victims diagnosed as multiple personality: A case study. *American Journal of Forensic Psychology, 9,* 13–17.

Opinion Research Corporation. (1968). *Police-community relations: A survey among New York City patrolmen.* Ann Arbor, MI: University Microfilms.

Orne, M. T. (1970). Hypnosis, motivation and the ecological validity of the psychological experiment. In W. J. Arnold & M. M. Page (Eds.), *Nebraska symposium on motivation.* Lincoln: University of Nebraska Press.

Orne, M. T., Dinges, D. F., & Orne, E. C. (1984). On the differential diagnosis of multiple personality in the forensic context. *The International Journal of Clinical and Experimental Hypnosis, 32,* 118–169.

Orne, M. T., Whitehouse, W. G., Dinges, D. F., & Orne, E. C. (1988). Reconstructing memory through hypnosis: Forensic and clinical implications. In H. M. Pettinati (Ed.), *Hypnosis and memory.* New York: Guilford Press.

Owings, C. (1925). *Women police: A study of the development and status of the woman police movement.* New York: F. H. Hitchcock.

Padawer-Singer, A. M., & Barton, A. H. (1975). The impact of pretrial publicity on jurors' verdicts. In R. J. Simon (Ed.), *The jury system in America.* Beverly Hills, CA: Sage.

Padawer-Singer, A. M., Singer, A. N., & Singer, R. L. J. (1974). Voir dire by two lawyers: An essential safeguard. *Judicature, 57,* 386–391.

Palmer, T. (1992). *The re-emergence of correctional intervention.* Newberry Park, CA: Sage.

Parry, C. D. H., Turkheiner, E., Hundley, P., & Creskoff, E. (1991). A comparison of respondents in commitment and recommitment hearings. *Law and Human Behavior, 15,* 315–324.

Partridge, A., & Bermant, G. (1978). *The quality of advocacy in the federal courts.* Washington, DC: Federal Judicial Center.

Passingham, R. G. (1972). Crime and personality: A review of Eysenck's theory. In V. D. Nebylitsyn & J. A. Gray (Eds.), *Biological bases of individual behavior.* New York: Academic Press.

Patrick, A. (1988). The crowding crisis: A global view. *Corrections Today, 50,* 110–115.

Patterson, B. L. (1992). Job experience and perceived job stress among police, correctional, and probation/parole officers. *Criminal Justice and Behavior, 19,* 260–265.

Paulus, P. B. (1988). *Prison crowding: A psychological perspective.* New York: Springer-Verlag.

Pelissier, B. (1991). The effects of a rapid increase in prison population. *Criminal Justice and Behavior, 18,* 427–447.

Pendergrass, V. E., & Ostrove, N. M. (1984). A survey of stress in women in policing. *Journal of Police Science and Administration, 12,* 303–309.

Pendergrass, V. E., & Ostrove, N. M. (1986). Correlates of alcohol use of police personnel. In J. T. Reese & H. A. Goldstein (Eds.), *Psychological services for law enforcement.* Washington, DC: USGPO.

Pennington, N., & Hastie, R. (1981). Juror decisionmaking models: The generalization gap. *Psychological Bulletin, 89,* 246–287.

Pennington, N., & Hastie, R. (1986). Evidence evaluation in complex decision making. *Journal of Personality and Social Psychology, 51,* 242–258.

Penrod, S., & Cutler, B. L. (1987). Assessing the competence of juries. In I. B. Weiner & A. K. Hess (Eds.), *Handbook of forensic psychology.* New York: Wiley

Penrod, S., & Hastie, R. (1979). Models of jury decision making: A critical review. *Psychological Bulletin, 86,* 462–492.

Perlin, M. L. (1991). Power imbalances in therapeutic and forensic relationships. *Behavioral Science and the Law, 9,* 111–128.

Perry, C. W., Laurence, J. R., D'eon, J., & Tallant, B. (1988). Hypnotic age regression techniques in the elicitation of memories: Applied uses and abuses. In H. M. Pettinati (Ed.), *Hypnosis and memory*. New York: Guilford Press.

Peters, D. P. (1987). The impact of naturally occurring stress on children's memory. In S. J. Ceci, M. P. Toglia, & D. F. Ross (Eds.), *Children's eyewitness memory*. New York: Springer-Verlag.

Peterson, J. L., & Zill, N. (1986). Marital description, parent-child relationships, and behavior problems in children. *Journal of Marriage and the Family, 48,* 295–307.

Pettinati, H. M. (1988). Hypnosis and memory: Integrative summary and future directions. In H. M. Pettinati (Ed.), *Hypnosis and memory*. New York: Guilford Press.

Petrila, J. (1992). Redefining mental health law. Thoughts on a new agenda. *Law and Human Behavior, 16,* 89–106.

Pinizzotto, A. J. (1984). Forensic psychology: Criminal personality profiling. *Journal of Police Science and Administration, 12,* 32–40.

Pinizzotto, A. J., & Finkel, N. J. (1990). Criminal personality profiling: An outcome and process study. *Law and Human Behavior, 14,* 215–234.

Platz, S. J., & Hosch, H. M. (1988). Cross-racial/ethnic eyewitness identification: A field study. *Journal of Applied Social Psychology, 18,* 972–984.

Pleck, E. (1989). Criminal approaches to family violence, 1640–1980. In L. Ohlin & M. Tonry (Eds), *Family violence* (Vol. 11). Chicago: University of Chicago Press.

Pliner, A. J., & Yates, S. (1992). Psychological and legal issues in minors' rights to abortion. *Journal of Social Issues, 48,* 203–216.

Podlesny, J. A., & Raskin, D. C. (1977). Physiological measures and the detection of deception. *Psychological Bulletin, 84,* 782–799.

Poland, J. M. (1978). Police selection methods and the prediction of police performance. *Journal of Police Science and Administration, 6,* 374–393.

Pontell, H. N., Jesilow, P. D., & Geis, G. (1984). Practitioner fraud and abuse in medical benefit programs. *Law and Policy, 6,* 405–424.

Popper, K. (1962). *Conjectures and refutations: The growth of scientific knowledge*. New York: Basic Books.

Poythress, N. G. (1979). A proposal for training in forensic psychology. *American Psychologist, 34,* 612–621.

Poythress, N. G., Otto, R. K., Darkes, J., & Starr, L. (1993). APA's expert panel in the Congressional review of the USS Iowa incident. *American Psychologist, 48,* 8–15.

Prentky, R. A. (1979). Creativity and psychopathology: A neurocognitive perspective. In B. Maher (Ed.), *Progress in experimental research* (Vol. 9). New York: Academic Press.

Prentky, R. A., & Knight, R. A. (1986). Impulsivity in the life style and criminal behavior of sexual offenders. *Criminal Justice and Behavior, 13,* 141–164.

President's Commission on Law Enforcement and Administration of justice. (1967). *The challenge of crime in a free society*. Washington, DC: USGPO.

Quay, H. C. (1977). The three faces of evaluation. What can be expected to work. *Criminal Justice and Behavior, 4,* 341–354.

Quinsey, V. L., & Marshall, W. L. (1983). Procedures for reducing inappropriate sexual arousal: An evaluation review. In J. G. Greer & I. R. Stuart (Eds.), *The sexual aggressor*. New York: Van Nostrand-Reinhold.

Radcliff, D. H. (1977). Pennsylvania child custody: The tender years doctrine. *Dickenson Law Review, 81,* 775–792.

Radelet, M. L., & Bernard, G. W. (1986). Ethics and the psychiatric determination of competency to be executed. *Bulletin of the American Academy of Psychiatry and Law, 14,* 37–53.

Rafky, D. M. (1974). My husband the cop. *Police Chief, 41,* 62–65.

Rafky, D. M., Lawley, T., & Ingram, R, (1976). Are police recruits cynical? *Journal of Police Science and Administration, 4,* 352–360.

Rafkey, D., & Sealey, R. (1975). The adolescent and the law: A survey. *Crime and Delinquency, 21,* 131–138.

Rafter, N. H. (1992). Criminal anthropology in the United States. *Criminology, 30,* 525–546.

Rahe, R. H., Mahan, J. L., & Arthur, R. J. (1970). Prediction of near-future health changes from subject's preceding life changes. *Journal of Psychosomatic Research, 14,* 401–406.

Rankin, J. H. (1957). Psychiatric screening of police recruits. *Public Personnel Review, 20,* 191–196.

Raskin, D. C. (1988). Does science support polygraph testing? In A. Gale (Ed.), *The polygraph test: Lies, truth and science.* London: Sage.

Regoli, R. M. (1976). The effects of college education on the maintenance of police cynicism. *Journal of Police Science and Administration, 4,* 340–351.

Regoli, B., Crank, J. P., & Rivera, G. F. (1990). The construction and implementation of an alternative measure of police cynicism. *Criminal Justice and Behavior, 17,* 395–409.

Reiner, R. (1992). Police research in the United Kingdom: A critical review. In M. Tonry & N. Morris (Eds.), *Modern policing.* Chicago: University of Chicago Press.

Reiser, M. (1973). *Practical psychology for police officers.* Springfield, IL: C. C. Thomas.

Reiss, A. J. (1967). Career orientations, job satisfaction and the assessment of law enforcement problems by officers. *Studies in crime and law enforcement in major metropolitan areas* (Vol. 2). Washington, DC: USGPO.

Reiss, A. J. (1992). Police organizations in the twentieth century. In M. Tonry & N. Morris (Eds.), *Modern policing.* Chicago: University of Chicago Press.

Reynolds, E. D., & Sanders, M. S. (1973, April). The effects of defendant attractiveness, age, and injury on severity of sentence given by simulated jurors. *Paper presented at the meeting of the Western Psychological Association,* San Francisco.

Rhead, C., Abrams, A., Trasman, H., & Margolis, P. (1968). The psychological assessment of police candidates. *American Journal of Psychiatry, 124,* 1575–1580.

Richard, W. C., & Fell, R. D. (1975, May). Health factors in police job stress. *Paper presented at the symposium on job stress and the police officer.* National Institute for Occupational Safety and Health, Cincinnati, OH.

Riflin, J. (1989). Mediation in the justice system: A paradox for women. *Women and Criminal Justice, 1,* 41–54.

Risin, L. I., & M. P. Koss. (1987). The sexual abuse of boys: Childhood victimizations reported by a national sample. *Journal of Interpersonal Violence, 2,* 309–323.

Roberts, E. F. (1961). Paradoxes in law enforcement. *Journal of Criminal Law, Criminology and Police Science, 52,* 224–228.

Roberts, J. V., & Gebobtys, R. J. (1992). Reforming rape laws: Effects of legislative change in Canada. *Law and Human Behavior, 16,* 555–573.

Robin, A., & MacDonald, D. (1975). *Lessons of leukotomy.* London: Henry Kimpton.

Roesch, R., & Golding, S. (1979). Treatment and disposition of defendants incompetent to stand trial: A review and proposal. *International Journal of Legal Psychiatry, 2,* 349.

Roesch, R., & Golding, S. (1980). *Competency to stand trial.* Urbana-Champaign, IL: University of Illinois Press.

Roesch, R., & Golding, S. (1987). Defining and assessing competency to stand trial. In I. B. Weiner & A. K. Hess, (Eds.), *Handbook of forensic psychology.* New York: Wiley.

Rogers, R., & Cavanaugh, J. L. (1981). Rogers criminal responsibility assessment scales. *Illinois Medical Journal, 160,* 164–169.

Rogers, R., Cavanaugh, J. L., Seman, W., & Harris, M. (1984a). Legal outcome and clinical findings: A study of insanity evaluations. *Bulletin of the American Academy of Psychiatry and the Law, 12,* 75–83.

Rogers, R., Wasyliw, O. E., and Cavanaugh, J. L. (1984b). Evaluating insanity: A study of construct validity. *Law and Human Behavior, 8,* 293–304.

Rohman, L. W., Sales, B. D., & Lou, M. (1987). The best interests of the child in custody disputes. In L. A. Weithorn (Ed.), *Psychology and child custody determinations.* Lincoln, NE: University of Nebraska Press.

Roper, R. (1980). Jury size and verdict consistency: "The line has to be drawn somewhere"? *Law and Society Review, 14,* 977–995.

Rosenbaum, R. (1991). *Travels with Dr. Death: and other unusual investigations.* New York: Penquin.

Rosenfeld, H. M. (1966). Approval-seeking and approval-inducing functions of verbal and nonverbal responses in the dyad. *Journal of Personality and Social Psychology, 4,* 597–605.

Rosenhan, D. L., & Seligman, M. E. P. (1984). *Abnormal psychology.* New York: Norton

Rosenkoetter, L. I. (1973). Resistance to temptation: Inhibitory and disinhibitory effects of models. *Developmental Psychology, 8*, 80–84.

Rosenzweig, M. R. (1992). Psychological science around the world. *American Psychologist, 47*, 718–722.

Rosner, R. (1989). Forensic psychiatry: A subspeciality. *Bulletin of the American Academy of Psychiatry and Law, 17*, 323–333.

Ross, D. F., Dunning, D., Toglia, M. P., & Ceci, S. J. (1990). The child in the eyes of the jury: Assessing mock jurors' perceptions of the child witness. *Law and Human Behavior, 14*, 5–23.

Ross, D. F., Dunning, D., Toglia, M. P., & Ceci, S. J. (1989). Age stereotypes, communication modality, and mock jurors' perceptions of the child witness. In S. J. Ceci, D. F. Ross, & M. P. Toglia (Eds.), *Perspectives on children's testimony.* New York: Springer-Verlag.

Rotenberg, K. J., Simourd, L., & Moore, D. (1989). Children's use of a verbal-nonverbal consisting principle to infer truth and lying. *Child Development, 60*, 309–322.

Rothman, D. J. (1971). *The discovery of the asylum: Social order and disorder in the new republic.* Boston: Little, Brown.

Rothman, D. J. (1980). *Conscience and convenience.* Boston: Little, Brown.

Rotter, J. B. (1954). *Social learning and clinical psychology.* Englewood Cliffs, NJ: Prentice-Hall.

Rotter, J. B. (1966). Generalized expectancies for internal versus external control of reinforcement. *Psychological Monographs, 80* (Whole No. 609).

Rotter, J. B. (1972). Beliefs, social attitudes and behavior: A social learning analysis. In J. B. Rotter, J. E. Chance, & E. J. Phares (Eds.), *Applications of social learning theory of personality.* New York: Holt, Rinehart & Winston.

Rottschaefer, W., & Knowlton, W. (1979). A cognitive social learning theory perspective on human freedom. *Behaviorism, 7*, 17–21.

Ruback, R. B., & Carr, T. S. (1984). Crowding in a woman's prison: Attitudinal and behavioral effects. *Journal of Applied Social Psychology, 14*, 57–68.

Ruback R. B., Carr, T. S., & Hopper, C. (1986). Perceived control in prison: Its relation to reported crowding, stress, and symptoms. *Journal of Applied Social Psychology, 16*, 375–386.

Ruback, R. B., & Innes, C. A. (1988). The relevance and irrelevance of psychological research: The example of prison crowding. *American Psychologist, 43*, 683–693.

Rubin, B. (1972). Predictions of dangerousness in mentally ill criminals. *Archives of General Psychiatry, 27*, 397–407.

Rubin, Z., & Peplau, A. (1973). Belief in a just world and reactions to another's lot: A study of participants in the national draft lottery. *Journal of Social Issues, 29*, 73–93.

Rubin, Z., & Peplau, A. (1975). Who believes in a just world? *Journal of Social Issues, 31*, 65–89.

Rubinsky, E. W., & Brandt, J. (1986). Amnesia and criminal law: A clinical overview. *Behavioral Sciences and the Law, 4*, 27–46.

Rumsey, M. G., & Castore, C. H. (1974). The effect of group discussion on juror sentencing. *Paper Presented at the Annual Meeting of the Midwestern Psychological Association*, Chicago.

Russell, D. E. H. (1983). The prevalence and incidence of forcible rape and attempted rape of females. *Victiminology: An International Journal, 7*, 81–93.

Russo, N. F. (1986). Adolescent abortion: The epidemiological context. In G. B. Melton (Ed.), *Adolescent abortion: Psychological and legal issues.* Lincoln, NE: University of Nebraska Press.

Russo, N. F. (1992). Psychological aspects of unwanted pregnancy and its resolution. In J. D. Butler & D. F. Walbert (Eds.), *Abortion, medicine, and the law* (4th ed.). New York: Facts on File.

Russo, N. F., Horn, J. D., & Schwartz, R. (1992). U. S. abortion in context: Selected characteristics and motivations of women seeking abortions. *Journal of Social Issues, 48*, 183–202.

Ryan, H., & Taylor, M. (1988). Information usage and cue identification as a function of experience in police officers. *Journal of Police Science and Administration, 16*, 177–181.

Rychlak, J. F. (1968). *A philosophy of science for personality theory.* Boston: Houghton Mifflin.

Rychlak, J. F. (1979). *Discovering free will and personal responsibility.* New York: Oxford University Press.

Sadoff, R. L. (1975). *Forensic psychiatry.* Springfield, IL: C. C. Thomas.

Sagatun, I. J. (1991). Expert witnesses in child abuse cases. *Behavioral Sciences and the Law, 9*, 201–215.

Saks, M. J. (1974). Ignorance of science is no excuse. *Trial, 10*, 18–24.

Saks, M. J. (1977). *Fury verdicts.* Lexington, MA: Lexington Books.

Saks, M.J. (1990). Expert witnesses, nonexpert witnesses and nonwitness experts. *Law and Human Behavior, 14*, 291–313.

Saks, M. J., & Hastie, R. (1978). *Social psychology in court*. New York: Van Nostrand-Reinhold.

Saks, M. J., & Kidd, R. F. (1980–81). Human information processing and adjudication: Trial by heuristics. *Law and Society Review, 15*, 123–160.

Saks, M. J., & Krupat, E. (1988). *Social psychology and its Applications*. Cambridge, MA: Harper & Row.

Saks, M. J., & Miller, M. (1979). A systems approach to discretion in the legal process. In L. E. Abt & L. R. Stuart (Eds.), *Social psychology and discretionary law*. New York: Van Nostrand-Reinhold.

Saks, M. J., & Ostrom, T M. (1975). Jury size and consensus requirements: The laws of probability vs. the laws of the land. *Journal of Contemporary Law, 1*, 163–173.

Sanders, G. S., & Simmons, W. L. (1983). Use of hypnosis to enhance eyewitness accuracy: Does it work? *Journal of Applied Psychology, 68*, 70–77.

Sandy, J. P., & Devine, D. A. (1978, September). Four stress factors unique to rural patrol. *The Police Chief*, pp. 42–44.

Santilli, L. E., & Roberts, M. C. (1990). Custody decisions in Alabama before and after the abolition of the tender years doctrine. *Law and Human Behavior, 14*, 123–136.

Sants, H. J. (1964). Genealogical bewilderment in children with substitute parents. *British Journal of Medical Psychology, 37*, 133–141.

Sappington A. A. (1990). Recent psychological approaches to the free will versus determinism issue. *Psychological Bulletin, 108*, 19–29.

Sarason, I. C., & Stoops, R. (1978). Test anxiety and the passage of time. *Journal of Consulting and Clinical Psychology, 46*, 102–108.

Sawyer, J. (1966). Measurement and prediction, clinical and statistical. *Psychological Bulletin, 66*, 178–200.

Schacter, D. L. (1986a). On the relation between genuine and simulated amnesia. *Behavioral Sciences and the Law, 4*, 47–64.

Schacter, D. L. (1986b). Amnesia and crime: How much do we really know. *American Psychologist, 41*, 286–295.

Schechter, M. D., & Bertocci, D. (1990). The meaning of search. In D. M. Brodzinsky & M. D. Sechechter (Eds.), *The Psychology of adoption*. New York: Oxford University Press.

Schlueter, M., Tubbs, F., & Ryan, K. F. (1991). *A profile of municipal police departments in Vermont*. Northfield, VT: Vermont Criminal Justice Center.

Schuller, R. A. (in press). The impact of battered woman syndrome testimony on jury decision processes. *Law and Human Behavior*.

Schuller, R. A., & Vidmar, N. (1992). Battered woman syndrome evidence in the courtroom: A review of the literature. *Law and Human Behavior, 16*, 272–292.

Schulman, J., Shaver, P., Colman, R., Emrich, B., & Christie, R. (1973, May). *Psychology Today*, pp. 37–83.

Schwartz, H. I., Vingiano, W., & Perez, C. B. (1990). Autonomy and the right to refuse treatment: Patients' attitudes after involuntary medication. In D. B. Wexler (Ed.), *Therapeutic jurisprudence*. Durham, NC: Carolina Academic Press.

Schwartz, I. M. (Ed.). (1992). *Juvenile justice and public policy*. New York: Lexington Books.

Schwitzgebel, R. K. (1974). The right to effective mental treatment. *California Law Review, 62*, 936–956.

Schwitzgebel, R. K. (1977). Professional accountability in the treatment and release of dangerous persons. In B. D. Sales (Ed.), *Perspectives in law and Psychology: Vol. 1. The criminal justice system*. New York: Plenum.

Schwitzgebel, R. L., & Schwitzgebel, R. K. (1980). *Law and psychological practice*. New York: Wiley.

Scott, J., & Derdeyn, E. (1984). Rethinking joint custody. *Ohio State Law Journal, 45*, 455–498.

Scully, D., & Marolla, J. (1984). Convicted rapists' vocabulary of motive: Excuses and justification. *Social Problems, 31*, 530–544.

Sechrest, D. K. (1989). Prison "boot camps" do not measure up. *Federal Probation, 53*, 15–20.

Segal, S., Watson, M., Goldfinger, S., & Averbuck, D. (1988). Civil commitment in the psychiatric emergency room: II. Mental disorder indicators and three dangerousness criteria. *Archives of General Psychiatry, 45,* 753–758.

Seligman, M. E. (1975). *Helplessness: On depression, development, and death.* San Francisco: W. H. Freeman.

Selkin, J. (1987). *Psychological autopsy in the courtroom.* Denver, CO: Author.

Sellin, T. (1959). *The death penalty.* Philadelphia, PA: The American Law Institute.

Selye, H. (1976). *The stress of life* (2nd ed.). New York: McGraw-Hill.

Serin, R. C. (1991). Psychopathy and violence in criminals. *Journal of Interpersonal Violence, 6,* 423–431.

Serin, R. C., Peters, R. D., & Barbaree, H.E. (1990). Predictors of psychopathy and release outcome in a criminal population. *Psychological Assessment: A Journal of Consulting and Clinical Psychology, 2,* 419–422.

Sewell, J. D. (1983). The development of a critical life events scale for law enforcement. *Journal of Police Science and Administration, 11,* 109–116.

Sewell, J. D., Ellison, K. W., & Hurrell, J. J. (1988, October). Stress management in law enforcement: Where do we go from here? *Police Chief,* pp. 94–99.

Shaffer, T. L. (1973). Introduction. *Santa Clara Lawyer, 13,* 369–376.

Shapiro, D. L. (1990). *Forensic psychological assessment: An integrative approach.* Boston: Allyn & Bacon.

Shapiro, M., & Tresolini, R. J. (1979). *American constitutional law* (5th ed.). New York: Macmillan.

Shaw, J. H. (1986). Effectiveness of the MMPI in differentiating ideal from undesirable police officer applicants. In J. Reese & H. A. Goldstein (Eds.), *Psychological services for law enforcement.* Washington, DC: USGPO.

Sheehan, P. W., & Tilden, J. (1983). Effects of suggestibility and hypnosis on accurate and distorted retrieval from memory. *Journal of Experimental Psychology: Learning, Memory, and Cognition, 9,* 283–293.

Sheehan, P. W., & Tilden, J. (1984). Real and simulated occurrences of memory distortion in hypnosis. *Journal of Abnormal Psychology, 93,* 47–57.

Shepherd, J. W. & Ellis, H. D. (1973). The effect of attractiveness on recognition memory for faces. *American Journal of Psychology, 86,* 627–633.

Sherman, L. (1992). Attacking crime: Policing and crime control. In M. Tonry & N. Morris (Eds.), *Modern policing.* Chicago: University of Chicago Press.

Sherman, L. W., & Berk, R. A. (1984). The specific deterrent effects of arrest for domestic assault. *American Sociological Review, 49,* 261–272.

Sherman, M. (1979). *Personality: Inquiry and application.* New York: Pergamon Press.

Shoemaker, D. J., South, D. R., & Lowe, J. (1973). Facial stereotypes of deviants and judgments of guilt or innocence. *Social Forces, 51,* 427–433.

Siegel, D. (1984). Multiple personality as a post-traumatic stress disorder. *Psychiatric Clinics of North America, 7,* 101–104.

Siegel, A.M., & Elwork, A. (1990). Treating incompetence to stand trial. *Law and Human Behavior, 14,* 57–65.

Siegel, L. J. (1992). *Criminology* (4th ed.). St. Paul, MN: West.

Sigall, H., & Ostrove, N. (1975). Beautiful but dangerous: Effects of offender attractiveness and nature of the crime on juridic judgment. *Journal of Personality and Social Psychology, 31,* 410–414.

Sigall, H., & Landy, D. (1972). Effects of the defendant's character and suffering on juridic judgement: A replication and clarification. *Journal of Personality and Social Psychology, 88,* 149–150.

Simon, R. J. (1980). The impact of pretrial publicity on the jury. In R. J. Simon (Ed.), *The jury: Its role in American society.* Lexington, MA: Lexington Books.

Simon, R., & Aaronson, D. E. (1988). *The insanity defense.* New York: Praeger.

Simpson, S. (1989). Feminist theory, crime and justice. *Criminology, 27,* 605–632.

Sims, V. (1982, July). Rural and small town police. *The Police Chief,* pp. 29–30.

Singer, M. T., & Nievod, A. (1987). Consulting and testifying in court. In I. B. Weiner & A. K. Hess (Eds.), *Handbook of forensic psychology.* New York: Wiley.

Skolnick, J. (1973). A sketch of the policeman's working personality. In A. Niederhoffer & A. S. Blumberg (Eds.), *The ambivalent force.* San Francisco: Rinehart Press.

Skouron, S. E., Scott, J. E., & Cullen, F. T. (1989). The death penalty for juveniles: An assessment of public support. *Crime and Delinquency, 35,* 546–561.

Slater, P. E. (1958). Contrasting correlates of group size. *Sociometry*, *21*, 129–139.

Slobogin, C. (1989). The "ultimate issue" issue. *Behavioral Sciences and the Law*, *7*, 259–266.

Slobogin, C. (1985). The guilty but mentally ill verdict: An idea whose time should not have come. *George Washington Law Review*, *53*, 494–580.

Slobogin, C., Melton, G. B., & Showalter, C. R. (1984). The feasibility of a brief evaluation of mental state at the time of offense. *Law and Human Behavior*, *8*, 305–321.

Slovenko, R. (1989). The multiple personality: A challenge to legal concepts. *The Journal of Psychiatry and Law*, Winter, 681–719.

Small, M. H., & Otto, R. K. (1991). Evaluations of competency to be executed: Legal contours and implications for assessment. *Criminal Justice and Behavior*, *18*, 146–158.

Smigel, E. O. (1964). *The Wall Street lawyer*. New York: Free Press.

Smith, B. M. (1967). The polygraph. *Scientific American*, *216*, 25–31.

Smith, C. E., & Felix, R. R. (1986). Beyond deterrence: A study of defenses on death row. *Federal Probation*, *50*, 55–59.

Smith, G. A., & Hall, J. A. (1982). Evaluating Michigan's guilty but mentally ill verdict: An empirical study. *Michigan Journal of Law Reform*, *16*, 75–112.

Smith, R. R. (1991). New study reports U. S. has highest incarceration rate in the world. *Correctional Psychologist*, *23*, 1.

Smith, V. L. (1991). Prototypes in the courtroom: Lay representations of legal concepts. *Journal of Personality and Social Psychology*, *61*, 857–872.

Sobeloff, S. G. (1958). From M'Naghten to Durham and beyond. In R. W. Nice (Ed.), *Crime and insanity*. New York: Philosophical Library.

Solomon, M. R., & Schopler, J. (1978). The relationship of physical attractiveness and punitiveness: Is the linearity assumption out of line? *Personality and Social Psychology Bulletin*, *4*, 483–486.

Solomon, R. M., & Horn, J. M. (1986). Post-shooting traumatic reactions: A pilot study. In J. T. Reese & H. A. Goldstein (Eds.), *Psychological services for law enforcement*. Washington, DC: USGPO.

Somodevilla, S. A. (1978, April). The psychologists' role in the police department. *The Police Chief*, pp. 21–23.

Somodevilla, S. A. (1978). The role of psychologists in a police department. In W. Taylor & M. Braswell (Eds.), *Issues in Police and Criminal Psychology*. Washington, DC: University Press of America.

Soskin, W. F. Influence of four types of data on diagnostic conceptualization in psychological testing. *Journal of Abnormal and Social Psychology*, *58*, 69–78.

Spiegel, D., & Spiegel, H. (1987). Forensic uses of hypnosis. In I. B. Weiner & A. K. Hess (Eds.), *Handbook of forensic psychology*. New York: Wiley.

Spielberger, C. D. (Ed.). (1979). *Police selection and evaluation: Issues and techniques*. Washington, DC: Hemisphere Publishing.

Spielberger, C. D., Spaulding, H. C., & Ward, J. C. (1978). *Selecting effective law enforcement officers: The Florida police standards research project*. Tampa, FL: Human Resources Institute.

Spielberger, C. D., Ward, J. C., & Spaulding, H. C. (1979). A model for the selection of law enforcement officers. In C. D. Spielberger (Ed.), *Police selection and evaluation: Issues and techniques*. Washington, DC: Hemisphere Publishing.

Spielberger, R. D. (1966). The effects of anxiety on complex learning and academic achievement. In C. D. Spielberger (Ed.), *Anxiety and behavior*. New York: Academic Press.

Spitzer, R. L., & Fleiss, J. (1974). A re-analysis of the reliability of psychiatric diagnosis. *British Journal of Psychiatry*, *125*, 341–347.

Stalnaker, J. M., & Riddle, E. F. (1932). The effect of hypnosis on long-delayed recall. *Journal of General Psychology*, *6*, 429–440.

Staub, E. (1978). *Positive social behavior and morality: Social and personal influences* (Vol. 1). New York: Academic Press.

Steadman, H. J. (1976). Predicting dangerousness. In D. J. Madden & J. R. Lion (Eds.), *Rage•hate•assault and other forms of violence*. New York: Spectrum.

Steadman, H. J. (1979). *Beating a rap?* Chicago: University of Chicago Press.

Steadman, H. J. (1985). Insanity defense research and treatment of insanity acquittees. *Behavioral Sciences and the Law, 3,* 37–48.

Steadman, H. J. (1992). Boundary spanners: A key component for the effective interactions of the justice and mental health systems. *Law and Human Behavior, 16,* 75–87.

Steadman, H. J., Callahan, L. A., Robbins, P. C., & Morrissey, J. P. (1989). The maintenance of an insanity defense under Montana's abolition. *American Journal of Psychiatry, 146,* 357–360.

Steadman, H. J., & Cocozza, J. J. (1974). *Careers of the criminally insane.* Lexington, MA: Lexington Books.

Steadman, H. J., & Hartstone, E. (1983). Defendants incompetent to stand trial. In J. Monahan & H. J. Steadman (Eds.), *Mentally disordered offenders.* New York: Plenum.

Steadman, H. J., McCarty, D. W., & Morrissey, J. P. (1989) *The mentally ill in jail: Planning for essential services.* New York: Guilford Press.

Steadman, H. J., McGreevy, M. A., Morrisey, J. P., Callahan, L. A., Robbins, P. C., & Cirincione, C. (1993). *Before and after Hinckley: Evaluating insanity defense reform.* New York: Guilford Press.

Steadman, H. J., Monahan, J., Appelbaum, P. S., Grisso, T., Mulvery, E. P., Roth, L. H., Robbins, P. C., & Klassen, D. (in press). Designing a new generation of risk assessment research. In J. Monahan & H. Steadman (Eds.), *Violence and mental disorder: Developments in risk assessment.* Chicago: University of Chicago Press.

Steinmetz, S. K. (1977). *The cycle of violence: Assaultive, aggressive, and abusive family interaction.* New York: Praeger.

Stephan, C., & Tully, J. C. (1977). The influence of physical attractiveness of a plaintiff on the decisions of simulated jurors. *Journal of Social Psychology, 101,* 149–150.

Stewart, J. E. (1980). Defendant's attractiveness as a factor in the outcome of criminal trials: An observational study. *Journal of Applied Social Psychology, 10,* 348–361.

Stier, S. D., & Stoebe, K. J. (1979). Involuntary hospitalization of the mentally ill in Iowa: The failure of the 1975 legislation. *Iowa Law Review, 64,* 1284–1458.

Stone, A. (1975). *Mental health and law: A system in transition.* Washington, DC: USGPO.

Stone, A. (1976). The Tarasoff decisions: Suing psychotherapists to safeguard society. *Harvard Law Review, 90,* 358–388.

Stoner, J. A. F. (1961). *A comparison of individual and group decisions involving risk.* Unpublished master's thesis, School of Industrial Management, MIT.

Stotland, E. (1986). Police stress and strain as influenced by police self-esteem, time on job, crime frequency and interpersonal relationships. In J. T. Reese & H. A. Goldstein (Eds.), *Psychological services for law enforcement.* Washington, DC: USGPO.

Stotland, E. (1991). The effects of police work and professional relationships on health. *Journal of Criminal Justice, 19,* 371–379.

Stotland, E., & Berberich, J. (1979). The psychology of the police. In H. Toch (Ed.), *Psychology of crime and criminal justice.* New York: Holt, Rinehart & Winston.

Stotland, E., Pendleton, M., & Schawartz, R. (1989). Police stress, time on the job, and strain. *Journal of Criminal Justice, 17,* 55–60.

Stratton, J. G. (1978, May). Police stress: An overview. *The Police Chief,* pp. 58–62.

Stratton, J., Parker, D., & Snabbe, J. (1984). Post-traumatic stress: Study of police officers involved in shooting. *Psychological Reports, 55,* 127–131.

Straus, M. A., & Gelles, R. J. (1986). Societal change and change in family violence from 1975 to 1985 as revealed by two national surveys. *Journal of Marriage and the Family, 48,* 465–479.

Straus, M. A., Gelles, R. J., & Steinmetz, S. K. (1980). *Behind closed doors: Violence in the American family.* New York: Doubleday.

Strawn, D. U., & Buchanan, R. W. (1976). Jury confusion: A threat to justice. *Judicature, 5,* 478–483.

Strodtbeck, F. L., & Hook, L. H. (1961). The social dimensions of a twelve-man jury table. *Sociometry, 24,* 397–415.

Strodtbeck, F. L., James, R., & Hawkins, C. (1957). Social status in jury deliberation. *American Sociological Review, 22,* 713–719.

Strodtbeck, F. L., & Mann, R. (1956). Sex role differentiation in jury deliberations. *Sociometry, 29,* 3–11.

Strube, M. J. (1988). The decision to leave an abusive relationship: Empirical evidence and theoretical issues. *Psychological Bulletin, 104,* 236–250.

Sue, S., Smith, R. E., & Caldwell, C. (1973). Effects of inadmissible evidence on the decisions of simulated jurors: A moral dilemma. *Journal of Applied Social Psychology, 3,* 345–353.

Suedfeld, P., Ramirez, C., Deaton, J., & Baker-Brown, G. (1982). Reactions and attributes of prisoner in solitary confinement. *Criminal Justice and Behavior, 9,* 303–340.

Suggs, D., & Sales, B. D. (1978). The art and science of conducting the voir dire. *Professional Psychology, 9,* 367–388.

Summit, R. C. (1983). The child sexual abuse accommodation syndrome. *Child Abuse and Neglect, 7,* 177–193.

Sutherland, E. H. (1939). *Criminology* (3rd ed.) Philadelphia: Lippincott.

Sutherland, E. H. (1949). *White collar crime.* New York: Holt, Rinehart & Winston.

Sutherland, E. H., & Cressey, D. R. (1974). *Criminology* (9th ed.). Philadelphia: Lippincott.

Sutker, P. B., Uddo-Crane, M., & Allain, A. N. (1991). Clinical and research assessment of posttraumatic stress disorder: A conceptual overview. *Psychological Assessment: A Journal of Consulting and Clinical Psychology, 3,* 520–530.

Swanson, J., & Holzer, C. (1991). Violence and the ECA data. *Hospital and Community Psychiatry, 42,* 79–80.

Swanson, J., Holzer, C., Ganji, V., & Jono, R. (1990). Violence and psychiatric disorder in the community: Evidence from the epidemiologic catchment area surveys. *Hospital and Community Psychiatry, 41,* 761–770.

Szasz, T. S. (1960). The myth of mental illness. *American Psychologist, 15,* 113–118.

Szasz, T. S. (1968). *Law, liberty, and psychiatry.* New York: Collier Books.

Tagatz, G. E., & Hess, L. R. (1972). *Police entry tests and their predictability of score in police academy and subsequent job performance.* Milwaukee: The Center for Criminal Justice.

Tageson, C. W. (1982). *Humanistic psychology: A synthesis.* Homewood, IL: Dorsey Press.

Tanford, J. A. (1986). An introduction to trial law. *Missouri Law Review, 51,* 623–740.

Tanford, J. A. (1990). The law and psychology of jury instructions. *Nebraska Law Review, 69,* 71–111.

Tanford, S., & Cox, M. (1987). Decision processes in civil cases: The impact of impeachment evidence on liability and credibility judgments. *Social Behavior, 2,* 165–182.

Tanford, S., & Cox, M. (1988). The effects of impeachment evidence and limiting instructions on individual and group decision making. *Law and Human Behavior, 12,* 477–497.

Tanford, S., & Penrod, S. (1982). Biases in trials involving defendants charged with multiple offenses. *Journal of Applied Social Psychology, 12,* 453–480.

Tanford, S., & Penrod, S. (1984). Social inference processes in juror judgments of multiple-offense trials. *Journal of Personality and Social Psychology, 47,* 749–765.

Tanford, S., & Penrod, S. (1986). Jury deliberations: Discussion content and influence processes injury decision making. *Journal of Applied Social Psychology, 16,* 322–347.

Tappan, P. W. (1949). Who is the criminal? *American Sociological Review, 12,* 100–110.

Terry, W. C. (1985). Police stress: The empirical evidence. In A. Blumberg & E. Niederhoffer (Eds.), *Ambivalent force* (2nd ed.). New York: Holt, Rinehart & Winston.

Thomas, N. H. (1978). The use of biofeedback training in alleviation of stress in the police officer. In W. Taylor & M. Braswell (Eds.), *Issues in police and criminal psychology.* Washington, DC: University Press of America.

Thurstone, L. L. (1922). The intelligence of policemen. *Journal of Personnel Research, 1,* 64–74.

Toch, H. (1982). The disturbed disruptive inmate: Where does the bus stop? *Journal of Psychology and Law, 10,* 327–349.

Toch, H., & Adams, K. (1989a). *The disturbed offender.* New Haven, CT: Yale University Press.

Toch, H., & Adams, K. (1989b). *Coping: Maladaption in prisons.* New Brunswick, NJ: Transaction Publishers.

Tonry, M. (1987). Prediction and classification: Legal and ethical issues. In D. M. Gottfredson & M. Tonry (Eds.), *Prediction and classification.* Chicago: University of Chicago Press.

Tooley, V., Brigham, J. C., Maas, A., & Bothwell, R. K. (1987). Facial recognition: Weapon effect and attentional focus. *Journal of Applied Social Psychology, 17,* 845–859.

Torres, A., & Forrest, J. D. (1988). Why do women have abortions? *Family Planning Perspectives, 20,* 169–176.

Trovillo, P. V. (1939). A history in lie detection. *Journal of Criminal Law and Criminology, 29,* 848–881.

Truax, C. B., & Mitchell, K. M. (1971). Research on certain therapist interpersonal skills in relation to process and outcome. In A. E. Bergin & S. L. Garfield (Eds.), *Handbook of psychotherapy and behavior change.* New York: Wiley.

Tucker, G. J., & Neppe, V. M. (1991). Neurological and neuropsychiatric assessment of brain injury. In H. O. Doerr & A. S. Carlin (Eds.), *Forensic neuropsychology: Legal and scientific bases.* New York: Guilford Press.

Tufts' New England Medical Center, Division of Child Psychiatry. (1984). *Sexually exploited children: Service and research project.* Final report for the Office of Juvenile Justice and Delinquency Prevention, Washington, DC: USGPO.

Turkheimer, E., & Parry, C. D. H. (1992). Why the gap? Practice and policy in civil commitment hearings. *American Psychologist, 47,* 646–655.

Tyler, T. R. (1990). *Why people obey the law.* New Haven, CT: Yale University Press.

Unger, C. A., & Buchanan, R. A. (1985). *Managing longterm inmates: A guide for the correctional administrator* (Report to the National Institute of Corrections). Washington, DC: U. S. Department of Justice.

Unikovic, C. M., & Brown, W. R. (1978, April). The drunken cop. *The Police Chief,* pp. 18–20.

U. S. Department of Justice. (1988). *Report to the nation on crime and justice* (2nd ed.). Washington, DC: USGPO.

U. S. Department of Justice (1990). *Census of local jails in 1988.* Washington, DC: USGPO.

U. S. Department of Justice (1991). *Correctional populations in the United States, 1989.* Washington, DC: USGPO.

U. S. Department of Health and Human Services. (1982). *National study of the incidence of child abuse and neglect.* Washington, DC: USGPO.

U. S. Department of Health and Human Services. (1988). *Study findings: Study of national incidence of child abuse and neglect.* Washington, DC: USGPO.

Ursin, H., Baade, E., & Levine, S. (1978). *Psychobiology of stress: A study of coping men.* New York: Academic Press.

Vago, S. (1991). *Law and society* (3rd ed.). Englewood Cliffs, NJ: Prentice-Hall.

Vander Zander, J. W. (1977). *Social psychology.* New York: Random House.

Vena, J., Violanti, J., Marshall, J., & Fielder, R. (1986). Mortality of a municipal worker cohort: III. Police officer. *American Journal of Industrial Medicine, 10,* 383–397.

Verinis, J. S., & Walker, V. (1970). Policemen and the recall of, criminal details. *Journal of Social Psychology, 81,* 217–222.

Vidmar, N. (1979). The other issues in jury simulation research: A commentary with particular reference to defendant character studies. *Law and Human Behavior, 3,* 95–106.

Vidmar, N., & Ellsworth. P. C. (1974). Public opinion and the death penalty. *Stanford Law Review, 26,* 1245–1270.

Violanti, J. M. (1983). Stress patterns in police work: A longitudinal study. *Journal of Police Science and Administration, 11,* 211–216.

Violanti, J. M. (1992). *Police retirement: The impact of change.* Springfield, IL: C. C. Thomas.

Wagstaff, G. F. (1982). Hypnosis and recognition of a face. *Perceptual and Motor Skills, 55,* 816–818.

Waid, W. M., Orne, E. C., Cook, M. R., & Orne, M. T. (1981). Meprobamate reduces accuracy of physiological detection of deception. *Science, 212,* 71–73.

Walbert, D. F. (1971). The effect of jury size on the probability of conviction: An evaluation of *Williams v. Florida. Case Western Research Law Review, 22,* 529–554.

Walker, L. E. (1979). *The battered woman.* New York: Harper Colophon Books.

Walker, L. E. (1983) Victimology and the psychological perspectives of battered women. *Victimology, 8,* 82–90.

Walker, L. E. (1984). *The battered woman syndrome.* New York: Springer.

Walker, L. E. (1989) Psychology and violence against women. *American Psychologist, 44,* 695–702.

Walker, T. G., & Main, E. C. (1973). Choice-shifts in Political decision making: Federal judges and civil liberties cases. *Journal of Applied Social Psychology, 2,* 39–48.

Wall, P. M. (1965). *Eyewitness identification in criminal cases.* Springfield, IL: C. C. Thomas.

Wallerstein, J. S. (1989, January 23). Children after divorce: Wounds that don't heal. *The New York Times Magazine,* pp. 19–21, 41–44.

Wallerstein, J. S., & Kelly, J. (1980). *Surviving the breakup: How children and parents cope with divorce.* New York: Basic Books.

Wallerstein, J. S., & Wyle, J. (1947). Our law-abiding law breakers, *Probation, 25,* 107–112.

Walters, G. C., & Grusec, J. E. (1977). *Punishment.* San Francisco: W. H. Freeman.

Walters, R. H., Callagan, J. E., & Newman, A. F. (1963). Effects of solitary confinement on prisoners. *American Journal of Psychiatry, 119,* 771–773.

Walters, R. H., & Parke, R, D. (1964). Emotional arousal, isolation, and discrimination learning in children. *Journal of Experimental Child Psychology, 1,* 269–280.

Warren, C. (1977). Involuntary commitment for mentally disordered: The application of California's Lanterman-Petris-Short Act. *Law and Society Review, 11,* 629–649.

Weinberg, M. M. (1967). Effects of partial sensory deprivation on involuntary subjects. *Dissertation Abstracts International, 28,* 2171B. (University Microfilms No. 67–14,558).

Weiner, I. B., & Hess, A. K. (Eds.). (1987). *Handbook of forensic psychology.* New York: Wiley.

Weis, J. G. (1989). Family violence methodology and design. In L. Ohlin & M. Tonry (Eds.), *Family violence* (Vol. 11). Chicago: University of Chicago Press.

Weisheit, R., & Mahan, S. (1988). *Women, crime, and criminal justice.* Cincinnati, OH: Anderson Publishing.

Weiss, J. M. (1968). Effects of coping response on stress. *Journal of Comparative and Physiological Psychology, 65,* 251–260.

Weiss, J. M. (1970). Somatic effects of predictable and unpredictable shock. *Psychosomatic Medicine, 32,* 397–409.

Weiss, J. M. (1971). Effects of coping behavior in different warning signal conditions on stress pathology in rats. *Journal of Comparative and Physiological Psychology, 77,* 1–13.

Weissman, H. N. (1991). Child custody evaluations: Fair and unfair professional practices. *Behavioral Sciences and the Law, 9,* 469–476.

Weiten, W., & Diamond, S. S. (1979). A critical review of the jury simulation paradigm: The case of defendant characteristics. *Law and Human Behavior, 3,* 71–94.

Wells, G. L. (1978). Applied eyewitness testimony research: System variables and estimator variables. *Journal of Personality and Social Psychology, 36,* 1546–1557.

Wells, G. L. (1986). Expert psychological testimony: Empirical and conceptual analyses of effects. *Law and Human Behavior, 10,* 83–96.

Wells, G. L., Leippe, M. R., & Ostrom, T. M. (1979). Guidelines for empirically assessing the fairness of a lineup. *Law and Human Behavior, 3,* 285–294.

Wells, G. L., Lindsay, R. C. L., & Ferguson, T. J. (1979). Accuracy, confidence, and juror perceptions in eyewitness identification. *Journal of Applied Psychology, 64,* 440–448.

Wells, G. L., & Turtle, J. W. (1986). Eyewitness identification: The importance of lineup models. *Psychological Bulletin, 90,* 320–329.

Wells, G. L., Turtle, J. W., & Luus, C. A. E. (1989). The perceived credibility of child eyewitnesses: What happens when they use their own words? In S. J. Ceci, D. F. Ross, & M. P. Toglia (Eds.), *Perspectives on children's testimony.* New York: Springer-Verlag.

Wenk, E. A., Robison, J. O., & Smith, C. W. (1972). Can violence be predicted? *Crime and Delinquency, 18,* 393–402.

Westin, A. (1967). *Privacy and freedom.* New York: Atheneum.

Westley, W. A. (1956). Secrecy and the police. *Social Forces, 34,* 254–257.

Wexler, D. B. (1981). *Mental health law: Major issues.* New York: Plenum.

Wexler, D. B. (1990a). Grave disability and family therapy: The therapeutic potential of civil libertarian commitment codes. In D. B. Wexler (Ed.), *Therapeutic jurisprudence.* Durham, NC: Carolina Academic Press.

Wexler, D. B. (1990b). *Therapeutic jurisprudence.* Durham, NC: Carolina Academic Press.

Wexler, D. B. (1990c). An introduction to therapeutic jurisprudence. In D. B. Wexler (Ed.), *Therapeutic jurisprudence.* Durham, NC: Carolina Academic Press.

Wexler, D. B. (1992). Putting mental health into mental health law. *Law and Human Behavior, 16,* 27–38.

Wexler, D. B., & Scoville, S. E. (1971). The administration of psychiatric justice theory and practice in Arizona. *Arizona Law Review, 13,* 1–250.

Wexler, D. B., & Winick, B. J. (1991) (Eds.), *Essays in therapeutic jurisprudence*. Durham, NC: Carolina Academic Press.

Wexler, J. G. (1985). Role styles of women police officers. *Sex Roles, 12,* 749–755.

Wexler, J. G., & Logan, D. D. (1983). Sources of stress among women police officers. *Journal of Police Science and Administration, 11,* 46–53.

Wheeler, S. (1961). Socialization in correctional communities. *American Sociological Review, 26,* 697–712.

Whitcomb, D., & Brandt, R.L. (1985). *Competency to stand trial. Policy Brief.* Washington, DC: U. S. Department of Justice, National Institute of Justice.

Widacki, J., & Horvath, F. S. (1978). An experimental investigation of the relative validity and utility of the polygraph technique and three other common methods of criminal investigation. *Journal of Forensic Sciences, 23,* 596–601.

Wiesner, W. H., & Cronshaw, S. F. (1988). A meta-analytical investigation of the impact of interview format and degree of structure on the validity of the employment interview. *Journal of Occupational Psychology, 61,* 275–290.

Wiggins, J. S. (1973). *Personality and prediction: Principles of personality assessment.* Reading, MA: Addison-Wesley.

Wilkins, L. T. (1979). Policy control, information, ethics, and discretion. In L. E. Abt & L. R. Stuart (Eds.), *Social psychology and discretionary law.* New York: Van Nostrand-Reinhold.

Williams, F. P., & McShane, M. D. (1991). Psychological testimony and the decisions of prospective death-qualified jurors. In R. M. Bohm (Ed.), *The death penalty in America: Current research.* Cincinnati, OH: Anderson Publishing.

Williams, G. (1963). *The proof of guilt* (3rd ed.). London: Stevens & Sons.

Williams, K., & Hawkings, R. (1989). The meaning of arrest for wife assault. *Criminology, 27,* 163–181.

Williams, R. N. (1992). The human context of agency. *American Psychologist, 47,* 752–760.

Williams, W., & Miller, K. (1981). The processing and disposition of incompetent mentally ill offenders. *Law and Human Behavior, 5,* 245–261.

Wilmoth, G. H., de Alteriss, M., & Bussell, D. (1992). Prevalence of psychological risks following legal abortion in the U. S.: Limits of the evidence. *Journal of Social Issues, 48,* 37–66.

Wilson, J. Q. (1968). *Varieties of police behavior: The management of law and order in eight communities.* Cambridge, MA: Harvard University Press.

Winick, B. J. (1991a). Competency to consent to treatment: The distinction between assent and objection. In D. B. Wexler (Ed.), *Therapeutic jurisprudence.* Durham, NC: Carolina Academic Press.

Winick, B. J. (1991b). Competency to consent to voluntary hospitalization: A therapeutic jurisprudence analysis of Zinermon v. Burch. In D. B. Wexler (Ed.), *Therapeutic jurisprudence.* Durham, NC: Carolina Academic Press.

Winick, C. (1979). The psychology of the courtroom. In H. Toch (Ed.), *Psychology of crime and criminal justice.* New York: Holt, Rinehart & Winston.

Wissler, R. L., & Saks, M. J. (1985). On the inefficacy of limiting instructions: When jurors use prior conviction evidence to decide on guilt. *Law and Human Behavior, 9,* 37–48.

Wohlmuth, P. C. (Ed.) (1990). Symposium: Alternative dispute resolution. *Journal of Contemporary Legal Issues* (Vol. 3).

Wolf, S., & Montgomery, D. A. (1977). Effects of inadmissible evidence and level of judicial admonishment to disregard on the judgments of mock jurors. *Journal of Applied Social Psychology, 7,* 205–219.

Wolfe, D. A. (1985). Child-abusive parents: An empirical review and analysis. *Psychological Bulletin, 97,* 462–482.

Wolfgang, M. E. (1958). *Patterns in criminal homicide.* Philadelphia: University of Pennsylvania Press.

Wolfgang, M. E. (1961). A sociological analysis of criminal homicide. *Federal Probation, 25,* 48–55.

Wolman, R., & Taylor, K. (1991). Psychological effects of custody disputes on children. *Behavioral Sciences and the Law, 9,* 399–417.

Wright, P. M., Lichtenfels, P. A., & Pursell, E. D. (1989). The structured interview: Additional studies and a meta-analysis. *Journal of Occupational Psychology, 62,* 191–199.

Wright, R. (1980). Rape and physical violence. In D. J. West (Ed.), *Sex offenders in the criminal justice system.* Cambridge, England: Cambridge University Institute of Criminology.

Wrightsman, L. S. (1977). *Social psychology* (2nd ed.). Monterey, CA: Brooks/Cole.

Wrightsman, L. S., & Deaux, K. (1981). *Social psychology in the 80's* (3rd ed.). Monterey, CA: Brooks/Cole.

Yarmey, A. D. (1979). *The psychology of eyewitness testimony*. New York: The Free Press.

Yarmey, A. D., & Kent, J. (1980). Eyewitness identification by elderly and young adults. *Law and Human Behavior, 4*, 359–371.

Yarmey, A. D. (1990). *Understanding police and police work: Psychosocial issues*. New York: New York University Press.

Yarmey, A. D. (1984). Age as a factor in eyewitness memory. In G. L. Wells & E. F. Loftus (Eds.), *Eyewitness testimony*. New York: Cambridge University Press.

Yarmey, A. D., & Jones, H. P. T. (1983). Is the psychology of eyewitness identification a matter of common sense? In S. M. A. Lloyd-Bostock & B. R. Clifford (Eds.), *Evaluating witness evidence: Recent psychological research and new perspectives*. Chichester, England: Wiley.

Yegidis, B. L. (1986). Date rape and other forced sexual encounters among college students. *Journal of Sex Education and Therapy, 12*, 51–54.

Yuille, J. C. (1980). A critical examination of the psychological and practical implications of eyewitness research. *Law and Human Behavior, 4*, 335–346.

Yuille, J. C. (1989). Expert evidence by psychologists: Sometimes problematic and often premature. *Behavioral Sciences and the Law, 7*, 181–196.

Yuille, J. C., & Tollestrup, P. A. (1990). Some effects of alcohol on eyewitness testimony. *Journal of Applied Psychology, 75*, 268–273.

Yunger, J. A. (1976). Is the death penalty a deterrent to homicide: Some time series evidence. *Journal of Behavioral Economics, 5*, 45–81.

Zamble, E. (1992). Behavior and adaptation in long-term prison inmates: Descriptive longitudinal results. *Criminal Justice and Behavior, 19*, 409–425.

Zamble, E., & Porporino, F. J. (1988). *Coping, behavior, and adaptation in prison inmates*. New York: Springer-Verlag.

Zeisel, H. (1971). … And then there were none: The diminution of the federal jury. *University of Chicago Law Review, 38*, 710–724.

Zeisel, H. (1974). Twelve is just. *Trial, 10*, 13–15.

Zeisel, H., & Diamond, S. (1978). The effect of peremptory challenges on the jury and verdict. *Stanford Law Review, 30*, 491–531.

Zeling, M. (1986). Research needs in the study of post shooting trauma. In J. T. Reese & H. A. Goldstein (Eds.), *Psychological services for law enforcement*. Washington, DC: USGPO.

Zellman, G. L. (1990). Child abuse reporting and failure to report among mandated reporters: Prevalence, incidence, and reasons. *Journal of Interpersonal Violence, 5*, 3–22.

Zilboorg, G. (1944). Legal aspects of psychiatry. In American Psychiatric Association (Ed.), *One hundred years of American psychiatry*. New York: Columbia University Press.

Zimbardo, P. G. (1973). The psychological power and pathology of imprisonment. In E. Aronson, & R. Helmreich (Eds.), *Social psychology*. New York: Van Nostrand.

Zimring, F. E. (1989). Toward a jurisprudence of family violence. In L. Ohlin & M. Tonry (Eds.), *Family violence* (Vol. 11). Chicago: University of Chicago Press.

Ziskin, J., & Faust, D. (1988). *Coping with psychiatric and psychological testimony* (4th ed.). Marina Del Rey, CA: Law & Psychology Press.

Zonana, H. V., Crane, L. E., & Getz, M. A. (1990). Training and credentialing in forensic psychiatry. *Behavioral Sciences and the Law, 8*, 233–247.

Zubek, J. P. (Ed.). (1969). *Sensory deprivation: Fifteen years of research*. New York: Appleton-Century-Crofts.

Zuckerman, M., & Gerbasi, K. C. (1977). Belief in internal control or belief in a just world: The use and misuse of the I-E scale in prediction of attitudes and behavior. *Journal of Personality, 45*, 356–378.

AUTHOR INDEX

SUBJECT INDEX